Fortunes of History

DONALD R. KELLEY

Fortunes of History

HISTORICAL INQUIRY FROM HERDER TO HUIZINGA

Yale University Press
New Haven &
London

Published with assistance from the Louis Stern Memorial Fund.

Set in Sabon type by Keystone Typesetting, Inc.
Printed in the United States of America by Sheridan Books, Ann Arbor, Michigan

Library of Congress Cataloging-in-Publication Data
Kelley, Donald R., 1931–
Fortunes of history : historical inquiry from Herder to Huizinga /
Donald R. Kelley.
         p.   cm.
Includes bibliographical references and index.
ISBN 0-300-09578-3 (hard cover : alk. paper)
1. History—Research. 2. History—Philosophy. 3. Historians—Europe.
4. History—Methodology. 5. Historiography. 6. Literature and history. I. Title.
D16 .K26 2003
901—dc21
2002153368

A catalogue record for this book is available from the British Library.

10 9 8 7 6 5 4 3 2 1

For Bonnie, who has accompanied me on these and many
other adventures, past and present, near and far, then and now

Contents

Preface

The great point is the history of history.
                                    — Lord Acton

If science begins with wonder, history begins with curiosity — not what, how, and why so much as who, where, and how long ago? "History" is the term we give to practices and associated theories traceable back, with extraordinary semantic continuity, to the pioneering contributions of Herodotus to the study of humanity's past. In a more general sense, it is true, the word applies to descriptive prose on almost any subject, and it was often kept separate from "antiquities" and matters of the deep past ("natural history"); yet the dominant meaning has become attached to inquiries into human actions and creations of ages gone by — to happenings and "antiquities" recorded since. This was the premise of my earlier book, *Faces of History: Historical Inquiry from Herodotus to Herder*, where, in a long perspective, in which remote objects tend to lose distinctness, I surveyed the earlier stages of historical inquiry through the conceit of two "faces" — namely, Herodotus and Thucydides, who directed their gazes, respectively, to a deep and mysterious cultural past and to the immediate background of a problematic political present. This is a gross oversimplification, of course, for an understanding of the accomplishments of these two early explorers "as they really were," but less so for their posthumous history, that is, their later reception (*fortuna* the ancients called it), in which they indeed came to offer models for later authors, who, consciously or not, carried on similar lines of inquiry and, deliberately or not, helped fashion, in this same long perspective, a genre, an art, a science, a discipline, and a profession. In this perspective they become one of "us."

In my earlier book I spoke of two faces, but I probably should have acknowledged at least one more, appearing later in the form of a story of a people, republic, church, or nation, as in the works of Livy, Josephus, Eusebius, and the "barbarian" historians; for these became even more powerful models, especially in the ages of modern nation-building, nation-expanding, and nation-inventing. In the wake of the histories of these essentialist constructs, history expanded into many areas of human activity, including the history of literature, philosophy, science, art, culture or civilization, history itself, and countless other fields and subfields within the encyclopedia of human knowledge, and inspired a new field (also with ancient roots), the "philosophy of history." With the emergence and proliferation of branches of historical study came also the so-called "auxiliary sciences" of history, including geography, chronology, paleography, diplomatics, numismatics, sphragistics, archeology, and other critical methods designed to gain access to sources of historical inquiry and to assist in interpretation. As a result of these developments "history" came to be regarded in modern times less as an art or a science than a method applicable to all areas of human endeavor — a foundational view according to which history, like philosophy and literature, could sweep all other disciplines into its intellectual orbit and, from a certain point of view, subsume them.

Discussions of history down to the eighteenth century were heavy with rhetorical convention — not only the famous Ciceronian topoi celebrating history as the messenger of antiquity, mistress of life, etc., but also the old tag of Dionysius of Halicarnassus, which was repeated by Bolingbroke and many others, that history was "philosophy teaching by example." Another, conceptually related, commonplace was the distinction between history, which dealt with the individual, and philosophy, which dealt with the general. Other incarnations of this duality were Meinecke's definition of historicism as a combination of the principles of individuality and development, in contrast with philosophical approaches, and Windelband's distinctions between idiographic and nomothetic methods. The two faces of history, Thucydidean and Herodotean, political and cultural, seemed to be replicated in a modern polemical context in the later nineteenth century in the *Methodenstreit* between the state-oriented disciples of Ranke and the upstart field of cultural history associated with Karl Lamprecht, a debate that has echoed over the past century. These persistent, or revived, dualities all helped give definition and structure to the practice, theory, and methods of history at our end of a tradition covering two and a half millennia.

Paradoxical efforts of historians to be "new" while looking back to a historical process are at once illuminating (the locus classicus of Cicero) and burdensome (the locus modernus, or postmodernus, of Nietzsche). Periodically, historians have laid claim to novelty, most famously in the sixteenth, eighteenth, and nineteenth centuries, and then more insistently in the early (and again in the late) twentieth century. There were good arguments for all of these innovationist movements, but there was also a danger that in superseding the defective old for the improved new product, the historian's office of understanding — and indeed "historicizing" — the background, forestructures, and semantic inheritance of his or her own condition might be forgotten. No doubt all history is present history, as Croce taught, but the reverse is also the case; and whatever strategies philosophers adopt, historians should not begin by suppressing undesirable memories in the name of better method. The dwarves-and-giants metaphor has not lost its relevance; and while the relationship between writers and their forebears may be uncomfortable, undesirable, or even (pace Harold Bloom) pathological, it is better to be aware of our disciplinary ancestors even if we want to repudiate them. One of the major problems with appreciating the study of history in these later times is the sheer quantity of materials — the vast amount of raw and half-digested scholarship and monographic works as well as the large number of multivolume masterpieces, or intended masterpieces, and life works which, in some cases, had considerable literary and intellectual impact even though their fame and fortune often did not survive their age. Intellectual quality aside, the phenomenon of historians' repeating the work of others, whether in the spirit of imitation, discipleship, or plagiarism, has condemned the vast majority of these publications to obsolescence and then oblivion. Yet some of these works were immensely influential and popular, rivaling novels and poems in the Romantic and Victorian ages. The authors of these historiographical creations deserve better, and I have tried to give notice to some of these forgotten creations of the Herodoto-Thucydidean community which transcend (we might like to think) the more recent flow of fashion and novelty.

This book takes up the story of historical inquiry where my former study left off — that is, in the later eighteenth century, when Herodotus and Thucydides were still intimidating presences.[1] The first chapter reviews the varieties of history in the Enlightenment period, with emphasis on the enhancing but also troubled relationship between history and philosophy, the theory and "art" of history, the advance of critical method, the shift from universal to cultural history, and the question, raised in later ages, of the rise of "historicism." The second chapter pursues these and related themes, including new forms of the philosophy of history, in the context of the French Revolution and its imprint on historical studies. Chapter 3 takes up the expanding horizons of history, including its convergence with other disciplines (especially literature, philosophy, law, and language), its relation to biblical studies, to hermeneutics, and to the new field of mythology, and the role of new geographical discoveries and the shock of ethnic alterity, all of which subverted Europeanist cultural assumptions and Christian chronology, and which established intellectual continuities with historical inquiry in the following century.

The next six chapters take up the complex story of historical thought, research, and writing in the major nineteenth-century national traditions — German, British, and French — with attention to scholarly and institutional conditions, schools of interpretation, auxiliary sciences, historical method, and questions of early and medieval stages of proto-"national" development. Among the topics discussed are the historical schools, philology and biblical scholarship, racial and ethnic differences, "constitutional history," as pursued according to different national styles, and ideas of primitive community. Among the major figures examined are Scott, Macaulay, Freeman, Stubbs, and Acton; Mommsen, Ranke, Burckhardt, Droysen, Waitz, and Treitschke; Guizot, Thierry, Michelet, Fustel de Coulanges, and the champions of scientific history — and many minor and forgotten figures as well.

Chapter 10 ventures "beyond the canon," taking up such professionally marginal topics as the emergence of "prehistory," cultural history, the Italian case, and various "mini-nationalisms" on the edges of Europe and their retrieved or fabricated history — Spain, Scandinavia, the Netherlands, Switzerland, the countries of Eastern Europe, and the Balkans. Still on the margins from a European standpoint, Chapter 9 takes up American parallels, with notice of American prehistory, the New England school (Bancroft, Prescott, Motley, and Parkman), later contributors to the national project, scientific history (White, Fiske, and Draper), and the work of Henry Adams. The last chapter treats the various "new histories" (German, American, and French — the British remaining for the most part in their unreflective Victorian mode) at the turn of the twentieth century, and returns, in this context, to a reconsideration of questions of hermeneutics and historicism (beyond the invidious stereotypes of "old" and "new" historicism, which have confused the issues) as the foundations and conditions of modern historical inquiry.

The orientation of this book is Western and Eurocentric, but only in the sense that it is necessarily bound to a local "point of view" and the horizon structure required by hermeneutics and historical interpretation and not because it rejects global or even comparative objectives. But unlike practitioners of other human sciences, who may aspire to an Archimedean position and universal range, historians work in a specific intellectual continuum and heuristic context and with what Hans-Georg Gadamer calls an "experience of tradition," and in a particular language, or set of languages, which constitute a semantic medium and which define a horizon of understanding and meaning. This is the hermeneutical predicament that limits historical inquiry. "For what man, in the natural state or course of thinking" — here Herder cites Jonathan Swift's *Tale of a Tub* — "did ever conceive it in his power to reduce the notions of all mankind exactly to the same length, and breadth, and height of his own?" By contrast the assignment of history is to keep lines of inquiry open and to follow provisional answers, however gratifying and useful, with further and more searching questions — a lowly job, perhaps, but someone has to do it (doesn't he or she?). And there are more things in the past of humanity than can be reduced to artificial measure (aren't there?). Such, in any case, are the main premises and aspirations of this book.

My first love was the history and literature of the nineteenth and twentieth centuries, contracted as an undergraduate in Harvard's department of that name, which, legend has it, was the first of such special divisions of the arts faculty. My senior thesis on Acton was the beginning of a long intellectual voyage, but afterward I was drawn farther back to early modern, medieval, and ancient aspects of historical tradition, and I worked my way up to the modern (and postmodern) world only a generation later. Of the colleagues who have shaped the course and direction of my intellectual interests over the years, I will mention especially Peter Burke, Ralph Giesey, Lionel Gossman, Anthony Grafton, Georg Iggers, Samuel Kinser, Reinhard Kosseleck, Joseph Levine, Wolfgang Mommsen, Peter Munz, Arthur Mitzman, Anthony Pagden, John Pocock, Peter Hans Reill, Jörn Rüsen, David Harris Sacks, John Salmon, Quentin Skinner, Bonnie Smith, Edoardo Tortarolo, Donald Verene, Daniel Woolf, and Perez Zagorin, as well as the late Herbert Butterfield, John Clive, Geoffrey Dickens, Wallace Ferguson, Hans-Georg Gadamer, Felix Gilbert, Leonard Krieger, Paul Kristeller, and Arnaldo Momigliano — and not to forget, especially, Robin Ladrach, my talented and irreplaceable associate on the *Journal of the History of Ideas.* For me these mentors, friends, interlocutors, and correspondents (epigones all of Herodotus, Thucydides, et al.) define for me the terrain of the *Respublica Historiographicorum,* of which this book is one small product.

Enlightened History

*An enlightenment without grounds, a historical Enlightenment without
documents, is no enlightenment at all.*

— *Friedrich Nicolai*

The Old Historicism

The Enlightenment was an age of history as well as philosophy. This fact
has not always been clear from classic studies of the eighteenth century. Paul
Hazard began the first of his two volumes on the "crisis of European consciousness" with an analysis of historical pyrrhonism but then launched into a
grand narrative featuring heterodoxy, deism, the "war against tradition," natural law, the achievements of science, and Enlightened "philosophy" in its
peculiar French sense.[1] Carl Becker celebrated the "new history" of the Enlightenment but identified it mainly with the old story of "philosophy teaching
by example" and the new (or, for Becker, not so new) agenda of the philosophes, which (like that of their scholastic prototypes) had to do more with
the future than with the past.[2] Peter Gay, while rejecting Becker's thesis concerning the religious archetype of the program of the philosophes, took the
ancient "pagan" heritage, scholarly tradition, and the "useful and beloved
past" as ancillary to the primary goal of Enlightenment, which he identified

with the "science of freedom" and "pursuit of modernity"; and for him (as for Voltaire and the philosophes), history was basically a solvent of old errors and a source of useful examples, while "criticism" was basically philosophical rather than historical in nature.[3]

Recent debates about the so-called Enlightenment project — whether "unfinished" or "failed" — also tend to evade or play down the presence of history in the eighteenth century in favor of the relentless and stereotypical rationality which Habermas, following Max Weber as well as Horkheimer and Adorno (and ultimately Kant), associates with the *Aufklärung*.[4] Nor have current discussions of a proto-Romantic "counter-Enlightenment" been of much help in this connection, creating as they do a different sort of dialectic in which the "philosophy of the Enlightenment" reconstructed by Cassirer is bifurcated, cast into two opposing traditions, again from the standpoint, presumably, of "our" cultural predicament.[5] J. G. A. Pocock's recent study of the background to Gibbon emphasizes the plurality of Enlightenments but, like Gibbon himself, avoids German aspects.[6] The eighteenth-century "mind" indeed seems divided against itself, especially in a post-revolutionary perspective; but from a philosophical, cultural, and especially historical point of view it resists this sort of analysis. The central issue of eighteenth-century thought was not reason against unreason, but rather the question: "What is reason?" — or, more famously phrased, "What is enlightenment?" or even "What is humanity?" One purpose of this study is to restore some balance to the understanding of the way these questions were asked and answered beyond the canon of formal philosophy and within the tradition of historical scholarship.

The historical character of the Enlightenment was made plain many years ago by Ernst Cassirer, whose *Philosophie der Aufklärung* (1932) located in that period "The Conquest of the Historical World."[7] More than thirty years earlier this thesis had already received classic expression in an article that Wilhelm Dilthey, like Cassirer a neo-Kantian, published in the *Deutsche Rundschau*.[8] In his survey of the "historical world" on which the eighteenth century drew, Dilthey noted the ancient and medieval roots, especially Polybius and Augustine; the "dynamic" views of Machiavelli and Guicciardini; the scholarship of Renaissance humanism and German Protestantism, including critical study of sources and biblical hermeneutics; the role of academies and universities in the advancement of historical learning; and, for him most essential, the notion of a unified "culture" or civilization. According to Dilthey, "History begins by taking up of the totality of culture." This totalizing impulse (the root, perhaps, of Dilthey's own idea of a "cultural system")[9] was the starting point of the "new history" of the Enlightenment (*neue Geschichtsschreibung*), beginning especially with the work of Voltaire, Montesquieu, and Turgot and continued by British and German scholars, including those teaching at the University of Göttingen and culminating in the groundbreaking work of B. G. Niebuhr, his followers, and his critics.[10]

But the historical aspects of the eighteenth century were hardly news even in 1901, since they had been celebrated and chronicled voluminously by scholars for almost two centuries, from the almost two-thousand-page historiographical survey of Ludwig Wachler (1812–16), to the more than one-thousand-page book by Franz X. von Wegele (1885), and followed by many others of this genre.[11] Indeed, champions of the Enlightenment were themselves aware of the role of history, for as the "popular philosopher" — Lessing's friend and Kant's enemy — Friedrich Nicolai wrote more than a century before Dilthey, "An enlightenment without grounds, a historical Enlightenment without documents, is no enlightenment at all."[12] Of course the *Aufklärung* envisioned by Nicolai (designed for those living in the world and not in a "Tübingen monastery")[13] was not that championed by Kant, not the *lumières* celebrated by D'Alembert and Condorcet, not the multiple "enlightenments" of Gibbon, and certainly not the controversial "Enlightenment" that received English recognition only in the nineteenth century. It was a larger, more human phenomenon, a chiaroscuro view of eighteenth-century thought, which embraced many aspects of reason and culture and which looked to history as well as rational thought for wisdom; and this is what locates the perspective of this study of modern historical thought and writing.

Unfortunately, even the perspective and the arguments of Dilthey and Cassirer are inadequate to the purpose of seeing the Enlightenment in the light of its historical enterprises; for their concerns remain in the context of philosophy and, specifically, neo-Kantian philosophy. Their attention was directed to public ideals rather than to the intellectual and scholarly practices of Enlightenment intellectuals, and they were oblivious or hostile to the inclination of many of these intellectuals and to that cast of mind called historicism. Curiously, this is also the case with historians like Friedrich Meinecke, who attempted to locate the roots of "historicism" in the eighteenth century but who deliberately restricted his vision to the "mountain tops" (the works of the great thinkers and narrative historians) rather than the "stones, the dirt, the soil out of which the mountains grew" (the positive achievements of historical erudition and criticism).[14] So, for example, while honoring Möser as "the first pathbreaker of historicism," Meinecke dismissed the prolific Rousseauist historian Johannes von Müller as unoriginal, despite an attempt to associate him with "early historicism"[15] — while, by contrast, Sismondi had called him "the first historian of our century."[16] On his tour of the intellectual heights, Meinecke constructed a curious canon that admits, as the *Vorläufer* of Ernst Troeltsch and himself, not only Vico and Ranke but also the arch-naturalist Leibniz, but that quite overlooks the linguistic, literary, and in many ways antiphilosophical orientation of historicism as it emerged in the age of the Göttingen school and proto-Romanticism. While giving due notice to Leibniz's metaphysical "law of continuity," Meinecke ignored the contributions of the nineteenth-century historical schools and the literary tradition as a whole. Goethe does figure prominently in Meinecke's book; but, revealingly, it is Goethe the naturalist, not Goethe the poet and critic. The result was that for Meinecke "historicism" was less an attribute of historical scholarship than a philosophical doctrine, which he reduced to the twin principles of individuality and development. The analysis of Peter Reill, following Hazard and Meinecke, of the "crisis of historical consciousness" has helped to restore the balance between thought and scholarship in the assessment of historicism, but he has not pursued these questions into the nineteenth century.[17]

Meinecke's formula for historicism was the substitution of the principle of individuality for generality and of development for static system, so that it was associated with organicist and evolutionary ideas and in this connection the particularity of the biological model. His conception is a later version both of the old idea that history treated the particular and philosophy the general and of Windelband's analogous conception of the natural sciences as "nomothetic" and the cultural sciences as "idiographic" — all of these echoing, perhaps, the still older problem of universals.[18] In any case in the past two centuries historicism, too, like the Hegelian view of history, has been philosophized — turned into a generalizing doctrine instead of an individualizing form of inquiry — and the result has been misunderstandings both historical and philosophical.[19] From a historical point of view, "historicism" has nothing to do, for example, with the claims of Popper, for whom historicism was a form of "scientific determinism," an approach to the social sciences that assumes that "*historical prediction* is their principal aim."[20] Nothing could be further from the intentions of historically grounded philosophers like Troeltsch and Croce, not to mention practicing historians like Ranke and, again, Croce. Nor does the imposition of the Kuhnian concept of disciplinary paradigm, employed by Ulrich Muhlack to historicism and by Horst Blanke even more narrowly to professional historical method (*Historik*), rescue such projects.[21] And the claims of "New Historicism" represent literary strategies rather than historical criticism. In general historical thinking and scholarship, torn as they are between literary and (in a general sense) scientific motives, resist notions of "normal science" and intellectual revolution. Historicizing impulses have always been interdisciplinary and even transdisciplinary, aspiring — like philosophy and science in their most imperialist modes — to a foundational position in the human (and to some extent natural) sciences; and it is these terms that the history of "history" needs to be understood.

In sum, historicism should be construed not as a concept but rather as an attitude, not as a theory but rather as a scholarly practice, not as a system of explanation but rather as a mode of interpretation; and it was part of an effort not to make history into a philosophical doctrine but rather to transform (or to extend) it into a foundational discipline to which philosophy itself would be subject.[22] In this spirit the "philosophy of history" after Herder proposed not to impose principles on but rather to discover them in recorded history. Nor can historicism be divorced from the accumulation of "mere" erudition produced by conventional and (as the philosophes would say) unprejudiced historical research, which promised the revelation of truth in the course of time— *veritas filia temporis.* These are some of the main features of historical inquiry in the late eighteenth century. This discussion, of course, cannot do justice to all the varieties, conditions, and contexts of history on the threshold of the revolutionary age. Even philosophers, while claiming often to be above the battle, even above the human condition, served the interests of state, church, and others; but historians were more manifestly engaged in political, social, and economic life. As they professed truth and impartiality, they also accommodated these values to another characteristic of history, which was its utility and which often required partisan commitment; and in this connection the relativism implied by historicist and hermeneutical attitudes served to give legitimacy to pragmatic lines of historical inquiry and interpretation. Obviously there are many ways of understanding the art and science of modern history—many traditions of scholarship and literature, many contexts, from the private and the psychological to the social and the public. History has inextricable ties to the character of its practitioners, to psychology, politics, religion, class, profession, and "ideology" (another neologism of this age); but it is the story of history as a discipline, as a form of knowledge, as the center of a larger conceptual field called, ambiguously, historicism, with its distinctive methods and ideals—and not history as *something else,* as doctrine, ideology, propaganda, or an emanation of the climate of opinion or spirit of the age— that is the subject of this inquiry. "Every thing is what it is, and not another thing," in the words of Joseph Butler quoted by Isaiah Berlin.[23]

The practice, theory, and philosophy of history differed of course in the various national traditions of Europe. In Italy, Vico joined philology, history, and philosophy into a "new science" that explored human experience from its genesis. In France, Voltaire, Goguet, Condillac, Turgot, and Condorcet opened up conventional narrative to the history of civilization, the last two in particular affecting to find material as well as intellectual progress, referring to the "four-stage" theory of human development.[24] In England, history, while celebrated by classical topoi, was also tied to common-law and parliamentary traditions and to the "Gothic bequest," which gave ancient pedigree to modern English society: the past was no doubt spoiled by mistakes, but its investigation was all the more useful for this reason. But it was in the German-speaking territories that history aspired to a position beyond the jurisdiction even of philosophy by claiming to understand the nature of reason in its development and so the phenomenon of "enlightenment" that gave its name to that age. Thus it is the study of history in Germany that marks the starting point for this discussion.

Philosophy and Pedantry

By 1800 the study of history in the West had itself a long — two-and-a-quarter-millennia — history that was complex, colorful, and contradictory.[25] Since Herodotus and Thucydides, who were still canonical figures at this time, history had generated truth and error and, in many languages, a large vocabulary and conceptual apparatus to distinguish one from the other and to disseminate both. It constituted a tradition, or set of traditions, of inquiry intended to satisfy private curiosities and increasingly to serve public interests; and as such it produced a variety of institutional forms — official posts and professorships, research teams and societies, outpourings of published books, reviews, journals, and expanding readerships.[26] It had become a prominent province in the Republic of Letters of late medieval and early modern times, and a dominant one in the "public sphere" of Enlightened Europe. States, churches, many cities, universities, and some families had their historians, official or self-nominated; and so did other human institutions with discernible and recorded pasts. In the process history had become an exclusive professional calling, a surrogate philosophy, an academic culture, and for some almost a religion.

Along with the professionalization of historical studies came the development and systematic training in the so-called auxiliary sciences (*Hilfswissenschaften*).[27] History itself had performed such an ancillary role, especially with respect to law, theology, and philosophy; but in the eighteenth century the subdisciplines of geography, chronology, diplomatics, paleography, numismatics, sphragistics, and statistics were arranged in an "encyclopedia" of practices that broadened and deepened historical scholarship as well as rendering it more technical and professional. Reinforcing these was a mounting mass of works of reference, editions of standard works and documentary sources, pedagogical manifestos, scholarly exchanges, textbooks, maps, scholarly journals, bibliographical listings of the "literature" of particular fields of study, and specialized books in the history of philosophy, art, the sciences, and history itself. This was the sort of erudition on which Gibbon drew, while at the same time deriding its more pedantic forms, and which philosophers like Kant and Hegel scorned as mindless and irrelevant empiricism and "pedantry."

In various ways history and philosophy were rivals in the eighteenth century: both claimed the status of a "science" and promised unique insights into the human condition. The major claim to philosophical hegemony was that of Immanuel Kant, who based his arguments on autonomous and "critical" reason.[28] "Was ist Aufklärung?" is the question Kant set out to answer in 1784 — "What is Enlightenment?" — and his answer was "Dare to know," Horace's *sapere aude,* that is, use your adult reason and, according to another Horatian motto repeated by earlier German Eclectic philosophers, "Never bind yourself over to the dictates of any master."[29] Humanity had lived under paternal and religious (Kant was careful not to meddle with political) authority long enough; now it was time to grow up and trust one's own enlightened reflection. Such was the timely — and timeless — message of Kant's *Critique of Pure Reason,* which was published three years earlier and which became the central and even authoritative text of the *Aufklärung.* As for history, it, too, could be rendered philosophical — that is, "universal," "conjectural," "reasoned," "a priori," and even "providential" — and understood as an expression of reason and the foundation of an idea of moral and political progress (as illustrated by the French Revolution, at least according to first impressions). Then as now, however, many historians avoided or scorned associations with philosophy, and not only because of its subversive implications.

Kant's was a radical version of the "philosophy of history" attempted by Voltaire and the "conjectural history" of Adam Ferguson and other Scottish moral philosophers, divorced as it was from any pretension to empirical research. Partly for this reason, even during the high tide of Kantianism, there were those who were skeptical of this line of argument. According to the adage of Cicero, repeated by Melanchthon and Bolingbroke, it was not philosophy but history that distinguished a child from an enlightened adult.[30] Among those who doubted that Critical Philosophy was the only road to understanding was Kant's old friend and sometime critic, J. G. Herder, who had suggested his contrary views in a work of 1774 entitled *Noch eine Philosophie der Geschichte,* that is, an alternative to the popular works of Voltaire and Robertson, whom he saw as celebrating human progress in naive and uncritically rationalist terms.[31] Twenty-five years later Herder gave more specifically philosophical, or antiphilosophical, form to his views in a crucial work which he called a *Metacritique* of the so-called Critical Philosophy, following the earlier "metacriticism" of Kant by Herder's older friend J. G. Hamann, who objected to eliminating tradition and use for purposes of philosophical "purification." "With me it is not so much the question what is reason," he wrote, "but far more: what is language?"[32] For Herder, similarly, the central question was not, "What is Enlightenment?" but rather, "What is humanity?" — and anthropology and the study of language, rather than theology, metaphysics, or epistemology, were the essential disciplines to answer this question.

In this metacriticism of the critical philosophy of Kant, Herder rejected his old friend's views of absolute space and time, a priori knowledge, and abstract reason and generalized experience — and by inference his neglect of the historically remote as well as the culturally different. To suggest the folly of philosophical schemes Herder quoted at length from Swift's *Tale of a Tub,* which situated philosophers in the "academy of modern bedlam." "For what man, in the natural state or course of thinking, did ever conceive it in his power to reduce the notions of all mankind exactly to the same length, and breadth, and height of his own?" asked Swift. "Yet [Swift answers his own question] this is the first humble and civil design of all innovators in the empire of reason."[33] Swift meant Descartes, but Herder turned the ridicule on Kant and his followers. Herder's metacriticism pointed out Kant's error in isolating reason from other faculties, in dealing not with words but with empty categories and senseless phenomenology. Nor did Kant ever ask the crucial historical question asked by Herder, "How did human concepts of understanding arise and develop?" For Herder, "The human mind thinks with words"; and reason was a process of experience in specific (not absolute) time and space, which was to say in history.[34] This was the background of Herder's own mature philosophy of history, which began appearing in 1784 and which was reviewed, needless to say, critically.

Herder, then, emphasized concrete, historical experience, and so established the conceptual grounds for historical studies. Yet even Herder sought laws in the historical process, and this was at odds with the prevailing "theory" of history as taught in the schools. As C. R. Hausen explained:

> History [*Geschichte*] in and of itself has no general principles. Only the historian knows how to give it systematic expression. This he must seek to realize through oral and written discourse, and he can accomplish this when he understands the theory of history [*Theorie der Geschichte*] . . . , [which] is expressed in the judgment, choice, criticism, and application of materials.[35]

This "theory" had little to do with formal philosophy, however, but rather with heuristics, the critical use of sources — "with the correctness, choice, criticism, and employment of events" — that is, with the modern counterpart of the ancient art of history (*ars historica; Kunst der Geschichte; Historik; Geschichtswissenschaft*).

In fact the roles played by historical studies in the eighteenth century illustrate the paradoxical character of the thought of that age about the nature and destiny of humanity. On the one hand history, in its reasoned and conjectural forms, aspired to the conceptual level of philosophy; yet on the other hand in its empirical and critical forms history rebuked the universalistic premises of formal philosophy. This is why one may speak of history as poised between erudition and philosophy, between posing small questions and proposing large answers, between the intellectual agenda of Plato and Aristotle and that of Herodotus, Thucydides, and their modern epigones. This is the starting point — or rather these are the starting points — of the story of historical studies in the past two centuries.

The German Art of History

German fascination with history had medieval roots and Renaissance flowering. It can be traced back to the first barbarian — retrospectively "European" and "national" — histories of Jordanes, Gregory of Tours, and Paul the Deacon, and more especially to the great tradition of universal chronicles culminating in the Augustinian interpretations of Orosius and Otto of Freising.[36] Both national and universal history were reinforced by the Lutheran Reformation, which produced a revisionist review of the medieval past and a reassessment of Christian tradition more generally. In this connection, too, the methodological issues of the Italianate *artes historicae* were taken up in a less literary and more practical and polemical fashion, since historical as well as religious "truth" was the alleged object of all confessional parties; and much the same can be said of the sensitive problems of biblical exegesis, with the parallel "art" of hermeneutics being expanded by German scholars, beginning with Flacius Illyricus.[37] Finally, the massive efforts of Renaissance scholarship were turned to ecclesiastical and medievalist questions, as in the project of Flacius and the Magdeburg Centuriators to review the documentary past of Christian tradition from a Lutheran standpoint. All of these initiatives were continued by rival confessional parties and were countered by Catholic scholars like Cardinal Baronius, who turned the same scholarly weapons to a defense of orthodox tradition. And in the seventeenth century Gottfried Arnold tried to raise the level of debate by introducing the conciliatory principle of impartiality (*Unparteilichkeit*) into historical inquiry.[38]

By the eighteenth century history had become a fundamental and even foundational discipline and, moreover, had found a solid institutional base. From the mid-seventeenth to the mid-nineteenth century there were more than twenty universities and forty professors offering nearly two hundred courses in some area of the study of history. Inaugural lectures, carrying on the old tradition of the *ars historica*, served to advertise and to celebrate the study of history. At first history was often combined with other subjects — in the formal title, "professor of history and — — —" (for example, metaphysics, rhetoric, poetry, ethics, public law, Greek, oriental languages, logic, or literature), and there were also courses given in antiquities, the auxiliary sciences of history, and the history of other disciplines, including literature, philosophy, natural science and, again, history itself.

The classical and Renaissance genre of the "art of history" found a new life in the universities of eighteenth-century Germany, with dozens of treatments — lectures, prefaces to books, essays, articles, reviews of books, chapters of textbooks, and systematic and "encyclopedic" treatises devoted to the praise and analysis of history.[39] Such publications, ranging from high erudition to elementary pedagogy, carried on the old Ciceronian commonplaces defining history ("the witness of time, the light of truth, the life of memory, the mistress of life, and the messenger of antiquity") and laying down its laws ("first that an author must not dare to tell anything but the truth and second that he must make bold to tell the whole truth").[40] So truth and utility continued to be the essential aims of historical study, but in an increasingly elaborate form in keeping with the standards of modern scholarship and criticism and adapted to the conditions and requirements of modern society and the state. As in the Renaissance but more systematically and professionally, the art of history (*historische Kunst*) was promoted to the level of a science (*Geschichtswissenschaft*) and a "theory."

Following the conventions of the rhetorical view of historical narrative, these new *artes historicae* had an acute sense of the difference between the "material," or sources, of history and the literary form (*Nachrichten; Erzählungen; Darstellung*) by which it was made intelligible, communicable, and perhaps useful. To emphasize this distinction between content and form, German scholars turned to the original Greek word "Historie," which became the standard term of the new arts of history. As S. J. Baumgarten wrote in his preface to the German translation of the great collective English world history, "History [*Historie*] is a well-grounded account of past events" (*geschehene Begebenheiten* — the "happenings," *res gestae*, of unreconstructed *Geschichte*). In recounting such events, truth (*Wahrheit*) or certainty (*Gewissheit*) continued to be the most important value of historical narrative.[41] The "fabulous" stories of Herodotus were often contrasted invidiously with Thucydides' insistence on firsthand testimony — "what he himself had seen or taken from trustworthy men or writings" — and his rejection of "archeology," that is, matters beyond the memory of contemporaries. But the attacks of historical pyrrhonism on the trustworthiness of history (*fides historiae*) made these ideals harder to achieve than in times of epistemological innocence. Tacitean impartiality, reinforced by that of Arnold, and avoidance of prejudice (*Vorurtheil*) were important; but as many scholars acknowledged, the certainty attainable by history was of a different order than that of mathematics. Thus history had to be empirical rather than demonstrative, since its brand of truth depended on the scholarly aids produced by three centuries of Renaissance learning and by the medium of print.

Another novelty among the German professors was a certain self-consciousness, or (not Socratic but Herodotean) irony, setting the historian apart as inquirer and giving new meaning to the old classical commonplaces about the truth and beauty of history (the *ars historica*), which continued to be rehearsed, though with a modern and more reflective significance. History was still *magistra vitae*, but the overtones of this tired old formula were epistemological and political as well as moral.[42] "My métier is history" (*Historie*), the Göttingen scholar J. C. Gatterer confessed in 1772. "My position in the world, my point of view, is historical. No wonder I prefer to see nations from a historical standpoint; no wonder I treat my own nation from this historical standpoint."[43] Gatterer went on to lament the unscientific notion of the intruding self — "my" métier, "my" nation, etc. — but such egocentricity was an essential condition of historical understanding (*historische Erkenntnis*), as few earlier historians knew or were prepared to admit. On the lowest level this involved merely the recognition of the author's role in shaping historical narrative and of the limited horizons of authorship in general, but it also indicated more reflective searches for the meaning of human history — whether for earlier examples of enlightened civilization or larger patterns and "principles" of historical development.

The German art of history also prided itself on its critical acumen. Now when Kant called his age a century of criticism, he was honoring his own logical and radically rationalist system, but of course historical criticism was something else again, harking back as it did to the scholarly tradition of the *ars critica*, which incorporated techniques of textual exegesis and "conjectural" emendation, literary analysis, and historical interpretation.[44] A prime example of this was the "higher criticism" of the Bible, established by the Göttingen scholar J. G. Eichhorn and others.[45] The extreme model of historical criticism was historical pyrrhonism, which denied the possibility of certainty to scholarly investigation but which, in a more "mitigated" form, raised the standards of historical studies. As many scholars came to acknowledge, historical truth was not absolute. "The truths of history cannot easily be compared with those of natural scientists," F. W. Bierling wrote,[46] and so historians often had to be content with a high degree of probability (*probabilitas; Wahrscheinlichkeit*); for such were the conditions of historical inquiry and that special sort of understanding which German scholars called historical knowledge.

A more sophisticated associate of the *ars critica* was the newer scholarly tradition of hermeneutics (*ars hermeneutica*), which also emphasized not rational or logical but human understanding.[47] A hermeneutical standpoint, implied by the remark of Gatterer quoted earlier, achieved more theoretical formulation in the work of J. M. Chladenius, professor of theology at the University of Erlangen, who also lectured on the art of history. "It is one thing to understand a proposition in itself," he wrote, "and another to understand it as being presented and asserted by someone."[48] In the latter case one must consider not only the "prevailing conditions" but also the position of the observer (*Zuschauer*) and the undeniable fact that "different people perceive that which happens in the world differently," a principle which Chladenius termed "point of view" (*Sehe-Punkt*).[49] As Chladenius explained, "We shall designate the term 'viewpoint' to refer to those conditions governed by our mind, body, and entire person which make or cause us to perceive of something in one way and not another." As Goethe wrote, "We see the world in one way from a plain, another way from the heights of a promontory, another from the glacier fields of the primary mountains . . . , but we cannot say that we see more truly from any one than from another."[50] For historians the result was aesthetic as well as psychological, producing differences not only in perceptions of one event (*Begebenheit*) but also in larger historical judgments, as in Jacob Burckhardt's very personal portrayal of Renaissance culture. The result was that such diversity of impressions would produce an endless series of debates and that phenomenon called "revisionism." Chladenius himself believed that hermeneutics would allow one to overcome these problems, but history has — that is, historians have — judged otherwise.

There is another novelty in eighteenth-century historical thought that deserves notice; and that is what Michel de Certeau has called "heterology," which directs inquiry to the Other," or rather "Others," of Western civilization.[51] "The course of history does not show us the Becoming of things foreign us," declared Hegel, "but the Becoming of ourselves and of our knowledge."[52] This is the philosopher's "point of view," however; for in fact, since Herodotus, the course of historical inquiry has violated this parochial philosophy, which would restrict knowledge to the self and to Eurocentric culture, and has opened up horizons of the alien and the exotic, including the past itself, which is indeed a "foreign country," but has focused even more conspicuously on the

New World. This centrifugal curiosity joined forces with the art of criticism and hermeneutics to broaden and to deepen the Enlightenment sense of the remote in time and in space, although this awareness continued to be informed by traditional primitivism and rhetoric of alterity — of the "Other."[53]

As history clung to the ideal of truth in the face of skeptical attacks and theological inhibitions, so it preserved its claims to utility, not only educational and moral but also social, economic, and political. German universities were founded to serve the interests of the particular states, and so was the new science of history, like the other sciences of government. Church and imperial history were the most obviously utilitarian fields; but universal, cultural, and "philosophical" history also ministered to official needs instructing the administrative personnel of the states in the *Staatswissenschaften* as well as *Statistik*. The study of history provided not only legitimacy for national and local traditions but also political (as well as social and moral) lessons and was in this old Polybian sense "pragmatic," as indeed it continued to be in the nineteenth century.[54]

The major types of historical study in German universities included universal or world history (*historia universalis; Universalhistorie; Weltgeschichte*), ecclesiastical history (*Kirchengeschichte*), imperial history (*Reichsgeschichte* or *Reichs-Historie*), European, national, local history (*Landesgeschichte*), and cultural history (*Kulturgeschichte*). There were many textbooks in these areas — at least thirty (surviving) world histories, for example, published in the eighteenth century, many of them of an elementary (and even a catechistic question-and-answer) character. Another medium of historical learning was that of the popular and professional journals started in the eighteenth century — 4,321 of them, of which 642 (15 percent) treated historical topics, published sources, and book reviews. This scholarship came not only from universities but also from the academies and local antiquarian societies founded at this same time.[55] The first historical institute was J. C. Gatterer's Historical Society of Göttingen (*Academic Historica Goettingensis*), dedicated to "history, antiquity, and the sciences."[56] Another project of Gatterer's was ecclesiastical history, contributing in particular to the tradition of *Germania Sacra* (1752).[57]

The history of the empire — "Holy Roman Empire of the German Nation," as it had been called since the fifteenth century — derived from a medieval genre continued, in altered form, in the Reformation.[58] One early example was Johann Sleidan's survey of the *Four Monarchies*, reprinted and translated many times as a textbook of imperial history, but not until the late seventeenth century did this tradition find a central role in the process of modern state-building. "At the beginning of this century," wrote a critic in 1773, "German history was not being cultivated, and there were no textbooks, still less a system, from which one could work"; but this situation changed radically over the next generations. "Imperial history," wrote Nicholas Gundling in 1719, "is a pragmatic narrative based on the records of the laws of the Emperor and of the state, how they arose, changed, and are today." This field was distinguished from German history, according to Johann David Köhler (who occupied the first chair of history in Göttingen), because the latter "treats the German people from their origins, their inherited freedom, from and under the Romans and Franks, and their own kings down to the remarkable events of our own times," whereas *Reichs-Historie* covers only the last part of this story, concerned with the transformations of Germany, "in head and members," from the Franks down to the present sovereign empire (*Königsreich*).[59]

Parallel to the study of imperial history in the eighteenth century was that of church history, and as the former was tied to the burgeoning field of public law, so the latter was part of the old tradition of theology.[60] Ecclesiastical history derived most directly from Lutheran academic reforms, themselves part of a larger effort to revise traditional church history in the light of evangelical religion. Through Melanchthon's reformation of the universities of the Lutheran territories, chairs of history were established at Marburg (1529), Tübingen (1530), Strasbourg (1544), and elsewhere, including Greifswald, Königsberg, Heidelberg, Rostok, and Jena. These professorships were devoted to classical but increasingly to ecclesiastical history, because "the profession of history [*opus historiae*] is above all in the church," as Melanchthon wrote in his preface to the *Chronicle* of Johann Cario (1530), which (in Melanchthon's revised version) became a standard textbook of history for Lutheran schools.[61]

In the eighteenth century the Protestant tradition of church history continued to flourish, still apologetic and anti-Catholic in character, yet at the same time dedicated to impartiality and truth. What was new was the effort to accommodate the Lutheran standpoint to standards of critical scholarship and enlightened reason and — in the spirit of Richard Simon, Spinoza, Reimarus, and the scriptural "neologists" of the Enlightenment — ideas of continuous human progress behind the "grand design of God."[62] The most distinguished practitioner of the new church history was the theologian Johann Lorenz von Mosheim, chancellor of the University of Göttingen, student of Leibniz, and "the Erasmus of the eighteenth century,"[63] whose *Ecclesiastical Institutes* (1737–41) traced both the "internal" and the "external" history of the Church, emphasizing the corruption of the Romanist tradition.[64] Although the Reformation appears as the turning point of modern history, Mosheim shows little interest in the theological issues behind the Lutheran schism; yet like Luther, Melanchthon, Flacius, and Arnold, he insisted, in opposition to both Pietism and defenders of Hellenistic influence, on the continuity between the primitive *ecclesia* and the modern Lutheran *Kirch* and hence on the legitimacy of the latter.

In the work of Mosheim and even more in that of Johann Salomo Semler, professor of theology at the University of Halle and teacher of Eichhorn, the "historicizing" of Christian religion becomes conspicuous, as both the institutional and the doctrinal dimensions of Christian worship came under examination and as the rational and enlightened tendencies of modern religious faith superseded arguments from tradition and an idealized "primitive church." Like so many secular historians at that time, Semler had a sense both of irreversible historical change and of the particularity of the Lutheran "point of view," but he hoped to escape the relativism implied by these modern insights through a critical understanding of the past. "Semler hoped to find deliverance in the historical enterprise," writes a contemporary scholar, and he was by no means alone in these devotional hopes.[65] Increasingly history was applied to for convincing and continuous "evidences" of Christianity — to the distress of more dogmatic or fundamentalist students of religion. Increasingly the history of religion and of dogma became a specialized field of research, tied still to biblical studies. The eighteenth-century school of scriptural exegesis pushed humanist criticism to a further extreme, accepting the premise that the Bible was the work of human authors and not of the Holy Ghost, which was the implication of the scholarship of Richard Simon, Reimarus, and others; and the upshot was a turn to philological and historical criticism in the form of hermeneutics, Eichhorn's "higher criticism," and the later mythological interpretation of David Friedrich Strauss. From this neohumanist, or Neologist, standpoint the old biblical chronology underwent revisions, as in the work of Schlözer, who also broadened the horizons of scholarship by his studies of Swedish and Russian history.[66] General historical scholarship, however, made a much more radical turn — away from the scriptural framework altogether and toward natural history, so that the question of origins came to be linked not with the fall from grace and expulsion from paradise but with the transition from a state of nature to a state of culture. The state of nature was mythical, too, but the new prehistorical disciplines of archeology and mythology suggested ways of historicizing even this hypothesis of moral and political philosophy.

But the dominant form of historical writing in the eighteenth century was universal history, a genre which was changing as fast as the horizons of the world and of the past. In a period of state-building and nation-inventing universal history was not universalist but rather national, especially in its late phases, following the fortunes of the various peoples who emerged in the wake of the Roman hegemony and who were granted recognition in the grand narrative of Western political competition and cultural development. With respect to this increasingly secularized continuation of the Polybio-Eusebian enterprise one may well, paraphrasing Carl Becker, speak of the "heavenly city of the eighteenth-century historiographers." In any case it was in this context that both the science of history and the philosophy of history assumed their modern forms.

Universal History

From the earliest creation myths to the most recent Western civilization textbooks, world history has been a popular field of study. To begin with, this field covered only a small part of our globe, but by the eighteenth century it had become a truly universal "world of nations," in Vico's phrase. The law of nations (*jus gentium*) originally referred to the *gentes* brought into the Roman Empire, but the "new law of nations" of medieval and early modern times accommodated many new peoples, and in the fifteenth century the discovery of the New World opened the door, in principle, to the rest of the world's population.[67] Temporal horizons were likewise expanded, and by the eighteenth century the biblical framework had been undermined by investigations into the human and the terrestrial past.[68] The written record of this past, which was gathered into the treasuries of "literary history" (*historia literaria, Literaturgeschichte*), was also universal in its reach, necessarily including not only the wisdom but also the myths and errors accumulated by human experience, memory, imagination, hopes, and duplicity.[69]

The career of universal history (*historia universalis; Weltgeschichte; Universalhistorie*) goes back to the Christian world-chronicle tradition of Eusebius and his medieval and Reformation epigones, including Sleidan and Conrad Cellarius, who established the ancient-medieval-modern periodization of Western history.[70] In Germany this genre was continued by Lutheran scholars, most notably in the succession of universal histories produced by professors at Göttingen, including Gatterer, Meiners, Schlözer, Schlosser, and Eichhorn, but also many lesser authors.[71] The world histories published by such scholars ranged from small textbooks to multivolume narratives, such as the translation by Baumgarten of the cooperative English universal history published in thirty-eight volumes (1736–65), on which Gatterer, Heeren, and Schlözer also worked. Earlier surveys were little more than chronological lists of rulers, according to the advertisement, while this work, "methodized" in the 1779 edition, "render[s] a system of History, hitherto unequalled in extent of useful information, and agreeable entertainment."[72] This new *Universal History* was based on "the most authentic documents of every nation," and moreover, "the clashing prejudices of the historians of different countries have been minutely examined, and their several degrees of credit scrupulously ascertained." Forgeries and fictions, partisanship and contradictions, and the loss of early accounts — except for that of the Jews — made the project more difficult; but adherence to the biblical story offered a sure path to historical truth.

One of the most curious early contributions to this genre was P. L. Berkenmeyer's *Poetical Introduction to Universal History,* covering the period from Creation to the Flood in mnemonic verse:

> Shem stayed in Asia. Ham went to Canaan.
> Japeth went on to settle Europe.
> What the Greek king Philip just began,
> Alexander went on to finish the plan.[73]

Johann Colmar's *World in a Nutshell* (1730) ordered the materials of world history according to a catechistic question-and-answer method, including derivative summaries on an elementary level.[74] In the early nineteenth century, for example in Eichhorn's *World History,* the general pattern remained much the same, except for scholarly amplification and efforts to show how history displayed, in Eichhorn's words, "unbroken, progressive development."[75]

Historical events occur in time and space, and so chronology and geography constituted the original auxiliary sciences. Histories of the New World discoveries and of colonization in particular insisted on the primary importance of the geographical and natural setting, and Montesquieu's more theoretical emphasis on factors of climate reinforced this tendency. Universal history in the Enlightenment continued to be Eurocentric, but the ever-expanding "new horizons" of the Renaissance (and the no less remarkable "oriental renaissance" of the eighteenth century) and experience and fascination with the exotic "Other" changed the assumptions as well as the orientation of historians.[76] This is especially the case with scholars like Christoph Meiners, who drew on travel reports as sources for the history of primitive and non-European societies — and indeed used them also for reflections on comparative history.[77]

If discoveries in both heaven and earth changed notions about the world of nations, the temporal dimension was less open to historical revision. In eighteenth-century Europe the time span of human existence was still defined by the Bible and the B.C.–A.D. convention which had been fixed by Bede.[78] The Christian era was divided by the ancient-medieval-modern convention created by humanists and formalized in the seventeenth century by Conrad Cellarius, and subdivided into centuries, or ages, marked by significant phenomena.[79]

One example is Hieronymus Freyer's introduction to universal history, which labeled each century (*seculum*) from the first to the eighteenth according to certain important political and religious features: 1. Augusto-Apostolicum; 2. Antoniano-Gnosticum; 3. Tyrannico-Novatianum; 4. Constantino-Arianum; 5. Migratorio-Nestorianum; 6. Gothico-Eutychianum; 7. Longobardico-Mohamedanum; 8. Francico-Iconiclasticum; 9. Carolino-Photianum; 10. Ottomano-Obscurum; 11. Henriciano-Hildebrandinum; 12. Suevico-Waldense; 13. Interregio-Scholasticum; 14. Electorali-Wiclefianum; 15. Fridericiano-Hussiticum; 16. Ferdinandino-Reformatum; 17. Leopoldino-Rixosum; and 18. Regio-Unitivum.[80]

Until the later eighteenth century, despite growing evidence about the "antiquity of man" as well as his earthly residence, universal history was generally locked into the biblical chronology as calibrated by J. J. Scaliger, Archbishop Ussher, and other pious scholars, Protestant, Catholic, and Jewish.[81] About the question of the age of the world, historians were literally of two minds; and Vico, for example, resolved the dilemma by limiting his inquiries to the gentile nations, leaving sacred history as an exception to the rule of his new science. In his handbook of 1792, Gatterer divided universal history into an "obscure" and a "historical" period (*tempus obscurum, tempus historicum*), the first — "prehistorical," it would later be termed — being an age of superstition and fable (*fabulosum; Sagengeschichte*) and speculation, the second, of human knowledge and historical truth (*fides historica*).[82] Like philologists and lawyers, historians were inclined to identify truth with written records and to limit history to scribal culture, for which the auxiliary sciences of diplomatics and paleography were essential. An exception to this was to be found in what George Kubler has called the "history of things," which forms the subject matter of other disciplines created by Renaissance scholarship, including epigraphy, numismatics, sphragistics, art history, and especially archeology, which was already making important, if unheralded, breakthroughs in "prehistory."[83]

But of course there were minority opinions about a longer history of the human race; and classical authors like Lucretius had speculated about primitive stages of humanity. The idea of pre-Adamite civilization, or cultures descended from "another Adam," inspired research into and speculation about prehistory, which were further encouraged by curiosity about humanity in its "state of nature."[84] The Social Compact may have been a fiction; but the notion that mankind had somehow made a transition from an animal to a human, that is, from a natural to a cultural condition, became a basis for conceptualizing universal history, beginning especially in the last third of the eighteenth century. By this time evidence from geology and paleontology was piling up to cast doubts on the biblical framework of history as fixed by Christian doctrine. Schlözer, for example, went beyond his predecessor Gatterer by admitting the evidence of natural history and geology concerning the extreme antiquity of the earth, though at the same time denying its relevance to critical history. However, A. A. Rhode, in a treatise on the excavation of burials, had already declared that such archeological finds were superior to such literary sources as Tacitus's *Germania;* and this was in accord with the spirit, if not the letter, of historical method, which likewise requires legible or tangible evidence for conclusions.[85]

Universal history continued to be taught and written in the nineteenth century, as illustrated by the lectures given by Schlegel in Paris in 1805–6, which took the story of humanity from natural and poetic origins down to the age of philosophy.[86] "History," he wrote, "is itself a true philosophy, the most essential link in that beautiful chain, which encompasses man's higher intellectual culture."[87] Yet Schlegel (recently converted to Catholicism) had no patience with the dogmatic and ungrounded "laws," false "epochs," and historical "metaphysics" derived by Condorcet from the logical and systematist prejudices of the Revolution, which neglected the disparities of intellectual and moral progress as well as the inertial force of evolution beneath human will.[88] For Schlegel, language was the key to the cultural process, and here he introduced the novelty of Indian origins, associated with his Sanskrit studies (following the lead of William Jones), on which he would publish his own manifesto two years later. The Germanic tribes originated in India, and even Africa began as an Indian colony, declared Schlegel, who went on to identify the first Indian hero, Manu, with Minos and Noah. Indian "influence" could be traced also in Egypt, Greece, Rome, Persia, Germany, China, and Japan. This line of research was intended to throw light on the obscurity of the Greco-Roman past in particular; for true history began only in the time of the Persian wars, with Herodotus, as "external history," in the form of international combat, was succeeded by the "internal history" of civil conflict. So Schlegel narrowed his focus back to the conventional European and German-imperial line, although he broadened the Eusebian framework in its prehistorical aspects.

One of the most popular world histories was that of Karl von Rotteck, who taught world history at Freiburg from 1798. His *General History,* which began to appear in 1812, was represented as a "pragmatic philosophical history" and a contribution to the "philosophy of history," eighteenth-century style. Rotteck, who supported the Revolution but turned against Napoleon, drew on the work of Herder and Meiners as well as the French philosophes in his opposition to despots like Alexander and Caesar and in his defense of constitutional liberty over the centuries. Rotteck distinguished the history of the world, which had a sort of chronological unity, from the history of mankind, which did not, since it rested on a wide range of changes and causes from a human standpoint. The chronological frame in any case was the old division of history "ancient" (Adam to the great migrations of the fifth century), "middle" (to the discovery of the two Indies), and "modern" (the three centuries since the discovery of America).[89] It was in the last, wrote Rotteck, marveling at the revolutions produced by human effort, that the hand of man transformed a "dismal wilderness" into "a blooming garden."[90] As he concluded, "The materials of the history of the world are, therefore, *art and science, religion and the constitution of states, morality and manner of life.*" The book went through twenty-five editions during the nineteenth century. Rotteck was also coeditor of the extraordinarily influential *Staatslexicon* (three editions, 1834–66), which promoted the liberal nationalism of the pre-1848 period.[91] Other surveys took a wider view of the "world," as in the case of Pölitz's handbook, published in 1805 and later editions, which treated the ages of myth (*Mythenalter*) before "the beginning of history" and which referred to the works not only of Niebuhr but also of Jones, Schlegel, and the Rosetta Stone before the decipherment by Champollion.[92] These works also disseminated the Enlightenment concept of culture, which was conscripted into the service of the state as well as put to use by historians.

The First Cultural History

Universal history was moving beyond the dated conventions of strict biblical chronology, the Four World Monarchies, and the Translation of Empire, and was also trying, in competition with philosophy, to be "systematic." Yet there was another, more modern approach to comprehensive historical understanding, which was based on the concept of culture and the resources of ethnology as ways of attaining a global view of humanity and its past. Among the pioneers of this culturalist approach was the Swiss historian Isaac Iselin, member of a "Society of Friends of Truth and Goodness," whose *Geschichte der Menschheit* (1764), directed in particular against Rousseau's idealization of the state of nature, celebrated the liberties of the German, Swiss, and English peoples and the progress of European civilization toward "pure reason" (*reine Vernunft*).[93] Iselin's work followed the pattern of biography, tracing the life of humanity from childhood to maturity. Yet, he noted, there was a major difference between humanity according to philosophers and humanity according to writers of history (*Geschichtschreiber*), the first being content with simple individual psychology, while historians had to confront the great diversity of human forms and the multitude of historical sources, including modern travel reports. Referring to Bodin and Machiavelli as well as to ancient authors, Iselin emphasized environment in the "revolutions" that humanity had passed through since emerging from the state of nature.

Among the first to signal this culturalist turn was William Robertson, who abandoned the spiritualist view of human creativity and argued that the capacity of human improvement beyond the natural state "depends entirely upon the state of society in which he is placed. To this state the human mind naturally accommodates itself, and from it receives its discipline and culture."[94] This passage was cited by another pioneering cultural historian, Karl von Irwing, who was among the first to adopt (in 1779) the terminology and conceptualization of "culture," a term derived from the Latin *cultura,* meaning the cultivation and mastery of material or spiritual activities. For Irwing, "Culture is the whole accumulation of improvements and increases . . . or sum of perfections to which man, from his rude condition, can raise himself." He posited a series of evolutionary stages from the state of nature to mature civilization, expressed most fully in the nation-state and the arts and sciences necessary for this institution.[95] The cultural value of the nation was fully appreciated by universal historians, as illustrated by C. D. Beck's introductory text (1787), which shifted the focus of "pragmatic history" from the world to national history (*Völkersgeschichte*).[96]

In late-eighteenth-century Germany "culture" (*Kultur*) came to replace "spirit" as a way of expressing the character of human society.[97] After Irwing, this usage was followed by J. C. Adelung (1782), J. G. Herder (1784), J. G. Wiggers (1784), C. D. Beck (1787), D. H. Hegewisch (1788), Karl von Pölitz (1795), J. G. Eichhorn (1796), Friedrich Maier (1798), Daniel Jenisch (1800), Friedrich Schlegel (1805), and others, as *Kulturgeschichte* emerged as a genre and even a discipline in the nineteenth century.[98] A similar terminological choice appeared also in Italy, where Juan Andres's "Origin, Progresses, and Present State of All Literature" (1782) introduced the terminology of "culture" (*coltura*) to express the conditions of human achievements preserved in writing.[99] The advantage of this culturalist vocabulary was that it encompassed not merely the static reason of high philosophical culture but its dynamic historical development, which alone made possible an answer to the question, not just "What is enlightenment?" but, "What is humanity?" and a critique of its rational state. As Pölitz argued in his "critical" history of humanity, "Cultural history confirms a posteriori what reason tries to establish a priori on the basis of a correct knowledge of human powers and abilities."[100] Unlike "reason" or "spirit," moreover, "culture" suggested the richness and variety, the contexts and the contingencies, of human experience in its temporal condition. This suggested, too, the wider context (*Umwelt*), the effects of outside "influences"

(*Einflüsse*, a key term in culturalist analysis), and the significance of local knowledge or reason (*Lokalvernunft* is an eighteenth-century coinage); and it was applicable to alien forms of society and thought — barbarism, exoticism, and myth — not shared by, or perhaps even commensurable with, modern Western rationality as a unified and immutable phenomenon.

In the most general terms the shift from universal to cultural history marks the movement from the grand design of God to human self-creation — from theodicy to anthropodicy. This is clear in the work of Daniel Jenisch, who was the first to formulate explicitly "a philosophy of cultural history" (1801). He began his work by discussing "anthropology"; but unlike Kant and Iselin, who were devoted to an idealist "theodicy" of reason, his purpose was to emphasize human history not as the progress of reason but as a conflict of instincts — not "What is Enlightenment?" but "What is Culture?"[101] Jenisch's answer is neither Rousseauean pessimism nor Kantian optimism; it is tempered and tragic, or tragico-comic, and best expressed in the "title-motto," drawn from Pope, representing man in terms not of his rational ideal but of his mixed historical record — "the glory, jest, and riddle of his world." Situated in "this Isthmus of a middle state," man is "a beeing [*sic*] darkly wise, and rudely great." "The animal is a creature of learning" (*ein Gelehrter*), he declared; "the human is being a genius with extraordinary capacities but no fixed knowledge or ready-made abilities." Humanity needed many generations to produce its Newtons, Leibnizes, Franklins, and Fredericks (the Great); and reason and perfectibility (*Perfektabilität; Vollkommung*) are properties only of the entire species, so that the "philosophy" emerging in the Enlightenment was the product not merely of individual genius but of "the collective wisdom of the thinkers of many centuries," who lived in former times on this little "earthball."[102]

Other cultural historians followed this historicist line. Like Kant, Meiners confronted the question of enlightenment, but for him "true enlightenment" was to be understood in the light not of pure reason but rather of the universal history of humanity and its culture.[103] For Meiners, "true Enlightenment" began not with rationalists like Descartes but with critics of traditional philosophy — in effect popular philosophers — like Petrarch, Erasmus, and Luther. Unlike the self-proclaimed critical philosophers, Meiners believed that the "history of the human spirit" and the accompanying "revolutions" in knowledge were not merely philosophical but were more fundamentally political, social, cultural questions, and that attention had to be paid to the external conditions of intellectual progress. Meiners did not ignore material culture — housing, clothing, decorative arts — but most important were the human spirit, understanding, and especially language and the use or abuse of these.[104]

Old-fashioned scholars were sometimes skeptical of the new *Kulturge-*

schichte, as for example was A. H. L. Heeren, an admirer of Montesquieu, in his critical review of K. H. L. Pölitz's *Outlines of Pragmatic World History* (1795).[105] The problem was that this historical study of the culture of humanity represented idealistic, "egoistic," and "reasoned history" (*Raisonnement über Geschichte*), like that of Kant a decade earlier, rather than empirical research; and as Heeren argued, "Without historical sources one cannot learn historical criticism." But of course cultural history drew on different sources than the conventional art of history, including especially travel literature, and this operated also to transform the modern study of history.

In 1796, J. G. Eichhorn published a study of modern European culture and literature which tried to raise history above the level of particular sciences to a more general level by joining *Kulturgeschichte* with *Literaturgeschichte.* According to Eichhorn:

> The history of arts and sciences, their origins, progress, and various transformations can never be separated from the history of the social conditions, for culture and literature are twin sisters, children of the same father, who continually provide support for each other. Culture, the first-born, prepares the birth of her younger sister, and thereafter they live and work together, inseparable and unseparated, and also die together. Without the history of one the life of the other is incomplete and incomprehensible.[106]

Eichhorn admitted that modern scientific culture (*Cultur der Naturwissenschaften*) dated only from the end of the Thirty Years War; but his main interest was in the earlier roots, and in this connection he focused less on internal, reasoned history than on the external conditions of culture (*Culturzustände*).

In explaining the emergence from medieval *Barbarey,* for example, Eichhorn laid special emphasis on the development of liberties in the medieval parliaments and in the Italian and German cities. "With this new beginning of culture," he remarked about these political phenomena, "there also began in Europe a new literary culture" — referring especially to Dante, Petrarch, and Boccaccio, but also to the liberating force of Lutheranism. He included philosophy and the sciences as well as the scholarship of the "humanists" and the "critical-historical spirit" which they had brought to literature. This "scientific" spirit reached its highest point in the Göttingen school, of which Eichhorn, too, was a distinguished member — and which was the center of modern German *Geschichtswissenschaft* before the founding of the University of Berlin in 1807 and the emergence of Leopold von Ranke and his more celebrated school.[107]

I have oversimplified and perhaps overdramatized this part of the story, since cultural history was of coursed practiced *ante litteram* — not only by men of letters like Turgot, Voltaire, Robertson, Goguet, and Condorcet but also by more conventional writers of universal history textbooks.[108] For Baumgarten, "historical knowledge" encompassed not only war and politics but also learning and the practical and fine arts; other universal historians recommended the study of laws, customs, and other human creations; and Hausen's "theory of history" required attention to manners, arts, sciences, laws, and constitutions.[109] This was the view also of students of the "history of humanity," from Iselin to C. A. Walckenaer, whose *Essay on the History of the Human Race* (1798) attempted to trace the progress of humanity from its natural to its civilized state. But such aims became more explicit, systematic, and philosophical, and in a sense more "scientific" in the emerging discipline of *Kulturgeschichte* and of discoveries about the antiquity of humanity.[110]

In the later eighteenth century, cultural histories began not merely with geographical background, a practice that goes back to antiquity, but also with astronomy, geology, and natural history. For Irwing nature was the first of four "grades" of culture, marked only by (1) self-awareness, to be followed by (2) the social stage, (3) the beginning of laws and property, and (4) the emergence of the nation, accompanied by industry, commerce, the arts and sciences, and finally the abstract knowledge of philosophy.[111] This was the "course of culture" (*Gang der Kultur*), as he and Herder called it, reinforced in its later stages by education (*Bildung*) and the wider public (*Publikum*) made possible by printing. Herder began his great survey by scanning, with the help of Buffon and Linnaeus, the "book of the universe" and the biological sphere populated by the animals — "the elder brethren of man" — which man surpassed by standing on two legs, looking up at the stars in wonder, and uttering sounds that were the making of intelligible speech. Thus Herder's "historicism" was supported by a naive evolutionism which, at least implicitly and potentially, replaced the rival, still prevailing biblical story. Cultural history has had an extraordinary *fortuna* since the time of von Irwing, Adelung, and Herder. The subsequent growth of cultural history in Germany was striking — at least twenty titles with the term "culture" appearing before 1800, fifty by 1820, one hundred by 1865, and the rate of publication increased thereafter in the heyday of *Kulturgeschichte*.[112] The topics of these publications were global and local, ancient and modern, general and special (including cultural histories of literature, medicine, commerce, and so on), and often designed for a general rather than merely a learned readership. Cultural history was promoted by university courses (given by at least eighteen professors in fourteen universities) and at least forty-four historical societies devoted to national cultural history and antiquities, attracting the participation not only of scholars but also of journalists, librarians, curators, lower-school teachers, doctors, lawyers, and even shopkeepers. Before mid-century, cultural history had indeed become part of a wider "popular culture" and — through university lectures, articles, monographs, textbooks, luxuriously illustrated volumes, museum collections, and the founding of its own specialized journal[113] — both a literary genre and a scholarly discipline. This was the context of the next, more invidious and political, and yet at the same time more scientific, stage of *Kulturgeschichte*.[114]

History between Research and Reason

Positive history describes, the philosophy of history demonstrates.
— *Giuseppe Ferrari*

Revolutionary Perspectives

French scholars took a quite different view of enlightenment (*lumière*, singular or plural). Theirs was more detached from religious concerns and closer to rationalism in the style of Descartes and Condillac, though with a later injection of Baconian, Newtonian, and Lockean ideas. They were also more confident of their cultural superiority, in keeping with the *petitio principii* that served as the prize topic set by the Academy of Berlin in 1777: "What has made the French language universal?"[1] Certainly French historians were more impressed with the arguments of skepticism, more excited by the old quarrel of ancients and moderns, and more attached to literary qualities in their historical writing; and moreover they had a coherent national tradition with its own set of constraints and conventions. They were also caught up in the more pressing issues of a crisis-ridden government soon to be overturned by a Revolution that subverted, along with society, many of these old premises and habits, at least for a generation. In all these contexts the question of history arose in one form or another, as problem or as solution. In the wake of the political ruptures and surrounding controversies, national traditions of scholarship, subverted or diverted for a generation between the fallen and the restored monarchy ("in the nineteenth year of the reign of Louis XVIII") emerged after 1815, and scholars set about restoring historical continuities, or at least finding a new sense of history, after old verities had ostensibly been lost.

France in the Old Regime was possessed by a sense of history; in the Restoration it was repossessed by it; and in between, history was the cynosure or target of all parties — whether to worship, escape from, control, or remake entirely. Ancients, Moderns, Royalists, republicans, revolutionaries, and Bonapartists alike wanted history, as well as God, to be on their side; and the history of Western history must be seen in the light, and felt in the heat, of these conceptions and hopes.[2] Yet the old but updated canons of scholarship continued in place, with history contrasted fundamentally with novels, and the work of "learned compilers" like Mabillon, Leibniz, Muratori, and Rymer added to narrative historians and chronologists;[3] and of course the requirements of religion, still the guarantor of spiritual continuity and the ideological concomitant of the monarchy and the nobility, continued to be served.

Religion was the surrogate of culture and the last resort of historical trust: "It is from history that the majority of religious opinions are derived," declared the Idéologue and reputed atheist C. F. Volney, so that "where religion is false, most of the actions and judgments based on it are also false and fail with it." Yet at the same time: "It is also from history that are derived most of the principles that guide, overturn, or consolidate governments."[4] This was the twofold wisdom offered by a leading revolutionary to the students in his course on history given at the short-lived Ecole Normale in the third year of the new calendar (1795). History was both the disease and, properly understood, the remedy — both a record of the crimes and errors of humanity, as Bayle, Voltaire, Gibbon, and other philosophes believed, and also the "mistress of life," as on similar exemplaristic grounds classical authors had taught. But there was a difference: for Cicero history had been a site of ancestor worship and a source of moral wisdom; for Volney and the Idéologues it was the basis of a "social science" (Hélvetius's phrase was *la science de la morale*) and legislative action — as well as veneration paid to certain selected ancestors.

In France during the Enlightenment, historical theory and practice was torn between several pairs of extremes, including: reason and research, doubt and certitude, impartiality and partisanship, nostalgia and utility, the local and the global, the nation and the larger world, literary art and social science, unfocused pedantry and lofty speculation, sin and salvation, theodicy and anthropodicy. In this it was not unlike the historiography in other parts of

Europe, but French historical inquiry had developed its own national style, and moreover it was uniquely shaped by the unprecedented historical experiences of a regime-toppling, society-shattering, and nation-creating Revolution, which called for reflection beyond the old categories of the art of history — and then by an overreaching empire presumptuously looking back to ancient and medieval imperial precedents. Behind these events notions of the "social," as distinguished from more clear-cut and reductionist views of politics and economics, and of the nation, as distinct from the regime and its institutions, conditioned historical interpretations of the age of democratic revolution. In other words the "People" took their place on the public stage recognized by historical writers.

By 1789, France had a long and rich tradition of historical studies. Medieval chronicles had been transformed under the influence of humanist scholarship and classical style into polished and didactic literary narrative, Latin and vernacular, and historical perspective had invaded other arts and sciences. Conventional national historical writing was tied especially to the charge of royal historiographer, a post which continued down to the Revolution and was revived in the Restoration, though with few distinguished occupants in the eighteenth century aside from Voltaire and Moreau; and in numbers the *historiographes* declined to nineteen from eighty-two in the seventeenth century.[5] As for its place in education during the Old Regime, history did not figure significantly except, following classical and humanist precedent, in support of literature and moral philosophy, as in a chair devoted to "histoire et morale" founded in the Collège de France in 1775.[6] Yet national histories continued to be issued on a grand scale, especially the thirty-volume survey of Velly, Villaret, and Garnier (1755–86), written "à la Pompadour," and the fourteen-volume pandect by L. P. Anquetil (1805), which replaced the popular publications of Mézeray and Daniel and which was often reprinted in the nineteenth century. Both Garnier and Anquetil carried their work over into the Class of Moral and Political Sciences established during the Directory in 1795. Even into this tired old genre enlightened views penetrated; and Velly, while emphasizing the value of history for statesmen, nonetheless — in what amounts to a historiographical topos — lamented the habits of his predecessors, with their "long descriptions of sieges and battles without mention of manners and the spirit of the nation."[7]

In the wake of the Revolution, history gained in prestige and moved nearer to the center of school and university curricula. Historical writing was also shaped by the agendas and enthusiasms of political parties, and virtually every author promised to reveal causes, underlying and immediate, obvious and "secret," and to demonstrate the meaning of the turning point of 1788–89 and the upheavals and reversals of the 1790s. In the fifth — the historical — section of the Class of Moral and Political Sciences of the Institute, the members were expected to teach and to write in the interests of the state, whatever condition it might be in. Yet Institute historians, who between 1795 and 1803 wrote memoirs and responded to prize questions in a wide range of subjects, also preserved interests in cultural history, and at least four of them planned a work which would elaborate Condorcet's progressivist vision.[8] If history could not be mastered, it could at least be appropriated for the benefit of the masters.

Under Napoleon, history seemed to thrive; by 1811 there were twenty-five chairs of history in the academies of the Napoleonic University, and others were added with the expansion of the empire. In alliance with "social science," however, history seemed ideologically threatening, and in the Bonapartist reorganization of 1803 the Class was suppressed, with history resurfacing in diluted form in the National Institute as the Class of History and Ancient Literature (for Napoleon history was not a "science" but an "art"). Idéologue influence, despised by Napoleon, did not prevent a conservative turn against radical and democratic doctrines, culminating in Anquetil's counterrevolutionary universal history (1801) and his French history (1805), in which he lamented even the abolishment of feudalism on the night of 4 August 1789, and in which he promoted the conspiracy theory of revolutionary origins maintained by Barruel and others. So in the First Empire historiography not only hewed to the official line but also reverted to old regime conventions, as apparent in the report of Bon-Joseph Dacier, former perpetual secretary of the Academy of Inscriptions, on the state of French historical studies in 1810.[9] This was in contrast to Germany, where the innovative work of Friedrich Wolf and Friedrich Creuzer was changing the face of historical scholarship, as reported by Charles de Villers, an émigré who, with Mme de Staël and other members of the exile Coppet group, served as an ominous and unwelcome promoter of German ideas and culture.[10]

Quantitatively the amount of publication on the level of general and textbook history was extraordinary, especially considering that these are the sort of materials not likely to survive in quantity. The *Catalogue de l'Histoire de France* (shelf-list of the Imperial Library in Paris in the nineteenth century), after chronological listings (from the incunabular age) of geographical and chronological surveys as well as "la philosophie de l'histoire de France," lists more than 150 general histories of France, many in multiple editions, down to 1815 and more than 70 "elementary histories" (more than 250 down to 1850), not to mention more than a dozen histories in verse.[11] To these must also be added geographic descriptions (some also in verse), statistical collections (beginning in the 1790s), chronologies, works on "the philosophy of history of France," histories of the provinces, cities, and chateaux, histories of particular institutions, disciplines, periods, and foreign countries, and biographies, many of them in translation.[12] The quantity, if not the quality, continued to increase under Napoleon, rising (from 1811 to 1825) from less than a fifth of all intellectual output to almost a third. Also increasing, of course, were the old practices of censorship, but the Restoration historians, many with political or journalistic backgrounds, made this a fighting issue.

The extraordinary mixing of the old and the new, the conventional and the critical, may be seen in the work of a professor of history at the military school in Fontainebleau. Chantereau's *Science of History* (1803), dedicated "à Bonaparte," presented a systematic set of chronologies and "tableaux synoptiques," which employed the work of the Académie des Inscriptions and Gibbon while at the same time preserving the biblical framework — creation in 4004 B.C. and all that (relying on the famous universal history assembled by a team of pious English scholars) — down to the fifth epoch, which began in 1789 and ended with the Treaty of Amiens.[13] Chantereau followed the dichotomizing "method" of Ramus and Bodin (the latter being invoked specifically in this connection) but also recommended the principles of Condillac's "art of conjecture in the matter of history." History was primarily for the benefit of *guerriers* and *hommes d'état,* Chantereau declared, and *Héros-Magistrats* like the First Consul had first call on the attention of historians. In general the book consisted of parallel columns aligning dates, "principal facts," and "historical sources," although he also, according to contemporary fashion, treated, in hierarchical fashion, notable individuals, authors, and achievements in the arts and sciences.

The persistence of the myths of monarchy and empire may be seen in the many-faceted image of Charlemagne, whose legend lay at the root of so many fictions and forgeries throughout the medieval and early modern periods. The author (according to Mably) of the first great "revolution" in French history,[14] Charlemagne was at once hero and barbarian, the source of absolutism and Germanic liberties, the restorer of empire and the model of constitutional monarchy. For Voltaire and Dubos he was an example of medieval violence and usurpation; for Germanists like Montesquieu he was an ideal ruler: "The prince was great, the man greater."[15] Charlemagne was seminal in the fictitious, legal continuity that allowed historians as well as jurists to project political and even national continuity back over three "races" of kings, and to select useful examples from the millennium of experience that was thus encompassed. Napoleon himself preferred classical and Byzantine models (especially Justinian) but was not above associating himself with Carolingian tradition by taking his imperial crown in his own hands from the pope, as imperialist legend had Charlemagne doing also, thus illustrating the divine origin of sovereignty — which in the Revolution devolved upon the nation and passed thence to Napoleon.

This was popular history, but more serious erudition also survived the institutional hiatus of the Revolution. The scholarly projects of the academies and monastic centers, which collected and published a large volume of historiographical documentary, were resumed in the nineteenth and twentieth centuries, most prominently the *Gallia Christiana* (1715–1920), *Ordonnances des rois de France de la IIIe race* (1723–1849), *Histoire littéraire de la France* (1733–1915), Sainte Palaye and Bréquigny's *Table chronologique des diplômes, chartes, titres, et actes imprimés concernant l'histoire de France* (1736–76; 1836–76), Dom Clement's *L'Art de vérifier les dates* (1750 and 1818), and what David Knowles called "the grandmother of all the great national collections," Bouquet's *Rerum gallicarum et francicarum scriptores* (1737–86), as well as critical listings of manuscript sources.[16] A similar conspicuous illustration of scholarly continuity in the face of ideological and institutional change was the lawyers' handbook, *Profession d'avocat*, which was a collection of canonical texts and essential bibliography of legal, institutional, and political history — in effect the shelf-list of the Library of the Order of Advocats, which was scattered during the Revolution. This book was published in 1780 by A. G. Camus, first director of the national archives, and — after the revolutionary suppression and Napoleonic revival of the Order — in amplified form in the Restoration by André Dupin.[17]

The institution that perhaps best illustrates the complex process of revolutionary change — an ostensible break with a hated regime, yet intractable ties with a glorious national past — is the national archives, which represented the entire institutional heritage of the monarchy, and yet was a creation, most directly, of the Revolution.[18] The archives were indeed "places of memory," and as such were vehicles of continuity reflecting the pathology of social tradition as well as the enduring strength of government. In France the archives dated back at least to the thirteenth century, and soon thereafter began a series of official (but largely ineffective) efforts to organize — "reform" — governmental records for practical legal purposes, "proofs" for various dynastic, territorial, and fiscal claims, including especially the work of Jean Du Tillet.[19] From that time, too, historical research was equally a beneficiary of archival labors, and it was commonplace for historians, long before Ranke, to privilege this sort of official, legalistic material.

By the eighteenth century these records had accumulated beyond the management of individual scholars, and networks of érudits — J. N. Moreau, H. L. J. B. Bertin, J. B. de la Curne de Saint-Palaye, L. G. de Bréquigny, and others.[20] In 1759, Moreau (royal historiographer from 1774), invoking the great tradition of French historians going back to Du Tillet, initiated a great project to organize and to centralize the public, private, and foreign archival sources of France — and more generally the "ancient monuments of history" discovered since the "renaissance of letters" — for purposes both scholarly and legal. In connection with this "ideological arsenal," as Keith Baker calls it, came efforts to formulate critical methods for studying and publishing medieval manuscripts.[21] His creation, the Cabinet des Chartes (or *Bibliothèque de Législation*), became associated with other major scholarly enterprises and publications; and though its operations were cut short by the Revolution, they were resumed by other hands in the nineteenth and twentieth and continue still in the twenty-first century.

These publications, designed for the schools and for a broad reading public and claiming to be "authoritative" in more than one sense, also represented part of the collective memory of the French nation. In the Old Regime, legitimacy was still tied to antiquity, and historical scholarship offered the most concrete and comprehensive basis for national ideology. Yet at the same time it opened a Pandora's box of interpretations that all parties and levels of society could draw on, or oppose. From the Renaissance arguing for the essentially Roman provenance of institutions implied a tradition of civility, or law and order, but it also suggested tendencies of paternalism and even tyranny, while a Germanist line connoted a fundamentally barbarian heritage, but also claims to racial purity and claims to inherited liberties.[22] In the debate over the historical pedigrees of the French monarchy and its institutions, the Abbé Dubos had enlisted the Romanist thesis in the service of the monarchy and was opposed by the Germanizing defense of feudal privileges and the nobility by Boullainvilliers, Mably, and especially Montesquieu, who had taken a long view of the French "constitution" of the Old Regime.

These debates continued throughout the nineteenth century. In 1814, Montlosier's treatise *De la Monarchie française* was one example of the belated renewal of the defense of the Old Regime. More striking was Mlle de Lézardière's extraordinary *Theory of the Political Laws of the French Monarchy*, which surveyed, in propositional fashion, the legal history of France through the Celtic, German, and properly French periods, with full documentation, and extensive juridico-historical "proofs" (*preuves*).[23] Lézardière's book, based on a lifetime's work in her father's library (which was burned during the Revolution), was a sort of summa of French constitutional history, following the Germanist line of Boullainvilliers. The first publication of the book, which was suspended in 1792, still seemed so timely in the July Monarchy that Guizot saw to its republication more than forty years later as an illustration of the longer history of the liberal and constitutionalist cause in France. So the scholarly and ideological issues of the Old Regime, especially those between Romanists and Germanists, continued, although the conceptual ground shifted from political legitimacy to that of historical continuity and change. If the words changed, the music of history remained much the same.

The French Art of History

Even in times of turmoil the criterion of truth remained at the center of historical inquiry. Yet the crisis of historical pyrrhonism had left its mark, and the divergence of opinions about the trustworthiness, meaning, and value of history reinforced conventional doubts. This was not merely an epistemological question, for historians had long suffered attacks by radical skeptics and were for the most part content to acknowledge the probable nature of historical knowledge. Moreover, in judging behavior, wrote the younger Portalis, one had to take into account "the genius and character of each age" in order to avoid error and prejudice.[24] By the eighteenth century the criterion of this probable truth, or moral certainty, was still the Herodoto-Thucydidean rule of autopsy, eyewitness testimony, but normally extended to include the written record of such evidence, and so incorporating the techniques of the auxiliary sciences of historical study. Crucial in this regard was the legal model of warranting conclusions, since it was above all legal sources — archives, governmental acts, laws, documentary evidence, and historical "proofs" (*preuves*) — that historians were most dependent on for their narratives. Otherwise, wrote Henri Griffet, the result will be only fiction (*romans*).[25] What could be proved in court was more than enough for a reading public, and this legalistic criterion was followed by historians in their own search for truth.[26]

The genre of universal history had not changed much over the ages, although there was in the eighteenth century a conspicuous turn to cultural and "philosophical history." One of the most popular works was the series of volumes on ancient history by the Jansenist Charles Rollin, which began to appear in the 1730s and which continued to be reprinted in the nineteenth century. Rollin also published a treatise on the "method" of teaching the humanities, and indeed his view of history was that of a pious and unimaginative pedagogue, who followed the Eurocentric and providentialist view of Bishop Bossuet and Archbishop Ussher and who wholly subordinated classical authors to the scriptural account of Judeo-Christian history. Let us, he wrote, not praise too much all "these great men, who were so much boasted of in profane history . . . [but] were so unhappy as not to know the true God and to displease him." Rollin's work was "intended more immediately for the instruction of youth," and he was not ashamed to plunder other authors without citation, and even to alter their language (especially those exhibiting the "superstitious credulity" of paganism).[27] Rollin preferred — and in this was more honest than many textbook writers, even though it was just a "humility topos" — the title of compiler to that of author. History was fuller of thorns than flowers, he admitted. Yet, following humanist convention and enlightened culturalist fashion, he attended not only to political and military narrative but also to "the genius, laws, and customs" of other nations; and in this spirit he offered "another knowledge," meaning "the manner in which arts and science were invented, cultivated and improved."

For Rollin the key to, or at least the common denominator of, universal history was religion, since every nation has acknowledged a supreme being, even if such belief, stemming from "a tradition as ancient as the world itself," became corrupted by superstition, false philosophy, or depraved manners. He begins his *Ancient History* with an account of geography, religious mysteries, games, and public theater before discussing the various epochs into which Jewish and Roman history were divided and then going on to political matters. Rollin rejected Egypt's "vain and fabulous claim" to antiquity, Herodotus's credulous reports, derived from Egyptian priests, and the fictions of Manetho, and used Scripture as an infallible guide through all this material, his critical remarks being limited to common sense and reason. Nevertheless, he accepted the high repute of Egyptian culture carried by these and other sources, corrected betimes by modern scholarship, such as publications in the Academy of Inscriptions, and travel literature. In general Egypt was not only "the cradle (if I may be allowed the expression) of the holy nation," and afterwards "a severe prison, and a fiery furnace," but also "the most renowned school for wisdom and politics, and the source from whence most arts and sciences were derived." After the succession of the kings (or their perhaps simultaneous rule, which would account for the impossible antiquity) Egyptian history, writes Rollin, merges with that of the Persians and Greeks, as do those of the other Eastern kingdoms; and these topics Rollin takes up (as Eusebius had done) in chronological order, and with better historiographical guides.

Voltaire, whose popularity also extended into the next century, went over the same ground as Bossuet and, in briefer compass and hardly less superficial scholarship, as Rollin; but he was even more intent on appreciating the advance of the arts, sciences, and other signs of precocious proto-enlightenment — the history of the arts being "perhaps the most useful of all." For Voltaire history begins in fable — that is, in memory and imagination — and fables grow in time, "whence it happens that the origins of all peoples are absurd," including the

Greeks and Romans.[28] All moderns can do is to rely on "incontestable monuments," such as the astronomical calculations of the ancients, and their own reason. Thus Herodotus is reliable only in matters close to his own time, and thus the superiority of Thucydides who deliberately limited both his geographical and his temporal horizons. Most noteworthy for Voltaire was the history of Rome, because of the survival of its laws and language — the Middle Ages being the time of a new order of things, the "barbaric *history* of people who became Christian, but not the better for it." Faithful histories came only with the art of printing and the restoration of the sciences; yet history — here repeating the established view — has (moral) utility but no (mathematical) certitude.

Voltaire complained against both Bossuet and Rollin for their narrowness and subordination of reason to faith — that is, to the idolization of Jewish antiquity ("despite our hatred and contempt for this people"), as if this history were intended only for *our* instruction. "There are about eighty different systems of calculating their chronology and even more ways of explaining the events of their history," Voltaire commented sarcastically. "We do not know which is the true one, but we are keeping our faith in reserve for it, hoping that some day it will be discovered." Nor were modern scholars immune from such myopia. There were, said Voltaire, already more histories of France than any man could read in a lifetime, and of course every nation and city in Europe had its histories, and with them their myths. Even monuments were not proof against the uncertainties of history — as witness one of the oldest of French antiquities, "the statue of St. Denis carrying his head in his arms."

History had lessons to teach, no doubt, but not necessarily those learned by modern scholars. "Charters of the time of Dagobert are dug up, most of them suspect and misunderstood, and it is inferred from them that the customs, rights and prerogatives which existed in those days ought to be revived today." This too was an abuse of reason. As for antiquarian research, "If you have nothing to say other than to tell us that one barbarian succeeded another on the shores of the Oxus and the Ixarte, what use are you to the public?" Yet history was essential for enlightened understanding. "Destroy the study of history," he concluded, "and you would very possibly see St. Bartholomew's Days in France and Cromwell's in England."[29] This search for truth and utility — and indeed beauty, the rare quality of literary artistry — was what Voltaire meant by the famous phrase he coined: "philosophy of history."

But for Voltaire and others of his generation, history was not merely philosophy "teaching by example," in the often-cited aphorism of Dionysius of Halicarnassus; it was philosophy in a larger sense of an intelligible (though not providential) scheme and indeed, for some, a "system," which reflected not only the past and the potential of human reason but also its future promise for social perfection. What Dugald Stewart called "conjectural history" inferred patterns and imposed schemes of periodization on the historical process, but aspired to end the conventional series of "epochs" in a transcendent age of moral, social, and political perfection.[30] The best known of these schemes was the so-called "four-stage theory" of cultural development first expressed by Turgot and Goguet (along with Adam Smith): the ages of gathering, of fishing and hunting, of agriculture, and of commerce underlying the shift from "barbarism" to full "civilization."[31] This enlightenment version of the idea of progress joined an economic base of material culture with a sensualist philosophy, derived from Locke, which rooted intellectual and scientific progress in experience, especially as formalized in education; and it joined easily to revolutionary ideas of political change and social engineering.

This sort of practical, but often also wishful, thinking received systematic formulation in the school of "Ideology," which aspired to move from a history of culture to a full-fledged "science of ideas" and to social engineering.[32] Devotees of Ideology, the "science of ideas," shifted their allegiance from Descartes to Locke and Condillac, taking sense experience as foundational and thought as a derivative phenomenon; and they inferred that human progress in a collective sense, like individual education, was a movement from the first to the second, from empirical experience to rational "analysis." In 1794, just before his death, Condorcet produced a comprehensive vision of cultural progress; and while he regarded history as in a way foundational, it was to be transcended in the positive science which would make possible the achievement of the new trinity of Enlightenment — "reason, toleration, and humanity."[33] Progress (like decadence, though Condorcet was disposed to reject this alternative in the light of the philosophy of his age) was a "law of nature," extending from the arts and sciences to society and government in general.

For the three generations of Idéologues, from Condorcet to Degérando, the past was prologue, history was preliminary, and the "science of ideas" was to be the master discipline of modern society as well as the Revolution. Three years before Condorcet wrote his famous essay on the progress of the human spirit, the Idéologue Volney, author of a study of Herodotus's chronology (1776), published his own meditations on history. His views were shaped by his travels in Egypt and Syria as well as participation in the Revolution as member of both the Estates General and the Constituent Assembly and as a near victim of the Terror. In *Les Ruines,* Volney reflected on the monuments and past glories of empires and, as a disciple of Helvétius and other secular-minded philosophes, sought the causes for these ancient "revolutions."[34] Was it blind fatality or celestial justice? Neither he nor the "pale apparition" who entered into dialogue with him answered. "Young man," said the apparition, "believe the voice of tombs and the testimony of monuments." These transformations were all due to human agency, and specifically from self-love, or selfishness, from which all evil and all good — war as well as property — had entered the world.

Volney traced the prehistory of humanity through a series of eight epochs defined not by material improvement but by the nature of religious worship: the elements, the stars, symbols (idolatry), dualist belief (white and black angels, the universe moralized), a future state (legends of the Fortunate Isles and the Elysian fields), an animated universe (pantheism), a world soul (sacred fire), and the universe as a machine (with God as supreme artificer). Such were the absurd cosmologies devised by the superstitious and by the theologians who extended them: "Such is the chain of ideas through which the human mind had already run at a period anterior to the recitals of history." After this, in the systems of Moses, Zoroaster, and Buddhism, Brahmanism, and Christianity, religion became mainly a political expedient for the ruling class and its apologists. Only in the past three centuries had reason begun to dissipate the vast heritage of superstition and to open up vistas of a society, or state, perfected by the new "science of man" and devoted to the welfare of humanity as a whole.

In 1795, after a few months in prison, Volney gave a course on history at the short-lived Ecole Normale in which he emphasized the social utility and not the literary glory of this discipline, recalling the advice of commentators on the art of history, especially Lucian and Mably. Volney recognized four types of historical writing: chronological, such as Thucydides and Tacitus; "dramatic," such as Herodotus; topical, such as Goguet on the origin of laws, arts, and science, Bailly on astronomy, Robertson on America, and Pluquet on fanaticism; and analytical, or philosophical, which proceeded synthetically and in terms of cause and effect and (pace Montesquieu) physical environment.[35] Despite occasional hyperbole — speaking of the "high mathematics of history" — history is for Volney indeed a repository of error, especially the errors of, and what Helvétius called the "acquired ignorance" of, traditional religion. Yet history had its uses. Although a "science," history differed from natural philosophy and mathematics in claiming only "moral probability" and in requiring the subject — the historian — to tell (*raconter*), to "resuscitate," and to give meaning to natural facts (*facts physiques*) through memory and imagination.

Volney emphasized the novelty of this study because of its association with the arts and sciences of civilization and especially because of its value, pedagogical and political, for the future, meaning the science of man and legislative policy based on a proper knowledge of history. He emphasized, too, the key role of printing in this process, especially in the new age of freedom of the press. As for the "labyrinth of origins," Volney returned to the topic of "ruins," that is, the monuments of antiquity, including inscriptions, medals, and manuscripts, which make possible a "complete history" of every nation on the way to the grander edifice of "universal history."[36]

Under the Empire, French proto-Romantic fascination with the remote past took a number of forms. Napoleon identified himself, variously, with Alexander, Caesar, Justinian, and Charlemagne.[37] As Volney looked back to ancient splendors, so Chateaubriand looked to the medieval church and J. F. Michaud inquired into the glories and the splendors of the Crusades. Pilgrimages have been common to all religions, he remarked ("whatever may be the opinion of an enlightened philosophy");[38] and like Volney he celebrated the stirring effects of looking on storied ruins: "the soul of the philosopher finds itself agitated at the sight of the ruins of Palmyra, Babylon, or Athens; what lively emotions must not the Christians have felt on beholding places which God had sanctified by his presence and his blessings?" For the French the capture of Jerusalem was as memorable as the siege of Troy for the Hellenes. Yet this event was properly the subject of the historian, not the poet, and Michaud lamented the anachronisms of Tasso, in whose *Jerusalem Delivered* "we discover much more of the manners of the times in which he lived than those of the end of the eleventh century."[39] Nor did the credulous seventeenth century or the over-critical eighteenth century do justice to the Crusades, which, if not successful in Christianizing the East, nevertheless opened the way for the destruction of feudalism, a "new order" in France, various sorts of political and cultural progress, and a "balance of power" in Europe.[40]

But it was Chateaubriand who tapped most directly into the nostalgic and antirevolutionary historicism of the early nineteenth century. His *Génie du Christianisme*, originally entitled *Beautés de la religion chrétienne* and published in the month of the Concordat and the *Te Deum* in Notre-Dame (April 1802), celebrated not only the poetry, art, and ceremonies of traditional religion but also, in an amateurish spirit, its dogma. The "genius of Christianity" was also favorable to the "genius of history," Chateaubriand remarked, though it also encouraged a new appreciation of myth.[41] His book seemed to substitute the *Golden Legend* for the *Encyclopédie*. Published "on the ruins of our temples," it opposed the influence of Voltaire, D'Alembert, Diderot, and Condorcet as well as the "anachronism" of the Napoleonic Empire.[42] It had an astonishing impact not only on conservatives and counterrevolutionaries but also on the post-Napoleonic generation of liberals. In a more scholarly way Chateaubriand continued his revisionist project in his later historical studies, although his perspective was superseded by a new generation of scholars who looked back with respect to their historiographical ancestors but who also looked forward to a newer vision of history.

The View from Coppet

French exiles had different views on the French Revolution, more bitter, of course, but also conceived in a larger perspective. Some of the émigrés, like the Bourbons, may have "learned nothing and forgotten nothing," but others found new ways of looking at the process of history in the wake of revolution. Aside from their bitter losses, they had a longer perspective on events, being critical of unreflective radicalism and absorbing historical and liberal, if not counterrevolutionary, attitudes and ideas from their German and English exile experiences. Of special interest was the circle gathered around Mme de Staël, née Germaine Necker, daughter of the last finance minister of Louis XVI and of Susan Curchod, who had been courted by the young Edward Gibbon in Lausanne in 1757.[43] At her family (Necker) estate in Coppet she established a circle, or salon, which seemed to engage in a "common mission" that included revisionist efforts in psychology, politics, philosophy, religion, literature, and (of course) history. The project of the "Groupe de Coppet" — in exile Mme de Staël and Sismondi called it a "prison"[44] — was to keep alive the old Republic of Letters and to preserve values of the Enlightenment, but in a religious (and especially Protestant) mode. To this "school," as Charles de Villers called it, came Benjamin Constant (1794), Wilhelm von Humboldt (1798), Sismondi (1804), and A. W. Schlegel (1804), as well as Chateaubriand and Prosper Barante, who all made significant contributions to history during the Empire and Restoration, partly in the shadow, or light, of their patroness's own wide-ranging writings.[45]

For Mme de Staël-Holstein recent French history was almost a family matter, her *Considerations on the French Revolution* (1818) being in large part a commentary on the career of her father, Jacques Necker, finance minister to Louis XVI in 1789. For Mme de Staël the pattern of French history was similar to that of England in that it was an interplay of three elements — the "nation" for its rights, the nobility for its privileges, and the king for absolute power. Referring to Dubuat-Nançay's *Maximes du droit public françois* (1775), Mme de Staël rejected the stereotypical view of Blackstone that France was a despotism. France indeed had the makings of a "constitution," since there were various limitations to royal authority, including the power of the parlement to register legislation and in the provincial customs, and history confirmed that there had always been a pact between nation and king.[46] Unfortunately, when the "nation" became a power, it was subject to corruption (not to speak of the crimes leading to emigration), and it was Jacobinism in particular that diverted the constitutional course into radicalism (shared even by Condorcet) and then true despotism. Her nemesis Napoleon Bonaparte did not understand history (though he plundered it) and took not only Charlemagne but also Attila, feudal law, and oriental despotism (meaning Justinian) as sources of inspiration for his new brand of absolutism, thus illustrating the thesis, which she shared with Constant, that "what is ancient is liberty, what is modern is despotism."[47] De Staël herself preserved her father's vision of a balanced constitution under monarchy in the style of England after 1688 and Montesquieu's idealization of it — realized perhaps in the French constitutional charter of the restored Bourbon monarchy in 1814.

As a disciple of Condorcet and Necker, Mme de Staël believed in the progress of science, both natural and (through statistics) social, and of political liberty. Her periodization of history was a function of her (and the Coppet circle's in general) understanding of the Revolution: humanity was moving from feudalism to despotism to liberty. Despite the primacy of politics, de Staël was more deeply attached to art and literature, which she defined as "the perfection of the art of thinking and of expressing one's self" and which she posited as a prerequisite of liberty. Unfortunately, progress in the humanities had not kept pace with that in science and philosophy, and in particular the moderns had still not equaled the ancients in the art of historical narrative. Mme de Staël herself was a philosophe and a writer (and even more, a talker), and she declared that "poetry, of all the arts, is closest to reason," though the novel was the preferred form of modern intellectuals. Her privileging of emotion and "enthusiasm" was all in keeping with the new "romantic" theories of her friends, the Schlegel brothers — the neologism "romantic" corresponding to the teutonic, and of course Protestant, culture of the north, best expressed (she still believed) by Ossian, and the other extreme, "classic," to the Greco-Latin culture of the south exemplified by Homer.[48] Her romantic ideas were derivative as well as à la mode, relying as she did on old racial stereotypes and racial theories to support her arguments about the mutual influences of literature on the one hand and religion, custom, and law on the other.

Mme de Staël elaborated on her ideas more intensively in her *De l'Allemagne* of 1813, which so offended Napoleon and which had so profound an influence on Restoration social and historical thought and, in a longer term, on the sociology of literature. The first edition, suppressed in France by Napoleon, appeared in French and then in English translation in London in 1813 and in Paris the year following Waterloo. This book, which surveyed all aspects of German culture and conversation as well as literature, philosophy, religion, and the arts, marks both the high tide of Germanism and a threshold of Romanticism — a name "recently introduced into Germany to designate that poetry whose source is the songs of the troubadours and which arose from chivalry and Christianity," wrote Mme de Staël.[49] In postrevolutionary and post-Napoleonic Europe it was "a political event," says René Wellek, "in purpose comparable to Tacitus' *Germania*."[50] Among historical scholars she pointed in particular to Herder, the Schlegel brothers, and especially the Swiss historian Johann Müller as expressions of the new spirit arising in the north of Europe.

The émigré Charles de Villers, also a member of De Staël's circle — "votre école," he called it — preceded his friend in the celebration of Germanism. He was also instrumental in disseminating her book in Germany through a review in the *Göttingische Gelehrte Anzeigen* and in an introduction to the second edition of the book. Villers, too, was devoted to celebrating the role of German thought in the growth of modern freedom. His best-known contribution was his work popularizing Kant in the Francophone world, a book which he compared to de Staël's on the relations between literature and social institutions.[51] In 1802, Villers, responding to a question posed by the French Institute, expounded his views on "the spirit and influence of the Reformation of Luther" on the various states of Europe, pointing especially to the "revolutions" begun in the liberation of theology and philosophy, followed by "the successive progress of enlightenment." Enlightenment (*lumières*) was not born of the Reformation, he declared, but rather — itself the product of the "renaissance of letters" — gave birth to it. The Reformation was the name given to the "revolution performed by Luther in Europe." In this effort poor Erasmus, who wanted to be a cardinal, was in effect a counterrevolutionary, although biblical scholarship and *herméneutique* was a force for the "liberty of thought" — and indeed the "revolution in philosophy" of Kant — which Lutheranism had inaugurated. Valuable in this connection, too, was the "philosophy of history" of such Scottish scholars as Robertson and Hume and of "l'Histoire de la culture" written by contemporary Germans.[52]

Another Swiss historian and a member of the Coppet circle was J. C. L. Simonde de Sismondi, émigré, philosophe, social scientist, and professor of history and philosophy in the Academy of Geneva. Sismondi was also a pioneering medievalist, who followed de Staël's line of inquiry into the social history of literature in southern Europe — the Romance as distinguished from the Teutonic nations (never realizing his plan to include that of English, German, and Slavonic languages).[53] This book, based on lectures given in Geneva in 1811–12, touched on historical linguistics, religion, and Arabic influences, reflecting his cosmopolitan interests and yet his awareness of the nationalist

passions which drew scholars back into the seminal period of vernacular poetry. Creative genius was to be found in all nations in their infancy, but in the
movement from barbarism to civilization this energy was lost, together with
the tendency to submit to authority. Cultural effervescence was succeeded by
critical reflection; and what was left, in the modern "age of analysis and
philosophy," in which "genius has lost its ways and its powers," was the
historical task of reviewing and celebrating "the progress of the human mind."
For Sismondi the sixteenth century marked the decline of Italy and inaugurated "that fatal period when chains were forged to subdue the intellect of
mankind and when genius, arrested in its course, was compelled to retrace its
steps."[54] In order to understand medieval authors, he wrote, "Let us study
their manners; let us estimate them not by their own rules, but by those to
which they themselves conformed"; and in the spirit of Herder as well as de
Staël, he added, "Let us learn to distinguish the genius of man [*esprit humain*]
from the genius of nations [*esprit national*]." Sismondi also carried over his
medievalist studies into contributions to Joseph Michaud's great collection,
Biographie universelle.

But like de Staël, Sismondi believed in the primacy of politics. In the spirit of
Coppet as well as the enlightenment science of man, Sismondi sought to celebrate the rise of liberty, and his first masterwork was a sixteen-volume study of
the role of the free communes of medieval Italy — a nation with a rich history,
though a state still unborn.[55] In this epic work Sismondi had been preceded by
his elder friend Johann Müller, who remarked that the Italian republics had, in
their struggles for liberty, "given the signal for all the great revolutions of the
following centuries" and who published his own history of the Swiss Confederation in 1780 as well as a universal history.[56] Sismondi's work appeared
simultaneously in French and in German translation between 1807 and 1818,
a worthy rival (some thought) of the masterwork written by the former suitor
of Germaine de Staël's mother — Gibbon's *Decline and Fall* — of which Sismondi was very critical, being inclined himself to the employment of history in
the service of "moral" or "political" science.[57] Sismondi's view of this history
of civic liberty was a bit naive, though understandably so given the sources
(chronicles and archives) which he employed, the sort of simple political wisdom which he sought, the sort of literary narrative (rather than erudite analysis) which he preferred, and perhaps the sort of readership he hoped to reach
(Benjamin Constant and Mme de Staël, for example, were both admirers of
the work).

It is true that Sismondi had a deep awareness of the economic dimension (on
which he would write a treatise while at work on his Italian history), but it was
state action that underlay material progress.[58] For Sismondi republicanism

and federal government (illustrated by Italian city leagues) were the best guarantee of liberty. Every Italian city had its own peculiar history, of course; yet
each exemplified in its own way the common theme of what he termed the
"revolution of public virtues" resulting from resistance to imperial and papal
authority. Civic virtue and bourgeois prosperity were an alliance which, according to "the general plan of providence," in which good often came from
evil, created the modern values of both liberty and "sociability."

Benjamin Constant was a French nobleman and a cosmopolitan intellectual
and not really a historian, but he drew on history for his rather simplistic
political views, which were based on a version of the old conflict between the
ancients and the moderns. According to Constant, the ancients were subject to
the spirit of conquest (most recently typified by Napoleon, whom Constant
alternately deplored and served) and the moderns to a spirit of commerce,
which was a new form of conquest that pursued wealth.[59] Similarly the ancients, including the French of the Old Regime, were bound to a collective sort
of liberty, still maintained by Rousseau and his illiberal General Will, and the
moderns to an unprecedented individualism and civil liberty. For Constant
progress was a trajectory from savagery to civilization, as war was becoming
outmoded in the postrevolutionary period.

The view from Coppet both drew on and reacted to the legacy of the Revolution, especially the idea of bourgeois liberty. For Sismondi, Mme de Staël,
Villers, Constant, and their colleagues, who all carried a heavy weight of old
regime philosophy, the Revolution, especially in its later stages, was largely an
unwelcome interruption to the progress of that liberty and the cultural values
which accompanied it. But of course the Revolution was not an aberration, it
was a product of the process that produced the liberties and cultural values of
the propertied classes, and as such it was the central historical problem of their
generation and the succeeding ones. Not "What is enlightenment?" but "What
is, or what was, the Revolution?"

Revolutionary Retrospectives

From the start the French Revolution set the question of history at center
stage. First came the problem, handed over to antiquarians, of what the Estates
General (the first to be held in France for 175 years) was like and how to call
and organize it, then whether to be guided in such matters by history at all, or
rather to put an end to it and turn to philosophy. Yet as always the question of
history remained, this time in the form of how to describe and to account for
the process transforming the Estates into a National Assembly and, as more
theoretical observers concluded, monarchy into nation.[60] From the vantage

point of the meeting of the three old Orders on May 5, 1789, some members looked back on an institutional tradition—an "Old Regime," as it would be called in a pejorative sense—covering almost four centuries, while others looked forward to a new process managed by reason and science. It was a new quarrel between ancients and moderns—transmuted in 1791 by Marat to a "parallel between the old and the new regime"—and historians had to accommodate both parties in grasping the world-defining event of modern times.

The concept and term "revolution" was itself far from new in 1789, having become familiar through the change of regimes in England in 1688. In France the term was applied rather indiscriminately to any major changes, usually political but also intellectual or cultural. In 1738, M. de La Hode published a massive study of "the history of the revolutions of France" down to the death of Louis XIV, making use of the work of such modern scholars as Mabillon and Fleury.[61] There were a "great number" of such revolutions, La Hode argued, beginning with the time of the "terror" of German raids and the conversion of Clovis and including many wars and constitutional changes, not to speak of disasters like the "horrible project" (the old conspiracy theory revived) of the massacres of St. Bartholomew. The last of these "revolutions" involved the defortification of towns and "complete submission" of the nobility under Louis XIV and the establishment of "absolute government," after which revolutions became impossible, at least from aristocratic sources. If not exactly prophetic, this book illustrates the wide and flexible use of the terminology of "revolution"—similar to the usage of Raynal, Voltaire, and Mably—before it was transformed in the social "effervescence" a half-century later and of *the* Revolution of 1789. Yet even then traditional meanings were preserved in the work of Condorcet, Villers, and Sismondi.

The Revolution was a lesson in and a paradigm of political and cultural rupture and discontinuity, showing intellectuals—men of letters, men of law, historians, and some just plain citizens—trying to stop or to change the course of history through their discourse. For a decade governments were overturned and established, new institutions were created (or old ones recreated, as in the case of the *juges du paix*), and new names were bestowed on the world of revolutionaries.[62] Historians drew upon this discourse, especially the debates of the assemblies and the outpourings of pamphlets, to create a narrative of the process of revolution. Sometimes they construed this in the light of old precedents—John Adams saw them as a repetition of the civil violence of the wars of religion[63]—but more usually they were caught up in the rhetoric of novelty and innovation, as were many young Germans and Englishmen.

The Revolution was sustained by innovating language, as abundantly illustrated by the *cahiers,* revolutionary oratory, and the avalanche of polemical literature that began cresting in the spring of 1789: "Pamphleteering opened its abysmal throat wider," said Carlyle; "never to close more." In this "carnival of words" — the newest form taken by the old Quarrel between Ancients and Moderns — the question of history was central, at least by implication. Had history come to an end, or was it fulfilled or renewed by the Revolution? Was it the enemy or the ally? On the one hand there was talk about the need for a "regeneration of French liberty" and restoration of the old constitution; on the other hand were complaints about the "errors of the centuries" to be rectified in the formation of a "new order." The ghosts of Rousseau and Montesquieu carried on a dialogue in the Constituent and Legislative Assemblies, as conservative, reformist, and idealist designs were debated. It was in this context that the notion of a "social science" was promoted from theory to practice, as French government became a laboratory for a series of constitutional and legislative experiments. "Antiquity," "honor," "custom," "liberty," "equality," "constitution," "the social," "property" — such key words were employed, often in the most contradictory fashion, and it was left to historians to make sense of the discussions and the political reality behind them. The term "revolution" itself was subject to the greatest ambiguity — Bergasse, for example, agreed that there should be an "absolute revolution" (*révolution absolue*), but he meant this in a gradual, planetary rather than a political sense.[64]

The review and revaluation of French history did not have to wait for the Revolution itself, and indeed the troubles and issues underlying that mega-event had already provoked discussion and research before the end of the Old Regime. Fantin-Désodouard's "philosophical history of the French revolution" had appeared in an earlier version in 1787, invoking the "Wigs and Tories" and the colors seen through the "prism" of their revolution — and yet he argued that the French phenomenon was "without model."[65] In the search for causes historians looked into the history not only of the monarchy and its institutions but also of the social orders, the legal system, corporations, and of course the church. Perhaps the most inflammatory topic was the role of the nobility and especially of "feudalism" (*féodalité*) in the predicament of French society as critics and scholars came to view it in the later eighteenth century. As "feudal law" (*ius feudale; droit féodale*) was a construct of the jurists, deriving from commentaries on medieval collections including the *Libri Feudorum* and the provincial customs, so "feudalism" — also known as the "feudal regime," "feudal government," or "feudal society" — was a larger fiction employed by scholars and polemicists to cover centuries of social relationships since the Merovingian age. Boullainvilliers defended feudal government as well as the superiority of the nobility, descended from the "free Franks," as Dubos asserted the priority of the monarchy; and this set the terms for the eighteenth-century debate and research agenda of later scholars.

Mythology of the racial superiority of the Germans and also of legendary feudal abuses, such as the lord's "first night" and "hunting the villeins," were widely believed. Except for the thoughtful treatment by Montesquieu, most of the early historical works on the subject were more polemical than scholarly in character, such as the physiocrat G. F. Letrosne's *Dissertation on Feudalism* (1779) and Simon Linguet's *Theory of Civil Laws* (1767), which lamented "feudal anarchy" and the noble "wolves" who preyed on the cultivators of the soil. Feudalism had of course its defenders, including some who associated its liberties with those generated by the Revolution.[66] Feudalism (and seigneurialism) and its own "liberties" were preserved in the grand tradition of customary law and the accumulation of charters, the embodiment of old regime abuses according to critics and the cahiers collected before the Revolution, and (in the case of the charters) the target of peasant vandalism and revolutionary action, whose aim was at one extreme to wipe away the past — renaming provinces, streets, and the calendar, the execution of the king, and the establishment of the Republic. The churches of both St. Denis and Cluny suffered revolutionary attacks. On the level of social action the culmination was the abolishment of feudalism on the extraordinary night of August 4, 1789. But such actions were merely temporary disruptions of the long-term historical process; not only were the monarchy and its legal continuity restored but even feudalism or its ghost was preserved in many ways after the Revolution, both in the work of historians and in social memory, unwritten customs, and judicial interpretation.

Parallel to and in rivalry with the feudal nobility was the Third Estate, which made its appearance in the rise of the medieval communes. One early historical study was L. G. O. F. de Bréquigny's "Recherches sur les communes," prefacing volume 11 of the *Ordonnances du roi* (1736), which described communal privileges derived from alliance with the crown as a form of self-defense against feudal "servitude."[67] Throughout the eighteenth century, as feudalism was the object of legal and moral criticism, so the "bourgeoisie" was lauded as the producer of national wealth and the champion of human liberty, and in the wave of propaganda accompanying the meeting of the Estates General it became identified with the "nation" as a whole and so the protagonist of revisionist history. This was the project that would be taken up by Guizot and Thierry in the Restoration.

Among the "origins" of the Revolution the printed book remains the most popular, at least with cultural historians. From Daniel Mornet to Roger Chartier and Robert Darnton the circulation of literary material has been examined in ever-increasing detail. Chartier can still ask the question, "Do books make revolutions?" (especially the "bad" philosophical books sought by the police), but in general the rhetoric of historical explanation has been scaled back from the ambitious search for the causal role of ideas — the *c'est la faute à Voltaire* approach of the royalist historians who produced the first conspiracy theories — to the more subtle configurations of "political culture," which is certainly more in keeping with the views of Mme de Staël and her friends.[68] In any case the radical and liberal approach was more apt to stress the pernicious effects of censorship and the "privilege" of publication, and historians like Volney and Sismondi took the position that only under conditions of a free press could ideas circulate — and history be written — without the pressures and prejudices of interests and attendant corruption.

The historiography of the Revolution, which is huge, amorphous, and contradictory, begins in 1789 in the midst of partisan polemic and censorship, and it goes through a number of revisionist stages corresponding to the phases of Revolution, from constitutional Monarchy to Republic to Terror to Consulate to Empire and then back to Monarchy again. The focus of historians of all sorts is concerned above all with questions of cause, or at least "influence," and again these correspond to ideological points of view. Causes could be underlying or immediate, spiritual or material, but could not be divorced from moral and political judgment. On one side is the work of Rabaut de Saint-Etienne, whose views emerged from earliest revolutionary times.[69] His authoritative and often reprinted *Précis historique* singled out the nobility, feudalism, and the clergy as the sources of the discontent — the "enemies of liberty" and the consequent uprising; and other similar works took the same apologetic line, including the twenty-volume history written by "two friends of liberty," which appeared between 1791 and 1802. More economically, Barnave singled out the question of property as most essential in the shift from a feudal to a bourgeois society.[70]

At the right extreme (following the political calibration of the seating in the National Assembly) was the royalist Abbé Augustin Barruel, whose conspiratorial history, inspired by an earlier work by the Edinburgh professor John Robison, exculpated the monarchy by focusing on three enemies of religion — Voltaire, D'Alembert, and King Frederick of Prussia, along with a fourth, Diderot. Through the impious agency of their "philosophical opinions," the "project of the *Encyclopedia*, and more especially the collective work of the academies, revolutionary societies, and the Freemasons, the monarchy and the church were subverted and destroyed."[71] J.-J. Mounier and the émigré Mallet du Pan rejected this idea on the grounds that, while the philosophes had sown seeds of discontent, they had actually failed to obtain reform for abuses. They created a language for the "passions and the interests," and their influence could be seen in the devising of the new weights and measures, the Conservatoire, the Institut, ideas of civil equality, and the reform of penal laws; but neither the events of 1789 nor the later excesses and "anarchy" can be attributed to them. For Mallet, writing in 1793, there had been a "social revolution" — which was misunderstood by most men over fifty who "only view the Revolution through the medium of antiquated habits" — but this was subverted by the "hideous society" of the Jacobins, not unlike the radical Anabaptists of Münster, the levelers, and peasant revolutionaries; and Mallet, too, wanted to stop the process of history at a particular point, which for him was before the regicide.[72]

So revolutionary historiography struggled between the bitter *j'accuse* of reactionaries, a few die-hard Bonapartists, the euphoric apologetics of radicals, the Anglophile ideals of émigrés like de Staël, Constant, and the young François Guizot, who was in England translating Gibbon before the Restoration. None of the various parties agreed on the fundamental question of causes, and more intensive and impartial study has never brought a consensus. A century later Lord Acton summed up the state of the question: "It was the deficit; it was the famine; it was the Austrian Committee; it was the Diamond Necklace; it was the pride of nobles or the intolerance of priests; it was philosophy; it was freemasonry; it was Mr. Pitt; it was the incurable levity and violence of the national character; it was the issue of that struggle between classes that constitutes the unity of the history of France."[73] This comment was written after the first centennial of the Revolution; it can not be said that historians are, a century after Acton, much closer to agreement.

With the collapse of the Empire the teaching of history entered into decline, at least until 1818, when several chairs were restored. One figure of transition who carried the values of the Enlightenment, and more particularly of Idéologie, over into the Restoration period was P. C. F. Daunou, a former Oratorian, editor of the *Journal des Savants,* and an associate of the old *Histoire littéraire de France,* to which he contributed entries on a number of medieval philosophers, including Albert the Great, Thomas Aquinas, Roger Bacon, Richard of St. Victor, Robert Grosseteste, authors of the lives of saints, and others. A member of the National Convention and author of the Constitution of 1795, Daunou followed Condorcet in his contributions to the founding of the National Institute of the same year, especially the classes devoted to the social sciences (and indeed became a member of the section on social sciences and legislation), which he hoped would be above political involvement, but which was eventually abolished by Napoleon for its alleged "Ideological" bias.

Yet Daunou himself was appointed director by Napoleon, and this led him to give documentary substance to his conception of history as the empirical aspect of a "sciences of manners" (*science des moeurs*) and a modernized encyclopedia of knowledge.

From 1819 to 1830, Daunou taught a course of lectures on history at the Collège de France, surveying all the conventional eighteenth-century aspects of the subject—sources (especially documentary and archival), methodology, criticism, geography, chronology, historiography, and the art of writing history.[74] Distinct from poetry, history was based on "positive facts," which were dead, so that the historian could not "resuscitate" the past but only "walk over its tombs"—in sharp contrast to Michelet, who served under him in the national archives after 1830. Daunou rejected the views of Wolf concerning the Homeric poems on the grounds that they merely substituted a hypothesis for probable facts about a single author. Daunou discussed the possibility of employing quantitative and the probabilistic methods of La Place on surviving testimonies, but in general he concluded that these were not easily applicable to remote antiquity or to the miraculous. He emphasized the rules of criticism, pointing to the deplorable defense of the *sainte ampoule* in the publications of the Académie des Inscriptions et Belles-Lettres and the recent refutation by Hallam of the old story of the discovery of the manuscript of the Digest at Amalfi in 1137. He also warned against forgeries of such enthusiasts as Cyriac of Ancona, while at the same time acknowledging his pioneering archeological efforts.

Yet though history "has no doctrine," "Clio is a muse," and Daunou reviewed the ideas of the old *artes historicae* from Lucian down to François Baudouin, Jean Bodin, and the collection made by Johann Wolf in the sixteenth century.[75] Above all, Daunou was concerned with the pedagogical value of history, which had been fundamental since the recitations given to the Greeks (assembled at Olympus) by Herodotus, who indeed, he told his students, gave the first and best course on the subject. In his third year of lectures Daunou offered an extensive survey of Western historiographical and archival traditions before tackling auxiliary questions of geography and chronology (technical, "litigious," and positive). Until the time of the July Monarchy, Daunou did his best to keep alive the intellectual traditions of Enlightenment, Ideology, and the revolutionary mentality which had nurtured them.

Another transitional scholar was Sismondi, who devoted the last twenty years of his life to his second masterpiece, his *Histoire des Français,* which was published ultimately in twenty-nine volumes (1821–42). Sismondi was among the first to exploit the great collections of medieval chronicles, though he did not venture into archival and manuscript sources, as the Idéologue archivist

Daunou complained. He hoped to avoid the extremes of speculation and pedantry displayed by his predecessors as well as the distortions which preceded a "free press." He made the conventional claims to novelty: he would treat the people, the "French," and not France, not the princes and the state; and indeed he did discuss the "manners," vices and virtues, of particular ages, as well as define particular periods according to the dominant power structures — feudalism, for instance, with concomitant psychological patterns. However, he avoided cultural and even literary subjects; and as before — and as a member of the Conseil representatif of Geneva — he took politics and government as the key. "History is the basis of all the social sciences," he declared.[76] He sought comforting precedents in earlier constitutional structures — modern federalism, for example, in feudal society under the Capetians — for representative government, and for signs of political liberty. He criticized his predecessors for naiveté and anachronism but was taken to task for the same faults by contemporary and later readers of his own indulgently detailed narrative, which was adorned with political and moral reflections. Sainte-Beuve called him the "Rollin of French history," though lacking earlier historians to translate; and indeed he was closer to his old regime predecessors than to the "new history" that was contemporary with his ambitious national history.

Philosophy of History

The philosophy of history, according to Voltaire's famous coinage, is not speculation but rather writing history, and especially universal history, as a philosopher (*en philosophe*). His approach was opposed to earlier historical reflections, from Augustine to Bossuet, which found a providential pattern in human affairs and which has retrospectively been admitted to the canon of Western "philosophy of history." Voltaire's contemporaries and successors, Turgot, Condorcet, Saint-Simon, and Comte, followed his enlightened lead; they also invoked the older tradition to the extent that they sought the future direction as well as the past course of history.[77] Yet these "prophets of Paris," while they affected to join the disciplines of philosophy and history, claimed to find the predetermined structures and stages of human experience in time not from doctrines, whether religious or philosophical, but from the a posteriori details, the "positive" substance, of history. For them enlightenment, *lumières*, was projected forward as well as backward, and so was the "conjectural history," as Dugald Stewart called it, which was itself a form of the philosophy of history.

Herder wrote two books on the philosophy of history, in which, like Vico, he opened up the poetic, mythological, and prehistorical dimensions of human experience. Like Kant he saw reason as the key, but he sought to understand it not through analysis but through its development in time and space, that is, its geographical and social environment; and so he identified it with "culture." Thus Herder turned to cultural history, human evolution, and the idea of progress for answers to the crucial question, "What is enlightenment?" No wonder Kant, for whom even the history of philosophy was a priori, took exception to his old friend's *Ideas for a Philosophy of History of Mankind* (1784). "His is not a logical precision in the definition of concepts or careful adherence to principles," Kant wrote, "but rather a fleeting, sweeping view, an adroitness in unearthing analogies in the wielding of which he shows a bold imagination."[78] But it was Herder's large vision of man in time and space rather than Kant's idea of pure reason that set the standard for the philosophy of history — if not for philosophy, which shunned "historicism" — in the following century; and in this connection his influence in France was especially powerful.[79]

In Restoration France the philosophy of history became a popular fashion, with Victor Cousin and his philosophy of Eclecticism, which gave history a central and even foundational role, taking the lead. In 1820, in aphoristic reflections added to the French translation of Dugald Stewart's survey of "metaphysical, moral, and political science" since the Renaissance, Cousin praised "that science of history, that philosophy of history," exemplified by Turgot, Schlegel, de Staël, Kant, and Vico (still largely unknown to French readers), who was the first since Machiavelli, he added, to trace the Polybian cycle of political change.[80] With Cousin's encouragement Vico and Herder were translated, by Michelet and his friend Quinet respectively, who carried on *la philosophie de l'histoire* in the style of these foreign masters. "Let us take care not to break the chain that links us with past ages," Quinet pleaded.[81] In 1829, Ballanche, who ventured into the philosophy of history in his *Social Palingenesis* (1823–30), published another neglected work of Vico, *On the Ancient Wisdom of the Italians*.[82] From this time, the late 1820s, the influence of Herder and especially Vico was remarkable in French and English intellectual circles.

The philosophy of history *à la française* was carried on in the Positivism of Auguste Comte, and while his own doctrine inclined to system rather than to history (the two contrasting modes of organization which he recognized), other authors directly or indirectly under his spell did follow historical, or metahistorical, form, among them Cournot, Renouvier, Barchou, and Bourdeau. In his "treatise on the linkage of fundamental ideas in the sciences and in history," Cournot rejected the cyclical views of Vico and Indian philosophy for the sort of absolute, linear progress exemplified in geological time and a "genealogical order" by which Cournot followed "scientific culture" from the Greeks to modern times.[83] For Cournot the key to social science and to the "philosophy of history" was to be found in statistics, where the "irregularity of fact" could be reduced to the regularity of law. Charles Renouvier, in what he called the "analytical philosophy of history," devoted himself to completing the Kantian critique of reason through a conjectural examination of "the experience which humanity has of itself," which was to say, history.[84] All of these are discussed in the remarkable work of Robert Flint on historical philosophy in France, Belgium, and Switzerland.[85]

In 1828, Friedrich Schlegel, converted twenty years before to Catholicism, published his lectures on the philosophy of history, in which he rather obscurely combined the pious providentialism of Bossuet with the expansive culturalism of Herder, expanded further by Schlegel's own Sanskrit studies. For Schlegel the first problem of philosophy and the primary object of the philosophy of history was "the restoration in man of the lost image of God," and this he expected to find by examining the course of history, especially in the light of recent discoveries by, among others, Champollion, the two Humboldts, and his own brother August.[86] Out of this, too, along with parallel works on the philosophy of language and of life, he hoped to construct "the foundations of a new general Philosophy." Schlegel's rule was that "the theological point of view is to be preferred in historical inquiries."[87] Despite these premises and goals Schlegel insisted that his ideas would not be imposed on but would be deduced from the facts of history. In the facts themselves, such as the wars and political events of the past, little remained of significance, except the conclusion that "internal discord" was innate in man, so that Kant's dream of "perpetual peace" was, to say the least, unhistorical. Schlegel repeatedly warned against "losing ourselves in the details" of history; his eyes were not on the trees but on the forest, and at a great distance, at that.

In general Schlegel preferred to defend the Mosaic story, though he admitted fossil evidence, and to refer natural calamities aside from the Flood to the time "when darkness was upon the face of the deep." There was no "state of nature" except cases of degeneracy. He rejected absolutely conjectures, based on "dead bones in an animal skeleton," linking man with lower forms of life. Man was to be distinguished not only by secular reason but also by language; for "to him alone among all other of earth's creatures, the word has been imparted and communicated."[88] After considering natural prehistory Schlegel turned to the four great early civilizations — the Hebrews, Egyptians, Chinese, and Indians. The last two were distinguished in their own way but were by no means comparable to Christianity, even India having fallen into the "aberrations of mysticism," from which Christians were protected. Then Schlegel proceeded to the familiar Eurocentric story, the succession of the four empires, and the miraculous coming of Christianity, on which, despite the ever-present problem of evil and its incarnation in the French Revolution, modern "social progress" was based, and from which Christian regeneration might still appear.

Two years after the lectures of Schlegel, Hegel gave his own lectures on the philosophy of history; but although religion formed a subtext to his discussion, he was not at all bound by the conventions of theology and the biblical story of mankind. Hegel began by distinguishing three sorts of history, starting with "original history," such as those of Herodotus and Thucydides, who depended on eyewitness material. Second is "reflective history," which goes beyond the present and is either universal (for example, Livy, Diodorus Siculus, and Johannes Müller), pragmatic (Polybius, because of his concern for political causes), or critical (a "history of history," for example, in Niebuhr's approach), which we might define as disciplinary (history of art, law, religion, and so on). This last connects with the final type, "philosophical history," which contemplates history in terms of reason, that is, Hegel's own kind of reason, which transcends individual consciousness and which avoids the alleged "impartiality" of professed historians.

What Hegel sought to show was nothing less than the ultimate design of the world as expressed in the spirit (*Geist*), which for him took the form first of man as such, displayed in "world-historical individuals," and finally of the state. History is "the development of Spirit in *Time,* as Nature is the development of the Idea in space."[89] Hegel's spirit was also identified with freedom, and here he revealed the Euro- and Germanocentric character of his idea of history. "The East knew and to the present day knows only that *One* is free," he wrote, implicitly invoking the Aristotelian triad of governments, monarchy, aristocracy, and democracy; and he continued, "the Greek and Roman world, that *some* are free; the German world knows that *All* are free."[90] World history is the working out of this idea of freedom in the realm of historical reality — so that, for Hegel, too, the philosophy of history is tied to historical facts, but only as the fulfillment of a preestablished goal. Hegel recognized the ancient distinction between history as facts and as the telling of these facts (*res gestae* and *historia rerum gestarum*) but claimed to end this division in the higher synthesis of the philosophy of history, and indeed the state, for written history reflected the "very progress of its own being" — a claim largely in accord with the assumptions of contemporary German historiographers.

Like Herder and other world historians, Hegel began with a discussion of geography, speculating on its spiritual effects, and then turned to an account of the states of the major civilizations — Oriental, Greek, Roman, and German —

which he accommodated to his theory of Spirit and its phases. He attended in particular to ancient art and mythology, especially as interpreted by Creuzer, to illuminate his view of the evolution of spiritual freedom out of subjection to nature. The interplay between the real and the ideal in modern history was for Hegel symbolized by Caesar and Christ, but it was in German political tradition that these principles converged into a new spiritual and, in Hegel's day, political form. For the Germanic stage Hegel posited another trinity of periods (which he, indeed, like Joachim of Flora four centuries earlier, compared to the Father, Son, and Holy Spirit): from the invasions to Charlemagne and the emergence of "Christendom"; from the Emperor Charlemagne to the Emperor Charles V, when the dialectic was between church and state; and from the Protestant Reformation, with its subjectivity and spiritual freedom, to the present era of Revolution and secular freedom — which "brings us to *the last stage in History, our world, our own time.*" So neo-Augustinian eschatology was transposed to the age of Napoleon and national liberation.

In spite of the secular categories, Hegel's creation was, like Schlegel's, a theodicy, a justification of God in history. Hegel left a gigantic heritage which had its own dialectic — between left and right interpretations, spiritualist and materialist orientations. Ranke and most German historians followed Hegel's idealization of the state but rejected his evasion of the "positive" side of historical reality. Marx and other "left Hegelians" criticized him on both grounds, and indeed Marx founded his own philosophy of history on the central "fact" overlooked by Hegel, namely, the materialist condition of the modern world and of humanity. On this insight and on a critique of the European legal tradition as a form of ideology, Marx built not only a vision of history but also a science of society; and yet in form if not in substance he remained a Hegelian.[91] Marx's was a "pragmatic" view of history, except that economics rather than politics provided the ruling methodology and revealed the prime causal factors, property, followed by labor, and especially the mode of production and accompanying class conflicts, which had been noted by Guizot, Thierry, and others. Intellectual, cultural, or spiritual factors were in general reflections of these primary socio-economic conditions, although in his later years Marx discovered the findings of contemporary anthropology and took a broader view of the historical process than the Eurocentric one inherited from his German and French antecedents.[92] His conception was still deterministic, but it was a technological rather than an economic sort of determinism.

Marx's periodization generally followed that of Hegel — the four stages, based not on spirit but on the nature of the economy of production — and included oriental (or patriarchal), antique (or slave), feudal (or serf), and capitalist (or bourgeois).[93] As Frank Manuel concluded, "Marx's four modes of production replaced Hegel's four world-historical cultures, as these had once ousted Daniel's four world monarchies."[94] Of course Marx, too, adopted a prophetic rather than a purely historical stance, his eyes, like Hegel's, fixed on the "end of history," although this end was not to be in his world, or his time. Marxism, too, was a theodicy, though a revolutionary one; and if it did not succeed in changing the world according to its own views, it did inspire and provoke historians to ask questions which went beyond and were deeper than those of the old, and continuing, conventional art and normal science of history. His analytical focus, more than his speculative ventures, have added immensely to the canon of Western historiography.

The nineteenth century saw countless contributions to the "philosophy of history" — as well as the "science" and "theory" of history — in all Western countries from every conceivable point of view between the extremes of Hegel and Marx. The neo-Guelf Cesare Balbo followed the conservative Catholic tradition of Schlegel, Bonald, and Joseph de Maistre (as well as Vico) in setting his conception of "philosophical history" (*filosofia storia*) within a providential framework, in which he projected the fate of a united Italy; and the rigorously orthodox Vicente La Fuente prefaced his vast survey of Spanish ecclesiastical history with the tag, "To God alone belongs honor and glory: this is the philosophy of history for Catholic truth."[95] Joseph Franz Molitor tried to bring *Philosophie der Geschichte* into the "metaphysical" orbit of Jewish tradition, including the Torah and Kabbalah; Frédéric de Rougement associated it with a complex periodization and a line of speculation leading from Augustine to Catholic authors like Schlegel and Lasaulx; Giuseppe Ferrari kept a Catholic position, rejecting the determinism (*fatalité*) of secularists but drawing also on the ideas and system of Vico; while the convergence with Darwinism and cultural history also acted powerfully to expand the field of operations of philosophers of history.[96] At the same time, however, the philosophy of history diverged from the field of historical research as such, as indeed it has continued to do. The difference was like that between induction and deduction, between facts and principles. "Positive history describes," Ferrari said; "the philosophy of history demonstrates." And seldom the twain would meet.

3

Expanding Horizons

History is not only a particular branch of knowledge, but a particular mode and method of knowledge in other branches.

— *Lord Acton*

A Wider World

Universal history had been an important part of the inventory of historical writing since antiquity — Polybius if not Herodotus — but this universality had always been Mediterraneo- or Eurocentric. The situation changed with the discovery of the New World, though the novelties in this hemisphere were at first also seen through European eyes and prejudices. It soon became evident, however, that the marvels and curiosities of the New World did not fit easily into the parochial categories of the West, whence the heterological impulse that accepted the facts of difference and the challenge of the "Other" — a historically and ethnographically concrete expression of Hegel's *Andersein* or *Anderheit* and the notion that self-consciousness depends on a consciousness of an Other.[1] Western values continued to shape historical interpretation, which likewise followed the course of empire; but by the eighteenth century historians realized that there was more at stake than conquest and expansion;

there was also the question of the economic, commercial, and industrial transformation of Western (and implicitly Eastern) civilization.

This was the point pursued in *The Philosophical and Political History of the Institutions and Commerce of the Europeans in the Two Indies* (1762), a popular and derivative work published under the name of G. T. F. Raynal but based on the writings of Diderot and other philosophes.[2] This book, which was much prized by Napoleon, described "the revolution in commerce, in the power of nations, in manners, industry, and government of all peoples" in the wake of the Columbian enterprise, which brought encounters between civilization and savagery. Claiming to write in Tacitean fashion, "without passion or prejudice," Raynal denounced the crimes of the conquerors and especially the institution of slavery. Yet for him as war and exploitation gave way to commerce, the expanding network of exchange produced new needs, new relationships, and new cultural "influences," moral as well as physical; and the long-term results were understanding, toleration, and progress.

In the Enlightenment cultural horizons expanded within the dimension of time as well as space. At first the historically remote was as mysterious as the geographically inaccessible, objects of inquiry being as dimly seen or imagined as Herodotus's "Scythians" or China and Japan before the Jesuit missions. Bossuet's *Discourse on Universal History* stayed with Augustine's City of God and "God's people," with only small gestures to the Scythians, Ethiopians, Egyptians, Persians, and others. At best the Eastern nations were the mysterious source of that primitive wisdom (*prisca sapientia*) which Pico, among others, had celebrated: "All wisdom has flowed from the East to the Greeks and from the Greeks to us." This was the "barbarian philosophy" which Diogenes Laertius had excluded from the history of philosophy, and indeed the prejudice remained, though scholars like J. J. Brucker did examine this prephilosophical tradition on the basis of conventional classical sources.[3] By the eighteenth century much knowledge had accumulated about these areas, as well as the "New World," but the "light from the orient" still shone dimly until the last quarter of the century, when the "oriental renaissance" burst on the scene to rival the first revival of learning four centuries earlier—and to form another sort of continuity across the revolutionary period.[4]

This growing awareness could already be perceived in the work of Voltaire, who boasted about his moving beyond the Judeo-Christian orientation of Bossuet, and in Gibbon, who allowed a glimpse of China and the East from his Mediterranean horizons. Herder also admitted Eastern civilization into his philosophy of history, first in a vague and conventional way and then under more direct contact with the new orientalist discoveries. Though likewise in derivative and amateurish terms, William Robertson contributed to the awareness of the orient in a late work which, it seems, helped spur Friedrich Schlegel to his orientalist studies.[5] By the early nineteenth century orientalism had invaded even the work of Idéologues like Degérando, whose comparative history of philosophy (1804) admitted this material into the canon, as did Victor Cousin in his famous course of lectures, in which he pointed to the East as "the cradle of civilization and philosophy; history ascends as high as that, and no higher."[6]

Of such pioneering efforts to transcend a Eurocentric perspective, Acton wrote, "The Romantic writers . . . doubled the horizon of Europe. They admitted India to an equality with Greece, medieval Rome with classical; and the thoughts they set in motion produced Creuzer's *Comparative Mythology* and Bopp's *Conjugations,* Grimm's enthusiasm for the liberty and belief of Odin's worshippers, and Otfried Müller's zeal for the factor of race."[7] The first stage of this second renaissance, as of the first, was the discovery and publication of essential texts, beginning with the translation of the so-called *Zen-Avesta* by A. H. Anquetil-Duperron, brother of the historian L. P. Anquetil. This work, the essential collection of Zoroastrian materials, was regarded by Schlegel as a missing link between Christianity and paganism.

The key to the oriental renaissance, however, was the uncovering of Sanskrit materials and the subsequent translations and analysis by William Jones, Charles Wilkins, Alexander Hamilton, Henry Colebrooke, and others. Although the English scholars, followers of the British Empire, were the pioneers in Indic studies, leadership of this scholarly enterprise was taken over by the French and especially the Germans. "During the 1790s," Schwab writes, "the impact of oriental studies in Germany was like a rapid-fire series of explosions," with poetic and legal texts made available and research results appearing in *Asiatic Researches,* the English journal founded in Calcutta. In France an orientalist school was established in 1795, with Silvestre de Sacy teaching Arabic and then Persian; and by 1814 there was a chair of Sanskrit in the university, which was assumed by a student of Sacy. It was to Paris that the Schlegels, Bopp, and other orientalist enthusiasts came to pursue their studies and to lay the foundations of a new "world history."

Friedrich Schlegel was a student of the Sanskritist Alexander Hamilton (as was Volney); and in 1808, after five years of studying Persian and Sanskrit, he published his famous manifesto *On the Language and Wisdom of the Indians,* which recalled Renaissance invocations of "ancient wisdom." As Heine later wrote, Schlegel "became for Germany what William Jones had been for England."[8] Both he and his brother August, who became an even better Sanskrit scholar, were attached at that time to the Coppet circle, and they shared their

Indic insights with Mme de Staël, Constant, and others. What Calcutta has to do with Rome was a live issue in these years of orientalist enthusiasm. What Schlegel emphasized above all was the spiritualism of the Brahmins, who were a caste of priests or even "philosophers" who believed in the immortality of the soul — "another life" — and indeed expressed "almost all the truths of natural theology."[9] In these years he was also giving his lectures on universal history and the history of literature and philosophy, both subjects enhanced by the flood of orientalist discoveries, which reinforced not only his own growing romantic medievalism and spiritualism — he was converted to Catholicism just a few days before the publication of his work — but also that of Chateaubriand and other romantic souls.

Orientalism never extricated itself from mythical constructs, as apparent in the "Aryan" and racialist speculations of Western scholars.[10] In details, however, orientalism passed, according to Schwab's fervent account, from the realm of imagination to that of science, as the study of language passed from speculation to historical inquiry. The central insight was expressed by William Jones in 1786 in this way: "The Sanskrit language, whatever be its antiquity, is of a wonderful structure; more perfect than the Greek, more copious than the Latin, and more exquisitely refined than either, yet bearing to both of them a stronger affinity, both in the roots of the verbs and the forms of the grammar, than could possibly have been produced by accident; so strong, indeed, that no philologer could examine them all three, without believing them to have sprung from some common source, which, perhaps, no longer exists."[11] As Burnouf declared in his inaugural lecture in 1832, "It is more than India, gentlemen, it is a page from the history of the human spirit that we shall attempt to decipher together."[12] The more general result of this line of discovery was the founding of the new disciplines of historical linguistics and comparative philology, which were central to the historical schools of the nineteenth century and to historicism more generally — and which were further reinforced by the support which Darwinist biology seemed to offer.[13]

An even more sensational aspect of the oriental renaissance was uncovering the mysteries of Egypt. Napoleon may have misread history, as de Staël charged, but he did draw inspiration from it, and moreover made important contributions to its cultivation. The Bonapartist interlude was not graced with historiographical masterpieces, but Napoleon did incorporate history in his educational projects, and moreover was himself at least the "unwitting architect" of the remarkable further advance of Egyptian, Roman, and Christian antiquities, stemming from his Egyptian campaign (1798), in which he was accompanied by intellectuals of various sorts.[14] One serendipitous result was the discovery of the Rosetta Stone in the Nile delta, leading to the decipherment of the language of the Egyptian priests concealed in the hieroglyphic script and to the consequent establishment of Egyptology as a discipline. The culmination came with Champollion's remarkable, if controversial, success (at the age of eighteen) in solving this puzzle, which had been the object of imaginative but fruitless study for centuries.[15]

Chateaubriand, who had included the Egyptians and Indians in his *Essay on Revolutions* in 1797, was struck by this achievement and concluded on the basis of linguistic connections, in the edition of 1826, that the Egyptians had originally come from India.[16] For Chateaubriand, too, the light from the Orient reinforced his pilgrimage back to orthodox religion expressed in his *Origin of Christianity* (1802), in which the hieroglyphs are again invoked as proof of the hidden mysteries of the universe.[17] In keeping with the conventions of Renaissance scholarship, Chateaubriand also claimed that the Trinity was known to the Brahmins and professed to see precedents to the ten commandments in the laws of the Indians, Egyptians, and Persians. All this added metahistorical context to Chateaubriand's major project, which was to rehabilitate the glories of the church which had suffered once again at the hands of pagans like Voltaire, who "renewed the persecutions of Julian" the Apostate (Voltaire was like a monk writing only for his order).[18] For Chateaubriand, Christianity was "sublime in the antiquity of its memories, which went back to the infancy of the world, ineffable in its mysteries, adorable in its sacraments, interesting in its history, heavenly in its morality, rich and charming in its rituals."[19] In the flamboyant interpretations of Chateaubriand we can see truly long-term continuities, from the old notion of a primitive wisdom and "perennial philosophy" to insights derived from the publications of the Asiatic society of Calcutta and other vehicles of the oriental renaissance.

The larger context of this centrifugal interest, beyond Napoleon's imperial designs (which extended as far as India), was the emergence of modern anthropology, in association with less politically motivated expeditions and institutions like the *Société des Observateurs de l'Homme* (1800), bringing together experts in natural and social sciences and Idéologues in a common ethnological and archeological project whose effects were also to expand historical perspectives by including "the natural history of man."[20] Human history takes place in the larger arena and longer time span of natural history, and the eighteenth century saw vast secular efforts to replace the creation myths of world religions, especially the Bible story. This is a large subject, taking different forms in different national contexts; but Buffon was a key figure in opening the horizons of history to the animal world. By the end of the century it was common to accommodate these expanding horizons of human evolution. Origins were still obscure, but to illuminate them natural history shifted attention to the environment and climate in the light of modern scientific discoveries, and moreover expanded the "four-stage theory" to a new universalism, an evolutionary perspective on human progress.

Mythistoricism

"Mythistory" (*mythistoria*), a coinage of Thucydides, applies not only to the tradition of myth and mythology but also to theories of origins and fictions accepted by Herodotus and scholars of his adventurous and often uncritical inclinations.[21] According to Nathan Bailey's dictionary of 1730, mythistory is "an history mingled with false fables and tales." "What was mythology to the ancients?" asked Herder: "Part history, part allegory, part religion, part mere poetic framework";[22] and it was up to the modern scholar to analyze these parts more critically. In the eighteenth century there were many competing theories of myth, and — like the theories of language — they were located between the extremes of natural and supernatural origins. In his *Philosophy of Mythology*, begun in the 1820s, F. W. J. Schelling listed the explanations of this mystery in a schematic, though by no means exhaustive way: "Mythologie" (that is, myth) is just the external covering of a historical truth (the idea of Euhemerus) or physical truth (C. G. Heyne), or it is a misunderstanding of a scientific truth (G. Hermann) or religious truth (William Jones and Friedrich Creuzer).[23]

By the eighteenth century mythology, while always mixing scholarship and speculation, was claiming for itself the status of a science. One early pioneer was Bernard Fontenelle, whose essay on the "origin of fables" (published in 1724 but written before 1700) identified poetry as "the philosophy of the first ages," though also a leading example of the errors to which the human mind was prone.[24] For Antoine Banier, writing in 1711, mythology was "ancient history disfigur'd by poets, who were the first historians"; but he appreciated the historical value of myth (as of etymology); for "How can we reduce to history what Grekes themselves did not know?"[25] In Vico's *New Science* all of these themes were joined in one gigantic structure: the problem of origins (*principia*), poetic wisdom (*sapienza poetica*), and "barbarism" (*barbarie*).[26] In linking modern reason with primitive forms of conceptualizing, Vico, too, was deliberately drawing on a long and familiar tradition of *prisca sapientia* and what Thomas Burnett had called "mythological philosophy."[27]

Taking a philosophical approach, some Enlightened scholars, from Bayle and Fontenelle to Hume and Holbach, looked down on primitive myth as the product of fear, ignorance, superstition, and error, not unlike orthodox criticisms, by Bishop Warburton and others, of myth as idolatry (thinking of the

Egyptian hieroglyphs) or animal worship. Charles de Brosses gained fame through his theory (1760) that myth was born of "fetish" worship, and like most other scholars assumed a correlation between an early state of barbarism and modern-day savages in the newly discovered parts of the world.[28] But the question always remained: what was the meaning (what were the meanings) of myth? If myth was a "veil" — the term used by Banier, Nicolas Freret, and Thomas Blackwell — what did this veil conceal? For Blackwell (1735) this understanding required a knowledge not only of the Greek context of Homer but also of the underlying primitive philosophy originating in Assyria and Egypt. Mythology was "a Labyrinth thro' whose Windings no *one* Thread can conduct us." Like Vico, Blackwell believed that knowledge of this labyrinth was available through an "original tradition" which, though perhaps corrupted, linked prehistory and history.[29]

Idealistic philosophy looked at mythology as an early stage, or collective aspect, of philosophy in a poetic, intuitive, symbolic, and unreflective condition. For Schelling (as for Vico and Herder) myth was a kind of concealed truth which held the secret to the primitive and perhaps the popular mind that only philosophy in alliance with history could reveal. Every age creates its own mythology, he believed, and "how a new mythology (which cannot be the invention of an individual poet but only of a new generation that represents things as if it were a single poet), can itself arise, is a problem for whose solution we must look to the future destiny of the world and the further course of history alone."[30]

Mythology and philology have at all times been linked, and they converged more directly in the later eighteenth century. Language itself was a "faded mythology," wrote Schelling, and indeed their fortunes were intertwined. Both myth and language were subject to inquiries about origins and about the transition of humanity from a state of nature to that of culture, both seemed to pass through homologous historical trajectories, both were subject to historical as well as comparative methods, and both were revolutionized by the oriental renaissance that threw new light on the Eastern background to Western civilization. This intersection between mythology and philology can be seen in various studies of the Homeric question, including that of Robert Wood (1767), who argued that these poems correspond to real historical facts, and especially in the influential work of Heyne, whose followers included Wolf, the Schlegels, Creuzer, Humboldt, and Coleridge — and, at greater remove, the biblical scholar David Friedrich Strauss.

Heyne was both a late agent of Renaissance humanism and a pioneer of the modern study of mythology.[31] At Göttingen he was not professor of law or theology but altogether humanist (*ganz Humanist*), rival of the best English and Dutch classicists. After Robert Wood he was the first to read Homer as grammarian and historian, and from this he went on to an interdisciplinary theory and practice of antiquities (*Alterthumswissenschaft*) and a poetically based mythology (*Dichtermythologie*) joined to history, geography, literature, and natural science. "The value and dignity of myth has been restored," he wrote; "it should be regarded as old sagas, and the first sources and beginnings of the history of peoples, or else as the first childish attempts at philosophizing." And: "Art, with its ideals mediating the nature and systems of the gods, has its first expression in myth and mythic images."[32] For Heyne, "In interpreting myth we must transport ourselves back into the manner of thought and expression which belonged to that remote period."[33] His purpose was to read back from poetic discourse on a preexisting set of myths — moving hermeneutically from letter to spirit, from *historia literaria* to *historia* "itself." Like Vico, Heyne granted a sort of protophilosophical status — "philosophemes" is his term, later adopted by Hegel and others — to poetic expressions of mythical beliefs.[34] And Heyne's views were popularized by a student, M. G. Herrmann, and his handbook of ancient mythology.[35]

These ideas were applied more specifically by F. A. Wolf (who also credited the work of Wood) to the controversial Homeric question. It was Homer's poems above all that "in a sense forced philological criticism into existence," and Wolf self-consciously continued the tradition of the ancient *grammatikoi* and *kritikoi*.[36] Moving back "in spirit," through the modern "art of interpretation and emendation," Wolf sought "the history which is hidden under the fable"; and he concluded that the Iliad and Odyssey were collective efforts reflecting not merely the work of one artist but also, and more profoundly, the oral culture of ancient Greece. As language was the creation of a people, so was the tradition of myth and philosophy. Niebuhr did much the same for ancient Rome as Eichhorn did for the more sensitive field of biblical studies. Textual tradition introduced corruptions into every surviving work of ancient literature, biblical as well as classical, and it was the task of philologists to try to restore the original state of both text and context.

Another approach to mythology was taken by Heyne's former student Friedrich Creuzer, whose aim was to create a sort of neoplatonic mytho-logic, not unlike Vico's "poetic wisdom." Creuzer's fascination with origins was evident in an early work which attempted to trace the Greek "art of history" back to its roots in the symbols of the priests as well as the writings of poets and logographers before Herodotus.[37] The "new symbolism" reflected in this approach placed Creuzer closer to Hegel and Friedrich Schlegel than to Wolf or Niebuhr, and it is not surprising to see his treatise *Symbolik und Mythologie der alten Völker*, which began to appear in 1810, praised by those classically

trained idealists like Schelling and Hegel. For Creuzer history was not limited
to written testimony; rather it was the expression of "a regular relationship
between consciousness and nature."[38] To retrace this relationship, to make the
leap backward from culture to nature, Creuzer proposed a method of interpretation through the symbol understood in a prehistorical, pre-linguistic, and
perhaps (anticipating Jung and Kerenyi) preconscious sense. In this effort
Creuzer also relied on art-historical sources, especially pictorial representations of gods and heroes interpreted allegorically. Creuzer assumed that nature
spoke to humanity through symbols, aural as well as visual, and myths were
the stories (*logoi*) told in this pre-verbal language, expressing the forces of
natures and the experiences of birth, acquisition, production, reproduction,
and death. In other words language was the product of apotheosis, or the-
ogony, and *logos* was a cultivated form of *mythos*.

For most nineteenth-century philologists and classical historians Creuzer
had, in search of self-knowledge, delved too deeply and credulously into what
Thomas Mann called "the deep well of the past."[39] Creuzer was not *historicos*
or *philologos* but rather, like Nietzsche and Bachofen after him, *philomythos*,
who raised Dionysian darkness above the Apollonian individualism and enlightenment, moving from metaphysics back to mysticism. After its initial
success his *Symbolik* became the target of criticisms aimed at its "mysticism"
and credulous speculation; and within a generation advances in philology, historical linguistics, art history, archeology, ethnology, and folklore had largely
discredited it. Yet admittedly rival theories did not fare much better, and the
modern science of mythology has repeatedly been led down the blind alleys, or
up garden paths, because of methodological or ideological excesses.

The resonances of Creuzer's symbolist thought were more positive in one
other area, which was that of the history of law. The combined influence of
Creuzer, Vico, and the oriental renaissance can be seen in one of Jules Michelet's ingenious, youthful work on the origins of law.[40] Michelet conceived of
his book as a treatise on the "poetic origins of European law" and a "symbolic of law," uncannily anticipating Cassirer's philosophy of symbolic forms.
Michelet's thesis was simple: God created man, and man created symbols. He
was *homo symbolicus*, and the language of symbols still reflected in the "poetry of law" preceded and subsumed written language. In this "juridical biography of man," Michelet ranged over the entire trajectory of human experience, from birth to death, from awareness of self to cooperation and conflict
with others, from the eternal *Moi* of ancient Roman and modern bourgeois
culture to the idealized *Nous* of primitive Germanic society and revolutionary
visions of fraternity. Questions of the status of women and children, of property and inheritance, of social structure and ceremony, or death and burial

were all reflected in ancient Indo-European law in terms not only of language but also of gestures, colors, devices, arms, and other sorts of silent symbolism.

Ten years later there appeared another remarkable essay on the "symbolic of law," this one by Joseph-Pierre Chassan. More comprehensive than Michelet's book, Chassan's work invoked Vico's three stages and Creuzer's belief in primitive religion; and it treated symbolic expression in art, especially sculpture, preceding the poetic language which was still detectable in legal monuments. Yet "philology alone can establish civil history," Chassan wrote. "Languages are a sort of intellectual cosmogony where the archives of the human race are deposited. Philology possesses the secret of reading these mysterious archives and sometimes of discovering, in the debris accumulated by the ages, certain expressions which, though meaningless to the layman, are for reflective scholars the revelations of an entire past."[41]

Chassan gave many examples of expressive but inarticulate symbolism, arranging them in hierarchical order. On the lowest level juridical symbols were natural—a bit of earth or stone, representing personal property and a branch, political authority, and parts of the human body, including the hand (for swearing, striking, or saluting) and the mouth (for kissing or libeling). Animal symbols were also common, such as the image of the white horse, the *cheval blanc,* which persisted from the fourteenth century down to Napoleon; and then of course there was woman, who was eternal and universal: "For woman was poetry itself," Chassan rhapsodized. In his quest for origins he could not establish a chronology of development, could not reach the bottom of the symbolic well. "Custom and symbols have no fathers," he wrote: "they are at once inside and as it were outside of time." Yet he did not reject historicism, or mythistoricism, and like his Romantic forebears he strained to hear the ancient voices, to see the primordial symbols resounding and reflected in the surviving texts, and to suggest continuities underlying the ruptures of a revolutionary age. "Modern France has undoubtedly broken with feudalism as a political system," he suggested, "but who can say that we do not continue to live at this very moment on the debris and in the bonds of the feudal regime, which organized Europe and created the landed property of the middle ages, an institution which is still evident today in our landed property?"[42] These continuities were at this very time being investigated by the new historians of that age.

Mythology emerged as a science in the later nineteenth century, especially in its comparative form, championed by Friedrich Max Müller, who was a student of Bopp and Burnouf, a friend of Ranke, Macaulay, Froude, and Freeman, and was strongly influenced by Jakob Grimm, and who from 1850 was professor of modern languages at Oxford. Rejecting the poorly founded concern for chronology of his older colleague Bunsen, Müller remained convinced of the value of philology for the study of "Aryan" antiquities, believing that myth was "an ancient form of language."[43] Max Müller was a dominant force in Indology and mythology for more than a generation, but his methods were challenged not only by historians but also by those who, like Andrew Lang, were suspicious of Müller's facile etymologies, analogies, and racial Aryanism, and who took an anthropological approach to myth (not that Lang's totemism has survived later criticism, either). Yet mythology, still ridden with interdisciplinary controversies and a succession of revisionist interpretations, remains an essential adjunct to historical inquiry.

Higher Criticism and Hermeneutics

Universal history was written within the biblical framework until the later nineteenth century (and even later), with all the supernatural and miraculous accompaniments that strict scriptural faith carried. Assaults of course there were, ranging from revived skepticism, pre-Adamite theories, Naturalism, Deism, and free-thinking to outright (if covert) atheism; but it was philology and biblical scholarship in the tradition of Valla, Erasmus, Spinoza, and Richard Simon that opened the Bible story and its temporal horizons to critical scrutiny. In 1860, Wilhelm Dilthey made a pioneering sketch of the history of biblical hermeneutics from Flacius Illyricus to Friedrich Schleiermacher, tracing its transformation into philosophical and especially historical modes. He gave credit to J. A. Bengel as the first to group biblical manuscripts into families and J. A. Turretini as the first to take ancient customs and opinions into account in biblical exegesis, but the key figures were S. J. Baumgarten and his students, J. D. Michaelis and J. S. Semler. According to the latter, Baumgarten's *Biblical Hemeneutics* (1769) was "the first German scientific plan for a hermeneutics."[44] The old hermeneutics was based on assumptions of divine inspiration and unity of text, while the new methods — loosely termed "neology" — took historical conditions into account and accepted the notion that Scriptures, too, were bound to time and place. With Semler, the real founder of the historical method, the biblical canon itself came into question (and not merely, as with Luther, on doctrinal grounds). With G. L. Bauer the "mythical" point of view was applied to the Old Testament, the extension of these views not yet reaching the New Testament.

Dilthey neglected to mention the scandalous and subversive incident which projected these issues into the public sphere when Lessing published the anonymous "Wolffenbüttel Fragments," later found to be the posthumous work of Samuel Reimarus, teacher of oriental languages in Hamburg and reader of the works of English deists like John Toland and Anthony Collins.[45] Reimarus applied the standards of reason to scriptural texts and concluded not that Jesus was an imposter (another radical theory of that period expressed in the mysterious treatise on the "three imposters") but that Christianity was the product of discipular deceit and fraud.[46] This conclusion was far too subversive for orthodox scholars, but it did suggest the extreme limits of the discussion of the significance of biblical texts.

The upshot for biblical criticism in any case was to fix attention not on the theological but on the philological status and meaning of the Old and New Testaments. Michaelis, professor of philosophy at Göttingen and one of the leading "neologists," published an introduction to the New Testament in 1750 and in three more editions down to 1788.[47] In this work, referring to the Wolffenbüttel fragments, Michaelis shifted from the question of inspiration to that of the authenticity and historicity of evangelical texts. In particular he subjected the first three, synoptic gospels to textual exegesis in the search for a common source; but he finally decided that Matthew, Mark, and Luke were authors working independently of each other. In 1793, Herbert Marsh, a pioneering Germanist in England, translated Michaelis's work and introduced into the Anglophone world not only this controversy but also the dangerous procedure of treating the Old and New Testaments in the same way as philologists treated Homer and Vergil, that is, as literary and historical source materials.

The phrase "higher criticism" was apparently coined by the Göttingen polymath, J. G. Eichhorn, who was the author also of many volumes of universal and cultural history. "Higher criticism" suggested the need for historical judgment about the world beyond the letter of the text — an updated version of the old *res-verba* topos, and, to this end, a critical history of the text and its early context. Eichhorn also preserved an attachment to a "natural" mode of explanation, though he objected to rationalists like Reimarus, who judged the past in the light of the present. Eichhorn began with the premise that the texts of the Old Testament were no less authentic than those of the *Iliad* and the *Odyssey*. "They come to us from no imposter," although they had indeed undergone many alterations in the course of human time.[48] "What Eichhorn did," concluded the translators of Wolf's book, "was to apply Heyne's method, more consistently than Heyne himself, to the material Michaelis has made available."[49] Eichhorn's work, especially his introduction to the Old Testament (1780), had a powerful influence on his younger colleague, Friedrich Wolf, in his groundbreaking and controversial study of the Homeric poems, their likewise collective authorship (not an identifiable Homer, like the Mosaic tradition), and the underlying texts. For Eichhorn this meant a possible original gospel (*Urevangelium*) on which the synoptic gospels (Matthew, Mark, and Luke) were arguably based.

The best-known figure in this tradition of higher criticism was Friedrich Schleiermacher, who added to it the Protestant tradition of hermeneutics and, moreover, in the context of nineteenth-century historicism, turned to the quest for the "historical Jesus." Schleiermacher lectured on the life of Jesus just after the biography of Paulus (1828). In general, while he likewise favored a natural mode of explanation, he found Eichhorn uncritical in failing to distinguish between the context of a modern critic and that of the primitive age of Christianity. Schleiermacher faced the old questions of inspiration and the presence of the divine spirit in the New Testament texts, but he distinguished between spirit in the eyewitnesses and that in the compilers, so that the question of authorship became central.[50] He rejected Eichhorn's thesis of a lost original gospel and focused on Luke as the source for reconstructing a biography, although he did not follow earlier critics in rejecting John as a witness as well as recorder. And indeed, while he insisted on treating Scriptures in philological, historical, and human terms, he argued also that conclusions must be compatible with the fundamentals of Christian faith. Schleiermacher's views were carried to England by Connop Thirlwall's translation of the study of Luke, although, moderate as his views seem, they were too drastic for the English churchmen of that day.

Much more radical than these mainstream higher critics were the members of the so-called "mythical school," whose point of departure was the work of Robert Lowth on the "sacred poetry of the Hebrews" (*de sacra poesi hebraeorum*), published in 1753 in Latin and later translated into English, for which Friedrich Meinecke included him, in association with Herder, in the tradition of European historicism.[51] Aside from Heyne, the key figures in this mythical school were J. P. Gabler, G. L. Bauer, who also brought hermeneutics, "from a mythical standpoint," to bear on "Hebrew myths of the Old and New Testament," and especially Eichhorn, teacher of Gabler and student of Michaelis (and his successor at Göttingen) and also of Heyne. These were the "precursors" of the more venturesome scholar David Friedrich Strauss, who in the next generation raised the level and the stakes of the discussion by taking the dangerous (and, for his own career, fatal) step of bringing religion and myth (*mythus*) together in the same field of inquiry. Even Vico had privileged Judeo-Christian history in the construction of his "gentile" "new science," and few scholars were willing to depart from the requirements of revealed religion. But following the lead of the mythical school Strauss deliberately and recklessly offered his own biography of Jesus as an expression of a "new point of view" that would discredit "the antiquated systems of supernaturalism and naturalism."[52] Among the other influences on Strauss were Ferdinand Christian Baur (whose *Symbolism and Mythology* appeared in 1824),[53] Schleiermacher, Schelling, and Hegel—and indeed Strauss was later enlisted among the left-Hegelians.[54] But Strauss turned away from philosophy back to the tradition of biblical criticism, where history figured more directly and positively. He rejected both the rationalism of the naturalists, which could not resolve the deeper puzzles of the gospels, and the naive fundamentalism of the harmonists, which resorted to supernaturalist explanation; and he repudiated the dogmatic position of Schleiermacher, whose posthumously published life of Jesus proceeded, he complained, "directly from faith."[55]

Between the extremes of regarding Christianity as a false creation by Jesus's disciples and a wholly supernatural explanation, Strauss proposed what he believed to be a novel and critical, yet moderate, third way, that is, the "mythic," or "genetic" view, which was to tell the story of the afterlife of Christ as the accumulation and progress of myth and legend—myth being the creation of a fact and legend, the seeing of an idea in a fact. Historically, there were a number of contradictions among the synoptic gospels, especially regarding the telling case of the resurrection, since it began the posthumous career of Jesus, connected with the legends and hopes of earlier messianic tradition, and suggested an explanation that led beyond the biblical text to historical context. For the life of Christ was the creation not just of the authors of the problematic gospels; it was a collective work over time. For Strauss myth was not just fable or error, and he rejected both the ancient allegorists and Euhemerists and the modern, neopagan naturalists and deists, including the views of the "Fragmentist" Reimarus, and Eichhorn. Hardly more acceptable was the moral interpretation introduced by Kant. The true mythological approach was made possible by critics who denied the eyewitness status of the gospels and who emphasized oral tradition, and it was begun more directly by (among many others cited by Strauss) Gabler, Schelling, Baur, and De Wette, who rejected the possibility of an access to truth behind the text. Mythological interpretations had been applied to primitive ages; it was Strauss's innovation to make them relevant to the period after the death of Christ. Strauss distinguished among historical myth, in which the mythical element predominated; mythical history, which is the reverse; and histories in which legend forms a part, where "we tread properly speaking on historical ground."[56]

"The boundary line . . . between the historical and the unhistorical . . ." admitted Strauss, "will ever remain fluctuating and unsusceptible of precise attainment." Yet the mythological method yielded probable knowledge of the past. As Herder had suggested and Wolf had argued, myths were not invented, not deliberate deceptions, but rather were the product of collective thinking over a long period of time. It was of course difficult for moderns to carry themselves back into a remote time when strange illusions were believed (like Livy's credulity about the Roman kings — or the Jews' belief in the coming of the Messiah?), but this is what Strauss's method made possible. His specific target was the evangelical myth, which was the product of the ideas of Jesus's followers and which was transmitted and transformed by oral tradition. The negative aspect of myth was that it was unhistorical; the positive side was that it produced its own narrative and so became part of the historical process. There was no "true picture" behind a "curtain of myth," as George Grote wrote of the ancient Greeks: "The curtain *is* the picture."[57] It is the subject of historical inquiry and not "something else."

Church History

The history of the church — *historia sacra, historia ecclesiastica* — ran parallel to biblical studies and likewise, while retaining a general belief in some sort of religious progress, was transmuted into a more critically historical state in the nineteenth century. Despite the precedent of Gottfried Arnold's "non-partisan history of heretics," the polarity of and polemic between Catholic and Protestant continued, as did Mosheim's distinction between external and internal history.[58] External history had to do with institutions — for Mosheim with the transformation of the church into a state — and of course Protestant scholars continued to emphasize the pre-Reformation degeneration of the church and its "abuses," while Catholics lamented the confusion produced by the Lutheran schism. Like his model and target Sleidan, Ranke was convinced that political and religious (external and internal) history could not be separated, and in the case of Germany he pointed to his own spiritual model, Martin Luther, as (though he would not use the term) the world-historical individual who was the principal founder of modernity in Europe and leader of a "mighty national movement."[59]

No less devoted to German nationality, the Catholic historian, Johannes Janssen, defended the later German Middle Ages as intellectually and culturally rich until the decay which set in with the advent of Protestantism, after which even popular songs shifted from a religious to a military tone. Not Melanchthon but the Jesuits were responsible for the revival of education from the sixteenth century. Janssen was especially critical of Protestant historiography, beginning with the partisan Sleidan, whose work was indeed based on documents, but only those of a public and not a private provenance, and including the gross attack made by the Magdeburg Centuries. He preferred the portrayals of contemporary violence given by Luther's polemical

Catholic biographer, Cochlaeus, despite his passion and exaggerations. Janssen followed the contemporary fashions of privileging cultural over political history, and in his survey of "historical writing" (drawing on the handbook of Wegele) he praised sixteenth-century German scholars, both Protestant and Catholic, for their contributions to documentary collections and archeology.[60] Janssen was fiercely protective of the fortunes of his work and answered in great detail the many criticisms of it.[61] His history was completed by Ludwig Pastor, whose history of the popes was intended, on a massive scale and with full access to the Vatican archives, to counter Ranke's youthful work and to assimilate German history to the new ultramontanism.

The internal history of the church was concerned less with biblical criticism and more with dogma, theological tradition, the principles separating Catholics and Protestants, and even (Leibniz's old dream) possibilities of reuniting the confessions. In the 1820s, during the debates surrounding Schleiermacher, Baur, and Strauss, the Catholic J. A. Möhler published a controversial book on the unity of the church in the time of the fathers (1825), which provoked criticism from Catholics as well as Protestants, including Strauss, who thought him soft on the evils of the church; and his last work, the often-reprinted and translated *Symbolik* (1832), which reviewed, in an ecumenical spirit, the non-Catholic theological traditions, caused an even greater uproar, including a polemic with Baur.[62] Möhler died soon after his move from Tübingen to Munich, but his work and his belief in the essential continuity of the church from apostolic times remained an ecumenical and conciliatory influence among liberal Catholics in an age of mounting ultramontanism.

In a critique of Möhler's *Symbolik*, Baur, working also for reconciliation between Catholics and Protestants, looked to the theology of Schleiermacher and the philosophy of Hegel as a way of defining a tradition which was historical, and indeed historicist, as well as spiritual and which could accommodate the major theological differences.[63] Although his theological proposals were not successful, Baur pursued his historical interests with reviews of the historiography and hermeneutics of Christian tradition and, in 1852, with a survey of church historiography.[64] For Baur the Reformation not only sent believers back to Scriptures but also led to a complete reevaluation of religious history. He awarded "high merit" to Flacius and his Magdeburg team of scholars for their exposure of ecclesiastical frauds and of the "dark side" of Catholic tradition, which had been penetrated by the "dualism" of God and history which was embedded in the Magdeburg Centuries and even the "mystical-Pietistic" work of Arnold, the "patron of heretics," which had placed dogma at the center of church history and which had overwhelmed the points of agreement between the parties. Baur discussed not only the ancient and medieval antecedents but also the contemporary works of Neander, Gieseler, Hase, Gfrörer, and others, whose multivolume narratives and monographs have been overshadowed by the national histories of that period and by the failure of the ecumenical program because of a revived ultramontanism. Perhaps the most influential of these works is that of Neander, who, although a Jew converted to Lutheranism, wrote his history of the Church in "the true Catholic spirit" — but also within the spiritualist framework in which "scientific theology" was set.[65]

Baur's argument led up to the overcoming of dualism and the external/internal opposition and especially to the centrality of dogma not only in theology but also in — and in some ways above — church history. This was the point of departure of Adolph von Harnack, whose massive history of dogma was published in 1884. His main predecessors in the study of dogma as a historical and changing phenomenon were Mosheim (the "Erasmus of the eighteenth century"), Walch, Ernesti, Lessing, and Semler; but not until "the great spiritual revolution at the beginning of our century" (especially Schleiermacher, Neander, and the Hegelians), did this antirationalistic genre reach maturity. For Harnack the key figure was Baur, who was "the first who attempted to give a general uniform idea of the history of dogma, and to live through the whole process himself, without renouncing the critical acquisitions of the 18th century."[66] Harnack followed and expanded on the Protestant line that credits Luther with being the first to join the issue of dogma (beginning as a "joyful message") with history and to set the goal which, in spirit as well as action, was still not fulfilled.[67]

The leadership of the Catholic school and Möhler's chair at Munich were taken over by Ignaz von Döllinger, who celebrated the "dawn of a new era in historical research" — referring to the Göttingen school as well as to Niebuhr, Humboldt, and Grimm, whom he called "heroes and representatives of the historic sense" — and he concluded that "the interest formerly taken in *Philosophy* has given place to that now taken in history."[68] Döllinger wrote extensively on the Middle Ages, especially in his multivolume handbook of church history (1833–38), but he turned increasingly to the Reformation, the critical period when the question of tradition and the role of history became central, and he sought, largely in vain, to correct the dark image created by Ranke's more popular histories of the popes and the German Reformation.

Döllinger had "an unlimited command of books," recalled Acton (who should have known), but he had a relatively slight interest in theology. He learned even less from Schleiermacher than from Herder, and he preferred the model represented by Savigny. Faith was beyond fruitful discussion, he thought: "we stand here upon the solid ground of history, evidence, and fact."[69] With Ranke he had scholarly and literary (and no doubt political) but no religious differences. Philosophically, he was attracted to Leibniz's "law of continuity" and, with Möhler, J. S. Drey, Newman, and others, in the currently popular idea of development in religion, introduced in Drey's "encyclopedic" textbook of 1819.[70] In his concern for Catholic tradition Döllinger always had ecclesiastical and political as well as scholarly goals, and as Acton remarked of his best book, "his *Reformation* was a treatise on the conditions of reunion."[71] He was also a forceful critic of anti-Semitism, as usual basing his argument on a long-term historical view of "the Jews in Europe."[72]

Döllinger was, according to Frederick York Powell, "the Sarpi of our time."[73] He was fascinated by the dark and seamy side of church history — frauds, fictions, fables, and forgeries as well as abuses and excesses — although for him none of this detracted from the spiritual continuity of the church. The false Donation of Constantine and the legend of Pope Joan, still accepted by modern Protestant historians like Mosheim and Luden, were among the targets of his researches.[74] Like Valla and Luther, Döllinger found this to be a peculiarly Roman practice. "History, in the form in which Germany received it from Rome," he wrote later, "has been crammed with myths and legends."[75] He praised Aventinus and especially Beatus Rhenanus for their critical view of German history, contrasting their works with "the adulatory, superficial historiography penned by writers like the Italian humanists, whom princes entertained at their courts that they might celebrate the deeds of their patrons."[76] He defended Aventinus — as likewise Dante — for his criticisms of ecclesiastical abuses and placed him in a moderate, middle position (not unlike Döllinger's own) between Protestant and papal extremes. He was especially interested in that problematic culmination of papal history, the Council of Trent, and tried to gain access to the still-closed archival sources, which he suspected would reveal further offenses, but he failed in this effort in the controversial atmosphere preceding the Vatican Council of 1870.[77]

All of Döllinger's values, scholarly commitments, and hopes came together at the crisis represented by this council, when the doctrine of infallibility was elevated officially to the level of dogma, thus — in the eyes of critics like Döllinger and his disciple Acton — excusing centuries of abuses and errors and joining them directly, and unnecessarily, to spiritual tradition. For both of these scholars and for other liberal Catholics this constituted a reproach to their conception of historical truth, which did not need protection by casuistry, refusal to admit errors and inconsistencies, official misrepresentation of the past, and concealment of historical records. For them there could be no conflict between religion and its tradition and historical fact, and in this they were in agreement with Ranke's dictum about the autonomy of history and "what really happened."

History and the Disciplines

"History is not only a particular branch of knowledge," noted Acton to himself, "but a particular mode and method of knowledge in other branches" — and so at least it had become by his time.[78] As Christoph Meiners wrote in 1802, "There is almost no science, no fine or practical art, no manufacture or trade, which has not found its historian during the last century, especially in our own generation."[79] In other words history had become a way of looking at all aspects of human culture, the medieval and Renaissance "encyclopedia" of the arts and sciences having in various ways been historicized, as had many of its disciplinary parts. Philosophy, religion, literature, natural science, and most disciplines of Renaissance learning had acquired histories, specialized "literatures," and even formal canons; and these vehicles of historical inquiry and historicist attitudes formed a bridge between the Enlightenment and the nineteenth century.

Classically, the art of history referred to actions accomplished, things done (*res gestae*); but from at least the sixteenth century it also reached out for words recorded, things written (*res literariae*), and especially works printed; and the upshot was a new discipline called literary history or the history of literature (*historia literaria; historia literaturae*). This inversion of the old humanist topos which subordinated words to things (*res non verba*) was linked directly to what was called the "renaissance of letters" (and in the nineteenth century abbreviated, abstractly, to simply the "Renaissance"). By letters or literature was meant not capital-L Literature ("good letters," *bonae litterae, belles lettres*), but anything set down in writing and, more especially, printing.[80] There was a series of handbooks devoted to the history and bibliography of literature in this sense from Jonsius's listing of 1659 down to Wachler's history of literature of 1793, which demonstrated the continuity between *historia literaria* and *Literaturgeschichte* and the new force of public opinion as an arena for historical writing.[81] According to G. J. Vossius, seventeenth-century philologist and historian of philosophy, "literary history treated the lives and writings of learned men and the invention and progress of the arts"; and as a recent scholar has commented, "what Vossius called 'literary history' was really what would now be called cultural history."[82] For Friedrich Schlegel, writing in the early nineteenth century, "literature includes all that circle of arts and sciences and faculties of representation which have life and man himself for their object"; and it reflected "nearly the whole of man's intellectual life."[83]

A subgenre of the history of literature was the history of philosophy (*historia philosophica*—the same terms being applied, confusingly, to "philosophical history"), and this was even more closely associated with the progress of enlightenment. "From a certain point of view," wrote A.-F. Boureau-Deslandes in 1737, "the history of philosophy may be regarded as the history of the human spirit, or at least the history of the human spirit in its highest form."[84] Like universal historians, historians of philosophy began not *ab urbe* but *ab orbe condita,* and of course within the biblical framework. This was the perspective of the two seventeenth-century founders of the history of philosophy, Thomas Stanley and Georg Horn, whose books both appeared in 1655. From this time the history of philosophy claimed status as a "science" and continued along many doctrinal and confessional lines, culminating in the exhaustive work of J. J. Brucker, on which were based the standard surveys of Tennemann, Tiedemann, Cousin, Zeller, and many others in the nineteenth century. The status of the new discipline of history of philosophy can be seen not only in textbooks and courses but also in the collection of miscellaneous lists, ordered bibliographies, biographical collections, and historiographical accounts of the philosophical tradition which was essential to the project of Eclectic philosophy.[85] This mass of erudition was added to and disseminated further by the academic theses which defended the methods and the promise of Eclectic method.[86] These theses, which remain to be explored in any systematic way, are concerned with a wide range of questions and keywords—including *historia, historia literaria,* and *historia philosophica*—that richly illustrate the dissemination of the key ideas and terms of early Enlightenment learning.[87]

Language, too, was increasingly a subject of historical inquiry, after so many centuries of theological and philosophical speculation.[88] By the eighteenth century the story of Babel did not function practically in the emergent fields of comparative grammar and philology. Instead emphasis was placed on the natural process of linguistic change and diversity that had been the subject of treatises on languages from the Renaissance down to the treatise of Olaus Borrichius, published in 1704, which emphasized factors of climate and geography, the influence of sounds, artificial changes brought by teaching, and such social phenomena as the migrations of peoples.[89] In this sense language invited the same arguments offered, often quite vaguely, to explain the great diversity of customs and opinions noted by historians. Public interest in these problems culminated in the two prize questions posed by the Academy of Sciences of Berlin in 1757 and 1769. The first topic was "What is the reciprocal influence of the opinions of a people on its language and of its language on its opinions?" and the second was "Would men left with only their natural faculties be capable of inventing language?" — and if so, how?[90]

In Condillac's pioneering explorations of the origins of language, including treatment of the first of these questions, both philosophy and history were relevant.[91] "Languages were precise methods as long as men spoke only of things related to their primary needs," he wrote; but after this state of simplicity men "went on to create needs out of pure curiosity, needs of opinion, finally useless needs, each more frivolous than the other."[92] In the period of recorded history languages had lost claims to such precision; for as he continued, "Commerce brought together people who exchanged, as it were, their opinions, their prejudices, as well as the products of their lands and their industry." For Condillac, as Hans Aarsleff wrote, "the progress of the mind becomes a question of the progress of language," though this progress was based largely on the "conjectural history" so common in the Enlightenment.[93]

More concretely historical was the approach of German scholars. The Neologist Johann David Michaelis, whose approach was that of a philologist rather than a philosopher, emphasized the changing nature of language. He noted the connections between particular languages and the historical experience of their speakers — the Bohemian language, for example, being "absolutely devoid of sea-terms, and the Russians [making] use of ours." What about new terms? "Every word was a neologism once," Erasmus had observed, and Michaelis accommodated this, too. "Language is a democracy where use or custom is decided by the majority," he argued, following a classical notion going back at least to the Roman grammarian Varro; and "it is from the opinions of the people and the point of view in which objects appear to them, that language receives its form."[94] In general, Michaelis concluded, "the right of creating [new words] . . . belongs only to classic authors, the fair sex, and the people, who are the supreme legislators."

Another historical (or metahistorical) aspect of language is etymology, and Michaelis was an enthusiast for this ancient area of speculation. "It cannot be imagined how much good is contained in etymology," he rhapsodized. "It is a treasure of sense, knowledge, and wisdom: it includes truths which most philosophers do not see into, and will one day immortalize the philosopher who shall discover them, without [knowing] that, from time immemorial, they have been in every body's mouth."[95] Vico had already, a generation earlier, propounded a similar view, proposing, through his "new science," to read his way back to the most primitive ideas formed by humanity in its formative, "barbaric" stages. As J. G. Sulzer wrote in 1767, "The etymological history of languages would indisputably be the best history of the progress of the human mind."[96]

More influential were the views of Herder, who likewise approached the question of the origin of language as a philologist and historian. Herder set a larger agenda than the Berlin Academy, extending the inquiry by asking significantly more refined questions:

> To what extent does the natural way of thought of the Germans also have an impact upon their language? And the language upon their literature . . . ? How much can be explained on the basis of their environment and their language organs? On the basis of historical evidence, to what extent can the richness and poverty of their language be said to have grown out of their way of thought and life? To what extent is the etymology of its words determinable by viewpoints held in common with other nations, or peculiar to itself? In matters essential, what revolutions did the German language have to experience? And how far has it come to date for the poet, the prose writer, and the philosopher?[97]

For Herder "each language has its distinct national character" and in turn represented a record of local conditions and experiences. Moreover, nations possessed no ideas without corresponding words — hence no thoughts, except perhaps in a spiritual world inaccessible to historians.[98]

Romantic scholars built on these Enlightenment ideas of the cultural significance of language. "There are cases," Coleridge wrote, "in which more value may be conveyed by the history of a *word* than by the history of a campaign."[99] The history of an entire language opened up a whole world of such value. As the historian of ancient Greece, K. O. Müller, put it, "Language, the earliest product of the human mind, and origin of all other intellectual energies, is at the same time the clearest evidence of the descent of a nation and of its affinity with other races. Hence the comparison of languages enables us to judge the history of nations at periods to which no other kind of memorial, no tradition or record, can ascend."[100] As a residue of verbal behavior, oral as well as written, language becomes the most fundamental vehicle for the history of ideas and culture.

Since the eighteenth century language has been a central concern to intellectual and cultural history, and the development of linguistic science (*Sprachwissenschaft*) in the nineteenth century confirmed this position.[101] Following the view of Herder but with a more extensive grounding, Humboldt regarded language as "a work of the spirit" and linked it historically to "the growth of man's mental power" (*die menschliche Geisteskraft*).[102] This work was the result of a long interplay between individuals and collective tradition. Geniuses like Dante and Luther, who were virtuosi of linguistic expression, stood on the shoulders not of giants but of many generations of speakers, singers, and writers. The further historians follow the chain of culture into the past, the less they are able to perceive the contributions of "great individuals" and the more they must attend to collective achievements, which makes it "evident how small, in fact, is the *power of the individual* compared to the might of language."[103] World history is the story of this collective effort, the "mental evolution of mankind," revealed by historical and comparative linguistics. Deciphering these large spiritual patterns hidden under the surface of history, "what actually happened," was the ultimate "task of the historian." Humboldt's views were continued in the next generation in treatises on *Historik,* modern counterpart of *ars historica,* such as those of G. G. Gervinus, Wilhelm Wachsmuth, and especially Johann Droysen, who all believed that the study of history should be placed in the service of the nation.[104]

Another discipline that turned to history for its foundations was the law; and Montesquieu's famous maxim, "History must be illuminated by laws, and laws by history," was a central issue of both legal and historical scholars in the eighteenth and nineteenth centuries.[105] The central debate, which persisted across the revolutionary divide, was located between two poles — the philosophical school, based on natural law ideas, and the historical school, based on custom, positive law, ideas of development, and criticism of the abstract theories of natural law.[106] The writings of J. S. Pütter (1725–1809) on legal and constitutional history rejected abstract systematizing in favor of the study of the customs and institutions of Germany, which he understood to be "deeply rooted in its constitution, partly in its climate, and in everything that was common to Germany's situation."[107] Yet Pütter seemed to be a throwback in an age of calculation and codification. In a general sense the Revolution and Napoleonic Code marked the ascendancy of the philosophical school — and "social science"[108] — while the historical school represented postrevolutionary efforts of restoration, if not reaction. There was nothing new in a historical approach to legal studies, but in a period of revolution and foreign intervention historical method was given an ideological and political dimension, which gave history a foundational role in German politics and legal reform after the turn of the century. The historical school arose nominally in the nineteenth century, and its leader was Karl Friedrich von Savigny; but its true founder was Gustav Hugo (1764–1844), who had studied with Pütter at Göttingen and who taught law at the University of Heidelberg.[109] Hugo, who was the translator of the famous forty-fourth chapter of Gibbon's *Decline and Fall* on the history of Roman law, regarded the history of law and a "juristic anthropology" as essential foundations for a legal system, or "encyclopedia"; and he saw law as a late stage of the long development of the customs of a particular society or nation. For Hugo an expert historical understanding of this evolution was necessary for any legal or political judgment; and this insight, though hardly reconcilable with contemporary revolutionary assumptions (and bitterly opposed later by Marx), seemed to be confirmed in postrevolutionary experience and attempts at "restoration" — which meant the reestablishment of continuity on many levels.

Enlightenment traditions were continued by many historians who turned to history for explanations of the extraordinary changes in the modern world. One of the most popular historians of the Restoration period was F. C. Schlosser (1776–1861), professor of history at Heidelberg, who preserved a moral and "philosophical" view in his many writings, both of them largely Kantian, on universal history and on the eighteenth century — and who specifically eschewed the pedantic archival focus of scholars like Ranke. According to Treitschke, Schlosser's *History of the Eighteenth Century* was "the most popular historical work of the day," far more influential than Ranke, despite its "antediluvian" (nonpolitical) character.[110] For Dilthey, Schlosser, in his "dictatorial sweep," was "the creator of universal history" (despite the tradition of sketchy Göttingen textbooks) and the first to see history as the means of educating the larger public.[111] A. L. H. Heeren, a student of both Heyne and Spittler (political and ecclesiastical historian and a pioneer of the seminar method), carried on the traditions of the Göttingen school and acknowledged the central importance of power politics by focusing on the European "state system" as the target of his historical investigations — a system, he wrote in 1809, which had been overthrown even as he was finishing his book.[112] For him the question of origins was conjectural and associated not with philosophy but with religion.[113] Heeren's influence was extraordinary, too, and among his American students were Bancroft (who was also his translator), Motley, Ticknor, and Longfellow.

Finally, the old tradition of *ars historica* was continued across the revolutionary divide, and with it the genre of history, especially with the comprehensive survey by Ludwig Wachler (1812–30), tracing the writing of history from the Greeks down to the Göttingen school and the early work of Niebuhr. In the age of Kant and Hegel, however, the study of history was shaped by idealist views of the past and of human nature. In 1803, Creuzer published his *Art of History of the Greeks*, which was indebted to Schlegel as well as Heyne and which approached history as an intellectual development linking nature and spirit (*Geist*). History grew out of myth, as poets were superseded by the Greek logographers, historians, and critics; and for Creuzer, referring to

Vossius as well as Heyne (though not Vico), it was the function of the modern scholar to retrace this process in reverse through "hermeneutical inquiry" (*hermeneutischen Versuch*).[114] As Hermann Ulrici wrote in his *Characteristic of Ancient Historiographie* (1833), while the historian dealt in facts, usually identified with deeds, spirit (*Geist*) was also a fact (*Faktum*), "a wonderful fact."[115] What distinguished modern history from ancient was that it took a form not only external but also internal and, moreover, universal — and for the pious Ulrici there could be "no pure, ideal truth without universal history," nor indeed the self-knowledge (*Erkenntniss seiner selbst*) which was the goal of historical studies. From Hegel to Croce and Collingwood the test of history was fundamentally this modernized version of the Apollonian motto, "Know thyself."

British Initiatives

It is not our purpose to intrude upon the province of history.
— *Walter Scott*

Conjectural History

David Hume described the highest aim of historical study in this way: "to see all human race, from the beginning of time, pass, as it were, in review before us; appearing in their true colours, without any of those disguises, which during their life-time, so much perplexed the judgment of the behold-ers."[1] Yet in the wake of the explosion of scholarship since the age of erudi-tion, how could modern scholars manage such a Herculean task? As Hume's friend William Robertson put it, "The universal progress of science during the last two centuries, the art of printing, and other obvious causes have filled Europe with such a multiplicity of historical materials, that the term of human life is too short for the study or even the perusal of them."[2]

The short answer to this question is "conjectural history," as Dugald Stew-art called it, and bound to it was a perspective that was not only comparative but also antiquarian — and indeed "conjectural" was often associated with "fabulous." According to Kant, conjecture is what makes it possible not only to fill in gaps in the historical record but also to understand the "first beginning of human actions," whether understood as expulsion from paradise or prog-ress from a state of nature to society. Whether conjecture of this sort applies to the future and to the "end of history" is, for philosophers if not for historians, a matter of debate. In any case Hume's project was both philosophical and historiographical, and the survey envisioned by him was made possible only through the sort of reasoned history (*histoire raisonnée* the French called it) that became popular during the Enlightenment. The premises underlying this kind of history included Lockean empiricism, itself a theoretical version of Baconian method adapted from individual psychology to collective action, from education to cultural progress, and the notion, defended by Scottish thinkers, of a distinctive moral sense which extended Lockean philosophy in order to give a rational basis to ideas of progress and perfectibility. To this was added, too, ideas of progressive enrichment, which was the business of politi-cal economy; but moral improvement was the ultimate goal. "Cultivate virtue, therefore, my dear young friends," exhorted Francis Hutcheson, "you who are the hope of the present age and who will, I hope, advance the future with your achievements."[3] This was the ideal of education and the goal of human his-tory, at least according to the hopeful, or wishful, thinking of many moral philosophers and conjectural historians.

"Cultivate," "cultivation," and "culture": these were key words of conjec-tural history in Britain and the continent; and attached to them was a sense of development from a "rude" to a "cultivated" or "refined" — from, in more conventional terms, a "barbarous" to a "civilized" — stage which, according to James Dunbar, underlay the histories of all human societies, leading to "the cultivation of real science, the love and study of the fine arts."[4] The assump-tion was also that this was the product not merely of great men or "inventors" but a collective achievement fixed by usages and custom. Attached to the culturalist terminology, too, was a consciousness of the significance of histor-ical context for such achievements and aspirations. Adam Ferguson accepted the idea of a general law of cultural progress arising from human effort but, concerning the individual, added that "his particular pursuits are prescribed to him by the circumstances of the age and of the country in which he lives," so that "the steps which lead to perfection are many."[5] And William Robertson found that the discipline and "culture" of a man "depends entirely upon the state of society in which he is placed."[6]

Robertson's first historical project was devoted to Scotland (1759), which shared with other northern nations the ignorance of that "dark and fabulous age" preceding the short period enlightened by "well-attested annals," which did not reach back even to the original possessions of the Scottish clans.[7] This situation was made worse by the policy of Edward I, who not only extended feudalism to this nation and made claims based on British mythology, but also "seized the public archives, he ransacked the churches and monasteries: and getting possession, by force or fraud, of many historical monuments, which tended to prove the antiquity or freedom of the kingdom, he carried some of them into England, and commanded the rest to be burned."[8] Only a few fragments were preserved, and later historians such as John Major, Hector Boese, and George Buchanan tried to assemble the story of Scotland, though without much regard for historical truth; and it was Robertson's hope to repair as much of the damage as possible. But of the four periods of Scottish history only three possessed authentic records. This was the problem with Scottish historiography throughout the eighteenth century: the resort to myth, as in Macpherson's Ossianic fabrications, versus the reliance on written remains, as in the criticisms of Whitaker's "genuine" history of the Britons.[9] Even Scottish feudalism had to be discussed without resort to written evidence, as contrasted with that in Germany and France, "In the former, the feudal institutions still subsist with great vigour . . . ," Robertson observed; "and though altogether abolished in the latter [writing in a later edition], the public records have been so carefully preserved, that the French lawyers and antiquaries have been enabled, with more certainty and precision, than those of any other country in Europe, to trace its rise, its progress, and revolutions."[10] So the Scots were reduced to conjecture.

In any case the patterns of later progress seemed to be discernible. Most fundamental in cultural progress was the economic base which was produced in modern times and which led, in the work of Smith, Turgot, and Y.-A. Goguet to the stadial conception of human history.[11] "The four stages of society," wrote Smith in 1762, "are hunting, pasturage, farming, and commerce." He explained these stages and the "origins of government" with the help of the ancient theory of three constitutional forms: "In the age of hunters there can be very little government of any sort, but what there is will be of the democratical kind. . . . The age of shepherds is that where government properly commences," followed by agriculture, property, and rule by a few rich men, and then by the emergence of chieftains, marking a monarchical government. "Arts and manufactures are then cultivated," as property arrangements and disputes are multiplied as well as civilized through writing.[12] As Rousseau and Herder tried to imagine how language arose in a state of nature, so Smith speculated on how these four phases of communal life would naturally arise if a group of Robinson Crusoes were shipwrecked on an island and forced to cope with their predicament — first by living off the fruits they could find and animals they could kill, then by cultivating vegetables, and finally by commercial exchange. Such was the progress of reason on the most fundamental level of human subsistence. By the end of the century this thesis, promoted also by Kames, Dalrymple, Millar, Monboddo, William Russell, Meiners, and others, had become commonplace in Britain as well as the continent.[13]

Ferguson's study of the history of civil society, published in 1767, was perhaps the most influential example of conjectural history in the English language. All nations were born in barbarism, including the Greeks and Romans as well as the Gauls, Germans, and Britons. The primitive state of society cannot be deduced from fables, Ferguson acknowledged; "but they may, with great justice, be cited to ascertain what were conceptions and sentiments of the age in which they were composed, or to characterise the genius of a people, with whose imaginations they were blended, and by whom they were fondly rehearsed and admired." There was also the secondhand evidence of travel reports, and like Vico (who, however, cited only Lipsius's comment on Tacitus) Ferguson used the work of contemporary explorers like Lafitau to argue that these savages "resembled, in many things, the present natives of North America; they were ignorant of agriculture; they painted their bodies; and used for clothing, the skins of beasts."[14] Like Smith, Ferguson made property the key to progress and the stadial progression to modern civilization.

The comparative and "sociological" approach of Scottish scholars led them to the study of class structure as well as stadial change — the Highlanders corresponding in a sense to the primitive stage of social development — as illustrated by John Millar's treatise on the origin of ranks in society. Millar saw, "in human society, a natural progression from ignorance to knowledge, and from rude to civilized manners, the several stages of which are usually accompanied with peculiar laws and customs."[15] What produced particular legislative "systems" was not fabled genius but rather commonsense efforts of men, for example, the Spartans, to fit laws to the "primitive manners of that simple and barbarous people" as well as climatic conditions. Millar was especially concerned with the lower grouping of society, especially the family, the status of women, sexual relations, paternal and political power, the progress of the arts and manners in successive social stages. In these terms history is written not about the deeds of heroic individuals but in the transformations in social groups or legal "systems," such as feudalism or slavery, and in society as a whole.

Another approach was taken by James Burnet, Lord Monboddo, who focused on the old question of language as the best illustration of social progress. Against Locke, Monboddo kept a distinction between sense and intellect and derived speech from the "political state," that is, the first of the four stages of development, in which society produced language, not vice versa, and language made possible the arts and sciences of civilization. Monboddo — who, notoriously, included the orangutan in the human species — regarded language as rooted in animal cries, arguing this from accounts of American Indian speech. He also clung to a version of the "primitive wisdom" thesis, which traced learning back to the Egyptians.[16] "The first great revolution of learning and philosophy was the conquest of Egypt by the Persians, and the destruction of the Egyptian college of priests." The second (recorded by Polybius) came when the Pythagoreans, preservers of this secret wisdom, were exiled from Italy; the third with the fall of Rome; and the current revival came from the Saracen restoration of Aristotle, through the Byzantine Greeks, to the West.

The conjectural discussion of "rudeness" and "barbarism" was carried on also by Monboddo's rival Lord Kames, who was named Historiographer Royal for Scotland in 1763 and who made use also of the works of Spelman, Mably, Dubos, and other scholars. Like Ferguson, Kames emphasized the central role of property in the progress of law and so of society.[17] Once the problem of subsistence was resolved for a significant part of the growing population, said Kames, men were finally "at liberty to cultivate the feelings of humanity: property, the main mark of distinction among individuals, is established; and the various rights of mankind arising from their multiplied connections, are recognised and protected."[18] It was this natural and rational process and not, as tradition and older historians had it, kingly "benefices" that lay at the roots of feudal tenures and accounted for the "natural progress of government" toward monarchy, democracy, and finally freedom, including the end of villeinage and of slavery, which for Monboddo arose from this material process rather than from the spiritual influence of religion.[19]

The last of the four ages, that of commerce, marked also the take-off of technical advancement and "the progress of knowledge." Dugald Stewart, the successor of Ferguson as professor of moral philosophy at Edinburgh and biographer of Adam Smith, wrote one of the "dissertations on the progress of knowledge" for the supplement of the *Encyclopaedia Britannica* (1815), tracing the history of thought (metaphysics, ethics, and political philosophy) "since the revival of letters in Europe."[20] Stewart, like Degérando, rejected the rigid separation of the faculties derived from Bacon and D'Alembert, since in practice reason, memory, and imagination were blended together. The subject of Stewart's essay was the way in which the "torch of science" (a conceit borrowed from Plato and Lucretius) was passed from antiquity to modernity and in which the "continuity of knowledge" was maintained.[21] For Stewart the "revival of letters" included the study of Roman and natural law but otherwise commenced not really with Italian humanism (except in its criticism of "Aristotelian doctrines") but rather with the Protestant Reformation, the invention of printing, "experimental" philosophers like Paracelsus and above all Bacon, and theologians like Melanchthon, who took the first steps away from dogmatism and toward "common sense." Thereafter Stewart reviewed the major French and English thinkers and, from his soberly progressivist stance, passed moral, political, and aesthetic judgment on them. In political philosophy Stewart emphasized the practical side, pointing out, for example, the extraordinary demand for agricultural books in the reign of James I, illustrating at once the taste for reading and the desire for national improvement. Stewart denounced Machiavelli at length (following Sismondi), and also Hobbes — "in their connexion with the circumstances of their times" — but praised Bodin as a predecessor to Montesquieu in their "common attachment to religious and civil liberty." The expansion of natural jurisprudence from a narrow and abstract system in the works of Grotius and Pufendorf to the superior views of the Scottish commentators, Carmichael and Hutcheson, and especially to Adam Smith. The result was the extension of legal science into the broader fields of the law of nature and the law of nations and even, with Montesquieu, of history and philosophy. Like his enlightened contemporaries in France, Stewart also envisioned not only a "moral" but also a "legislative" science devoted to the improvement of particular nations and humanity as a whole, lest we be reduced to "mere *spectators* of the progress and decline of society" — mere "historians of the human mind," we might say, in the phrase Stewart applied to himself.[22]

The larger rubric under which conjectural history falls is that of the question of periodization — in the sense of dividing the historical process, not in the old sense of putting an end to it.[23] Dividing history into periods was as old as historical writing, the Four Monarchies, the Ages of Man, cyclical patterns, and other devices being employed by authors since "antiquity" — itself the label for a general span of time. By the eighteenth century the ancient-medieval-modern convention was well in place, but the new conjectural history, especially the four (more or less) stage theory, was a more ambitious effort to find a secular pattern in human experience — whether seen as progress or decadence or an alteration of the two — and this ongoing search for a universal trajectory continues to be part of the project of historical inquiry.

After Gibbon

Gibbon, who himself drew on the Scottish school, left a mighty legacy, and indeed some people today still think him the greatest of modern narrative historians. But there is a negative side, too. In Germany the *Decline and Fall* began to appear in translation as early as 1779, gained some popularity, and was drawn on by authors like Meiners and Hegewisch. Yet it was less cordially received by more expert scholars, the Göttingen historian Spittler, for example, arguing in 1788 that it did not meet the standards of German scholarship, especially regarding its uncritical use of sources, and it was further eclipsed by the work of Niebuhr a generation later.[24] What most distressed Gibbons's English contemporaries and immediate posterity, however, was not his ignorance of German learning but his attitude toward revealed religion, which was located somewhere between sarcasm and contempt; and this provoked reactions from a number of pious critics, including East Apthorp, James Chelsum, Henry Edwards Davis, David Dalrymple, William Jesse, and Joseph Priestley. Their chief complaint was Gibbon's failure to appreciate the true — that is, the spiritual and the miraculous — causes of the triumph of Christianity. Apthorp took Gibbon to task for his superficial method, and in a little excursus on the art of history chided him for following the tradition of Herodotus rather than that of Holy Scriptures.[25] Chelsum charged Gibbon, misled by friends and wrongheaded authors, with falling into "ancient credulity" and with neglecting the evidence of the miraculous progress of Christianity, adding later that Gibbon's "embellished" style was a sign of disregard of truth.[26] Somewhat surprised by these reactions, Gibbon made a few alterations but did not change his opinion of the role of the Christian religion in the decline and fall of the Empire.

Criticism of Gibbon continued for a generation and more and still echoed in the annotated edition prepared by Henry Hart Milman, who was a frequent breakfast companion of Macaulay and who ended his life as Dean of St. Paul's. Milman complained that Gibbon's negative judgments of Christianity at the beginning of chapter fifteen were the result of confusing its origin as an apostolic propagation with its later career, so that "the main question — the divine origin of religion — is dexterously eluded or speciously conceded."[27] He also objected to Gibbon's unmanly and "insidious and sarcastic description of the less pure and generous elements of the Christian character as it appeared even at that time," his views about the principle of a community of goods in the New Testament, and his "disgraceful" extenuation of the Roman persecutions of the Christian martyrs in chapter sixteen.[28] Milman's other obiter dicta, beyond corrections based on more recent scholarship, follow the same orthodox line, including defense of miracles in the primitive church.

Milman's own conception of Christian tradition, informed by his knowledge of modern German scholarship, was exhibited in his *History of the Jews* and *History of Latin Christianity*. Although he wanted to construct a continuous narrative, Milman was closer to Paley than to Gibbon in his outlook, retaining a providential framework and the accompanying theodicy. He declined to parade his learning in extensive footnotes, though he declared his familiarity with the great tradition of scholars from the Magdeburg Centuriators and Baronius down to Döllinger and Bunsen (unfortunately not including any distinguished Englishmen).[29] Milman did question the authority of the chronology somehow implanted on the margins of the English Bible, and he showed skepticism about some of the numbers in the Old Testament, though the same could be said about classical authors.[30] But as a prominent high churchman he avoided the dangerous opinions carried by the new learning of his age (such as those of Renan and Strauss), and like Gibbon he suffered criticism, though in his case on the part of "authors hostile to Revelation."

One follower of both Gibbon and the "lamented Milman" was Charles Merivale, whose apologetic history of imperial Rome began to appear in 1850. He opposed ancient critics of the Empire such as Tacitus and Suetonius and projected Gibbon's admiration for the Antonine period back to the Flavians. Merivale wanted to tell a story, not offer critical proofs (*historia scribitur ad narrandum non ad probandum,* he quoted), but he also wanted to disassociate himself from the "Romish creed," including perhaps Ozanam, who, with Broglie, he mentioned as adding to the Gibbonian tradition.[31] Merivale claimed admiration for Thomas Arnold, whose work was a popularization of Niebuhr; but in fact Merivale's work was, like Gibbon's and Milman's, based on literary sources and was largely innocent of the new critical history represented by Mommsen as well as Niebuhr.

In fact new opinions about religious and biblical history were making headway in England even before Milman's publications, especially those of the "higher criticism" in Germany, which itself had been given impetus by an earlier generation of freethinkers in England. After Herbert Marsh, translator of Michaelis's introduction to the New Testament, the pioneers of German scholarship in England were Connop Thirlwall and Julius Hare, who represented, in the 1820s, a sort of Germanist avant-garde, both in biblical scholarship and in ancient history. Yet it was also a conservative movement: Thirlwall despised Hegel and his devotees; and as Hare wrote, "Men have often been warned against old prejudices: I would rather warn them against new conceits."[32] Thirlwall was a prodigy in a class with John Stuart Mill, studying Latin at three and Greek at four and publishing his first book at eleven. By 1818 he was already reading Niebuhr's history of Rome, and the next year in Rome he met Niebuhr's friend Bunsen, the great statesman and Egyptologist.[33] In 1825, switching from law to theology, Thirlwall translated Schleiermacher's study of St. Luke. At Cambridge, where he was one of the "Apostles," Thirlwall called for admission of dissenters to degrees, and as a result he lost his tutorship (though he ended up as Bishop of St. David's). Macaulay congratulated him on his ill treatment and said he would rather be treated in this way than be Master of Trinity.[34]

In 1828, Thirlwall's friend and collaborator Julius Hare published, with his brother, a reflective and aphoristic (Pascalian rather than Nietzschean) work, dedicated to Wordsworth, called *Guesses at Truth,* in which, also following Schleiermacher, he called for a philosophical outlook that drew its positive strength not from a false transcendence but from the new, Germanic philology. In 1828, Thirlwall and Hare published their translation of Niebuhr's Roman history and in 1831 launched their short-lived *Philological Museum.* They were criticized by Established scholars for both of these ventures. Niebuhr was associated with the youthful violence of that decade and charged with unbelief as well for comparing the biblical story with classical myth — a "pert *dull* scoffer," wrote John Barrow anonymously in the *Quarterly Review* (and his conclusions about early Roman history were based neither on argument nor on evidence). Nonsense, Hare replied. Niebuhr stood with Burke against the social contract, and his real target was the United States. But most of Hare's "vindication" (with Thirlwall's postscript) was devoted to defending the philological innovations of Niebuhr as well as the notes added by the translators.[35]

Another pioneering Germanist of this generation was Thomas Arnold, whose own *History of Rome* was designed "to make Niebuhr known" and to transform his findings from awkward "dissertations" into narrative.[36] Like Niebuhr, Arnold treated the early legends and stories of the later kings, but he was not comfortable with conjectures and preferred the period of true history, when documentary sources were available and when he could discuss more tangible questions of race, language, and society. Arnold seemed to accept Niebuhr's ballad theory, but in fact the empirical and skeptical tendencies of British historiography soon ended the Niebuhrian fashion, especially with the assaults of George Cornwall Lewis, who concluded, "His history teems with cases where he has built a vast imaginative superstructure upon a foundation of error."[37] Lewis also congratulated Freeman on his classicist critique of continental views of ancient astronomy — for "upsetting all the Egyptian and Babylonian dreams." Despite talk about myths, history was still history, as Mr. Gradgrind might have said, and fiction was fiction.

Gibbon's successors carried on his explorations into other areas of ancient history, and indeed it was under Gibbon's encouragement that William Mitford wrote his *History of Greece,* which appeared in five volumes between 1784 and 1805. Mitford wanted to explore antiquity, and he welcomed the new discoveries made in natural history; but he depended heavily on Homer, and he stopped short of "that state of man, wholly untaught and unconnected, which philosophers have invented for purposes of speculation." What struck Macaulay was Mitford's love not only of the singular detail or person, which helped to restore life to antiquity, but also of tyranny and oligarchy, which put such knowledge to bad use. Mitford's Tory prejudices were called up by the Revolution, and he became a severe critic of the despotic democracy which was exemplified by ancient Greece and again by "John James" Rousseau. Yet Mitford celebrated the cultural achievements of the Greeks, whose oldest traditions, unlike those of the Romans, treated not war and conquest but "the invention or introduction of institutions the most indispensable to political society, and of arts ever the most necessary to human life."[38]

Superior to Mitford in scholarly terms was Thirlwall's *History of Greece* (1835–47), which was written under the inspiration of the emancipation of Greece in the early nineteenth century and in which, as his friend Hare commented, "the Greeks have at least been called out of their graves by a mind combining their own clearness and grace with a wealth of modern learning and thought."[39] Thirlwall was indeed endowed with a deep knowledge of continental philologists, mythologists like Creuzer, as well as historians like Niebuhr. He opened his narrative, in classic fashion, with a sketch of the geographical and social background. Like Niebuhr (and unlike Mitford) he made an effort to separate legend and historical fact; and he employed his footnotes to make criticisms, often severe ones, of contemporary historians such as Schlosser, Droysen, and Curtius over points of detail and judgment. At the end of his book Thirlwall celebrated the second revival of philology which made possible an understanding of the classic age of Greek liberty.

But the best parallel to Edward Gibbon's Rome was surely George Grote's Greece, which appeared in twelve volumes from 1846 to 1856 and which Thirlwall himself acknowledged as superseding his own. Grote noted the remarkable progress in historical knowledge between the uncritical work of Mitford (which he had criticized in the *Westminster Review*) and that of his good friend Thirlwall. His own volumes, informed by his reading of Boeckh, Niebuhr, and Müller, marked a turn back to mythology and Homeric sources; for in his view (differing from Thirlwall) it was impossible to draw aside the "curtain" of myth, and indeed epic poetry and legend formed the very essence of early Greek history, or prehistory.[40] Grote professed Socratic doubt about finding historical facts behind surviving myth, and he found it absurd to criticize Homeric descriptions from the standpoint of modern history or (as in the case of Napoleon) military science — probably also geography (as Heinrich Schliemann was soon to do). Nevertheless, it was for Grote essential to understand this sort of "historical faith, as distinguished from the later age of historical reason," as well as to compare it with the mentality of early modern Europe; and it was "unphilosophical" to confuse the early period with "the historical age," beginning with the first Olympiad (776 B.C.) and moving through six periods down to the death of Alexander.

The first volume and a half of Grote's history treated the legendary period in which the "real" battle of Troy, for instance, was not what historians tried to discover but what the Homeric texts represented: this account, not the vain inquiries of historians without sources, was all that generations of Greeks and classical scholars could know of that putative event. Grote's aim was to think back, through the poetic remains of an oral and as it were childlike society, to its "mental system"; and in this connection he invoked not only Wolf, Niebuhr, Müller, and the Grimms but also the newly appreciated work of "that eminently original thinker" and predecessor of these scholars, Giambattista Vico, who (Grote noted) "points out the personifying instinct (*istinto d'animazione*) as the spontaneous philosophy of man."[41] Grote subjected Herodotus and Thucydides to this same contextualist approach, noting that, despite their incipient "historical sense," both of them "had imbibed that complete and unsuspecting belief in the general reality of mythical antiquity, which was interwoven with the religion and the patriotism, and all the public demonstrations of the Hellenic world." In this sense, despite the provocative interpretations of Wolf, who sought a long oral tradition behind the later assembled texts, Homer was indeed "real."

Varro had saved the historical process by dividing theology into mythical, civil, and natural types; and Grote preferred this separating of legend from history to the later "rationalizing" and "historicizing" (his word) of poetic wisdom by historians and philosophers (Vico and others excepted) and neo-Euhemerists, including Warburton, Creuzer, Hermann, and Homer's translator Voss, who assumed that each mythical personage, each mytheme, corresponded somehow to a historical fact. These literal-minded scholars misguidedly carried on the business of "accommodating the old mythes to a new standard both of belief and of appreciation."[42] However, the trouble with this sort of historicist skepticism, or solipsism, which made the poets the only "real witnesses" of the Trojan story, was that it prevented Grote from seeing the possibility of attaining a Rankean sort of "reality," such as determining the actual location of Troy, which Schliemann and other archeologists, however naive their reading of Homer, were in the process of doing.

After Arnold published his Roman history and while Grote was publishing his Greek history, the horizons of the preclassical past were expanding marvelously. The study of Sanskrit and Persian and the deciphering of the Egyptian hieroglyphs were followed by assaults on other aspects of Near Eastern civilization. The cuneiform script of ancient Persia and Assyria was the first to yield, and Henry Rawlinson took his place beside Champollion, father of Egyptology, as the "father of Assyriology."[43] As in the case of Champollion, of course, there was a significant prehistory, including most notably the copies made in 1765 by Niebuhr's father, Carsten, of the trilingual inscriptions at an Achaemenid site known at least since the fifteenth century, the attempt at decipherment by the rabbinic scholar O. G. Tychsen in 1798, and the more successful effort made in 1802 by the philologist G. F. Grotefend, who had studied with Heyne and Heeren at Göttingen. But it was the English traveler and self-made scholar Henry Rawlinson who by 1851 had put the finishing touches on this long enterprise. The next steps were interpretation, historical synthesis, and construction of the new field of Assyriology — which were followed by similar assaults on other "lost languages," such as Hittite, Cypriot, and Etruscan.

These discoveries, though at first marginal to historical inquiry, soon had an impact that wholly transformed the old genre of universal history. This can be seen by comparing the "general history" of Karl von Rotteck, which began to appear in 1812, with Heeren's "historical researches," published three years later — the first tied closely to the old biblical narrative and familiar classical sources, and the second employing recent investigations of ancient sites, archeological finds, and linguistic breakthroughs. In particular Heeren referred to the work not only of Niebuhr but also of his own pupil Grotefend on cuneiform.[44] And compare this with the study of the "five great monarchies" of antiquity by Henry Rawlinson's brother George, which — with heavy reliance on his brother's work, "the latest results of modern comparative philology," and a rich selection of archeological and architectural illustrations — supplemented the story of Israel with parallel histories of Chaldea, Assyria, Media, Babylonia, and Persia.[45] When Ranke began his historical career, this new knowledge was only beginning to appear; by 1880, when he began publishing his own universal history, he was able to draw on a vast amount of research that had produced the new sciences of Egyptology and Assyriology.

Meanwhile the temporal horizons of universal history were broken open in even more sensational fashion by the rise of another new science, that of archeology, and its companion, anthropology, which were, according to Glyn Daniel, "born in the two decades between 1850 and 1870."[46] Scandinavian researches were key here, as in medieval history and inquiries into "mark" organization.[47] Before the discovery of Neanderthal man in 1857 there had been scattered fossil finds, but not until this period was there anything like a paradigm shift in the human sciences. In 1844, Robert Chambers's *Vestiges of Creation* gave public impetus to such a shift — going back in a sense to the speculations of Lucretius and conjectures of Lord Monboddo, but on the basis of positive evidence for "prehistory" (a coinage of Daniel Wilson in 1851, though twenty years earlier M. Tournal had spoken of *préhistoire*).[48] Arguments for the "antiquity of man" were also reinforced by advances in geology, especially the work of Charles Lyell, who published a book under that title in 1863, and two years later by the equally stunning books by John Lubbock (*Prehistoric Times*) and Edward Tylor (*Researches into the Early History of Mankind and the Development of Civilization*). By this time, of course, the paradigm shift was finding firmer ground in the new doctrine of Darwinism and the start of a new phase of the study of prehistory.

The Anglo-Saxon Inheritance

"The love of history seems inseparable from human nature," wrote Bolingbroke, "because it seems inseparable from self-love"; and this might well be the motto of what Herbert Butterfield called the "Whig interpretation of history," which is a sort of "glorification and ratification of the present" — and indeed of "our" present and the ancestral lines leading up to it. The views of English historians have followed channels cut by the development of the institutions, laws, and myths associated with the patterns of their government. The "immemorial" character of common law, Magna Carta, the Glorious Revolution of 1688 (archetype of this phenomenon before the American and French uprisings a century later), and other idols of English veneration were the defining features of historical interpretation and debate, as the Norman Yoke, Roman and French "absolutism," and royal Prerogative were the taboos of Whiggish history. Magnified in retrospect, these themes were used to reinforce the insular and exceptionalist premises that informed English legal and historiographical tradition for centuries. In the Renaissance these ideas intersected with critical erudition, including the work of William Camden, John Selden, Henry Spelman, and the "learned group of worshipful men" of the later seventeenth and eighteenth centuries, whose labors have been described by David Douglas.[49] As Germanists in France emphasized the Frankish, or Franco-Gallic provenance of French institutions, so Saxonists, beginning with Richard Verstegan in the early seventeenth century down to Edward Freeman in the nineteenth, carried on the same primitivist lines of argument against Romanist interpretations and on behalf of a distinct national character.

The "Gothic bequest" of the Anglo-Saxon past provided standard material for eighteenth-century British historians, including Bolingbroke, who, at least rhetorically and exemplaristically, located British liberty and forms of government in the Saxon past.[50] Saxonism was a source of strength for defenders not only of feudal institutions and aristocracy but also, in its more radical form, of democracy; and both positions assumed a natural continuity over the centuries. The popular republican history of Hume's rival, Mrs. Catharine Macaulay, also drew on the myths of the Norman Yoke and Anglo-Saxon liberties, and she moreover marked England's decline from the time of Henry VIII, when political and ecclesiastical power undermined this ancient heritage, except for the brief and bright interlude of the Commonwealth before Cromwell.[51] Many readers such as Joseph Priestley saw her work as an antidote to Hume's mainly Tory interpretation, though neither of these writers made any serious claim on critical scholarship.[52]

Other writers of English history strove for attention in an age still dominated by Hume. "The greatest number of our historians have given us only a detail of our civil, military, and ecclesiastical affairs," wrote Robert Henry in his history of Great Britain; "a few of them have inserted occasional dissertations on our constitution, government, and laws; but not one of them hath given, or so much as pretended or disposed to give, any thing like a history of learning, arts, commerce, and manners." "Does not the ingenious scholar who hath enlarged and enlightened the faculties of the human mind . . . deserve a place in the annals of his country; as well as even the good prince, the wise politician, or the victorious general?"[53] Henry's history, "written on a new plan," tried to remedy this through a topically organized text — seven chapters for each of ten books, devoted to civil and military history, religion, the constitution, learning, arts, commerce, and manners. He attended, for example, to the "manners of the Saxons in their pagan state" the progress of learning, especially under the encyclopedic and "enlightened" genius-king Alfred. He also offered a critical review of the Arthur story and its sources, carefully seeking the facts behind the texts, and opposing both romancers like "Jeffry" (Geoffrey of Monmouth) and those, like Milton, "unfriendly to his fame," that is, who doubted his existence, and accepting the testimony of Giraldus Cambrensis and William of Malmesbury, who saw the bones and inscription discovered in the abbey of Glastonbury in 1189.[54]

As suggested by the publications of Hume, Macaulay, Henry, and Priestley the cooperation between English intellectual traditions and modern scholarship lagged behind that of the continent; and Gibbon, for one, lamented the lack of a "Scriptores rerum Anglicarum" to set beside the great collections published in Germany, France, and Italy.[55] Sharon Turner was among the first who tried to bring narrative English history into contact with the erudition of "an enlightened age"; and in his study of the Anglo-Saxons, first published from 1799 to 1805, he promised that "the authentic will be distinguished from the conjectural" — though for the Germanic background he still relied on antiquated works such as those of Bebel and Mascou.[56] Thomas Percy's distinction between Celtic and Gothic tribes, he wrote, "laid the foundations for the true history of ancient Europe." Turner rejected the ancient myths about various original races, holding that population patterns were the result of emigration. He accepted the notion of a universal deluge, though he called on modern geology to testify on behalf of this ancient belief; and he stayed within the framework of biblical chronology. He invoked ideas of social progress but counterbalanced these with reminders of the corruptions of even modern "cultivated" nations and the Germanizing thesis that it was the infusion of barbarian virtues and liberty that rescued civilization from its vices — referring in particular to the Saxons, Franks, Burgundians, Goths, Northmen, and especially to his own forebears, who were, if not learned, then at least "mentally alert."

Though no Romantic, Turner was, like Volney, led to reflect on the fortunes of ancient and modern empires, moved by the ruins of the ancient Near East, that is, the Egyptian monuments in the courtyard of the British Museum brought from a site of veneration to the "gaze and criticism of public curiosity." "When Egypt was in her splendour, England was barbaric and unknown," he remarked. Yet "England has now reached one of the highest summits of human civilization; and Egypt has sunk into our ancestors' darkest state."[57] Turner felt sorrow at the "melancholy sublimities in this revolution of human greatness, yet soon changing into a feeling of triumph, that were Egypt now in her proudest state, she would not be, in any thing, our superior."

The beginning of this national pride was one theme of Turner's book. After a survey of the ancient background, as usual depending mainly on classical sources, Turner took up the "revolution" that brought the Anglo-Saxons into England, "than which history presents to us none more complete" — nor, he added, more enduring, for "our language, our government, and our laws, display our Gothic ancestors in every part; they live, not merely in our annals and traditions, but in our civil institutions and perpetual discourse."[58] Though at first applied to a confederacy of nations, the Saxon name became identified with a single "state," given further definition by the affinity of ancient languages — here with reference to modern linguistic scholarship and controversies, much of it antiquated, including Pontano, Bebel, Krantz, Cellarius, Mascov, and Leibniz. And in general, argued Turner, referring to the Saxon Emperors and to Luther's Reformation, "The rise of the Saxon nation has been, therefore, singularly propitious to human improvement."[59]

Turner's groundbreaking work was succeeded, and indeed superseded, by John Lingard's *Antiquities of the Anglo-Saxon Church*, which, based on extensive manuscript study, began to appear in 1806. Rejecting Henry's new plan, Lingard followed a strict and classical chronological arrangement and declined to discuss mythical subjects like Brutus; nor was he impressed by the "fictitious glory" of Arthur, whose strictly historical presence was no more substantial than other chieftains (not "kings") of the Britons. Lingard was a moderate Catholic who, though he did not deny his primary aim of "serving religion," carried on the Counter-Reformation tradition of scholarship but without, he claimed, the associated partisanship, which had been inherited by both modern Protestants and modern Ultramontanes. In this, as well as in his rejection of "what is called the philosophy of history," he resembled his contemporary Ranke.[60] Yet he did manage to undermine the Protestant view of a primitive anti-papalism among the Anglo-Saxons that was restored in the English Reformation.[61]

In the spirit of Ranke, too, Lingard did further archival research on the continent before turning to his major work, his *History of England (1819–30)*, which was translated into French, Italian, and German. In good empiricist fashion — Dr. Johnson kicking the stone to repudiate the presumption of philosophy — Lingard disclaimed any interest in the "philosophy of history," which he renamed "the philosophy of romance," which is a literary way of disfiguring historical understanding.[62] Whether or not it produced, as a French admirer claimed, seconding Lingard's own judgment, "a revolution in men's minds,"[63] it certainly provoked reactions from both sides in the Catholic emancipation question of that day, who saw in the work echoes of both the skepticism and the style of Gibbon. And perhaps his pessimism as well: "History," interjects Lingard in his discussion of Roman Britain, "is little more than a record of the miseries inflicted on the many by the passions of the few."[64] One controversial point was Lingard's opposition (based on contemporary sources, especially a later "Vindication" against Protestant critics) to the popular theory that the massacres of St. Bartholomew had been premeditated. For many readers Lingard, despite his contempt for philosophy, had replaced Hume as the national historian of England — as he would be replaced by Macaulay (whose own history, however, for Lingard would "not do").[65]

The progress of scholarship, together with the continuation of Whiggish history, is best illustrated by the career of Francis Palgrave, who continued the work of Turner on Anglo-Saxon antiquities and made even more valuable contributions in editing public records, beginning in 1821 and more formally from 1838, when he became Deputy Keeper of Her Majesty's Records until his death in 1861. In 1832, year of the Reform bill, he published *The Rise and Progress of the English Commonwealth*, in which he traced the modern state back to Roman precedents, following the line of John Allen, who denied, however, that English government resembled those on the continent.[66] Under the influence of Savigny, Palgrave increasingly took the Romanist side and even reverted to the old notion of Four World Monarchies as background to emergence of the English polity and laws. Despite what a modern scholar calls his "residual Gothicism," Palgrave, in the perspective of the Fourth Monarchy, defended the Roman origins of royalty, nobility, feudality, villeinage, feudal jurisprudence, civil law, corps, great councils, parliaments, romance, chivalry, arts, architecture, and civilization in general. Nor was there a rupture caused by "dark ages" — still less (*contra* Thierry) by the Norman Conquest — so that, he wrote hyperbolically, "We, therefore, all live in this Roman world."[67]

The insular character of English medievalism was countered by the work of German historians, beginning especially with J. M. Lappenberg, whose history of "the unmixed German race in Britain" began to appear in 1834. Lappenberg, who worked also in continental sources, including those of his own in Hamburg, found modern writers (excluding perhaps Palgrave and C. P. Cooper) industrious but uncritical. Despite differences in vocabulary, there was a remarkable "agreement between the public and private legal institutions of the Germans and those of the English Saxons," although these were a far cry from existing notions of property and other artificial products of many centuries.[68] So Lappenberg set English history in a broader European context, as later did at least a few English historians, including Kemble, Stubbs, and Maitland. His work, which contained a critical review of sources and historiography, was translated into English in 1845 by Benjamin Thorpe, who had published a vital collection of the *Ancient Laws and Institutes of England* in 1840.

The work of J. M. Kemble drew on such Germanist influence, especially that of Jakob Grimm, Turner, Hallam, and Palgrave; and he taught the same lessons of social continuity from an essentially Germanic past.[69] As an editor of Beowulf, he was much interested in the "heathen" legends of the Anglo-Saxons, which he found passed easily into the sphere of Christian faith. Yet he also turned to the study of Anglo-Saxon charters to give access to the historical reality behind the chronicles and poems — the "Mythos and Epos" — on which earlier historians had relied so heavily. He was Stubbs's "pattern scholar," and for J. W. Burrow, his work was "in the line of radical ancient constitutionalism."[70] In his *Codex Diplomaticus* (1835–48) and in his *Saxons in England* (1849), Kemble was following the lead of Spelman, Selden, Rymer, Hearne, and others; but to this erudition he added a deeper knowledge of Anglo-Saxon, and the tools of modern philology. Like his Renaissance predecessors Kemble was a Germanist and derived most British institutions (except for the Church) and virtues from the Anglo-Saxon "forefathers" — although he had the further inspiration of the legal scholarship of Eichhorn and Grimm, from whom he took the idea of the Mark-community as the fundamental unit of society.[71]

Roman or German, Protestant or Catholic, in their cultural indebtedness the English formed their own distinctive customs and character, and their scholars have insisted on it. The main difference between English and continental scholarship was the inclination of the former to exceptionalism and insularism in judging national traditions. The result has been to exaggerate the differences between English and continental feudalism, parliamentary institutions, and customary law, despite their common origins. This is altogether in keeping with the habits of insularism, nominalism, and, more recently, the ever-narrowing focus of revisionist history; but it underplays the parallels suggested by a long perspective and comparative (and conjectural) methods. For example, the similarities between the career of English common law and the unwritten customs of France and Germany are striking, especially in earlier periods, as are the "constitutionalist" aspects of French government, which English polemics since John Fortescue have denied. By contrast French and German scholars have emphasized these common features and even, as in the case of the jury system in postrevolutionary France, tried to imitate them.

"Continuity," which was so apparent in other national historiographies, was even more central to English history; and again it was the law that provided the cohesion. Central to the mythical tendencies of English scholarship has been the tradition of common law from Fortescue and Edward Coke down to William Blackstone, whose purpose was to give systematic and methodical form to this tradition. But the position of Blackstone in his *Commentary on the Laws of England* (1765–69) was closer to Coke's than to that of an enlightened philosopher (though he did indeed invoke Montesquieu). Blackstone indulged in his own sort of conjectural history, though grounded in the Bible story, especially concerning the natural right of property—the "dominion upon the earth . . . and everything that moveth upon the earth"—which furnishes the foundation of civil society and which was generalized by the English Parliament through the laws of property, inheritance, testaments, and criminal laws designed to protect this feudal heritage. For Blackstone the "natural" character of English law referred not to its rational perfection but rather to its organic relation to the development of national character. Modern (post-1688) liberties were not "natural" in the sense that continental jusnaturalists used the term but rather as outgrowths of "the ancient customs of the realm" (modern natural lawyers would say "privileges"). So the idea of English legal tradition—along with that of the English "constitution"—regarded by common lawyers as "the accumulated wisdom of the ages" was carried over into the Whig interpretation of history.

The political catalyst that gave a modern polemical edge to ingrained Whiggery was the example of the French Revolution, and it was Edmund Burke who gave classic expression to the conservative line of argument in protest over the French radicalism of the early 1790s. The fashion for destruction exemplified by Rabaut de Saint-Etienne was typical of "the machine now at work in Paris," which turns against experience, prudence, and especially history. By contrast, according to Burke, "our revolution [of 1688] was made to preserve our *antient* indisputable laws and liberties and that *antient constitution* which is our only security for law and liberty." The "spirit of the [English] constitution" was not a theoretical vision but "*an inheritance from our forefathers*"; and it preserved the old sense of ideals and words—"liberty," for example, and "constitution"—which the French were trying to subvert.[72] This legacy, going back to extreme antiquity, was marked by the "first reformation" of Magna Charta and the Petition of Right as well as the juridical pedigree and "liberal descent" endorsed by Coke and Blackstone. This pedigree has "its records, evidences, and titles," which it is the business of historians as well as jurists to study in a respectful spirit.

"The history of law is the most satisfactory clue to the political history of England," wrote Francis Palgrave. "The character of the people mainly depends on their law." Henry Hallam began his *Constitutional History of England* (1827) by declaring that "the government of England, in all times recorded by history, has been one of those mixed or limited monarchies" characteristic of Celtic and Germanic tradition—and utterly irreconcilable with the Austinian and Benthamite conception of law.[73] Following common law conventions going back to Coke and Fortescue (though rejecting the myth of an "ancient constitution"), Hallam recognized a number of "essential checks upon royal authority," including parliamentary consent for taxes and new laws, due process of law, and guarantees of individual liberties, all of which was nonsense as far as John Austin was concerned. For Hallam the English constitution, though it had a common origin with those of other European nations, had an exceptionally fortunate career, producing a unique sort of security and liberty which had been "the slow fruit of ages" and reached its present height through the "democratical influence" which Hallam, very much like Guizot, attributed to "the commercial and industrious classes in contradistinction to the territorial aristocracy." Hallam declined to take his history beyond the accession of George III because of his "unwillingness to excite the prejudices of modern politics."[74] But his own views were plain, and his adherence to the principle of continuity led him to oppose the democratic reforms leading to the Reform Act of 1832.

Except on this issue Macaulay was largely in agreement with Hallam's line of argument. In his review he found Hallam's history not only "judicial" (if somewhat prosaic and unimaginative) but also eloquent, in a legalistic way.[75] "The Constitution of England was only one of a large family," he wrote in his own *History of England,* which he began publishing more than twenty years later. "In all the monarchies of Europe in the middle ages, there existed restraints on the royal authority, fundamental laws, and representative assemblies."[76] Such were the institutional conditions of that "progress of civilisation" which was so obvious to Macaulay in his own day. England was especially fortunate in escaping the fate of other continental states, which had fallen into absolutism. For Macaulay the lessons taught by history were not the power of reason and calculation but rather the vital force of the unwritten English "constitution," the continuing spirit of common law, the growth of ancient and modern liberty, and the preeminence of the revolutionary model of 1688.

Hallam, who had practiced law for a few years before turning to scholarship, had preceded his constitutional history of England with a survey of the European Middle Ages (1818). In this work he drew on both the older and the newer scholarship, reaching back as far as Etienne Pasquier and François Hotman in the sixteenth century and citing a wide range of contemporary scholars, including Savigny, Guizot, and Thierry as well as the reigning English medievalists. He relied often on Muratori, the French Academy of Inscriptions, and the histories of Sismondi and Michelet, though at one point he admitted a preference for the fuller narratives of Velly and Garnier. He was a great admirer of Sismondi — whose two histories "will, in all likelihood, never be superseded" — and yet he criticized his tendency to find liberal precedents in medieval times and his suggestion that Charlemagne should have issued a constitutional charter, finding it "difficult not to smile at such a proof of his inclination to judge past times by a standard borrowed from the theories of his own."[77] Hallam came rather late to think of history as a "progressive science" like chemistry or geology; but in the second edition of his work, published thirty years later (1848), he made a serious effort to update his knowledge, though he remained quite innocent of German scholarship, except for Sarah Taylor Austin's translation of Ranke.

In general Hallam followed the line of Gibbon and Robertson, appealing to the interest of "a philosophical inquirer" and taking the "philosophy of history" in a restricted sense of treating the manners, language, literature, culture, and commerce of medieval society. Yet he opposed the conjectural history of the Scots, which assigned institutions in a general sense to particular stages of social development. So he rejected the view of a certain "ingenious and philosophical writer" — identified in a footnote as John Millar — that the

frank-pledge was common to all barbaric nations, and argued that this "peculiar system" was peculiar to Anglo-Saxon society, though it indeed passed
through discernible stages.[78] No foreign customs alleged by Millar "fully re-
semble the Saxon institution of which we are treating." In another case regarding the Saxon distinction of bocland and folkland Hallam again preferred the
specific judgments of Anglo-Saxon lexicographers over the theory of John
Dalrymple. In general Hallam was much more concerned with finding differences in national traditions than with making conjectural analogies.

As a Whig and as a lawyer Hallam was interested largely in institutional
history. His purpose was "either to trace the civil revolutions of states during
the period of the middle ages, or to investigate, with rather more minute
attention, their political institutions"; and he denied the "advantage of crowd-
ing the memory with barbarian wars and assassinations" and, for instance,
praised Velly (on whose history he relied extensively) for devoting a whole
volume to the administration of St. Louis. Like Mitford and Palgrave, he was
fond of singularities and the telling of detail — "The truth is, that the accidents
of personal character have more to do with the revolutions of nations than
either philosophical historians or democratic politicians like to admit";[79] and
he loaded his Gibbonesque footnotes with castigations of the errors, small and
large, of other historians, pointing out, for example, that Hume was filled with
"glaring prejudices," compounded by his ignorance of the law, and Michelet
was "more studious in effect than minute in details." Hallam himself relied on
certain historical generalities, such as associating the accumulation of customs
with a cohesive English "constitution" and recognizing, with due attention to
the debate between Romanists and Germanists, a "feudal system." Yet even
here he was careful not to extend "feudal principles" to Scotland, Poland, or
Russia, and he rejected the extremes of Roman analogies (such as vassalage
with the patron-client relationship) and the Gothicist myth of the earlier
Whigs and the radicals. In the *Libri Feudorum* Lombard lawyers argued that
feudal law originated in their country, but by contrast "the ancient customs of
France and England . . . were fresh from the fountain of that curious polity
with which the stream of Roman law had never mingled its waters."[80]

Hallam took a Whiggish view of English history, focusing, like Sismondi in
his study of the Italian republics, on the rise of liberties, especially in the
Parliament. The keys to English history were the gaining of "civil liberties,"
equivalent to the *isonomia* celebrated by Herodotus,[81] the use of representation, first perhaps in a charter of Henry III in 1254,[82] and the rise of the
House of Commons to legislative status. Hallam was well aware of the mythical element in this construction of history, including the "pretensions to antiquity" of the Commons in tracing its origins directly to the Anglo-Saxon

witenagemot ("the immemorial organ of the Anglo-Saxon aristocracy in their relation to the king"),[83] the tales of Alfred, the imaginary laws of Edward the Confessor, and the fabrication of the "Method of Holding Parliaments in the Time of Ethelred" — not to speak of the exaggerated view of Magna Charta, which Hallam himself held.[84] Scholars like Camden and Spelman had criticized such antiquarian excesses, but they kept a grip on the popular imagination. Hallam, who located the essential English liberties in the time of the Plantagenets and tried to avoid vulgar idealizations, acknowledged that English liberties were not so much "bought with the blood of our forefathers" as purchased by money.[85]

Despite his lawyerly background Hallam spread his interests far beyond the English constitution. He inquired as well into areas of social and cultural history, including chivalry, moral improvements, the arts, literature, and philosophy, relying heavily on French and Italian, if not German scholars. Romantic authors had delved deeply into the vernacular literature of the medieval period but had largely avoided the central topic of scholastic philosophy. This was the case with Meiners and even Brucker, whose discussion was mainly a denunciation, and in 1814 Hallam commented that he knew only four Englishmen, including Turner and Coleridge, who had explored that arcane subject, though in a later edition he noted the work of Tenneman (through Cousin's French translation) and Degérando.[86] This chapter in Hallam's *Middle Ages* led him to his larger study of medieval intellectual history published in 1837, which surveyed the whole field of "literature" in the old encyclopedic sense, trying to draw a balance between philosophical reflections and the "minute details" of the antiquary.

The Wizard of the North

There was another path to historical understanding, the one followed by Walter Scott, whom Hallam recognized as one of the "masters of literature" and a fellow cultivator of the history of literature in particular. Scott was a child of the Scottish Enlightenment, having studied with Dugald Stewart among others, but he was also a rebel against it, sharing the veneration of his Romantic contemporaries for the remains and relics of the medieval European and especially national past. Like Hallam and so many other men of letters he was drawn away from the legal profession by literature and fascination with the Border ballads. In 1805 Scott was established already as a poet (as well as a lawyer) with the publication of "The Lay of the Last Minstrel," a work which suggested Scott's romanticized view of his calling:

> The last of all the Bards was he,
> Who sung of Border chivalry;
> For welladay! Their date was fled,
> His tuneful brethren all were dead;
> And he, neglected and oppress'd,
> Wished to be with them, and at rest.

But Scott was a bold pioneer as well as late-coming troubadour, as he turned to the novel, that sister of history and dominant genre of modernism. He began this phase of his career in 1814 as "the Author of Waverley," a work devoted to the lost world of the Highlands "sixty years hence"; and he did not publicly remove his mask of anonymity until 1827.[87]

So began Scott's great series of novels, drawn from "an ocean of reading without compass or pilot" and then more systematic study of "histories, memoirs, voyages and travels, and the like, events nearly as wonderful as those which were the work of imagination, with the additional advantage that they were at least in a great measure true."[88] In the Waverly novels Scott revealed a distinctive sense of history, based on the cultural traditions of Scotland preserved in histories, popular literature, oral tradition, and his own recollections (though he was admittedly weak on names and dates). He made extensive, if desultory, use of chronicles, such as Commines, of broadsides and newspapers, manuscripts, inscriptions,[89] oral communications, and secondary studies; and in a later edition of his novels he added explanatory notes concerning terms and events, many of them, characteristically, derived from his uncertain memory. Though he avoided the serious study of grammar, he was something of an amateur archeologist and self-taught philologist, at least in his employment of Scottish dialects and annotations, some attributed to Dr. "Dryasdust," though he also cited such modern scholars as Barante, Robert Henry, Turner, and Palgrave. Scott also had his own three-fold periodization of history over three generations: "WAVERLEY embraced the age of our fathers, GUY MANNERING that of our own youth, and the ANTIQUARY refers to the last ten years of the eighteenth century."[90]

Not that Scott claimed to be a true historian, for "it is not our purpose to intrude upon the province of history."[91] For Scott the aim of history was not moral instruction but the resurrection of bygone life. In the introduction to the *Chronicles of the Canongate* Scott tells a little anecdote about Mrs. Policy, housekeeper of Queen Mary's Apartments in the castle of Canongate, who was showing the rooms to a "cockney" visitor from London. This young man was a commercial traveler, selling various items, including an "Infallible Detergent Mixture." Mrs. Policy told the story of Mary Stuart and her lover,

David Riccio ("Rizzio"), and showed him the two-hundred-and-fifty-year-old blood stain marking his assassination, adding that "neither water nor anything else will ever remove them from that spot." Thus challenged, the man went "down on his knees . . . but neither in horror nor in devotion." Promising to fetch out the stain in five minutes with his elixir, the man fell to scrubbing, while the poor woman tried to drag him away from his "sacrilegious purpose." Hearing the ruckus, Scott came into the room and explained to the "zealous purifier of silk stockings, embroidered waistcoats, broadcloth, and deal planks" that "there were such things in the world as stains which ought to remain indelible on account of the associations with which they are connected." The vandal left, muttering about the "nasty" Scots, and Scot (the author) himself was rewarded with permission to wander through the historic castle, hoping to "light upon some hidden crypt or massive antique cabinet, which should yield to my researches an almost illegible manuscript, containing the authentic particulars of some of the strange deeds of those wild days of the unhappy Mary." This anecdotes might be glossed as a parable of Scott's own vocation as bard, novelist, revealer of (apocryphal) manuscript revelations, and (in his own way) conjectural historian.

At first he worked mainly within the horizons of personal and vicarious memory, but later he turned to the medieval and especially crusading past, where — drawing on "the great picture of life" — it was his imagination rather than his memory that wandered. In rendering dialogue he strove for authenticity, and regarding the Scottish peasants, for example, he tried to reproduce "the antique force and simplicity of their language."[92] He was interested in the Scottish terrain, the history of families, including his own, but especially clans which traced their lineage back into the medieval period; and he tried to include all classes of society, representing their ways of life and speech, in his tales and long-winded digressions. Scott was fascinated with and solicitous of the particularities of history and what he called the *vie privée;* and though (like Shakespeare and Fielding) he took considerable license with individual characters, he made a special effort to avoid anachronism and defended himself against charges of violating this standard. Without being "obsolete or unintelligible," he tried to "admit, if possible, no word or turn of phraseology betraying an origin directly modern"; and so he bowed to his British readership by trying to "explain our ancient manners in modern language" and to avoid "the repulsive dryness of mere antiquity."[93] Yet he was very conscious of the drastic changes in language and manners, pointing to the Beggar in *The Antiquary,* "as it formerly existed in Scotland, though it is now scarcely to be traced"; moreover the Scottish mendicants in that novel "were by no means to be confounded with the utterly degraded class of beings who now practice that wandering trade," and indeed (referring to Martin, *Reliquiae Divi Sancti Andreae,* 1683) these "Jockies" might even be "descended from the ancient bards, who earned their bread."

Geographically, Scotland itself reflected Scot's sense of chronology.[94] As a young Waverley moved from his home into the lowlands and into the highlands, he also moved back in time into the Scottish Middle Ages. In *Rob Roy* Scott remarked on "the strong contrast betwixt the civilized and cultivated mode of life on the one side of the Highland line, and the wild and lawless adventures which were habitually undertaken and achieved by one who dwelt on the opposite side of that ideal boundary" — an ideal boundary which might be said to stand as well between modernity and antiquity. With Hume, Ferguson, and other philosophical-minded historians Scott believed that human nature was basically the same in all classes and all ages, but only in a general sense; and in fact his emphasis was indeed on singularity and change and the "influence" of a "peculiar state of society." This awareness of individuality and development admitted him to Meinecke's pantheon of historicism.[95]

In the 1820s Scott turned from Scottish to English history and faced more directly the growing criticisms of mixing fiction and history, though half-facetiously. Under the name of "Lawrence Templeton," Scott wrote a fictitious letter to the antiquary "Dr. Jonas Dryasdust" in defense of his ventures into English medieval history and in particular against the charge that, like Macpherson and his spurious *Ossian,* he had drawn on recent history to give false authenticity to his work.[96] Scott admitted that, within human memory, "the whole north of Scotland was under a state of government nearly as simple and as patriarchal as those good allies the Mohawks and the Iroquois"; but he also argued that the past of England, though its comparable period was four centuries earlier, was not beyond the grasp of memory and historical imagination. Of course one could not write in Anglo-Norman French or Chaucerian English, but the language and art of a modern historian need not produce anachronism: "His language must not be exclusively obsolete and unintelligible; but he should admit, if possible, no word or turn of phraseology betraying an origin directly modern." If he confused the manners of two or three centuries, Scott added, this was no worse than "modern architects falling into Gothic style." Finally, Scott affected historical warrant — mocking "severe antiquaries" like Dryasdust — for work on the basis of the sort of legitimacy offered by historians in that (Ranke's and Michelet's as well as Scott's) generation, which was invocation of the "precious pages" of the imaginary "Wardour Manuscript."[97]

Scott did make one serious effort of conventional history, though it was still the marvelous that engaged his fancy. In the preface to *The Betrothed,* describing a meeting in 1825 of the joint-stock company behind the Waverley novels, the chairman notes his intention to write "the most wonderful book which the world ever read — a book in which every incident shall be incredible, yet strictly true — a work which shall be read by our children with an admiration approaching to incredulity. Such shall be the LIFE OF NAPOLEON BUONAPARTE, by the AUTHOR OF WAVERLEY." One prefers to think that this prediction was made in the spirit of Scott's frequent facetiousness.

Scott left a small mark on the discipline of history but had a vast influence on nineteenth-century historians, even those who were suspicious of imaginative reconstructions of past life.[98] Scott, said Carlyle, had taught the truth, or truism, "that the bygone ages of the world were actually filled by living men, not by protocols, state papers, controversies and abstractions of men . . . but men, in buff and other coats and breeches, and the idioms, features and vitalities of very men."[99] Ranke admitted his value even as he distinguished it from his own source-based method. For Sismondi *Waverly, Guy Mannering,* and *The Antiquary* were "the best books written in England in many years."[100] Thierry linked Scott with his own new history, and Scott was Michelet's favorite novelist. But Scott's greatest beneficiary was probably Macaulay, who preferred him to the Romantic poets.[101] In general Scott presided over narrative history, while being the target of scholars closer to the spirit of Scott's own "Antiquary" or his and Carlyle's "Dr. Dryasdust."

Macaulay and the Whig View

Growing up a prodigy in an evangelical family and devoted in early manhood to journalism and reform politics, Thomas Babington Macaulay was nevertheless a born historian. He had a solid classical education and was an obsessive reader of literary and historical, if not philosophical, works in several languages (though acquiring German fairly late). As a young child his imagination was fired by reading Scott, and "he took it into his head to write a compendium of Universal History."[102] He and his favorite sister, Hannah, often read together, reported his nephew G. O. Trevelyan; and "when they were discoursing together about a work of history or biography, a bystander would have supposed that they had lived in the times of which the author treated, and had a personal acquaintance with every human being who was mentioned in his pages. . . . The past was to them as the present."[103] Here the theme of narrative history is introduced: a primary duty of the historian was "to make the past present"; and yet the precise relationship between past and present — in effect between history and politics — was a continual problem for Macaulay; for on the one hand it was a grave error to judge the past by the present (if not vice versa), but on the other hand he chided Mitford because he "judged of antiq-uity by itself alone."[104] On the one hand the historian "attributes no expression to his characters [sic], which is not authenticated by sufficient testimony"; but on the other hand "by judicious selection, rejection, and arrangement he gives to truth those attractions which have been usurped by fiction." These were all variations on the classical themes of the old *ars historica*.

Macaulay lived, acted, and wrote between extremes — between past and present, between literature and history, between reason and imagination, be-tween Scott and Ranke, between the reactionary views of Mitford and the radical ones of James Mill and Jeremy Bentham. In his political career and thinking he was, as Joseph Hamburger argued, not so much a Whig, as his reputation indicated, as a "trimmer," following the moderate and practical lead of Halifax.[105] Except for three years in India on the Supreme Council, Macaulay was a member of Parliament from the campaign for the Reform Act of 1832 until his (welcome) defeat in 1847. From then on he was "liberated" for the great historical work, which he had begun planning from 1839 — or even from 1835, when he was "half-determined to quit politics and to give [him]self wholly to letters."[106] He preserved this liberty by declining the regius chair of history at Cambridge as offered him by Prince Albert, for (aside from the pitiful income) "I cannot bear the collar."[107] As a historian Macaulay prided himself that, like Thucydides, his active public life sharpened his politi-cal instincts and judgment. Even before entering politics he had gained a literary reputation through the articles he wrote for the *Edinburgh Review* and other general journals. In all aspects of his career the strength and talent of "Mr. Babble-tongue Macaulay" (as he was called by his enemies on the *Times*)[108] derived from his oratorical, rhetorical, and indeed poetic skills ("his-tory is compounded of poetry and philosophy"),[109] and these carried over also into the eloquent, if not long-winded narrative of his *History of England*. Macaulay set his sights high, hoping to construct a narrative after which it would no longer be necessary to seek the actions of the Puritans half in Claren-don and half in *Old Mortality*, or the character of James II, half in Hume and half in *The Fortunes of Nigel*.[110]

Macaulay was a formidable researcher but not deeply touched by new cur-rents of historical scholarship. He worked little with manuscripts, preferring pamphlets, which is to say journalistic sources; and indeed Ranke criticized him on this score. Unlike his friend Ellis he was not "Niebuhr-mad," and while he acknowledged that the Roman history marked "an era in the intellectual history of Europe," he criticized Niebuhr's overconfidence and the "ridiculous presumption" in his assertions.[111] The major impact can be seen in Macaulay's best-selling *Lays of Ancient Rome*, published in 1842. Macaulay saw merit in modern historians such as Hume, Robertson, Voltaire, and Gibbon and in general recognized that "[the] writers of modern times have far surpassed those of antiquity." Yet despite their advantages they were still epigones of the ancients. In fact he admitted that "I admire no historians much except Herodotus, Thucydides, and Tacitus." "Of the romantic historians Herodotus is the earliest and the best" — not unlike "children and servants" — but Thucydides, who wrote about what he had experienced firsthand, "is the greatest historian that ever lived."[112] Macaulay's famous 1828 essay on "History" was conceived mainly within this classical paradigm, although not even the greatest of ancients were above criticism in the light of his vision of the ideal historian.

Macaulay had conceived his grand design, his *History of England from the Accession of James II*, at least by 1839, and by the time of his death twenty years later had carried the narrative down to the death of William. His interpretation was connected in many ways with his politics, but it was also planned to contribute in a scholarly way and indeed to correct the traditional story told by Hume, Lingard, and lesser historians. It centered on the significance especially of the Glorious Revolution of 1688 — and so of "revolution" in a general sense — but it set this seminal phase of English history in a longer perspective, drawing on Germanist (Anglo-Saxonist) notions, the Whig view, and Enlightened ideas of material progress and the rise of the middle classes, and the desire — associated with the later work of J. R. Green — to enhance political with social and cultural history and matters of government with human interest.

Like Thucydides, Macaulay took little interest in the earliest period of national history, since early Britain, unlike the barbarians of the continent, lacked historical figures and could boast only of "mythical persons, whose very existence may be questioned."[113] Hengst and Horsa and Arthur were the Hercules and Romulus of English history, and Macaulay had no desire to indulge in Livian or Niebuhrian speculations about concealed historical meanings. Macaulay could see significance only after "the darkness begins to break; and the country which had been lost to view as Britain reappears as England" — and when Christianity began to exert its civilizing influence. Extending the Whiggish principle of religious tolerance to medieval beliefs, he rejected the false liberalism of the philosophical writers of an earlier generation, whose attitudes "were, in truth, as narrow-minded as any monk of the dark ages, and whose habit was to apply to all events, in the history of the world, the standard received in the Parisian society of the eighteenth century." Like Michaud and others he also rejected the fashion of ridiculing "the pilgrimages, the sanctuaries, the crusades, and the monastic institutions of the middle ages." In the "evil time . . . of darkness and tempest . . . and deluge" the Church was indeed the ark which preserved some continuity with antiquity.

For Macaulay the exception to the principle of continuity of English history was the Norman Conquest, which brought to the English nation a subjugation even worse than the despotisms of the Orient. "During the century and a half which followed the Conquest there was, to speak strictly, no English history." English history began only with the Great Charter of 1215, after which the national character began to take form; and it was preserved by the Parliament, which unlike the representative assemblies of the continent continued to grow even in the face of absolute monarchy. The House of Commons was the basis of "the present constitution of our country," which grew over five centuries from sapling to tree, from boy to man, as "with us, the precedents of the middle ages are still valid precedents."[114] Even the influence of the Church was on the whole beneficial, although coming to need Reformation, and receiving such "in the fullness of time" following the Council of Constance.[115] The defining element of English tradition, however, was "that ancient constitution which the majority of the people had always loved," and which would be restored in the later seventeenth century.[116] From that period, which was the focus of Macaulay's concern, the story of England was largely that of "improvement."

What always stood in the way of such improvement — and here Macaulay drew on his political experience — was extremism, enthusiasm, and "party spirit." For the persecution of the Albigensians and Lollards, despite his Protestant sympathies, he had little regret. Papists and Puritans, absolutists and republicans, Tories like Mitford and radicals, including the elder Mill, Bentham, and the "philosophical radicals," all helped to produce crises, or "conjunctures." Men like James I, Filmer, and Laud were the villains of the *History;* "trimmers" and moderates such as Cranmer, Halifax, and even Cromwell were the heros. In general revolution was an evil, wrote Macaulay in 1830 in his unpublished "History of France," except for "defensive" ones.[117] The English needed a revolution, but that of 1688 was their last one, except for the social "revolution" of 1832, which was in keeping with moderation as well as progress.

"Revolution" was a word that Macaulay used often and easily, but of course it applied best, in his flexible usage, to the seventeenth century, which located many of the transformations of the modern age. In his third chapter on "the state of England in 1685" Macaulay sketched the background and foreground of these changes — from the expansion of wealth to the crime and filth of London, from diplomatic and military matters to private life and religious practices, from the political side of religion to the poor condition of the lower clergy, from high literature to low journalism and the scandal sheets that proliferated in the time of civil war and after, including rumors (such as those of Cavalier cannibalism during the Civil War), and from the divisive "party-spirit" to the formation of "national character" in the wake of civil war. He celebrated material and intellectual progress, while noting the failure of its benefits to reach "the poorest class." His sources included statistics (based on contemporary political arithmeticians), state and private papers, correspondence, poetry, earlier historical and popular writers, and especially newspapers preserved in the British Museum; but he employed them in the most unsystematic and impressionistic ways. On the topic of the country gentleman, for example, he pleaded that the sources were "too numerous to be recapitulated" and left judgment to "those who have studied the history and lighter literature of that age."[118]

The term "revolution" was in general born out of the seventeenth-century English experience before being exported to the French and various intellectual contexts, including the idea of a "scientific revolution"; and this usage was reflected in Macaulay, too.[119] "It is a remarkable fact that, while the lighter literature of England was thus becoming a nuisance and a national disgrace," he wrote, "the English genius was effecting in science a revolution which will, to the end of time, be reckoned among the highest achievements of the human intellect." He was referring in the first instance to Bacon, the "Verulamian doctrine" of inductive method, and its reception, which Macaulay thought depended on "the civil troubles [which] had stimulated the faculties of the educated classes, and had called forth a restless activity and insatiable curiosity, such as had not been known before among us." Yet, Macaulay suggested, it may well be "that the increase of wealth and the progress of science have benefitted the few at the expense of the many."[120]

Macaulay's explanations had more to do with what he called "the noble science of politics," it might seem, than the ancient art of history; and even his efforts to evoke the "spirit" of an age or the surrounding "circumstances" of action were pictorial rather than analytical, as in the famous third chapter, which was an extraordinary model for a generation or more of historians even though it has been almost entirely superseded, if not discredited. He wrote in the style of his speeches, and he allowed no room for doubt or mere probability; nor was he inclined to acknowledge errors.[121] Treating institutions and classes in a conventional way, his interest lay in tracing the course of events and judging the characters and motives of individual actors. He was not, nor did he intend to be, a professional historian in the manner of a Ranke or even a Michelet; he wanted to achieve the literary status of a Hume, a Gibbon, or even a Scott, whose popularity he sought to surpass—and indeed did so. Macaulay was extraordinarily solicitous of his readership and sales. Within a generation after its appearance more than 140,000 copies of the *History* were sold in Britain alone; Lord Acton reported another 100,000 in America (with Macaulay preferred to Hume); and while it fell out of favor with more demanding scholars, it has never fallen out of print.[122] The same cannot be said of the volumes published by Phillip Stanhope, Lord Mahan, which, though in part written earlier, serve as a continuation of Macaulay's history.[123] Macaulay called Stanhope a "violent Tory," but also "agreeable" and a "very good scholar" and, despite political differences, a "very great favorite."[124] For Stanhope the era of the Georges, like that of the Antonines, was a "golden period," filled with happiness and glory, owing to England's ancient and free institutions and its Revolution; and despite loud and angry complaints, improvement was making "gigantic strides." Yet Stanhope also admitted that this was mixed with corruption, producing a "mingled mass of national wisdom and national folly."

Stanhope has remained in Macaulay's shadow. Macaulay himself, who displayed some of this same intermingling, left a monument which, despite its rhetorical excesses, scholarly deficiencies, and naive and insular view of progress, became and remains a literary classic. As John Kenyon noted, he was "the first literary peer" and perhaps the first literary millionaire as well.[125] In scholarship he was soon surpassed by Ranke and Gardiner, who denied him "any real historical knowledge"; but his Whiggish and triumphalist desire, in the spirit of Polybius, Livy, Eusebius, and many other national and confessional historians down to the time of Guizot, to tell the story of the winners caught the fashion of optimistic evolutionism, which itself was an echo of Scottish conjectural history, before the appearance of *The Origin of Species*. "For the history of our country during the last hundred and fifty years is eminently then history of physical, of moral, and of intellectual improvement." Scholars like Ranke and Döllinger were not impressed with his flamboyant rhetoric and political partisanship; but Döllinger's disciple, Acton, could not avoid Macaulay's spell; as a youth he read the history four times and, while disapproving Macaulay's "violent Liberalism," never lost his admiration. For Acton, Macaulay, though "utterly base, contemptible, and odious" in political terms, was (especially since he created a historical masterpiece such as Acton never produced) "one of the greatest of all writers and masters."[126]

German Impulses

History speaks.
— *F. A. Wolf*

The Return of Philology

Not even philosophy outshone history in early nineteenth-century Germany. "Without a knowledge of the mighty past," declared Friedrich Schlegel in 1810, "the philosophy of life . . . will never be able to carry us beyond the limits of the present, out of the narrow circle of our customs and immediate associations."[1] He continued: "It is the great merit of our age to have renovated the study of history and to have cultivated it with extraordinary zeal. The English had the honour of leading the way in this noble career. The Germans have followed them with success." The upshot in both cases was renovated traditions of national historiography, but foundational to these old projects was the critical and revisionist exploration of remote antiquity and the origins of "our" civilization. Out of this imagined cultural birth and genealogy and search for proto-European cultural and ideological ancestors there appears another sort of "Whig history," raised now to the level of a concept of general progress, which both inspired and misled scholars in the heroic age of antiquarian scholarship in Restoration Europe.

In Germany philhellenism began in the eighteenth century with Winckelmann and art history, but the critical study of ancient history arising in the early nineteenth century was rooted above all in philology. By the sixteenth century philology had emerged from the arts of grammar and rhetoric as a science and had become part of the "encyclopedia" of sciences in the German universities by the later eighteenth century, when it moved into biblical and vernacular scholarship and joined forces with auxiliary sciences such as epigraphy, archeology, and numismatics. Like Vico, Schlegel and Humboldt wanted to join philology and philosophy into a science of culture which gave primacy to language and its history and which offered access to remote antiquity, but the true pioneers of the assault on the earliest ages of Greek and Roman history were Heyne, Wolf, and Niebuhr. Wolf in particular took a revisionist stand on the Homeric poems, arguing for collective rather than individual authorship—for him, between Homer's lines, "history speaks"— and this was an inspiration and a provocation to a generation of classicists.[2] The epigones and critics of these pioneers carried on their work on two fronts which represented the divided legacy of philology — divided according to the classical *res-verba* topos, corresponding to the philology of things (*Sachphilologie*) and the philology of words (*Wortphilologie*). In the early nineteenth century there appeared another methodological division, one of which was the "symbolic" school — "men of darkness," Treitschke called them[3] — of Creuzer (supported by Hegel and Schelling), and the other from the more orthodox approach of scholars like P. A. Boeckh, who was a student of Wolf as Wolf was of Heyne, and who was the leading Hellenist of the Restoration period and a dedicated "philologist of things."[4]

Boeckh's conception of philology was indeed "encyclopedic," for it included matters of private life as well as the arts, sciences, and language, and he opposed the literary and romantic idealizing of Greek culture.[5] In 1817, in a book dedicated to Niebuhr, Boeckh investigated the material base and economic life of ancient Greece with due attention to revenues and expenditures, prices and wages, and the role of slavery in the decline of the polis. In this work he made use of inscriptions and in 1815 proposed a systematic collection of these, of which, beginning in 1824, he became chief editor. His work was criticized by the *Wortphilolog* Gottfried Hermann, but it was essential for further critical studies, most notably those of his best student, K. O. Müller, who became professor at Göttingen in 1819. Müller turned also to archeology and especially mythology, but he rejected the mystical tendency of Creuzer's symbolism, as did the translator of Homer, Johann Voss, and other philologists.[6] Müller envisioned a synthetic work on Hellenic races and cities, beginning with the Dorians and the Minyae, for which he used Boeckh's corpus of inscriptions, but he died before he could carry out his plan. He published a comprehensive history of ancient Greek literature, in which he pointed to language as the key to prehistory; for "the comparison of languages enables us to judge the history of nations at periods to which no other kind of memorial, no tradition or record, can ascend."[7] Ignoring the thesis of Wolf, Müller accepted Homer as an individual artist, creating epic unity out of earlier mythical traditions. Surveying all genres, he remarked on the slowness of the Greeks, in contrast to the oriental nations, to cultivate historiography. He represented Herodotus, "the Homer of history," as the first of the logographoi, concerned with things divine as well as human and assuming an "ancient enmity" between East and West. On the other hand, he represented Thucydides as the creator of an entirely new sort of writing, confined to human deeds but seeking out the underlying causes.[8] A scholar with Romantic leanings, Müller died a romantic death in 1840 in Athens on his first field trip to Greece.

Among Boeckh's and Müller's disciples was Ernst Curtius, who was with Müller at his death, who succeeded to his chair at Göttingen (later moving to Berlin), and who continued Boeckh's work on the *Corpus Inscriptionum Graecarum*. Curtius's best work was done in the fields of archeology and geography, but his fame rested on his immensely popular history of Greece (1857–67), which, published in the same series as Mommsen's Roman history, was the counterpart to Grote's work, though unlike Grote he believed that historical reality could be detected behind the curtain of myth. Curtius was more interested in culture than politics, however, and his best work was done in the fields of geography and archeology. Most important of all was his controversial championing of the effort to excavate Olympia itself to enhance German philhellenism — as contrasted with the Roman tradition which Germans, and especially German Protestants, had always, from the time of Arminius to Bismarck, opposed — which for him was almost a religious quest.[9]

The accomplishments of professional scholars like Boeckh, Müller, and Curtius were overshadowed by one unlikely romantic triumph, which was Heinrich Schliemann's uncovering of ancient Troy and "Priam's gold." Schliemann himself, though his sensational work resolved a long-standing puzzle, remains a mystery. His was a heroic career after he turned from the pursuit of wealth to his quest for the true site of the city of Homer's *Iliad*, which he finally located at Hissarlik — and this despite charges not only of incompetence (on the part of scholars like Curtius and Mommsen as well as modern archeologists) but also of falsifications both at Troy and at Mycenae. Troy was an amalgam, or archeological palimpsest, of several cities, whose layers, carelessly dug through by Schliemann, were distinguished and analyzed in the next century (unlike whatever reality lay beneath the Homeric poems). But whatever his faults and whatever the opposition of classicists (if not anthropologists), Schliemann in fact discovered what he rightly called "a new world for archeology," and he remains what a recent biographer calls "the emblematic archeologist of all time."[10] And as another recent scholar writes, "The discovery of Troy was the beginning of the end of philological hegemony over the study of ancient *Kultur*."[11]

But Schliemann was on the margins of professional scholarship, and philology continued to reign in the schools. Another of Boeckh's students was J. G. Droysen, who turned to later and more eventful aspects of Greek history, which he called "Hellenism," referring to the achievements of Alexander the Great and his successors. "I am an admirer of movement and advance," he admitted to a friend in 1835: "Caesar not Cato, Alexander and not Demosthenes is my passion."[12] Politics not philology, one might say of his own career, though he began as a student of Boeckh as well as Hegel. For Droysen, Alexander was the first "world-historical figure," a supreme exemplar of universal state-building, whose Macedonian realm represented a model, perhaps, for the Prussian-centered unification movement in Germany — which, like Greece, was a land of individual liberty, lacking only unity to achieve cultural perfection. Such was Alexander's mission to the disunited Greek states. Indeed he was the incarnation of history, and the world has never been the same after the historical fact and posthumous spirit of Hellenism, which was for Droysen what Rome was for Hegel — and India for Schlegel.

Boeckh and Droysen both illustrated the expansion of philology into larger historical areas and into an encyclopedic and a hermeneutical mode. For Boeckh philology was not just criticism but also a form of knowledge and of interpretation. The target of encyclopedic philology was "verbal tradition . . . fixed through written record," and the accompanying exposition involved four sorts of interpretation of texts, or historical sources: objectively, grammatical and, depending on context, historical; subjectively, individual and, relating to other subjects, generic. Authors who express the spirit of an age, like Cicero, require objective interpretation, while poets and sophisticated historians like Tacitus demand more subjective interpretation. In any case such understanding is caught between reading of individual texts and general linguistic usage, that is, other examples which cannot be identical, since (here Boeckh cites Gorgias) "nobody thinks like another man . . . and the speaker and the auditor do not have the same idea."[13] This is the basis of the famous "hermeneutical circle," which traces the course of historical as well as textual understanding.

Droysen also lectured in this encyclopedic and hermeneutical mode, which was rooted in Lutheran traditions; and he summed up his views in his popular handbook of historical method, his *Historik,* which carried on the work of Flacius Illyricus, Jean Bodin, and other writers on historical method. "The realm of historical method is the cosmos of the moral world," Droysen wrote, and history was the "know thyself" of humanity in general.[14] The moral world was the arena of individual and collective wills, which was given shape by memory ("mother of muses," citing Aeschylus's *Prometheus*); and so history, set apart from philology and philosophy, was the place of consciousness, so that "the knowledge of history is history itself." The task of the historian was to find the human cause, the individual or collective will, underlying the historical sources. This was "psychological interpretation," which went beyond pragmatic interpretation and the study of historical conditions and which led to the "interpretation of ideas" and to the making of the whole of moral life and the social world. Like Vico, Droysen believed that this historical or hermeneutical understanding "arises from the kinship of our nature with that of the utterances lying before us as historical material."[15] Both the historian and the human object of his studies represent an "I" — a historically mediated "I" at that — and so the "process of understanding is as truly synthetic as analytic, as truly inductive as deductive."

Yet history was for Droysen as it had been for Herodotus, a matter of endless inquiry — "not," alluding to John the Baptist, " 'the light and the truth' but a search therefor, a sermon thereupon, a consecration thereto."[16] For Droysen history was a spiritual process which included present and future as well as past, and so it is not surprising that he joined his pious erudition to the cause of national (*kleindeutsch*) unification. Nevertheless, the point of departure of historical inquiry within any hermeneutical tradition remained source material, and the basis of "method" was the choice and criticism of this material, including remains, sources, and monuments — "heuristics" — and so the whole range of auxiliary sciences cultivated in the eighteenth century, especially at Göttingen. This was *Historik,* and from it came the process of interpretation — "interpretation of ideas" — that led to an understanding of the intentions of the most remote agents and institutions of antiquity.

The interpretation of collective life, however, needed categories grounded in sources and monuments, and Droysen measured human horizons through the concentric social circles of the family, the neighborhood (*Nachbarschaft*), the tribe (*Stamme*), and the people (*Volk*). Associated with the family was marriage, paternal authority, and blood-vengeance, and with the neighborhood, the elders and allocation of land. The tribe was a conventional (political) and not natural institution, and the people provided the basis of government, religion, and nationality. In this context there developed the chief forms of human culture (language, art, science, and religion) and of social order (property, justice, and authority), leading to the state — and thence to a federation of states, a "state-system," and perhaps a "world-system of states" (*Weltstaaten-system*). Out of this process — here the Hegelian structure becomes evident — arises self-consciousness and freedom on an ever higher level of social, national, and international life; and this in turn gave warrant for Droysen's conviction that "history is humanity's knowledge of itself."[17]

Penetration of the Greek past led to exploration of Near Eastern and Egyptian backgrounds, especially in the wake of Champollion's controversial decipherment of hieroglyphic texts. This breakthrough was extended by the archeological investigations of Baron Bunsen, Richard Lepsius, and F. A. F. Mariette, confirming the work of Champollion. Lepsius had studied with Bopp, Herrmann, and Boeckh as well as Müller at Göttingen and held the first chair of Egyptology at the University of Berlin. As further hieroglyphic texts were discovered and chronology was established, Egypt took its place in the canon of Western history, beginning with Bunsen's general survey, which located Egypt between the Semitic and Indo-European traditions in the mainstream of universal history. This book, dedicated to Niebuhr, again invoked language as "the oldest authentic record of mental development in the primordial epochs of the human race."[18] Egyptology was followed by Mesopotamian languages, hieroglyphics by cuneiform — with Henry Rawlinson as "the Champollion of Assyriology" — as a new specialty of ancient history; and from here the ancient Near Eastern civilizations, celebrated remotely in the Eusebian tradition and within the framework of biblical chronology, took their place in general and more critical surveys of ancient history, such as those of George Rawlinson and Max Duncker, who drew on these often sensational discoveries, carried on still under the aegis of an expanded practice of modern philology.[19] The first great synthesis was that of Eduard Meyer, which appeared between 1884 and 1902, when he became professor at the University of Berlin, and it began with an introduction on the "elements of anthropology" and carried the complex narrative down to the fall of the Athenian Empire.[20] Unlike Duncker and other predecessors, Meyer was adept at several oriental languages as well as Greek history, and his book, published in many later editions, was the standard survey in the early part of the twentieth century.

Niebuhr and the Lure of Antiquity

In an age of state-building and nation-inventing, however, it was not Greece but Rome that served as the principal model of politics — and target of philology — and this was the project undertaken by Niebuhr, who not only was a distinguished statesman but also, according to Heinrich von Treitschke, had "the glory of being the first among all men of learning."[21] As Niebuhr wrote in 1826, "It is certainly incontestable that philology now stands many degrees higher than it did thirty years ago."[22] The work of Heyne, Wolf, Boeckh, and of Niebuhr himself all contributed to that convergence between philology — classical scholarship and antiquities — and the art of history, which prepared the ground for the critical science of history emerging in the nineteenth century. Of this historical science (*Geschichtswissenschaft*) Niebuhr was a founding and an exemplary figure, "the true reformer of our historiography," as Wegele put it, "to whom Ranke himself deferred."[23] Although little has been noted in the vast and growing literature on "historicism," Niebuhr was indeed one of the founders of this attitude toward knowledge and experience.[24]

Born in the year of the American Revolution, of the first version of Goethe's *Faust,* and of the first volume of Gibbon's *Decline and Fall,* Barthold Georg Niebuhr, son of the Danish explorer Carsten Niebuhr, was a prodigy and a largely self-taught, classical scholar by the age of twenty — much later, he lamented, than Grotius, Scaliger, or Salmasius — but he spent much of his life as a businessman, diplomat, and statesman. Like Petrarch and other humanists Niebuhr preferred the company of the ancients to that of the moderns, in 1794 already complaining, "I long to get back to my ancients, my friends, to whom I owe all my thoughts."[25] His ego-ideal was Scaliger, "who stood at the summit of universal solid philological learning, in a degree that none have reached since; and so high in every branch of science, that from the resources of his own mind he could comprehend, apply, and decide on whatsoever came his way," Niebuhr wrote. "And why does not France set up the name of Scaliger to match that of Leibnitz?"[26] Niebuhr was himself a *philologus* in the old sense: "O how would philology be cherished," he exclaimed in 1812, "if people knew the magical delight of living and moving amid the most beautiful scenes of the past!"[27] Even during the periods of his public service he continued his classical studies and search for manuscripts. Not that he ignored philosophy, especially Kant and Fichte, who encouraged his idea of history as a "systematic" field of study, though in a practical rather than theoretical sense — a view distinguishing him from Enlightenment as well as humanist scholars. Yet if his reading was omnivorous and polyglot, his focus was still Eurocentric, "following the order and limits of Justin," that is, the four monarchies and the Greco-Roman tradition, though on a more solid base than Voltaire, Rollin, Gatterer, or Gibbon could find, but interpreting history not as a form of theology but rather as a "branch of philology."[28]

This distinction reflected Niebuhr's assumption that there were two basic approaches to history — the theological one of Bossuet, following the Old

Testament and the fortunes of Israel, and the philological one involving a focus on the texts of classical literature, non-Roman as well as Roman. Of the first, non-Roman, stage the story of Greece was the "noblest part"; but it was mainly to the Roman, the "second half of ancient history philologically considered," in which the earlier traditions were joined in an imperial unity, that Niebuhr devoted his scholarly energies. He was at once a backward-looking representative of the old humanist tradition of historical scholarship and a forward-looking pioneer of the new historical "science" which, though it made larger claims, took the literal reading of texts as its basic method. He likened the study of ancient history to exploring a mighty river. "As rivers are received into the sea," he wrote, "so the history of Rome receives into itself that of all other nations known to have existed before her in the regions beyond the Mediterranean." But it was not possible to trace the whole course of the river: "No man can mount up to the fountain-head of those streams by which the tribes of the human race have been borne downe," he wrote.[29] In another metaphor Niebuhr admitted that, as regards origins, "poetry has thrown her many-coloured veil over historical truth."[30] Yet at the same time poetic sources, even at second or third hand, could yield some insights into the earliest ages.

In 1829–30, in lectures on ancient history given at the University of Bonn, Niebuhr celebrated the new discoveries which were transforming the discipline of history and making it the "true *magistra vitae*." "Egyptian antiquity will be laid open before our eyes," he declared, alluding to the work of Champollion: "we stand at the very threshold of a new era in the history of antiquity."[31] Yet Niebuhr himself, in the name of science, wanted to narrow the horizons of history, setting aside not only natural history and the earlier stages of humanity but also questions of race, the physical condition of man, and the history of diseases, not to mention the significance of China, Japan, India, Islam, and other largely unconnected cultures. Niebuhr's Eurocentric orientation reduced the horizons opened up by the conjectural history of the Enlightenment and represented in a sense a step backward; the positive aspect of his point of view, however, was that this narrowing of vision permitted him, drawing on the erudition of past generations, to achieve a critical depth denied to more philosophical historians.

In a general way Niebuhr's renowned critical method was a sophisticated version of the procedures of Herodotus, especially his second book, which was on Egypt and which tried to stick to reliable testimony; before him "the primordia of Greek history are to us a real chaos." "Whoever is engaged in philological studies," he wrote, "must make Herodotus his daily companion."[32] But Niebuhr, drawing on humanist and encyclopedic scholarship, attempted to go beyond naive Herodotean reporting by attending to the fact that surviving narratives overlie older ones and by the critical study of myth and poetical sources. Unlike many contemporary poets, who were intimidated by their classical heritage and bemoaned their neoclassical — epigonal — status, Niebuhr hoped to surpass his forebears. Niebuhr's task was to undo the efforts of Cicero and Livy to go beyond the scanty annals, as indeed Renaissance historians had tried to do, and "to throw rich dress over the story of Rome," that is, "to restore the ancient tradition, to fill it up by reuniting such scattered features as still remain, but have been left out in that classical narrative which has become the current one, and to free it from the refinements with which learning has disfigured it."[33] The first principle of historical criticism was that the more ancient traditions are full of contradictions, while more recent ones are coherent but also further from original truth; but unfortunately seeking this original truth from texts like Ennius and Fabius Pictor was a matter rather of informed judgment than of reason. Traditions could be corrupted by national vanity, but they could also be confused by differing systems of chronology. Some ancient historians used historical records, but little of their work has survived, and it was the goal of modern historians to reconstruct the most probable story.

Among critics who thought Niebuhr had gone too far was Auguste Schlegel, who published a review of the first edition of Niebuhr's history, objecting to his excessive reliance on poetic sources (*Sagen*) and mere "shadows of testimony" in classical texts. Poetry came late to Rome, and "the good Ennius was certainly no Homer"; and it was the Greeks who began Roman historiography. Schlegel offered many detailed criticisms of Niebuhr's conjectures and chided him for his excessive distrust of Livy, Dionysius of Halicarnassus, Plutarch, and others. Schlegel also pointed out his neglect, or tardy recognition, of the work of Beaufort and Cluver as well as of contemporary scholarship. "The study of antiquity," he wrote, paraphrasing Bacon's notion of science, "is not the work of an individual."[34] Yet despite his haughty self-confidence, Niebuhr was far from unaware of the progress of scholarship, especially in the earlier stages of humanist tradition. He paid tribute to antecedents such as Sigonio, one of the last scholars to treat Roman history before "ordinary historians" such as Machiavelli and Montesquieu; Perizonius, who "advanced far beyond his age"; and Johann Voss, "with whom a new age for the knowledge of antiquity begins." Niebuhr also mentioned Beaufort, though he was overskeptical and no philologist. Niebuhr had small respect for superficial and half-learned authors like Gatterer and Heeren; and even Wolf he criticized for neglecting, in his Homeric studies, comparisons with the East, especially Egypt — though of course it was only with the work of Champollion in the

1820s that new vistas were opened on this subject. As for Rome, it was Niebuhr himself who stood at the heights of scholarly tradition. "I do not hesitate
to say, that the discovery of no ancient historian could have taught the world
so much as my work," he wrote to Savigny in 1827; "and that all that may
hereafter come to light from ancient and uncorrupted sources, will only tend
to confirm or develop the principle I have advanced."[35]

Niebuhr's calling was the study of Roman history, or rather prehistory
(*Vorgeschichte*), that *tempus obscurum* which Vico had called "poetic wisdom" — though Niebuhr apparently did not know Vico's work, and certainly
did not cite it — and which had been neglected, at least until the time of Heyne
and Wolf, in the wake of the historical pyrrhonism of Bayle, Beaufort, and
Voltaire. Antiquity, wrote Niebuhr, "is like an immeasurable city of which
there is not even a grand plan extant."[36] Niebuhr wanted, through philological
penetration, conjecture, and divination, to restore this plan, to fill in the gaps
left in "the most important of all histories," especially the famous "lost" books
of Livy (as well as those of Varro). His strategy, his so-called ballad theory, was
to resurrect historical characters from myths and legends, on the analogy of
the study of the recently discovered *Nibelungenlied*.[37] In effect a hermeneutical reading going back through surviving poetical texts would reveal at least
something of "the night of remote antiquity." Niebuhr said of his enterprise
what Renaissance humanists had said of their philological efforts, that "he
who calls departed ages back again into being, enjoys a bliss like that of
creating."[38] And some critics thought that this was precisely what he was
doing.

For Niebuhr Roman history represented a sort of intellectual continuum
divided into three stages: an age of myth, an age in which myth and history
were mixed, and an age of true history.[39] In the first, figures and events were
confused and chronology indeterminate; in the second, myth paralleled and
overlapped (sometimes revised) historical records, with memory of the past
caught between the two; in the last, chronological measurement and "arith-
metic outline" appeared, to be filled in by later scholars. As he explained,
"Between the purely poetical age, the relations of which to history are altogether irrational, and the thoroughly historical age, there intervenes in all
nations a mixed age, which, if one wishes to designate it by a single word, may
be called the mythico-historical" — and which corresponds to the notion of the
Middle Ages, as in Spain and Scandinavia, if not Italy. In any case Niebuhr
himself belonged to the last stage, except that philology provided tools of criticism for the task of filling in lacunae in the historical record and even ways of
using myth to throw light on the historical process. Although Perizonius had
extraordinary insights into poetic sources, he was a child of his century, and

lacked the sort of comparative knowledge available to Niebuhr's generation, that is, the Spanish, Scottish, Scandinavian, and German lays and sagas, which all displayed historical features to informed and critical scholars.[40]

Niebuhr's interest was not in events and personalities but in the social conditions, institutions, and movements of the early peoples of the eastern Mediterranean — not "who was the builder, or the lawgiver of Rome, but . . . what Rome was, before her history begins, and how she grew out of her cradle [as inferred] from traditions and from her institutions."[41] Myth told of founding fathers; history suggested the formation of states through the incorporation of families, as in the comparable cases of the communes of medieval Italy and (referring to the work of Johann Müller) Zurich.[42] Nor was it possible to argue, on the basis of myth, the existence of a Trojan colony in Latium, which no proof could confirm centuries afterwards; it was rather to determine whether the Trojan legend, which "has not the least historical truth," was exported from Greece or homegrown. Scattered references to the Trojan exiles led Niebuhr to conclude that it was the latter, but in any case numerous nations claimed descent from Troy and attached themselves to the Homeric tradition, thus altering the original story, as Aeneas did for the Roman state. The transmogrifications of the Trojan legend could not give human reality to the great names memorialized in poetic tradition, but they could suggest the connections between various national groups who came into contact with the Trojans, whom Niebuhr was inclined to identify with the original "Pelasgian" inhabitants.

What could be inferred from myth about the origins of Rome? Like Livy, Niebuhr was at pains both to honor sacred traditions, which held that the majesty of Rome demanded nothing less than a god at its conception, and yet at the same time to give priority to the more human and answerable question of "what people the first Romans belonged to." Whatever the historical facts behind the story of Romulus and Remus, the twins did reflect the two tribes — the Romans and the Quirites — making up the original population of Rome, which was always the site of a "double people" well into the historical age.[43] Beyond this Niebuhr suggested that, looking back to ancestral origins, the inhabitants of "Roma" called their founder "Romus," or "with the inflexion so usual in their language, Romulus," and then — what is peculiar to Roman tradition — attributed of their rivals in Remuria, an analogous founder, Remus, twin brother who was slain by Romulus. This story, associated with local legend of the savior she-wolf, was memorialized by "the oldest and the finest work of Roman art," the bronze figures set up in 458 B.C. near the Ficus Ruminalis. It also received many modifications in the course of later repetitions and interpretations, including that of Livy, who "tells the tale of these times like a history, without meaning it for one." Some parts of this had even been preserved by oral tradition down to Niebuhr's time.

But the mythical tradition was corrupted, lost from memory, first by a decline of faith, then by poetic distortion (such as that of Ennius), and finally by a turn to "real history," whose devotees, rationalists and naturalists as they were, paradoxically perverted the old traditions in the style of euhemerism, hardly better than the opposite fallacy of "belief in goblins." "The wish of these historians was to gain the whole of the mythical age for history: their assumption, that the poetical stories always contained a core of dry historical truth: and their system, to bring this core to light by stripping it of everything marvellous." In the wake of this came the metamorphoses of Livy and then the exaggerations of later forgers and such anachronisms as making Numa Pompilius the disciple of Pythagoras. Or was this an error? For Pythagorean influence indeed penetrated as far as Rome, as shown by the statue of Pythagoras erected by the Roman Senate. In any case Numa, unlike Romulus, was a figure of real history, or real institutional accomplishments (especially the securing of landed property), behind the embellishments of myth. Nor unfortunately did the hypothesis of an original language help the ancient historian, since it was belied by his researches, which showed that the richness and diversity of dialects increased the further the historian penetrated into antiquity.[44]

With the annals, despite later revisions, began the period of history and efforts to establish a regular chronology. Here begins the tradition culminating in the work of Scaliger, who labored to restore the seminal work of Eusebius. For Niebuhr, Scaliger "stood at the summit of universal solid philological learning, in a degree that none have reached since." The Romans were always a "double people": Romulus and Remus, Romans and Quirites, but also patricians and plebeians, patrons and clients — the origins of none of which admit to a strictly historical account. In the historical period names are not imaginary but refer to real persons. The foundations of this history, however, were weak and uncertain — the annals being "restored" and the poetic traditions turned into new forms of poetry, as with Ennius, or prose; and the problem, the hermeneutical task, was to read back into the original forms, in however a general way, though always with attention to chronology along the lines set by Scaliger, but without the biblical baggage.

Niebuhr's example inspired many later historians, including Michelet and Thomas Arnold, not to speak of Macaulay's "Lays of Ancient Rome." With Macaulay history, having descended from poetry, returned again to this literary source: every society — not only the Romans but also Celts, Germans, Danes, Scots, Welsh, Spanish, Serbians, Africans, and Peruvians — passed through a ballad stage, which could only be restored by a "reverse process" of history; and his effort of antiquarian "imitation" was intended to revive (as Ennius, perhaps, had revived, and with the help of Walter Scott) the old spirit of primitive poetry. His "Horatius," a lay set "in the brave days of old" (394 B.C.), invoked the old days of Roman glory:

> Then none was for a party;
> Then all were for the state;
> Then the great man helped the poor;
> And the poor man loved the great:
> Then lands were fairly portioned;
> Then spoils were fairly sold:
> The Romans were like brothers
> In the brave days of old.

Thus was Niebuhr's historical sense received and idealized by one of his most attentive readers.

Mommsen and the Turn to Science

Yet Niebuhr's metaphilological method was not acceptable to many scholars in an age of empirical science, represented most famously by Ranke but championed by many scholars, philologists and historians alike. The poetic sources were inferred by Niebuhr from only a few hints in much later classical authors (Cato, Varro, Horace, Cicero, et al.), depending indeed on another sort of conjectural history and vulnerable to the old arguments of historical pyrrhonism, such as those of George Cornwall Lewis, which was revived from the work of Louis Beaufort. Lewis applied the judicial model of evidence — first-hand evidence and not hearsay (*auritis testis*) — and came to his conclusion about "the futility of Niebuhr's ballad-theory" on this basis.[45] Lewis's stand was representative not only of narrow British empiricism but also of the hypercriticism which flourished among the enthusiasts for "scientific" method.

More authoritative were the criticisms of Theodor Mommsen, who joined Ranke in the promotion of scientific history. Though he gained an international reputation for his narrative history of Rome, he turned his back on such literary pastimes for technical and systematic study of the sources — the result, surmised Arnold Toynbee, of the intrusion of the Industrial Revolution into historical thought.[46] Mommsen deplored the proliferation of "pseudodoctores," many of whom went to America, as defectors from this professional community. For Mommsen history was bound to texts and other tangible remains, and he opposed the literary and occult conjectures of his predecessors. Indeed he had wanted to work on Roman legal texts before he had thought of, or was enticed into, writing narrative history.[47] He paid homage to both Niebuhr and Savigny, who brought an end to the dilettantish stage of antiquarian study, but he declined to follow them down the unlit path of what Thucydides called "archeology."[48] Once again we see the Janus-faces of history: Niebuhr admired Herodotus both for his attempts to distinguish history from myth and for his honest reporting of the latter, while Mommsen took as the first motto for his *Roman History* Thucydides' famous disparagement of "archeology," on the grounds that it was impossible to get clear information about earlier periods because of the lapse of time and that, moreover, such antiquities were not really very important.

So Mommsen turned to the later period of Roman history. Like Niebuhr, he studied at the University of Kiel, made his *italienische Reise,* was involved at various times in public life, but returned always to Roman antiquities. He had been trained in law as well as philology, and this reinforced his attachment to authentic written sources, as did his lifelong devotion to the study of inscriptions, which he began, with Savigny's support, in collaboration with Otto Jahn. Mommsen taught briefly at Leipzig, Zurich, and Berlin. His reputation was made in 1854–56 with the publication of his literary masterpiece, the *Roman History,* which showed the influence of Macaulay and his own journalistic work and which, though it preceded his major publication in epigraphy and Roman law and remained unfinished, brought him a Nobel Prize for literature at the end of his life.

Ancient history for Mommsen was a complete cycle of civilization, with modern history a second wave; and both, at least in the West, had a general pattern in common, which was a progression from "that cantonal individuality, with which the history of every people necessarily begins, to the national union with which the history of every people ends or at any rate ought to end."[49] For Rome this process was one of successive incorporation, or unification (*synoikismos*), from family and paternal household to nation and sovereign state.[50] Like Niebuhr, Mommsen hoped to know Rome better than Rome (Livy and even Tacitus) knew itself; but following Thucydides, he largely gave up on trying to recapture individual life in the earlier ages, "which are, so far as history is concerned, all but lost in oblivion." There was no "Italian Homer" to describe the early conflicts and system of incorporation out of which Rome arose; and even the Trojan legend (here Mommsen contradicts Niebuhr) was imported from Greece. So Mommsen turned instead to inquiring "how the real life of the people in ancient Italy expressed itself in their law, and their ideal life in religion; how they farmed and how they traded; and whence the several nations derived the art of writing and other elements of culture."[51] Trained as a jurist, Mommsen had little use for Niebuhr's ballad theory and questions of prehistory, and concentrated instead on the legal records and constitutional and social forms.

Mommsen followed this story of *synoikismos* from Roman origins through the fragmentary and revised records, distorted further by myths, homegrown and imported from Greece, down to successive "constitutions," as inferred mainly from legal sources, which in the case of Rome had already lost their symbolic character. By the mid-fifth century the rule of Rome in central Italy was complete, though the Social Question was only just beginning to disturb the process of state building and subsequent Latinizing of Italy, and Hellenism was only just beginning to exert its influence. Just beginning, too, were the records of the magistrates and pontifices, but everything earlier than 509 B.C. "remains, chronologically, in oblivion."[52] The largely fictitious connections between Rome and Greece were the work of Hellenic authors, especially Timaeus of Sicily, who mixed their tales with indigenous stories. The substance of history must be sought in authentic records, beginning with the law of the Twelve Tables, which according to tradition was modelled on Greek legislation. Yet Mommsen's was a work of literature as much as scholarship, in keeping with his view that "the imagination . . . is the author of all history as of all poetry."[53]

The common belief in the inexorable drive of the Romans to establish an empire was for Mommsen an exaggeration. Rather, they were compelled by the need to defend themselves against the intrusions first of Africa, then of Greece, and finally of Asia. Expansion was also energized by the "mercantile spirit" of capitalism, which took possession of the nation.[54] The study of history was in a sad condition, at least concerning Roman origins, as the national story, linking Rome with Alba, competed with the Greek version, linking it with Troy. Parts of the Roman story were told in the third century by the "national" poet Naevius and the "anti-national poet" Ennius, in whom the "Hellenic contagion" left its epic, unhistorical mark. When Roman historiography came into maturity, it was the work of a Greek author. Polybius, in his "pragmatic" analysis, depended on the most mechanical explanations. Yet he employed original sources and threw aside legends, anecdotes, and worthless chronicles: "His books are like the sun in the field of Roman history."[55] In a later, imperial age and under Greek influence, the national focus widened into universal history.

Mommsen did not gloss over the bloody periods of Roman history, but he regarded such excesses — with many parallels in modern European history — as an unavoidable byproduct of a "law, that a people which has grown into a state absorbs its neighbors who are in political nonage, and a civilized people absorbs its neighbors who are in intellectual nonage." What he called the "lower grades of culture" (Libyans, Iberians, Celts, Germans) could not resist the power, and indeed the right, of an unrivalled nation like Rome — "just as England with equal right has in Asia reduced to subjection a civilization of rival standing but politically impotent, and in America and Australia has marked and ennobled . . . extensive barbarian countries with the impress of its nationality."[56] Unlike Thierry, Mommsen had little sympathy for the losers. Of the Celts he wrote: "In the mighty vortex of the world's history, which inevitably crushes all peoples that are not as hard and as flexible as steel, such a nation could not permanently maintain itself" — just as, he added, their kinsmen, the contemporary Irish, were being overcome by their Anglo-Saxon rulers.[57]

While Mommsen had to downplay individual agency in his early volumes, he embraced this level of explanation when he came to the last century of the Republic and that "rare man" and "genius" Caesar, as Droysen had done in his book on Alexander. As Alexander had created a "system" and an extraordinary legacy, "Hellenism," so Caesar and "Caesarism" were world-historical phenomena. Mommsen saw a larger design to this triumphal story, in which ploughshare and sword went "hand in hand"; for in the long run — the analogy with Prussia was obvious — it was "not decided by provoking chance, but was the fulfillment of an unchangeable, and therefore endurable, destiny."[58] Although Mommsen did not finish his story, he did offer a summing-up that showed the significance of Rome in general and Caesar in particular for his own age:

> That there is a bridge connecting the past glory of Hellas and Rome with the prouder fabric of modern history; that Western Europe is Romanic, and German Europe classic; that the names of Themistocles and Scipio have to us a very different sound from those of Asoka and Salmanassar; that Homer and Sophocles are not merely like the Vedas and Kalidasa attractive to the literary botanist, but bloom for us in our own garden — all this is the work of Caesar; and, while the creation of his great predecessor in the east has been almost wholly reduced to ruin by the tempests of the Middle Ages, the structure of Caesar has outlasted those thousands of years which have changed religion and policy for the human race and even shifted for it the center of civilization itself, and it stands erect for what we may designate as eternity.[59]

So rhetoric was joined to erudition in Mommsen's version of scientific history.

Mommsen was "the Caesar of the contemporary establishment in classical studies."[60] Even more than Niebuhr and not less than Ranke, he epitomized, or at least symbolized, the scientific — legalistic and positivistic — history that achieved high professional status in the nineteenth century. This insistence on documentary sources was reinforced by the narrowing of the classical canon which occurred in nineteenth-century universities. Together the result was to promote the "scientific" aspect of history by requiring both specific textual evidence and testimony within the recognized, authoritative European tradition — the external threats being conjectures from alien traditions and inferences from nonliterary — mythical or art-historical — sources. One example was K. O. Müller, who (according to one critic) showed his classicist bias by rejecting as "barbaric" all that fell outside Greco-Latin tradition.[61] Yet Müller drew parallels from Germanic folklore and was not nearly so narrow as some contemporaries.

Nevertheless, this was a deep methodological disagreement. The insistence on documentary and epigraphical sources, which for Mommsen replaced Herodotus's method of "autopsy," and the literal reading of texts by conservative philologists, seemed narrow and inadequate to many scholars of prehistory, who, like Herder, Creuzer, Görres, and David Friedrich Strauss, turned to myth, religion, and symbol in order to shed light on the earliest ages. Along similar lines Nietzsche hoped to capture the mythical spirit of Greece in the images of the opposing gods, Apollo and Dionysius, who, however, he warned, could not be approached by a scholar "with another religion in his heart";[62] and he was in effect excluded from the orthodox, Greco-Roman philological canon for his conjectural presumption. Nietzsche's fellow Basler J. J. Bachofen, defecting from the study of Roman law, conceived a contempt for self-proclaimed critical scholars like Niebuhr and Mommsen, "who believed in their self-conceit that the great epochs of the ancient world could permanently be reduced to the petty proportions of their own minds" — that is, to "pragmatic" explanation and to the "facts" of geography, chronology, and such modern measures — and turned instead to metahistorical and mythistorical sources and more conjectural interpretations in search of the spirit of antiquity.[63] This new mythology followed the lead of Friedrich Wolf, in that it regarded myth as a product not of an individual fabricator but rather of an unconscious impulse on the part of a whole community in time. One reason for resistance to this idea is "that this mythicizing tendency has no analogy in the present mode of thinking," suggested Müller (quoted by Strauss). "But is not history to acknowledge even what is strange," asked Strauss, "when led to it by unprejudiced research?"[64]

National History

Across the revolutionary divide there continued to be an outpouring of world histories (the number cannot even be estimated because of the short life and existence of textbooks), but these were increasingly rivalled by national histories in all the established European states and in those still in the process of becoming. "It was Herder who first taught the German nation to think historically," wrote Treitschke, meaning that he had rejected the unnaturalness of natural law, discredited by revolutionary associations, and turned to national traditions.[65] It was also Herder who, in 1795, asked the question "Why do we still have no history of the Germans?" (discounting such amateurish attempts as that of Michael Ignaz Schmidt, director of the Viennese archives, who published a Voltairean *History of the Germans* from 1778) with attention to the manners, laws, sciences, arts, and commerce of the Germans within each stage of the development of "culture" — "the historical house-Bible of our great-grandfathers," Karl Lamprecht called it.[66] A generation later this picture was changing dramatically, as, in the words of Acton, "a movement began in the world of minds which was deeper and more serious than the revival of ancient learning" — that is, "the renovation of history" taking place especially in Germany.

"Historical writing was old, but historical thinking was new in Germany when it sprang from the shock of the French Revolution," wrote Acton in 1886, adding that "the romantic reaction which began with the invasion of 1794 was the revolt of outraged history."[67] In this statement Acton was endorsing a myth which German scholars were then in the process of undermining; for the study of history was indeed a central feature not only of the Enlightenment but also of the Lutheran tradition and German erudition in general since the Renaissance. Yet it is still the case that new impulses were given to historical curiosity and understanding by German medievalism, and especially the wars against France beginning in 1813. This historical — or "historicist" — turn can be seen in the developmental ideas of Goethe, in the dialectic of Hegel, in the scholarship of Savigny and the Grimms, in the proliferation of local historical societies and the founding of the first historical association recommended by Savigny in 1819 (*Gesellschafte für ältere deutsche Geswchichtskunde*),[68] and especially in the nationalist program of Fichte as asserted in his *Addresses to the German Nation* of 1807. As Meinecke concluded, "A perspective is opened here that looks directly toward Ranke's concept of history."[69] In any case it suggests the agenda of German historiography from the Wars of Liberation onwards which was to project this national principle back into the German, and with it the European, past.

The Wars of Liberation were a test of the objectivity of professional historians. Consider emulating Herodotus in his recitation of his history at Olympus, remarked Friedrich Dahlmann, and how little pleasing the account of the German movement will be to partisans on either side.[70] These wars in Germany, following those of America and Poland, covered three "unforgettable" and "glorious" years, recalled Droysen in his still-impassioned lectures of

1842–43, which saw both the fall of the *Reich deutscher Nation* and the rise of the German *Volk* to political prominence and virtual statehood with a rationale that was far from that "utopian abstraction," the law of reason (*Vernunftsrecht*) of France.[71] This marked the true "Revolution," and its result was "a direction, a goal, a plan" for the German people, who had found their — "our" — own general will and calling (*Berufung*). What the French Revolution and Empire had awakened was the German *Volk* and *Vaterland* — the historical foundations of a nation which would surely (Droysen predicted) produce a modern state to join the "new order" (*Neugestaltung*) of Europe.

This resurgence may be seen in the work of Heinrich Luden, a follower of Johann Müller, who came as professor of history to the University of Jena in 1806, after its days of glory with Fichte, Schiller, Novalis, Hegel, and the Schlegels.[72] Luden had several conversations with Goethe, holding court in nearby Weimar; and among other things they discussed the subject of Luden's calling, with frequent references to Goethe's, and in particular to his *Faust*. Why, wondered Goethe, do you want to be a historian (*Historiker, historicus*)? What do you find in your sources? The truth, perhaps? And do you also aspire to the office of a poet? Luden answered that his quest was for a critical understanding of the people, their spirit and character, and the state. "That will be a great enterprise" (*Operation*), Goethe commented, "but what the historian takes from this labor is always only subjective truth; objective, indisputable truth it is not." Fichte had quoted Pilate in this connection ("What is truth?") and had offered an answer, that truth was something that was thought and could not be thought otherwise; but Goethe responded that this was only Fichte's truth — "for everyone has his own truth." What held for mathematics did not apply to "historical things." Still, Goethe concluded in his exchanges with Luden, "Go on and live in your History, make bold to depict bygone ages untouched by the confusions of the present. . . . I hope you and Jena are good for each other." And Luden did have the distinction, according to Treitschke, of first preaching the power, liberty, and moral force of the state.[73] In 1808 he gave an enormously popular course of lectures on "the study of the history of the fatherland," lamenting its ruin under Napoleon and dedicating himself to the memorialization of the German past.[74]

But the defeat of the Prussian forces at the battle of Jena in the fall of 1806, when the city was burned and plundered, made it impossible for Luden to remain "objective," though he retained the claim to be purely scientific (*reinwissenschaftlich*). In the confused time of defeat and reforms of Stein he followed the notion of truth represented by the political and not the philosophical Fichte. "In Germany all culture comes from the people," and so he lamented "the evil associations and seductive power of vanity [which] have swept the growing nation into spheres which are not its own." Like Fichte,

Luden could not be silent in a time of "misfortune and our shame." In 1814 he founded a journal of politics and history called *Nemesis,* which was devoted to the cause of the Germans (*Teutschen*). In the past few years the life of the people and the folk seemed to have lost its foundation, but now there were signs of change: "The year 1812 showed that the laws of nature could not be changed, that life still ran in its old, bounded course, which formerly determined the relations between persons . . . , and that the destroyer, who had contempt for everything, would himself be destroyed." The next task—so history became prophetic and "subjective"—was national rebirth and unification, in which fatherland, folk, and state would all be the same.

In 1814, too, Luden published the first volume of his *General History of People and States,* in which he joined his own universalist designs to Fichte's idealist philosophy—moving from the individual subject (the *Ich*) to the state and the nation (the *Volk*) in space and time—in terms, that is, of geography and chronology and all aspects of "culture." In 1825 he began publishing his twelve-volume *History of the German People,* which projected the story of the liberation of the fatherland back to the Middle Ages, salvaged from the assaults of uniformed critics of the previous generation, and which reached the time of the Emperor Frederick II. As a teacher Luden wanted to spread the same message, to bring together *Volk* and *Wissenschaft,* hoping to see "not only the auditorium . . . but also the anteroom, the stairs, and even the courtyard full of students"—and indeed he did have an impact on the younger generation in the *Burschenschaften.*[75]

Luden belonged to the first generation of national historiography. Two other students of Müller who contributed to this enterprise were Friedrich von Raumer, who came to Berlin in 1819, published a *History of the Hohenstaufen* in 1823–25, and founded the *Historisches Taschenbuch* in 1830 (and over whom Ranke was chosen for the Prussian Academy), and Gustav Stenzel, whose *History of Germany under the Frankish Emperors* appeared in 1827–28 and *History of Prussia* in 1830–37.[76] In 1830, Dahlmann published his valuable bibliography of sources of German history, which (with the collaboration of Georg Waitz) went through many editions down to the present. Other national histories of this pre-Rankean age were those of Friedrich Wilken (1810), Friedrich Kohlrausch (1816–17), K. A. Menzel (1815–21), J. K. Pfister (1829–35), and Hans von Gagern (1825–26).[77] These were all of course overshadowed by the more critical, if no less nationalistic, work of Ranke, Sybel, and Treitschke.

These early efforts, however, were made on a scholarly base hardly more extensive than that of the eighteenth century, and they were rendered obsolete by the organized erudition of the post-Napoleonic period, beginning especially with the *Monumenta Germaniae Historica,* which was sponsored by

Stein and supported also by Goethe, Savigny, and Grimm. The Society for Germany's Oldest Historical Sources was founded in 1819, and after many difficulties Georg Heinrich Pertz was appointed editor and Johann Friedrich Böhmer secretary, later to be joined by Ranke's student Georg Waitz, Wilhelm Wattenbach, and Philipp Jaffé. The first volume (on Carolingian chronicles) appeared in 1826, featuring the famous motto, "Sanctus amor patriae dat animum." From then on experts edited volumes devoted to five sorts of source material: chronicles, laws, charters, letters, and antiquities.[78] The *MGH* is one legacy of the period of German liberation which continues today, surpassing the shelf-lives of the popular histories of the age of Ranke, Michelet, and Macaulay. This was also the period of the opening of the archives to scholars like Pertz and Ranke and the reinforcing of one critical aspect of the art, and now increasingly the professional science, of history.

Yet erudition did not remain objective. Already in 1846 in Frankfurt, two years before the Parliament, representatives of the fields of law, history, and language met to discuss their agenda; and Grimm addressed them on the value of these "inexact sciences" for the political future of their fatherland.[79] Early-nineteenth-century historians were prodigious researchers and writers, but they were also drawn, many of them, to the active life in pursuit of national or liberal aims. This was true even of medievalists like Georg Waitz, Wilhelm Giesebrecht, and Heinrich von Sybel, who were all devoted students of Ranke. Many historians of the *Vormärz* period alternated between scholarship and political activism. Whether resisting Napoleonic imperialism or following their own plans of state-serving and building, they looked at history as an extension of politics and, increasingly, economics. Droysen, Gervinus, Dahlmann, and Waitz were members of the Frankfurt Parliament in 1848.[80] Some of the best known historians were actually publicists or journalists, such as Mommsen, G. G. Gervinus, and Ludwig Häuser, whose *Deutsche Zeitung* served scholarship as well as national politics, not to mention F. L. G. von Raumer, whose *Historisches Taschenbuch* (1830) was the first professional historical journal and predecessor of the *Historisches Zeitschrift*.[81] They also joined the general move from the cosmopolitan ideals of the Enlightened Republic of Letters to the competitive and invidious nationalisms of the Romantic period — and of course to the "scientific" history that preached objectivity even as it served national ideology.

Ranke and World History

Leopold von Ranke was the leading professional historian of the nineteenth century, certainly from the retrospective view of his legacy and legend. Leonard Krieger goes so far as to compare him with Copernicus in astronomy

and Kant in philosophy, a judgment which does justice at least to his ambitions.[82] After classical and theological training and his thesis on Thucydides at
the University of Leipzig, Ranke taught ancient and medieval history before he
found his calling, which was the study, teaching, and writing of modern European history, beginning especially with his *Latin and Teutonic Nations* of
1824, which led to his professorship at Berlin. Ranke found inspiration in the
work of Niebuhr, whom he acknowledged as a mentor; but he was much more
of a literary artist (despite his ambivalence toward Scott), and his writings
are full of more color and moral judgment than his later reputation would
suggest. They are also fuller of theology and philosophy than later epigones
acknowledge—except that the rational and spiritual features of those disciplines were transferred to the study of history in often ingenious ways.

Ranke moved close to the shapers of German history and, for example,
acted as tutor to Frederick William IV, but he shunned the role of advisor. "I
lived so completely in the sixteenth century," he wrote, "that it would have
been hard for me to consider it."[83] Yet Ranke fashioned his historical thinking
in the context of contemporary religious and philosophical thought, in effect
claiming the missionary's role for the professional historian. Like Luther just
four centuries earlier Ranke experienced a religious conversion in 1817, but he
recognized the deep divide between himself and his Protestant forebear and
hero, for concerning the belief in Christ, along with the moral obligations
linked to this, Ranke commented, "We cannot take this in the same way that
Luther took it."[84] The spirituality of Ranke's age was less innocent and more
philosophical than Luther's, though Ranke continued to believe that humanity
could reach a spiritual dimension and move from the real to the ideal, from
appearance to higher truth. Indeed this was precisely the office of the historian
and the reverse of that of the philosopher—to find the universal in the particular and to find spiritual and intellectual meaning in things and events. Yet
Ranke had little use for the "new scholasticism" of political theory and indeed
established his own journal with the intention of investigating the "public
sphere" in terms of historical science.[85]

Ranke constructed his own sort of idealism—refashioning Fichte's "I" as
the historian's "eye," for which history represented the hermeneutical Other
(Fichte's "not-I"). Ranke inherited the eighteenth century's concern with point
of view (*Sehe-Punkt*) and the realization that, as Goethe had also noted, "history must always be rewritten."[86] History was a collection of facts, but it was
also a subject- (or author-) centered vision that found meaning in these facts
through selection and trained intuition. The historian had to confront the
individual persons and events—"History is an empirical science"[87]—but also
had to reach out for the general. As in language the individual was part of a
larger community, so particular persons and actions had to be placed in a

larger process to find meaning — historically, if not teleologically, since the historian was no prophet — and it was the historian who took the position of a surrogate, backward-looking god. As Luther read the Bible and Kant, the conditions of human reason, so Ranke read the historical process, in order to expound, according to his own materials, methods, and lights, God's plan.[88] For Ranke indeed invoked Providence, and sometimes Fate, in creating the general syntheses out of the chaos of particular happenings, intended and unintended — and identified God with the general unity of things which the historian sought. Ranke's sense of the spirit could also be expressed in the view that God was truly in our consciousness. In a sense historical interpretation was an analogue of Lutheran consubstantiation, in which human substance brought the subject into contact with the spirit, and in this sense, the divine.

Other philosophical, or theological, themes inform Ranke's work, among them the hyperbolic claim that states were ideas in the mind of God and the notion that every epoch is immediate to God. In this latter notion Ranke is not so much establishing a principle of historical relativism as invoking an Augustinian conception of God's time, which cannot be grasped by humans, though scholars may approximate through the extension of memory produced by historical penetration. As for the statist claim, while Ranke was not an activist, he was of course swept up by the national enthusiasm that gripped the German states during and after Napoleonic domination; but his celebration of nationality went deeper than such political commitment; his belief was that national (linguistic) groups were the divine unities, or collectivities, which drew together individuals and gave them meaning and purpose. On a universal level the communities that develop into states could themselves be seen as individuals, growing not merely out of their soil but also through the experience of great events and rivalries; and in his last years Ranke returned to the Enlightenment project of *Weltgeschichte* and the divine ideal that transcends the history of particular states in the larger progress of "culture or civilization, by whichever name we choose to call it."[89]

Yet it was on the individual that Ranke concentrated his attention and extraordinary powers, and here it is that the old, much misunderstood question of so-called objectivity arises. The negative side of this principle came in the Thucydidean form of Ranke's criticism relegating early modern historians to the level of secondary — non-eyewitness and largely untrustworthy — sources.[90] "Guicciardini," he admitted, "is the basis of all later work about the beginnings of modern history and easily has precedence";[91] but he offered no firm foundation for the modern historian. The positive side appeared in his famous phrase, echoing the sentiments of Lucian, Thucydides, and other champions of historical method: "To show how things really happened." This is the principle that Ranke stated in his first major work, *The History of the Latin and Teutonic Nations* (1824).[92] What he meant, despite later misconstructions by positivists innocent of philosophy and desirous of claiming a status for history quite different from Ranke's understanding of "science" (*Geschichtswissenschaft*), was not the hope of transcending a human "point of view," of surveying human behavior *sub specie aeternitatis;* on the contrary he surrendered the roles of superhuman judge and prophet, which historiographical rhetoric had so long preserved.

More to the point, however, is the question immediately following, which clarifies the context and foundation of Ranke's method: "But from what sources could this [reality] be newly investigated?" Ranke's answer serves both as a summation of the historical science and pedagogy of the previous century and as a manifesto for a more subtle and critical historical epistemology and employment of sources (*Quellenforschung, Quellenkritik*), which would throw light on the old problem of historical knowledge. History indeed treated the probable, the realm of opinion, and yet there were practical ways of maximizing probability and approximating historical truth and moral certainty. Here is Ranke's solution: "The foundations of the present writing, the origins of its subject matter, are memoirs, letters, diaries, reports from embassies, and original narratives of eyewitnesses."[93] Now in one way this repeats the old wisdom about "autopsy," which goes back to Herodotus and especially Thucydides and which was further developed in the Renaissance "arts" and "methods" of history; but there is a new emphasis introduced by Ranke, deriving not just from his epistemological acumen but, more directly, from his seminal, extensive, and sexually charged experience in the archives of Berlin, Austria, and especially Venice, which opened up more fully in the 1820s.

The essential and novel point (though it had not gone wholly unnoticed by earlier scholars) was the crucial value of sources that were private, or secret, as well as official. Of course "God alone knows history," and yet "it is not opinions which we examine" — it is existence and the "stuff" of human action.[94] The implied distinction was between writings designed for public consumption, or outright propaganda, and those designed for policy and decision making, created by observers who had no ostensible motive to distort the truth and every reason to produce accurate intelligence for political use. "Objectivity" existed at least on this practical level, and could presumably be achieved by later scholars as well. To Ranke this seemed to be the peculiar virtue of, in particular, the Venetian *relazioni* produced in the age of Machiavelli and being opened up just in Ranke's day. Of course the Vatican archives would no doubt have yielded even more forthright intelligence, except that neither the Protestant Ranke, nor any other nineteenth-century historian could gain access to these dangerous treasures. Contemporaneous with Ranke in the 1830s, Michelet also came to appreciate the value of archival evidence, but he was perhaps more interested in colorful detail and curious motivation, and in any case there is little evidence of systematic exploitation of the French archives by Michelet even before he was denied access.

In fact even Ranke's use of archival sources was unsystematic, part of a very eclectic mixture of available testimonies and placed in the service of Ranke's quasi-religious intuition; but he was conscious of the larger possibilities in such manuscript materials. Moreover, he made an unprecedented effort to compare and to criticize familiar historiographical, that is, secondary, sources of sixteenth-century history — Guicciardini, Machiavelli, Sleidan, Sarpi, and other authorities. Ranke's assumption was that such comparative source criticism, combined with an attempt to uncover the errors and contradictions of historians (including eyewitnesses), would bring the modern scholar closer to the "facts," even though these had still to be expressed from the modern author's standpoint, and certainly were closer to a synthesis than any earlier observer or participant could hope to reach.

Ranke's first book, his *History of the Latin and Teutonic Nations* (1824), set the scene for his later intellectual travels. His starting point was not the old myth of universal Christendom but a post-Lutheran recognition of a Europe divided by competing nationalities evolving into "great" and small powers, or groups with no power at all. "What is it that exalts nations, and brings them low?" Ranke asked: not merely their "natural development, their growth and decay, as is the case with human beings," he answered; for "external circumstances often marvellously co-operate to accomplish this end."[95] Nor was it some "divine and predestined fatality for destruction and prosperity." Whence Ranke's determination to return to the history of political actions and interactions — *l'histoire événementielle,* as it would later be called.

Ranke's story, centering on a generation that, historically, "was the most remarkable that [has] ever existed," involved what has become familiar as the origins of modern Europe and its "state system," following the fondness for "system" of historians — even Niebuhr — as well as philosophers in the later eighteenth century. The collapse of Italy, the rise of the national monarchies, especially Spain and France, and the continued threat of Turkey, which itself joined the diplomatic system in 1536 — this is the material of Ranke's narrative. Yet the story breaks off in 1514, when history was about to change its course and when the national divisions were about to be deepened by movements of religious reform in Germany, which would bring him back to the theological roots of his life work and political commitment. Ranke's second work, *The Ottoman Turks and the Spanish Monarchy,* followed the decline of these powers within the international framework, making extensive use of the Venetian relations for these developments on the edge of Europe. His secondhand *History of the Serbian Revolution* also pursued the affairs and search for liberty on the periphery of the European scene.[96]

The next major effort of Ranke to "read the book of history" was his *History of the Popes* (1834–36). Here his focus was on Rome and her traditional position at the center of events, except now, in the sixteenth century and after, as target rather than as leader. Again he invoked, if only rhetorically — "if we dare thus to express ourselves" — the notion of "the plans of God in the government of the world," and the conceit of Augustine and Lessing of "the education of the human race."[97] The pattern displayed was "a universal tendency to the circumscription of the papal power" and the expansion of national traditions, both under conditions of the new force of "public opinion."[98] In his preface Ranke gave detailed attention to the archival collections he had visited, and from which he had received inspiration, in the preceding decade not only in Berlin but also in Vienna, Venice, and (though without free access) Rome; and he appended a large number of original documents and a powerful critique of Sarpi, Pallavicino, and other contemporary authorities. He also acknowledged that his national and Protestant point of view led him to approach his subject in a very different spirit from that of an Italian or a Catholic. In his account Ranke included not only the sequence of events and striking portraits of the popes and other leading figures but also matters of constitutional, institutional, fiscal, and intellectual history, and the arts. This was an ideologically inflamed age, and he confessed some puzzlement as to whether political doctrines, such as the subversive ideas of the Jesuits, arose out of the facts or were the originators of events.[99] Nor have any of Ranke's successors, whatever their point of view or access to documents, resolved this perhaps badly posed question.

Ranke's next work was a case in point of this problem. In 1836 and 1837 he began to study the archival records of the Empire, Prussia, and Saxony to extract from "lifeless paper" remnants of "our national life" more direct than the work of historians who were not eyewitnesses.[100] On these he based his *History of Germany in the Reformation,* which brought him back to one of his main sources of inspiration, Martin Luther. Although he disdained the work of Johann Sleidan, Ranke opened his own book with a virtual quotation of the main theme of Sleidan's *De statu religionis et reipublicae* (1555), which was that ecclesiastical and political history are "indissolubly connected, or rather fused into one indivisible whole."[101] Yet Ranke's perspective was indelibly secular, as contrasted, for example, with the five-volume history of Jean Henri Merle d'Aubigné, who sought the "soul" of the Reformation as well as of

Luther.[102] In Ranke's story of the rise of modern Europe (though reaching back to Carolingian origins) the duality was expressed in the moral force of religion and the political reality of nationality — Church and State — and of course Luther had also devoted his energies to the German Nation as well as to the evangelical faith. The struggle of nation versus empire was another example of universality, both in religion and in politics, being opposed by individuality — tyranny in effect against liberty, which was represented by the German people, whose national consciousness was awakened by the resistance to Roman-inspired theocracy. This resistance was not begun, but only renewed, in the Lutheran Reformation.

Ranke continued his two-track narrative from the late fifteenth century, following the deliberations and acts of the Diets from the efforts of constitutional reform at Worms in 1495 to the final break between imperialists and "protestant" princes at Speier in 1529, and intellectual and religious issues before and after Luther's confrontation with ecclesiastical authority. Erasmus was "the first great author of the modern opposition, the champion of the modern views" and a pioneer of "public opinion," which "adorned him with her fairest wreaths."[103] Luther's dramatic career received even more hyperbolic praise, as the only person to represent the interests of Germany in this crisis and to take a "stand"; and like Erasmus, he rode the new wave of printed books, whose increase after "Luther's appearance before the public was prodigious." From Luther's inner and outer struggles Ranke pursued the dual theme of the politicization of religious reform through the convergence with the princes and cities moving to establish national churches and to resist imperial claims and ecclesiastical tradition.

In his *Nine Books of Prussian History* (1846) Ranke narrowed his focus from the Empire to one of the principalities that followed the national path. Beginning, for example, in the case of Henry the Lion, as oppositional forces, the princes came to supplant the Emperor in the role of political leadership and anticipated — and reinforced — the religious defection of Luther, who made Germany "the first to break through the pale of hierarchy which encircled western Europe."[104] Thereafter diversity became the order of the day and was responsible not only for catastrophes like the Thirty Years' War but also the "great political truth signified by the balance of power." The story of Brandenburg-Prussia in particular reflected this pattern, which was continued in Ranke's day in the form of the *kleindeutsch/grossdeutsch* conflict, setting Prussia against Austria, which dominated German history before unification in 1870, and the *Kulturkampf* against the Catholic church which arose afterward.

After 1848 Ranke turned to the study of other national traditions of western Europe, still employing documentary sources, especially official acts and the Venetian relations, but (in contrast to Michelet and Macaulay) none of the rich pamphlet literature. In 1852 he published his study of the French monarchy, mainly in the sixteenth century, and the civil wars which became a "universal religious war."[105] He took up the contorted question of the massacres of St. Bartholomew, the motives of Catherine de Medici, and the aftermath, which (in the work of François Hotman and "Junius Brutus") produced the proto-revolutionary idea of "the sovereignty of the people."[106] Ranke followed a similar line in his study of England and its constitutional-religious wars (1859); and again he relied on documentary sources and historiographical criticism of Clarendon, Burnet, and others, displaying these supplementary materials in appendices.[107] In both of these works Ranke admitted that he could bring no comparable expertise or empathy, but only his investigative virtuosity, critical eye, and historical intuition.

Despite his investigations of national traditions within a European framework, or "system" of "great powers," and his own political commitment, Ranke's first and last field of exploration was the old genre of universal history, *Weltgeschichte;* and to this subject he devoted his last work, which began to appear in 1880. With most other German historians Ranke retained a Eurocentric view and endorsed what a recent scholar has called "the disqualification of non-Europeans from historical inquiry."[108] Nevertheless, Ranke brought into this global arena his usual critical and concrete view of history as — no less than the law — tied to written documentary evidence. For him the historian, despite the recent discoveries of archeology and linguistic science in the "vestibule of History," cannot penetrate the mysteries of prehistory and the relation of mankind to nature, not to mention divinity, which are the objects of scientific and theological study. "History begins at the point where monuments become intelligible and documentary evidence of a trustworthy evidence is forthcoming," he declared, "but from this point onwards her domain is boundless."[109] In modern times, he continued, historians dispensed with the old theory of the Four Monarchies and continued the secularizing tendency exhibited in the mid-eighteenth-century *Universal History* assembled by English scholars and continued by German historians. National traditions, when worthy of notice to a universal perspective, are important and constitute empirical grounds of investigation, Ranke wrote, but Universal History went far beyond politics and war to culture and civilization, which was the true goal of universal history. Was capturing this vast and panoramic story beyond human powers? Perhaps, Ranke admitted, but — speaking from the heights of the profession which he had come to dominate — it was worth the effort.

Historians had to begin in the "vestibule" of poetry, since conceptions of religion counted for more than particular events in understanding the life and culture of people. Ranke indeed treated the religions of Egypt, Assyria, Persia, and the Greeks, but he evaded questions of the historicity of mythical figures and turned as quickly as possible to "history proper," meaning politics and war but also literature, philosophy, and history, which constitutes evidence about "the spirit of man." He considered at some length, and with his usual critical asides, the foundational works of Herodotus and Thucydides, which together spanned the range of Ranke's ambitions — Herodotus with his "sympathetic insight into universal history" and Thucydides with his concreteness, chronological accuracy, and respect for records. Over the nine volumes of the *Weltgeschichte* Ranke himself, though he referred occasionally to modern authorities, tried to practice what he preached about primary sources, with the result that he departed little — less, indeed, than Niebuhr had done — from the standard classical and biblical story, and that he moved back closer to the theological sort of history which had inspired him more than sixty years earlier, after his religious awakening, to take up the historian's calling.[110]

6

French Novelties

The philosophy of history had its Copernicus and Kepler; now what is needed is its Newton.

— Jules Michelet

The Generation of 1820

Born in the revolutionary period, coming of age in the Empire, and entering the public sphere with the return of the Bourbons, the "generation of 1820" was exposed to extremes of political and social change, and so was drawn to the study of history in order to understand these shattering experiences.[1] This was the basis of what Renan called "the revolution which since 1820 has completely changed the face of historical studies, or rather has founded history among us."[2] The leaders of this revolution included especially Guizot, Thierry, Mignet, Barante, and Michelet, whose work in the 1820s opened a "new school of history," as a voice of an earlier generation — the last to hold the title of *historiographe du roi* (1817–24) — testified in 1831.[3] This was Chateaubriand, who himself was not without erudition, as Sismondi had remarked in 1810, but lacked critical ability, impartiality, simplicity of style, and method, which were the marks of the new history.[4]

The age of revolutions, at once exhilarating and disillusioning, forced these scholars to look at history with new eyes, as Lamartine wrote in his history of the Restoration. Before he reached the age of sixty at mid-century, he "had already lived under ten dominations, or ten different governments, in France and witnessed ten revolutions" from Louis XVI to the Second Republic. Even in their antiquarian explorations members of the generation of 1820 owed many of their insights to what Thierry, in 1840, called "the previously unheard of events of the past fifty years which have taught us to understand the revolutions of the Middle Ages."[5] Add to this the new appreciation of the more distant past, reinforced during the 1820s by the opening of the medieval, Renaissance, and Egyptian galleries of the Louvre. "Like the humanism of 1520," remarked Camille Jullian, "the romanticism of 1820 was a humanism."[6] What it produced was a new "Pléiade" which did for the Romantic period what the poetic fivesome did for the French Renaissance.

With changes of regimes and constitutions came changes in ideas and mentalities and a sense of eternal motion, to which even the most stable values and concepts were subject. In a famous essay published in 1825 the Eclectic philosopher Theodore Jouffroy offered a sort of conjectural history of such change on the level of doctrine — not only religious (one may infer) but also political. "How Dogmas Come to an End" shows how articles of faith rise, gain acceptance, face criticism, provoke controversy, and finally are replaced by other concepts.[7] Dogmas arise because they seem true; thereafter they are accepted uncritically by later generations; then they become corrupted and error-ridden, while remaining the basis for social and political control. Against this appears a new faith, which begins as a negative and skeptical critique and which subsequently is subject to censorship and persecution; later it enters a stage of satire and mockery, as common people watch and suffer from the division. A final crisis occurs before the "revolution of ideas" which brings a "new generation" that sees the errors of both the defenders of the old faith and its skeptical opposition and that understands what a revolution truly is and what it is designed to accomplish in material as well as spiritual terms. "Thus the ruin of the party of the old dogma is completed, and the new one introduced," concluded Jouffroy. "As to the old dogma itself, it has been dead for a long time."

Such a paradigm might seem to fit the history of the Christian church (from a Protestant standpoint like that of Guizot), perhaps of philosophy (as seen by the Eclectic Jouffroy), or, more immediately in 1823, when the article was written, of the revolutionary ideal (as envisioned, for example, by a critic of Jacobinism). In any case it seemed to suit the generation of 1820, and more particularly its view of recent history. The old dogmas had been undermined by skeptics, they had been demolished despite the resistance of the Old Regime, and now they were being replaced by new conceptions of what a revolution was truly meant to be in social terms — and how history ought to be read.

The historiographical Pléiade of the generation of 1820 were all, by that date, beginning or launched into their life work.[8] Guizot (b. 1787), already known as a politician as well as a journalist, teacher, and editor of Gibbon's work (1812), was starting his lectures on the history of representative government. Thierry (b. 1795), having served his apprenticeship under Saint-Simon and gained a reputation as a journalist for opposition journals, published the first of his revisionist "Letters on the History of France." Barante (b. 1782) was already well established, having published a survey of French literature under Napoleon, and was working on his great history of the Burgundian dukes, which began to appear in 1824. Mignet (b. 1796) received a medal from the Academy of Nimes for his study of the national restoration of the fifteenth century under Charles VII (and Joan of Arc) and was beginning his study of feudalism in the reign of St. Louis. Michelet (b. 1798) had finished his two doctoral theses, on Plutarch and on Locke, and was beginning his "Journal of My Ideas," outlining future projects. That year he moved into learned society and met Villemain (b. 1790), who had published his biography of Cromwell the year before. Michelet's life-long friend Quinet (b. 1803) was also beginning to write, turning from literature to history and to study Herder. These were all, in one way or another, representatives of the "new history" which emerged in Restoration France.

The primary object of study for these historians, direct or indirect, was the French Revolution, its immediate and deeper background, its products and byproducts, its later transformations, and its future; and the primary focus was political — questions of monarchism, constitutionalism, republicanism, representation, and of course "revolution" itself. From this conventional position, however, the new history expanded in at least three ways. First it moved back in time, exploring the medieval and old regime background to the Revolution and contemporary predicament in France. Second it broadened its horizons to include the European states, especially England, medieval and modern, with particular attention to the Puritan and "glorious" revolutions of the seventeenth century, often in a comparative way. Third it moved from political and institutional to social and cultural questions, including problems of material interests and class conflict as well as intellectual and ideological controversy. In historiography, too, the "People" came upon the stage of history, sometimes eclipsing the usual movers and shakers of the Old Regime and increasingly, sad to say, divided against itself.

These novelties are all, in a general sense, familiar to Western historiographical tradition; but in the early nineteenth century another humanizing element was added to this mix — that is, the concern with the substance as well as the structure of the history of society and culture. Most obviously, this entailed concentration on neglected classes and peoples, beginning with the Third Estate, or rather the middle class, with its passion for property, but coming also to include peasants and workers, with emphasis shifting from property to labor, as economic factors received increasing notice after 1848. However, new historians like Thierry were also fascinated with devices for evoking the quality of life of bygone ages, including not only the employment of chronicles and documents but also dramatic and painterly techniques to represent the passions and colors of the past in all of its human dimensions and at the same time according to its own lights and values.

This last goal required something more than the methods which the old art of history could supply, and here it was that history and literature once again came into alliance. In 1820, two months before his first letter on French history, Thierry published a review of Walter Scott's *Ivanhoe* (1817), which suggested a powerful corrective to the vacuity of conjectural history, the tedium of French national history, and the aridity of historical erudition. In this work Scott moved from Scotland "sixty years hence" to the relatively unfamiliar territory of medieval England, which had been illuminated by Sharon Turner and others, to the neglect, however, of private life (*vie privée* is Scott's term). The materials for this were scant, but the combination of fictional techniques and care to employ suitable, that is, non-anachronistic, language and plausible illustrations of past sentiments and customs in all classes of humanity in order to draw "a true picture of old English manners" and yet at the same time to express this in terms intelligible to modern readers. The popularity of Scott's novels in France called for some ten thousand copies per year, considerably more than the popular works of history.[9]

These enthusiasts of the new history of the Restoration all looked into the deep past of France before the Revolution and indeed before nationhood; yet they were also active in politics, and they could not keep their present concerns out of their narratives. In 1820 Guizot had a position in the Conseil d'Etat until the reaction following the assassination of the Duc de Berry, after which he retired from politics; and in 1822 he was banned from lecturing at the university until 1828, when he gave his famous course on the history of civilization. Meanwhile, Thierry became a historico-political journalist for the *Censeur Européen* and (after its demise in 1820) for the *Globe* and the *Courrier Français,* as did Mignet.[10] Like Guizot, both of them (despite Thierry's supposed Carbonari associations) were deflected into scholarly pursuits in which their political views could be disguised behind studies of medieval and English history. Michelet was more single-minded in his scholarly career, but he, too, sought a philosophical understanding of history that would illuminate the political process of his own age. All of these men found the realization of their euphoric vision first in their teaching and then in the Revolution of 1830 — and disenchantment about the distinctly illiberal Revolutions of 1848, which led them to question and modify their early faith in liberal progress and hopes for the fulfillment of revolutionary promise — so that their dogmas also "came to an end."

Guizot and the History of Civilization

François Guizot had a remarkable, many-tracked career, in which historical scholarship figured significantly, if unevenly.[11] He came to Paris in 1805 and moved from the study of law to literary and philosophical circles, including Royer-Collard, De Gérando, Cousin, Maine de Biran, and (in a visit to Geneva) Mme de Staël.[12] Guizot was inspired to the study of the medieval past not only through the questions provoked by the Revolution (of which his father had been a victim) but also by the positive aspects of the Middle Ages evoked by the work of Chateaubriand, especially *The Martyrs,* which (like the *Génie du Christianisme*) created a sort of Christian mythology.[13] As Joseph de Maistre wrote in this spirit, "The modern world was born at the foot of the cross."[14] The project of Chateaubriand was continued later by Catholic scholars like Ozanam and Montalembert, who likewise wanted to distinguish a creative "middle age" from a corrupt "old regime." Guizot was praised by Montalembert for recognizing, thirty years before his *Monks of the West,* "the social *rôle* of the Church, of which he had not the good fortune to be a son."[15]

Guizot had his own reasons for looking back into the medieval past. Rejecting the "insane pride" of eighteenth-century philosophy, Guizot continued to seek rational foundations but in historical experience, not philosophical speculation.[16] As a young man he also became familiar with English and German literature and scholarship (including Heyne, Herder, and Kant), which shaped his political and historiographical thinking, and he studied Arabic with the great orientalist Sacy. This broad knowledge, combined with his experiences during the revolutionary period, gave him an unusual awareness of the diversity and mutability of human experience and the restrictions of individual perspective. The historian, such as Guizot himself, was "the observer [who], while himself continually changing his point of view, has been the witness of a spectacle which changes as often as he." For this reason, he continued, "we may speak of the past as changing with the present."[17] These comments, which were made in his lectures of 1820, certainly applied to the historiographical as well as the political career of Guizot.

During the Empire, Guizot became a prolific journalist and educational writer, gaining his reputation for erudition in his edition and translation of Gibbon's *Decline and Fall,* as again later in his publication of documents concerning the history of France and seventeenth-century Britain. During three separate periods (1812, 1820–22, 1828–30) Guizot was professor of history in the University of Paris, and his lectures became the basis for his most famous books, which surveyed the history of civilization in Europe and in France. He also had an active political life, first after 1815 in lower ministerial posts and association with the doctrinaire party, which tried to steer between revolutionary and counterrevolutionary extremes, and then again after the Revolution of 1830 as minister of education and then as prime minister (1840–48). After the Revolution of 1848 he retired again to private life, politically discredited and exiled in London, where he returned to his didactic writings on English and (with his wife) on French history.

On December 11, 1812, Guizot gave his first lecture on modern history, in which he refused to honor the convention of referring to the Emperor. Guizot asserted the impossibility of full knowledge of the past and yet rejected the conclusions of skepticism that an understanding of its laws was beyond human grasp. Research may not reveal the exact date of Constantine's birth, but it does allow for the understanding of the results of his conversion and the political and religious principles of his Empire. For Guizot there were two pasts — one dead and without interest and the other enduring forever in its influence over posterity. "History presents us, at every epoch," he declared, "with some predominant ideas, some great events which have decided the fortune and character of a long series of generations."[18] Through surviving "monuments" historians can, with the application of reason, find their way through the labyrinth of facts deposited by public experience. From the self-satisfied standpoint of postrevolutionary modernity — "from the midst of the new political order which commenced in Europe in our own days" — Guizot thus proposed to review the history of the human race, which was to say the development of liberty in Western civilization from a French perspective.

Guizot was a child of the Enlightenment but not of its rationalist phase or of the "insane philosophy" that spoiled the promise of revolution. He later referred to the "unjust contempt for ancient institutions" characteristic of revolutionary excess, illustrated by the proposal in Cromwell's time (similar to those in France in the 1790s) "to deliver up to the flames all the archives in the Tower of London, and thus to annihilate the existence of England in former ages."[19] As a politician and "doctrinaire" Guizot wanted "not to destroy but to reform and to purify [the Revolution] in the name of justice and truth," while paying "equal respect to intellect and to social order"; as a historian he wanted likewise to understand the past with appreciation both of reason (and its limits) and to the social process (and its ungovernable aspects). "Against our will, and without our knowledge," he said, "the ideas which have occupied the present will follow us wherever we go in the study of the past."[20] And then there were more direct pressures. "I have lived in an age of political plots and outrages," he wrote later, "directed alternately against the authorities to whom I was in opposition and those I supported with ardour."[21] He remained a moderate even when, as in 1822, he was dismissed from his university post (giving the lectures which he had prepared while residing at the estate of Condorcet's widow) for his "dangerous" beliefs and when he was denounced as reactionary for his service to the July Monarchy and the Bourgeoisie, whom he advised, notoriously, to "enrich" themselves.

From his first statements (his lectures begun at the age of twenty-five) Guizot had a coherent vision of history, and it was founded on a critical theory of progress which tried to situate spiritual achievement not merely in the march of ideas but also on a material base. A remarkable image of this union was the Greek community, where "social existence is in full vigour, and the human mind is in a state of excitement [and where] Herodotus reads to the Greeks assembled at Olympia his patriotic narratives, and the discoveries of his voyages" — not, perhaps, unlike Guizot's own equally patriotic lectures, expounded to a "numerous and diversified" audience, "youths and experienced men, natives and foreigners."[22] From Greco-Roman beginnings every epoch had something to contribute, but the major impulse appeared in the fifteenth century, in the form of the social energy of the Italian city republics enhanced by classical learning, the invention of printing, and the rise of the intellectual class, after which "books became a tribune from which the world was addressed," and then the Reformation, which "struck a deadly blow against spiritual supremacy."[23] Thus began "the march of human nature," which Guizot set out to survey, encouraging his students to take "even a few steps on the road which leads to truth."

The subject of Guizot's researches and lectures centered on the ideals of 1789 — constitutional monarchy, representative government, and individual liberty — but traced, in a European perspective, from their deep origins in late antiquity. In 1812, Guizot located the origins of representative government in "the forests of Germany," following the formula to which Montesquieu had given authority; but by 1820 he had become suspicious of this old cliché.[24] The idea of representation had in a sense "constantly hovered over Europe," reappearing at different times and in different places; and it was up to the modern historian to find its surviving traces in his own, that is, the European, cultural tradition. For Guizot this was a four-part story, moving progressively through the epochs of barbarism, feudalism, royalism, and (from the sixteenth century) the emergence of representative government.[25]

It was in England that representative government first emerged, and Guizot began to lecture on this subject in the fall of 1820, this time (unlike 1812) in a relatively free climate. Guizot's interest was not in narrative history but in social conditions and institutions, and here the past seemed to have a "double history"—that is, local communities, which prevailed in the earliest period, and political organizations, which followed power, wars, and conquest—corresponding, in modern terms, to civil society and the state and to the trajectory of national histories. Representative government did not arise out of local institutions, nor was it reflected in the national assemblies which had been described by Tacitus and which in Anglo-Saxon England took the form of the Wittenagemot; it came into being only with the election of proxies who were authorized to speak for others at the great council, and with Magna Carta and later "charters" which have always been a mark of constitutional government.[26] In general such a system of representation was "the work of ages"—and one aspect of the natural law of progress which Guizot saw in the double history of European and English society.

Thus Guizot offered his own sort of conjectural history—a rationalized mixture of political theory and a progressivist account of political organization, which usually arose under the aegis of great men (like himself?) appearing at crucial times. Representative government required three principles for realization—division of powers, election, and publicity.[27] King and curia, empowering of representatives, and communication of political actions within a public sphere: these were the essential elements of European history from the point of view of Guizot as publicist, as professor, and as (to his glory but ultimate discredit) politician. This was also a movement from fact to law, from force to justice, and from the political to the social; and it could be seen not only in the English case but also, though delayed, in the other European nations. This, in outline, was the triumphalist and Whiggish view of history which Guizot urged on his students and the wider middle class audience to which he was devoted.

During the administration of Villèle (1822–28) one of the essential ingredients of representative government, publicity, was placed under severe restrictions, and Guizot (with Villemain and Cousin) was dismissed from his professorship. He returned to his scholarly pursuits and published documentary collections in French and English history as well as a history of the English revolutions of the seventeenth century. In 1828 he resumed his teaching, taking as his subject the progress of civilization in Europe and in France, which, as for Bossuet, followed a sort of providential plan "according to the intentions of God."[28]

"Civilization is a fact like any other," declared Guizot, and indeed "the fact par excellence" — though in a very general sense defined by particular principles less general than the "fact" which encompassed them.[29] In studying this fact Guizot turned away from narrative to a kind of conjectural social and cultural history. Earlier civilizations had displayed a remarkable unity, each of them emanating from a single fact, idea, or principle — theocracy in Egypt and India, for example, and commerce in the ancient Mediterranean republics. What distinguished European civilization was the diversity of its principles and the complexity of its conflicts. Guizot began his analysis with the collapse of Rome, which was governed by a municipal order and potential representative government that, though it was impossible to maintain, was nevertheless, along with the idea of empire, "bequeathed to modern Europe."[30] With the emergence of the Christian church as an institution came another "great fact," the separation of spiritual and temporal power, which was the course of the idea of liberty of conscience. European history, properly speaking, began with the barbarian epoch succeeding the fall of Rome, but historians have never agreed upon the origins of this "system."[31] One school, represented by Boullainvilliers, identifies it with the nobility; another, led by Dubos, looks rather to the principle of royalty; still another, following Mably, finds it in the system of free, republican institutions; and then there were also the "theocratic pretensions of the church." Ultimately all these systems were rooted in force, and all claim legitimacy based on a prior moral existence; yet none of them prevailed in the barbarian period of early European history but were rather mixed together. As always Guizot saw the underlying causes of this barbarian system as twofold: "the one material, arising from without, in the course of events; the other moral, originating from within, from man himself."[32] This version of the old external-internal distinction was the remote ancestor of Marxian material-base superstructure. To these primary causes were added two others, the Christian church and the impact of "great men" such as Charlemagne.

The second epoch of modern history was defined by the "feudal system," and Guizot was careful to defend this way of organizing society as necessary for times of violence and disorder.[33] Liberal ideas and practices were hard-won and long in appearing, and could not be attributed to the ancient Germans merely on the basis of a sentence of Tacitus. People always hated feudalism because of these associations, but the brutal features were moderated over the ages, especially through the influence of chivalry and Christian morality, which shifted emphasis to the smaller family, domestic manners, and individuals, including women. In evaluating feudalism Guizot again took a dual perspective, trying to steer between the extremes of fanatics, who were content with general ideas divorced from social reality, and freethinkers, who conversely judged merely in terms of immediate circumstances.

The influence of religion in the feudal period was extraordinary for one overriding reason, according to Guizot, that was: "The clergy was associated with all human conditions. From the miserable habitation of the serf, at the foot of the feudal castle, to the king's palace itself, everywhere there was a priest, a member of the clergy."[34] Moreover, the church lessened the evils caused by the separation between the governing and the governed. It was of course a power structure and as such not much concerned with the development of the individual, but it did provide a field "open to talent," and it worked against slavery and many barbarous customs, especially in penal law. In general, Guizot argued, "the moral and intellectual development of Europe has been essentially theological."[35] Yet one had to be cautious in making such judgments and especially not to judge earlier centuries by later standards — not to forget what Guizot called the "moral chronology" underlying the continuing process of civilization.

The third and most dynamic element of civilization was the "boroughs" (William Hazlitt's translation of *bourgeoisie,* or *tiers état*). The new towns were scenes of embryonic "liberty," though not in a fully modern sense. "The enfranchisement of the commons in the eleventh century was the fruit of a veritable insurrection, a veritable war . . . declared by the population of the towns against their lords."[36] This "contest of classes" — "the contest which constitutes the fact itself and which fills modern history" — would produce still greater revolutions, especially those of England, the English colonies, and France, and which was still upsetting Europe in Guizot's day. But the achievement of liberty marked an almost unimaginable difference between the burghers of the twelfth and those of the eighteenth century, when Siéyès virtually identified the Third Estate with the "nation." Guizot invoked this remarkable transformation of "moral chronology" by representing it through the eyes of a medieval town-dweller transported into Guizot's time and, conversely, a modern city-dweller returned to the twelfth century.[37]

For Guizot the history of civilization was defined by the interaction between two great forces — society in its influence on government and government in its power over society. The circle of the three estates — nobility, clergy, and burghers — was overshadowed by the dialectic between people and its government; but progress from primitive to modern Europe demanded something more; and it was the Crusades, "the first European event," that opened up the new period of development. "The people rushed into the crusades as into a new existence . . . , which at one time recalled the ancient liberty of barbarism, at others opened out the perspective of a vast future."[38] The results included "a great step towards the enfranchisement of mind, a great step towards more extensive and liberal ideas."

A central shaping force in European history was that of royalty, which went through (often overlapping) barbarian, imperial, religious, feudal, and modern phases and which at all times embodied the principle of legitimacy. What was characteristic of modern society was the fusion of royalty with the other elements of society into a state; and efforts, republican and mixed, to construct this institution dominated European history down to the fifteenth century, when "modern history" properly speaking commenced, as nationality fused with states, as a public came into being, and as the Reformation brought "the emancipation of the human mind" and diversity to European civilization — all essential ingredients of "the revolution of the sixteenth century" and of progress.[39] The next step was taken in the English revolution of the seventeenth century, which began as a movement of legal reform and moved on, through regicide, to the creation of constitutional monarchy.[40] To Guizot and his generation France seemed to have recapitulated this trajectory almost a century and a half later, and it is not surprising that it was a subject much on their minds — Guizot himself having already written a book on the subject.

In his second set of lectures Guizot narrowed his focus to the national tradition and intensified his patriotic stance, asserting the superiority of France even to England and Germany. Beginning with the collapse of the Roman Empire, he traced a variety of "reformations" and "revolutions" down to the establishment of the Carolingian Empire, which likewise collapsed after the demise of the great man, Charlemagne, whom Guizot compared with Napoleon in his military and institutional achievements. As for the causes of this creation, Guizot disagreed with his friend Thierry that it was due merely to the diversity of races under Charlemagne's rule; for there were other, political reasons for its dismemberment.[41]

Once again Guizot distinguished between an internal view, which attended to "moral chronology," and an external view based on determinable facts. In establishing these facts and inferring moral progress he employed the great collections of the old regime as well as the work of scholars such as Mlle de Lézardières and Savigny, and at one point he invoked Walter Scott's *Old Mortality,* which portrayed the archeological efforts of Robert Patterson in tracing the remains of Scottish Puritans, comparing these with the antiquarian aspects of the saints' lives collected by the Bollandists in the seventeenth century, in which massive literature, not only miracles and marvels, but also "morality bursts forth."[42] On the internal and spiritual side, too, was medieval

philosophy and poetry, which Guizot quoted from and commented on extensively, praising John Erigena for his turn from theology to human and philosophical arguments, and citing St. Avitus's *On the Beginning of the World* at
length to show that he was not only an influence on but even in some respects
superior to Milton.[43]

According to Guizot, French national unity began to appear — in a spiritual
and social if not factual and political sense — from the end of the tenth century,
replacing the foreign names of Roman, Gallo-Roman, Frankish, and Gallo-
Frankish civilization. This is apparent especially in the provincial customs of
the feudal period and in vernacular literature. Thenceforth, Guizot tells his
students, "the middle ages are quite other than a matter of learning to us . . . ,
[for] they correspond to interests more real, more direct than those of historical erudition and criticism, to sentiments more general, more full of life than
that of mere curiosity."[44] Voltaire erred when he associated medieval fables
with "error," for the "poetical side of these old times" had a sort of truth, even
if it was not philosophical. The eighteenth century undervalued both imagination and antiquity. "We are now in the reaction against the tendency of the
age which preceded us," Guizot continued, suggesting that there might be
"great advantages in this historical impartiality, this poetic sympathy for ancient France."

On the "factual" side, Guizot examined the feudal system from the eleventh
through the thirteenth century, defining it as an institution based on the union
of sovereignty and property. In keeping with the premises of eighteenth-
century conjectural history, he likened early German social relations to those of
present-day American Indians. He also criticized the views of German scholars, including Savigny, about the origins of feudalism on the grounds that they
used sources, such as the *Libri Feudorum*, which had been assembled by jurists
reflecting a later period.[45] There were good as well as bad aspects of feudalism,
including rule by consent and the right to resistance; but in any case it was a
necessary step in the emergence of modern society. So was the development of
royalty, which, through a number of stages, came to legislate and to administer
the principles of order and liberty. Most essential, however, was the rise of the
Third Estate as reflected in the charters of the early communes, such as that of
Laon (which had been studied by Thierry), which marked a revolution and the
"birth of modern legislation" in social matters. The French Charter of 1814
also alluded to the enfranchisement of the medieval communes, but only to
celebrate the authority of the restored Bourbon monarch.[46]

Guizot's lectures extended only to the fourteenth century, and he finished
the narrative only many years later in the popular history which he wrote in
his last years and which carried the story down to 1789. The Revolution of

1830 drew him back into politics and into the service of the July Monarchy: he was minister for a few months, then minister of public instruction, and finally prime minister from 1840 to 1848. For Guizot history was always an extension and a justification for his political ideas and actions, with the revolutions of 1688 in England and 1789 in France as models of his idealization of representative government as realized in constitutional monarchy — and the July days in Paris promising this ideal at the end of the historical process as envisioned by him in the 1820s. After 1830 he continued his contributions to historical scholarship not only by his continued writing on English history and his biography of a successful revolutionary, Washington, but also by founding, or refounding, the Academy of Moral and Political Sciences, which had been suppressed a generation earlier by Napoleon and which included the likes of Talleyrand, Siéyès, Degérando, and Daunou, and by establishing the Society for the History of France, which resumed the task of publishing the sources of history which he and others had already begun in the Restoration.[47]

Under the July Monarchy, Guizot was a prisoner of his progressivist view of history, which emphasized the success of the *Bourgeoisie conquérante* at the expense of the levels of society which it conquered. But after 1803 the theme of Progress was joined, and for some even replaced, by the Social Question; and Guizot had no answers for this. He was surprised by the Revolution of 1848 (accompanied as it was by cries of "à bas Guizot") and the renewed hopes of turning the course of history; but then so was Marx and others who opposed him: history did not move in the way they expected and even demanded, either. Guizot went into exile in London to lick his wounds and watch historical change from a distance. Later he settled in his estate in the Val-Richer, returning to journalism and scholarship, especially to the study of the English Revolution, which was always more gratifying to his political ideas and sensibilities.

Was Guizot a "failure"? It has been conventional to say so; but while his metahistorical vision was flawed (whose in that age, or any other for that matter, was not?) and his political career was ruined by the revolutionary storms of the mid-nineteenth century, he has remained a major intellectual presence. He was a historian of the first magnitude who incorporated an appreciation for modern social and cultural history into his interpretations. From him Marx learned about the role of classes in the historical process, and from him many others learned about the great "fact" of civilization beyond the small facts of politics and war. His was in many respects "conjectural history," but it was updated and refurbished from the Enlightenment speculations through his inquiries into the phenomena of revolution which periodically transformed the state of society and the state.

Thierry and the New History

Augustin Thierry was the champion of the "new history" of this generation, although the novelty in his case was somewhat different from Guizot's
doctrinaire variety.[48] A graduate of the Ecole Normale, Thierry gave up a
teaching career and accepted an offer from Saint-Simon, with whom, as an
"adopted son," he collaborated for several years (1814–17) on projects of social reform. The main idea, following the Congress of Vienna, was the reorganization of Europe according to the English parliamentary model, which had
emerged in the fifth, postrevolutionary age of political evolution. In 1817
Thierry pursued a journalistic career, shifting progressively from political to
historical topics, displaying his interests in English history and Scott's novels,
and developing his revisionist views of historical writing. As a political polem-
icist in *Le Censeur européen* he attacked the conservative and censoring government of the Restoration; as an aspiring historian in *Le Courier français*
he sought "Proofs and arguments" for his "constitutional opinions."[49] "The
study of liberty is almost everything in the study of history," he decided, and
(following Sismondi and Guizot) he turned especially to the history of England
and of the French communes as the most direct entry into this epic theme.[50]

Thierry began to publish his revisionist "Letters on the History of France" in
1820 before the groundbreaking works of Sismondi (on France), Guizot, and
Barante had appeared, beginning his labors in the "frigid galleries" of the
Bibliothèque National in the great documentary collections of the history of
the monarchy.[51] It is true that Velly had claimed to have created a "new
history"; but Thierry had contempt for "our historians," that is, for the French
historiographical tradition stretching from Bonapartist historians back to the
Chronicles of St. Denis; and he was proud of the label of "new school," which
Chateaubriand had attached to the work of him and other members of his
generation. Thierry himself distinguished three schools of history-writing: the
medieval chronicles, which were at least valuable as source material; the Italian school of the Renaissance (beginning with Du Haillan), which, despite its
boasts, was full of prejudice and error; and the abstract and partisan philosophical history of the previous century, which had its own way of misconstru-
ing the substance of history.[52] In the coming "revolution in the way of writing
history,"[53] Thierry did not mean to avoid the impulse of patriotism, but only
to give it a better grounding, to move from the slanted generalities of conjectural history to the colorful substance of detailed narrative, from the emphasis
on great personages to the masses and classes of humanity, as Scott was doing
in his own more freely imaginative way.[54]

For Thierry the aim of the historian was not to confound and confuse but to distinguish and to differentiate. His attitude was that of a sense of distance and a sort of historical irony. Telling of a miracle in Merovingian times after the death of a murdered queen, Thierry commented that "tales of this kind may make us smile, who read them in old books written for men of another age; but in the sixth century . . . people became pensive and wept when they were told."[55] The primary target of Thierry's methodological criticism was anachronism, especially the gross sort of linguistic ignorance that identified the fifth-century Franks, already a mixed people, with the modern French. Clovis (or rather "Chlodio") was not the founder of the French monarchy (which was the product rather of feudalism under the Capetian—the first "French"— dynasty), nor was Louis VI the founder of the free communes, as official historiographers from Du Tillet and Du Haillan to Velly and Anquetil had believed, for there was already a communal regime, or "revolution," before the charters bearing his name.[56] The "Franks" were not French, "Francia" not France, and the correct title was "King of the Franks" (*rex Francorum*), not "King of France." History should not present simplistic variations on a single society, as Hume had done; for there were many social groups and interacting "races" involved in the evolution (and nomenclature) of nations like France and England. A close study of languages and their transformations and an avoidance of imposing modern terminology and classifications on earlier history were essential to all historical judgments. "It is impossible, whatever the amount of intellectual superiority we possess," he wrote, "to see beyond the horizons of our century, and therefore every new epoch opens for history new points of view and imprints on it a particular form.[57] This was an article of faith of all the "new historians" of this generation.

Yet Thierry himself toyed with anachronism when he launched into his project of tracing modern liberty from the "communal revolutions" of the eleventh and twelfth centuries through the "national revolution" of the eighteenth century.[58] Both were in a sense victories of the bourgeoisie over feudal power, the result of a "debate between the people and the royal power," and both were expressed in charters, from which Thierry quoted at length. "My imagination applied to the towns of France what I had read about the Italian republics of the middle ages," he later wrote, referring to Sismondi's volumes. For Thierry the medieval commune was a counterpart of the modern "Constitution"; and the insurrection of Laon was "a prototype of modern revolutions," although the liberty it achieved was of a material and not political character, and of course there were other cultural differences.[59] But the category of "bourgeois" was one which seemed to span the centuries, being the carrier not only of communal liberties and "revolutions" but also of the national assemblies which constituted modern liberal government.

In his first decade of serious historical scholarship Thierry treated a wide range of theoretical and practical subjects. He reviewed Villemain's biography of Cromwell, Scott's *Ivanhoe,* and Hallam's *Constitutional History of England;* he described the courses given by the old philosophe Daunou in history and the young Eclectic Cousin in philosophy; he wrote on questions of medieval and English history; he criticized various errors of historians, arising especially from their ignorance of language, orthography, etymology, of proper names and titles; and he also studied more deeply the historiographical tradition (from Gilles, Paule-Emile, and Gaguin to Mézeray), which he hoped to revise and surpass.[60] But while liberty was a splendid theme for a historian, liberty of the press was still too restricted to allow a full treatment of the subject in sensitive areas of French history; and for this reason (as well as the attractions of the English model of constitutional government) Thierry turned his attention to the origins of English society and politics, and did so with due attention to the demands of a narrative style that was colorful and concrete as well as instructive.

Like Guizot, Thierry took a broad perspective on the European past and regarded the medieval period as formative, though not wholly constructive. European civilization was composed of a mixture of racial and social groupings which appeared more diverse the further back the historian penetrated. Depending on primary sources, especially legal sources, the historian had to distinguish these collectivities and refrain from being misled by current ideas, manners, and politics; eighteenth century authors violated this rule, but the new history of the present century, said Thierry, would not allow it and demanded especially an understanding of the language of different epochs of the past. In *Ivanhoe* Walter Scott had been sensitive to this requirement, too, except that as a writer of imaginative fiction he took care to modernize the language, if not the manners, of the past. Thierry was in agreement with Scott not only in awareness of cultural anachronism, however; he also appreciated the value of literary sources, and in his study of medieval England he turned in particular, like his friend Claude Fauriel in his work on Greek songs, to popular legends, ballads, and other such remnants of oral culture in recreating the mentality of that age.[61]

From 1821 Thierry began working on his *History of the Conquest of England by the Normans,* which dramatized and analyzed the themes of racial, and so social, conflict, conquest, and public crimes which were so central to European history. This was a classic story not only of class struggle but also of the losers as well as the winners, which qualified and undercut the progressivist views of the generation of 1820. Thierry rejected the habit of earlier historians, who "transported the ideas, the manners, and the political position of their own time to former ages."[62] His own age was not content with history written for a single idea; it needed "everything" to be told, and told moreover from original sources and in terms of the language of bygone times. Although modern political conflicts were between governments, in earlier times they were between races; and nations were rooted in violence and usurpation alien to Christian conceptions of morality and justice.

What was "new" about Thierry's historiography beyond the claims? One thing was the emphasis, appropriate to the postrevolutionary concern with the social, on "collectivities" over movers and shakers — kings, nobles, battles, and all that. Another even more subversive feature was the focus on conquest and criticism of conquerors. To a large extent, in contrast to Guizot, who concentrated on the "bourgeois conquérants," Thierry told the story of the losers in history — Scots, Irish, Welsh — who were overrun and victimized successively by Germanic tribes and then, more permanently, by the Normans. He was, as Sismondi put it, a "genealogist of misfortune," to the conspicuous neglect of the fashionable themes of progress and civilization.

As Hume had said, early periods of history had to be understood in terms not of noteworthy events but of long-enduring laws, manners, and customs; and to this agenda Thierry added an intense concern for languages and place names, residues of successive waves of barbarians in the wake of Roman conquest. Like Niebuhr and Romantic scholars like his friend Fauriel, he also turned to literary remains to capture the spirit of the tribes that left their traces in Britain. As Thierry wrote, "The ancient Britons lived and breathed in poetry. The expression may seem extravagant, but not so in reality: for in their political maxims, preserved to our own times, they place the poet-musician beside the agriculturalist and the artist, as one of the three pillars of social existence. Their poets had but one theme: the destiny of their country, its misfortunes and its hopes. The nation, a poet in its turn, caught up and adopted their fictions with earnest enthusiasm, giving the wildest instruction to their simplest expressions: that which in the bard was a patriotic wish, became to the excited imagination of the hearers a national promise."[63] Nor did the racial conflict end with the conquest, and here the comment of Walter Scott might stand for Thierry's interpretation: "Four generations had not sufficed to blend the hostile blood of the Normans and Anglo-Saxons, or to unite, by common language and mutual interests, two hostile races, one of which still felt the elation of triumph, while the other groaned under the consequences of defeat."[64] Yet the split and "great national distinctions" were preserved, for "French was the language of honour, of chivalry, and even of justice, while the far more manly and expressive Anglo-Saxon was abandoned to the use of rustics and hinds, who knew no other."

During the 1820s, driven by literary ambition as well as political partisanship, Thierry began toning down his subversive criticism that, if only indirectly, offended the current regime; and like Guizot and Michelet, he turned
to a more positive estimate of the historical process, especially in terms of the
contributions of the Third Estate to progress and civilization. For him as for
other liberals the Revolution of 1830 marked not only the triumph of the
Orleanist party but also the culmination of this movement and of the "new
history" associated with it. It was the French counterpart to the "glorious
revolution" of 1688 in England: "Our minds were full of the English Revolution of 1688," Guizot later wrote.[65] Among those who benefitted from the
"July Days" were Thierry's friends Villemain, who became a peer of France;
Fauriel, who got a chair in the history of literature; Michelet, who became a
director of the archives under Daunou; and Guizot, who held ministerial positions in the governments. Thierry, despite effort to receive recognition and
position, remained in the shadow of these colleagues (denied even a place in
the restored Academy) until Guizot, in 1834, appointed him editor of the
collection of documents concerning the history of the Third Estate; and it was
in this connection that he turned to an early interest that became the basis for
his last major work.

Thierry's *History of the Progress and Formation of the Third Estate* (1853)
was an introduction to the collection of documents illustrating the principal
vehicle of French liberty and civilization which reached its climax in the Revolution of 1830 and in the regime of precarious order presided over by Guizot
in the early 1840s. "What is the Third Estate?" the Abbé Siéyès had famously
asked in 1789. "Nothing," was his answer — and "What does it want to be?
Something." After 1830 the Third Estate had indeed become "something,"
and, with Siéyès's question in mind, Thierry set about reconstructing, and
celebrating, this history of this cornerstone of the French nation which had
emerged from the fires of revolution to absorb, according to Thierry, the old
orders. The history, as reflected in the documentary records of the communes,
was one both of an "immense evolution" and of a series of particular "revolutions" involving the non-noble class — *la Roture, la bourgeoisie* — in its striv-
ing over a millennium and more against the obstacles of feudalism for *liberté
et lumières*. In teleological fashion and abandoning his emphasis on racial
conflict, Thierry told a story of the growth, shown in communal charters, of
elective and popular government, of civil and political liberty, and in this
connection of a "new class," and ultimately a "new nation" in the making.
Although he was aware of the vast distance between the liberated peasants of
the twelfth century and the proud bourgeois of his own day, Thierry could not

resist the identification, citing the poetic formula, of "original equality" expressed in the *Roman de Rou*, that "we are men like them" (their feudal lords).

Aside from communal charters the major expression of "the spirit of reform and progress" of the Third Estate was the Estates General, which was the locus of the "sovereignty" and "will" of the people and the "ascendant march of French civilization." The discourses and protests in the assemblies of the Estates, such as that of Tours in 1484, produced political maxims, such as the subversive formula that "it is the sovereign people that first created kings" and moreover opened the space of modern "public opinion."[66] In the progress of the Third Estate, too, could be seen what Thierry called "the aspiration toward the civil equality, judicial and commercial unity, and industrial liberty of our days."[67] From Etienne Marcel to the Frondes and down to 1789 the history of the Third Estate was one of the "constant march of revolutions."[68]

While emphasizing the collective source of liberty, Thierry also recognized individual contributions over the centuries and the common effort suggested by certain parallels — Bodin as a "precursor of Montesquieu," for example, and Henry IV as "L'Hôpital armed" — the sixteenth-century chancellor Michel de L'Hôpital being himself the son of a bourgeois.[69] But Thierry's enthusiasm for the *bourgeoisie conquérante*, expressed in articles written in 1846, was tempered by the depressing events of 1848 and their aftermath, and again he took a moderate turn toward greater appreciation of the nobility as participant in the revolutionary evolution of the nation and its "civilization." And in his last years Thierry moved, in another turn, further back to old regime values and tradition, this time to religious faith.

It should not be forgotten that Thierry's comrade in his historiographical quest was his brother Amédée, who produced a remarkable body of work, dedicated to Augustin and likewise employing techniques of modern criticism. Like the other historians of this generation Amédée Thierry regarded peoples as "collective persons" making up the human family.[70] "In the human race," he asked, following his brother's lead, "do families and races exist as individuals do in races?" An affirmative answer led Thierry to consider the national character of the Gauls throughout the four epochs of their history, from the nomadic to the sedentary to internal conflicts to the formation of the Roman province; and his conclusions about the distinct character of the Gauls (the two races of Gauls, specifically not including the Basques) were philological as well as historical, using both classical and native sources, which allowed access to what he called the "intellectual archeology of the Gauls."

Amédée Thierry worked in his brother's shadow his whole life, and it was Augustin who received credit for his historical conceptualizations. In agreement with Guizot and Mignet, Augustin Thierry sought a philosophical sort of history not in enlightened conjecture or the sort of "spiritualism" promoted by their colleague Victor Cousin and his Eclecticism but in human and material conditions and factors of race and social class. Mignet in particular was associated by critics with "historical fatalism," which saw in feudalism as well as the Revolution a necessary stage in cultural progress, in which race and class were supposed to fuse into a unified nation. Following the line of argument popularized by Montesquieu, Mignet concluded that "from the origins of the monarchy, it is less that events [choses] were made by men than that men were made by events."[71] This attitude was in keeping not only with the view of literature taken by Mme de Staël and Vicomte de Bonald, that "literature was an expression of society" but also with the more theoretical outlook of Karl Marx, who acknowledged the contribution of Thierry in particular to dialectical materialism. It was in keeping, too, with the ideology of the "Bourgeois Monarchy," which came to disappoint the French historians and to provoke revolutionaries like Marx and insurrectionists of 1848. In the wake of that "turning point where history failed to turn," all parties, scholars and activists alike, were disappointed in their interpretations of the historical process, though without giving up their hope in the didactic power of history.

Michelet and the Poetry of History

What the great sixteenth-century humanist Guillaume Budé said of philosophy, Jules Michelet said of history, that it was his "second wife."[72] Michelet became what so many earlier scholars, from "Paule-Emile" to Sismondi, had aspired to be, the national historian of France. He wanted to be a modern Livy and beyond that a philosopher of history, and in many ways he succeeded in these undertakings, with all of the drawbacks which such ambitions brought in the eyes of other authors. For Roland Barthes, Michelet was an "eater of history," and today it is his appetite, his capacity, and especially his culinary taste that most impress later readers, including epigones like Lucien Febvre and Fernand Braudel.[73]

The son of a failed Parisian printer, Michelet had a solitary and unhappy childhood, scarred by the death of his mother when he was sixteen and soon after by that of his closest friend, Paul Poinsot. "I have loved death," he remarked, with characteristic hyperbolic concision, looking back over his life's work; "I lived for over nineteen years at the gate of Père Lachaise."[74] Over the years he spent many hours walking, first by himself and later with his children, among the "permanent Parisians" in this cemetery — this "necropolis-amphitheater."[75] "To love the dead," he confessed to his students, "that is my immortality."[76] He also had an old-fashioned classical education which drew off his extraordinary energies, gave him a vicarious life, and filled his extravagant imagination. Michelet was not yet seventeen at the time of Napoleon's second abdication, in 1815, when a new world opened up, bringing to France, as he later told his students, Goethe, Scott, and Byron. In 1817 he graduated from the Collège Charlemagne; in 1819 he submitted his two doctoral theses, the French one on Plutarch and the Latin one on Locke's idea of the infinite; and a year later he took his aggrégation, ranking third.

From 1818 he applied his enthusiasm for history to himself by starting a journal of his readings — "to record his sentiments, thoughts, and actions"[77] — later another one (partly in English) of his "ideas," and most conscientiously of his travels in the French provinces and western Europe, on which he grounded many of his historical writings, especially the "tableau of Italy" in his Roman history[78] and "tableau of France" (c. A.D. 1000) in the third volume of his history. Geography was the essential base of history, and Michelet criticized Thierry for neglecting this in his fascination with factors of race (Guizot had neglected it, too).[79] In 1822 Michelet began his teaching career at the Collège Sainte-Barbe, and in this connection he wrote a number of textbooks on modern, medieval, and ancient history. He also established important contacts among prominent Parisian intellectuals, especially Villemain (his former teacher), Guizot, Cousin, and Thiers, who later assisted him in his rise to literary and professional prominence.

Like Gibbon and Sismondi, Michelet spent much time reflecting on a subject that would be adequate both to his talents and to the unique character of the postrevolutionary age. Among the topics which he considered were histories of Greek literature, of French literature in relation to politics, of an aspect of sixteenth-century France, of the republican spirit, and especially "a history of civilization found in languages."[80] In any case he took a philosophical view based on the concept of "the history of the world as a system." As he told students in 1825, "Science is one: languages, literature and history, mathematics and philosophy, and knowledges apparently most remote are actually joined, or rather form a system, of which we in our weakness [can only] consider separate parts in succession." So the "civilization" being studied by Guizot, Cousin, and Villemain appeared to this young "eater of history." To this heaven-storming goal, however, Michelet was inspired by more than the revolutionary and Enlightenment projects of his elder colleagues, for by 1824 he had found a philosopher of history equal to the plan of a unified "science." By 1821 Michelet was reading the Scottish moralists, especially Adam Ferguson and Dugald Stewart, the latter in French translation; and in 1824 he discovered, in the third volume Stewart's survey of metaphysical, ethical, and political philosophy since the Renaissance (with a supplement on the philosophy of history by Cousin), an account of the work of Giambattista Vico.[81] For Michelet this was an epiphany, and he hoped, as he told Cousin, that it would be possible to translate Vico's work. Deeply involved in the philosophy of history, Michelet also went on to address to Cousin a series of questions on the subject, on which Cousin had given lectures.[82] What should he read concerning historical criticism? Should he consult Sismondi—whom he called "the father of this generation of young historians"[83]—and Daunou on the subject? Sismondi was a stranger to philosophy, Cousin apparently replied, and Daunou was "mediocre." (Unlike Michelet, Daunou did not believe that history was capable of resuscitation, but could only "march over the tombs of the dead."[84]) Have Plato or Descartes, whose works Cousin edited, anything to say about the philosophy of history? (Answer: "Nothing.") What about Montesquieu, his disciple Ferguson, and Grotius? Also Comte, Creuzer, Herder, Ancillon, Priestley, and Niebuhr? And where could he find new books to read or borrow?

In 1827 Michelet's translations of Vico appeared, as did the translation of Herder (through the English version of Churchill) by his new friend Edgar Quinet, likewise with the encouragement of Cousin. In Vico and Herder, he wrote to Quinet (as a challenge?), "the philosophy of history had its Copernicus and Kepler; now what is needed is its Newton."[85] Michelet had planned a "history of the philosophy of history" but gave it up because of his ignorance of the German literature. In the next two years, besides his teaching and Vichian studies, Michelet pursued two new lines of investigation. One was ancient Roman history, which he also taught, and the other was his interest in German scholarship, both of which were furthered by his Italian and German voyages, as his reading of Gibbon, Hallam, et al. was by his English trip. In 1828 these interests converged in his study of Niebuhr, whose work he later compared with that of Vico on Italian prehistory. At the same time he made the acquaintance of Creuzer, Grimm, and other German scholars, and began work on various German projects, including a study of Luther. Michelet's association with the "poetry of law" of Savigny's disciple Grimm and the "symbolist school" of Creuzer underlay his book on the origins of French law and his nickname, "M. Symbole."[86] Of this book Sainte-Beuve asked, "It is poetic but is it historical?"[87] Taking a more positive tone, Victor Hugo celebrated Michelet as both poet and historian—although he denied either title to Voltaire.[88]

In ancient Roman studies Niebuhr had certainly begun a revolution, Michelet admitted in a review of 1831, two years after beginning his own course on Roman history at the Ecole Normale. "Niebuhr knew antiquity as antiquity did not always know itself," Michelet admitted, and yet his work was no more than a beginning.[89] One could better understand the primitive age of Rome with comparative reference to other poetic texts which had undergone transformations, such as the Alexander story, the Nibelungen, and the Eddas.[90] What Niebuhr lacked was the "philosophical genius" to see the course of early Roman history as a whole and the key to this history in the "symbolic language of antiquity." But then, he added, who could at once be Niebuhr, Hegel, and Creuzer? In fact the real originator of the sort of critical view proposed by Michelet was "poor Vico, on whom German scholars had apparently commented, usually without naming him, for half a century." Such was the canon of modern Roman studies which had yet to reach its culmination, although Michelet — whose own *History of Rome* came out two weeks after his review of Niebuhr — suggested his own role by claiming that the scholarly reform begun by Germans would be completed by the French: "this reform has had its Luther: now comes its Calvin."

Michelet's fascination with historical origins was not merely a reflection of Romantic fashion (or "chaos," as he would call it); it followed also from and was reinforced by his study of Vico, Wolf, Niebuhr, Creuzer, Grimm, and Burnouf, and their various ways of inquiring into prehistory. While drawn to myth as a valid expression of history, Michelet also looked back to Perizonius, Louis de Beaufort, and Niebuhr in examining the "uncertainties of the history of the first centuries of Rome" and in trying to separate legends from the factual basis of early history.[91] The historian was at once inspired poet (*vates*) and critic.[92] Following Wolf, Creuzer, and Görres, he read poetic sources as expressions of a people and heroic figures as symbols of the period of myth. Michelet wanted to avoid both the "fatalism of race," to which Thierry had surrendered, and the "legendary fatalism of providential men" — Romulus, Hercules, Siegfried — preserved by myth. Roman history had to be analyzed between the falsities of early myths and the later ones that were calculated for reasons of state, that is, "Caesarism." "Humanity is its own work" (*l'Humanité est son oeuvre à elle-même*), as Michelet liked to quote from Vico;[93] and his account of Roman origins was carried out in the spirit of the "little pandemonium" that was Vico's *New Science*. It should be added that Michelet also noted a classical source for this formula, that "man makes his own destiny" (*fabrum suae quemque fortunae*).[94]

While Michelet was still lecturing on Roman history, the Revolution of 1830 broke out, marking a caesura in historical writing as well as political life. Old Chateaubriand understood the significance of the event. "I was writing ancient history when modern history knocked at my door," he wrote in 1831. "In vain I cried, 'I'm coming to you.' It passed by and took with it three generations of kings."[95] The "Three Glorious" days of July represented a turning point in the life of Michelet—"I began to exist, that is, to write, at the end of 1830," he recalled forty years later[96]—and indeed of the whole generation of 1820. Guizot, for whom 1688 had finally come to France, became minister of the interior, later of public instruction (as were Villemain and Cousin), Thiers was appointed to the ministry of finance and then Conseil d'Etat, Fauriel became professor of foreign literature, Mignet became director of the archives of foreign affairs, and Daunou director of the National Archives, with Michelet head of the historical section. "Come join the competition," Michelet wrote to Quinet on August 10; "everything is being organized, and positions are going fast." Barante was already in the Académie (as Cousin soon would be), and of the "new historians" only Thierry (Sismondi was Swiss) was left out. For Michelet, finishing his lectures on Roman history, life and history itself had become an "eternal July"; and it was in this spirit that he launched himself into his life's project, his *Histoire de France*.

Even before the epiphany of the July Revolution, Michelet had conceived a grand and philosophical (crypto-Hegelian, neo-Cousinian?) vision of the historical process. History was an epic struggle between fatality and liberty that found expression in many contexts and on many levels: man liberated from nature, spirit from material, the Persians from India, the Jews from Egypt, Christianity from paganism, the barbarians from the Roman Empire, Protestants from the Roman church, Italian cities from feudalism, and France from the Old Regime. At the same time Michelet's horizons narrowed concentrically from universal history (to which he wrote an "introduction" in 1831) to Europe, to France, to Paris, and finally to himself, as the authorial microcosm of the historical world which he surveyed and declaimed upon from his chair of *histoire et morale* at the Collège de France, secured finally, after several applications, in 1838, and enhanced by his election to the Académie des Sciences Morales a few months later. For Michelet these positions certified his commission not only to tell the truths of history but also to interpret their moral meanings and to give instruction not only to his students but to all the French people.

Michelet's preparations for his history were both deep and broad. His goal was "resurrection"—in invidious contrast to Thierry's "narrative" and Guizot's "analysis," as well as the "galvinism" of Dumas, who dug up corpses and made them "grimace."[97] First, however, came the preliminary work of excavation.[98] In 1834 Michelet was appointed by Guizot, whose assistant (*suppléant*) he was at the Sorbonne, to the National Archives, which for him was not merely masses of papers but the biographies of men, and indeed the nation—"intimate method," he wrote in his journal: "simplify, biographize [*biographier*] history."[99] Before the Revolution archival researchers were in-terested only in kings and nobles, Chateaubriand noted, while modern histo-rians were concerned as well with the rest of the people and social transforma-tions.[100] The archives, which "returned [Michelet] to the Middle Ages,"[101] joined Père Lachaise as a locus of Michelet's internal dialogues with the dead. Much of the next two decades he spent in the company of those he called "Messieurs les morts," whose testimonies were essential in his project of "res-urrection" and of "biographizing history." The archives, though at first under attack by revolutionaries, were in fact enriched by revolutionary efforts to pre-serve and to centralize monastic and provincial deposits; and in 1835 Michelet received from Guizot a commission to visit the major deposits and prepare a report on the condition of the records. From this time Michelet's travel journal include comments on these researches as well as his impressions as a tourist and connoisseur of art, architecture, and archeological remains. In his report he recommended further centralization of the archives and the appointment of experts trained at the Ecole des Chartes to examine those relating to the history of the old regime.[102]

   "My life and my science are one and the same," Michelet told his students in 1841.[103] His life work and surrogate autobiography, the *History of France,* was conceived at the height of his fascination with the "philosophy of his-tory" and in the "brilliant morning of July"; over the next ten years it was carried down, in six volumes, to the late medieval period; and then, after a ten-year break, it was completed, in another eleven volumes, over a dozen more years. During the intervening decade, covering the extinction of "July," which he attributed to materialism, the Revolution of 1848, and its darkening aftermath — "A century has passed in a month," he declared on April 1 of that year[104] — Michelet published the seven volumes of his *History of the French Revolution,* these largely without access to the archives, not to mention other works, scholarly and popular, historical and naturalistic, and his unfinished *History of the Nineteenth Century*. Michelet's book was an "act of faith"; it was also his life, and his aim, as in the courses he taught at the Ecole Normale and, as *professeur de l'histoire et morale,* at the Collège de France, was not just a learned, eloquent, and even poetic account of a dead past but, in one of the vitalist conceits that informed all his writings, "the resurrection of the whole life" of the French nation.[105] "My hero," he wrote, "is the People." And as Jullian concluded, his work was "a masterpiece of historical and literary an-thropomorphism."[106]

   Michelet paid tribute to the great "pleiade" of historians already on the scene when he began his studies, Barante, Guizot, Mignet, Thiers, and Au-gustin Thierry, as he counted them;[107] but he hoped to surpass them and to avoid their errors, especially Thierry's lack of geographical background and racialist determinism (*fatalité*). Michelet's own themes were the rise of liberty and the growth of national unity, culminating in and defined by the Revolution of 1789. Like humanity in general, France was a "person," indeed an immortal person with a soul, that had "made itself" according to Vico's formula, just as, through his books, Michelet had made himself.

The process of national self-making was complicated. The character of the nation in its Celtic stage arose in the crucible of war, the Gauls running through the world sword in hand before Christianity arrived. Seen in such teleological terms, France was the product of successive waves of influence — Greek, Roman, Iberian, Islamic, and Germanic. The "primitive genius" of France in its "Helleno-Celtic" stage was seen in the theology of Pelagius, which, emphasizing free will above divine grace, marked the appearance of the self and the independent personality. Opinions of later scholars to the contrary notwithstanding, French culture was not merely an extension of the Roman or the German; it was rather an amalgam of a number of "systems," which were all transcended in the progress from the chaos and servitude of feudalism to liberty and civil order. "The middle ages are the battle, the modern age the victory": here is one version of Michelet's heedless historicism. He insisted on the importance of geography, and he illustrated this at length in the "Tableau de la France" (an anticipation of the great work of Vidal de la Blache) included in his second volume; but he argued, too, that the determinism (*fatalité*) of environment was overcome in the "victory" of modernity.

In the course of a detailed narrative that was largely political and military Michelet kept his focus intermittently on the emergent personality of France shown by the formation of the language, the institution of property, and the building of the state against the "counterrevolution" of feudalism and the mysticism and symbolism of opposing forces such as the Templers and the Roman church ("la poésie mystique de l'*Unam Sanctam*"). He attended especially to what might be called marks of nationality: the oaths of Strasbourg, after which one could speak of "français"; the career of Abelard, "son of Pelagius, father of Descartes . . . and precursor of the *human and sentimental school*," followed by Fénelon and Rousseau; the founding of the university; the Estates General of 1302, where the "People" first appeared; and the story of Joan of Arc, which marks the end of the Middle Ages and the beginning of the Modern Ages (as well as a "moral revolution").[108] In volume 3 Michelet offered an excursus on the national archives, their history, and the work of its administrators (Budé, Du Tillet, Dupuy, Camus, Daunou, and Michelet himself), which reflected the pervasive theme of political centralization. In the preface to volume 4, Michelet described the process in this way: "To the priests and the knights succeeded the lawyers, after faith came the law";[109] after the epic came the chronicle, and again Michelet stood at the end of these developments.

In his course at the Collège de France Michelet went over some of the same ground. In his first lecture on April 23, 1838, he invoked his Parisian predecessors, beginning with Peter Abelard — the "father of method" in the twelfth century as Descartes was in the seventeenth — and including Peter Ramus, who advanced liberty of thought toward modern philosophy, and more specifically, in the chair of history, Daunou and Letronne.[110] "It is Paris that I have been teaching," he told his students. Paris was both France itself on a small scale and "the center of the world." Like Niebuhr, Michelet began with mythical prehistory, including the image of St. Denis carrying his head in his hands, which Michelet explained as a misinterpretation of a rhetorical conceit picturing martyrs confessing their faith even as their heads were being cut off — even as the severed head of Orpheus, floating down the Hebrus, continued to call out the name of Euridice, suggesting also a suppressed pagan memory of Dionysius, or Bacchus.[111] In later lectures Michelet drew not only on his own early volumes but also on Thierry's letters on the history of France, focusing on the rise of liberty as seen in the emergence of the communes from feudalism, the elevation of women in chivalry, and the foundation of the university, when Paris became "the true center of the world" — as indeed it still was.

In the wake of these egocentric and melodramatic invocations of the medieval past of France-Paris-self, Michelet was plunged into three years of emotional turmoil and crises which changed the direction and character of his historical efforts. Between the death of his wife, Pauline, in July 1839 (which made him wish that he really believed in the principle of immortality that he taught)[112] and that of his new friend Mme Dumesnil in May 1842, Michelet began taking a new interest in women and the family and a new view of the dead world of the Middle Ages, which were the subject of the first three volumes of his *History of France* (1833–37) as well as his first courses at the Collège de France. He moved from the death of his wife to the death of France in the fifteenth century, on which he wrote what he called "the only serious and *well-founded* history."[113] In these years history really became his "second wife," but it was also a "violent moral chemistry," transforming his passions into general ideas, his "people" into his self, and vice versa.[114]

What Michelet was discovering, in his ego-historical approach to understanding, was modernity, rethinking in historical terms the process of philosophy: "The heroism of the modern age — what is left of it?" Descartes: "I think, therefore I am" (individually). Leibniz: "I cause, therefore I am" (individually).

Vico: "I cause, therefore I am (as humanity); that is, not only my individuality but also my generality is caused by me."[115] In 1839 (he recalled in 1842) he had finally come to terms with life, and death, as "the synthesis and analysis of God." Michelet had his own idea of "how dogmas come to an end." "The history of philosophy kills philosophy," he remarked later; "Royer-Collard kills Maine de Biran"; and so it was, too, with the history of art.[116] And yet it was the historian's task to restore, or at least commemorate these dead. "Let the present not kill its father but bury him with respect."[117]

In any case, through this crypto-Hegelian (or Cousinian) dialectic, "history appeared to me as it were for the first time."[118] That is, it appeared from "a thousand points of view at the same time." So Michelet moved from a philosophy to a religion of history, with himself as priest and chief prophet — and indeed as a Vichian maker — and his *patrie* as chief object of worship.[119] "Humanity is its own work" (Michelet recalled Vico's formula at this time of his own autobiographical reflections), and so was Michelet. He also recalled an older adage, that "to be ignorant of history is forever to be a child." His course of 1840 treated an "eternal Renaissance," comparable to the "eternal July," which was his political inspiration.

But this new point of departure was also a personal break. Like Volney, Michelet was drawn to ruins, especially at this point, when his heart was also devastated.[120] As he wrote in his journal in August 1843: "Adieu to the past, adieu sweet solitary years, adieu Adèle, [his daughter, just married to Alfred Dumesnil], adieu Pauline. All is finished, including my dreams of the middle ages. What is left to me is the future."[121] On this emotional basis he began to take a larger — not only a philosophical but also a social, political, and prophetic view of his professorial responsibilities. He would be not just a seer but a maker of the future.[122] In his lectures, carried on from 1838 to 1851, and in his published works during this same period, Michelet undertook to educate not only successive generations of students but the whole nation — the "People." This was the subject of a more popular book which appeared in 1846 and which was even more of an ego trip: "This book is more than a book," he wrote in his preface to Quinet; "it is myself" — and also "you." In 1843, Quinet and Michelet joined forces in a crusade against the Jesuits and their corruptive doctrines and on behalf of the liberty of education. Ranke himself, as well as Quinet, Mickiewicz, Sacy, and Letronne, was present at one lecture in May, often interrupted, on education as an imitation of Providence and Jesuit distortions of French history and the honored dead of an earlier (Napoleonic) generation.[123]

Of the Jesuits he wrote as he had of feudalism: "They are the enemies of the modern mind, enemies of liberty, and of the future."[124] "Ask anyone on the street, 'Who are the Jesuits?'" Michelet proclaimed in 1843, "and he will answer, 'the Counter-Revolution.'"[125] He continued, "History (according to my definition of 1830, which I retain) is the progressive victory of liberty . . . , [which] should be made not through destruction but through *interpretation,*" and more specifically the interpretation of "tradition." This was not the tradition of the Roman church, however, but that of the Revolution and of liberty — and once again Michelet resorted to self-dramatization, identifying himself with the process: "Tradition is my mother," he concluded, "and liberty is myself." *Moi-Paris, Moi-Histoire, Moi-Liberté:* these are the angles from which arose Michelet's profound, pretentious, bombastic, "resurrectionist" view of history.[126]

The question of tradition was much complicated by the Revolution — not that of 1830 but those of 1789 and 1848, which Michelet respectively began to write about and to live through. Michelet's father, who "was tradition," died in November 1846 while his son was writing the first two volumes of his *History of the French Revolution,* which were finished on New Year's day 1847.[127] Having moved out of his emotional as well as his scholarly middle ages (his psychological crisis past and *History of France* suspended after reaching the fifteenth century), Michelet had been lecturing on the subject since the previous January, proclaiming to his students that the Revolution, when France seemed to "lose" its traditions, was the defining moment and indeed — with usual hyperbolic synecdoche — *was* France, as well as a whole philosophy of history. But like the French People, the French Revolution did not know either itself, its past, or its future; and it was Michelet's poetic-prophetic-pedagogical-philosophical duty over the next six years to explain this phenomenon, which, also as usual, was entangled with his own quest for self-knowledge. So Michelet moved from archeology to the living process of history, and from abstract liberty to economic reality and the "social question," and, like France itself after 1789, came to what at first seemed to be full self-consciousness.

Michelet's new book was born in the archives (where he spent much time from 1845 to 1850), and on this basis, as well as his own empathetic insights, he claimed it to be superior to the exactly contemporaneous works of Thiers, Lamartine, and Blanc.[128] At first the Revolution of '89 — like its younger *soixante-huitard* sister — was "credulous, fraternal, and peaceful." It was a continuation of Christianity, though it substituted law and justice for faith and mysticism. "The Revolution is on her march, with Rousseau and Voltaire still in front," he wrote with characteristic hyperbole. "Kings themselves are in her train; Frederick, Catherine, Joseph, Leopold."[129] Women, too, would soon join in, as the "immortal" Third Estate was transformed into the nation, and as, with the destruction of feudalism on the night of August 4, the Middle Ages ended (again!), and the nation began its "spontaneous organization."[130] Then, however, the "holy period" of the nation was over; the "power of love" was lost; peace was broken; and soon "France is a soldier."[131] So the Revolution was "plunged into night and winter," as Michelet saw the ruins of a world in the documentary remains of the Terror in the "catacombs" of the archives and felt himself to be the "last man."

After mid-century Michelet began losing his revolutionary euphoria. In 1849 he found a new wife and, for a short time, emotional euphoria. He continued teaching, though in a very irregular and polemical way, following his agenda of combining his courses and his life, which was instructing the French people in his (still) revolutionary vision. "Education, that is the way," he told his journal.[132] "*Love, love-and-create by education*"; and in this spirit he conceived his *Bible of Humanity,* which restored the universal, especially oriental, context to his historical thinking.[133] For him history was still centered on his *Moi* — "not the egoist Moi," however, "but the harmonized and sympathetic Moi."[134] But in August 1850 he and his troubled young wife lost their child less than two months after birth, and his old thoughts of death returned with new force. In 1851 his course was suspended, soon after he lost his chair, and the next year, at odds with the contemptible republican regime, he lost his position at the archives as well. ("Suspension," he wrote tersely, "Enterrment.")[135] It was a period of decline — as indeed was that of the Revolution, whose fall into Terror he was chronicling.

After concluding his history of the revolution he turned to more popular subjects — nature, women, democracy — and back to the later volumes of his history of France, left hanging a decade before at the threshold of modernity. The starting point was the "Renaissance," which for him centered not on Petrarch and Giotto but on Columbus, Copernicus, and Luther — "the discovery of the world and the discovery of man," but also of a new faith, although these novelties came three centuries too late. Returning to his old project, Michelet recovered his optimism. Reversing the Romantic idealization of the Middle Ages and rejecting them as grotesque, violent, and dark, Michelet turned to the invasions of Italy by Charles VIII and Louis XII, which brought discoveries "not less astonishing than those of Christopher Columbus," implying the Italian roots of this cultural revival. For Michelet the result was a world transformed, "a world of humanity and universal sympathy," promoted thereafter by "the *human* party," which however took the nation-state as the vehicle of progress.

The Reformation, to which Michelet's next volume was devoted, represented a further step toward republicanism and democracy, to the extent that

Protestantism brought a victory over papal despotism (converging at this time with the rise of the Jesuits). In France this was the work of the Huguenots, especially after the terrible massacres of St. Bartholomew, whose resistance "anticipated" the French Revolution. The best literary expression was the book published by François Hotman: "Gaul and France, *Franco-Gallia,* is the title of this book which, out of Geneva [where it was completed], invaded all of Europe and was translated into all languages. Before the *Contrat Social* no book had such a success." Ironically, Hotman was a master of Roman law, but "he wisely doubted that at a distance of two thousand years the law of the Empire could suit a world so deeply changed." Like Charles Dumoulin, moreover, Hotman turned to French customs as a basis for a unified system of law. Did Hotman, asked Michelet, know the work of La Boétie? "The book was called *Le contr'un.* That of Hotman could have been called *Le Pour Tous.*" It was, Michelet concluded, "a profound, true, and luminous book, which identified barbarian liberty with modern liberty, connected races with the times and the historical consciousness of France and the world."

In the later volumes of his history of France, Michelet did not have access to the archives; and in any case, beyond what was a fairly conventional political narrative — sometimes thin and not infrequently pompous — he was absorbed in his role as poet-prophet-pedagogue. Sismondi had criticized his French prejudices, in contrast to his own (Swiss) impartiality,[136] and Michelet would not disagree. "This history is not impartial," he wrote — not a balance between good and evil but devoted to right and truth, with an eye always on the coming Revolution — which was precisely "the coming of Law, the resurrection of Right, and the reaction of Justice." The enemy continued to be Roman Catholicism, especially as represented by the Jesuits; but after the wars of religion even the Protestants forgot their republican inclinations and fell back into royalism — not that this prevented their expulsion by the revocation of the Edict of Nantes, which for Michelet was the seventeenth-century equivalent of the Revolution, sending perhaps as many people into exile. In these unhappy generations the major factors were family interest and economic distress. Opposed to them, the *credo* of the eighteenth century, was the principle of action. This was the motto of Montesquieu and Voltaire (as well as Vico), and it was joined to reality in the events of 1789.

After mid-century Michelet seemed to wander from his historical calling. He was distracted by personal, physical, and especially marital problems with Athénaïs. Increasingly, he surrendered not only to his philosophico-poetico-prophetic urges but also joining these to a social program aimed at educating the People, transforming society through Love, and even establishing a sort of secular religion not unlike the aspirations of contemporary Socialists and

Positivists and his friend Quinet.[137] For the historian was, or ought to be, at once interpreter of the past, leader of public opinion in the present, and standard bearer for the future of humanity. That this role had not worked out before the disasters of 1848 did not divert Michelet from his vision of national history and national destiny.

The expression of this vision was to come in a work, conceived in 1853, never completed, but published posthumously, called the *Banquet,* which invoked a secular sort of communion as well as the revolutionary celebrations of 1848 and displayed a spiritualist and utopian agenda. "Dreamed of a book, the *Banquet,*" he reported to his diary on December 30.[138] "Very cold, and I lay down next to my wife." In execution this was his work, but in conception it was an outgrowth of historical ideas shared with Quinet. "We, Quinet and I, for fifteen years (1830–1845), Herder and Vico," he wrote on April 13, 1854. "Vico is Christian, but he transcends Christianity by a Pythagorean and Virgilian grandeur." "The banquet according to Vico: hearth, altar, city. Quinet makes the city with the gods; I make the gods with the law and the city."[139] It was the historian's version of the eucharist, uniting the spirit of humanity with material progress, and it went beyond the "new history" of the generation of 1815. It was unknown to Guizot and Cousin, who accepted conventional religion; to Robespierre; to the Socialists of 1830; to the pantheism and communism of Pierre Leroux; and to the atheism of Feuerbach. In 1833, Michelet, transcending these limited views, posited a "temporary death" of Christianity and advanced beyond established religion and "infant socialism." His views were developed in *The Priest and the Woman, The People* (giving "a scientific base" to the revolution), and his volumes on the French Revolution. Michelet omits to mention his and Quinet's attack on the Jesuits, but the "Banquet" does propose to do without the priesthood as well as socialism and Jacobinism. Nor did 1848 or "the cruel experience of 1852" destroy this vision. (Meanwhile his wife, *ma mie,* was again indisposed.)

Yet it was his history of France that continued to absorb "M. Symbole," and in 1854 he returned to the last volumes. Into this book, he wrote in the preface to the last volume in 1867, "I have put my life." Like Marx, Michelet was disappointed not in himself and his lack of foresight, especially concerning the events of 1848, but rather in the course of history itself, in which the French nation had made itself, but unfortunately not in the image of concord and harmony with which Michelet had begun his quest. And yet he could say in 1867 at the end of his history of France, in the words of a famous popular song, "Je ne regrette rien."[140] In any case Michelet's historiographical virtues outlived his vices, and in French scholarly as well as literary tradition he remains an icon and participant in another "new history."

7

German Ascendancy

The chief creation of more recent history is the Great Power, the life form of the most significant peoples.

— Jacob Burckhardt

In the Shadow of Ranke

Like ancient and medieval philosophers, historians in nineteenth-century Germany were divided, by themselves and others, into various "schools," according to different professorial followings, universities, regions, religions, politics, philosophies, and methods. Catholic and Protestant, Austrian and Prussian, *grossdeutsch* and *kleindeutsch*, empirical and conjectural historians all cultivated the common ground of a national past — "the world-historical development of our people," in the words of Heinrich Luden — but they quarreled over this legacy in general and in detail. What were the origins, provenance, positive forces, underlying continuities, social bases and structures, political leadership, institutional and legal traditions, and cultural achievements as well as the future destiny of the German nation as it took shape in the wake of the Revolutions of 1789, 1848, and 1870? Who were the heroes and villains, the saints and sinners, the makers and destroyers of the German history? What are the important questions facing the historian? What are the sources of history, and how should they be understood, taught, criticized, and debated? And, in the background, what constituted the main tradition of the coming German nationhood, the medieval German Empire or the upstart principality of Prussia which was becoming so threatening?

In retrospect the so-called Austrian and Catholic schools seem outside mainstream historiography, although they did feature some major scholars, especially Julius Ficker and Ignaz von Döllinger, the mentor of the liberal Catholic English historian, Lord Acton, and they were rivals of the Prussians in documentary research and auxiliary sciences (*Hilfswissenschaften*).[1] In 1880 a Catholic historical journal, dedicated to the ideas that Christ was the "mid-point of history" and that the Catholic Church was "the education of the human race," was founded.[2] Another rival was the Heidelberg school, including Schlosser, his pupil Georg Gervinus, and Ludwig Häusser. Schlosser was the author of widely read and translated works on eighteenth-century and world history. A member of the famous "Göttingen Seven" (professors expelled for political opposition), Gervinus, like Droysen, wrote a treatise on historical method (*Historik*, 1837), following the idealism of Wilhelm Humboldt, although he was better known for his history of German poetry, his study of the great "Germanic" poet, William Shakespeare, and his massive history of the nineteenth century. Häusser, a protégé of Dahlmann, published a survey of medieval German historiography in 1839 and a German history which actually aligned him more closely with the Prussian party.[3]

Among the founders of this *kleindeutsch* school were J. G. Droysen, classicist and national historian, and F. C. Dahlmann, a member (with Droysen, Gervinus, Waitz, Sybel, and Duncker) of the National Assembly in Frankfurt in 1848. Except for his early classical studies, including his monograph on Herodotus,[4] Dahlmann wrote histories of the English and French revolutions, and in 1830 he published his bibliography of German sources (on which Waitz later collaborated). Droysen turned from the Hellenistic period to the history of Prussian politics (1855–86), at once charged with nationalist ardor and based on documents in the Prussian archives, of which he was director after Dahlmann and before Sybel. Other applicants to the Prussian school included Gustav Stenzel and Johannes Voigt, at least on the grounds of their large-scale surveys of Prussian history. It was Ranke, however, who was the doyen and leader of this school for two generations and more, as well as the source and symbol of an extraordinary posthumous legend, positive and negative, in Anglo- and Francophone as well as German and East European areas, and a large professional progeny. As he wrote in 1884, "I am still astonished at the talent and application of the young men who gathered around me"—among them Giesebrecht, Sybel, Burckhardt, Gniest, Jaffé, Duncker, Wattenbach, and Waitz.[5]

Like Droysen, Mommsen, and others, Ranke was the father — the *Doktor-vater* — of a great extended family of scholars, of disciples, grand-disciples, and great-grand-disciples over at least five academic generations.[6] This credentialed elite came to monopolize chairs of history in more than fifty German universities and to establish a scholarly continuity that was broken only (and even then only occasionally) by the upheavals of the third Reich. Despite debates and revisionist moves this scholarly community preserved social and intellectual coherence over space and time and imposed a certain methodological and ideological orthodoxy on the interpretation of European as well as German history.

Many of these scholars were medievalists associated with the *Monumenta Germanica Historica,* although some turned to modern history, especially after 1848, and were swept up into the movement for unification. Waitz, whom Ranke had predicted would be "the Muratori of German history," had also been one of the Göttingen Seven and was drawn into the political turmoil of 1848, before returning as professor of medieval history to Göttingen, where he attracted many more doctoral students than the master himself (almost sixty to Ranke's thirty or so).[7] One of these was the French scholar Gabriel Monod, founder of the *Revue Historique,* whose friendship with Waitz survived the Franco-Prussian War. In 1876, Waitz also became director of the *MGH,* but his major work was his great *German Constitutional History* (1844–78), three successive editions of which he dedicated to Ranke.

Perhaps the major celebrator of the Prussian school was Heinrich von Treitschke, son of an ennobled Saxon general, who was no less a national historian-prophet than Droysen and Sybel.[8] While writing poetry, Treitschke turned to politics and economics through the influence of Dahlmann and Roscher respectively. In 1857, Treitschke founded the *Preussische Jahrbücher,* and for it wrote essays on history, literature, and politics; and two years later he accepted a position as lecturer at the University of Leipzig, from which he entered actively into national politics, eventually becoming a supporter of Bismarck and, moving to Berlin in 1874, was given free access to the Prussian archives and eventually succeeded Ranke in the chair of modern history. Invited to write a history of the German Confederation as early as 1861, Treitschke later expanded the plan into a history of the whole nation, his much-delayed and much-criticized masterwork, which was published between 1879 and 1894 and translated during the First World War.

Treitschke's *History of Germany in the Nineteenth Century* is a panoramic view of German politics and culture from the end of the Thirty Years' War down to the period of unification. The long duel between the Habsburgs and the Hohenstaufen, projected into the *grossdeutsch-kleindeutsch* polarity of his own day, was won by the latter as a result of the "pitiless and cruel German realism," the central role of the military in Prussian tradition, the reforms of Stein, and the warlike spirit generated by the wars of liberation. But Treitschke emphasized also the remarkable cultural revival of that period of anti-French militancy and "the beautiful sunset glow of philosophy." "For the first time since Martin Luther, the ideas of the Germans once more made the round of the world"—thanks to (among other things) Goethe and the "invisible church" gathered around him, to the efforts of Germanophiles like Mme de Staël, and to the new University of Berlin, which "soon outsoared all others." University professors began to play the roles assumed by the lawyers in France. "Almost simultaneously appeared the epoch-making writings of Savigny, the brothers Grimm, Boeckh, Lachmann, Bopp, Diez and Ritter; whilst Niebuhr, the Humboldts, Eichhorn, Creuzer and Gottfried Hermann went vigorously along the paths they had already opened."[9] That "Boeckh and Creuzer had idled, revelled, and caroused so many nights with the enthusiasts of Heidelberg romanticism" showed that the expanding *Volksgeist* went beyond the narrow circle of men of science, spreading to other parts of society and to the next, even more zealous generation of Young Germany.

Into his colorful, opinionated, and sometimes intemperate account Treitschke (who disapproved of the comparatively neutral stance of Ranke toward public issues and concern for the history of foreign countries) brought interpretations of the German historians, who, from Luden's time, had played so important a role in the national movement. On many scholars Hegel, with his "well-developed historical sense," left his imprint even on historians like Droysen and Ranke, "who detested the philosophers' interpretation of history."[10] The notion that "the rational is real and the real is rational" was comforting to intellectuals set upon realizing their political ideals and especially to historians locked into the teleology of national unification—the "dream," dreamed first in St. Paul's Church in Frankfurt in 1848, "of the Prussian Empire of the German Nation."[11] Treitschke pointed out in particular the advances in politics and political history due to the work of Rotteck, Dahlmann, Leo, Schlosser, and others; and he endorsed Luden's view, expressed in the time of the *Freiheitskriege,* that the morality of the state was to be prized above private morality. In general Treitschke recognized the central position of Ranke in setting the political agenda of historical inquiry and especially in securing "world-wide renown for German historians."[12]

Heinrich von Sybel's first book was a history of the Crusades (1841), which he called "one of the greatest revolutions that has ever taken place in the history of the human race," and he hoped that it would supplant the uncritical old book of Michaud.[13] His second publication was a study of early German kingship (1847), but the events of the next year turned him to modern history. Sybel expressed sorrow that he could not maintain a scholarly level in this contemporary area, but he knew that he could never rely on the relevant archives "for the simple reason that there was not the slightest prospect that a petition to make use of them would be granted."[14] Combining literary sensationalism with the heavy artillery of scholarship, Sybel, like Droysen, turned to the revolutionary experience of France in his *History of the Age of the French Revolution,* and then to contemporary history in the making in Germany, associated with a vision of a unified German nation and state. "Germany will always be one," he quoted the poet Arndt as writing, "as long as German speech rings out"; and he cast his history of the German Empire (1889–94), including the setbacks under the old Holy Roman Empire as well as advances under the post-Napoleonic Reich, in the light of this divine process, foreseen by Fichte, Arndt, Dahlmann, and others.[15]

In 1859, Sybel founded the *Historische Zeitschrift,* which was both a manifesto of the German historical profession and an expression of national self-consciousness and which featured introductory appreciations of German historiography by Ranke, Droysen, Giesebrecht, and Waitz, who denounced the "dilettantism" of much contemporary writing.[16] "This periodical should, above all, be a scientific one," Sybel wrote. "Its first task should, therefore, be to represent the true method of history and to point out the deviations therefrom."[17] The historical discipline had to avoid the extremes of the antiquarian and the partisan (and the nineteenth century surely saw fantastic examples of both these extremes). The journal was to study "the life of the people, governed by the laws of morality, [appearing] as a natural and individual evolution" and "organic development"; and so feudalism, radicalism, and ultramontanism would be excluded. Yet the study of the past had to connect with the public concerns of the present, and so emphasis would be on modern over ancient history and German over foreign. At the same time discussions of "the characteristic differences between German and foreign ways of writing history in our days, will be most welcome." This was descriptive as well as prophetic of the controversies of nineteenth-century historiography as they evolved along with the "life of the people." French historians like Charles Seignobos noticed the intensified nationalist and imperialist tone of Sybel's review and others and the conspicuous political bias (*arrière-pensées*) of their university teaching after 1870.[18] Other periodicals appeared with more specialized functions, such as that founded in 1878 by the Historical Society of Berlin to keep up on the scholarly publications across the whole spectrum of Western history, including (from 1888) prehistory (*Urgeschichte*).[19]

In the postrevolutionary period there was a remarkable shift of emphasis from world history to the history of national groups.[20] One reason for this was the flowering of national — and anti-national — sentiment in the revolutionary age, but another more subtle element was a tendency to privilege fundamental matters of legal, social, and institutional structures above political action. Increasingly, in the wake of Herder, historians turned away from the turbulent surface of politics and legislation to the underlying social nature and will of the people, the nation, the folk, as expressed in age-old customs, long-term social arrangements, and cultural continuities. The result was a sort of historiography that was essentialist, but also that probed deeply into the documentary sources of history below the political level. The kings had not departed, but they were overshadowed by *Nation* and the *Volk*.

The Historical School

Historians writing in the wake of the Wars of Liberation looked not to the defunct Empire or the foreign Church to construct their history but to the people, the *Volk*, and the political and institutional expressions of its inarticulate will. This meant above all the Romano-Germanic legal tradition, which represented centuries of experience and jurisprudence and, at least indirectly, the substance of German social history in local and national terms. It also represented the starting point of the historical school of law, whose foundations had been laid by legal scholars, first at the University of Göttingen, especially in the work of Gustav Hugo, and then at the new University of Berlin founded in 1807 by Wilhelm von Humboldt, who was himself a pioneer of nineteenth-century historicism — the "Bacon of the historical sciences," as Droysen called him.[21] He corrected the emphasis of the old "arts of history" by declaring, anticipating Ranke's much-repeated motto, that "the historian's task is to present what actually happened."[22]

One of those to be called to the new Prussian university was Karl Friedrich von Savigny, who became head of the historical school of law. This was in 1810, eight years before the arrival of his colleague and rival Hegel.[23] Savigny's major work, his *History of Roman Law in the Middle Ages,* began to appear in 1815; but already another colleague, Karl Friedrich Eichhorn (son of the great Hebrew scholar), had begun to publish his pioneering history of German law and institutions in 1808 and had come to Berlin in 1811. His work, which portrayed a national life going continuously back to Frankish times, was supplemented by that on German legal antiquities by Savigny's pupil Jakob Grimm, and especially by the systematic collection of historical and legal sources, the *Monumenta Germaniae Historica,* which began appearing in 1826 under the auspices of the German Society for the Sources of Ancient History of Germany, founded in 1819 by Stein and others, supported by Savigny and Grimm, and directed by G. H. Pertz and J. F. Böhmer, who were later joined by graduates of Ranke's seminar, begun in 1833, including Giesebrecht and Waitz. Such publications formed the basis of the efforts to reconstruct a national past paralleling and reinforcing the movement toward political and legal unity of a new German state which many of these scholars envisioned. The famous motto of the *MGH* was *Sanctus amor patriae dat animum,* but it has served as a great treasury for all of European history.

The historical school came into prominence with the appearance of the new journal edited by Savigny and Eichhorn, the *Zeitschrift für geschichtliche Rechtswissenschaft,* and especially the following year with Savigny's manifesto, the *Vocation of Our Age for Legislation and Jurisprudence,* of 1814. In the eighteenth century, Savigny wrote, "Men longed for new codes, which, by their completeness, should insure a mechanically precise administration of justice"; and the upshot was that Bonapartist creation, which "broke into Germany, and ate in, further and further, like a cancer."[24] Moreover, "As soon as Napoleon had subjected everything to a military despotism, he greedily held fast that part of the revolution which answered his purpose and prevented the return of the ancient constitution."[25] According to Savigny, "Only through her [history] can a lively connection with the primitive state of a people be kept up," he declared; "and the loss of this connection must take away from every people the best part of its spiritual life."[26] It was the legislative violation of history that provoked Savigny's critique and led him to a key question for both historians and jurists: "What is the influence of the past on the present?" is the way he posed it, "and what is the relation of what is now to what will be?" Leaders of the Philosophical School like Hegel sought answers in reason, but Savigny and Eichhorn turned back to history.

Savigny had many disciples in the first half of the nineteenth century, such as G. F. Puchta, whose book on customary law argued, in the spirit also of Herder, that custom was really the creation of the jurists rather than the *Volk,* yet no less an expression of national spirit.[27] Others moved beyond the legal tradition, such as the historical linguist Jakob Grimm, who had studied with Savigny at Berlin, and the political economist Wilhelm Roscher, who applied Savigny's premises to their own lines of inquiry in the effort to enhance the defense and illustration of the life of the people — the *Volk* being the German counterpart of the emergent French *Nation.* Politically, the historical school resembled the philosophical school — Savigny's influence resembled that of

Hegel, his rival at the University of Berlin—in that both had left- as well as right-wing offspring; and historical interpretation, too, was torn between these ideological extremes energized by the legacy of the Revolution.

For the interpretation of German history and its origins the work of Jakob Grimm was central, for it was he who sought a solid basis for prehistory, that is, the period before extant documentation, in etymology and folklore. After the "Fairy Tales" compiled with his brother Wilhelm, he followed Humboldt into the badly charted field of the history of language, starting with his German grammar published in 1819 and including especially, under the influence of Creuzer, his study of the symbolism (or grammar) and the "poetry of law," which inspired Michelet's work on the origins of French law.[28] Grimm turned away from the Romanism of his mentor Savigny and plunged into the sources of German customary law.[29] Most fundamental was his imaginative investigation of legal antiquities, the *Reichsaltertümer* of 1828, that represented his patriotic duty (*vaterländische Arbeit*). Some of these judicial records dated from the thirteenth century, and they threw light on literature and language as well as the law as it was reflected in the lives and mentality of the people.

The influence of the historical school even reached the New World, which was ostensibly free of the burdens of the feudal past of Europe and yet which displayed a similar pattern of development. "American law was the growth of necessity, not of the wisdom of the individuals," wrote George Bancroft (who had studied in Germany) of the period of the American Revolution. "It was not an acquisition from abroad; it was begotten from the American mind, of which it was a natural and inevitable but also a slow and gradual development. The sublime thought that there existed a united nation was yet to spring into being."[30] Bancroft acquired many of the rhetorical habits as well as the scholarly dedication of the historical school.

An offshoot of the historical school of law was the historical school of economics, which had its roots in the practical and empirical cameralist science of the eighteenth century and which was also suspicious of the abstractions of natural law.[31] In the nineteenth century the leader of this school—who was a counterpart and in some ways follower of Savigny and Eichhorn—was Wilhelm Roscher, who studied under Heeren, Gervinus, Dahlman, and K. O. Müller as well as Ranke, and who taught at Göttingen and Leipzig. Roscher's aim was both to place economics in historical and social context—beyond the conventional political view of the *Staatswissenschaften* and Rankean historical science—and to provide an empirical base for political economy. He was seconded in this effort by Bruno Hildebrand and Karl Knies.[32] The members of this "older historical school" wanted, too, to transform the old categories of cameralism into developmental stages—like historical jurisprudence, of course, all in the service of the national state. In the later nineteenth century economic history, in the work of K. W. Nitzsch, K. T. Von Inama-Sternegg, Gustav Schmoller, Julius Beloch, and Karl Lamprecht, emerged as a parallel and even a rival to political and "racist," or national, history — and was given further reinforcement by Marxist theory and scholarship.[33]

German historicism also made a powerful imprint on Restoration France, where Savigny's followers hoped for a time that his doctrines would be a way of completing the unfinished "social revolution," while others associated the historicism of Savigny exclusively with the formation of the authoritarian national state.[34] The journal *Thémis* carried the message of Savigny's intellectual "revolution" to French scholars, and indeed it received a favorable notice in Savigny's own journal. Hugo commented that this historical "revolution" had actually begun in 1789, when the first volume of his course had appeared. Many other French scholars were enlisted under Savigny's banner, among them Eugene Lerminier, originally from Strasbourg, who wrote his thesis on Savigny before giving his lectures and writing his books on the history of ideas and legal philosophy, in which, invoking Montesquieu, he tried to act as mediator in the "war" between the historical and the philosophical school. "The Code is at once a system and a history," he commented about the "Code of the French People" created by Napoleon. Of course the French had had their own "historical school," for as Edouard Laboulaye recalled, "Let us take, or rather restore from Germany that excellent historical method which they have taken from [the great sixteenth-century jurist, Jacques] Cujas."

In nineteenth-century France law and history were both shaped, and then haunted, by the ideologies and realities of the French Revolution. They regularly defined their ideological positions in terms of the Revolution, whether the seating arrangement in the National Assembly or the chronological extension of this represented by the successive stages of revolutionary government, from constitutional monarchy to republic to despotism and back to constitutional monarchy, with various shadings in between. What was increasingly apparent in retrospect was not so much what the Revolution destroyed but the survivals and continuities that emerged in the Restoration as a product of the old legal tradition, which managed to persist first unofficially under the Revolution and then in Bonapartist revival and which carried with it much of the mentality of the legal practice and theory of the Old Regime. In many ways legal scholars such as Portalis, P. P. N. Henrion de Pansey, Charles Toullier, and J. P. Proudhon reestablished, or reinforced, juridical continuities with the feudal, corporatist, and parlementary traditions of the Old Regime, while historians such as Augustin Thierry, François Guizot, and Jules Michelet carried on parallel projects in the realm of historical scholarship and (in Michelet's term) "resurrection."[35] In all of this German impulses were of central importance.

Before the Revolution lawyers were joined by historians in celebrating the glories and continuities of French history. One of the most extraordinary expressions of this traditionalism was the erudite summation of French constitutional history assembled by the erudite noblewoman Marie-Charlotte-Pauline Robert de Lézardière. In her *Theory of the Political Laws of the French Monarchy* (1792) Lézardière assembled a vast array of "proofs" to illustrate the first three epochs of the history of France, that is, the Merovingian, Carolingian, and Capetian dynasties. She celebrated the Germanic heritage of the French monarchy and (in a style similar to that of Montesquieu and perhaps of Edmund Burke) its "political constitution."[36] She made extensive use not only of standard medieval authors but also of modern collections of critical scholarship, including Bouquet's *Recueil;* and she took to task Moreau especially because of his denial of the originally elective character of the Frankish monarchy. Seldom has a book been more unfortunately timed, stillborn as it was in the first year of the French Republic. However, a half-century and two revolutions later it received new life during the constitutional monarchy of July, when Guizot had it republished. It is a nice symbol of the paradoxical combination of the political rupture and social continuity which characterized the inter-revolutionary period of modern European history.

Historicism was associated with the historical schools, and so with other disciplines of law, language, and economics; but it was also tied to the old tradition of the *ars historica*, Germanized as *Historik;* and indeed Horst Blanke, endorsed by Jörn Rüsen, would enclose both within a Kuhnian paradigm.[37] The standard expression of this historiographical model was the handbook of Eduard Bernheim, published first in 1889, which hearkened back to earlier works in this genre, including Droysen, Chladenius, Köhler, Vossius, and Bodin; but he was also immersed in the contemporary literature of philosophy, the natural and human sciences — Windelband, Rickert, Simmel, Durkheim, Croce, Berr, Flint — and so-called cultural history, represented especially by Karl Lamprecht. Bernheim recognized three stages of historical science: narrative, or "referring," which included myth, inscriptions, and memorials, and was represented by the Greek *logographoi* and Herodotus; "pragmatic" history, which had to do with political utility and civic life, and was represented by Polybius, Thucydides, and Tacitus; and "genetic," or developmental, history, which introduced selection and criticism of sources, organic ordering of materials, and philosophical reflection — *Historik*, and problems of geographical and chronological division.[38] The question of "periodization" (*Periodisierung*) had progressed from the Four World Monarchies concept to the ancient-medieval-modern convention fixed by Conrad Cellarius in the seventeenth century; but it had become more complex, especially with the addition of a "prehistorical" (*prähistorisch*) stage.

This "encyclopedic" genre, in the tradition of Boeckh and Droysen, also opened up questions of "method" (in a modern, scientific, and not pedagogical, Bodinian sense) and the relation of history to other sciences — philology, politics, science, art, anthropology, ethnography, etc. These contacts had enriched history, and historical method, drawing on philological "inner" and "outer" criticism, was itself a protection against skepticism and the "hypercritical panic" that had seized some extreme practitioners of *Heuristik* and *Quellenkritik;* but historical methods had not expanded it to the extent that made "universal history" really possible. History could be objective as well as subjective — as represented respectively by Ranke's first great work on the Roman and German peoples and Schlosser's study of the eighteenth century, both appearing in 1825 — but it could not reach beyond the particular cultural circle of the inquiring and interpreting historian.[39] Even Mommsen, speaking of scientific objectivity, added that this was an "ideal goal which every scientist sought but never reached or could reach."[40] Within those limits, however, scholars could move toward "comparative history" and the philosophy of history in a modern sense, though with awareness of providentialist precedents and "prototypes" in Augustine and Otto of Freising as well as Voltaire, Condorcet, Schlegel, Hegel, Marx, and many others.

For this consciousness of intellectual ancestors was also part of *Historik* and *Historismus,* and indeed another byproduct of the upsurge of historical scholarship since the later eighteenth century was the blossoming of the history of history.[41] The genre of *Historiographiegeschichte,* with roots in the old tradition of *historia literaria,* was promoted by the work of Wachle, Lorenz, Horawitz, Waitz, and especially Francis X. von Wegele, whose massive survey of the predecessors of the master historians of his generation — the "brave men before Agamemnon," as Acton called them — and the "founding of the German science of history" was published in 1885, four years before Bernheim's handbook appeared. A great trinity of factors underlay this great canon, he concluded: "Science, humanity, German Nationality."[42] What the historical schools did was to shift emphasis from the nation to the people, from politics to institutions.

The Germanic Constitution

The question of origins continued to be pursued in the nineteenth century, although along rather different lines. Historians of the school and the age of Ranke were divided between the demands of the contemporary and the lure of antiquity, but their national sentiments colored their work in both areas, and their attitudes were shaped as well by the sources, assumptions, and arguments of the historical school. In general the concern of national historians was to defend the German character — and the German "constitution," understood in a social as well as a political sense — from charges of barbarism, drawing on the accounts of Caesar and especially Tacitus, reinforced by modern scholarship and conjectures. This led to a renewal of the old battles between Romanists and Germanists, traceable back to the disputes between medieval and Renaissance jurists and historians, about the provenance of European society, institutions, and culture more generally.[43]

The researches of Germans into their own antiquity began essentially with the rediscovery of Tacitus's *Germania* in the fifteenth century and the massive commentary inspired and provoked by that classical text of anticlassicism, although some themes could be taken as well from barbarian laws and medieval chronicles.[44] For Tacitus and the Tacitists the ancient *Germani* displayed a variety of features, mostly positive (aside from a tendency to violence and drink): racial and moral purity, piety and integrity, constancy and fortitude, opposition to usury, natural nobility, and especially a love of liberty. These features, or topoi, carried over into the writings of German (and sometimes of French and English) historians for the next four centuries, from Andreas Althamer and Beatus Rhenanus to Sybel and Treitschke. In the search for Germanic origins Tacitus (and to some extent Caesar) marked ground zero of the national story, at least before the sciences of linguistics and archeology found access into the new underground territory which nineteenth-century scholars began to call "prehistory" (*Vorgeschichte*).

The question of origins — origins of humanity, civilization, agriculture, property, etc. — had fascinated eighteenth-century scholars, but they tended to approach such matters in conjectural ways, that is, in terms of the emergence from a state of nature, beginnings of speech, first occupancy, and even social contract. Increasingly, however, empirical history was brought into play, especially in Germany, as in the case of Justus Möser, who investigated the Westphalian peasantry and projected their customs back into earlier times.[45] Möser tried, as Meinecke put it, to read the effaced writing of the past in the palimpsest of the present.[46] The historical school reinforced this line of inquiry and, in reaction to revolutionary and "philosophical" ideas, emphasized social forces above individual actions and underlying continuities above political events, turning, within the framework of historicism, from politics to laws and customs to determine national character and its transformations over the centuries.

According to Möser, agrarian history began with individual homesteads (*Einzelhöfe*) that marked a golden age of freeholders transformed later into communal settlements, that is, the Mark-system (*Markgenossenschaft*), which seemed to be referred to in Caesar and Tacitus. The confusion between social and legal history was as influential as it was objectionable to later scholars. As Alfons Dopsch summed it up, "Thus the fundamental observations which J. Möser had drawn from nature itself were reshaped by legal arguments into a Mark-association theory, which was something quite different."[47] Möser's views were continued by later scholars, especially Karl Friedrich Eichhorn, whose seminal study of the legal history of Germany (first edition 1808) likewise opened the discussion of Caesar's and Tacitus's impressions of the barbarian tribes and traced the primitive constitution (*aelteste Verfassung*) of the German *Volk* and its persistence into modern times. At first sight the Germans were in a period of transition between a nomadic and a settled, agrarian society, between war and peace, and the essential question was that of their "constitution," that is, not just the state, which came in a much later stage of development, but also family, kindred, lifestyle, and primitive forms of social organization. Differences arose about the cultural level of the "barbarians," and Tacitus offered opinions on both sides of the debate. Were the Germans in general wild, violent, and disorganized, as classical scholars like Niebuhr tended to infer? Or were they superior in their simplicity, liberty, and moral character, as Tacitus suggested?

For Eichhorn, German "constitutional history" began with the social condition of these tribes, for only with the Frankish monarchy did something like a state appear. Drawing on older scholarship, including Montesquieu, Macou, Adelung, and Möser, he rejected a philosophical state of nature, arguing that during the "so-called wandering of the people" (*sogenannte Völkerwanderung*) — in fact they were pressured by tribes further east — the early Germans brought with them a collective form of social organization, which was the famous Mark (*Markgenossen*). With Möser he agreed that this was based on individual holdings and that survivals could be found in modern Germany. Out of this first Mark constitution (*Markverfassung*), defined so as to exclude nonparticipants (*Ausmärker*), developed the larger collectivities, including the *Gau* and its formal organization (*Gaugemeinde*), which Tacitus called *concilium* and which was the first political constitution of the *Volk*. After this fairly schematic analysis and a discussion of the relations between the Germans and the Romans, Eichhorn proceeded according to the Roman legal system comprising the main rubrics of private law, including persons, family, property, and other features of civil society.

In the next generation Germanism became the reigning dogma in France and England as well as Germany, Tacitus the tutelary founding author, and Jakob Grimm the modern champion. Of many lesser-known examples, one is Davoud-Oghlou's study, published in French in Berlin and dedicated to Grimm, of the legislation of the ancient Germans. What he offered was a survey, based on early Germanic laws but not Carolingian capitularies, of the "purely German" legislation of eleven of the Germanic tribes, based on the argument that these laws reached into high antiquity and were preserved in (runic) writing that did not require formulation in the Latin language. Indeed German was ill suited to the formalism of Roman law and traced its own trajectory from earliest times.[48]

The major champion of the Germanist thesis at this time was Georg Ludwig von Maurer, professor of law at the University of Munich and later Göttingen and Bavarian statesman. Maurer pursued this search for the continuity of social forms, following the lead of Eichhorn and Savigny, but Maurer rejected Möser's view and settled upon the Mark as the original form of Germanic settlement succeeding the nomadic period of barbarian invasions; and he posited instead original cultivation by families or communal brotherhoods and associations (*Freundschaften* and *Genossenschaften*), each occupying a bounded district called a *Mark*.[49] The communal organization, the *Markgenossenschaft*, which was social and economic rather than political in character and had nothing in common with the Roman corporation, was from the beginning the form displayed by the first settlements of the German tribes; and it was extended also to villages, manors, churches, and provinces in later times. "Constitutional history" treated not only the state but also the ways in which a people was tied to the land (*Grund und Boden*), and it was the Germanic Mark, not Roman forms, that linked the Germanic tribes and families (*Stämme* and *Geschlechter*) to the earliest agrarian cultivation. The concept and terminology of the *Markgenossen* appeared especially in the legal records of the *Weistümer*, which Jakob Grimm had been collecting, and survivals could be detected even in Maurer's day in parts of Denmark.[50] The collective form of the Mark was attached not only to the *Land* but also to manors, villages, and cities, and not until later was it associated in legal terms with the Roman corporation. For Maurer, moreover, the Mark system was virtually universal, leaving traces in Japan, China, and Mexico as well as western and eastern Europe.

The second half of the nineteenth century was the heyday of Mark-theory in Europe as applied not only to Germanic but also to "Indo-Germanic" traditions. The Romantic proposition that, in contrast to Rome, German society was based on communal possession was embraced by Marx and Engels as evidence of primitive communism, though for purposes of invidious contrast rather than national pride. "It is necessary to contrast the misery of the agricultural labourers of the present time and the mortgage-servitude of the small peasants," Engels wrote, "with the old common property of all free men in what was then in truth their 'fatherland,' the free common possession by all by inheritance."[51] The notion was taken over by English historians, including Kemble and, in a more restricted and hypothetical way, by Stubbs, as the basis of the "primitive polity" of Anglo-Saxon England, if not of later constitutional principles.[52]

In 1847 Sybel made his own contribution to these conjectural and controversial historical inquiries, still relying mainly on the authority of classical authors and of Möser, Eichhorn, and Grimm, which assigned "the most ancient division of people first to the association of the Mark, next to the higher organization of the Gau, and then to territorial districts."[53] The Mark was bound to have the deepest influence not only on divisions of the land but also on relations within the family and on private and public matters. The German Mark, like German gods and kings, was aboriginal, but there were differences as well as continuities. According to Sybel, the earliest representatives of "our people" did not possess culture but only had the capacity to develop culture; and he inferred that the barbarians derived their institutional and political arrangements mainly from the Romans.

Sybel's friend Georg Waitz had a higher opinion of the cultural level of the ancient Germans, and he devoted his life to an enormously scholarly but also essentialist "constitutional history," which traced the social and institutional continuities of German society over several centuries. Waitz's book, as an American admirer wrote, "records every scrap of knowledge in regard to it which the world possesses."[54] Waitz's constitutional history of Germany (1855), dedicated to Ranke, was a counterpart to Bishop Stubbs's narrative of English constitutional history and followed the path opened up by Eichhorn and Grimm in seeking the roots of Germanic customs, legal institutions, and political life. He offered a systematic analysis of the German constitution from its barbaric roots to its flowering in the age of Bismarck.

Like Möser, Eichhorn, and other predecessors, Waitz relied heavily on the testimony and interpretations of Tacitus and presumptions of social continuity, supported however by the massive scholarship of his generation, including the *Monumenta Germanica Historica,* on which he also worked. He opposed the Romanist bias of classical historians such as Niebuhr, who regarded the early Germans as "uncultivated peasants" (*unkultivirte Landleute*), and sketched a rich portrait of national character, family life, free institutions, and inclinations toward local associations, meaning especially the Mark in its various forms, class divisions, and military and political leadership. "The state is not a natural creation, not an invention, not a machine," Dahlmann wrote in 1835. "The state is primordial. The family is the primitive state."[55] As Waitz argued, "The nation and the state grow out of the family"; and with a wealth of reference (but heavy reliance on Tacitus) he followed this growth through arrangements of property, estates, social groupings, princes, kingship, and other steps on the way to nationality.[56] As for nationality, this too displayed a complex developmental pattern, "The German people, as it entered into history, enjoyed a juridical and political order, in which were displayed its higher moral dispositions, which could in the same way be developed further, as foreign elements were adopted and developed to accommodate the cultural world of antiquity, and so to begin a new period of history, in which it came to know its transformed meaning but in which its old principles were preserved and from which a diverse and rich life would emerge."[57]

A more limited phase of the German national story was told by Giesebrecht, a Prussian even though he taught at the Catholic University of Munich and was fairly moderate in his views. In his popular *History of the German Imperial Age* (1855–88) he sought signs of national character in the opposition between Franks and Romans in the Carolingian period. "It has often been noted," he wrote, "that only through constant foreign pressure on us Germans arose the need to bring national unity to consciousness."[58] The original "wars of liberation" (*Freiheitskriege*) of the Germans were directed against the world empire of Rome, and the final triumph came with the founding of the "Holy Roman Empire of the German Nation." For Giesebrecht the origins of "our national life" (*unseres deutschen Volksleben*) lay in the tenth century; and what remained was the diffuse story of its institutional expression through the Holy Roman Empire of the German Nation.

On one point many Germans and French historians, sharing a common institutional heritage from Merovingia and Carolingian times, could agree. Waitz, Droysen, Heinrich Brunner, Henri Martin, Ferdinand Lot, and others saw, in the seminal act of the Treaty of Verdun in 843, which divided Charlemagne's territories into three parts, including the German Empire and French kingdom, the origin of their respective national traditions. In Germany in 1843 and again in 1943 the thousandth and eleven-hundredth anniversaries of this act were celebrated in Germany, reinforcing the nationalist myths and legal fictions which nineteenth-century historians had inherited — for the most part uncritically — from their historiographical and juridical predecessors.[59]

In the later Middle Ages the national story moved into a conflict between Empire and territorial states, and the essential question, as in the nineteenth century, revolved around the question of "national" leadership. The question was the subject of a polemical exchange between Sybel and Ficker in the years between 1859 and 1862 over the significance of the old thousand-(and six)-year Empire. In a contribution to a volume honoring King Max II of Bavaria, Sybel celebrated the "new future" of the German nation after the Enlightenment and the French Revolution, on which he published a detailed study

(1853–58); and he condemned the "false path" to national unity taken by the medieval empire, including a long series of Italian misadventures, which earlier historians like Stenzel and Raumer had applauded. The Empire, like its modern descendent, not only lacked a "national base" but it was "half-spiritual," referring to the dependency on the Roman Church. It was clear to readers that Sybel wrote out of a Prussian — *kleindeutsch* — commitment; and his anti-Romanism, which anticipated Bismarck's *Kulturkampf*, further undermined his impartiality.[60] Privately, indeed, he favored a "war for healthy, just German purposes."[61]

The imperial case was presented at some length two years later by Ficker, an Austrian historian, who criticized Sybel's unscrupulous "Borussianism" of the Prussian-led unification movement and opposed to it the *grossdeutsch* — and Catholic — line, traceable to Leibniz and represented by such contemporary scholars as A. F. Gfrörer, J. F. Böhmer, F. E. Hurter, Döllinger, Johannes Janssen, and later Ludwig Pastor. Ficker's aim was to counter the Borussianism of the unification movement of that period.[62] However, Ficker also deplored the "unhistorical" character of this position, taking the line of Sybel's *Doktorvater* Ranke and arguing that historical facts (*geschichtliche Dinge*) were not to be measured by contemporary views (*von modernen Anschauungen*). Nor were any of the notions expressed by Sybel to be found in the medieval sources. In a review of this exchange, Georg Waitz, though he disagreed with Ficker's view of imperial history, agreed that Sybel had undermined scientific history by his politics and had compromised his politics by placing them above principle and judging everything by the consequences. Not even Gibbon and Schlosser had been so "teleological" and so "subjective."[63] For Waitz the old Empire had nothing to do with the Prussian-Austrian competition of the nineteenth century, and the science of history had nothing to do with contemporary political problems and goals. Romanist interpretations, encouraged by Savigny's great history of Roman law in the Middle Ages, presented an obstacle to Germanist enthusiasm. This obstacle was reinforced by the work of Paul Roth, beginning especially with his history of the institution of the benefice in 1850, which criticized the Germanist arguments of French and German historians from Dubos, Lézardière, and Guizot to Eichhorn and Maurer, and emphasized Roman influence in the foundations of feudalism, which was tied to the distribution of benefices in the Frankish monarchy.[64] The Merovingian state itself had Roman roots, and the allod continued to be part of law despite the appearance of feudal relationships, in which, through vassalage, freemen came under the control of seigneurs. This line of argument was furthered by the anti-Germanist work of Fustel de Coulanges.

One conciliatory and even ecumenical thesis was propounded by Ernest

Theodor Gaupp, whose study of German settlements in the Roman provinces was dedicated to the growing unity of Europe and the Romano-German family produced by the Middle Ages.[65] For him, Ranke's "Roman and Teuton nations" were determining the fate of world civilization. Not only had modern Roman law evolved in Germany, whose story had been told by Savigny, but the alliance between German and French scholars reinforced this convergence, in which "Germans and Romans have become the carriers of the new culture." Gaupp celebrated the colonial expansion of European culture opened up by the discovery of the New World. He invoked the description of the beautiful climes of Asia Minor by the *Altvater* of history, Herodotus, and wondered why they might not also be colonized by present-day Romans and Germans. "Why should we not hope that it belongs to the spirit of recent times to do what the feudalism of the twelfth and thirteenth centuries could not do on these coasts and on these islands, which is through colonization to connect them with the western life of Europe?"

In the nineteenth century German scholars sought continuity in their national tradition not only in the spirit and character of the people but also in the persistence of institutions, and here they were divided, as indeed they had been for centuries, between the poles of Romanism and Germanism — *Juristenrecht* and *Volksrecht*. At these extremes Roman law indicated absolute government, private property, paternal power, cities, revolutionary legislation, and more recently the Napoleonic Code, while Germanism suggested a free and communal rural society under popular government and native customs. This rather vague duality underlay several of the scholarly quarrels of the century, including that between Georg Waitz and Paul Roth over the origin and nature of feudalism; that between Sybel and Ficker over the significance of the Empire for German nationality; and that between Georg von Maurer and Fustel de Coulanges over the Mark system and the question of private property.[66]

The corporatist ideas of German scholars were extended by Otto von Gierke into larger social theorizing in his monumental history of *Genossenschaftsrecht*, which imputed communal organization to Germanic social traditions, though such local customs were eventually destroyed by ideas of sovereignty.[67] Although without adding much evidence, he gave a more theoretical and juridical formulation to these Germanist-organicist ideas of folk associations and fellowships, following the development through five periods from social to political organizations. The first period, down to Charlemagne, was one of popular freedom, followed by the emergence of patrimonial and feudal structures, and then of higher forms of organization and, with the help of Roman law, territorial sovereignty, to be joined with modern forms of free association. Gierke extrapolated from the Mark to a theory of national and indeed world history that deserves comparison with that of Hegel, except that Gierke joined to the idea of freedom that of community — history itself being a battle between these principles. "As the progress of world history unfolds inexorably," he wrote, "there rises the unending arch of the noble edifice of those organic associations which, in ever greater and increasingly broad spheres, lend external form and efficacy to the coherence of all human existence and to unity in all its varied complexity."

The new field of economic history represented an expansion, or even a fulfillment, of old-fashioned legal and institutional history. Though "not yet written," as Karl Inama-Sternegg wrote in 1879, it was more fundamental than other kinds of historical study. "Social economy [*Volkswirtschaft*] is the Summa of the life activities of peoples," he wrote, "through which the idea of material well-being can be realized."[68] It was a higher form of the Darwinian "struggle for existence" (*Kampf um das Dasein*) underlying the development — not the political but the "inner development" — of a people. Whence a new specialty, since "as legal history must be written by jurists, so economic history must be the charge of political economists" (*Nationalökonomen*); and in the next century indeed economic history became a professional field associated both with the academic study of history and the formation of policy.

Burckhardt and Cultural History

Jacob Burckhardt was essentially an amateur historian even though he taught history at a university, wrote books, and was a master of source selection and criticism. Though a historian should have a specialty, he should also be "an amateur at as many points as possible, privately at any rate, for increase of his own knowledge and the enrichment of his possible standpoints."[69] Burckhardt had studied theology at the University of Basel and history at Berlin with Boeckh, Grimm, Droysen, and Ranke; but contact with Franz Kugler, his real mentor (whose course he took in preference to that of Ranke, scheduled at the same hour), turned his interests to art history not only because of its subject matter but also because of its value as a model of historical research and expression.[70] Vaspasiano's lives of the artists, which he read in Rome in 1847, was his main source of inspiration. As usual, however, books were not his only teachers. While studying in Paris his habit was to spend three hours in the Bibliothèque Nationale and the rest of the time exploring the city, its cafés and its museums.[71] A skilled draftsman, he recorded his impressions, especially on his Italian tours.

Burckhardt's appointment as professor of art history in Zurich was a great "turning point" in his life.[72] One result was his choice of cultural history over the scientific variety associated not only with the scientistic claims of the professionals but also with the concerns of the great powers of the later nineteenth century; another was his later refusal to move from Basel to Berlin as the successor to Ranke. Two of his first books were devoted to art history, but all of his works were in the mode of impressionistic portrayal and interpretation of culture, illustrating general themes with striking examples and anecdotes. This was the case with his early study of the age of Constantine, which focused on the transition from pagan antiquity to Christian modernity, and with his great portrait of civilization (*Kultur*) in the Italian Renaissance as well as his posthumously published lectures on Greek culture. Seeing "the sudden devaluation of all mere 'events' in history" in 1870 — for him Rousseau's *Social Contract* was a greater "event" than the Seven Years' War[73] — he decided that "from now on I shall emphasize only cultural history, and retain nothing but the indispensable external scaffolding."[74]

Beginning his career in journalism, Burckhardt wrote voluminously and apparently with literary ambitions; but in his chosen line of scholarship he preferred reading and lecturing to writing and publishing. He also preferred the light touch in historical narrative to the heavy treatises of his contemporaries, especially in Germany. "History is actually the most unscientific of all the sciences."[75] Without the "shining example" of the theologian and historian Heinrich Schreiber, Burckhardt wrote in 1839, "it probably would not have occurred to me to seek my vocation in the study of history, although very early on I was determined never to lose sight of history my whole life long."[76] Yet it was immersion in the sources and teaching that absorbed him; and in 1863, four years after the success of his *Civilization of the Renaissance in Italy*, he wrote, "I now consider my literary career as finally closed, and feel much better and more content in reading sources, as I only study and make notes for teaching and not possible book-making."[77] Nor did he try to keep up on recent historical literature.

For Burckhardt the key to historical understanding was not the "bogus objectivity" of Ranke and company but rather the subjectivity which arose in the Renaissance and Reformation. He rejected the egoism which accompanied the incessant emphasis on the "We" of modern times and the "utterly ridiculous self-seeking [which] first regards those times as happy which are in some ways akin to our nature."[78] Yet Burckhardt himself, very much like Voltaire, looked back with affection on certain ages of high culture, especially of the Greek "enlightenment," of early Christianity, and of the Italian Renaissance. Moreover, he was extraordinarily sensitive to the problem of the "point of view," which had been incorporated into the art of history in the eighteenth century and which Burckhardt assumed in his own aesthetic-historical views, carried over from his art-historical studies. Of Hamlet, he noted, "every reader sees a different picture of it, and a new one at each reading."[79] So it was also with historical periods. He admitted to "a great deal of subjectivity in the selection of material" for his Greek cultural history;[80] and at the outset of his study of the Renaissance in Italy he wrote: "To each eye, perhaps, the outlines of a given civilization presents a different picture, [so that] it is unavoidable that individual judgment and feeling should tell every moment both on the writer and on the reader."[81] The result was a principle, or premise, of relativism that applied to the study of history itself, since "each age has a new and different way of looking at the more remote periods of the past."[82]

In his early years Burckhardt had been attracted to the "philosophy of history," especially that of Droysen, so popular in the early nineteenth century; but he turned against this even more sharply than against Ranke. He was not attracted by the philosophical fashions of Hegel and Schelling; and he never really appreciated even the often antiphilosophical declarations of his colleague and neighbor Nietzsche.[83] "I have never, my whole life long," he wrote in 1886, "been philosophically minded."[84] The philosophy of history was an illusion, "a centaur, a contradiction in terms."[85] As he noted already in 1842, "History, to me, is always poetry for the greater part."[86] History did not speak directly to the modern condition; for "even to the scholar and the thinker, the past, in its own utterance, is at first always alien, and its acquisition arduous."[87] Even humor — Aristophanes, Rabelais, Cervantes — may seem tedious because they did not write for the modern reader. For such reasons Burckhardt's own age, especially in America, was profoundly unhistorical. Americans have largely "foregone history . . . and wish to share in the enjoyment of art and poetry merely as forms of luxury."[88]

Between 1830 and 1848 Europe was deluded into believing that history developed toward happiness: "For we judge everything by that standard of security without which *we* could no longer exist." Burckhardt did not himself share this idea of progress nor in "the arrogant belief in the moral superiority of the present." This was a fundamental violation of historical understanding. "Morality as a power . . . stands no higher, nor is there more of it, than in so-called barbarous times."[89] Nor did modern culture change this rule. "Who are we anyway to demand of Luther and the other reformers that they should have carried out *our* programs?"[90] The fact that Lutheran ideals were wedded to the process of state-building did not change the situation. On the contrary, Burckhardt argued, "It is a ridiculous assumption that power which otherwise, in all of world history, makes men neither particularly bad nor particularly good, should have accomplished this miracle with the German governments of the sixteenth century just because they were Protestant."[91]

What characterized modernity for Burckhardt was money-making and power politics. "The chief creation of more recent history," he wrote, "is the Great Power, the life form of the most significant peoples."[92] His reaction to the emergence of the German Empire in 1870 was to reject even more forcefully the subsequent obsession with money-making and especially the focus on the power and action of states fashionable among the learned professionals — *Viri eruditissimi,* he called them.[93] "Gentlemen," he recalled Ranke's saying in 1840, "nations are God's thoughts!" But states, allegedly the highest form of nationality, were always founded in force ("force always comes first") and were thereafter preserved by power, which "is in itself evil."[94] Nor has history, "the breach with nature caused by the awakening of consciousness,"[95] changed this amoral foundation of human destiny. Not progress but strife is the pattern of history, "for the life of the West *is* struggle."[96]

Burckhardt was not attracted by the Romantic search for origins, neither "the hypothetical original state of all mankind," such as imagined by Lucretius, nor the "'Alt Germania' nonsense" of medievalists.[97] Yet he insisted on "the intellectual necessity of studying ancient history," on the grounds that "we can never cut ourselves off from antiquity unless we intend to revert to barbarism."[98] Nor can modern times be understood apart from antiquity, which at once "gives rise to the concept of the state" (the *polis*) and is "the birthplace of our religions" and of the most permanent elements of our culture, including individualism. Although the Greeks had a deeply tragic history, our debts to them are incalculable, for "we see with their eyes and use their phrases when we speak."[99]

Three phases of Greek culture can be identified: "that of Homer and Hesiod, that of the time of the nation's greatness, and lastly that attained by the reflections of the philosophers" — the heroic and agonal ages and the fifth-century Enlightenment.[100] Each of these intellectual epochs Burckhardt describes in terms of general characteristics inferred from literature and art. Even the historical writers he treats in terms less of the facts alleged than of the underlying mental presuppositions. "No matter whether it really happened" wrote Burckhardt in a nice inversion of Ranke's famous formula, "they convey a knowledge of the Greeks and their perception of the external world as well as their inner habits of thought."[101] In these terms Burckhardt surveyed, through a gallery of impressionistic paintings, the leading traits of Greek life from the age of Homeric myth to the heyday of the polis and the period of Hellenistic decadence. He portrayed the lights and darks, the ups and downs, of social life (pessimism, suicide, vengeance, superstition, deceitfulness) as well as the chief traits of Greek character (individualism, competitiveness, love of fame, heroism, liberty). Again mere "events" were downplayed, as the

Greeks came to interpret their own disasters, mankind (according to Alcinous in the *Odyssey*) being doomed to ruin by the gods, "so that all this should be a *song for future generations.*"[102] And Burckhardt was himself more concerned with the song than with the underlying actions.

In *The Age of Constantine the Great* Burckhardt again avoided *l'histoire événementielle* for a highly selective and "integrated description, from the viewpoint of cultural history," of this important transition period that introduced the earliest stage of modern history. With barbarians "crashing in . . . from several directions" and republican memories and terms on the decline, the late Roman Empire was marked by militarism, periodic revolution, and extremes of good and evil leadership, including "a true Saint Louis of antiquity," Alexander Severus.[103] Despite what Gibbon had said, this was a time not of "enlightenment" but of superstition, especially in its extreme Neoplatonic incarnation, and "theocracy," the intermingling of gods, as well as their "demonization." In a world of magic it was hopeless to inquire into "objective actualities," as pagans, Jews, and Christians alike believed in spirits and an accessible realm of the dead. Nor, behind new religious forms, was myth overcome. Among many others the "great goddess," Mother of Life, and Mithras, the sun god — Constantine's *Sol Invictus* — reappeared in many local guises.[104] The "senescence of ancient life" was covered by the "cloud of delusion" of mystery religions and the imperial ambition which discredited Constantine (who "had no real theological convictions"), while it benefitted the new religion superseding decadent paganism.[105] It is against this colorful and confusing background, in which "Christianity was bound to conquer in the end because it provided answers that were incomparably simpler," that modern history had to be understood.[106]

Like Ranke, Burckhardt was attracted in his major works to the beginning of modern times, but from a wholly different perspective. While Ranke focused on the emergence of the "great powers" from the late fifteenth century, Burckhardt took a broader view of the cultural background in Italy, which in political terms was a victim of the national power politics that defined the modern world but which socially, intellectually, and artistically represented the heights of human creativity from the fourteenth to the sixteenth century. Both historians felt the imprint of Machiavelli; but while Ranke viewed the state and its military actions as expressions of power, Burckhardt looked at both as "works of art," Italian style. Long before the invasions of Italy by Charles VIII and Louis XII, northern rulers, and especially German Emperors, had been drawn to the peninsula; and indeed it was there that Frederick II, "the first ruler of the modern type who sat upon a throne," established his centralized government and modern system of administration and taxation.[107]

Burckhardt's view of the Renaissance was born of his art-historical studies and reading of the biographies of Vespasiano da Bisticci in Rome in 1847, but it was just after his Basel appointment that he began to take notes on "Renaissance-Renaître: The revival of a fallen world of civilization or at least its forms."[108] The term "renaissance," originally applied to the revival of antiquity, was "one-sidedly chosen as a name to sum up the whole period" from the fourteenth to the sixteenth century. Beyond the fascination with Roman ruins, the rise of humanism, the study of the classics, and efforts to reform education on the basis of the liberal arts, this period had other defining features, which Burckhardt laid out with characteristic impressionistic boldness. Most important was the rise of individualism and the "subjective side" of humanity, beginning with Dante and based on the desire for glory (*fama*) — and illustrated earlier by the careers of Renaissance despots. Related to this was the "discovery of the world and of man," which emphasized interests in the natural environment and the physical side of humanity expressed in literature and the visual arts. A section on "society and festivals" takes up matters of popular culture, including family life, etiquette, the place of women, and entertainment (music, carnivals, triumphs, etc.). Finally, Burckhardt surveys morality and religious life in the age of Luther and, moreover, of both the survival of ancient superstition and the rise of secular doubt. A portrait, from Burckhardt's eccentric eye, as far as can be imagined from Ranke's political narrative, but it has left an indelible imprint on our understanding of the crucial period of European modernity.

If Burckhardt rejected the "philosophy of history," he did not in his reflections avoid questions of larger metahistorical patterns in Western history. In 1868 he gave introductory lectures on the study of history in which he reduced the large-scale changes in the European past to the interaction between three powers, treating the permutations and combinations of the state, religion, and culture — each as being determined by the other two. The state is the product neither of a contract (Rousseau) nor of purely racial origins but of a violent fusion, criminal perhaps but later developing "a kind of justice and morality."[109] Religions are "the expression of human nature's eternal and indestructible metaphysical need," established by individual leaders followed by a priesthood. "Culture may be defined as the sum total of those mental developments which take place spontaneously and lay no claims to universal or compulsive authority."[110] It is disseminated by the "miracle of mind" that is speech, and in the nineteenth century it came "into possession of the traditions of all times, peoples and cultures, while the literature of our age is a world literature."[111]

As for narratives concerning historical change, Burckhardt did not venture far beyond conventions defined by these three powers and the subordinate rubrics of "crisis" and "great men." Again, he did not venture into prehistory or even the crises underlying the barbarian invasions.[112] Wars represented a type of crisis, destructive of course but also, periodically, a sort of natural condition that acted as a remedy for decadence. The famous Polybian cycle of governments — monarchy, aristocracy, democracy, despotism — also described crises, social as well as political. Some crises, such as the fall of the Roman Empire, seemed to Burckhardt unavoidable, while others, including the Reformation and the French Revolution, could have been checked or mitigated. As for crises in his own day, Burckhardt attributed them mainly "to the influence of the press and of commerce."[113] In the uneven process of history "great men" — discoverers, rulers, artists, even historians — achieve their stature usually in cultural terms, although sometimes history (as in the case of Alexander or Napoleon) seems to be concentrated on a single figure, "who is then obeyed by the world": "their relationship to their time is a *hieros gamos* ('a sacred marriage') . . . , consummated in times of terror."[114] Rarest of all, Burckhardt added, is "greatness of soul," but all of these were lacking in Burckhardt's age, although crises — the Franco-Prussian war in particular — were still in evidence. At least he had realized one dream of his youth: "We may all perish," as he wrote in 1846, "but at least I want to discover the interest for which I am to perish, namely, the culture of old Europe."[115]

French Visions

There is therefore a revolution to be mounted in history analogous to that pursued in the political sphere.

— *Louis Bourdeau*

Public History

During the Second Empire and the Third Republic French historiography became increasingly involved with the state, which was not only its chief subject but also its main supporter and guide.[1] Though some were still statesmen, historians were for the most part no longer men of letters, critics, or journalists; they were pedagogues and professors, with responsibilities toward their political patron. They criticized their predecessors and one another, but they approached the political heritage of their nation with respect and veneration. They might indeed pass moral judgments on individual kings and public figures but not, for the most part, on the institutional vehicles of political decision and action. The king and his officers, churchmen, judges, military men, tax-collectors, the Estates General, all were described in terms of the official records left in the archives, and other kinds of sources, literary and artistic, served as background and context for matters of national and public import. The study of history in nineteenth-century France was pursued along several tracks: low-level textbooks for the schools and university, grand and detailed narratives in the styles of Anquetil and, less derivatively, Sismondi, and collections and studies of documentary sources — not only chronicles but also charters and the records of administration and justice — continuing the erudite publications of the Old Regime. To the revived *Histoire Littéraire de la France,* founded by the Maurists in 1733 and taken up again in 1807, the *Recueil des historiens des Gaules et de la France,* begun by Dom Bouquet in 1738 and continued by the Académie des Inscriptions in 1840, and the *Ordonnances des rois de France,* in which Bréquigny's great *Table chronologique* (1769) was taken up by J. M. Pardessus (1841), were added, among others, Petitot's *Collection complète des mémoires* (1819–29, 79 vols.), Buchon's *Collection des chroniques nationales* (1826–28, 47 vols.), Michaud and Poujoulat's *Nouvelle Collection des mémoires* (1836–54, 32 vols.), Cimber and Danjou's *Archives curieuses de l'histoire de France* (1834–40, 37 vols.), Guizot's *Collection des documents inédits* (1835–1900, 206 vols.), and the *Patrilogiae* (Latin, 1844–64, 221 vols.; Greek, 1857–66, 161 vols.) of J. P. Migne, "God's plagiarist," as Howard Block called him, rivalling those of Muratori, the *Acta Sanctorum,* the *Monumenta Germaniae Historica,* and the *Rolls Series.* The mid-nineteenth century in France was also the great age of inventories, especially of the archives and the Bibliothèque Nationale (including the voluminous work of Leopold Delisle), not to speak of bibliographies and exhaustive footnotes tracing the "literature" of major questions. "The hunt for documents [*la chasse aux documents*] was in effect," wrote Louis Halphen, "the favorite and almost only occupation of the historians of 1830."[2]

Paralleling these monumental productions were dozens, if not hundreds of volumes of textbooks, some illustrated and some in verse or mnemonic — for elementary history depended heavily on memory-training — to indoctrinate the young in the political traditions of the nation. Since the sixteenth century so-called abbreviated histories (*histoires abrégées*) had proliferated in many editions over many years — that of La Ragois (1687–1853) in more than 100 editions, for example; that of Letellier (1811–1850) in at least 28 editions; and that of Saint-Ouen (1830–54) in at least 38.[3] After 1830 the production of textbooks became an industry; and scholars like the Roman historian, Bonapartist, and former student of Michelet (himself the author of one "précis"), Victor Duruy, before he became minister of education under the Second Empire, joined in promoting history among the youth of France — rejecting the fetishism of facts and dates and shifting emphasis, though his own reputation rested on his work in ancient history, to contemporary history. After 1870 the influence, positive as well as negative, of Germany — which had far more teachers and students of history — encouraged further modernization, including the substitution of disputation by dissertation, an effort to emphasize contemporary matters, introduction of the seminar system, and in general, "the birth of historical pedagogy."

There was little contact between these products of low pedagogy and the high erudition of historical science, although late in life (1869) Guizot, joined by his wife, published an eight-volume history of France as told originally to his grandchildren, but supported by references to the scholarly work of himself and others and interspersed with some of his own accumulated wisdom and prejudice. Guizot noted the fable of Trojan origins, which was not only mythical but also historical, in the sense that (citing Fauriel) it was devised in the fifth century "with the idea of popularizing the Frankish kings amongst the Gallo-Roman subjects."[4] In general Guizot preferred the poetry of the people to the records of the court, and he preferred to illustrate French antiquity with "a fragment of an old chronicle" than with a modern description, yet his own attention remained fixed on the modern nation and "government." Guizot repeated the conventional view that as a separate kingdom France was a product of the Treaty of Verdun in 843, although the name "Francia" first appeared on the fourth-century map published by the German humanist Conrad Peutinger (*tabula Peutingeri*), covering various tribes of Franks, or "freemen," all of the German race. After the initiatives of Charlemagne and the feudal chaos of the medieval period, Guizot and his wife settled into a conventional narrative that followed the fortunes of the monarchy reign-by-reign down to the time of his own political emergence and the "unknown future" opened up by the disappointing events of 1848.

Public interest in history was spurred by the growth of provincial and Parisian societies, which included amateur scholars as well as historians and which also promoted such associated fields as geography, ethnography, and archeology. State support increased, especially during the Third Republic, as history continued to be the target of rivalries between the political left and right and between secularists and Catholics. To judge from the quantity of books, histories of the church and of kings and their officers were on the decline, while studies of classes, commerce, industry, and agriculture were on the rise.[5] After 1870, there was a remarkable increase in students and faculty, including professorial chairs, in historical training. As in Germany, history was regarded as a political tool or weapon of the state — monarchy, republic, empire, and republic again — and as Jules Ferry told a group of professors, "God forbid that there should be in your teaching no ideology."[6]

In the promotion of historical studies, Victor Duruy, Michelet's former pupil and Fustel's successor at the Ecole Normale, was a central figure. Duruy was the author of several books on Roman, Greek, and French history on a textbook and a scholarly level. As a student of Michelet, Duruy had dreamed of writing a history of France in eight or ten volumes, but studying the Celtic period led him to the "Roman foundation" and then to Greece.[7] His history of Rome (1843–44), building on Niebuhr, Schwegler, and Arnold, gained him the attention of Louis Napoleon, who appointed him minister of education.[8] During the Second Empire he led the reorganization of education, in which history was given a primary role; and in 1868 he was responsible for the creation of the Ecole des Hautes Etudes, which was intended to bring France up to the scientific standards of Germany. His public career and textbook-writing dissipated his energies, but he continued his scholarly work. During the Third Republic he published the later volumes of his Roman history, which celebrated the imperial tradition and which rivalled Mommsen in popularity. His Greek history followed two lines: socio-political facts and the arena of ideas and art. Both works he published in elaborately illustrated volumes.

The first of Duruy's protégés was Gabriel Monod, who took the advice of Taine to pursue his historical training in Germany, where he studied especially with Waitz in Göttingen and came to admire the German seminar system. Nor did the Franco-Prussian War undermine either his friendship with Waitz or his enthusiasm for German *Geschichtswissenschaft*. Back in France, Monod began his teaching at the Ecole Practique des Hautes Etudes and Ecole des Chartes, where he gave lectures based on Merovingian sources and worked also to modernize — or Germanize — historical studies in terms of both depth of research and breadth of vision.[9] To this end Monod founded, in 1876, the *Revue Historique,* several years after the establishment of the Catholic journal the *Revue des Questions Historiques,* which claimed to pursue "historical truth" but which, alluding in the first issue to Joseph de Maistre and Montalembert as well as Martin and Thierry, seemed to identify this with apologetics for the history of the church.[10] Monod despised this Catholic partisanship and devoted his new journal to educating the public about the national heritage as well as keeping up with proliferating research and professional publication. "The Review will accept only original contributions, based on original sources," he declared in the first issue; yet he hoped to find a reception "not only by all those who make a special study of history but also by all those who are interested in intellectual affairs" — with the aim of contributing to the "unity and moral strength" of the nation. The first article in the review (reprinted a century later) was Monod's critical survey of French historiography from medieval and Renaissance times down to his own day. In 1888 he published a critical listing of French history along the lines of Dahlmann-Waitz's famous bibliography.

A colleague and classmate of Monod was Ernest Lavisse, who also studied with Waitz in Göttingen, although he later confessed that "Michelet was my master."[11] His first work was a study of the origins of the Prussian monarchy and the reasons for its extraordinary military and political success, which he published five years after the disastrous war with France, followed by other works on contemporary Germany and how it evolved out of Prussian political tradition to become a modern state. Lavisse taught at the Ecole Normale and the Sorbonne in the chair formerly held by Guizot. Like Guizot, Michelet, and Duruy, Lavisse was concerned with making the study of history central to public opinion as well as university education. His major influence came in the three great series he edited on ancient, modern, and contemporary history.

Among Lavisse's students were Charles Seignobos and Charles-Victoire Langlois, who both began as medievalists but were less attracted to German-style research than their elders, even though Seignobos studied with Ranke and Sybel in Berlin. They regarded the German "science" of history, especially in the medieval area, as narrow and pedantic. Seignobos, a committed anti-clerical, wrote his doctoral thesis on feudalism in late medieval Burgundy, though he later turned to contemporary history. He taught at the Sorbonne and contributed three volumes on the period 1848–1914 to Lavisse's series. Seignobos defended the old-fashioned, essentially positivist historical methods of French scholars like Lavisse against the new-fangled collective approach of Emile Durkheim and François Simiand, although he wanted to go beyond the narrow legalism of institutional history, and he was critical of the German combination of pretended "science" with political and national bias.[12]

Langlois also made late medieval Burgundy, the paradigm of a failed state, the object of his researches, later the Parlement of Paris and a volume on the last of the Capetians in Lavisse's series. Langlois had a reputation as a strict positivistic documentarian because of both the volume on historical method he wrote with Seignobos and that on the archives he wrote with Henri Stein.[13] Yet he also wrote extensively on medieval literary and cultural history: to give a true picture of contemporary society, he argued, it was necessary to consult newspapers, novels, comedies, caricatures, art, and photography; and to view the Middle Ages fully it was essential to turn to comparable sources, notably the *chansons de geste*. In 1890, with the support of Lavisse, Langlois succeeded Achille Luchaire (himself the successor of Fustel) at the Sorbonne but later took over as director of the National Archives.[14]

Not only textbooks, popular histories, and periodical publications but also the old narrative genre of history carried on this pedagogical task, though on a higher level, most notably by Michelet's efforts to teach the whole people their political and cultural heritage. Down to the time of Ernst Lavisse's series,

Michelet's only rival as the national historian of France was Victor Martin, whose theme likewise was "the progressive development of national unity."[15] He worked in the tradition of Mézeray and Velly, and acknowledged debts to Sismondi, Thierry, Fauriel, but none of his predecessors had, in his opinion, produced anything adequate either in base or in plan despite a "sterile abundance" of footnotes. Only after the Revolution could the design of French history be seen, and this, Martin's narrative, stretching from Caesar to the Constituent Assembly, was intended to display. A member of the "Gallic party," whose historiographical traditions went back to the Renaissance, he summed up his view of the national story in this way:

> Children of the Gauls by birth and character, children of the Romans by education, violently ravished by the mixture of German barbarians, then infused by the vitality of ancient civilization, united by the old alliances with Iberia and Greece, we can today understand that it is not by chance that our Gallic blood has been mixed with that of all the great races of antiquity, which has guided the slow formation of the French people on the Gallic soil set in the middle of Europe, making contact with all peoples. Such was the theatre prepared by Providence for a nation destined to be the European assembly point and the starting point for modern civilization.[16]

Gesta Dei per Francos: France had saved Europe from Islam, crushed the papal theocracy, become the birthplace of Catholicism and philosophy and the cradle of liberty and equality, and now was taking on a new mission for the benefit of European civilization.[17]

Institutional History

So in an age of national zeal, political and institutional historians came to terms with the Old Regime and indeed drew on its accomplishments as a basis for further progress and expansion in the future. Professional historians, though they all celebrated aspects of the national past and the continuity of French society, worked for different goals and according to different lights. In the wake of the great documentary publications and works of erudition modeled on German scholarship, emphasis was increasingly shifted from individual actions — the old notion of history as *res gestae* and the telling thereof — to social patterns and movements, which, given the nature of the sources, meant especially political structure and development. For this is where the modern meaning of history resided. As Sismondi had written, "The study of the development of the character of the institutions of nations is the true philosophy of history."[18]

The "generation of 1820," including Guizot, Thierry, and Mignet, had included institutions in their field of inquiry, especially those associated with feudalism, which, for revolutionaries, had been the repository of all the evil customs and practices of the Old Regime. One early treatment that drew on the new scholarship while still retaining a polemical orientation was that of Mignet, for whom feudalism had legalized private wars and, under cover of hierarchy that subjected men to men and lands to lands, had prepared the way for anarchy.[19] Rejecting the old views of Dubos and Mably, Mignet argued that all the elements of feudalism were present at the founding of the Carolingian monarchy. Nor had feudalism entirely disappeared in the France of the restored monarchy.

In France the influence of the German historical school of law reinforced this emphasis, as did the social and economic questions of the postrevolutionary period, especially those of private property and with labor. Among the pioneering historians of law in France were L. F. J. Laferrière, C. J. B. Giraud, E. R. L. de Laboulaye, and Henri Klimrath, who all applied the views of Savigny to the history of French law. As inspectors-general of legal education Laferrière and Giraud emphasized the importance of law in legal studies. Laferrière argued that French history could not be separated from its Roman legacy, yet also that French law was a unique product of national development.[20] Giraud was an admirer of the "new history" in France but deplored the ignorance shown by Guizot and Thierry of legal history; and while recognizing the value of German scholarship, he pointed to the great native heritage represented by Cujas, Pasquier, Dumoulin, and the parlementary tradition in general.[21] La Boulaye was Savigny's major disciple in France as well as his biographer, though he also lauded France's own historical traditions in legal scholarship (France borrowed from Savigny as Savigny had borrowed from Cujas), and was likewise concerned with the reform of legal education.[22] Klimrath, France's leading Germanist, turned to provincial customs as the most fundamental expression of French character and continuity, but also employed all the resources of modern German and French scholarship.[23] Despite the grand tradition of scholarship going back to the sixteenth century the history of French law remained to be done, he lamented, and despite his preliminary efforts, so it remained at his early death in 1837 at the age of thirty.

Another early example of the turn to institutional history was J. M. Lehuërou, who published two volumes on the institutions of the Merovingians and the Carolingians in 1842 and 1843.[24] Drawing on the recent work of Laboulaye, Giraud, and Laferrière, Lehuërou explored the "great political revolution" of feudalism. He thought that earlier erudition had taken a wrong direction, with the partial exception of Montesquieu, who had — in the face of scholarly opinion — recognized the deep roots of feudal institutions. The study of institutions, he added, should not be carried on in isolation but be integrated with the facts of general history. His purpose was to show:

> that what is called feudalism in the tenth century and following is fundamentally just the simple and natural play of principles and customs by which the German family had been governed from time immemorial beyond the Rhine; that feudal laws were only the continuation or regular development of an order of things before the conquest and that the conquest itself had never been interrupted; that these domestic institutions of the German tribes, when they were still encamped on the other side of the Rhine, can be found at the foundations of the *civil* and *political* institutions which governed Gaul under the first two dynasties; and that under the half-Roman cover of Clovis and Charlemagne were hidden — as a flower in the seed — wholly feudal traditions, form, and institutions.[25]

Lehuërou was concerned with the primitive institution arising not from state action but from family structure and customs before the rise of the Frankish state. Like all recorded barbarian peoples the Germans held possessions, women as well as land, in common; but by the end of the invasions it was clear from the barbarian laws that both the institution of property and ideas of "appropriation" and succession had arisen — although traces of the old communal regime were preserved, as in rights to unclaimed land (*terres vaines et vagues*). These were the years before the Revolutions of 1848 when private property was an inflammatory issue, idealized by liberal scholars and denounced by radicals as the source of class conflict and the Social Question. Siding with the former, Lehuërou represented property as a mark of civilization and a precondition of morality, and he disassociated his historical views from the "theories of modern socialists."[26]

The priority of law and society over politics and war led to more complex and sensitive lines of inquiry and conceptualizing. Feudalism should be considered not merely as an obstacle to state-building but as a factor in the history of landed property. The prime role of the aristocracy was overshadowed by the famous question of the Abbé Siéyès — "What is the Third Estate? — and that question in turn was problematized by the problem of the rest of the "People," especially the "dangerous classes," so that in social history "labor" took its place beside "property" as a central historical (as well as "social") question. Historians had to consider, too, the structure of government, administration, taxation, judicial and ecclesiastical matters, and indeed all the institutions which left traces in archival repositories and which led to historiographical specialties. The shift to social history was especially prominent in the study of the earliest periods and "origins" of French political tradition, but it was pursued as well in the turn to administrative history of the monarchy, as illustrated later by Langlois's history of Philip III (1887) and Luchaire's history of institutions under the first Capetians (1883), tracing the "progress of royal power" over the nation, as well as his posthumous study of social France under Philip Augustus (1909), long before anyone knew of the "social question."

Officially, history was still seen from the top down, and the emphasis was on the process of the advance of the monarchy to political power. In 1847 Dareste de la Chavanne was given a prize by the Académie des Sciences Politiques et Morales for his study of French administration from Philip Augustus to Louis XIV.[27] Like Fustel a generation later, Dareste preferred an analytic to a synthetic (and confused) method, treating in turn the royal council, the Estates General, the nobility, church, universities, municipalities, police, justice, and finance—like many treatises on government in the Old Regime. He drew on manuscript sources, but his was the old story of political centralization emerging out of feudal anarchy. In his later survey of the history of France he placed the story of "national institutions" in a larger framework, making use of modern German scholarship, especially on barbarian society, agreeing with Waitz, for example, about the common institutional heritage of the Franks and other Germanic tribes, much of which was in place by the fifth century, and with Roth in identifying the fief with the Merovingian benefice.[28] Dareste accepted the idea of the *Markgenossenschaft,* which he called *commune,* yet at the same time insisting on the early existence of private (allodial) property.

Dareste's rival for this prize was Adolphe Cheruel, who unfortunately, as a disciple of Michelet, chose a historical and chronological over an analytical approach and so, despite Mignet's support, received only a medal.[29] That same year Cheruel published a dictionary of French institutional history, following the tradition set in the sixteenth century by Pasquier, the Pithous, Loisel, Coquille, and others.[30] The definition of "administration" Cheruel took from Guizot and opposed it sharply to feudalism, which confused sovereignty with property in land. Cheruel divided his story into four parts—the royal struggle against feudalism under the last Capetians (with the help of the bourgeoisie and the "communal revolution"), the victory of the monarchy down to the end of the fifteenth century, administrative organization down to the accession of Louis XIV, and the "triumph" that followed. "In sum," Cheurel wrote, "during the seven centuries following the fall of the Roman Empire France lacked unity: it had received from Rome cities, law, and the principles of regular organization, from Germany the rich seeds of liberty in judgment and liberty in political assemblies, and from Christianity the end of slavery, peace between hostile races, and moral purity in a period of anarchy and violence."[31] Feudalism, though it partly destroyed the work of Charle-

magne, had overthrown the barbarians, while the communes, asylum of liberty, raised up a bourgeoisie that, in alliance with royalty, created a nation that
struggled toward a higher unity from the time of Philip Augustus onward.
Cheruel's second volume finished his account of French administration with a
celebration of modern progress from the "new mission" of the sixteenth century to Louis XIV, when political unity was "solidly established."

In 1856, Edgard Boutaric won a (Bordin) prize for his contribution to the
story of centralization, especially through legislation, in this case centered on
the reign of Philip IV.[32] This period marked both the arrival point of feudalism
(and its defeat by the king), he argued, and "the point of departure of the
modern world." In this study of the moral and physical progress of the French
monarchy Boutaric, like Dareste, followed an analytical method, focusing on
royal power and domain, the Estates General and clergy, and the growth of the
administration, the judiciary, and finances. Like Dareste, too, he grounded his
work in archival and manuscript sources in the national — now imperial —
repositories as well as the earlier collections. According to Boutaric, Philip IV
had created a truly "absolute government" out of the feudal inheritance. This
conclusion was reinforced not only by the arguments of the Capetian legists
but also by the recent publications of the parliamentary series ("Olim") and
Pardessus's study of judicial organization as well as the old collection concerning the "difference" between Philip and Pope Boniface VIII assembled in the
sixteenth century by Pierre Dupuy. Philip was not an ideal king; indeed he
often acted tyrannically and, as clear from the evidence in poetic sources,
caused suffering to his contemporaries. Yet in such an "age of transition" he
should not be judged like an ordinary man, Boutaric concluded: "All in all his
was a great reign, and his name should be inscribed next to those of Charlemagne and Louis XIV as the founders of France."[33]

Gabriel Monod established his reputation with a study of the sources of
Frankish history in the Merovingian period, specifically the chronicles and
more especially Gregory of Tours, but he was a disciple, too, of Michelet,
leaving a discipular biography to be published after his death; and this part
of his heritage led him to a synthetic view of history, emphasizing not only
narrative sources of history but also documents, juridical texts, letters, and
poems, such as those produced during what he called "the Carolingian Renaissance."[34] This is one example of the central methodological issue in "scientific history," that is, whether to follow an analytical procedure determined
by specific institutions considered in isolation and according to the relevant
sources, or to follow a chronological and narrative plan bringing all available
sources into play.

One of the standard institutional histories of France was that of Ernest

Glasson, whose perspective was comparative — he wrote also on English and German constitutional history. Glasson accepted the need of periodization for general history but not for the study of individual institutions, and so he combined synthetic and analytical methods, in effect historical interpretation with the examination of documentary evidence. For Glasson, who was a professor at the faculty of law, the essential division was the Romanist categories of public and private law, corresponding to that between political and social history. He admitted a "true communism in land" (*véritable communisme de la terre*), but only in the earliest stages of Germanic society (judging from the evidence of old Scandinavian laws); and he regarded private property as an "immense" progress from that state, through feudalism, to modern civilization.[35] The nation was fundamentally Celtic, but with many cultural admixtures that left imprints on French institutions and culture. In general, Glasson concluded, "the race is Celtic or Gallic, the institutions Roman or Germanic, and the language Latin."[36]

Paul Viollet, also a law professor, added an anthropological and evolutionary dimension to the study of French "primitive institutions," citing the recent works of Henry Sumner Maine and Herbert Spencer, among others.[37] Disclaiming any theoretical motive in his work, Viollet still claimed to see "laws" not only of the "progressive centralization" of the monarchy but also of the division of labor and function. "Every society is in perpetual evolution," he wrote, and in general the direction of evolution was from monarchy to "self government"; and he kept the old periodization — Gallic, Gallo-Roman, Frankish, feudal, and the dynastic succession — as well as the conventional lawyer's date 843, which marked at once the end of the Frankish empire and the beginning of the "new world." He also kept a political and administrative focus, while acknowledging in "constitutional and social" history a shift of focus from "great men" and actions to collective patterns. The common people had been the victims of the old monarchy, Viollet admitted; but — here Michelet's message resounds again — the future belonged to the disinherited.

Jacques Flach, professor of comparative legislation at the Collège de France, invoked the great tradition of "jurisconsult-historians" in his study of the role of seigneurialism, a term he preferred to "feudalism" (*féodalité*), in the origins of ancient France in the tenth century. He meant the Pithous, Godefroys, Baluze of the Old Regime but also Pardessus, Laboulaye, Giraud, Klimrath, and others of his time. He was still looking for a new and better history, especially in his use of medieval charters, a source exploited earlier by Benjamin Guérard, a director of the Ecole des Chartes. "The materials are abundant," he wrote, "the edifice remains to be constructed"; and he fancied himself one of the architects.[38] Flach's project was the work of a lifetime, his master Laboulaye warned, and he agreed, devoting himself, with the help of Léopold Delisle and others, to the riches of the Bibliothèque Nationale, just then being catalogued for modern use. For Flach, French "origins" meant the family, Roman, Celtic, and Germanic; and he then turned to questions of patronage, immunities, vassalage, the benefice, and other aspects of feudal society, only in the second part considering royal institutions and the cornerstones of monarchy, protection, and justice.[39] In any case French history was rooted in law: "Feudal law, religious law, and communal law are all founded upon royal law, for this is the symbol at once of social unity and national unity, and it is, or should be, the expression of public interest."[40]

The greatest of the nineteenth-century investigators of French institutions was Numa Denis Fustel de Coulanges, who also began as a classical scholar, one of the first French students at the French school at Athens, whose first work was a study of Polybius. In his study of the ancient city (1864) Fustel, following the "symbolic" path of Creuzer and his translator Joseph Guigniaut, found the origins of the city in "the religion of sacred fire and dead ancestors," a religion that appeared not only in Greece and Rome but also in India — at this stage Fustel being a proponent of a comparative method.[41] Essential to this family religion, too, was the institution of private property, derived from god as "primitive proprietor." Private property figured in all of Fustel's scientific inquiries from the *Ager publicus* to the medieval allod to the *propriété privé* sanctioned by the Napoleonic Code. So the god Terminus guarded the territory of Rome and, symbolically, all of its cultural descendants. Fustel's indulgent first work was assaulted by Charles Morel, who had studied at the University of Bonn; and while he rejected the Germanic basis of this critique of his inadequate documentation, he came himself to a similar sort of positivist erudition.[42]

By the time of the Franco-Prussian War, Fustel had turned his attention to France's own medieval past, and the result was a six-volume, posthumously published, institutional history of France. Despite his anti-German impulse, Fustel displayed an inclination to an extreme objectivity like that of Polybius, who wrote "without regret or hate."[43] Fustel would "neither praise nor condemn the ancient institutions" of France, which in any case were not the product of individual wills but rather were formed "in a slow and gradual manner," as indeed the Germanic invasions had progressed.[44] Refusing even to cite the opinions of modern scholars — except when he disagreed — Fustel rejected theories, especially those due to racial or ethnographical preoccupations (and he hated the word "sociology" for its pretensions), conclusions drawn from poetic sources, not immediately inferrable from the documents, especially laws and charters, and even comparisons from Scandinavian customs.

Nor was there talk of national assemblies or nobility of birth in the sources to which Fustel restricted himself. So, Fustel concluded, "I have not spoken here of the spirit of liberty of Frankish warriors, nor of elective kingship, nor of national assemblies, nor of popular juries, nor of the confiscation of the vanquished, nor of allods distributed to the victors."[45] These were all anachronisms not to be found in the sources, as also was the assignment of patriotic or xenophobic motives to the Germanic tribes (as if they were Prussians from the start), who entered the empire as Roman subjects. For a day of such synthesis (in a formula later repeated by Henri Berr), years of analysis were required. Yet Fustel himself was capable of uncritical synthesis, as in his imputation of long-range (and so extra-documentary) continuities in, for example, institutions of landed property and forms of administration.

Unlike many contemporaries Fustel was largely unimpressed by the German science of history because of its ideological thrust — referring here not only to Maurer, Waitz, Sohm, and Lamprecht, but also to such French Germanizers as Laveleye and Viollet. Even Mommsen, despite his massive erudition, remained modern in his ideas and sentiments, writing of Rome but thinking of Germany; and Fustel preferred the notions of Livy to those of Niebuhr. Fustel also rejected the impressionistic inclinations of the so-called new history of Thierry and Barante, who took painting or novels as their model of interpretation. Nor did Fustel accept the approach of Gabriel Monod, who, instead of explicating Gregory of Tours's text, linked it in a comparative and vague way to the Salic Law: this was not "true analysis." And in his survey of French historical scholarship prefacing the first issue of the *Revue Historique* (1876), Monod failed to cite the names of great legal scholars like Cujas and Dumoulin as well as Pardessus, Laferrière, Giraud, and other moderns.

The science of history was indeed a creation of French scholars — not the Walter-Scottisé "new history" of the previous generation but rather the model procedure of early modern scholars such as Godefroy, Mabillon, Guérard, and Pardessus — "of our Benedictines, of our Academy of Inscriptions, of Beaufort, Freret, and so many others" who prepared the ground for the erudition of Fustel's day.[46] Following this tradition Fustel took a line that was not only nonpartisan but also severely literalist, based on a detailed and narrowly focused examination of the texts (though his rigid neglect of context was pointed out by later critics), a refusal to introduce any elements not found in these texts, and a strict elimination of modern issues and ideas. "The analysis of a text such as a charter, a letter, a historical account, or a simple phrase, consists in establishing the meaning of each word and extricating the thought of the writer."[47] Avoid the seductions of interpretation and stick to words and facts was his teaching to his young students as well as to his critical colleagues on both sides of the Rhine.

What Fustel abominated in particular were the Germanist theories beginning with Maurer and including French scholars, which attributed the institution of communal property to the migrating Germanic tribes. The idea of primitive communal ownership in Indo-European society was wholly without documentary foundation, so that: "M. Viollet has not offered a single [document] to prove that the Greek cities had ever practiced agrarian communism; M. de Jubainville has demonstrated that not one shows this regime among the Celts; Maurer and Lamprecht have none to prove that the *Mark* signified communal territory. As for the comparative method about which there has been so much talk, this name has been given only to a bizarre accumulation of isolated facts, taken on all sides, often ill-understood, and have cast aside facts unfavorable to this system."[48] This was a theory deriving from the speculations of Rousseau and unworthy of a scientific study of documentary facts — not to speak (as Fustel did not speak) of the values of modern bourgeois civilization, which Guizot, Thierry, and others had introduced into the premises of historical inquiry.

Fustel continued his criticism of the comparative method — despite the fact that he had himself practiced it in his *Ancient City* — in exchanges with Gabriel Monod, who reviewed Fustel's work on French institutions and concluded that it was inferior to the old study of his master Waitz on the German constitution. For Fustel, Monod was guilty of the Germanist fallacy as well as an "unscientific" substitution of comparison for analysis in his Merovingian investigations. "Instead of seeking the meaning of each phrase and the thought behind it," Fustel complained, "he comments on each phrase with what he has learned from Tacitus or the Salic Law."[49] Monod's errors arose from his neglect of the words of his sources and his substitution of his own commentary for careful *explication de texte*.

So Fustel, who had established his reputation by conjectural and comparative history, shifted to the narrowest Francocentric positivism. In his study of early Frankish institutions he insisted that there were virtually no trustworthy sources, all of them deriving from Latin authors, sufficient for only the vaguest of notions. Again criticizing Monod, he denied that Gregory of Tours had access to popular German poetry — "pure conjecture" — and even Tacitus he thought praiseworthy more for eloquence than for accuracy.[50] Fustel denied, too, ideas of German unity in the early period, and above all he rejected the German identification of science with patriotism, as with Giesebrecht, though in separating history from nationality he admitted that it became the subject of

partisan debate.[51] For him in any case the great tradition of historical learning was not German but French, deriving from Mabillon and érudits of the
seventeenth and eighteenth centuries. He turned entirely against the subjectivism of the new history of Thierry and "M. Symbol," Michelet, who worked
in the shadow of Walter Scott. History was not the work of individuals or even
the "people" but of evolving institutions. Fustel embraced instead a scientific
method in which not only God but also historical truth resided in "details,"
especially textual details which recorded this evolution. Not that he was above
error himself, and Jubainville deplored his myopic acceptance of false di-
plomas; but his example and his self-assured teaching had a powerful influence on the French historical profession well into the next century.

The anti-German sentiment provoked by the Franco-Prussian War was revived in the early twentieth century in the build-up to the world war and much
intensified by the long conflict itself. In 1915, Ernst Lavisse, biographer of
Frederick the Great, joined Charles Andler, author of a study of German state
socialism (1897), and published a protest against pan-German militarism and
war atrocities; and others, such as the historian of Protestantism, Imbart de
la Tour, turned the attack on German intellectual tradition going back to
Fichte.[52] Another writer, René Pichon, even assigned blame to the great
Mommsen for his Caesarist views, while Fustel's distinguished disciple Camille
Jullian — defending his Gaul against Mommsen's Rome — went so far as to cast
doubt on (German) science, which he represented as inferior to "ancestral
traditions." Jullian carried his patriotic fervor into his erudite studies of ancient Gaul as the source of these traditions.[53] But of course nationalism survived and thrived, hardly less than in the time of Fichte, on all sides of this
murderous intercultural conflict.

Scientific History

In France the revolutionary and postrevolutionary search for a science of
society turned to history as an auxiliary and empirical — a "positive," and
"positivist" — base. From Condorcet to Comte the study of history again allied
itself with philosophy and took a conjectural form, seeking large patterns and
periods, like the "epochs" of Condorcet's *Esquisse,* and the emphasis was on
social and economic forces rather than political and legislative control — on
collective rather than individual behavior. Saint Simon's view of history took
the form of a modern trinity (industry, science, and art) and on the four stages
of fetishism, polytheism, deism, and "physicism"; and in this he was followed
by Fourier and others. The thought of these socialists was systematic and
encyclopedic as well as utopian; its religious tendency suggested that the quest

for the "Heavenly City" (in the phrase of Carl Becker) was still in progress; and as Saint-Simonian social science became a sort of theology, so history became a sort of theodicy leading to a New Christianity based on the principle not of struggle or competition but of cooperation and love. Saint-Simon's vision moved many young historians of the postrevolutionary generation, including Guizot, Thierry, Michelet, and Lerminier, as well as theorists like P. J. B. Buchez and Auguste Comte.[54]

In 1833, Buchez published an introduction to the "science of history," which was devoted to the determination of "causes," but final and not efficient causes, according to a sort of Catholic socialism.[55] What he preached was a doctrine of progress and a teleology envisaging a future of utopian socialism. Buchez was also keen on "method" and the inference of a "law of variations" which would make it possible to predict this future, but behind these high "scientific" ideals Buchez's view of history remained with the framework of the Adamic story and seems closer to Bossuet than to Condorcet. With Le Roux, Buchez also published in 1834 a standard source collection of the French Revolution, to which was prefixed a survey of French history, representing the Revolution as the necessary culmination of modern civilization, or at least its next-to-last stage.

Auguste Comte's "sociology" was "positive" because it was based on history, or at least a theory thereof. With the "new history" of Thierry, Comte agreed that the Middle Ages had been undervalued and needed to be taken seriously to understand the organic growth of society. For Comte "positive" was the opposite of "conjectural," and yet his idea of history was little more than a rehearsal of the ancient (and medieval) ages-of-man idea — the famous law of three stages, theological, metaphysical, and positive, corresponding to childhood, youth, and manhood. In its theological phase (drawing here on Creuze's *Symbolik*) history began with fetishism — and ended there, too, as some critics would say with respect to Comte's own worship of natural science. In a global as well as European perspective humanity progressed from polytheism to monotheism, and like Bossuet, Comte celebrated the contributions of Catholicism to progress.[56] Metaphysics, "the ghost of dead theologies," arose from Protestantism and went into decline because of its alliance with secular power; but the spirit of positivism already appeared especially in the work of Descartes, Bacon, and Galileo, although the necessary base was already in place in the fourteenth century in the Saint-Simonian triad of industry, science, and art. This eclectic scheme represented no more than an updating of the conjectural history of the previous century conscripted into the service of the new theology, new fetishism, and new mythology constructed by Comte.

"Socialist" was a qualifying term that applied to anti-rationalist and anti-"Jacobin" thought by parties from right to left — from Metternich to Marx — and the new science of society, "sociology" in Comte's coinage, shared the premise that civil society took precedence over political, juridical, and economic actions. Revolutionary thinkers from Proudhon and Marx stressed these new priorities — but then so, without the activist and utopian agenda, did the historians of that time. Thus Thierry turned away from the dramatic deeds of individuals recounted in the chronicles to an analysis of class struggles and the bourgeois liberties preserved in urban charters and other documentary sources; and historians of a later generation turned to the still less familiar sources reflecting the condition of the lower and "dangerous" classes and of "labor history." This shift of emphasis, reinforced by the historical school of economics, headed by Savigny's disciple Wilhelm Roscher, led to the development of economic history as a subdiscipline, exemplified by the work of Emile Levasseur in France (winner of the prize question posed in 1858 by the Académie des Sciences Morales et Politiques on the history of the working classes) and Karl Inama-Sternegg, Karl Nitzsch, and the young Karl Lamprecht in Germany.

As Louis Bourdeau wrote, "Let us finally appreciate the role played by the masses, who have been sacrificed to civilization, of which the best part is their creation and would be nothing without them," he wrote, and continued: "There is therefore a revolution to be mounted in history analogous to that pursued in the political sphere. . . . Citizens of modern democracies, let us close the book which has for so long told the story of royalty and the nobility of the court. Let us concentrate on the masses and write about the doings of the newly liberated peoples . . . and the history of humanity."[57] But this, too, required a shift from individual action to collective behavior — the methodological equivalent of the political principle of democracy. This shift from the individual to the group was reinforced by the alliance with sociology, signaled by the impact of Emile Durkheim, François Simiand, and Paul Lacombe, whose *History Considered as Science*, which first appeared in 1894, called for historians to search for social laws.[58]

There was another way of envisioning "science," and this was best expressed by Ernest Renan's view of its future in 1848. Renan himself came out of the seminary, but he approached religion in a comparative and mythological way; and while he supported social reform, he rejected the notion of a new theology fashioned for modern spirits. He applauded the rejection of "prejudice" by philosophers of the Enlightenment, and he celebrated the "revolution" brought about by the "new history" which appeared around 1820, especially in the work of Guizot, Thierry, and Michelet.[59] For his own "scientific" tradition, however, he invoked not the abstract philosophy of Descartes or the positivism of Comte but the tradition of humanist criticism going back to Petrarch and Boccaccio, to the Protestant Reformation, which "was born in the midst of philology," and especially to seventeenth-century *érudits* like Mabillon and Muratori, followed in later times by Vico, Herder ("my king of thought"), Wolf, Niebuhr, Burnouf, Grimm, and Strauss. No philologist, Comte missed all this sort of positive learning, and so his doctrine pointed back to religion rather than to the future of science.[60]

Renan's first interest was in the secularist influence of Aristotle and Averroës on Christian thought, but his lifework was devoted to the history of Christianity, and here he showed the literary side of his scientific method. In his *Life of Jesus* he followed Strauss, except in the excesses of his "exclusive system," in pursing the legendary aspects of the gospels, agreed that "absolute faith is incompatible with sincere history," and disallowed the acceptance of miracles and the supernatural.[61] Memory changes with lapse of time (so that Napoleon, for example, became liberal in the recollections of his companions in exile), and Renan distinguished three stages in the gospel story: the original documentary phase (primary collections which no longer exist), the state of simple mixture (Matthew and Mark), and "the state of combination or of intentional and deliberate compiling (Luke), with later distorted interpretations (John). But in his story Renan also made use of supplementary sources, including the Talmud and Philo, "elder brother of Jesus," whose writings allowed the reconstruction of contemporary states of mind.

Unlike Renan, whom he otherwise admired, Hippolyte Taine adopted the model of physical science rather than philology and took chemistry and biology more seriously than the other two. He argued that it was necessary to bring *nature* into moral philosophy and history in order to understand the substance and the "causes" of human behavior, following the scientific lead of Cuvier, Saint-Hilaire, Linnaeus, and Darwin. In this way he approached his *History of English Literature*, in which he employed the famous, apparently deterministic — "fatalist," as Chateaubriand had called it — trinity of "race, moment, milieu."[62] The inherited dispositions of national character, the pressures of the natural environment, and the periods of cultural development encompass the external "causes" of historical change and even natural laws analogous to those of natural science. At the same time Taine did not neglect what he called "facts of the highest kind," that is, modes of feeling and thought which only literary efforts could reveal — the "revival of imagination" associated with the names of Lessing, Chateaubriand, Scott, Thierry, and Michelet.[63] Thus Taine hoped to join together the old incompatibles of external and internal history, which was the essential task set for the writing of cultural history. Taine was not without a historical sense of individuality, a sense he shared with his friend Sainte-Beuve, who wrote: "One can indeed show all the relations they have with the time in which they are born and live . . . , but one cannot tell in advance that [the age] will give birth to a particular kind of individual or talent. Why Pascal rather than La Fontaine?"[64]

But the "science" of Comte and his followers and of Taine (if not Renan) was a world apart from the "scientific history" (*Geschichtswissenschaft*) which was spreading from Germany into the practices and theories of French scholars, beginning especially with Michelet and Quinet. After Savigny and the historical school it was the influence of Niebuhr, Ranke, and their students that had the greatest impact on French history, especially in medieval studies, where the common Frankish and Carolingian past drew German and French scholars together on a common terrain and in a common, though divergent, tradition. As German scholars had come to Paris to work in the libraries, so French students traveled to Göttingen and Berlin to the seminars of German professors. Among these German-trained scholars were Gabriel Monod, Ernst Lavisse, and Charles Seignobos, who carried the scientific to members of the next generation.

All of these men — and others, such as Victor Duruy, Charles Langlois, and Fustel de Coulanges — representing the elite of the French historical profession were involved in the reform of education, under the influence of, or (especially after 1870) in competition with, German historical science. In 1897 Langlois and Seignobos published a standard manual of historical method, rivaling and criticizing the famous treatise by Eduard Bernheim, which appeared in 1889. Langlois and Seignobos had little use for the philosophy or so-called laws of history. They found the "metaphysical" discussions of Bernheim "devoid of interest" and the "heavy, pedantic" arguments of Droysen obscure and useless.[65] Nor did they have respect for the "literary" approach to history, although they did emphasize the value of poetic sources for social and political history. "The historians work with documents," they proclaimed at the beginning and the end of their textbook; and this "positivist" credo was the warrant for their claims for history as a "science."

Although French positivists, in their elaboration of the old *ars historica*, had contempt for the idealist philosophy of German scholars, their view of "scientific history" resembled conventional German *Historik*, not only in its insistence on "method," "criticism," and the auxiliary sciences but also in its acceptance of the lessons of hermeneutics. In this connection, however, they cited not Schliermacher or Droysen but Fustel and his injunction against reading one document in the light of another, so that hermeneutics was in effect *explication de texte*. At the same time texts opened up a large world of human action and "facts," and Langlois and Seignobos recognized six classes of the conditions of these facts: material conditions (including biology, geography, and demography), intellectual habits (arts, sciences, philosophy), material customs (food, clothing, private life), economic customs (transport, commerce, distribution), social institutions (family, education, classes), and public institutions (state, church, administration) — a range comparable to the controversial German *Kulturgeschichte*. Of these only the last was "obligatory," while the second and third were "not obligatory." And all of these features of the science of history, they argued (with a singular lack of historical sense), has been developed only in the previous half-century.

The move into social history was made from another angle by more popular writers, of whom the Goncourt brothers, Edmond and Jules, were a conspicuous example. In the *Journal* which these learned aesthetes began in 1851 (and which Edmond continued until his death in 1894), they displayed their interests in elite and popular culture, and they pursued these pastimes into French history, especially since the eighteenth century.[66] They offered a new view on the revolutionary past by shifting attention from politics, law, and institutions to the life of the people — or at least people like themselves. The culture of salons and cafés ("the speaking press of the Revolution"), art and caricature, fashion and conversation, the theater and music, eating and drinking, women and prostitution, popular entertainment and pornography, and above all journalism (themselves being the founders of a series of literary journals), "the arena of great battles" — here were all the materials of another "new history," although the Goncourts did not make this boast directly. But they did open up a new vision of the Revolution, which "began with eighteenth-century public opinion, began with the salons." The agency of history itself shifted to the people: "Hardly born, the Revolution pushed men against other men, assembled them, set ideas against ideas, words against words; for from these associations and shocks burst forth flames, enlightenment, and liberty."[67] For the Goncourts, at least, as for Michelet, the Revolution signaled an end to business as usual for alert historians and a search for new sources of understanding.

Interpreting the Revolution

A specter was haunting historical scholarship in France, and indeed in Europe as a whole, during the nineteenth century — it was the ghost, or rather the continuing reality, of the French Revolution. This was true even for antiquarians and students of the deep past, in which the institutions of the Old Regime were born and shaped. Historians tended to identify with one stage of the revolutionary process or another. The positions of scholars ranged from royalism to regicide and from idealization or rehabilitation of the Old Regime to glorification or exoneration of the Terror; but most historians, even republicans under the skin, favored constitutional monarchy as restored under the Charter. Yet the demands of history, too, had to be met. The first question for historians, according to "scientific" goals embedded in the old "pragmatic" historiography, was that of causes of the "revolution," a term inherited from English experience and usage that itself went mainly unexamined. The Restoration period was devoted especially to the publication of sources, memoirs of survivors, and the first generation of historical accounts, to be succeeded by a flood of narratives, beginning with the books of Mignet and Thiers published in the 1820s, and revisionist studies which have continued down to the present.

The first popular history of the Revolution to appear in the Restoration was that of François Mignet — "the Bible for liberal revolutions," it has been called[68] — whose first publication was on the government of St. Louis and whose main concerns thereafter were directed to the sixteenth century. In 1824, however, he published a hasty survey of the Revolution which was aimed, in a veiled way, against the Bourbon monarchy. Mignet did not make use of new sources, but he did have access to the recollections of Daunou and Talleyrand. What Mignet sought was to present a unified and idealized account of the Revolution in terms of its underlying causes, following the earlier views of Mme de Staël and Toulongeon that the Revolution was surely no accident, nothing like a hurricane or an earthquake, or an effect of the whims of the people.[69] He regretted the violence of particular parties but regarded it as necessary in the face of absolutism and later of external threats to Jacobin rule — the will of the people being at all times the ultimate standard of judgment. For Mignet the major cause of revolution was the struggle not of ideas but of classes.

Complaints of "fatalism" and "fatality" were common in the Restoration, and both Mignet and Thiers were accused of this resort to determinism in explaining the phenomenon of revolution. Sainte-Beuve charged Mignet with this fallacy — while defending Thiers from the same complaint. For while Mignet sought social causes, all Thiers wanted to do was, like Barante and Thierry, to impose order on his narrative of human actions — he was quite aware of the principle of Cleopatra's nose, and realized that, despite the "ideal of historical perfection," in human events the causes often escape us.[70] The only "fatality" was the revolutionary passion of the people, which was a necessity but not a "law of history" — although like Mignet he also saw in the revolutionary quest for liberty the working of "Providence." Thiers, who had been a founder, with Mignet (and Carrel), of the oppositional journal, *Le National,* published, with his colleague Felix Bodin, also author of a brief survey of French history, the first volume of his history of the years before Mignet's (1823); his was not a "précis," however, but a detailed account in ten volumes (to 1827). If Mignet was a "philosopher," Thiers was a "painter," but he also took reason of state (the stance of his "hero" Machiavelli and Talleyrand) as his measure. He deplored the excesses of the older generation and yet recognized his position as inheritor and pledged to remain objective in his judgments, even as he celebrated the success of the Third Estate and its liberties, which would triumph again, with his and Mignet's help, in the July Revolution of 1830.

Historians of laws and institutions had their own take on the Revolution; and while they admitted the destructiveness of the Revolution in its early stages, when not only laws but the legal profession itself was ostensibly suppressed, they also took into consideration the surreptitious survival of customs, legal practices, and the legal mentality itself. The Order of Advocates was revived by Napoleon, and so in effect was much of the substance of the law of the Old Regime. "The Code was not founded on an exclusive system," wrote Laferrière; "it was the product of time and manners; it was the product of the historical school and not of a school purely dogmatic, that is, the school of Montesquieu and not of Rousseau" — and indeed he was tempted to call his book, "the spirit of the laws of the Revolution."[71] Many of the words had changed, but the music, to a professional ear, remained the same. So continuity and not destruction was the underlying and final theme of the Revolution for Laferrière and scholars with his deep perspective.

In the year before the Revolutions of 1848 three studies of the French Revolution began to appear — those of Lamartine, Louis Blanc, and Michelet, republicans all, and idealizers of the Revolution. Lamartine was a poet, and his history of the Girondins had the best and worst qualities of a novel, being at once highly colored and highly inaccurate. His book started with the death of Mirabeau and focused on a small party, "men who, cast by providence into the very centre of the greatest drama of modern times, comprise in themselves the ideas, the passions, the virtues of their epoch."[72] Lamartine claimed to be impartial but, invoking two of the oldest topoi of Western historiography, remarked that history's "impartiality" was that not of a mirror but of a judge and that his account of that bloody era was to be "an example to mankind." Besides telling what had happened, he wanted also to teach "what the Revolution might have been."[73]

Louis Blanc, a journalist and a socialist, whose *History of Ten Years* was an indictment of the July Monarchy, celebrated the Revolution — *l'honneur de la Révolution défendue* — as a work of the entire human race, and he emphasized the modern conjunction of liberty and fraternity.[74] The trajectory of history was from authority, which prevailed in ancient and medieval times, to individualism, born in the Reformation, and fraternity, begun by Hus and the Anabaptists and represented by the Mountain—though it would not be achieved until another, truly social revolution. As Lamartine idealized the Girondins, so Blanc idealized Robespierre, and set Rousseau above Voltaire—the champions of fraternal and social ideals above bourgeois individualists.

In the 1840s Michelet took time out from his history of France to write his history of the Revolution, a book "born in the archives"—unlike the books of Thiers, Blanc, and Lamartine, which relied on printed sources like the *Moniteur*—but also featuring the most extreme hyperbole, sometimes verging on hysteria, straining for dramatic effect with his one-sentence paragraphs, and engaging his own emotions and psyche in the history of the People. "This subject is the ocean," he wrote in 1846—but also a "refuge."[75] The turning point came on the astonishing night of 4 August, when seigneurialism was abolished—given up in an extraordinary display of humanity initiated by the nobles. After that marvelous night, "no more classes for the French," Michelet concluded; "no more provinces, just a single France."[76] (Thiers had been a little more temperate, remarking on the aftermath and practical struggles following that euphoric night.) Though it represented the birth of the Nation, the Revolution had few monuments, having been overwhelmed by Napoleonic memorials, but it resided in the very souls of the French—Michelet here extending his "moi-histoire." Indeed, continuing and at the same time opposing Christianity—Michelet himself was fresh off a combat with the Jesuits—the Revolution was a church, a "communion," which drew on the strength of "the People," and Michelet was its high priest.[77]

In 1865 Michelet's lifelong friend Edgar Quinet published a philosophical survey of the Revolution, likewise emphasizing its intellectual side, against the materialism and focus on property of many of his contemporaries, beginning with the generation of 1820. The fiscal interpretation—Necker's "errors" and all that—was wholly insufficient to explain such a complex phenomenon. Do not ask of economists or meteorologists more than they can give, he argued: "Woe to those who hope to discover in this way the revolutions either of the heavens or of humanity."[78]

As a common European heritage the Revolution was a favorite object of study of many non-French scholars as well. The only history of the French Revolution more extravagant than Michelet's was that of Carlyle, published a decade earlier (1835)—replacing the popular survey of Archibald Alison, which began to appear in 1833. Like Michelet, Carlyle regarded the Revolution as a new church, passing this judgment in connection with the night of 4 August: "Miraculous, or semi-miraculous, some seem to think it," he wrote.

"A new Night of Pentecost, shall we say, shaped according to the new Time, and new Church of Jean Jacques Rousseau?"[79] Like Michelet, too, though with a critical twist, he thought that "the French Revolution lies in the heart and head of every violent-speaking, of every violent-thinking, French Man." Even less than Michelet could Carlyle be accused of "fatalism," for he denied that the Revolution had simple and intelligible causes: "Man cannot explain it," he admitted, and gloried in the admission.[80] But then Carlyle, dragging along his readers, was always much more interested in individual exploits and in declamation and exhortation than in explanation and analysis.

One major history of the Revolution that was critical was that of Heinrich von Sybel, whose experiences in the Frankfurt Parliament drove him to the right. What began as a conservative pamphlet turned into a multivolume life work, which was based on archival research (carried on after Michelet had been denied access).[81] Sybel turned to the social dimension of the revolutionary process as well as its impact on the rest of Europe. He had little respect for any of the revolutionary leaders, their naive ideals, and their absurd goals, including the Rights of Man; and like Burke he held the Revolution up as a negative example for the nations of post-1848 Europe. Sybel, as Lord Acton wrote, "uses the Revolution to exhibit the superiority of enlightened and conservative Germany."[82]

Alexis de Tocqueville was a French nobleman and statesman who made a name for himself with the publication of his *Democracy in America* in 1835. Tocqueville had the instincts not only of a comparative historian but also of a political scientist, or prophet, searching for a "new science of politics." His study of the United States, drawn from books but even more from his experiences as a traveller, was intended to provide insights for the French, who — though they had been moving toward social equality for centuries — were behind Americans in the able and "alarming" bent toward democracy. According to Tocqueville, "in the past seven centuries, we shall scarcely meet with a single event, in the lapse of seven hundred years, which has not turned to the advantage of equality."[83] Such was the prospect for the future, too, and this belief also informed his view of the past, especially under the impact of the events of 1848, of which Tocqueville was an insightful chronicler.

Turning to the central event that brought democracy to the fore and inaugurated the modern age, Tocqueville directed his intellectual energies to the French Revolution, exploring a number of provincial archives (Tours, Normandy, Languedoc). His book, appearing in 1856, was concerned above all with class structure and relations. What 1789 represented was "the greatest effort ever undertaken by any people to disassociate themselves from their past"; and yet, though the Revolution surely "gave birth to modern society," the break with the past was far from complete.[84] Looking at the old society across the watershed of revolution, Tocqueville found that many feelings, habits, and ideas had survived into his own century; and so the basic theme of his work was continuity. Under this overarching argument his history followed not a narrative but a sequence of propositions designed to revise conventional notions of revolutionary change, beginning with the argument that the aim of the Revolution was not to destroy religion and weaken the state but to continue the process of centralization begun by the medieval monarchy. In *Democracy in America* Tocqueville had already made this argument — that it is "incorrect to say that centralization was produced by the French revolution: the revolution brought it to perfection, but did not create it" — citing a memo written by his great-grandfather Malesherbes to Louis XVI on the right of every citizenry to administer its own affairs.[85]

Tocqueville lived through two revolutions and wrote about another — and more thoughtfully than Thiers. Unlike other so-called revolutions, that of 1789 went beyond a particular national territory, and it resembled more the transformation brought about by the rise of Christianity. Religious in character, the French Revolution did not initiate but only confirmed the process which, in the quest for freedom, individualism, and social equality, accompanied the collapse of the feudal class and the institutions of the Old Regime — though without eradicating the old governmental and bureaucratic powers. "The men of '89 had knocked down the building," he wrote, "but its foundations had remained in the very souls of its destroyers, and on those foundations it was possible to rebuild it again, and to construct it more solidly than ever" with the "debris" of the old order.[86]

By the time of the Revolution the intellectuals had become leaders in politics, as they were in Tocqueville's time, and were responsible for the old idea, or fallacy, of ignoring old wisdom, including religion, and building a society on the basis of principles of reason, rather than the English way — so Tocqueville read the complaints of all three of the estates in their *cahiers*. In this context, as an imaginary society was imposed on the "real" one, the nobility proceeded to self-destruction, while the masses were radicalized and the king lost control to public opinion. After 1780 things did not go from bad to worse; and though they were in an improving condition, the masses were inflamed and contributed to the revolutionary dream. In the end, however, the Revolution did not live up to its hopes and dreams. It did not really destroy the old world, nor create a new one; it merely brought misplaced idealism, violence, and revolutionary rhetoric to a process that was essentially evolutionary.

Hyppolyte Taine was a distinguished man of letters with inflated philosophical pretensions who turned in his last years to a vast, ultimately unfinished, survey of the "origins of contemporary France," which focused on the causes and results of the Revolution. Taine was as far as possible from Tocqueville in his social analysis and from Michelet in his moral judgments. As in his study of English literature Taine affected a scientific approach with affinities rather to biology than to geometry, but the upshot is rather patches of scientistic rhetoric than any systematic analysis of his materials. Taine indeed searched archival sources, but rather to find colorful illustrations to adorn his detailed narrative than to seek causes beyond commonplace opinions of old regime abuse and superficial and utopian philosophy leading to violence and horrible atrocities — a series of old-fashioned *jacqueries* — provoked by extreme distress but lacking any human purpose, although from these experiences of oppression peasants did achieve a sense of commonality.[87]

The first phase of revolution was the work of destruction, the attempt to eliminate an infection also acting to destroy vital organs of the body politic. The work of construction was lamentably undertaken by the Jacobins, "men of unstable class," he characterized them, who formed a party whose inspiration became the "homicidal idea." Much of Taine's story consists in following first their "conquest," their descent into "moral perversion," and the substitution of government by law into government by force, as clubs became a mainstay of social organization. The Revolution was, concluded Taine, "a specious mask with a hideous visage beneath it, under the reign of a nominally humanitarian theory, covering over the effective dictatorship of evil and low passions" — and from the intellectual emerged the executioner.[88]

Taine's work was an uneasy combination of intellectual and social history. Much of it was devoted to descriptions of mob violence and the formation of the clubs, parties, and journals around the assemblies and constitutional experiments, and yet it was ideas that generated movement and conflict. Taine grounded his explanation on the combination of two "spiritual" elements, classicism and science, and the ideas of intellectuals, which took a political and a social form in revolutionary legislation and the Jacobin program of national regeneration. As Egyptians had worshiped crocodiles, so French radicals revered the false philanthropy of the followers of the "speculative" theology of Rousseau. Yet Taine also saw the crucial and indeed growing importance of material factors, so that "whatever the force of the great names of liberty, equality, and fraternity with which the Revolution decorated itself, is was in essence *a translation of property*." Moreover, it was under Bonapartist rule, starting under the guise of preserving the revolutionary tradition, that the elements of modern France really took shape.

In the nineteenth century the French Revolution took on a life of itself inseparable from its narratives. It was not part of the dead past that Michelet

worshiped or merely a modern myth that took its place beside the other elements of the national story; it was the beginning of a "new man"—a new age,
a "new people," and a new language—and a promise (or threat) of a future
that historians have envisioned in many different ways.[89] It has been a locus
and a focus for the imagination, for utopian (and dystopian) dreams, and for
emotions ranging from reactionary anger to activist euphoria to revolutionary
prophecy. It is not surprising that the temptation has been to treat it as a
literary phenomenon, an adjunct or dimension of fiction; and indeed this is
one way to view the history of historiography.[90] So we come back to the
ancient Pindaric formula, "longer than deeds liveth the word," for this is
indeed the epistemological condition of the scientific scholar as well as the
literary artist.

9

English Observances

Knowledge of history means choice of ancestors.
— Lord Acton

National History

In late-nineteenth-century England there was, after Macaulay (b. 1800) and Thomas Arnold (b. 1795), a generation, almost a cohort, of historians devoted to the national history. Situated between amateur and professional historical practice, these scholars were in most cases refugees from a religious vocation; and yet they were, even when estranged from Christian doctrine, deeply concerned with the role of faith, morality, and ecclesiastical institutions in history. They were also involved in journalism and polemic and in the teaching of history, especially on the university level, for future statesmen as well as professional scholars. Many of them were themselves active in political and colonial affairs. Of the most prominent of these magisterial English historians born between 1820 and 1850 were James Anthony Froude (1818), Edward A. Freeman (1823), William Stubbs (1825), James Gardiner (1829), Lord Acton (1834), J. R. Seeley, (1834), J. R. Green (1837), W. E. H. Lecky (1838), Mandell Creighton (1843), and F. W. Maitland (1850), who all produced their major work in the last half of the century.[1]

After Macaulay these professional, or semi-professional, scholars took up the project of researching, writing, and revising national history, with the growing advantage of sources published in the tradition of Rymer and Wilkins as well as the Journal of the House of Commons and the Statutes of the Realm, but now on the model, if not the level, of the *Monumenta Germaniae Historica* and Guizot's documentary series begun in the 1830s. They built on or contended with the interpretations of Hume, Hallam, and Macaulay, and on materials provided by, among others, the Record Commission (1802), the Public Record Office (reorganized by an Act of 1838 and headed by the first deputy keeper, Francis Palgrave), the Camden Society (1838), and the Rolls Series (which began publishing in 1858, in which William Stubbs later became the dominant figure), and Stubbs's own *Select Charters* (1870 and many later editions).[2] All of this contributed to what David Knowles called "the great revolution in academic history, which has sprung primarily from medieval constitutional and institutional history."[3]

This generation of scholars tended to follow Macaulay's tradition of the gentleman scholar, some even while holding university chairs, but increasingly, they were forced to take seriously the task of teaching and training scholars or future statesmen and the standards of professionalism.[4] The regius professorships of history were established at Oxford and Cambridge in 1724, but few of the tenants had serious pretensions to scholarship for a century and more. The first distinguished regius professor at Oxford was Thomas Arnold, but he died less than a year after his appointment in 1841. Arnold was succeeded by Henry Halwell Vaughan and then Goldwyn Smith, who resigned in 1866 for a position at Cornell and then Toronto. The "Oxford" school really begins with the next tenants of the regius chair, Stubbs, Freeman, and Froude. To these should be added the name of Freeman's lifelong friend, John Richard Green. The "Cambridge School" begins essentially not with Charles Kingsley (regius professor, 1859–69, and brother-in-law of Froude), as lightweight as Goldwyn Smith, but with Seeley, Acton, and J. B. Bury (1902–27), and including Creighton, Dixie Professor of ecclesiastical history (1884–91) and first editor of the *English Historical Review,* and Maitland, professor of law, who turned down an offer of the regius chair, as did S. R. Gardiner. These were the dominant scholars in the writing, revising, and wrangling about English history down to the turn of the century.

All of these historians had deeply religious backgrounds, entering orders (like Froude and Green) and some moving into the Anglican hierarchy, like Stubbs (Bishop of Oxford) and Creighton (Bishop of London), while Acton was a liberal Catholic layman deeply involved in ecclesiastical politics surrounding the Vatican Council. The "broad churchman" Seeley, with his political and imperial emphasis, was the only one who had a straightforward academic career, though he also wrote on theology. In his famous *Ecce Homo* (1865), which made his reputation, he had denied the divinity of Christ, but in 1888 he wrote that he was "still a believer," not being able to account for the success of Christianity by any ordinary cause.[5] The Oxford movement influenced their views, and so did the extraordinary career of Newman, who pushed "historicism" to its ecclesiastical limits when the "ideas of development" and "the wonderful revivals" of the Church sent him back to Catholicism.[6] Not only for the poet and the historian but also for the theologian truth could be the daughter of time.

But in English historical scholarship Newman represented an aberrant movement, and the influence of dogmatic religion was largely negative, since the abhorrence of Romanism persisted and was even intensified by historical studies. As Charles Kingsley wrote of Newman's casuistic sense of history, "Truth, for its own sake, has never been a virtue with the Roman clergy. Father Newman informs us that it need not, and on the whole ought not to be." In any case all of these historians saw history as an important part of religious and moral instruction.[7] Some of them, of course, fell away from scriptural faith; and as Froude wrote in 1849 in his novel *The Nemesis of Faith*, "The great Bible which cannot lie is the history of the human race."[8]

Religion was central to their conception of history, too. Kingsley saw "God working everywhere in history," so that the historian's business was to seek only "effective not final causes" — and yet he assigned Gibbon as the text in his course.[9] J. R. Green originally planned to write the history of the Church of England before deciding to be "the historian of England" — "indifferent" to modern ideas as he was.[10] In his inaugural lecture in 1859 Goldwyn Smith, perhaps an extreme example, celebrated the religious dimension of historical study and the triumph of free will over the vulgar materialism of the "necessarians" and the Positivists. In general Smith distanced himself from the enlightened tradition, including not only the "fearful mischief" done by Voltaire and Rousseau but also Gibbon's skeptical approach to history. "Gibbon's shallow and satirical view of the church and churchmen," he said, "has made him miss the grand actions and grand actors on the stage."[11] Smith's successor, Stubbs, who could not have been much impressed with Smith's scholarship, nonetheless, in his own inaugural in 1867, paid tribute to Smith's "learning, acuteness, earnestness, and eloquence" employed "on the behalf of Christian Truth against philosophic sciolists."[12] Of Stubbs himself the story is told of his first meeting with Green, when, under pretense of borrowing and with the aim of protecting Green's intellectual innocence, he confiscated the young man's copy of a volume by Renan.[13]

Related to religion was the question of moral judgment in history, and here opinions were divided by the invasion of "scientific" attitudes — whether Comtean or Rankean — into historical interpretation and by the requirements of Victorian education. In a way professional history became more moralistic because of the pedagogical need to form the character of young Christian students caught between Newman's bold choice and dissent — or worse. Even Freeman, immersed in the sources of history, heard the "voice of Arnold" and celebrated the professor of history's "high calling" to teach virtue. Acton and Creighton, founders of the *English Historical Review,* debated the question of the duty of the historian to make moral judgments, with Creighton taking the negative side. Yet increasingly Christian religion became historicized, and historians like Lecky and Leslie Stephens made it the problematic object of their researches. For Green the progress of the "Race" was marked by the falling away of dead religions from human thought.[14]

The influence of continental scholarship — "the great hive of German workers," Stubbs called them in 1867 — was crucial for professional history in England.[15] Thomas Arnold was one of the early English Niebuhrianer: he learned of Niebuhr's *Roman History* through Julius Hare, corresponded with Baron Bunsen about it, reviewed it in 1825, and drew on it extensively for his own work, especially his idea of "the unity of history,"[16] a principle which Freeman likewise championed. Freeman also regarded Niebuhr's work as "wonderful," though Mommsen, his superior as a writer, he judged to be "the greatest scholar of our time."[17] One dissenting voice was the sour and skeptical George Cornwall Lewis, who was appalled by the presumption of Niebuhr, whose *Roman History* "teems with cases where he has built a vast imaginative superstructure upon a foundation of error" — but then he found Hallam's constitutional history "dry, meagre, and ill-written" and Macaulay's comments on Bacon "shallow and ignorant in the extreme."[18] But in biblical, antiquarian, legal, constitutional, and institutional studies it was the Germans who introduced English scholars to modern methods of criticism and to attitudes associated with historicism and transmitted through many translations, especially from the 1840s.[19]

The history professors of the Oxford and Cambridge schools had much to say about method and history as a science — "on the level of other sciences," argued Freeman[20] — but they fell short of the subtleties of Droysen and even Ranke. Not that they entertained a faith in absolute truth. "I am beginning to think that there is not, and never was, any such thing as truth in the world," wrote Freeman in 1858, but then adding: "At least I don't believe that any two people ever give exactly the same account of anything, even when they have seen it with their own eyes, except when they copy from one another."[21] They could display a certain sense of anachronism, which is implied in Creighton's remark: "My method is to take up questions as they present themselves and to view them as they might have presented themselves to an intelligent member of the Curia."[22] They could also acknowledge a certain relativism not only in history but also in historiography, and Freeman cited Mark Pattison's view that "every age has its own fashion of writing history."[23]

Yet on the whole the "science" of English historians was situated between the vulgar positivism of eccentric scholars like Buckle, whom most of them scorned, and the empiricism — and what Macaulay called "that great intellectual revolution"[24] — attributed to Lord Bacon, whom many of them turned into another sort of "idol." "Science" was collecting the facts, getting them straight, and putting them together properly (without reflecting much about what that involved). For his masterpiece, the *History of the Norman Conquest*, Freeman hoped that he had "thrown life into some things into which nobody since the Chroniclers [had] thrown life" — or "translate[d] Stubbs into thunder and lightning."[25] Some historians, including Kemble, Palgrave, Stubbs, Maitland, published documentary sources as well as interpretive studies. But the sign of historical achievement was a master narrative, and such was the common aim of this heroic generation of national historians — Stubbs and Freeman (for the Middle Ages), Froude (for the sixteenth century), Macaulay and Firth (for the seventeenth), Lecky (for the eighteenth), and Green for the whole range of English history — who all continued, he told Freeman, "on the old traditional line of English historians."[26]

The one scholar who might be judged the equal of the major continental historians was Stubbs — "that modern Mabillon," as Green called him.[27] Stubbs hardly denied his English heritage, but he thought poorly of it. "To speak with the utmost respect of my early predecessors," he declared in his inaugural lecture in 1867, "I do not find that they were men to whom the study of History, either English or foreign, is in any way indebted."[28] On the other hand Stubbs invoked his great seventeenth-century antecedents, including Hearne and Dugdale, in celebrating the "new studies" constituting the future of this great tradition. He envisaged "the founding of an historical school in England . . . which shall build, not upon Hallam and Palgrave and Kemble and Froude and Macaulay, but on the abundant collections and arranged materials on which those writers tried to build whilst they were scanty and scattered and in disorder."[29] Moreover, it was essential to make use of the British Museum and the Bodleian as well as recent German scholarship based on such sources — implicit rebukes to Freeman, who avoided manuscript research, and Green (a charter member of the "Freeman school"),[30] who hated libraries and never bothered to learn German.

Nineteenth-century English historians were deeply concerned with the large patterns of history, but for literary and ideological rather than philosophical reasons. The Romantic impulse to seek out origins was still apparent, even though such quests could seem illusory — being "lured into cloud-land" by "those Welsh chaps" (such as Gildas), as Green told Freeman.[31] Freeman found the "new and fascinating doctrine" of Max Müller — that is, comparative philology and mythology — a possible access to this "cloud-land."[32] In general Freeman recognized four kinds of statements in English history: historical, based on evidence; romantic, legendary and anecdotal (like Plutarch); traditional (received stories); and mythical. Freeman himself preferred chronicles as closest to historical truth — William of Malmesbury, for example, being superior to Hume on these grounds.[33] Stubbs, citing Waitz, Maurer, and other German medievalists, accepted the idea of the "barbarian" and Germanic origins of the English nation, though he concentrated on the institutional traces described in Tacitus and Caesar as the beginnings of the "primitive polity" and national tradition, connecting the *comitatus* with modern representative assemblies and the allod with private property.[34]

With Freeman, Stubbs shared an interest in comparative method, remarking that "it is quite lawful to work back, through obvious generalisations and comparisons with the early phenomena of other nations, to the primitive civilisation of the Aryan or the Indo-Germanic family."[35] Freeman extended such comparativism into a wider range of political reflection, especially in his projected but never completed study of federal government from ancient times to the present.[36] Although he was an enthusiast of geography, archeology, and even anthropology, Freeman preferred Thucydides (who was oriented politically to the future) to Herodotus (who was an antiquarian whose view was directed toward the past).[37] He was almost as much the political historian as Seeley, to the extent indeed that his beloved "Johnnikins" Green rebuked him for ignoring matters of "culture," which by no means were limited to literature, of which Freeman admittedly knew little, not even Shakespeare (nor was he informed about finance).[38] His favorite motto, "history is past politics, politics present history," enshrined along with his portrait in the Johns Hopkins history department seminar, does justice to his public life as well as historical writing. So he did not mind making rather more detached comparisons than Stubbs, for example, the return of the Saxon Godwin in 1052 with the Petition of Right almost six centuries later, and more theoretical judgments, as admitted that federations in general were more inclined to civil wars than other forms of government.[39]

One principle that all of these historians agreed about was that of continuity, whether legal, institutional, social, cultural, or all of these grouped under "the unity of history." For Green this was illustrated by "the unbroken row of Registers on the Lambeth shelves"; but of course he extended this insight into many aspects of his "history of the English people," which traced the fortunes of a single community over a dozen and more centuries.[40] So even more elaborately and minutely did Freeman, for whom the Conquest was, famously, "not a beginning but a turning point," and the "good old cause" lived continuously from Harold to the Petition of Right,[41] and Stubbs, for whom the English "Constitution" was the product of a slow and largely gradual process of growth—a "continuity of life," "rooted and grounded in the past."[42] It was a common view. As Creighton's wife wrote, "He was always anxious to impress upon his hearers the continuity of history, the truth that people in the past were like people in the present, that nothing was inevitable."[43] Yet for Creighton this principle did not violate revealed religion, for "the acceptance of evolution only explains, but does not overthrow, the divine creation of the world to the religious mind."[44] In the nineteenth century the principle of continuity, essential to the old historicism, applied across doctrines and confessions, from Bishop Creighton and Cardinal Newman to the most subversive Darwinist.

Periodization was a matter of concern for these historians, although the question usually took the pedagogical issue of the dividing line between "ancient" and "modern"—the charge of particular historical chairs—if not, more naively, "past and present." In his inaugural lecture at Oxford, attended and reviewed by Green, Stubbs set forth his vision of his duties. "Here came the crackers," Green told Freeman. "The chair was not to be a chair of Politics, but of simple, sheer work."[45] Stubbs went on to distinguish ancient from modern history: "The one was dead; we were living in the other." But where did "modern" history begin? With the "call of Abraham," the Flood, the fall of the Western Empire, the coronation of Charlemagne, or the French Revolution? Green, who believed in "the rule of reading the past by the present" (as Charles Lyell read geology) deplored the "ignorant fling" of Seeley for urging "present history" as the only study for sensible men.[46] This was the most vulgar sort of utilitarianism. As for Freeman, though for practical purposes he began his lectures with the invasion of Gaul by the barbarians in A.D. 407, he actually rejected, in the name of continuity, the distinction between ancient and modern.[47]

A primary mark of the coming of age of scientific history in the nineteenth century was the founding of a professional journal, although the *English Historical Review* followed its German and French counterparts, the *Historische Zeitschrift* and *Revue Historique,* by ten and thirty-seven years respectively. In the prospectus of the English periodical its first editor, Mandell Creighton, having consulted with scholars like Bryce, Seeley, Gardiner, R. L. Poole, and especially Lord Acton, laid out a modest agenda, appealing to general readers as well as professional students, invoking impartiality and a balance between Herodotean and Thucydidean extremes — between Freeman's "past politics" and a history that would attempt a "picture of the whole past." The *EHR* would privilege politics but at the same time take notice of all the arts and sciences as well as notable private persons. Creighton proposed as a motto a quotation from Sydney beginning, "Not professing any art, the historian, as his matter leads him, deals with all arts."[48] Emphasis would be placed on "new" facts rather than "allurements of style," and indeed Creighton privately decided to leave Froude's name off the publisher's list of possible contributors. On the other hand, he told Acton, "I should like some ladies." Of the review's public image Creighton added, "We do not wish to look ornamental or gaudy," and in this he surely succeeded.

Nineteenth-century historiography in Britain was produced by what was a community of scholars almost comparable to that society which created seventeenth-century science. It was hardly so coherent, but it was the work of intellectuals with a common education, social background, terminology, assumptions, and purposes. The difference was that, whereas the scientists agreed generally about the nature of truth, English historians, despite similar rhetoric about evidence and inference, worked within different ideological and religious frameworks which shaped their conclusions about historical meaning, and moreover they carried on discussion of historical themes not merely in order to reach a consensus but rather to succeed in a competition for literary as well as scientific success, applause, and authority. "Criticism" was a weapon of offense as well as defense to be employed in reviews as well as texts and footnotes. Like poets and novelists, historians sought friendly reviews and feared hostile ones; and historical literature not only displayed accumulations of knowledge but also defined battlegrounds. Yet these writers were also very conscious of carrying on a grand tradition, of being part of a great community, extending back to the eighteenth century and perhaps earlier.

Between Medieval and Modern

Despite the "oriental renaissance" (and England's key role in the teaching of Sanskrit in the generation after Jones and Colbrooke),[49] the example of Gibbon, and the expanding empire, English historians were unabashedly Eurocentric, and most of them remained within the biblical framework as well. Froude was a close friend of Max Müller, as was Freeman, but shared little of his scholarly interests. Like Eusebius, English historians studied ancient Greece and Rome as antecedents of Judeo-Christian tradition; and continental scholarship, as in the work of Niebuhr, Guizot, and the historical schools, reinforced this parochialism. The Anglican view, a bit more liberally construed, appeared also in the history of the late medieval and early modern papacy of Mandell Creighton, who, picking up where Gibbon and Milman had left off, followed the secular, or Erastian, line of Marsilius of Padua, William Ockham, and John Wyclif (following Stubbs), and, leaning heavily on ecclesiastical polemic, the story of "national resistance to papal distortion," in which England took the lead from the fourteenth century.[50] The crucial points in Creighton's account were the "revolution" brought about by Conciliarism and more especially the Reformation. Bishop as well as professor, Creighton hoped to keep a balance between religion and science. He accepted the idea of tradition but avoided the Romanist fate of Newman, he wrote, because he avoided theology.[51]

As for the political and institutional history of Europe, the story began with the invasions of the "barbarian" tribes, which formed the national bases of a Christianizing society. The broad narrative of this transformation was told in the massive work of Thomas Hodgkin, friend of Creighton and subject of the biography of Creighton's wife, whose Italian travels led to a lifelong fascination with the invasions of Italy from the fifth century.[52] The history of the primary creation of Germanic political organization was given by James Bryce's *Holy Roman Empire,* which began as a small monograph that won the Arnold Prize in 1862 and which grew into the standard nineteenth-century survey of the thousand- (and six-) year Reich. In his account Bryce conspicuously avoided citation of Gibbon (though not of Sismondi's derivative study of the fall of Rome). "Gibbon seems to me to have won by his style rather more credit than he deserves as a historian," wrote Bryce in 1920. "He does not see far below the surface, and often fails to ask the right questions; but of course history was a different thing a hundred and fifty years ago."[53] Yet Bryce himself, widely read as he was, relied extensively on seventeenth- and eighteenth-century scholarship and cited few contemporary authors, except for a few German scholars, including Ranke and Döllinger.

For Bryce the Holy Roman Empire was a major link between the Victorian and the ancient world; for "just as to explain a modern Act of Parliament or a modern conveyance of lands we must go back to the feudal customs of the thirteenth century, so among the institutions of the Middle Ages there is scarcely one which can be understood until it is traced up either to classical or to primitive Teutonic antiquity."[54] Christianity became a political force when, clinging to the departed "nationality" and institutional traditions of Rome, it became allied with the state and later renewed this alliance with the

Frankish rulers. The coronation of Charlemagne in A.D. 800 — surely a calculated move — was the "central event of the middle ages," declared Bryce, and
without it the history of the world would have been different.[55] Bryce traced
the fortunes of the Carolingian, Italian, and German Emperors, their expansion and struggles with the papacy, and especially the idea of empire, over the
next millennium down to its dissolution by Napoleon in 1806. In concluding
he noted the nineteenth-century controversy between Prussian historians such
as Sybel and Waitz and Austrians like Ficker over the national significance of
the medieval empire, and he deplored the contemporary Austrian Empire,
which, unlike its Holy Roman forebear, sinned not "in the dim twilight of a
half-barbarous age" but "in the noonday blaze of modern civilization."[56] The
medieval empire was too recently dead to judge its meaning for European
civilization, but it left a valuable legacy of Roman jurisprudence, a tradition of
antipapal politics, and an ideal of a European commonwealth, while self-
destructing and "in effect abolishing the need for a centralizing and despotic
power like itself."[57]

Even as they traced European traditions back into medieval and ancient
times, British historians were mainly contemptuous of antiquarianism and
kept their eyes on the question of modernity. William Stubbs was regius professor of "modern history," and he gloried in the epithet. "Compared with the
study of Ancient history," he declared, modern historical inquiry — which for
Stubbs included medieval — "is like the study of life compared with that of
death, the view of the living body compared with that of the skeleton."[58]
Present reality was "rooted and grounded in the past" through the rule of the
"continuity of life." According to this continuity, Stubbs continued, "history
could be read either backwards or forwards"; the latter was the procedure of
politicians and popular writers and the former for scholars and teachers, who
needed to avoid partisanship and controversy.[59] Historical continuity was the
product not of individual actions, not of the *res gestae,* the memorable deeds,
of classical historical narrative but rather of institutions passed on over the
generations as tribal, or national, customs and patterns of social organization.
The "English Constitution," which was the rubric under which social institutions, national character, and the transformations of these were grouped, was
the subject of Stubbs's great, if flawed survey; and individuals were subordinated to these historical constructs.[60] English history began when these social
ingredients of the "primitive polity" merged with national self-consciousness
to reinforce the "growth of national character" and "continuity of national
life."[61] Such imputed continuities were the basis of what he called "constitutional precedents." Stubbs saw not only continuities but also uniformities, and
he repeatedly used the term "system" to emphasize social, institutional, and

constitutional formations — the "mark system," the "Anglo-Saxon system," the "national system," the Norman "administrative system," etc.[62] He also found a "uniformity of principle in feudal law" which extended across centuries and national traditions.

The larger European context was defined in general by a struggle between imperialism and nationality, of papal north and imperial south, but beneath these conflicts large patterns of local growth could be detected; and Anglo-Saxon England was an instance of an almost pure development of Germanic principles into feudal forms. In the centuries-long debate between Romanists and Germanists, Stubbs was definitely, and derivatively, in the latter camp — though he admitted Roman influence in the religious unity afforded by the church. In particular he followed the interpretations of early legal and constitutional history of Waitz, Grimm, Brunner, Gniest, and von Maurer, who themselves took their own lead from the invidious contrasts between Romans and barbarians in Tacitus's *Germania*. He inferred "common German sources" — or even, following Henry Sumner Maine, Indo-German sources — for a number of institutions, the hundred, the *comitatus,* limited and elective kingship, the right of deposition, the principle of counsel and consent, which was "the traditional theory of all the German races" and which in England was the basis of the national assembly, the *Witenagemot,* which evolved into the national Council and finally the Parliament.[63] Stubbs also imported into English history von Maurer's views of the *Mark* and accepted the idea of common property in land in the earliest period.[64]

Like Guizot, Stubbs focused in particular on the theory and practice of representative government. The *Witenagemot* preserved its form after the Conquest despite the introduction of new feudal practices and legal and administrative machinery.[65] For Stubbs the great turning point was not the Conquest but the Great Charter. It was both "the united act of a nation that had been learning union" and "the watchword of a new political party" — to which, indeed, Stubbs was a member.[66] Magna Carta, based on an earlier charter of Henry I in 1100 as an amplification of his coronation oath,[67] was a treaty between the king and his subjects, including a provision reaffirming the principle of a common counsel taken in a national assembly, which was at once a feudal court and a stage toward the representation of the three estates and which by the time of Henry III was called "Parliament." The "system" of juries, whether or not instituted by Henry II in its English form, was another step toward representation, and it, too, was reinforced by "the growth of a burgher spirit," the triumph of the "mercantile" over the "aristocratic spirit."[68] With the Great Charter England became indeed "a self-reliant and self-sustained nation."[69]

Like Guizot, too, Stubbs was interested in the comparative dimension invited by Germanist premises. English parliamentary development occurred in a period, the twelfth and thirteenth centuries, when other European states — Aragon (1162), Castile (1169), Sicily (1232), Germany (1255), and France (1302) — were experimenting with representative assemblies. Only England had continuous success, however, and this was because representation was combined with local machinery which implemented the rights of all "freemen" to be represented in Parliament. Whence arose, too, parliamentary powers in matters of taxation, justice, legislation, and "general business" — reflected in the famous motto "What touches all must be approved by all" (*Quod omnes tangit, ab omnes [ab]probetur*), which also contributed "to produce unity of national action."[70] Unlike the continental states, moreover, English government did not, finally, allow the lawyers a constitutional position as a virtual Fourth Estate, while the clergy gained in influence by meeting separately, from the thirteenth century, in Convocation.[71]

For Stubbs the story of the development of the English Constitution and its supporting institutions and social groupings, which he carried down to the age of print and the accession of Henry VII, was uneven but largely progressive, especially in its theory. He quoted from the works of John Fortescue and Thomas Smith, no less celebratory than Stubbs himself of common law and parliamentary tradition. Stubbs was "clerical and conservative" in his outlook, and yet as a teacher of "modern history" he was unabashedly Whiggish — didactic — in his sympathies, and yet he claimed, in the most pretentious and "moralising" terms, to be a fair and impartial judge who offered "the truth, the whole truth and nothing but the truth."[72]

The other major work of this generation on the English Middle Ages was the account of the Norman Conquest by Stubbs's friend Freeman, who was no less attached to the principle of continuity and to Germanist interpretations, which for him stretched back to the "early Teutonic constitution" down to survivals in nineteenth-century Switzerland, which he saw at first hand. Freeman's aim was to combine the half truths of his predecessors Thierry and Palgrave, of whom the first exaggerated the break and the racial divisions brought by the Conquest, and the other overestimated the Roman and then German continuities of English history. The Conquest was not a break, argued Freeman, but only the most important turning point, "the temporary overthrow of our national being."[73] Drawing extensively on printed chronicles and geographical knowledge, Freeman dispensed with manuscript sources; and in contrast to Thierry's concern for class and ethnic conflict, he attended to politics, personalities, and individual actions — the Danish kings and Norman Dukes, Edward the Confessor, Godwin, and Harold. Yet like Stubbs, Freeman was also concerned with institutions, and he traced the "Constitution," from its "early Teutonic" form down to the parliamentary monarchy of later modern times. In language, institutions, social character, and "community of blood," English history displayed a unique and coherent pattern that underlay the violent events reported by chroniclers and repeated by superficial historians.

"In Britain everything is different," Freeman aphorized.[74] Yet Freeman was also intensely aware of the common heritage of European political traditions and indeed, through the comparative philology of Grimm and his own friend Max Müller, of the whole Aryan family of nations. For Freeman comparative philology marks a stage in the progress of the human mind "at least as great and memorable as the revival of Greek and Latin learning," which formed the basis of Freeman's own scholarship and which he defended fiercely against Philistines like Froude.[75] Comparative philology (anticipated, Freeman suggested, by Roger Bacon) was a true science, an "absolutely universal solvent," which led to an otherwise inaccessible prehistory of Western society. Much less certain was the companion discipline of comparative mythology, although myths, too, may be inferred to belong, at least in part, to a common Indo-European stock.

Freeman shared the views of Vico and Herder (though he did not cite them) about the unmixed nature of national traditions. This is evident in his fascination with another area of comparative method—the "third, as yet nameless, science," which was the "scientific inquiry into manners and customs" and indeed into "culture itself," and which drew on the insights of scholars like Edward Tylor and Henry Sumner Maine.[76] Classicist tradition and its comparativist extension are what produced the "unity of history," as Freeman argued in his Rede lecture of 1872, published with his lectures on the new discipline he called "comparative politics." This "unity" underlay that Eurocentric view that situated "Greek, Roman, and Teuton" — "brethren of one common stock," Freeman called them — in a linear master narrative, linking the Achaians of Homer not only with the Germans of Tacitus but also the Anglo-Saxons and free villagers of the Alpine valleys of Uri and Unterwalden, in which Freeman and most other nineteenth-century historians operated.[77] Kingship, council, representative assemblies, property, analogous social groupings (including the *Markgenossenschaft*), and finally the State itself—these all helped to preserve the continuity of this great Aryan tradition in which England figured so centrally and which for him made the old distinction between "ancient" and "modern" so misguided in a pedagogical as well as a scholarly sense: all history is modern history. His Norman studies turned his interests to his last major work, also unfinished, which was the history of Sicily as a part of universal history.[78]

So the English Middle Ages were given narrative form by two regius professors of "modern history," but it was their younger friend, and essentially amateur historian, J. R. Green, who told the whole story of English history. Green published his *Short History* in 1874, featuring neither individual agents ("drum and trumpet history") nor enduring institutions but rather, romantically, the "People" — a book translated into French in 1888 and introduced in a laudatory way by Gabriel Monod. A carryover from his missed ecclesiastical calling appeared in the religious dimension of Green's history, tracing English religious faith from superstition to freedom. Green's interpretation began with his paper on St. Dunstan given in 1862, which brought him to Freeman's notice and began a lifelong friendship between Freeman and his "Johnnikins."[79] In his *History* Green represented Dunstan as "first in the line of ecclesiastical statesmen who counted among them Lanfranc and Wolsey, and ended with Laud."[80] Following Stubbs, Green gave special reverence to the Great Charter, "the earliest monument of English freedom which we can see with our own eyes" — "with the royal seal still hanging from the brown, shriveled parchment" in the British Museum — and he celebrated the "social revolution" leading to the establishment of Parliament.[81] He celebrated, too, the "new monarchy" and the "new learning" of the sixteenth century and another "great revolution" carried out by Thomas Cromwell; and he represented the Puritan Revolution as the result of "national resistance" following "the earlier struggle for Parliamentary liberty."[82] Green's book, only slightly less popular than Macaulay's, was a classic summary of the Whig interpretation of British history.

The history of law and institutions was turned in a more comparative and theoretical direction by Henry Sumner Maine, who took the history of Roman law as his model, but who extended his interpretations into the larger field of Indo-European, or "Aryan," history — refusing, unlike McLennan, Bachofen, and Morgan, to include "promiscuous" examples from unrelated traditions.[83] Maine's comparativist studies were strongly influenced by the work of Max Müller in comparative philology, but he also drew on the Mark theory of Maurer and endorsed the idea of primitive communalism.[84] For Maine kinship and not individualism was the condition of prehistory, and the later pattern was a shift from blood relations to territorial rule and "from status to contract." Maine's anthropological turn was important for English historical scholarship, although his speculations about primitive communism were discredited by professional historians, especially F. W. Maitland.

Maitland was, by common consent, the greatest of English medievalists. He moved from a legal to a scholarly career and devoted himself to bringing together the study of law and history, and indeed to rewriting the history of English law. His grandfather, S. R. Maitland, was also a medievalist, author of *The Dark Ages*, in which he criticized Gibbon and Robertson for their ignorance of the Middle Ages.[85] What turned Maitland toward the history of law was not only his discovery of Stubbs's constitutional history but also his exposure to the historical school, especially Savigny, Gierke, Brunner, and Grimm, which encouraged his sympathies with Germanist ideas (and turned him against the enthusiasms of Celticists), so that, for example, he accepted Brunner's suggestion that English law was a "daughter" of Frankish law — although Alfred's legislation, so similar to the Carolingian, came much later — and moreover he was willing to admit deeper "Aryan" origins of some institutions. But Maitland was uncomfortable with "antiquities," such as the prehistorical family and ideas of collective ownership (antedating modern "corporations"?); and he was unwilling to deviate from textual tradition on which he did pioneering work (as a moving spirit in the Selden Society, founded in 1887), from the law and lawyers beginning with Bracton (whose notebooks were discovered in 1874 by Vinogradoff) and including the law reports, and here the record was consistently and characteristically English.

Like German scholars, too, Maitland insisted on the continuity of English legal history, going back at least to Alfred the Great.[86] Despite the invasion of the French language — much more gradual, taking perhaps a century, than that of the Normans themselves — the Conquest was not really a break, as narrative historians like Freeman argued, but rather a "confluence" of traditions, and indeed Latin was not "dislodged" until 1731. In fact Anglo-Saxon laws and customs persisted and were revived, as shown by the laws of Henry I published by Felix Liebermann; and indeed the Great Charter was itself mainly "restorative."[87] Nor were Roman (largely canonist and ecclesiastical) imports a sign of foreign contamination, for unlike continental states England resisted a "Reception" of Roman law; on the contract, while European nations were incorporating "the ultimate of Roman legal history, England was unconsciously reproducing that history," that is, developing a system of protection against Romanist influence and a guarantee of England's exceptionalist status.[88] In other ways Maitland showed his revisionist inclinations, as, in exploring the role of common law, shifting emphasis from self-congratulatory Parliamentary concerns to the monarchy itself: "In England the law for the great men has become the law for all men," he argued, in another tradition of self-congratulation, "because the law of the king's court has become the common law."[89]

For several reasons Maitland was unhappy with the unhistorical temper of his English colleagues, protesting that they had not caught up with continental scholars in publishing their records, that they — jurists and historians — had little appreciation for the value of legal sources for social and economic history, and that they tended to fall into absurd anachronisms by failing to read "the law of the time in the language of the time." Like his lawyerly predecessors Maitland regarded philosophy as marginal, if not irrelevant, to common law; and for him historical semantics was at all times a key to understanding the ways of men and their laws, "for language is no mere instrument that we can control at will; it controls us."[90] He also deplored the influence of Bentham, "scornful as he was of the past and its historic deposit," and ready as he was to draw up a code at a moment's notice.[91] He was an extraordinarily acute critic of careless scholarship, like that of Maine; but he also disliked the nationalist exchanges on "the battlefield of scholars" fighting over Merovingian territory and the attacks of Round, Freeman, and others (Round in particular was extraordinarily uncivil in his criticisms of Freeman and Maitland's protégé Mary Bateson). For Maitland the sources were the proper object of scholarly energies, and they had yet to be exhausted, or indeed even assembled, so that, as he proclaimed famously, the history of English law had yet to be written. Yet he also felt deeply about the larger significance of the story of the great line of lawmakers who, as he wrote in the last sentence of his (and Pollock's) history, "were making right and wrong for us and for our children."

Between Science and Literature

In a famous essay published in 1913 George Macaulay Trevelyan reviewed the previous half-century and saw a rivalry between a historical science seeking causes and effects in human affairs and a historical art aspiring to remove prejudices, breed enthusiasm, and bring pleasure (ideals that both had roots in antiquity).[92] His own preference was on the side of art, following Thomas Carlyle, whose essay "On History" opened with an invocation of "Clio . . . , chief of the Muses" — yet lying, he added, "at the root of all science."[93] Nor was this merely a matter of taste, for Carlyle also pointed out the "fatal discrepancy between our manner of observing these [events] and their manner of occurring." It is perhaps curious that while "literary," or "mere literature," became a term of reprobation, literary historians often brandished the epithet "scientific" to grace their work. For Trevelyan, "science" was often humbug, and he placed himself squarely on the side of artists like Gibbon, Scott, Carlyle, and of course his revered uncle, rather than on pedantic works like those of Ranke, the *Cambridge Modern History*, edited by

Lord Acton, which began to appear in 1902, and even Creighton's "excessively dispassionate" account of the Reformation. For Clio was not a doctor, in Jacques Barzun's term, but "a muse." Equally famous was J. B. Bury's retort on "The Science of History," though what he meant by this was closer to old-fashioned empiricism than to modern speculations about natural laws.[94]

Illustrations — almost caricatures — of history as art and as science can be seen in the cases of Carlyle and Henry Thomas Buckle. Even before Macaulay, Thomas Carlyle, who had lost his faith reading Gibbon and broadened his horizons reading German authors, entertained a larger public with his *French Revolution,* in which, in grotesquely affected style, he tried to "splash down what I know in large masses of colour that it may look like a smoke and flame conflagration in the distance."[95] Carlyle lamented the fact that so much history, "interpreting events," had been left not to the Shakespeare and the Goethe but to the "Dryasdust" (*Gelehrte Dummkopf*), a "hapless Nigger gone masterless" but affecting to read the ways of God. Carlyle's life of Frederick the Great (Hitler's favorite book) was a very extended account of "the *last* real *king* that we have had in Europe," who was since quite submerged by the French Revolution, and displayed the same sense of color, drama, and disdain for the methods of Niebuhr and Ranke.[96] The heroic Frederick "lived in a Century which has no history and can have little or none," declared Carlyle, a century "opulent in accumulated falsities," and notable only for "that grand universal Suicide" called the French Revolution. Carlyle was an importer of German literature into the Anglophone world, but this included no part of the philosophy of history that emerged in the wake of Hegel — although the "world-historical individual" did have a superficial similarity with Carlyle's rough view of history. For Carlyle individual, not collective, actions were the target of the historical artist; for universal history was a compendium of biographies, accounts of "great men," and stories of heroes.[97] It was a "magical web," whose appearance changed with time. "Thus, do not the records of Tacitus acquire new meaning, after seventeen hundred years, in the hands of a Montesquieu?" he asked; and, "Niebuhr must reinterpret for us, at a still greater distance, the writings of Titus Livius."[98] History might be "philosophy teaching by example" for the political historian, he admitted, but life is too rich and complex to be captured by scientific formulas. For Carlyle, too, Clio was not only the "eldest daughter of memory" but also "chief of the muses."[99]

For Buckle, at the other extreme, history not only sought causes and effects but adopted the terms and claims of modern natural science. This meant not only the collecting of dates, ranging from statistics and physical geography to ethnography and linguistic, but also the study of the physical aspects of history — climate, food, soil, and "general aspects of nature."[100] Unlike most of his English contemporaries Buckle drew widely on French and German scholarship and theories in his search for a synthetic and "philosophic history" that would shift the focus of inquiry from "metaphysics" to positive grounds. What Buckle sought was the laws of man and nature and the ways in which mind surpassed nature in the European, and especially English, tradition. So Buckle would reduce the "civilization" which Guizot and so many others talked about to a process accessible to the methods of a true science of history. In the course of his work Buckle also traced the history of this science from its skeptical origins through its largely French career, including Voltaire (who "anticipated Niebuhr"!), Helvétius, Condillac, and the rise of "democratic" physical science before the French Revolution.

In England (unlike the continent) "modern history" was at first conceived as beginning with Constantine, or Charlemagne, or "1066 and All That," and only later as succeeding the centuries of medieval darkness rather than, as for instance with Green, Stubbs, and Freeman, the ancient world—contrasting the living with the dead aspects of history. But the fascination with the "modern" as something more dramatic than the mere opposite of antiquity and more appropriate to Victorian triumphalist values made an indelible imprint on historians despite the emphasis on continuity inherited from legal and political tradition; and of course the Anglican break with Roman "popery" in the sixteenth century gave further ideological impetus to the distinction. "For, indeed, a change was coming on the world, the direction of which even still is hidden from us, a change from era to era," wrote Froude in the first chapter of his epic story of Tudor England. "The paths trodden by the footsteps of ages were broken up; old things were passing away, and the faith and life of ten centuries were dissolving like a dream."[101] This "most memorable era" was marked in particular by the Reformation Parliament meeting in 1529—and its consequences, too, were revolutionary: "Monastic life in England was at an end, and for ever."[102]

For Froude, who was certainly to be numbered among the "literary historians," this religious transformation constituted a great "revolution," as indeed did the conversion of Henry IV in France and the achievement of Joan of Arc; and it was to this seminal experience that he devoted his major work. Froude had been a journalist and editor of *Fraser's Magazine* before his appointment as regius professor at Cambridge. Like his brother Hurrel (who died in 1836), Froude was a product of the Oxford movement and the influence of Newman, and he even took orders in 1845.[103] This was a time of religious and emotional crisis: while Newman was defecting to Rome, Froude, under the counterinfluence of Carlyle (whose *French Revolution* he read in 1842) and Kingsley, fell away from High Church ideals and into the skeptical turn described in his *Nemesis of Faith,* which was begun in 1847, and which was intensified by the revolutionary events of the next year. Froude's crisis of conscience led him to a more serious study of history and the anti-Romanist edge of his view of the English past. After his marriage in 1850 and a three-year residence in Wales, where he began to read intensively in Elizabethan history, Froude turned to the legal records of the Tudor monarchy as an entry into the social conditions of England in the age of Henry VIII.

Froude wrote of the beginning of modernity, with its morally mixed legacy, but he wrote also of a world he, and we, have lost. It was hard to understand fanaticism and superstition as well as the depth of faith of that period which had created monsters of persecution as well as the marvels of martyrdom. Henry had asserted the principle of freedom of speech for the Parliament, he wrote;[104] but there was no "liberty of conscience" in the sixteenth century, though it had become a "law of modern thought."[105] On the other side of the ledger were the efforts of exploration and expansion, which Froude also followed in other books. The sixteenth century was for Froude the planting ground of national genius, though the harvest of individual creations came a bit later, so that "Shakespeare's plays were as much the offspring of the long generations who had pioneered his road for him, as the discoveries of Newton were the offspring of those of Copernicus."[106] "And now it is all gone — like an unsubstantial pageant faded," he wrote of sixteenth-century England; "and between us and the old English there lies a gulf of mystery which the prose of the historian will never quite bridge. They cannot come to us, and our imagination can but feebly penetrate to them."[107]

Struggling against religious uncertainty, Froude was not immune to the vision of scientific history, at least on the level of commonsense empiricism. "It is not for the historian to balance advantages," Froude also wrote, in a rough paraphrase of Ranke's famous formula. "His duty is with the facts." Like Macaulay, Froude was especially fond of journalistic sources — the so-called informations preserved in the Record Office — and the anecdotes which they contained; but he also, like Ranke (and unlike Freeman, who avoided manuscripts), prized archival sources; and indeed he was the first, for example, to explore the archives of Simancas.[108] Yet Froude acquired a reputation as an extremely careless and (like Carlyle) lamentably "literary" writer — largely through the invidious efforts of Freeman, who not only called him "the vilest brute that ever wrote a book" but also elevated his discovery of errors in Froude's publications to a general judgment about what Charles Langlois and Charles Seignobos, in their handbook of historical method, called "Froude's Disease."[109] But Freeman himself was entirely innocent of manuscript knowledge and endured severe criticisms for his pedantic excesses.

Froude's highly dramatic narrative depended on a careful and colorful selection of the "facts" at his disposal, and moreover sharp judgments of these facts. He distinguished between "noble" and "ignoble" Catholics, for example;[110] he concluded that Wolsey "loved Rome better than England," that the Marian exiles were "a band of heroes," and that ("Bloody") "Mary's epithet will cling forever."[111] To portray the extremes of the Reformation debate Froude dramatically described the exchange, in Convocation in the presence of Cromwell, "lording over the scowling crowd," between Cardinal Pole, whose vision was based on the Catholic world across the channel, "bound under an iron yoke, and sinking down in despair and desolation," and the "heretic leader" Latimer, whose sermon treated the "children of light" and the "children of this world" still struggling in darkness.[112]

In contrast to Stubbs, Freeman, and Green, Froude rejected the argument from continuity — the sort of argument that led Newman back to the Romanist fold — and took "revolution" as his model of explanation, or depiction, of the Reformation Parliament. "And this one body of men, dim as they now seem to us . . . ," he declared, "had commenced and had concluded a revolution which had reversed the foundations of the State."[113] Subsequent events were also part of this revolutionary pattern, so that, for example, "the sermons at Paul's Cross breathed of revolution."[114] Like his friend Carlyle, he was inclined to place "great men," and women as well, near the center of the historical process; and later he also wrote biographies of Caesar and Erasmus as well as Carlyle. In contrast to his medievalist contemporaries, too, he concentrated not on institutions and factors of *longue durée* but rather on human agency and heroism. "Periods of revolution bring out and develop extraordinary characters," he wrote; "they produce saints and heroes, and they produce also fanatics, and fools, and villains."[115] Froude's portraits of Henry VIII, Pole, More, Knox, Anne Boleyn, Cromwell, Elizabeth, and Mary Stuart often dominate his narrative.

So rupture not flow was the pattern Froude found at the threshold of modernity: " 'breaking the bonds of Rome' and the establishment of spiritual independence" represented "the greatest achievement in English history." As a result he revised the common opinion about the Tudor monarchs, arguing that it was better not to complain of the "tyranny" of Henry and Elizabeth but "rather admire the judgment . . . which steered the country safe among those dangerous shoals."[116] Indeed Henry VIII seemed in retrospect "formed by Providence for the conduct of the Reformation."[117] Like his newfound friend J. L. Motley, Froude pressed the thesis of religious emancipation from papal and medieval servitude, and — though he denied that there was such a thing as "liberty of conscience in the Reformation period" — he extended credit for this national liberation to both government and people in the sixteenth century. Not that the Protestant battles had been won, for the "magical theory of priesthood" was the cause of the contemporary conflict with modern science as well as Reformation controversy.[118]

Though secular-minded, Froude had nothing but contempt for scientific history as preached and practiced by Buckle, who "does not believe (as some one has said) that the history of mankind is the history of its great men" — Froude was here alluding to Carlyle, whose biographer he was.[119] History can be invoked to support any theory, he added — progress, corruption, or even the social contract — but theories themselves were subject to the erosion of time, so that "the temper of each new generation is a continual surprise." Despite its currency, the idea of progress was no more sacrosanct than other theories. "The world calls all this progress," Froude wrote about the material advances of his age. "I call it only change."[120] And moreover, "I hate all historical theories."[121] Among professional colleagues who would agree on this point Froude's reputation was never high, and even his successor in the regius chair, Frederick York Powell, saw in his work "the demon of inaccuracy" and wrote that "he handles his authorities as a wilful baby does her dolls."[122]

Between Froude and Macaulay the work of transition was another of those mammoth creations of Victorian scholarship, Samuel Rawson Gardiner's narrative of the Stuart period and the English civil wars. Gardiner (an Irvingite Nonconformist) was director of the Camden Society and later editor of the *English Historical Review,* but he held no academic appointment, turning down the offer of the regius professorship after Froude to finish his book. Like Froude, he did extensive archival research on the continent and emphasized social and economic as well as political history. But in his study of the "Puritan Revolution," Gardiner made a serious effort to rise above the Whig-Tory partisanship of Macaulay's generation, and he argued, on commonsense rather than philosophical grounds, that sources should be "read in the spirit of the times in which they were drawn up."[123] His *History of England from 1603 to 1660,* which began to appear in 1863, was more self-consciously "scientific" than Froude's — hoping even, as he commented in his obituary of Ranke, "the father of modern historical research," as he called him, "to do for history what Darwin did for science."[124] But in fact Gardiner's "science" hardly rose above common British empiricism. His devotion to factual, chronological narrative, seeking to uncover the diverse motives of the principal actors, was such as to minimize interpretation as well as repudiate teleology, a sense of development, and even (as Lytton Strachey thought) a point of view, not unlike the revisionists of the past century.[125] He preferred to view the trees and not the forest, and he failed to interest such a reader as Maitland. His work was continued a generation later by his pupil and executor Charles Firth.

John Seeley, an admirer of Gardiner and successor of Kingsley as regius professor at Cambridge, shifted the emphasis of national history back to politics, beginning with a biography of Stein, reformer of the Prussian state. Without contact with politics and the laws which political science offered, history was narrowly chronological and "mere literature."[126] Through Comte and especially Buckle, Seeley derived ideas, nominally positivist, about the "scientific" nature of historical study. But Seeley's impact was mainly pedagogical. His biography of Stein was massive but derivative, and his other historical works were based mainly on popular lectures and articles.

Seeley had a strong classical background but turned to modern history as the best way of educating British statesmen. "The Roman Empire is the greatest political fact in the past history of man," by which all subsequent history was determined; but from the eighteenth century Britain had surpassed this great model. For Seeley, British history had taken center stage—or rather (recalling Aristotle's view that while drama ends, like the history of Holland or Sweden, epic only leaves off, as historians of British expansion must do) it had become the central theme of the modern epic of the European past.[127] But Seeley was not satisfied with vague invocations of "civilization" of the previous generation of historians, which amounted to "flinging over the whole mass [of historical phenomena] a *word* which hold[s] them together like a net." A painting or scientific discovery, he wrote, was not an "event." To avoid such vagueness Seeley proposed to return to the practice of authors like Thucydides and focus on the state and its actions. Only by selecting one factor can a historian expect to make explanatory progress—which at the same time allowed Seeley to celebrate the triumphs and future of British "Colonial Empire."[128] Of the five major empires—"greater Spain, Portugal, France, Holland, and Britain"—only the latter survived, avoided revolution, and remained significant.

The gap of eighteenth-century British history was filled by Lecky, who was a historian of opinions and ideas, of morals and of rationalism, as well as politics and society. He was also a product of the age of religious crisis and doubt and like Newman did not think theology could be divorced from history—except that, under the spell of liberating secularism, he believed that "Catholicism is rapidly becoming incredible to all intelligent minds."[129] He was enthusiastic in his attitude toward Darwin, and at first toward Buckle as well, calling his book "the *very* best history I have ever read." Later he changed his mind and contrasted "Carlyle, who resolves all history into the acts of individuals . . . , and Buckle, whose idea is history, leaving out the men and women."[130] But he liked Carlyle and Froude and with the latter argued about Irish history, which he thought Froude had treated so unfairly. One of his purposes, in his history of the eighteenth century, which began to appear in 1878, was to correct this negative image.[131] He became friendly with H. C. Lea and with him, as with Froude, shared a love of archival research, though he wanted always to include social, cultural, and intellectual matters as well as politics. The book was well received, though Acton was critical. Lecky thought that here, as elsewhere, Acton was more interested in revealing the extent of his own reading than in the subject at hand.[132]

Lord Acton and the Great Point of History

Lord Acton was a cosmopolitan and polyglot historian, a sometime politician, and a nobleman twice-over — through his father and grandfather (prime minister of the Kingdom of the Two Sicilies during the French Revolution), going back eight generations, and his mother, of the German house of Dalberg, going back several generations more than that; and through his stepfather, Lord Granville, he had further aristocratic and political ties, including a close friendship with Gladstone.[133] At the age of twenty-one he had already made the acquaintance of Macaulay, Grote, Savigny, Ranke, Boeckh, Bopp, Montalembert, and Thiers, among many others.[134] By then, too, he was already building his library with the purchase of basic source collections. Acton was moreover a Catholic and, with properties variously in Germany and France as well as England, had further connections that encouraged European travel and broad horizons. Yet as a Catholic he could not attend an English university (until his appointment as regius professor at Cambridge in 1895), and his hopes for an English Catholic university were never realized. As a scholar he felt out of place and out of his time; as an author he had no specific readership beyond his fellow Catholics, a small minority in England, and the smaller elite of European scholars, primarily Germans, interested in his rarefied erudition and particular brand of ecclesiastical politics.

Acton was educated at the University of Munich, but more specifically under the tutorship of the great German scholar (and later Cardinal) Ignaz von Döllinger, who had, Acton thought, followed the theological historicism of Möhler and, leaving behind the romantic, conjectural school of Creuzer, the scholarly historicism of Savigny. ("Möhler's *Symbolik* is wonderful," wrote Acton to Döllinger in 1855, signing himself "your loyal student"). "As a historian, Döllinger regarded Christianity as a force more than as a doctrine, and displayed it as it expanded and became the soul of later history."[135] Döllinger became his model in a number of ways, especially in this historical idealism and in the omnivorous pursuit of the sources of history and their criticism. He was, said Acton, "an accomplished bibliographer, who knew the hidden resources of printed books better than other men."[136] Acton shared with him the tendency to identify Catholic tradition with history — reinforced by Newman's theological evolutionism, which had led him back to orthodoxy and which both fascinated and repelled Acton. For Acton history revealed both the ideals of religion, morality, and freedom and the darker human and institutional side which needed not only to be admitted but also to be explored with the methods of modern historical science. But Döllinger was of an older generation: "He had begun when Niebuhr was lecturing at Bonn and Hegel in Berlin; before . . . Ranke had begun to pluck the plumbs for his modern popes," Acton wrote. "Guizot had not founded the *Ecole des Chartes,* and the school of method was not yet opened at Berlin."

By contrast, Acton grew up at the high tide of the "revolution in method," as different from Gibbon's time as astronomy before and after Copernicus. "There is an interval, as it were," Acton commented in 1863, "of centuries which divides Cuvier from Buffon, Gibbon from Niebuhr, with a distinctness almost as great as that which separates chemistry from alchemy, astronomy from astrology, history from legend."[137] This new learning, which Döllinger tried to master late in life, Acton could only compare in impact to the first Renaissance of learning four centuries earlier. The radical representative of the new discipline was Ranke, for whom "history is a science complete in itself, independent, borrowing no instruments and supplying no instruction, beyond its own domain."[138] From Döllinger and Ranke he learned to prize the archives as a source of privileged knowledge that would allow a true account of the events of the past — and correction of the errors that historians committed and were still committing, including Catholics who wanted to "get rid" of embarrassing or incriminating evidence. After the opening of the archives, Acton remarked about the divorce of Catherine of Aragon and Henry VIII, "the old story [of Wolsey] which satisfied Hallam will never be told again."[139] "By going on from book to manuscript and from library to archive," he noted, "we exchange doubt for certainty, and become our own masters."[140] This is the belief intended by Ranke's famous motto, *wie es eigentlich gewesen,* which was less an epistemological credo than a heuristic premise.

This pursuit of hidden and secret knowledge underlies one of the passions of Acton's life, also contracted from Döllinger, which was the bibliomania he indulged until he reached bankruptcy, buying books and manuscripts and hiring copyists. His notes and correspondence are filled with reports of his finds and his quarries, which he hoped would give him special knowledge of and insight into European history, as would his visits to more than forty continental archives, unfortunately not including those of the Vatican, to which he never gained access. Like the Renaissance humanists Acton called for a return *ad fontes.* "The Germans have a word: quellenmässig = ex ipsissimis fontibus, and another: wissenschaftlichkeit." "I might know Gibbon or Grote by heart," he told Richard Simpson, "I should yet have no real, original, scientific knowledge of Roman or Grecian history."[141] That the Church had, in his view, so much to hide made this quest more than ever necessary, though, with Döllinger, Acton was confident that revealing ecclesiastical errors and scandals would not touch the true tradition of the Church any more than the "fables" which Döllinger had surveyed.

Acton shared one of the excesses of nineteenth-century scientific history, and this was hypercriticism. Not only was he fascinated by historical puzzles and mysteries, which he hoped could be resolved by the appearance of still-hidden sources, but he was ever on the lookout for errors and oversights in published historical works. Not even the greatest of historians, not Ranke, Macaulay, or even Döllinger, were above reproach, whether on scholarly, political, or ethical grounds; and of course such criticism came easier to Acton seeing that he did not himself venture far into the arena of published and reviewed books. Not that he was himself above error. Having offered a critical and condescending review of Carlyle's massive study of Frederick the Great, Acton published a forged eighteenth-century work on the Prussian ruler entitled *Royal Mornings, or the Art of Reigning,* claiming that there were no conclusive arguments against Frederick's authorship (!).[142] In an essay on Paolo Sarpi, Acton carelessly charged Pope Pius V and Charles Borromeo, saints both, for supporting a decree promising pardon for the murder of heretics — confusing Pius IV with Pius V and the date and the meaning of the decree.[143]

Some of Acton's best years, when he was building up his contacts and his learning, were spent as a journalist, writing for the short-lived Catholic periodical the *Rambler,* continued as the *Home and Foreign Review.* This would keep him "hard at work," he told Döllinger, and at the same time "give me a position and an influence among Catholics."[144] Although he never distinguished much between his devotion to his faith and to historical scholarship, his first readership was indeed the cause of liberal Catholicism. Although Acton embraced the new historical science, he deplored the "prevailing mood of infidelity" (1859), and he warned that history could lead to Protestant heresy as science could to infidelity. The work of Henry Buckle was an example of each. "Setting aside the theory, the learning of the book is utterly superficial and obsolete," said Acton of Buckle's history of civilization in England. "He is altogether a mere humbug and a bad arguer."[145] But capping ignorance, "unreason" and derivative philosophical pretensions were "the monstrous and absurd results" of his "infidel philosophy." Like Döllinger, Acton took an increasingly ecumenical view of Protestantism, but he continued to believe that Catholic tradition, reinforced by modern critical learning, represented the best way to historical understanding.

Although tolerance, along with liberty the product of true religious tradition, was a central theme of Acton's writings, he was himself a rigid moralist and in personal and historical judgments, as even Döllinger admitted, was markedly intolerant; and this was also the impression of Henry Charles Lea and especially Mandell Creighton, with whom Acton had a famous interchange about the question of moral judgments in history. Acton admired Ranke's scholarship but not his evasion of this duty, and of Sybel's book on the French Revolution, it was "the best political history of that age I have ever seen, but [it] admits no purely theoretical elements." Romanticism, according to Acton, has "established the theory that every age must be understood and judged on its own terms," and this was significant for historical criticism — "the rule distingue tempora," he called it — but it did not relieve the historian of his moral duty. To Creighton, whose book on the late medieval church he reviewed severely, he offered one of his lists of precepts about the need of the historian to confront questions of good and evil with a moral code that was as far beyond the vicissitudes of time as was religion itself. And of course this was his position with regard to the church, too, in connection with the corruption and vice in its history — the massacre of St. Bartholomew, in which he thought the papacy complicit, being a paradigmatic case, although the evidence was only indirect.[146] Even more sensational, perhaps, would be the full story of the Council of Trent, when and if the Vatican archives were opened. Like Döllinger, Acton was always drawn to the dark, sometimes distorted, and controversial aspects of Church history.

The central — the life-shaping and disillusioning — event of Acton's life, as of Döllinger's, was the Vatican Council of 1870, which was long anticipated in those times of controversy between Ultramontanes and liberal Catholics. He reported on, analyzed, and deplored it in many journalistic and polemical publications, and discussed it with many friends, including Döllinger, Newman, and Gladstone.[147] For Acton (unlike Newman) proclaiming the dogma of infallibility implied the blanket exculpation of the church from unmistakable errors apparent in the historical record. He reviewed a work of Döllinger declaring that both popes and councils were capable of erring, though he believed that the cardinal had not gone far enough in his arguments. Pointing out the frauds that had been committed for the interests of Rome and the religious orders, he judged the principle of infallibility, with the attendant inclination to "get rid of the evidence" (*suppressio veri*), to be a "great calamity." The Ultramontanes ignored morality and denied truth, he told Döllinger, with the result that in order that "men might believe the Pope it was resolved to make them believe that vice is virtue and falsehood is truth."[148] Like his old teacher Acton refused to accept it as dogma though as a layman he avoided the excommunication that fell on Cardinal Döllinger. The Council cast a shadow over the rest of his life, but did not deter him from his historical calling and ideals and especially from his emphasis on making moral judgments in history.

To what, then, should Acton devote his immense learning, privileged position, and considerable talent? Like Gibbon, he gave this much thought. A history of the popes, a study of James II and VII (last Catholic king of England and Scotland), the Reformation, a biography of Pole, a history of the Council of Trent, another on the papal Index, and, most insistently, his "Madonna of the Future," the history of liberty—these were some of the subjects which he considered.[149] Acton spent much of his life reading not only the proliferating source collections but also the mass of monographs and multivolume narratives of universal, national, and church history; and yet, though his writings and lectures fill six or more large volumes, he never wrote a conventional book. He certainly prepared himself for such a project, as the tens of thousands of notes in the Cambridge Library attest, but they served only to promote his legend as the most learned man of his generation. Perhaps, as he once said of Döllinger, "he knew too much to write"; or perhaps, as Toynbee speculated more remotely, it was the tragic "sterilizing influence of Industrialism upon historical thought"—but then Toynbee was a man who specifically decided not to let reading interfere with his writing.[150] But aside from internal weakness and external "influence," the fact is that writing more than reviews, essays, and lectures was not a priority for him; and like Burckhardt (hard as it may be for some academics and deans to understand) he was finally more interested in reading and talking than in producing a published commodity (also encouraged by "Industrialism").

Acton was a political and cultural as well as a historical critic, and after his death he was credited with being something of a prophet. It is true that he was suspicious of power and absolutism, and his famous aphorism, that "power tends to corrupt and absolute power corrupts absolutely," did guide his historical judgments; but it was also an indication of his own frustrating condition of powerlessness and marginality. From the beginning he was also an insistent critic of nationality, but this was perhaps less a sense of the future than of the revered past, for as he argued, "this theory of nationality, unknown to the catholic middle ages . . . , is inconsistent both with political reason and with Christianity."[151] His political sensibilities also allowed him to regard the

Austro-Hungarian Empire as a model state, to side with the American South during the Civil War (as his correspondence with General Lee indicates), and to exalt John Calhoun as one of the great political thinkers.[152] Twentieth-century admirers like Ernest Barker carried on this tradition of decentralism in the form of "pluralism."[153]

Acton finally achieved recognition in his last years with the regius professorship at Cambridge, for which he received support not only from Henry Sidgwick but also Creighton, whom he had criticized so severely, who called him "perhaps the most learned Englishman."[154] His reputation rested mainly on personal connections, his four libraries, the largest at Aldenham, his friendship with Gladstone, and a few impressive essays, of which the best is probably that on "German Schools of History," the first article in the first issue of the *English Historical Review,* which he helped to found in 1886. At Cambridge he gave two famous courses, one on modern history and another on the French Revolution, which were both printed. In 1868 Michelet expressed the wish "that a capable hand would sketch the history of history, that is, the progress which has occurred in our studies of the Revolution"; and this is precisely what Acton did in his volume.[155] Finally, before his death in 1902, he planned and began the editing of the *Cambridge Modern History,* which was a standard work of reference for more than half a century. This series was to be another contribution to the old genre of universal history, but now a definitive one, since, as Acton told his contributors, "we approach the final stage in the conditions of historical learning" and can overcome "the long conspiracy against the knowledge of truth."[156]

Acton's essay on nineteenth-century German historians is a marvel of scholarship. Cryptic, allusive, aphoristic, judgmental, hyperbolic, compulsively driven by name-dropping, it documents and perpetuates the legend of the historical revolution in the wake of the French Revolution. There had been "brave men who lived before Agamemnon" (referring to Wegele's survey), he admitted, that is, critical scholars before Niebuhr; but it was a different order than that of his century. "The romantic reaction which began with the invasion of 1794 was the revolt of outraged history," he declared, referring in particular to the historical school of Savigny. "Forty years after Savigny's *Vocation* had made Germany a nation of historically thinking men, every branch of knowledge had felt its influence" — language (Grimm), geography (Ritter), philosophy (Hegel), art (Schnaase), theology (Baur), and civil law (Stahl). "History is not only a particular branch of knowledge," Acton set down in one of his private notes, "but a particular mode and method in other branches."[157] For this, he lamented elsewhere, "the depressing names historicism and historical-mindedness have been devised."[158]

Acton also invoked the classicist breakthroughs of K. O. Müller and August Böckh, followed by the amazing output of Ranke — author "of a larger number of mostly excellent books than any man that ever lived" and hailed by Döllinger as *praeceptor Germaniae*. Nor did Acton fail to mention the contributions of philosophers, theologians, and biblical critics to whom he had been introduced by Döllinger, though it was the archival sources and their explorers that held first place in Acton's esteem. "By going from book to manuscript, from library to archive," he wrote, "we exchange doubt for certainty, and become our own masters."[159] But there was more to come, and Acton ended by alluding to the new work in social and cultural history.

Acton's most famous production was his inaugural lecture on the study of history, which, with its multiple themes, its tangential dissertations, and its encyclopedic mass of citations in several languages, could well have been turned into a book.[160] The story still hinged on the revolution in historical science started by Niebuhr but not completed until Ranke. Niebuhr's role was preliminary and negative, Ranke's positive and fulfilling; for "whilst Niebuhr dismissed the traditional story, replacing it with a concoction of his own, it was Ranke's mission to preserve, not to undermine, and to set up masters whom, in their proper sphere, he could obey." "History is a choice of ancestors," he also noted, but for him this meant above all a choice of historiographical predecessors.[161] As Acton remarked, in a phrase that might stand for his own bibliomaniacal efforts and for the historiographical views of such followers as G. P. Gooch and Herbert Butterfield, "The great point is the history of history."[162]

10

Beyond the Canon

The whole life of humanity, insofar as it has been explored in time and in space consists in the struggle between Culture and Unculture.

— *Otto Henne am Rhyn*

Prehistory

For access to the deep past scholars had usually been restricted either to philological and etymological speculation or to analogies with savage cultures of modern times. Even Kant acknowledged that "one of the ways of extending the range of anthropology is *traveling,* or at least reading travelogues."[1] And as the Baron Degérando wrote, "We shall in a way be taken back to the first periods of our own history. . . . The philosophic sailing to the ends of the earth, is in fact traveling in time. Those unknown islands are for him the cradle of human society."[2] Philology promised a more direct access, especially in the nineteenth-century search for an original language, whether Hebrew or, with the more sophisticated methods of historical and comparative philology, a lost Indo-Germanic, Indo-European, or "Aryan" root language. Such methods were still practiced by linguistic scholars in the nineteenth century, as suggested by the work of Gregor Dankovsky, which, on the basis of similarity of words and grammar, argued that Slavic languages could be traced back to

Greek.[3] But philological and analogical speculation was increasingly challenged and corrected by harder sorts of evidence, which underlay a new historical discipline.

"Prehistory" (*Vorgeschichte; préhistoire; preistoria*) was an international creation of nineteenth-century scholarship, and it drew especially on two new disciplines with old names, that is, "anthropology" (the philosophical study of human nature) and "archeology" (Thucydidean prehistory).[4] Monuments, memorials, and material objects offered historians access to a deeper past than afforded by written records. Graves, sepulchral urns, runes, and stone implements uncovered from the seventeenth century threw light on the life (as well as the death) and migrations of "barbarian" peoples, while fossil remains forced Christian scholars to confront, and finally to acknowledge, the notion of a humanity older than Adam. John Frere published such evidence from a site in Suffolk in an archeological journal in 1800, although its significance was not appreciated, or accepted, for another generation, as even the great geologist Cuvier, who died in 1832, declared that "fossil man does not exist." In 1813 James Pritchard had already held out, in a speculative way, the possibility of the nonbiblical principle of polygenesis;[5] and by 1846 Boucher de Perthes — "the founder of prehistory," as a later French philosopher called him[6] — was already publishing his findings about "antediluvian man," though these were not generally accepted in England until 1859; in 1857 the controversial Neanderthal man was unearthed; and in the 1860s John Lubbock was celebrating Frere's discoveries, adding some of his own and those of Perthes. About the old biblical chronology he wrote, "The whole six thousand years, which were until lately looked on as the sum of the world's existence, are to Perthes but one unit of measurement in the long succession of ages."[7]

Prehistory had its own prehistory, for materials for this "new science" had been accumulating for three centuries and more, without the accompaniment of a theoretical framework but with a substantial constituency in the Republic of Letters.[8] The works of George Agricola and Conrad Gesner on fossils were followed in the seventeenth century by state-supported efforts, notably in Denmark and Sweden undertaken for the glory of the fatherland, and the establishment of societies of antiquities (such as that of London in 1717 and the Dilettanti in 1732), journals (such as that of A. A. Rhode in 1719 — the first — and *Archaeologia,* in London in 1770), and other publications and marks of professionalization. The discovery of Chilperich's grave in 1653 marked a starting point of French archeology. Another inspiration to archeological inquiry came from the study of the ruins of Pompei and the study of ancient art history associated with Winckelmann. The interest in prehistory grew in circles at least marginal to scholarship, and in the view of A. A. Rhode, expressed in his publication on north German antiquities, material remains furnished a much better access to the ancient Germans than Tacitus and all the associated commentary and derivative historiography.

Despite these unsettling discoveries, irreconcilable with the "evidences of Christianity" still being celebrated by William Paley in the early nineteenth century, the big picture, the Eusebian chronology, remained long in place, but it was fading. As one historian of British antiquities wrote of prehistory, "We must give it up, that speechless past; whether fact or chronology, doctrine or mythology; whether in Europe, Asia, Africa, or America; at Thebes or Palenque, on Lycian shore or Salisbury Plain: lost is lost, gone is gone forever." In his *Pre-Historic Times* (1861) Lubbock quoted these words of Palgrave to dramatize the revolution of archeological science in that generation, and he painted a glowing picture of the progress of understanding the prehistorical past.[9] Reviewing this progress, Lubbock, who had made his own tours of archeological sites, including those of Denmark, described the periodization which archeology had established (though anticipated by Goguet in the eighteenth century): stone (which he divided into old and new — paleolithic and neolithic), bronze, and iron ages, which replaced or gave solid reinforcement to the "four-stage" system of eighteenth-century conjectural history, by connecting it with more precise chronological, that is, stratigraphic, calibrations.

The English came late to this understanding, for continental scholars — French, German, and especially Scandinavian — had appreciated the high "antiquity of man" (Lyell's phrase) for almost half a century.[10] One pioneering archeologist was the Danish professor of literature Rasmus Nyerup, who was appointed head of a committee for the preservation and collection of national antiquities.[11] One result of Nyerup's efforts was the founding of a national museum in Copenhagen in 1819, which was directed by his follower Christian Jurgensen Thomsen, who was one of the formulators of the three-age system — "archaeology's first paradigm." This convention, already in use by other Scandinavian, French, and German scholars, was included in his influential guide to Nordic antiquities (1836), a work translated soon after into German (1837) and English (1838). A variation on the new periodization was offered by Sven Nilsson, professor of zoology at Lund — savage, barbarian, agricultural, and (taking over the rubric of historians) civilized. Nilsson's work on the primitive inhabitants of Scandinavia, published in 1834, was translated in 1868 by Lubbock, who drew on other Scandinavian researches and publications.

A central — pioneering as well as popularizing — figure in nineteenth-century prehistorical studies was J. J. A. Worsaae, whose work accompanied and ornamented the formation of the Danish state (1849). Worsaae, who prepared himself by traveling to Germany, France, England, Scotland, Ireland, Hungary, and Russia, ended up as both professor of archeology at the University of Copenhagen and head of the Royal Museum of Nordic Antiquities. Worsaae's first book, which was on Nordic antiquities, was published in 1843 and soon translated into German and English. The antiquities of Greece and Rome had long been under scrutiny, he wrote, but not those peoples who had never been conquered and overlaid by classical civilization, although materials were now available, such as those collected by Thomsen in the Royal Museum.[12] Here stone-, bronze-, and iron-age artifacts could be examined, and Danish, Swedish, and Norwegian cultures could be compared with others — and moreover the transition from warlike to agrarian societies could be traced in more than a conjectural way. For Worsaae the "progress of culture" was measured not by writing but "as indicated by the appearance of pile-dwellings and other remains."[13] However, though cautious in expanding temporal horizons much beyond the conventional limits, he was convinced of the global range of the human species through the cultural continuum divided into the stone, bronze, and iron ages. At first he stopped short of Charles Lyell's estimate of the age of the human race as about 100,000 years. "Yet this much is certain," Worsaae later wrote, "the more our glance is directed to that epoch-making point of time, when the Creator wakened man in all his nakedness into life, and therefore most probably under a warmer sun in some more genial clime, the more does that point recede into an endlessly distant undefinable past."[14]

As Worsaae argued, Europe was settled late, and Scandinavia even later, after the human race had already spread elsewhere. The evidence for this was above all stone-age antiquities, as exemplified by India, where these were regarded with "superstitious awe." From here humanity migrated northward, eventually moving as far as the Bering Straits, across to America, and from the Western hemisphere to the islands of the South Seas (an assumption which was still guiding Thor Heyerdal more than a century later). They also moved to the Mediterranean, and Worsaae found the great Mommsen wrong in denying settlements in Italy before agriculture: "The museums of Italy tell a different story and might have warned so careful an archeologist from roundly asserting a negative."[15] (Mommsen, in his epigraphical enthusiasm, had little respect for what he regarded as the amateurism of field archeology.) Stone-age peoples migrated northwards, between the "so-called ice ages," arriving in Scandinavia after "the Mammoth or Reindeer period or the 'Paleolithic Age.'" Worsaae distinguished between the Danish population and those "higher dominant people" arriving from the north, although they shared the same global paleolithic culture, as the evidence of graves indicates.

But the story told by scattered archeological evidence was incomplete,

Worsaae admitted, and needed to be filled in by comparison with modern savage culture beyond the European and Aryan context. This was the argument, too, of Lubbock and others, who turned to the evidence of modern ethnography to supplement what tradition, history, and prehistory could provide. The idea of the "antiquity of man" was confirmed by the evolutionary ideas that emerged and began to prevail in the wake of Darwin, whose *Origin of Species* appeared in 1859. Darwinism, preceded by the naive evolutionism of Spencer, Chambers, and Darwin's own grandfather Erasmus Darwin, gave systematic and scientific basis (as in Spencer's "laws of evolution") to age-old organistic and biological analogies that joined all human races, however defined, in one general process and so extended the field of comparisons to the entire globe, which had been the scene of the stone, bronze, and iron ages. The uses of archeology diminish, however, with the emergence of written culture, so that "monumental records and ancient relics," as Worsaae acknowledged, "become mere illustrations of the internal and external contemporary conditions of civilisation, the main features of which are already known in history."[16] Later archeologists, such as Gabriel de Mortillet, likewise insisted on the priority of cultural over narrowly paleontological criteria.

Scandinavian history drew extensively on archeology as well as philology, medieval chronicles, documentary collections, and Latin scholarship, which, as in the cases of the major states, had been published since the sixteenth century; and some of it was translated into German, French, and English. In 1832 Eric Geijer, professor of history at the University of Upsala since 1817, published his history of Sweden, in which he drew on "relics" as well as tradition, mythology, and medieval and classical sources.[17] More directly relying on archeological sources was Thomsen's guide to Nordic antiquities, published in 1837, which included illustrations of graves, ships, tools, medals, and runic inscriptions, with comparative asides about American antiquities culled from Alexander von Humboldt's discoveries. In 1852 P. A. Munch published a study of "Norse Folk History," dedicated to Rudolf Keyser (himself later the author of a comprehensive book on Norse social history)[18] and making use of the work of Worsaae as well as Grimm and German explorations of the "mark" organization apparently shared by Germans and Scandinavians.[19] C. F. Allen's pioneering history of Denmark, inspired by a competition of the Society for Posterity (*Selskabetfor Efterslaegten*) and supported by a massive bibliographical foundation, inquired into Danish prehistory, mythology, language, and runes to illuminate the early phases of national culture (including manners, customs, domestic life, laws, institutions, literature, and above all language).[20] This is only a sampling of a vast bibliography which happened to have a European currency.

In 1870 Louis Figuier could still argue that the science of prehistory did not yet exist, but rather was a "chaos" of geology, paleontology, ethnology, archeology, and history.[21] Forty years earlier, he wrote, the "antiquity of man" and the ages of stone, bronze, and iron were still being denied, even by men of science; but the growing mass of evidence, such as that of Frere at the beginning of the century, drove even the cautious Cuvier to admit the possibility. In the meantime there appeared a large accumulation of books, popular and scholarly, polemical and academic, addressing and trying to give historical and scientific form to this "chaos" and to the notion of pre-Adamic culture, about which Renaissance scholars had also speculated.

All of this historiography was shaped by the intellectual and political currents of Europe before and after the traumatic experiences of 1848 — and then of 1870. Allen in particular took part in that linguistic nationalism which fired European states in the nineteenth century. In the storied Schleswig-Holstein question the Danes, as a minority in the Duchy of Schleswig, were menaced and eventually conquered by the new German state; and in 1848 Allen had already published a book on the deep background of the underlying *Sprachkampf*.[22] The "fanaticism" of the Germans had deep roots, and so did their tendency to overreach their natural, that is, national bounds, as in their conflicts with the Slavs. In the mid-nineteenth century this linguistic (underlying a poorly concealed political) imperialism was threatening not only the equally old and rich Danish language but also the culture of which it was part. So Allen, like other representatives of small nationalities, invoked cultural history against the new state politics of his age — in vain, of course, except for the outer reaches of European historical understanding.

The Italian Way

Italian historiography in the eighteenth century participated in the Enlightenment in several ways. Of particular significance were the subversive *Civil History of the Kingdom of Naples* by Vico's contemporary Pieto Giannone and Muratori's great collection of medieval Italian sources, both published in 1723, just a year before the first edition of Vico's *New Science*.[23] While Muratori published a vast amount of documentary sources and what Gibbon called "curious dissertations to illuminate the medieval period (500–1500)," Giannone, a jurist and a "civil humanist," told the story of the interplay between papacy and empire; and he was forced into exile for tipping the balance too far toward the secular power and for his skeptical emphasis on secular historical factors in general.[24] Retrospectively, of course, it was the virtuoso scholarship and speculations of Vico which were most significant, beginning with the question of the emergence of mankind from a state of nature, over which the Vichian Emmanuele Duni and the Dominican G. F. Finetti had an inconclusive controversy. Vico had other followers in Italy later in the century, including F. M. Pagano, who was concerned with "the philosophical history of nations and the mythology of poets" (and who was a victim in the Neapolitan revolution of 1799), and especially Vincenzo Cuoco, who published a work on that revolution in 1801 and who drew Vico's ideas into the service of the embryonic national cause, although it was in France that Vico's presence was first restored to European historical theorizing and philosophizing.[25]

The "new historiography" of Italy, as Croce called it, was created by the generation of Italian patriots, especially liberal Catholics reacting against the superficial rationalism of Enlightenment writers and, as activists and politicians, hoping to place history in the service of national unification. Among the most prominent of these Neoguelf historians were Carlo Botta, Pietro Colletta, Cesare Balbo, Gino Capponi, Carlo Troya, Carlo Cattaneo, Cesare Cantù, Michele Amari, Luigi Tosti, and Giuseppe Ferrari. There was also a Neoghibelline school of historians, but inferior in scholarship as well as politically off the mark in the unification movement. Italian scholars were coming into contact with the new history in France and the new erudition in Germany, as illustrated by the international review *Antologia,* founded by Capponi and Vieusseux in 1821, modelled on the *Edinburgh Review,* and predecessor to the *Archivio storico italiano.*[26] Yet their historiographical ideal was rather a fusion between Vico and Muratori, philology and philosophy Italian style. While they pursued Muratori's antiquarian efforts, for political as well as religious reasons they remained within the orthodox framework of biblical chronology, and they looked with suspicion on secular ideas of progress and German "philosophy of history."[27]

The older generation was first to make its mark on what Croce called the "new historiography" of the Restoration. Carlo Botta, born in 1766, was a physician and Piedmontese politician who published in 1809 a history of the American Revolution, replete with errors and "discourses" but which he claimed to be historically authentic for the most part. America, "having been discovered by the genius and intrepidity of Italians," was a leader in modern liberty and national unification; and Botta told the story in great, undocumented detail, drawing on him the criticism of Prescott for neglecting the intellectual, economic, and social context.[28] During the Restoration he went into retirement and turned more directly to the writing of history, and in 1824 his major work appeared, a history of Italy from 1789 to 1814, which drew on his own unfortunate experiences in that "age of violence, of ambition, and of pride" under the Bourbons and the "geometric governors" of Bonapartist rule.[29] This was followed by a survey of Italian history from 300 to the Revolution and then a continuation of Guicciardini's pioneering history of Italy, which he published in ten volumes in 1832.

As a historian Botta rejected both the abstractions of the Enlightenment and the imaginative indulgences of Romanticism as well as current trends in foreign erudition and philosophy with national (and anti-French) emphasis. He worked within an Italian canon, beginning with Livy, "prince of patriotic historians"; and he carried on the project, broken off after Guicciardini, of a truly national history.[30] His "purist" models were classical and humanist historians, whose lessons were patriotic (Livy and Bembo), moral (Tacitus), and "positive" (Machiavelli and Guicciardini). But Botta himself had little sympathy for the new science, for Italian political culture in general, and still less for the new historiographical currents of the Restoration. Neither in intellectual nor in scholarly terms was his work well received. This was also the case with his contemporary Pietro Colletta (born in 1775), former general and politician, who attempted to continue Giannone's history of Naples in a work published posthumously by the blind Capponi, who himself wrote a comprehensive history of the Florentine republic.[31] The old humanist tradition had worn thin, and the project of a national history had to be taken up by a younger and broader-minded generation.

Like other European scholars of the Restoration period, the younger Italians turned especially to their medieval past in order to establish a sense of national identity and political destiny. One pioneer was Giuseppe Micali, who published a history of the ancient Italian peoples in 1822 and followed it a decade later with a collection of supporting documents.[32] Although not an admirer of the work, Niebuhr did find some useful points, such as Micali's comparison between Etruscan painting and that of the Renaissance.[33] Another original scholar was the poet and dramatist Alessandro Manzoni, who in 1822 set a major question of medieval Italian history with a discourse on the Lombards, in which he lamented the loss of Italian liberty under these barbarian invasions, which broke off the tradition of Roman law and civility.[34] This interpretation was continued by his follower Cantù and by Troya, Balbo, and Tosti against the authority of Savigny and Leo.

The major figures and comrades in the enterprise of remaking Italian history were Balbo and Troya, inspired in part by the career, if not the political agenda, of Dante, who combined the active with the contemplative life and added to it a seminal control of the Italian language.[35] Yet while defending the tradition of erudition preserved by Muratori and Vico, they tried also, from the 1820s, to benefit from French and German scholarship; but they had little use for what Balbo, in his own contribution to the *ars historica*, called the sterile objectivity (*obbiecttività eunuca*) of historians like Droysen and Ranke.[36] History needed more than poetry and erudition; it required a commitment to civil life; and from 1824, Balbo wanted in a sense to be a "Christian Voltaire." In a letter to Troya, Balbo claimed for his own work, published in 1830, "the glory of being the first among the Italians of that courageous school of critics founded or at least raised up in Germany by Niebuhr, Savigny, Luden, and many others, followed or imitated in France by Guizot, Thierry, and neglected, not appreciated, or until now not followed by us."[37]

In later writings on the modern art of history Balbo continued this celebration of French and German scholars as well as Muratori and of the source collections being published at the time, especially for Italy, which had for too long suffered under the oppression of Austrian imperial claims ("AEIOU").[38] Ranke's rival Heinrich Leo had indeed studied medieval Italy, but he was no Italian. In the same cause Troya published his own history of medieval Italy, which entered into the "vast argument" about the origins of the migrating barbarians, including even the notion of the Greek origins of the Slavs.[39] For Troya, India marked the origins of the Celts, Germans, and Slavs, although he kept faith with the Mosaic story and biblical chronology (beginning in 6000 B.C.), which was followed in the margins of his book as well as printed editions of Scriptures, the "great document," as Balbo called it. "Scanza" might be the *vagina gentium,* as Jordanes had written, but there was no "Scandinavian Noah." In any case the central theme of Balbo's story and the direction of history was — even more than liberty — independence.

This was the theme of his *Hope of Italy* (1845), which appealed to Providence as the guarantee of "Christian progress" and so of Italian unity.[40] In his *Historical Meditations*, Balbo raised his scholarship and political aspirations to the level of the philosophy of history, following the line of Machiavelli, Vico, and his contemporaries Romagnosi, Manzoni, Gioberti, and Cantù, who all opposed "fatalism" and insistence on natural causation and supported the notion of providence in history. Balbo also aligned himself with the restorers of modern Christianity, including Chateaubriand, Bonald, Guizot, Cousin, Villemain, Schlegel, Leo, Voigt, Ranke, Raumer, Lingard, Wiseman, and his Italian colleagues. In these meditations, though he was aware of modern discoveries such as those of Champollion, he clung to the biblical story and to conventional periodization and to the existence of miracles and mysteries.[41]

Another champion of Italian independence was Cesare Cantù, who was a great admirer of Pope Pius IX and friend of Montalembert and even more orthodox in his religious views.[42] One of his works was a survey of heretical threats to the Church down to Protestantism.[43] Cantù situated himself in the great tradition of universal historiography leading from Bossuet down to

Johann Müller, but broadened by the opening of the Orient to historical inquiry. He also wrote a multivolume history of Italy, which showed passing
acquaintance with authors such as Niebuhr and Creuzer but which otherwise
was a conventional survey, including a discussion (though not acceptance) of
the myths of the Trojan origins of various Italian cities.[44] He approved of the
"philosophy of history" to the extent that he wanted to join fact and theory,
but he rejected the "school of progress" associated with the Enlightenment
and the *Encyclopédie*. He also indulged in the popular pastime of periodization, calculating eighteen "epochs" from the beginning to his own time. For
Cantù, Christianity was the unifying factor in history, making all men brothers; and he adhered to the Genesis story, invoking the authority of Cuvier to
argue that "the truth of the account of Moses, which gives 7000 to 8000 to
mankind, is confirmed by the progress of science."[45] Yet Cantù also drew on
Vico and the work of Jones, Creuzer, Bopp, Schlegel, and Champollion as well
as recent advances in the history of law, geography, chronology, archeology,
and numismatics.

Like the Germans and the French, the Italians sought to enhance national
traditions by reviving past glories, and of these one of the most illustrious was
the war of the Sicilian vespers, of which there was no comprehensive account
until the nineteenth century. Such at least was the claim of Michele Amari,
who was also a great Islamic scholar, a rival of Renan, and who published a
major study of the Arabs in Sicily. Unlike Ranke, who was a foreigner to
several of the national histories he undertook, Michele Amari took pride in his
Sicilian condition and in this celebrated episode of Italian nationality.[46] The
war against the French occupiers was no conspiracy but was caused "by the
insolence of the ruling party," the revolution being not from the nobles but
from the people, and this glorious tradition was bequeathed to Italians of
Amari's own day. No "diviner of the past," Amari respected facts as reflected
in contemporary writings and documents, and he imputed large meanings to
national tradition and even larger ones to religion, since for him "Christianity
is the only source of light."

Another pioneering medievalist was Luigi Tosti, an abbot in Monte Cas-
sino, who published a heavily documented history of that monastery. Tosti
painted an unhappy picture of the church in the eleventh century and defended
the papacy against the empire — Guelfs against Ghibellines — as the positive
force in Italian history down to his own day.[47] He was a true "man of the
middle ages," although he also appreciated the art and culture of the Renaissance. In 1848 he published a history of the Lombard league, which reflected
the "ancient glory" of the Italian city-states and which held up Pope Alexander
III as a model for the newly elected Pius IX. Tosti also wrote a favorable and

again well-documented biography of "the Italian" Boniface VIII, which he dedicated to Dante, in order to "remove the infamy" that had attached to his name because of his foreign entanglements.[48] Despite his defeat his pontificate marked the beginning of the modern world of national politics. But the shattering events of 1848 sent Tosti into exile and undermined his faith in the Neoguelf program.

Giuseppe Ferrari was a radical, an anti-Catholic, and an exile in France for most of his life, and he was strongly influenced by French social theory. In France in the circle of Domenico Romagnosi he came into contact with Thierry, Fauriel, Michelet, and Quinet as well as Leroux and Buchez; and shifting to the French language, Ferrari wrote on a wide range of subjects, including Machiavelli, Cousin and his influence, modern revolutions, and the philosophy of history. His major contribution, however, was in promoting the work of Vico, especially in publishing the first critical edition of his writings (1835–37). In a study published first in Italian and then in French Ferrari was one of the first to attend to the role of Roman law in the historical thought of Vico and as a model for the interpretation of later history. Vico's contemporaries did not appreciate his insights, Ferrari wrote: "It is to our century that Vico owes his posthumous glory."[49] Ferrari also wrote on the question of periodization, that is, on the concept of generations, which became so prominent during the Restoration.[50] In this curious, highly original book he tried to calculate the length (and "comparative velocity") of generations in different periods of history, in different civilizations, and under different sorts of regimes as indicators and measures of historical "mutation" down to the "thinking generation" (*la generazione pensante*) of 1815. It was as if Vico's cycles were calibrated according to smaller-scale life cycles discernible in Ferrari's own turbulent experience.

Cultural History Continued

Born in the late Enlightenment as a form of philosophical history and even an antidote to philosophy, cultural history became a major field of investigation and interpretation in the nineteenth century as it drew not only on history and philology but also on the new sciences (which assumed the old names) of archeology and anthropology and which also adopted the new culturalist terminology.[51] Anthropology was now not merely the study of human nature which the faculties of medicine, law, and philosophy all regarded as preliminary to their higher discipline but a systematic extension of ethnology in which field research was essential to its method. Pioneering anthropologists followed the early ethnographers in drawing on historical writing, ancient and modern, to fill in the gaps in their own materials; and so Edward Tylor, for example, referred in particular to Klemm's conception of "Culture-History," which he substituted for the more conventional term "civilization," which was preferred by English and French writers.[52] And the concept was shared by anthropologists and cultural historians, so that when the cultural historian J. J. Honegger in 1882 asked the question "What is Culture?" he offered a simple paraphrase of Tylor's famous definition of 1865: "*Culture* or Civilization taken in its wide ethnographic sense is that complex whole which includes knowledge, belief, art, morals, law, custom, and any other capabilities and habits acquired by man as a member of society."[53]

This was also the arena of cultural history, an incredibly popular field of study and entertainment in the mid-nineteenth century. As T. K. Penneman facetiously put it, "It is probable that every German who was not writing an *Allgemeine Culturgeschichte* in ten volumes was writing *Die Völkerkunde* in twenty."[54] Cultural history overlapped with the older tradition of universal and world history, and in some cases cleaved to the biblical narrative and chronology into the twentieth century. Schlosser's "universal view of the history of the ancient world and its culture" (1826), Wilhelm Wachsmuth's "outline of the general history of peoples and states" (1826), "European social history" (1831), and "general history" (1850), J. G. A. Wirth's "fragments of cultural history" (1836, second edition), R. Lorentz's "general history of peoples and their cultures" (1837), G. Klemm's "general cultural history of mankind" (1837), G. F. Kolb's "history of mankind and its culture" (1843), C. F. Apelt's "historical-philosophical sketch" (1845), W. Drumann's "outline of cultural history" (1847)—these are only a few of the contributions to this popular genre before mid-century, all of which stand closer to eighteenth-century histories of humanity and of civilization than to the scientific history taught in the universities.[55]

Such popular, often elaborately illustrated efforts were continued in the second half of the century, some retaining a fundamentalist basis, others acknowledging the "antiquity of man," to one degree or another, and still others accepting the biological perspective of Darwinist evolution. In the Anglophone world Christian faith continued to protect cultural historians from contemplating a pre-Edenic world, as in the cases of W. Cooke Taylor, whose "natural history of society" (1841) took the Pentateuch (confirmed by recent discoveries, he argued) as still the best account of the origins of civilization; William MacKinnon, whose scope was international and whose focus was religious; Alexander Alison, who proposed, in his study "the philosophy and history of civilization" (1860), to make an improvement on Guizot and Buckle, while at the same time remaining within the Christian framework; and Amos Dean, whose history of civilization (1868) relied on the earlier works of Prichard, Bunsen, and Rawlinson.[56] Other scholars, including J. W. Draper, his admirer John S. Hittell, and E. A. Allen, accepted the idea of cultural evolution over a vast period of time and still operating in their own day, and in 1854, Daniel Wilson introduced the term "prehistorical" into the discussion of the origins of civilization.[57] All of these writers tied their knowledge and beliefs to the reigning dogma of human progress, whether under the aegis of Providence, natural evolution, or a combination of the two.

Cultural history in the nineteenth century was unreservedly interdisciplinary, proposing to include not only all aspects of human behavior beyond politics and war but also to subsume the political and the military aspects in a wider social field. At first philology and mythology, especially in their new comparative forms, seemed to provide access to prehistorical culture, and indeed Herder retained followers in the nineteenth century, such as Lazarus Geiger, who with Heinrich Steinthal was one of the founders of *Völkerspsychologie,* a new discipline that one scholar has traced back to Christoph Meiners.[58] Geiger regarded language as a kind of tool and a way "to gain . . . an idea of the condition of mankind" in its earliest times.[59] For empirical-minded historians, however, such approaches seemed too spiritual, too speculative and conjectural, for positive conclusions, and the social and economic sciences were brought into play as well. The point was that culture had a "material" as well as an "intellectual" side (material base and superstructure, in the more famous formula of Marx and Engels), and an understanding of both was needed for a full understanding of the human condition. Positivism in a general sense was the rule of science in every field, and so, for example, the "younger" historical school of political economy criticized the older school of Roscher, Knies, and Hildebrandt (followers of Savigny) for theoretical excesses. So the drift of cultural history — even in the elitist writings of a scholar like Burckhardt, whose point of departure was the history of art — was toward the concrete, the particular, the tangible, and the local.[60] This was the case also with the popular and prolific writer Gustav Freytag, who presented, in historical as well as fictional form, "pictures from the German past" to illustrate "the good old times" and "the soul of the folk."[61]

Wilhelm Wachsmuth and Wilhelm Riehl were two of the leading practitioners of cultural history, although, despite their empirical thrust, they did not move conceptually far beyond Enlightenment histories of humanity. Wachsmuth was professor of ancient and modern languages at the University of Halle and then Leipzig (1825). Rejecting not nationalism but the state-fetishism of contemporary professional historians, Wachsmuth wrote prolifically on Greek antiquities (1826), in which he surveyed the whole life and character of

the Greek "nation,"[62] and then on "general cultural history," which he identified with "historical ethnography." For him the essence of a nation was its
social and cultural life, which brought it out of a natural condition into a
civilized state and which created a national character, that is, the distinctive
features of a *Volk*. Although Wachsmuth investigated these features in micro-
historical terms, he nevertheless organized his materials within a holistic manner, with the help of general categories like — not the State but — society, culture, and especially *Volkstum*.

A generation younger, Riehl followed much the same line. He was a journalist and lecturer at the court of Maximilian II of Bavaria who, following the line
of Tacitus, Saxo Grammaticus, and Justus Möser, devoted himself to the "natural history of the German people." For him folklore (*Volkskunde*) was a science and cultural history was a history of the *Volkstum*, and like Wachsmuth
he pursued his researches beyond the state and its institutions into the classes
of society and family life. His "natural history," appearing in four parts between 1851 and 1869, was divided into four parts, which treated civil society
(*bürgerliche Gesellschaft*), land and people (*Land und Leute*), the family, and
even a travelbook (*Wanderbuch*).[63] Although Riehl was a conservative, he
was, for his apolitical views, organistic conception of society, and support of
women's emancipation, regarded as a sort of socialist. In fact he was a champion of the "good old times" (and virtues), and his romantic vision of the *Volk*
gained him posthumous popularity under the Nazi regime.

Meanwhile the genre of cultural history was moving toward the status of
"science." This is apparent, if not in being welcomed into the universities, then
at least in the founding of its first journal: the *Zeitschrift für deutsche Kulturgeschichte* in 1856, which included among its first sponsors Wachsmuth and
Klemm (but no professional historians). As the prospectus declared, the life
of the *Volk* was also the object of science and so needed a scholarly vehicle
to discuss methods of study and other practical — rather than theoretical —
questions. It was not merely the sum of such fields as (the history of) literature, law, art, religion, philosophy, and history itself but a transcendent whole
(*ganz*) subsuming all of these and more. Leaving its "dilettante" prehistory
behind, cultural history would become "the science of the future." This journal continued to appear in a number of series, the fourth of which, under the
direction of Georg Steinhausen, expanded its field of inquiry by dropping the
"deutsche" in the title and becoming simply the *Zeitschrift für Kulturgeschichte*.[64] By this time the field had become a full-fledged discipline accepted,
though controversially and grudgingly, into the universities, and indeed had
found its historiographer in the survey of Friedrich Jodl.[65]

One of the pioneers of the new cultural history was Gustav Klemm, who regarded himself as successor not only to such enlightened authors as Herder and Voltaire but also to such Christian historians as Paulus Orosius and Johann Cario, and who nevertheless also insisted that cultural history should be undertaken from an entirely "new standpoint," to which he himself contributed significantly through his extraordinary ethnographic collection — realizing an early museological "fantasy" — in Dresden, which served as a model for the Smithsonian Institution.[66] Like other cultural historians of this generation, Klemm was drawn to the projects of prehistory, especially the study of "material culture" (*materielle Kultur*) and "material bases" (*materiellen Grundlagen*). What Klemm wanted to investigate were the "original conditions of humanity" (*Urzustände der Menschheit*).[67] "What were the oldest tools of the human race?" he asked, and "how did early man eat, drink, shelter and clothe himself?" — and his works were filled with illustrations of these means of coping with nature. He rejected biblical accounts of human origins and progress through the various stages of culture.

G. F. Kolb, a south-German liberal, who was involved in journalism and parliamentary activity before the Revolutions of 1848, published a pioneering ten-volume history of culture in 1843–52.[68] More than forty years later, in the third edition of his work, he looked back on this youthful effort and the political turmoil through which it and he had passed. By then he had added not only the stone-bronze-iron-age periodization (and "ice-age," introduced by Agassiz in 1840) but also Darwinian evolution, which he regarded as the "first key" to historical understanding — although he was well aware that evolutionism long antedated Darwin. By then, too, Kolb was also fully abreast of the work of Thomsen, Nilsson, and others in archeology and paleontology, and duly employed them in his arguments for the antiquity of man. His version of the archeological periodization was "primordial," paleo-, meso-, and neolithic, and "anthropological" (quarternary age to the present). Kolb had small respect for the light provided by theologians, philosophers, even archeologists, and turned to the scientific, especially biological, disciplines of paleontology, medicine, and anatomy (as well as statistics), which permitted insight into questions of demography and race. He rejected notions of immortality and the "mystical darkness" offered by scholars like Döllinger — especially in comparison to the work of Strauss — arguing that history had learned to move beyond theological obscurantism and adding that a "history of historical writing" would be a useful addition to the advancement of science in general.[69] Yet he also believed in free will and moral improvement in the historical evolution of humanity.

One rival of Kolb was Friedrich Hellwald, a Prussian scholar whose cultural history of 1875 was dedicated to Ernst Haeckel and who was a radical naturalist and "social Darwinist." Fully abreast of the ideas and periodization of prehistory, Hellwald drew on the work of philologists like Geiger, social theorists like Bagehot, and anthropologists like Lubbock; but he was essentially a biological determinist or "fatalist," as Kolb called him, and to biology he added geography and labor as causes of human behavior. Hellwald applied the brutal notion of "struggle for existence" (*der Kampf um's Dasein*) directly to the historical process and indeed he celebrated the virtues of war above those of peace.[70]

Kolb disagreed violently with the brutal "Junker" Hellwald, who denounced all his predecessors, including even Buckle (despite the similarity of their views), and who regarded everything as subject to necessity and without moral value. As a historian Hellwald was, like Mommsen, a "Caesarist," whose attitudes reflected an inhumanity leading to "brutal despotism" and a racism worthy of American slaveholders.[71] Hellwald sought explanations of cultural development in the "Causalnexus" of historical forces rather than in the achievements of "great men," who were more like comets, which changed the face but not the frame of the skies; they could not alter the inertial forces of *longue durée*. Founders, kings, and princes could not fundamentally transform their social and cultural situations (*gesellschaftliche Zustände; Kulturzustand*).

There were many other cultural historians who were less biologistic and reductionist than Hellwald and who granted some role to human efforts, especially labor and economic efforts, beyond biological inheritance and environment. Among these were Otto Henne am Rhyn, Karl Grün, J. J. Honegger, and Julius Lippert.[72] Derivatively and eclectically, these authors drew on biology, paleontology, geology, archeology, anthropology, economics, sociology (especially Comte's Positivism), philology, psychology (including *Völkerpsychologie*), philosophy of history, philosophy, and (at least surreptitiously) theology. With the help of these theoretical structures and the accompanying data, they tried to steer between the Scylla of nature and the Charybdis of culture. They were champions of the idea of progress, which they expressed, invidiously, as the cultured vs. the uncultured. "The whole life of humanity, insofar as it has been explored in time and in space," wrote Henne am Rhyn, "consists in the struggle between Culture and Unculture."[73] The latter was barbarism; the former consisted in an ascending scale of social institutions and cultural forms from the family to the state, from primitive tools to modern technology, from basic needs to high cultural achievements. This was the evolutionary process which cultural historians undertook to understand, and it is hardly surprising—with the attendant political and religious implications—that they never reached a consensus on the answers or indeed even the questions involved. They still represented a form of "conjectural history"; and not surprisingly, because few of their works met the standards of the new

Geschichtswissenschaft of Ranke, their works were barred from the major pedagogical vehicle of this "science of history," the university seminar, until the end of the century — although in the next generation it more than made up for its former low status, especially through the efforts of Karl Lamprecht.[74]

The most extravagant (and wholly unprofessional) proponent of universal cultural history in the early twentieth century was the Quixotic and indeed Joachimite interpretation of the decline of the West by Oswald Spengler, who continued the tradition of Hegelian and Schlegelian philosophy of history, but in an eschatological mode. Spengler's immensely popular book, a product of eclectic reading (in the classical tradition but especially Goethe and Nietzsche) and the experience of the First World War, offered a grand theory of — not the progress — but the "morphology" and destiny of "cultures" (equivalent to the *Kulturvölker* of the anthropologists). Of these he recognized, not altogether originally, eight traditions: Egyptian, Chinese, Ancient Semitic, Indian, "Apollinian" (Greco-Roman), "Magian" (Iranian, Hebrew, and Arabian), "Faustian" (European, not including Russia), and Mexican.[75] For Spengler (as for Vico), cultures were self-generating and hermetic though sometimes could weigh heavily one on another, as classical antiquity did on Magian culture. Adapting the contemporary contrast between culture and civilization, Spengler interpreted the latter as a degenerate for the former — whence the Gibbonian theme of decline in Spengler's ornate modernist conceptual framework. In describing Western culture Spengler drew on metaphysics and mathematics; but for him, history was a matter not of rational thought but of penetration to superhuman and metahistorical mysteries — not of conjecture but of intuition. Spengler was only the best known of early-twentieth-century authors (such as Egon Friedell) who, under the impact of the trauma of the war and its aftermath, sought a deeper meaning — theodicy or anthropodicy — and found in it a pessimistic and tragic, but still Eurocentric, perspective.

Among cultural historians, some of the most important were women, although they did not emerge from an amateur status until the late nineteenth century. From the eighteenth century, women scholars wrote about great ladies — *de mulieribus illustribus* — especially queens, but they were also drawn to social and cultural matters, and in that connection their "own" history, especially questions of the condition over the ages. They were also active as translators, such as Sarah Taylor Austin, who translated Ranke's works. Before the turn of the twentieth century, a few women had reached professional status and recognition — Acton's friend Lady Blennerhasset, Maitland's protégé Mary Bateson, Celia Ady, daughter of Julia Cartwright, and distinguished historians of Renaissance Italy Eileen Power, Lucy Maynard Salmon, and Mary Beard, are only a few examples from a vast field, still largely uncharted from the standpoint of the history of history.[76] It is more than time for women's historiography (and that of amateur traditions) to be associated with the old, self-constituted Herodoto-Thucydidean canon, from which only historical ignorance has excluded them.

On the Margins

The general theory of the nation, the *Volk*, was taken from or confirmed by the work of Herder, who indeed offered a sensitive survey of the little peoples of the "Republic of Europe," who had become such an "object of astonishment and dread" for the rest of the world: the Basques, alone among Spanish tribes with a claim to high antiquity; the Gaels, Gauls, or Celts, who had resisted Rome; the Cimbri, whose language Herder thought had survived in Wales and Brittany; the Finns, related by language to the Hungarians, who alone of this race became conquerors; the Germanic nations; and the Slavs, sunk into "slavery" but on the way to awakening—and moreover, he commented, very much in need of a history of their own on the basis of rich materials.[77] To these aboriginal nations Herder added the conquering but also scientific Arabs; Turks, who were still strangers; Jews, who were to be regarded as "parasitical plants"; Armenians, merely travelers; and that "foreign, heathen, subterranean people," the Gypsies, originally a "reprobated Indian caste." But for Herder the original inhabitants of Europe had been driven into the mountains and other remote quarters; and more fortunate Europeans were called on—without playing favorites, for Herder was an internationalist in this regard—to inquire into their languages and manners before they suffered the inevitable fate of all peoples, which is the "gradual extinction of national character." In the field of historiography the small, interstitial nationalities— "mini-nationalisms," as Louis Snyder called them—both imitated and were threatened by the larger national models.[78] Like them they faced the dilemma of reconciling nation and state, liberty and independence, but of course they had to deal with encroaching larger states and traditions, so that "conquered" nationalities, such as Czechs, Slovaks, Vlachs, Slovenes, Ruthenians, Finns, Danes, White Russians, and even Luxemburgers had to confront such "conquering" and imperializing powers as Sweden, Poland, and Hungary, as well as Germany, France, England, Turkey, and Russia. Among the smaller domains nationalism originated normally as a cultural movement and "awakenings," which were marked by linguistic, literary, lexicographical, and folklorist efforts—what Benedict Anderson has called "philological" or "lexicographical" revolutions—and which were given form by the remembered, constructed, and imagined pasts, as well as "invented traditions" assembled by the labors of national historiography.[79]

In the nineteenth century historical writing was dominated by nationalist impulses, but nationalism took different forms. That is, there were not only revolutionary, liberal, Catholic, and imperialist but also marginal, overshadowed, repressed, or as it were interstitial, national traditions, which looked to the great powers — France, England, Germany, and to some extent Italy — as both models and menaces; and historiographical schools followed the same intellectual patterns.[80] Iberian, Scandinavian, East European, and Balkan nations and states, or potential or would-be states, fell in this category. They all followed a similar trajectory of development, looking back to a mythical past, to medieval chronicles, Latin histories, collections of primary sources, and assemblages of bibliography in the early modern period, the shift from Latin to vernacular, attempts at syntheses in the Enlightenment, Romantic efforts of national revival or even invention of tradition, the rise of critical, "scientific," and professional history, and the professionalization and institutionalization of historical research, teaching, and writing. These interstitial traditions also had their literary masterpieces, though they were hardly known outside their particular cultural spheres except through translation into at least one of the major languages.

The Scandinavian countries were deeply involved in their prehistory, that is, in questions of the first settlements and the cultural priorities of Norway, Denmark, and Sweden, which claimed great-power status in the eighteenth century and so a place in the canon of European historiography.[81] Critical historiography began in the eighteenth century with Ludwig Holberg's history of the Danish kingdom in the 1730s, Gerhard Schöning's history of the Norwegian kingdom (1771–73), Olaf Dalin's eighteenth-century histories, and Sven Lagerbring's history of the Swedish kingdom. In the nineteenth century Rudolf Keyser and Peter Andreas Munch were leaders of the Norwegian historical school, the "folk-history" edited by the latter (*Det Norske Folks Historie*), taking as its motto a statement from Niebuhr, that its aim was not the finding of answers but "the searches themselves" (*die Untersuchungen selbst*) — although the ideological stakes became even higher in the conflict between Danish and Scandinavianist theories of national origins, the former looking to the north and the latter, with better archeological evidence, to the "Aryan" south.[82] Eric Gustav Geijer published a history of the Swedish people (1832–36), and C. F. Allen's history of Denmark appeared in 1842.[83] In all three countries historical societies and journals reinforced the systematic and professional study and teaching of history and antiquities, carried on in the midst of linguistic conflicts and rivalries which further marginalized these mini-nationalities.

Torn over the centuries among Swedish, Russian, and German forces, Finland has usually been assigned to an eastern, perhaps Mongolian, origin, and their Finno-Ugrian language certainly sets them apart from their Indo-European neighbors. Finnish scholars also tried, first in Swedish and then in Finnish, to construct a national tradition. This included the efforts of the eighteenth-century "father of Finnish history," Henrik Gabriel Porthan, following the lead of Schlözer, who severed the old connections with the Hebrews and Greeks and regarded the Finns as an independent tradition, perhaps Eastern in origin, and those of Yrjö Sakari Yrjö-Koskinen, who introduced critical methods into Finnish historiography, who (as a promoter of "Fennomania") regarded the Swedes as foreign, and who located Finnish origins in the Turanian race, including Mongolians, Turks, and Finno-Ugric peoples.[84] On this still-controversial question the orientalist thesis was continued by German and Scandinavian scholars like the Norwegian historian P. A. Munch, who classified the Finns with other non-European "barbarians."[85] National awakening also reached the former Danish territories of Iceland, which achieved independence in 1849 on the basis of the historical arguments of Jon Sigurdson linking Iceland to medieval Norway; the Faroe Islands, whose language received a grammar by V. U. Hammerschaimb in 1854 and whose earlier history was reviewed by N. C. Winther in his *Ancient History of the Faroe Islands* (1875); and Greenland, whose language was recognized in its first periodical in 1861 and in its first grammar by Samuel Kleinschmidt in 1871.[86]

The nations of Eastern Europe in the nineteenth century had mixed and conflicted pasts, having been divided between barbarian north and civilized south, Catholic west and Orthodox east, and subjugated by a number of imperial powers — Rome, Byzantium, the Ottoman Turks, Russia, and Austria.[87] Poland invoked a glorious republican heritage and dreamed of independence against eighteenth-century partitions and Russian rule. The most influential historian was Joachim Lelewel, who published an essay on the modern art of history (*Historyk*) as early as 1815 and who promoted the Polish myth of "being the first" in the European tradition of republican liberty.[88] From 1818 he was professor of history at the Universities of Warsaw and Vilna and then took active part in politics and the Revolution of 1830, taking refuge afterward in Paris and Brussels. Before the Revolution of 1848 he served with Marx on the International Democratic Society. Lelewel wrote widely on Scandinavian literature, numismatics, medieval geography, and bibliography as well as on the theory of history and on Polish history, which for him began in a communal and democratic period (which he celebrated in tones reminiscent of Michelet) and which declined under pressures of external despotisms.[89] Lelewel's work came under attack by the later generation of historians, especially the conservative and Catholic Warsaw school, which was led by Michal Bobrzynski, who died in 1935, and which took a pessimistic view of Poland's history and destiny. In opposition was the rival, liberal Cracow school, which supported the program of national liberation and which was led by Szymon Askenazy (later a contributor to the *Cambridge Modern History*), who also died in 1935.

Hungary had an even more complex historical tradition, beginning with medieval legends of Eastern origins and medieval chronicles before conversion to Christianity and absorption into the tradition of Latin historical writing and scholarly source collections, beginning in the eighteenth century by the Protestant Matthias Bél and by later Jesuit scholars, especially György Pray and István Katona, author of a forty-two volume "critical history of the kings of Hungary" (1779–1817). Hungarian historiography shifted from Latin to German with Ignácz Aurél Fessler's and János Engel's multivolume histories published in the restoration period. These German syntheses were paralleled by the Magyar works published by Benedek Virág and Esiás Budai. The leading historians of the next generation were Mihály Horvath and Lazlö Szalay, both involved in the Revolution of 1848 and both writing history in the spirit of liberal nationalism as well as of modern critical scholarship underlying the establishment of history as a profession, marked by the foundation of the Historical Commission of the Hungarian Academy of Sciences in 1854, the publication of the *Monumenta Hungariae Historica*, rival to the *MGH*, in 1857, the formation of the Hungarian Historical Association in 1867, the organization of the national archives in the 1870s, and the influence of the German (and Austrian) scholarship in the writing of history that was at once national and scientific.[90] In particular, Hungarian scholars followed the Germans in the twentieth century in the pursuit of *Kulturgeschichte* and, especially in the work of G. Szekfü, *Geistesgeschichte*.

Czechoslovakia looked back, too, to a glorious — and mixed, especially between Catholics and Protestants — national past in its medieval legends and chronicles, in the kingdom of Bohemia, and in the Hussite revolution, contrasted especially with the political dreadnought of Germany. As early as 1781 history was taught in the University of Prague, and the new critical history was inaugurated by Joseph Dobrowsky, who was also the "father of Czech prehistory."[91] The first great national historian was Frantisek Palácky — "father of the Czech nation," as he was styled, and official historiographer — who began publishing his survey of Czech history in 1836 after a study of earlier Hungarian historiography and research in the archives. Influenced not only by German scholarship but also by Robertson, Gibbon, and Bolingbroke, Palácky's history of the Czechs, as R. W. Seton-Watson remarked, "brought them back to life."[92] His story, reaching only the post-Hussite reformation, centered on national tradition and the struggle for liberty and autonomy against imperial forces and especially German tyranny. Here, too, the next generation, led by Jaroslav Goll, reacted to Palácky's romantic idealism in the name of critical, professional history. Archeology added to the "romantic synthesis" with the publication of Erazim Vocel's *Prehistory of Bohemia* (1866–68).

Romania has been torn between East and West, having suffered Turkish domination but clinging to its Romance language and "Roman" heritage and seeking cultural identity in mainly Western terms. This was the aim of the "Transylvanian" school of the Enlightenment. In 1812, Petru Major published a study of Romanian origins in the Roman province of Dacia, arguing for the continuity of Roman influence in Transylvania down to his own day, and so contributing to the shaping of national consciousness leading to the union of Moldavia and Wallachia in 1859 and full unification in 1877, and with these the establishment of history as a professional field. The greatest of modern Romanian historians were Alexandru Xénopol, who studied history in Germany before becoming professor at the University of Iasi and who lectured also in Paris, and his pupil Nicolae Iorga, who also studied in Germany as well as France and who taught world history at the University of Bucharest, both of them maintaining scholarly contacts with the West. Xénopol wrote a general history of Romania (1888–93) and an influential contribution to the positivist philosophy of history (1899), published in French and Spanish as well as Romanian.[93] Iorga was a man of letters as well as a historical scholar and published even more widely during his academic and political career, not only on Romanian history and East European institutions but also on literature, Byzantine studies, the Crusades, institutional history, and historical method and theory.[94] Iorga's distinguished career ended tragically with his assassination in 1940 under the Nazi domination of Romania.

Similar patterns can be traced in the writings of national history in the marginal ethnic groups of the Balkan and Baltic areas. All of these groups experienced national awakenings and efforts at state-building (or rebuilding), attended by historiographical research and celebration, beginning with Romantic traditionalism succeeded by more critical, source-based, and institutionalized history in pursuit of the national mission. Modern Croatian historical writing (in Latin) began in the seventeenth century, was continued in more "scientific" form, following the German lead, in the later nineteenth century, and was accompanied by the establishment of a modern Croatian literary language by Ljudevit Gaj.[95] Serbia had a medieval tradition, based on folk songs and chronicles, and it also passed into a scientific stage, especially in the work of Ilarion Ruvaric and his followers, again concomitant with a linguistic and literary revival led by Vuc Stefanovic Karadzic and George Danicic.[96] Latvian and Estonian history was carried on mainly by Baltic Germans and

Russians, and it was given professional form somewhat later, after the national awakenings of the 1860s and before the establishment of independence in 1918. Lithuania looked back on a much grander, indeed imperial, heritage of medieval and Latin histories, being associated with Polish history and included in the works of Schlözer and Lelewel as well as major nineteenth-century histories such as those of Theodor Narbutt (1835–41) and Simonas Daukantas, who was the first historian to publish in Lithuanian, starting in the 1820s.[97]

Spanish historiography was in a state of decline since the seventeenth century, and Portugal's even more so, and both were far inferior to that of other European traditions.[98] The best Portuguese national history was that of Alexandre Herculano de Carvalho Araújo (1846–53), who modeled his work after those of the new history in France; but he carried it down only to the thirteenth century and then turned to a history of the Inquisition. The Spanish scholar and former secretary of the Inquisition, Juan Antonio Llorente, had already published a work on the Spanish Inquisition in 1817, which was based on the archives of the supreme council and of the holy office and which was highly critical, though not in a scholarly sense — denouncing the "detestable knavery" of the Inquisitors who had concealed the truth and undermined Spanish power.[99] The standard survey at the beginning of the nineteenth century was the "critical history" of Father Juan Francisco de Masdeu, published from 1781 and translated also into Italian, though filled as it was with "enormous errors."[100] Spanish historians were strong on investigating ecclesiastical history and on publishing original sources — from the great collection *Historia Sagrada* (1754–1879) to the *Collección de documentos inéditos* (1842–95) — and from the mid-nineteenth century, professors composed many textbooks, elementary and advanced, surveying the national history. In fact there was no major synthesis of national history until La Fuente's thirty-volume history (1850–67), and even then his work, glorifying monarchy and church, was uncritical and highly derivative of the earlier study of Eugène Saint-Hilaire. What made Spanish historical writing even more marginal was the fact that much of the important historical work was done by German, French, English, and even American scholars — although Menéndez y Pelayo's *History of the Heterodox Spanish* (1880–81) marked the beginning of a scholarly national tradition.[101]

Yet Spanish historians of the nineteenth century, following their French and German colleagues, did develop their own views about a "new history" (*nueva historiografía*), as Manuel Moreno Alonso has shown.[102] In 1847, the Real Academia de la Historia was founded, or rather reorganized, and scholars such as Martinez de la Rosa, Lopez Ballesteros, Zaragoza, San Miguel, and

Flórez gave discourses praising and analyzing their art, which was on the way to becoming a science. Thus, according to Martinez, it was essential for scholars to "consider past actions in relation to their times and circumstances in order to avoid a kind of *anachronism* that judges in terms of our preoccupations."[103] Following the lead of French and German historians they carried on the search for sources, the discussion of periodization, antiquities, the philosophy of history, and the history of historiography. Increasingly Spanish historians turned against the reigning way of falsifying history of that century, that is, "politico-mania," and toward a view of history that included not merely kings and wars but also the "people," the arts of peace, and culture, and that tried to cover, in Ballesteros's words, "the whole of social existence" (*toda de la existence social*).[104]

In Switzerland, Johann Müller's great history of the Swiss confederation and its contributions to liberty (1786–1808) was surpassed by the more critical works of younger scholars, including J. von Arz's history of St. Gall (1810–13) and the documentary collections of J. E. Kopp (1832–51), who was converted from the Romantic idealism of Müller, from whose work he published popular selections, to a more critical view. On his later work were based the histories of Switzerland by Karl Dändiker (1884–87) and, in French, by Louis Vuillemin (1875–76). Historical studies in Switzerland were also promoted by cantonal societies and other institutional support.[105] In 1911 the Swiss scholar Eduard Fueter published his standard survey of modern European historiography.[106]

The Dutch had, from the sixteenth century, a distinguished tradition of classical scholarship and historical writing, and the Enlightenment saw a number of national surveys, including Jan Wagenaar's history of the fatherland (1749–59), Simon Stijl's history of the Dutch Republic (1774), and Adriaan Kluit's "critical history" of Holland and Zeeland, followed by the Romantic interpretation offered in the posthumously published lectures of Willem Bilderdijk in the 1830s. Bilderdijk, an admirer and translator of Ossian, believed that Dutch was the closest language to the original Indo-European speech that was still the object of the quest of nineteenth-century linguists. The turn to modern scientific history was made by Bilderdijk's pupil Guillaume Groen van Prinsterer, who published a handbook for the history of the fatherland in 1846, celebrating the role of the house of Orange, whose correspondence he also published from the private royal archives, of which he was keeper. Reinier Cornelis Bakheisen von den Brink also contributed to the critical study of national history. The acknowledged "father of Dutch history" was Robert Jacobus Fruin, who held a professorship in history at the University of Leiden and who published many scholarly papers promoting German methods of research and teaching. His defense of "impartiality," similar to Shakespearean drama, was opposed to Wagenaar and Bilderdijk, as his "liberal-positive" approach to national history was opposed to the conservative Calvinist view of Groen van Prinsterer. For Fruin, historical science, too, had to be "free," and moreover, "impartiality is liberal."[107] Fruin, who never himself wrote a large-scale work, was succeeded in this conciliatory task, and also in his chair, by Petrus Joannes Blok, whose magisterial national synthesis of Dutch history began to appear in 1892.

Belgian "national" history began in the eighteenth century under Austrian rule and, as in Holland, was adapted to modern critical methods in the nineteenth century. In 1834, after the establishment of the monarchy, a royal commission for history was founded, supplemented by journals, research centers, and source publications from the archives which were organized by Louis-Prosper Gachard. Belgian history entered the mainstream of European historiography with the work of Henri Pirenne, who published a national bibliography in 1893 and whose classic survey of Belgian history began to appear in 1900, showing the influence of Lamprecht, with whom Pirenne had a correspondence and whose ideas he supported.[108] Not surprisingly, Pirenne's application of a nationalist interpretation of history to the modern, monarchical descendant of the old Burgundian territory, without a national language and divided politically only since the Eighty Years' War, was challenged in the twentieth century by Blok, Johann Huizinga, Pieter Geyl, and other Dutch scholars, who took a more integralist view of the Netherlandish cultural past and a more skeptical view of the national unity of Belgium which Pirenne, with his inclinations toward economic determinism and the search for material foundations of liberty, projected back into the medieval past.

If Pirenne was at first Belgo-centric in his perspective, he vastly transcended this limitation in his studies of economic history, which shifted the focus of the investigations of Thierry into French communal history to the cities of the Netherlands from their origins down to the seventeenth century and their role in generating liberty and modern institutions of democracy (1910) — taking special exception to the racialist views of earlier historians and in particular the *Markgenossenschaft* theory.[109] "The birth of cities," Pirenne continued to argue, "marked the beginning of a new era in the internal history of Western Europe."[110] Unlike the municipal democracies of antiquity, the medieval communes were independent of and even hostile to the state, while welcoming the influx of "foreigners," who were admitted to communal rights — and all of this, he argued, quite independent of medieval political theorists. Pirenne's researches were projected onto a larger stage in his interpretations of European urban history and the revival of trade, and especially his controversial thesis about the break between ancient and medieval history, arguing that it was not barbarism (or Gibbon's "barbarism and religion") that marked the end of the ancient world but rather the Islamic mastery of the Mediterranean.[111] Such post-Gibbonian efforts at revisionism have still not found a consensus among European scholars. As for Pirenne, though he reached out for a global range, his partiality continued to be evident not only in what John Mundy called his "economism," but also in his insistence on the primacy of the Netherlandish urban (rather than the French-English-German statist or the Italian civic) legacy.

The one fallacy shared by historians of both large and small nations was the tendency to claim exaggerated antiquity for their origin — corresponding to what Vico called the conceit of nations, which alleges absurdly ancient origins for various peoples, and the conceit of scholars, "who will have it that what they know is as old as the world."[112] Formerly this often amounted to being associated with the old Trojan myth; in the nineteenth century, when it was not a form of mythologizing, it meant ransacking chronicles and archives for proof of foundings and continuities, whether of nations or of their political, social, and educational institutions. Charlemagne was no longer regarded as founder of the University of Paris; but on the basis of capitularies and charters, he was claimed as founding father of both "Germany" and "France" and their legal and institutional genealogies, and perhaps even of the European Economic Union, a modern form of the Vichian conceit.[113]

With nationalism, too, came the other side of ethnic awakening, which is xenophobia. An important ingredient of historical perspective among the smaller states was hatred of the larger occupying or oppressing powers, including not only the Turks, Austrians, Germans, British, and Spaniards but also Magyars, Poles, and Russians. The various national linguistic and literary awakenings of the nineteenth century were all directed against nationalizing policies of centralizing states, as in the cases of Greeks against Turks, the Danes of Schleswig against Germans, Serbs (clinging to Latin before the revival of Serbian), and Romanians against the Hungarians. These disputes all had, and indeed still have, their effect on the attempt to shape and master the European past. Seeking a grand and unifying narrative, historians of the great powers have resisted the obverse "Balkanizing" efforts to recover lost and hidden faces of European history, but they have never succeeded in these conjectural attempts to find unity and destiny in diversity, and at the beginning of the third millennium they seem farther than ever from this utopian, imperialist, and globalist (not to say universalist) goal.

II

American Parallels

One sought no absolute truth. One sought only a spool on which to wind the thread of history without breaking it.

— *Henry Adams*

Prehistory in the New World

How did the New World fit into the prehistorical perspective that was emerging in the nineteenth century? The discoveries of Columbus and his followers and the imperial extensions of the Conquistadores were incorporated without much difficulty into the "universal histories" of European tradition, although at first the political and cultural categories of the colonial intruders were imposed indiscriminately on the original inhabitants.[1] The old theme of the Four World Monarchies was replaced by the modern succession of Empires — Spanish, English, Dutch, French, and American — as a way of periodizing the grand narrative of Western history; and historians of all of these offered interpretations of the consequences of the opening of the new hemisphere. The old stereotypes of barbarism and civilization, too, were employed to distinguish not only the vanquished from the victors but also the primitive stages of historical development from those produced by material and spiritual culture, whether governed by laws of Providence or of secular Progress.

There was a tradition of pre-Columbian history, too, though it was largely expressed in old rumors, prophecy, and poetic visions going back to Dante and Petrarch; and not until the seventeenth and eighteenth centuries did scholars pass beyond myth and ungrounded speculation to ethnological inquiries into the origins of the Indian populations of the Americas, such as arguments for the Israelite origins of the Indians and Grotius's choice of the Scandinavians.[2] Indeed, wrote Justin Winsor, "there is not a race of eastern Asia — Siberian, Tartar, Chinese, Japanese, Malay, with the Polynesians — which has not been claimed as discoverers, intending or accidental, of American shores, or as progenitors, more or less perfect or remote, of American peoples," and none of them, he added, without some plausibility.[3] These were not questions investigated by early national historians such as George Bancroft and Richard Hildreth, but other scholars had long discussed them. The Asiatic theory of American origins, upheld by Lafitau, Alexander von Humboldt, and Charles Lyell, among others, was the most popular, although specific tall tales of Chinese discoveries were discredited; and this theory was reinforced by the fact of the narrowness of the Bering Strait and its frozen condition in winter. Long before Thor Heyerdahl's ideas of Polynesian contacts were defended, at least indirectly even by Tylor; and so were Irish and Welsh claims, based on legend. Less plausible but no less long lasting were arguments for Jewish migrations to the New World, based on speculations about the Ten Tribes of Israel, a theory, assisted by ingenious linguistic analogies, which was apparently accepted by Roger Williams and William Penn. The vast work of William Prescott's predecessor, Lord Kingsborough, otherwise a useful scholarly collection, was a late effort — "moonshine theory," Prescott called it — to prove the Jewish origins of Mexican civilization.[4]

At first American antiquarian studies were locked into biblical chronology and ethnological speculations drawn from the Old Testament. In 1833, for example, there appeared Josiah Priest's work on American antiquities which begins on Mount Ararat after the Flood, which he tries to explain in natural terms rather than as an effect of "God's power."[5] Priest proceeded through conjectures about linguistic connections and about ancient discoveries attached to many scattered archeological finds (drawn from antiquarian journals). He described the remains of mammoths (which Jefferson believed still existed) in awestruck terms and associated them with the behemoth mentioned in the book of Job, and his ethnographic interpretations are likewise tied to scriptural passages. Although Priest believed that the peopling of America was antediluvian, he was especially interested in finding possible Jewish connections — but also Roman, Greek, Phoenician, and of course Scandinavian. Another devout study of American antiquities was published in 1841 by

Alexander Bradford, who claimed to spurn such conjectures and to rely on the most trustworthy authorities. Geological evidence, monuments, mythology, and traditions (some "as old as the deluge") were, through such scientific publications as the transactions of the American Philosophical Society and *Archaeologia Americana,* the means to extricate historical fact from the "folly and superstition" of earlier ages.[6] Bradford affected to see traces of traditions about the New World in Plato and Proclus. He examined the various theories of origins—Hebrews, Carthaginians, Egyptians, Hindus, Chinese, Tartars, Malays, Polynesians, Northmen, Welsh, and even the Indians themselves—and judged them in "moral," not "demonstrative" terms, that is, according to the degree of probability but also admitting comparisons and analogies, including physical similarities, as the basis for plausible argument. His conclusion was that racially the Indians may be traced to almost all of these, although the question of earliest origins remains a mystery; and history must now, he concluded, turn to the time "when a new race, and the Christian religion, were appointed to take possession of this soil."[7]

As for pre-Columbian contacts, the major debates have been over the contacts made by the Scandinavians over several centuries, testified to mainly by the traditions preserved in Icelandic sagas and later historical writings, especially those collected in the *Landnamabók.*[8] The sagas had been put into writing by the thirteenth century, and Scandinavian scholars have tended to give them great credence, beginning with the seventeenth-century historian Olaus Magnus and including the later works (cited by Winsor) of P. H. Mallet, E. J. Geijer, P. A. Munch, K. Keyser, Henry Wheaton, and Maurer. Part of the story is the colonization of Greenland by Eric the Red and Leif Ericson, based on materials collected in the *Antiquitates Americanae,* edited by C. C. Rafn (1837).[9] Legendary accounts were supplemented by archeological finds, which at first were hardly less difficult to interpret. Most controversial was the story of the voyages to Vinland, whether region or island, mentioned in Adam of Bremen and Ordericus Vitalis as well as in a number of manuscripts.[10] Wheaton argued that Vinland should be sought in New England and Humboldt somewhere between Newfoundland and New York, and Daniel Wilson accepted the view in general; but Bancroft and Hildreth remained skeptical. Arguments for the thesis have been linguistic, ethnological, physical, geographical, and from the evidences of archeology, only the last of which were very persuasive, but even these (e.g., the Dighton Rock) seemed to be of Indian origin. The Norsemen did meet American natives (*Skraelings*), but they were probably Eskimos.[11]

The problem was proving such claims, many of them arising from national pride, and the criteria for such proofs came to depend on increasingly strict and scientific standards of historical linkage. Arguments were supported by interpretations of myths and legends, similarities of customs and rituals, intuitive etymologies, comparative linguistics, physical and cultural anthropology, and archeology (later to be supplemented by radiocarbon and DNA testing); and though the standards and techniques change, the results are still coming in. The question of the "antiquity of man" raised by Charles Lyell, a recent convert to Darwinism, in his book of that title published in 1863, was imported into America and at first encountered the same sort of religious resistance as it had in Europe, especially in England. But the work of Tylor, Lubbock, Bastian, and Theodor Waitz, based on studies of the American Indian, shifted the opinion in the scientific community; and in 1896, Andrew Dickson White could celebrate the victory of Darwinism and the findings of comparative ethnology and comparative philology over the obscurantist theological champions of the "fall of man."[12]

White's work represented the victory of evolutionism in some intellectual circles, but refinement of questions of prehistory was pursued along more sophisticated lines drawing on the "New Science of Anthropology" and, even more persuasively, on archeology. As in Europe the fact that human remains were found along with those of extinct mammals forced acceptance of the antiquity of man in America and, as C. C. Abbott concluded, adopting the paleontological evidence introduced by Scandinavian scholars, his existence, specifically, in paleolithic times in America. And proofs, assembled by Winsor, continued to accumulate, especially with the collective efforts reflected in the proliferation of archeological museums and periodicals, beginning with the transactions of the American Philosophical Society (1769), whose president, Thomas Jefferson, was himself a pioneering archeologist, the American Academy of Arts and Sciences (founded in part "to promote and encourage the knowledge of the antiquities of America"), the publications of the American Antiquarian Society (1812), the American Ethnological Society (founded by Albert Gallatin), the proceedings of the American Association for Advancement of Science (begun in 1848), the publications of the American Geographical Society (1852), the *American Naturalist* (1867), the *American Antiquarian* (1878), the Archeological Institute of America (1879), the *American Journal of Archeology* (1881), the American Folk-Lore Society (1888), the Smithsonian Institution (1846), the Peabody Museum (1866), and others.[13] The assault on the remote past was concerted and broadly based, and yet, as in Europe, the efforts were mainly descriptive and analytical, with no stable synthesis — except the macro-doctrine of Darwinian evolution — appearing before the twentieth century.[14]

American antiquarianism was created in the pious old European image. The

American Antiquarian Society called its proceedings *Archaeologia Americana,* in memory of the English *Archaeologia,* founded in the later eighteenth
century, and was associated itself with a grand tradition going back to Charlemagne, under Alcuin's aegis (if not the legendary Irish society founded seven
centuries before Christ), the English Society of Antiquaries of the later sixteenth century, and the recent foundation in Copenhagen. In 1813 the Rever-
end William Jenks gave an address in which he remarked on the "high antiquity" which infidels like Dupuis and Volney had assigned to the Egyptians,
but he was pleased to add that such "pagan fictions" had been disproved
by "learned Antiquaries" acquainted with the truths of revelation (citing
Georg Horn and Robertson, among others).[15] The society was especially solicitous about collecting books, but it also sponsored fieldwork, for example,
on the "Western mounds of earth," which promised enlightenment on pre-
Columbian America. But of course over the next two generations, as the thesis
of the "Antiquity of Man" gained support, the society was itself drawn into
infidelity and even Darwinist ideas, as were other organizations. In its first
annual report (1881), for example, the American Bureau of Ethnology, directed by J. W. Powell, showed itself fully committed to ideas of evolution, at
least in language.[16]

What effect did these inquiries and discoveries have on the writing of American history? Pioneering authors like George Bancroft, Richard Hildreth, and
John Gorham Palfrey preferred to skirt the question with a few references to
earlier speculations, but of course they were writing when the issues were in a
state of massive confusion and deadly controversy. In 1843, Prescott, confronting the question in the context of Mexican civilization (in an appendix to
his book), surveyed the myths and theories deriving from discredited notions
of the unity of the human race, including the transplantation of animals,
whether by angels or men, to the New World. The key question for him was
precisely where men reached America.[17] Religious analogies, including the
deluge, communion, and baptism, had been invoked, as had those in science,
art, architecture, and language, especially Mayan hieroglyphics, and physical
structure and appearance; but in the end Prescott was skeptical of the findings
of those who set out to find similarities; and on the whole he found differences
more striking. His conclusion was to reject Hebrew, Egyptian, Chinese, or
Tartar origins for East Asia — but in a period "so remote, that this foreign
influence has been too feeble to interfere with the growth of what may be
regarded, in its essential features, as a peculiar and indigenous civilization."
Prehistory was largely a matter of speculation in other words, and scholars
had to get on with periods that were recorded and accessible. This, too, was a
premise of nineteenth-century historicism.

The National Project

Questions of origins aside, American historiography began with a variety of the English Protestant view of the past, incorporating the New World into an Augustinian and Puritan framework, with the help of authors like John Foxe and Walter Raleigh. John Smith's history of Virginia, New England, and the Summer Isles (1624), William Bradford's history of Plymouth Plantation (though not published until 1856), Cotton Mather's *Magnalia,* an ecclesiastical history of New England (1702), Thomas Hutchinson's history of the Massachusetts Bay Colony (1754), and the history of New York by William Smith, friend of William Robertson, who himself wrote a history of America, were among the most successful efforts of British colonists to establish their own traditions.[18] Their efforts were continued in the revolutionary and early national period by the histories of the Revolution by David Ramsay (1789) and Mercy Otis Warren (1805), Noah Webster's history of the United States (1787), Ramsay's history of South Carolina (1809), Jeremy Belnap's history of New Hampshire, and the biographies of Washington by John Marshall, Washington Irving, and, especially, Jared Sparks, who held the first American professorship of history, established at Harvard in 1839, and who, with Peter Force, was one of the pioneers in collecting national records.[19]

Like the English, but somewhat later, Americans discovered European and, having read Mme de Staël, especially German culture and scholarship. This began with their own "generation of 1820," most notably Washington Irving, George Ticknor, George Bancroft, William Hickling Prescott, Richard Hildreth, John Gorham Palfrey, Sparks, and Edward Everett, all Harvard-educated, and the last two, presidents of that university.[20] As Coleridge made a pilgrimage to Germany (especially Göttingen) in 1798 and Henry Crabb Robinson in 1802, so in 1815 George Ticknor went to that university and likewise made contact with many of the major German scholars and writers, on whom he reported to American friends, including Jefferson. In America, Puritanism was yielding "before the advances of social civilization," he wrote, though "not yet strenuously attacked, either by the influx of a foreign population bringing with it its own foreign creed, or by the cold scepticism of what is called modern thought."[21] In 1814, Ticknor quit the law for a career in letters, which he began with an extended tour of England, France, Germany, Italy, and especially Spain — during which he associated with many prominent intellectuals, including Byron, Mme de Staël, August Schlegel, Wolf, Michaelis, Eichhorn, Heeren, Creuzer, Humboldt, Goethe, Sismondi, Chateaubriand, Barante, Constant, and Villemain, returning in 1819 to become Harvard's first professor of modern languages. A few years later Ticknor's younger friend George Bancroft also came to Göttingen, where he met many of the same figures, adopted continental fashions, and indeed took a doctorate (as did Everett) before moving to Berlin and then returning in 1822 to teach briefly at Harvard. Another American student at Göttingen and then Berlin was John Lothrop Motley, who came to Germany a decade later to study law, though he, too, turned away from this subject. These historians were all in close contact with European and especially English writers through visits and correspondence.

Bancroft, deciding not to enter the ministry and never succeeding as a poet, became the American national historian with the publication in 1834 of the first volume of his history of the United States, the tenth and last volume appearing forty years later, the whole based on extensive manuscript research and revised in time for the first Centenary. In Göttingen, Bancroft was at first attracted to philology and orientalism, that is, biblical criticism, mainly under Eichhorn; in Berlin he met other distinguished professors, including Boeckh and Wolf, though he was unfavorably impressed with the aged Homeric scholar.[22] Like other American student-tourists he also paid his respects to Goethe, and in Paris he made the acquaintance of Alexander Humboldt, Cuvier, and Constant, in Italy Lord Byron, and in England Hallam, Milman, and Macaulay (whom he particularly admired); but despite his veneration of Old World culture his expressive patriotism was never diminished. Bancroft's esoteric scholarly ambitions, however, did not survive his return to America, nor did his interest in teaching survive his short and unsuccessful stay at Harvard as Greek tutor. Bancroft was also active in politics and diplomacy and was ambassador both to England, where he met Macaulay, Carlyle, Hallam, Milman, Mahon, and to Germany, where he met Mommsen, Ranke, Droysen, and Bunsen. In Bancroft's work, Romantic sensibility and nationalist fervor competed with German ideas and standards of scientific history, all of which he tried to import into his own democratic culture. Bancroft also translated two works of the Göttingen historian Heeren and wrote widely on literary topics, including medieval and modern German literature, and on questions of culture, progress, and national character in history, following the lead in particular of Herder and Mme de Staël. Bancroft believed that "the moral world is swayed by general laws" and that these laws can be revealed through the "science" of history, that is, through careful research into facts, "which become of themselves the first links of a brightly burnished chain, connecting events with their causes, and marking the line along which the power of truth is conveyed from generation to generation."[23] The main law of "universal history" was that of human progress, which had been understood by Vico and Bossuet but even better by Jonathan Edwards, for whom "the new creation is more excellent than the old." Thus Bancroft sought underlying principles as well as dramatic actions and heroes in the national past, but his was a very derivative and providential philosophy of history, further diluted by theological concerns, nationalist excesses, and extravagant oratorical indulgences.

For Bancroft the U.S. was an essential part of a great "political system" (Heeren's term),[24] which included the entire world of nations centering on Europe, and which by his time, hardly two centuries after the first colony had begun to transform the "unproductive waste" of pre-Columbian America, inhabited only by "a few scattered tribes of feeble barbarians," had reached the front rank of civilized states.[25] Bancroft's first hero was of course Columbus, who led "the most memorable maritime enterprise in the history of the world [which] formed between Europe and America the communication which will never cease." "His great discovery was the triumph of free mind," and yet it could not have been done "without the favor of heaven." Columbus's goal was, Bancroft exalted, "not merely to open new paths to islands of continents, but to bring together the ends of the earth, and join all nations in commerce and spiritual life."[26] But spiritual life meant competition, too; and soon the French entered into rivalry for the New World, followed by the English, who introduced first liberty and then "the unjust, wasteful, and unhappy system" of slavery into their colonies. Down to the Glorious Revolution, Bancroft traced the fortunes of the English colonies "almost exclusively from contemporary documents and records" (but without footnotes)[27] and celebrated both the colonial isolation from the monarchical institutions of the Old World and the (anti-Roman) spirit of freedom brought by Calvinists and Quakers — Protestantism being "the seed-plot of democratic revolutions."[28] Bancroft also devoted several chapters to the culture and languages of the American Indians, and on the basis of their connections with Mongolians he concluded that "the indigenous population of America offers no new obstacles to faith in the unity of the human race."[29] This unity, reflected in the ideals of Christianity, was also furthered by the American Revolution, whose aim, in accord with "Divine Wisdom," was the "welfare of all mankind . . . and the service of their own and of all future generations." There was often a large gap between Bancroft's boasted scholarship and the romantic indulgences of his judgments.

William Prescott was a younger classmate of Sparks, Bancroft, and Ticknor, who indeed, beginning in 1824, gave him instruction in Italian and Spanish after his tour of Europe, when, having likewise given up the idea of a career in the law, he sought an appropriate historical subject to which to devote himself.[30] Like Bancroft he was concerned with religion but, like him, too, did not think this suitable for a literary career, which, for him as for many others in his group, began with articles to the *North American Review,* "that old watchdog of our American literature," as Oliver Wendell Holmes called it, edited first by Sparks, then Palfrey, and later Henry Adams.[31] Prescott prepared himself carefully for his literary calling, for "poets may be born, but historians are made."[32] His journals are filled with reports on his readings in several languages and anxious promises not to waste time and to improve his writing habits and speed, taking popular authors like Gibbon, Barante, even Scott ("master of the picturesque"), Irving, and his friend Bancroft as standards of quality and quantity — hoping to avoid their defects but to emulate their success. He never learned German but studied Italian, French, and Spanish literature and, after considering and rejecting Roman and Italian topics, turned to the latter as the most promising and least cultivated area. He felt the competition of Washington Irving, "the Devil may take him," who had made pioneering researches into the primary sources for his massive but hastily assembled life of Columbus, published in 1828.[33] Nevertheless, on 3 July of that year he decided "finally and for the hundredth time" on the Spanish monarchs Ferdinand and Isabella as the focus of his scholarly and literary effort, on 6 October began to write the first chapter, and on 26 June 1536 finished the book.[34] This eminently successful effort set Prescott on a course that took him through a series of volumes on the Spanish conquests of Mexico and Peru and the reign of Philip II, and that brought international fame and honors.

Whether he exaggerated his "blindness" or not, Prescott did work under severe handicaps. Like two of his correspondents who were also hampered by loss of eyesight, that is, Augustin Thierry (whose *Norman Conquest* gave Prescott a narrative model) and Gino Capponi (who had Prescott's first work translated into Italian), he depended on friends, including his Harvard friend Sparks, his "brother Antiquary" Bancroft, and Washington Irving as well as Friedrich von Raumer (who arranged for a German translation), but especially Pascual de Gayangos to locate and copy documents and other secretaries to read them to him, so that, as his friend and biographer Ticknor put it, he could "make his ears do the work of his eyes."[35] Prescott also depended on documentary collections, especially that of Martín Fernández de Navarette, for his largely political, institutional, and military narrative.

Following the tracks of Peter Martyr, Gerónimo Zurita, Mariana, Hererra, Antonio de Solís, and Robertson as well as a wide range of primary sources, Prescott surveyed, in stately, Latinate, and laudatory fashion, the story of Castile and Aragon, their political, institutional, and literary heritage, and their struggles with the Moslem invaders, down to the union of crowns under Ferdinand and Isabella. The wars first of Granada and then of Italia monopolized Prescott's attention, but he also observed other major topics, including the role of the Inquisition ("the most humiliating triumph which fanaticism has ever been able to obtain over the most civilized portion of the world"), the expulsion of the Jews, the reforms of Cardinal Ximenes, and the creations of literature and scholarship in Spain's "golden age," as well as portraits of major protagonists. In 1492, with the simultaneous beginning of the long conflict between France and Spain over Italy and the enterprise of Columbia, Prescott's narrative entered upon the "memorable epoch" of political modernity, with the opening up of European and global horizons.[36] He was on the whole even-handed in his treatment of the ups and downs of Spanish history, admitting both the "outward show of glory" and the hidden seeds of decay, the interplay between which heightened the dramatic tension of the book.

Prescott was self-consciously solicitous of his style, but he also prided himself on his critical abilities, and like Ranke, he offered severe estimates of his sources and predecessors. It was an unspoken (but privately acknowledged) rule in the circle of Prescott, Ticknor, and Bancroft, who all promoted each other's published work, to set friendship above criticism; but Prescott implicitly censured his older friend and rival, Washington Irving, for surrendering to "the dramatic brilliancy of coloring denied to sober history." In general Prescott hoped to combine the virtues of Ranke and of Macaulay, and in the second he succeeded, certainly with contemporaries, as reviews and private opinions were almost all favorable and even flattering. This was even more the case with the two sequels to his first book, which continued the story but narrowed the focus again, this time to the Spanish imperial enterprises, following the Crusade against the Moslems, in Mexico and Peru, which were much less cultivated territories — especially since he no longer had to worry about competition with Irving. While the demands of colorful and dramatic narrative remained, source problems were heavier, and added to these was the great difference in moral standards between the nineteenth and sixteenth centuries, which required Prescott to avoid the extremes of partiality — showing either overindulgence (like Solís) or over-severity (like Las Casas) toward the actions of the heroic-murderous Conquistadores.[37]

Prescott's masterpiece, the *Conquest of Mexico*, opens with a survey of the geographical and social background and the mythic, religious, scientific, and literary remains of the Aztecs; but he refrained from taking up the subject of "the origins of Mexican civilization" in depth, citing the view of Humboldt that the question of the origins of the inhabitants of a continent is beyond the limits of history and perhaps even philosophy — and indeed the findings of anthropology and archeology were largely beyond Prescott's purview. Yet he did append some remarks on this largely speculative question through analogies with Old World cosmogonies, physical characteristics, architecture, and hieroglyphics.[38] Prescott's conclusion was to accept a belief in the "influence" of East Asian civilization, but in a period too remote "to interfere materially with the growth of what may be regarded, in its essential features, as a peculiar and indigenous civilization." But Prescott's major concern was with the story of Mexico after the Spanish discovery and the spectacular conflict between Montezuma and Cortés, and indeed his fascination with the personality of the latter led him to extend the natural limits of the drama to the end of Cortés's life, concluding with a largely positive assessment of the character of the Conqueror of Mexico. This book, which was praised by scholars such as Guizot, Mignet, and Milman as well as many American friends, was followed by the less spectacular story of Pizarro and the conquest of Peru, and a study of Philip II, a topic on which his friend Motley was also engaged. They came from the same Boston intellectual milieu and Harvard-educated elite with literary ambitions, and yet Motley took a strikingly different approach to the early modern European scene than Prescott. Like Bancroft, Motley — though he, too, gave up his legal career — was drawn not only to public life but also to political ideals which were largely irrelevant to Prescott's impartial literary impulse; and, denouncing the "splendid empire of Charles V . . . erected upon the grave of liberty," he glorified the new Republic of the Netherlands, even more than Florence, as the leader of "the resistance of chartered liberty to foreign despotism" and as the teacher of "that great science of political equilibrium," forming in its revolution, together with those of England and America in later centuries, "links of one chain."[39]

Motley had begun his career as statesman (serving a term in the Massachusetts legislature), novelist and, more successfully, contributor to the *North American Review,* and by 1850 had chosen the vehicle for his historiographical calling, namely, the rise of the Dutch Republic and its heroic leader, William of Orange.[40] In this enterprise he was encouraged by his older colleague Prescott. From 1851 to 1856, Motley explored European archives, made scholarly contacts, and employed copyists; but his way of life was far different, especially during his diplomatic service in Russia, Austria, and England. As Prescott labored at home and in the dark with his noctograph, so Motley, with the help of Ticknor's letters of introduction, made social and literary contacts and endured the distractions of endless rounds of dinner parties with the likes of Macaulay, Thackeray, Hallam, Milman, Stanhope, higher nobility and, later, of official duties, which activities monopolized his correspondence to his wife and parents. Yet through it all Motley "worked like a brute beast," and achieved a success not inferior to Bancroft's and Prescott's. His *Dutch Republic* was acclaimed by American friends, including Prescott, Bancroft, Ticknor, and Holmes, and Europeans alike, Froude being especially warm in his review of 1856, while Guizot arranged for a French translation and Bakhuizen van der Brink for a Dutch one.[41] For the *History of the United Netherlands,* which, he lamented, lacked a hero like William the Silent, he explored the Public Record Office and the archives of Brussels, the Hague, and Paris, though he feared to be overwhelmed by the materials.[42] This work, too, was favorably received, with its characteristic combination, noted by Prescott, of the styles of romance and sober history.[43] Dutch critics like Groen van Prinsterer were less approving, especially of his last work on Barneveldt, and even Guizot protested his partisanship.

The Rise of the Dutch Republic, after sketching the social, religious, and political background of the Netherlands and noting the enduring principles of love of liberty and self-government of its people, opens with an account of the abjuration of Charles V (recently de-romanticized by the modern scholarship of Gachard and Bakhuizen van der Brink) and then plunges into a narrative of the mounting conflict between Phillip II and the "Machiavellian" policy underlying the persecutions of his Dutch subjects at a time when toleration was "the deadliest heresy of all."[44] The succeeding wars and "municipal revolutions" are described in flamboyant detail, employing not only the newly printed sources but also manuscript diplomatic reports, pamphlets, and Huguenot songs. As Prescott placed Cortés at the center of his narrative, so Motley did with William of Orange, whose story culminated in Dutch independence proclaimed in the Act of Abjuration, "by which the united provinces threw off their allegiance to Spain, and *ipso facto* established a republic which was to flourish for two centuries."[45] The book ends with the assassination of "Father William," and a remark quoted from a manuscript source: "As long as he lived, he was the guiding-star of a whole brave nation, and when he died the little children cried in the streets."[46]

The youngest member of the heroic generation of American historians, Francis Parkman, descended from a long line of New England divines and graduated from Harvard in 1844, returning much later as professor of horticulture. He entered Harvard Law School and even received a degree but was much more interested in Indian ethnology and literature, and like Motley he made an unsuccessful attempt at writing novels and poetry. But unlike Motley, Prescott, and Bancroft, though he made the obligatory European trip (and stole a branch as a memento from Virgil's tomb), he loved nature, scenery, and even hardship, and he turned not East but West to complete his education and to seek his literary and scholarly fortune.[47] After his *Oregon Trail* (1846), which chronicled his adventurous trip across the Rockies, Parkman set out as an explorer of an "uncultured and unreclaimed" field of history, starting with *The Conspiracy of Pontiac* (1851), dedicated to Sparks, president of Harvard. That Parkman shared European horizons with his elder colleagues is evident from his remark that this first book tells how "began that memorable war which, kindling among the forests of America, scattered its fires over the kingdoms of Europe . . . , the war made glorious by the heroic death of Wolfe, the victories of Frederick, and the exploits of Clive; the war which controlled the destinies of America, and was the first in the chain of events which led on to her revolution with all its vast and undeveloped consequences" — while the "forest hero" Pontiac lies beneath a city as the descendants of his enemies "trample with unceasing footsteps over his forgotten grave."[48]

Despite poor health and the loss of his wife and a child, he completed his career with a brilliant eight-volume series on *France and England in North America* (1865–92), which filled in the story begun with the dramatic tale of Pontiac and the Indians, caught like a cloth between the points of the American-French shears in the "old French war." Parkman's great epic treated whites and savages, Papists and Huguenots, priests and Puritans, forest life and military conflict, and a variety of heroes and villains, as well as the institutions of New France, as a broad prelude to the American Revolution. The story, set in the panoramic scenes of Canada and the wild American West, was the conflict of white Anglo-Saxon liberty against French (and Jesuit) absolutism and a non-Germanic sort of barbarism; and to that extent, while operating on the margins of European history, he shared the Eurocentric values of his English and continental colleagues. His heroes were La Salle, Frontenac, Montcalm, and Wolfe; his scenes were the wild forests, uncanny visions such as that of "the imperial cataract" of Niagara, displayed "in primeval solitudes unprofaned as yet by the pettiness of man."[49] Behind the artistry and the rhetoric lay the careful search of original records, such as the Jesuit relations and archives, and indeed his *La Salle and the Discovery of the Great West* was rewritten on the basis of new French discoveries, though it confirmed his intuitions in all but matters of detail. Parkman was also an amateur archeologist, and in this book he also determined the site of the "Great Illinois Town" of the Indians.

Though "literary" in their ambitions and approach, Parkman, Prescott, Motley, and to some extent Bancroft were pioneers of scholarly historical writing and, despite their Harvard and New England point of departure, preserved European horizons in their inquiries and interpretations. Their narratives were dramatic, their backgrounds colorful, and their stories dominated by heroic figures who created the conditions of change, whether for good or for evil. At the same time they shared with their continental colleagues a conviction that their histories ought to be founded on an exhaustive exploration of archival sources, which alone could reveal motives and causes in the historical process. Implicitly they all supported the notion of universal history and national histories and, moreover, the goal of contributing a critical and definitive piece to the master narrative of the story of the human race from a Eurocentric vantage point.

American History in a Scientific Mode

As the heroic generation of American historians was completing its masterworks, the character of history was changing in America as in Europe. The private collections of books by Obadiah Rich, Sparks, H. H. Bancroft, John Carter Brown, and others, the massive publication of sources by Sparks and others, the founding of historical periodicals and societies, the turn to institutional and social history, the rise of "scientific history," the employment of ethnology and archeology, the influence of Positivism and Darwinism, and the introduction of history into the university curriculum and the German seminar system into its teaching: these all acted to transform American historiography and place it in the hands of modern experts who have at best a secondary interest in the "literary" qualities of historical writing.[50] As amateurs were replaced by professionals, so the old "art of history" was replaced by historical science — and yet the old genre of multivolume narrative continued, and with it many of the old literary conventions and habits of thought and explanation.

After Bancroft, the project of writing a national history of the United States was still carried on by non- or pre-professional historians, most notably by Richard Hildreth, the Harvard-educated author of the first antislavery novel (1836) and a six-volume survey of the history of the United States down to 1821, and also the more derivative Southern scholar, George Tucker, whose four-volume survey appeared in 1856, as well as the more restricted history of New England published by Palfrey in 1858 and dedicated to Sparks. Tucker, who taught at the University of Virginia, brought a Southern viewpoint, not defending slavery but rejecting Northern interference; but he died in 1861. Palfrey, with his more restricted horizons, laid emphasis on racial character, including not only the homogeneous, "unmixed" character of New England settlers but also the inferior Indian population, cunning, false, and "destitute of mental culture."[51] Hildreth, although Bancroft's volumes had begun to appear, claimed priority in publishing a synthesis of national history that represented the American founders "without stilts, buskins, tinsel, or bedizzenment."[52] Hildreth's work, which Lecky preferred to Bancroft's, began with Columbus's "scientific heroism" and had a theoretical underpinning that treated the theory of morals, politics, taste and criticism, economics, psychology, education, justice, and law, and which turned to the social dimension. "Is there never to be an *Age of the People*," he asked, "of the working classes?"[53]

Such indeed was the ambition of the first great American social historian, John Bach McMaster, who followed the lead of Green's popular history in viewing not merely the actions of the politicians but also, and more closely, the life of the people apart from the public movers and shakers. The national project was continued by a great line of cooperating and competing historians. Among others the immigrant German scholar Hermann von Holst published eight volumes on American political and constitutional history (1877–92); in 1887 James Ford Rhodes, inspired by Hildreth, began writing his history of the United States from the Compromise of 1850; Hubert Howe Bancroft, with collaborators, published a series of volumes, appearing from 1882, on the American West, Mexico, and Central America; Theodore Roosevelt contributed his *Winning of the West* (1889–96); John Fiske published several works on early American history; Herbert Levi Osgood's institutional study of the American colonies came out in 1904; in 1907 G. L. Beer began his analysis of the British colonial system; and Edward Channing's history began to appear in 1905. In these works the historiographical focus was narrowed, as sectional research was deepened and patriotism turned into exceptionalist arguments, represented especially by the "frontier thesis" presented by Frederick Jackson Turner in 1893.[54]

National preeminence and manifest destiny might be enough to carry along a gratifying story, but for stronger conceptual structure American scholars unsatisfied with providentialism turned to contemporary science, first to Positivism and then to Darwinism. Hildreth, Henry Adams, Roosevelt, and Turner were among many who drew on these doctrines for their conjectures and interpretations; and so, in a more doctrinaire fashion, did J. W. Draper, Andrew Dickson White, and John Fiske. In this way the expanding mass of published records, sources, and narratives was given a framework for an updated sort of conjectural history in which "science" established not only the methods of collection and inference but also the larger patterns of interaction and change, generally in the direction of progress and improvement.

An evolutionist before Darwin, Draper was a chemistry teacher at New York University who applied his "physiological argument" (presented first at the British Society for the Advancement of Science in 1860) to his ambitious narrative of the "intellectual development of Europe" from ancient times to the "age of reason," with a glance ahead at the bright future of civilization. Draper followed Stephen, Lecky, and Buckle in tracing the "progress of the human mind" from myth and medieval obscurantism to scientific enlightenment and an understanding of the laws of nature and history. "Individual development is the model of social progress," declared Draper, following the lead of Enlightenment historical thought and indeed going a step further, for "nations, like individuals, die."[55] In a detailed but derivative way and with no reference to sources, Draper sketched out the natural background of world history, but soon narrowed his focus to the Greco-Roman tradition, mainly philosophical and religious, with a "digression" on Indian and Egyptian civilizations. He deplored the medieval "Italian Church system" and celebrated the Arabs for reintroducing a "scientific" element in Western culture, leading eventually to open conflict between theology and reason. Draper saw four revolts against ecclesiastical authority—the Albigensian, the Wycliffite, the Reformation, and the French Revolution—and the reactions of the Church were indications, as sure as astronomical observations, of its changing position from strength to exhaustion.[56]

The preparations for the European "age of reason" (similar to that of Greece) reached back to scholastic philosophy, especially to Albertus Magnus and Roger Bacon, and were advanced by the discovery of Columbus, even though it was made under the aegis of the "hideous skeleton" of the Spanish monarchy, and especially by Vasco de Gama's world-encircling voyage. For Draper, Progress then found another arena in the New World on which to work its laws, repeating, though independent of, their operations in the Old. Draper celebrated, too, the impact of printing, which allowed enlightenment—the old plea of philosophes like Condorcet—to be extended from "the leading, the intellectual class" to humanity as a whole, yet which also, in the excessive multiplication of works, doomed individual authors to quick extinction.[57] In any case these were the conditions which led to the victory of the "astronomical party" over the "ecclesiastical party" in the seventeenth century, and to other triumphs of science over obscurantism and anthropocentrism, most recently in geology and biology (referring to his own but not Darwin's or Lyell's work).[58] These were also the conditions, Draper concluded, making possible a philosophical understanding of the past acts of nations and even "a prophetic monitor of their future."

White agreed with Draper about the underlying pattern of the history of civilization, especially the conflict between reason and authority, except that he took dogmatic theology rather than religion as the enemy of science. First president of Cornell, diplomat, statesman, and an admirer of Guizot and Thierry as well as Gibbon, White had traveled in Europe as a tourist-student, had heard the lectures of, among others, Boeck, Raumer, and Ranke (though he could not follow his mumbling), and had introduced continental pedagogical methods to Cornell, with particular emphasis on history—the "best of all methods . . . [for] political and social life."[59] White's own scholarly, doctrinal, and ideological position was made clear in the major work, begun as a popular and tendentious lecture and published in two volumes during his residence in St. Petersburg, on the warfare between science and theology in Western history — the victory of the former being in effect the agenda of White's Cornell. Even more polemically than Draper, and now with the arguments of Darwin and Lyell, White wanted to bring scientific enlightenment to the American population at large concerning Creation and its history.

The enemies of science always outnumbered its champions, and much of White's account is taken up with the defenders of ecclesiastical authority and unreason, beginning especially with "the war upon Galileo" and his posthumous victory over the "theological view."[60] A similar pattern could be seen in the disputatious advances in physics and chemistry and, more especially, in the earth and the human sciences, for here the priority of biblical chronology and supernaturalism was even more directly challenged. Genesis was overcome by geology, divinely created man by biology, and biblical chronology — already subverted by Egyptology and Assyriology — by paleontology. Invoking the names of Draper, Lubbock, Tylor, Spencer, Buckle, and Max Müller (and the higher critics of the Bible, but not Strauss), White gave special praise to "Anthropology and its handmaids, Ethnology, Philology, and History [, as] proofs of the "upward evolution of humanity since the appearance of man upon our planet."[61] He ended by celebrating the Bible but in the light of the new revelation not of the "Fall" but of the "Ascent of Man" — an ascent tied also to advances in medicine, psychology, public health, social policy, politics, and a religion that had laid down its ecclesiastical arms and come to terms with modern science.[62]

John Fiske was an ambitious and self-indulgent intellectual of religious temperament who was swept up in the new sciences, not only geology and Darwinian biology but also comparative philology and history, as well as scientistic system-building in the style of Comte, Buckle, and especially Herbert Spencer, the first result being his competitive, but also derivative, *Outlines of Cosmic Philosophy* (1874). Refusal to continue a law career and failure to obtain a Harvard appointment in history led to lecturing and journalism as a way to carry on his "struggle for survival" as well as to make his name.[63] In his lectures he kept his global and geological framework, commenting on Europe before and after the arrival of man, but his main interest was the light thrown on the origins of human culture by the comparative philology of Grimm and Bopp, the "legal archeology" of Maine, the discoveries of Egyptology and Assyriology, the "doctrine of survivals" of Tylor, and "the geological proof of the enormous antiquity of the human race" confirmed by the work of Darwin.[64] He was especially fascinated by "this mighty talisman," the Comparative Method, which Cuvier carried into paleontology but which had its greatest victories in linguistics.[65] Following Schlegel, Bopp, and especially Max

Müller, Fiske spoke to popular audiences of the appearance of "our Aryans forefathers" (a term he preferred to "Indo-Europeans"), and the linguistic basis of their supposed unity and differentiation from other linguistic groups conquered or replaced by them.

Fiske's approach to history followed a conjectural line, and he contrasted, unfavorably, Carlyle's "great-man" thesis, followed by Froude and even Freeman (whom he very much admired), with the ideas of Spencer and the work of Mommsen, who was "saturated in every fibre with 'science,' with 'sociology,' with the 'comparative method,' with the 'study of institutions.' "[66] Along with the advancement of science, and as a consequence, of Protestantism, Fiske saw the overthrow of anthropocentrism — "man . . . rudely unseated from his imaginary throne in the centre of the universe"[67] — and at the same time a decline in dogmatism, intolerance, and persecution, and he celebrated the works of Renan and Buckle as both champions and beneficiaries of this tendency. These were also consequences of the universal and many-levelled law of evolution.

Within this grandiose framework Fiske made his own contributions to the great project of national history, which he investigated during his time as Harvard librarian (failing to secure the appointment to succeed Henry Adams in the history department) and on which he gave popular lectures before embarking on serious scholarship, in which he was encouraged by Parkman. In his effort to set "America's place in history," he shifted his enthusiasm from the cosmos and Aryan linguistic roots to America's destiny as suggested especially by its early history. In his volumes on the discovery of America (which he dedicated to Freeman), Fiske recalled his study of the "Aryan forefathers" which led to his interest in aboriginal America.[68] He reviewed the ground which Justin Winsor had gone over so thoroughly with reference to recent archeological and paleontological discoveries, Fiske himself noting the work of Lubbock, Tylor, and Lewis Henry Morgan. This was followed by a series of volumes on New England, Virginia, the Dutch and the Quakers, the Revolution, and the Civil War.

These hastily written works, based on the surveys of Bancroft, McMaster, and even Irving, and on Fiske's reading in the "American room" of the Harvard library, were concerned not with scientific source criticism but rather with underlying principles and "the meaning of America," manifested especially in the evolution of self-government, and not with historical accuracy, as professional critics like James Ford Rhodes, bound to a very different sort of "science," pointed out. Fiske took his "lamented friend" J. R. Green as his model, and he took the Germanism and "comparative" approach to politics of his and Green's friend Freeman as his guiding idea. As Freeman denied that

English history started with the Norman Conquest, so Fiske argued that "our American history does not begin with the Declaration of Independence, or even with the settlement of Jamestown and Plymouth; but it descends in unbroken continuity from the days when stout Arminius in the forests of northern Germany defied the might of imperial Rome."[69] So Fiske's conception of "science" easily accommodated, and transported to the New World, one of the central and time-honored myths of European historiography.

Until the end of the nineteenth century, American historians remained in many ways in the shadow of the European tradition and the historiographical canon going back to the foundational figures, and the "faces" of Herodotus and Thucydides continued to preside over discussions of the art of history. In his presidential address before the American Historical Association in 1899, James Ford Rhodes pointed to Thucydides, Tacitus, Herodotus, and Gibbon as the still-reigning masters. In modern times, however, historical methods had so improved "that they may be called scientific"; and in this regard it was the first two of these that came closest to this ideal. By contrast, Carlyle and Macaulay, and probably Green as well, belonged among the "literary historians"; and among contemporaries Rhodes's preference was for Gardiner, the "peer of Thucydides."[70] In his sketch in 1908 of a portrait of an ideal—American!—historian, Rhodes, still at work on his magisterial history of the United States since 1850, told students at Harvard, Yale, Columbia, and Western Reserve that a knowledge of Latin, French, German, and perhaps Greek was essential to their training.[71] A younger generation would take a different view of its priorities, its relationship to European historiographical tradition, and the shape of the national project with respect to past and future.

Henry Adams between the Old and the New

In nineteenth-century America, the greatest historian, or at least the greatest man of letters who wrote history, was Henry Adams, who, like Ticknor, Bancroft, Motley, and Prescott, rejected a career in the law for more intellectual occupations—although he did study the history of Roman and German law enough to write about and teach it later at Harvard.[72] Like Augustine, Petrarch, Vico, Mill, and so many others, Adams took autobiography as the most fundamental sort of history, and his letters and other writings are part of the self-reflection that grounds all of his work. In retrospect Adams viewed himself with an eery, third person (or "one") objectivity, posing consistently as a "failure," in part by comparison with his presidential forebears. No sane man would call Adams a "failure," Carl Becker later remarked, and could give no simple reason for this self-"debunking."[73] Adams's rueful humor and heavy irony — heavier even than Gibbon's — impede historical judgments about his achievement, even if we take his self-deprecatory rhetoric to be an extreme example of the use of the "humility topos." The story he tells about himself in *The Education of Henry Adams,* almost a *Bildungsroman* despite its factual base, is one of learning sought but missed, or squandered, but never given up. Adams was a successor to the "generation of 1812" — Harvard class of '58 — and he followed their tracks to Europe, where he, too, found a society congenial and even familiar. "The Paris of Louis Philippe, Guizot, and de Tocqueville, as well as the London of Robert Peel, Macaulay, and Mill, were but varieties of the same upper-class *bourgeoisie* that felt instinctive cousin-ship with the Boston of Ticknor, Prescott, and Motley."[74] In spite of his studies and travels he felt himself only a "tourist," and still an uneducated one at that.

In Rome, Adams recalled Gibbon's epiphany in the Temple of Jupiter inspiring his great Roman project, which, however, Adams remarked, did not in any way solve the mystery of the decline and fall.[75] Adams returned home, filled with historical images but still with "no education." During the Civil War he was plunged into politics as private secretary to his father, the American ambassador in London, where he learned little but the negative and mendacious aspects of diplomacy; and in 1867 — the Church "gone" — he came home again to start a "new education," now with some appreciation of both Marx and Darwin and of the sciences associated with them. After a short stay in Washington as a sardonic political observer and journalist (and urged by his brother Charles), he accepted an assistant professorship at Harvard and at the same time the editorship of the *North American Review;* and with this dual commission — and another "failure" as he looked back on it — he served his apprenticeship in history.

In teaching medieval history, Adams was able to draw on his knowledge of German scholarship in law and institutions — his "lost two years of German schooling" — though he concentrated on England. In his characteristically self-deprecating way, Adams told how he led, or rather joined, his students in following the track of "primitive man, and came down, through the Salian Franks, to the Norman English."[76] Adams introduced German ideas, methods, and the seminar to Harvard, however briefly; and he also attempted to link American federal institutions to a remote Anglo-Saxon, and therefore "Teutonic," heritage, in this way "to trace, through two thousand years of vicissitudes and dangers, the slender thread of political and legal thought . . . back until it leads him out upon the wide plains of northern Germany."[77] In such vulgar Germanist tones he introduced the volume that issued from this seminar, in which Adams's own contribution was a study of the Anglo-Saxon courts of law. He addressed the question of communal origins, but unlike

Maine, Tylor, McLennan, Buckle, and Comte, he could find no appropriate evolutionary theory to assist him, and he believed (like Maitland) that an ignorance of the law had led English historians, even Stubbs, unlike their German counterparts, astray.[78] Adams himself, finding history a century behind other empirical sciences and regarding German methods as beyond him (though in fact he urged them on his younger colleague Henry Cabot Lodge),[79] he let simple textual study and factual inquiry suffice for the common quest with his students, pretending that he was a failure in teaching as in life. His students, including Lodge, Edward Channing, Ephraim Emerton, A. B. Hart, Henry Osborn Taylor, and Barrett Wendell, thought differently ("the greatest teacher I ever encountered," said Channing); and the Germanizing *Essays in Anglo-Saxon Law* arising from his seminar also support this view.[80]

Through his family Adams was at the center of the American political experience, and it was inevitable that he should turn to the study of national history, first in his Harvard course, then in a collection of Federalist documents and a biography of Albert Gallatin, and finally in his massive survey of the United States in the age of Thomas Jefferson and of Adams's great-grandfather John Adams. Following the fashion set by Green, Adams opens with a portrait of American society and culture in 1800. Boston was poor in history and "still poorer in science," and while a few citizens might speak French, "Germany was nearly as unknown as China"; and of course New York was further behind (Washington Irving was seventeen and Fenimore Cooper only eleven).[81] But the youthful, active, and ambitious American figure compared well with the "decrepitude" of Europe, and certainly had a brighter future — although the "American ideals" (and associated features of "national character") which Adams represented in his introductory chapters could hardly survive intact in the turmoil of the first decade of the nineteenth century. Yet it was at this time that America began to diverge from Europe and to follow its own destiny; and it was the beginning of this epic national story, so intermingled with the fortunes of his own proud family, that Adams, after trying his hand at novel-writing, took ten years out of his life to tell — although his only purpose, he claimed in his *Education,* was "to fix for a familiar moment a necessary sequence of necessary movement" — and, as Joseph Levenson suggested, to pay off a debt to his forebears.[82] But his was a major contribution to the project of national history, which (he told Parkman in 1884) was to follow the lead not of Bancroft but of his lamented friend, J. R. Green: "Democracy is the only subject for scientific history."[83]

In 1871 Adams "stopped his education" — and indeed there is a twenty-year gap in the *Education,* including his Harvard period, his novels, his wife's suicide, and the preparation for his works in American history.[84] Having, he claimed, "failed even to educate the generation of 1870," he was yet, almost thirty years later, still "passionately seeking" more education; and in this late, "twilight" phase he made a curious move, the exact reverse of Michelet's.[85] Leaving the chaos of modernity, he turned to the unity of the medieval period, as he had learned to appreciate it in his many pilgrimages, seeking a Hegelian "synthesis" in Russia but then more fundamentally in thirteenth-century Europe — the culmination of the education of a man "who had dabbled in fifty educations all over the world: whence the conception both of the 'Education' and of 'Mont-Saint-Michel and Chartres.' "[86] Here modern science and medieval unity — Darwin and St. Thomas, "the dynamo and the Virgin," the New and the Old — would find reconciliation in the reflections of a not-yet fully educated traveler and writer, who had become, though he would never claim it directly, the most insightful historian of his age, at least in the New World. He had started out "doubt[ing] neither presidents nor churches," but now he contemplated a new century in which "the stupendous failure of Christianity tortured history," and all he could do was to pass on what he had so intermittently learned.[87] "One sought no absolute truth. One sought only a spool on which to wind the thread of history without breaking it." The result, in partial cooperation with his brother Brooks, was his "Dynamic Theory of History," although this dated contraption concerning the process of history and its quasi-physical laws (harking back to Turgot and Condorcet) has been overshadowed by his work on the tenuous thread whose traces, modern and medieval, he had followed in a lifetime as an eternal "tourist-student."

Mont-Saint-Michel and Chartres was as much an autobiography and a travel guide as the *Education,* except that it attempted to illuminate a moment in history more remote than that of Adams's own disappointed and delayed Romanticism. It was the product of a dual discovery — one, shared with Brooks, arising from his obsessive reading in the literature of popular science, and the other, his voyage of emotional awakening through the cities of Normandy in 1895.[88] The former stimulated him to speculate rather grandiosely about the philosophy of history, the latter to think more critically about historical understanding. "Our age has lost much of its ear for poetry," he wrote, "as has its eye for colour and line, and its taste for war and worship, wine and women"; and it was one of Adams's aims to revive this lost sense of beauty and life.[89] One of the requirements was to appreciate the role of Mary and of the superiority of women in general — "The superiority of the woman was not a fancy, but a fact" — and so, "if you are to get the full enjoyment of Chartres, you must, for the time, believe in Mary as Bernard and Adam [of St. Victor] did, and feel her presence as the architects did, in every stone they placed, and every touch they chiselled."[90] And parallel with Mariolatry

(*Notre-Dame* was a battle cry as well as an appellation of many churches) was Scholasticism, especially that of Abelard and St. Thomas, who forged the intellectual unity that (as Adams argued before Panofsky) was the counterpart of the majestic, perhaps "too ambitious" Norman and French cathedrals. Adams's was a portrait of the high Middle Ages that has not been undone by generations of less personalized research in the style of his own earlier work.

Despite his professional teaching at Harvard and his infatuation with the idea of a science of history, Adams was essentially an amateur historian; and his last works, designed for private circulation, appeared in an atmosphere dominated by professional concerns, signaled by the establishment of the American Historical Association in 1884. There were still distinguished amateurs writing history, including George Bancroft (who lived until 1992), A. D. White, H. C. Lea (friend of Döllinger, Acton, and Lecky, and historian of the medieval church and the Inquisition),[91] H. O. Taylor (a student of Adams's and historian of ancient, medieval, and early modern thought), and Theodore Roosevelt — who were all presidents of the association, as was Adams himself (not to mention nonscholars such as his brother Charles Francis Adams and his friend John Jay). The major issue debated in the early presidential addresses was that of the utility of history, on which public figures like White, Jay, and Roosevelt insisted, but which Lea and scholars like Justin Winsor resisted.[92] Poised as always between the old and the new, Adams wanted both; and in his own presidential address given in 1894, he remarked on the overloaded and under-conceptualized condition of history, although Darwinism still held out hope from which a true and politically useful philosophy of history might emerge.

But Adams's faith in the ramshackle notion of science he shared with his brother Brooks, whose *Law of Civilization and Decay* moved still further from historiographical orthodoxy, was wavering. In his contribution to the very first issue of the *American Historical Review*, Adams took a negative position on the question; his "world-weary satirizing of historical accuracy and fact-finding starkly contrasted with the optimistic hopes and scientific aims of the fledgling historical profession in 1895," a recent professional historian commented a century later, adding, "this *fin de siècle* piece could have been written today."[93] Was it another "failure" for Adams? But then of course he was not alone, and at the end of his *Education* he dreamed, with his characteristic sense of history in the long term, of returning with his friends on his centenary "to see the mistakes of their own lives made clear in the light of the mistakes of their successors."[94] At any rate much of what Adams wrote can be and indeed still is read today. Of all the American parallels to the European historiographical canon, that of Adams, though less professional, was most profound, provocative, and, in its ironic and backward-looking way, philosophically original. And he well knew that historiography, like history, life, and the earth itself, "moved"; and he wrote to Parkman as early as 1884, referring to the parallel growth of democracy and science, that "the more I write, the more confident I feel that before long a new school of history will arise which will leave us antiquated."[95] He still felt that way at the end of his life.

New Histories

> 'The time has come,' the Walrus said, 'to speak of many things. . . .'
> — Lewis Carroll

Die Neue Geschichte

The idea of a "new history" was at least four hundred years old when it was reinvented at the end of the nineteenth century.[1] It rebegan with the attack of Georg von Below in 1898 on Karl Lamprecht, for his presumptuous and subversive "new method of history," a charge which was given a favorable spin in an article in the *American Historical Review* that same year praising "the new history," and so the phrase passed into American usage, to be taken up later by James Harvey Robinson.[2] Lamprecht's new history was actually a continuation of the old tradition of cultural history (*Kulturgeschichte*), which he pursued along two lines: that of material culture, to which he contributed in his massive study of medieval German economic and social history, and second, a Burckhardtian sort of art history, emphasizing "spiritual" factors, which were combined in his *German History* (19 volumes, 1891–1909).[3] Under the aegis of Lamprecht and his protégés cultural history emerged at the turn of the century to challenge the professional hegemony of the Rankean school. The upshot was a methodological conflict, a *Methodenstreit*, even a *Kulturkampf*, that occupied historians for a generation and more.[4]

The first exchange in this academic quarrel had occurred a decade earlier, just after the deaths of both Ranke and Waitz in 1886, and it featured Dietrich Schäfer and Eberhard Gothein. Schäfer, who had studied in Berlin with Waitz and Treitschke, had become a professor of history at the University of Tübingen in 1888, and in his inaugural lecture he began an assault on the field of cultural history, which was so popular at that time. "So-called cultural history" turned attention away from politics and the state to the study of everyday customs and usages — the study of lowlife (*Kleinleben*) in its most minute details — rather than the spiritual and moral character of the people. This could be seen especially in the history of "little peoples," and Schäfer pointed to a recent work on Scandinavian history which treated not nation-building but "tables and chairs, cupboards and beds, pots and pans" and which, despite its trivial focus, had gained popularity even in Germany through translation and illustrated a fashion current among nonprofessional authors.[5] By contrast the office of the historian was to follow historical development from beginning to end, and to do this moreover in the context of a growing folk, nation, and state. In support of his thesis, Schäfer offered a survey of the course of German historiography from medieval times down to the school of Ranke, associating the major authors — Otto of Freising, the newly discovered Tacitus, Sleidan, Melanchthon (Johann Cario), Flacius Illyricus, Pufendorf, Möser, Schiller, and others — with the national project of the nineteenth century and the rise of the critical "science" of history. The "new era" of history was marked by the work not of the *Kulturhistoriker* but of Niebuhr and Ranke.

"Without political life there is no growing historical consciousness and no historical process" (*geschichtliche Arbeit*), Schäfer declared. In the nineteenth century the belief (however unwarranted) arose that every nation had the right to become a national state, whence the search in history and prehistory for national identity — as with the Finns, Estonians, Poles, Czechs, Croats, Slovenes, and Irish. It was, he wrote, "the office of the historian to raise to consciousness the state, its origins, its development, the conditions of its being, and its goal" — meaning the historian's own state, given the difficulty of penetrating the political life of a foreign country. The distinction between history and cultural history was false, in that the latter was really a function of the former in its highest, political form. The cultural achievements of Winckelmann, Herder, Savigny, and Grimm were significant for a number of disciplines; but like the actions of individuals, they found meaning only in political life and through critical scholarship. For none of this were the unfocused pretensions of "popular cultural history" needed; for "the true territory of history is political history." This was the protest of the entrenched professional, reminiscent of complaints of eighteenth-century philosophers against the "popular philosophers."

This manifesto for Rankean (and Thucydidean, or Livian) history was answered the next year by Eberhard Gothein, a historian of Italian culture teaching at a lower school in Karlsruhe, who set about explaining "the tasks of cultural history."[6] His main premise was "the unity of method" as applied to the human spirit, but he shifted from Hegel's metaphysical to Dilthey's historical approach, and he denied that political history was adequate for this task. He defended "the good word *Kulturgeschichte*" and offered as representatives of this practice Burckhardt and Gustav Freitag—and indeed some of the work of Ranke—whom Schäfer would do well to consider in his attack. The domain of cultural history included the study of religion, art, law, and economics, all of which were aspects of the higher unity of cultural history. "Political history should accept the expansion resulting from the careful study of cultural history, if it wants to reach its goal of establishing the general causal process of political life."[7] Political history as such was too thin to capture cultural life in trying to explain the French Revolution, for example, or to accommodate both Pietist emotionalism and Enlightened reason in eighteenth-century Germany.

Like Schäfer, Gothein presented a review of German historiography in support of his case, but he found a wealth of concern for cultural subjects, especially in the Renaissance, when the territory of history was greatly expanded and when historical writing joined with philology in the formation of a critical science of history. Among later contributors to cultural history were Möser, Johannes Müller, Schlözer, Meiners, and especially Herder; and to these should be added historians of literature, art, philosophy, theology (up to Strauss), and the "positive sciences" of nature as well as the sciences of law, linguistics, and political, or national, economy, which received historical form in the work of Savigny, Grimm, List, and Knies. The seventeenth century had its polyhistors, Gothein remarked, but their encyclopedic knowledge was arranged on the "mechanical" basis of metaphysics, while cultural history—which in its pure form was the "history of ideas" (*Ideengeschichte*)—provided organic unity.[8] What marked the nineteenth century was the fulfillment of this dual heritage, the fruitful intersection of the study of political life (*Staatsleben*) and cultural life (*Kulturleben*)—State and Nation—as apparent in the work of Treitschke. The recognition of a "higher unity" (than the state) expressed by cultural history, which was implicit in Herder's plan, was made explicit in Burckhardt's great essay.[9]

The continued rise of cultural history was signaled by such discussions, by the circulation of popular books and the journalistic organ, the *Zeitschrift für Kulturgeschichte* (formerly *Zeitschrift für deutsche Kulturgeschichte*), which was taken over by the librarian at Jena, Georg Steinhausen, who oversaw the omnivorous collecting of bibliographies in the field and its associated subfields. The primary constituency consisted of librarians, archivists, members of local societies, and secondary school teachers, but there was also a push for entry into university education. Connections were stronger with economists and sociologists than with historians, and the ideological implications of "material" culture made it suspect among many conventional scholars in the universities — echoes of the *Materialismusstreit* of the previous generation.[10] Constitutional history was threatened by the new and perhaps reductionist "paradigm" of economic history, which was beginning to achieve professional status in the work of Inama-Sternegg and others in the 1870s, including both the "older" historical school of economics, led by Roscher, and the "younger" school, led by Gustav Schmoller and Karl Knies, while Karl Julius Beloch brought statistical methods into the study of ancient history.[11]

The neo-Rankean school, with its own official organ, the *Historische Zeitschrift,* remained in command of the political and "scientific" history and the professional establishment; but the challenge on the part of the "new history" became remarkable in 1891, when Lamprecht, after teaching briefly in Bonn and Marburg, moved to Leipzig, where he took over the historical seminar, turned it toward *Kulturgeschichte,* and made it a power to be reckoned with in the academic and indeed in the political world. In that year, too, the first volume of his German history appeared, with four more appearing by 1905. Lamprecht, who had also studied with Waitz, among others, had made his mark as a medieval economic historian, and indeed "material culture" was the key to his early interpretation of history. He accepted contemporary notions (already under fire) of the Mark community, while at the same time displaying knowledge of recent archeological and ethnological work (including Lewis Henry Morgan's matriarchal thesis). But ideas of high culture, spiritual or aesthetic rather than material, were more important for his changing periodization, which he defined as successive stages of symbolism, typism, convention, individualism, and subjectivism.[12] His central theme was the rise of individualism under the impact of commercial and psychological forces expressed not in political or "constitutional" but in social forms and artistic and literary creation, in the hope of revealing not "how it really was" (in the famous Rankean formula) but "how it really became" (*wie ist es eigentlich geworden*).[13] After a break the rest of the volumes appeared between 1904 and 1909, offering Lamprecht's "alternative to Ranke."

During the 1890s the *Methodenstreit* reached a crest, as Lamprecht's work was attacked by a succession of conventional historians, including Georg von Below, Felix Rachfels, Heinrich Finke, Max Lenz, Hermann Oncken, and Friedrich Meinecke, with Eduard Bernheim and Otto Hintze taking a more moderate position, and Steinhausen, Kurt Breysig, and Walter Goetz carrying on the mission of *Kulturgeschichte*. Out of piety for the *kleindeutsch* school and the standards of the *Historische Zeitschrift,* of which he was editor, Meinecke declared himself against Lamprecht's innovative but unclear materialism.[14] Below, whose analytical and political cast of mind contrasted sharply with Lamprecht's drive to synthesis and to the social, reviewed both Lamprecht's work on medieval economic history and the *German History* in the most unsympathetic and polemical terms, and moreover from the forum of the *Historische Zeitschrift* — although as editor Meinecke took a milder stand and refused to sponsor a "war to the death" in his pages, and in addition he was a supporter of Walter Goetz, who succeeded Lamprecht as head of his historical institute.[15] Below emphasized Lamprecht's errors and confusions, but underlying this were deep ideological, political, theoretical, and of course methodological differences; and Lamprecht, responding even more venomously, took the debate to new depths.

After Lamprecht's death the contentious Below carried on the controversy in his survey of German historiography published in 1916.[16] The war continued on several fronts, beginning with the defense of political and constitutional history against Lamprecht's cultural and social variety, suggesting to some "socialist" leanings (reinforced by favorable comments from the Marxist scholar Franz Mehring), the opposition to the "positivism" of Lamprecht's invocation of historical laws, and including a defense (especially by Heinrich Finke) of the Catholic over the national point of view, but involving increasingly the incidence of errors of fact in the *German History* (Lenz and Oncken), resulting, in the opinion of Roger Chickering, in the complete destruction of Lamprecht's professional reputation. According to Alfons Dopsch, writing in 1927, none of the contributions to this "new history," including those of Breysig, Steinhausen, and Franz von Löher as well as Lamprecht, "satisfy what today science demands in this field of research."[17]

Yet Lamprecht's influence and popularity grew, especially as he was drawn into theoretical questions. Lamprecht emphasized the novelty of his approach, though he also recognized that he was part of a tradition. "Herder," he told an American audience in 1904, "was the first to admit the importance of the socio-psychic demands for the proper historical comprehension of all human communities — nations — and to draw from them the necessary conclusions."[18] Ranke's "mystical" doctrine of ideas (*Ideenlehre*) was in no way new, and indeed, like historians of the state, "constitution," and political "centralization," represented a step backward from the insights of economic and cultural history, which underlay the "new science of history" (*die neue Geschichtswissenschaft*).[19] Though called a "positivist," Lamprecht also regarded as one-sided and obsolete the naturalistic efforts of Comte and Buckle and the voluntaristic ones of Marx, Hellwald, and Lippert. In contrast Lamprecht offered his own modernizing program, drawing on advances in linguistics, archeology, art history, economic history, and especially recent psychology. For Lamprecht "psychology must be the foundation of all scientific history"; but this was not the rationalist, individual psychology of the Enlightenment, it was the social or collective psychology (*Völkerpsychologie*) of his equally controversial colleague at Leipzig, Wilhelm Wundt, which offered the best approach to cultural history.[20]

In open rivalry with Berlin, Lamprecht promoted his "new history" in the "historical seminar," the central institution of professional instruction, which was dedicated entirely to cultural history.[21] In 1909 he replaced this with a more ambitious Institute for Cultural and Universal History, which, though much resented by his orthodox colleagues, attracted many students in the years before the First World War.[22] In the years before his death in 1915 he tried to extend his already extensive, if bitterly contested, influence into politics with the idea of a "cultural foreign policy," which inclined to cosmopolitanism, if not pacifism.[23] It is hardly surprising that, alienating most of his colleagues and taking an unpopular political position on the eve of the war, he died in disrepute, nor perhaps that cultural history—a failed "paradigm," as Chickering calls it—shared some of this discredit and went into decline. The "new history" in Germany came to a sad and abrupt, if only temporary, halt, as the conflict between German *Kultur* and French and English *civilisation* became involved in the national rivalries leading to the Great War of 1914–18, when Hellwald's notion of war as a necessary part of the historical process—as a higher form of the Darwinist "struggle for existences"—seemed to reach fulfillment.[24]

The point was made, famously, by the remark of the disillusioned veteran in Hans Johst's *Schlageter:* "When I hear the word 'culture,' I reach for my revolver." In fact World War I had been fought in the name of this "culture" but had violated its spirit and provoked attacks by the Allies on the pernicious character of German *Kultur*.[25] This invidious view infected scholarship, too, in the editions of the *History of German Culture,* where Lamprecht's follower Georg Steinhausen glorified, in a "scientific and systematic" way, the development of German *Kultur*, which (he wrote in 1904) joined "inner strength" with political power in its twentieth-century "rebirth."[26] In 1920, however, disillusioned with political and economic failure, Steinhausen began to emphasize the "inner strength" and drive toward *Wiedergeburt* reflected in cultural history.[27] These themes persisted in the 1936 edition edited by Eugen Diesel, who celebrated the new form of *Volkskultur* under Naziism and the "rebirth" associated with the "unified political will pulsing through the land."[28] This was "culture in the service of life," as one old warrior and follower of the new Führer proclaimed, and it was soon to be, once again, conscripted into the service of war.[29]

Yet cultural history persisted in its older and more civilized modes, and Rankean history was hardly the winner in this conflict of methods: Meinecke himself conceded that Lamprecht had helped to broaden the horizons of history; and late in life, in order to suggest the cultural dimensions of history, Meinecke elevated Burckhardt (certainly not Lamprecht) to a place next to that of Ranke.[30] Cultural history has preserved its claims to novelty even while repudiating or forgetting the labors of Karl Lamprecht and while resuming the tradition of Burckhardt. This was conspicuously the case with Johan Huizinga, who himself was associated for a time with Lamprecht's great project before he defined for himself, in the interwar years, "the task of cultural history."[31]

The New History

In 1884, just as the American Historical Association was being established, Henry Adams wrote to Francis Parkman congratulating him on the publication of his *Montcalm* — "an honor to our historical school," he declared.[32] Compared to Parkman, Bancroft lacked completeness even in a dozen volumes ("as I often tell him"). The English, too, were not well off, except for Gardiner, Lecky, and "the old war horses Freeman and Froude," J. R. Green being gone. Adams himself was midway in his American history, but this was also a voice of the past. "The more I write, the more I feel that before long a new school of history will arise which will leave us antiquated," he continued. "Democracy is the only fit subject for scientific history." Less than a decade later, before Adams had finished his history, the evidence for this was already visible.

In the United States the New History is dated conventionally from the appearance of James Harvey Robinson's book of that title published in 1912; but as usual there was a significant prehistory, related in this case to the "new history" of Lamprecht. Reports of this had reached American readers as early as 1898 in a review of Lamprecht's book in the *American Historical Review* by William E. Dow, and in 1902 and 1903 the label was also displayed by Edward Eggleston and William E. Dodd in the same national journal.[33] Moreover, in 1904, Lamprecht himself came to the United States to advertize his product at St. Louis in the presence of Robinson, Woodrow Wilson, and Charles Homer Haskins, among others.[34] The American version, however, found a much more receptive audience, and two generations of New Historians carried on the effort to enlarge and perhaps to replace the conventional political-institutional historiography modeled on nineteenth-century "scientific history" as taught, notoriously, in German and French seminars and in their American offspring.[35]

But the "new history" had deeper roots that were associated with the conditions of the New World and, more particularly in late nineteenth century, the New West, which was being treated by amateur historians like Parkman and Theodore Roosevelt but which was also attracting formally trained scholars. The American historical profession, while drawing on and imitating its continental European counterparts, had to establish its own direction, sense of nationality, and original "covenant," and — as John Franklin Jameson, one of the founders, told Henry Adams — "proper development of historical work in America."[36] For Jameson, who had his own perspective on Western tradition, this meant the "need of emancipation from the traditions and conventions of European historiography" — as indeed, from his experience at the University of Chicago, Americans were already doing.[37] His own "prophecy" was that this meant looking West. That his view was presentist as well as exceptionalist is suggested by his further comment that this did not mean questions of origins or the Indians, which were "most remote from present affairs." "Time is the basic dimension of history," Richard Hofstadter remarked, "but the basic dimension of the American imagination is space."[38]

Jameson's prophecy was already being fulfilled by the young historian from Wisconsin, Frederick Jackson Turner, a student of W. F. Allen, who himself had studied at Göttingen with Heeren, and later of H. B. Adams at Hopkins, who was a disciple of Freeman. Turner followed the progressive views of the first, largely rejected the Eastern conservatism of the second, and built his career, as Lee Benson wrote, on a certain "present-mindedness."[39] As a "progressive historian," Turner associated at least indirectly with the New History. "It is a familiar doctrine that each age studies its history anew and with interests determined by the spirit of the time," Turner wrote; and for him this relativism and drive for novelty was not only temporal but also spatial, and he was inclined to believe that American experience was incommensurate with those of the Old World. "Whatever be the truth regarding European history," he wrote, "American history is chiefly concerned with social forces." He rejected in particular the Germanist doctrine still being promoted in "the holy temple of the Teutonists" at Johns Hopkins University, presided over by Herbert Baxter Adams.[40] In 1891, writing on "the significance of history," Turner gave his own sketch of earlier traditions of historical writing, reviewing the literary, political, metaphysical, and religious approaches before "Herder proclaimed the doctrine of growth in human institutions" and so "paved the way for the study of comparative philology, or mythology, and of political evolution," followed by Wolf, "applying Herder's suggestions to the Iliad" (!), Niebuhr, and Ranke—"but to him also history was past politics."[41] So in the earlier nineteenth century, "the study of history became scientific and political," while yet following the Apollonian formula of Droysen, of which Turner very much approved, that "history is the 'know thyself' of humanity"—"the self-consciousness of mankind."

In Turner's day, however, the character of the quest had changed; and he repeatedly emphasized the new economic over the old, English and German, constitutional history, and on this basis introduced his thesis of the seminal and crucial import of the frontier and of the sections for American history. In keeping with the views of the New History in Germany as well as the United States, Turner sought the vital social and economic forces which lay "behind constitutional forms and modifications," meaning the attraction of the Great West; and even issues like slavery, which Von Holst emphasized, were tied to this central phenomenon.[42] For Turner the frontier represented not only a continuation of an old thrust but also an "escape from the bondage of the past . . . and scorn of older society." The first challenge to historians of his generation was "the Problem of the West," a problem not understood by Easterners still under the sway of European ideas and habits. Turner's position, taken up by a generation of students, was one of many encouragements to beliefs in "the birth of a new nation," manifest destiny, ideas of exceptionalism, and rejection of European historiographical tradition.[43] Strongly influenced by contemporary scientific thought, especially economic and environmentalist ideas, Turner transmitted his program from Wisconsin to Harvard, and through teaching even more than writing he brought about a reorientation of American history with regard to the European background.

The locus classicus of the New History American style was the agenda of James Harvey Robinson, who had studied at Freiburg with Hermann von Holst before beginning to teach intellectual and cultural history at Columbia in 1904. Like Lamprecht, Robinson rejected the old political school—Freeman's motto of history as "past politics" appearing then on the wall of the history seminar room at Johns Hopkins—which had represented only one strand of Western historiographical tradition but which had prevailed in the nineteenth century. Not, of course, that this entailed a return to old "literary" historians like Gibbon, whom Robinson scolded for uncritical use of sources, as for example, relying on the ignorant and derivative Jordanes for his imaginative description of the death of Alaric.[44] What Robinson wanted was to establish the broad meaning of history not merely "as it really was" (*wie es eigentlich gewesen*), in the famous Rankean phrase, but "as it actually developed" (*wie es eigentlich geworden*), in Lamprecht's also famous modification, and to do this with the help of the "new allies of history," including anthropology, sociology, economics, comparative religion, social and animal psychology, physical geography, and climatology. As a representative of the hostile Old History, Robinson referred to the presidential message delivered by George Burton Adams at the 1908 Meeting of the American Historical Association, who represented these relations as "attacks" on history by "aggressive and confident workers in the same field."

In 1908 Robinson offered an interpretation of "the growth of historical-mindedness," referring to the program of Daunou as evidence of the strength of the literary tradition, though also pointing out history's independence from poetry by its focus on politics, as exemplified by Thucydides, Polybius, and Tacitus. As classical history was associated with poetry, so Christian history fell under the dominance of religion from Orosius to Bossuet and beyond, with Reformation scholars like the Magdeburg Centuriators and Baronius descending further into partisanship. Enlightenment authors like Bolingbroke, who repeated the old saw "philosophy teaching by example," subordinated history to moral philosophy. But these old habits were changing, Robinson wrote: "Since the middle of the eighteenth century, new interests other than the more primitive literary, political, military, moral, and theological, have been developing." Beginning with Hegel (whom Robinson claimed not to understand) a national trend appeared, giving impetus to source collections such as the *MGH* and the patriotic writings of Ranke, Dahn, Giesebrecht, Waitz, Droysen, and many others. Despite the accumulation of sources, old-fashioned historians like Thomas Hodgkin unreasonably inflated his materials, which deserved a single volume instead of the eight he finally delivered. At the same time the mutable "Muse of History . . . began to fall under the potent spell of natural science," with the crude interpretations and "laws of Buckle, Marx, Draper, and others, unsupported by adequate evidence."[45]

This perspective on the Old History was Robinson's way of setting the stage for the New History, with its interdisciplinary reach. For him the influence of the "newer sciences" — which gave new meaning to old terms such as "race," "religion," "progress," "the ancients," "culture," and "human nature" — was "infinitely more revolutionary than all that Giesebrecht, Waitz, Martin, or Hodgkin ever found out about the past."[46] Most remarkable were the discoveries of anthropology, paleontology, and "prehistory," which created a new perspective, so that "we have outgrown the scale which served for Archbishop Ussher," and we have outgrown also the "shallow talk about our relation to 'the ancients' who are in reality our contemporaries."[47] Through the new human sciences, "prehistory" had been admitted to the domain of history and had become essential in "the whole perspective of *modern* change." This was alien to even the greatest of the older generation, and Robinson remarked that Solomon Reinach told him that when Mommsen visited the collections of the Museum of Saint-Germain-en-Laye, "he had never heard either of the ice age or of totemism!"[48] The New Historian must be abreast of all these areas of historical inquiry even if they appear from outside the historiographical canon. Robinson's agenda was later drawn out more extensively by his disciple, Harry Elmer Barnes, who claimed Herodotus — in explicit contrast to Thucydides, as a model of the Old History who (Barnes writes) was the Ranke of antiquity — a founder of modern cultural history, which reached its "triumph" in the work of (among others) Berr, Lamprecht, Robinson, Becker, Beard, Toynbee (!), and Barnes himself, though of course "in the light of twentieth-century knowledge and methods."[49]

Charles Beard and Carl Becker were the leaders of the second generation of New Historians, both moving between European and American history and sharing Turner's New World relativism, and both beginning their major work before and during World War I.[50] Beard went to Oxford, where he became an activist and published a popular book on the Industrial Revolution (1901) before completing a thesis on the English justices of the peace, "their origins and development," and coming to Columbia in 1904, where he collaborated with Robinson on a textbook in European history. Becker was drawn to the study of history by Turner and Haskins at Wisconsin, did graduate work at Columbia under Robinson, Burgess, and Osgood, and finished his thesis on New York political parties (1909) before moving from Wisconsin to Kansas, and later to Cornell. Beard made his mark in 1913 with his radical (rather too radical for Becker) economic interpretation of the American constitution, while two years later Becker published his book on the origins of the American people with a similar, pragmatic, skeptical, and ideologically deflating line of argument.

Like Turner (and in the spirit of Herodotus), Beard and Becker regarded history not as a system of knowledge but rather as a form of open-ended inquiry — after the fashion, indeed, of the frontier itself — dependent on changing historical conditions. According to Wilkins, Becker is "the connecting link . . . between the 'historicism' or 'presentism' of Turner (and Burgess) and the 'relativism' of the late Becker."[51] At least part of this was derived from Turner, who, rejecting easy answers and little interested in narrative explanation, told his students that he was "not God."[52] In 1910, Becker, writing on the "detachment" of the historian, already rejected the idea of Rankean "objectivity," since "the historian cannot separate himself from the process he describes." Becker's sense of doubt about the ideals of history was intensified by his experiences with the war, and especially with the naive program, which he once supported, of his — and Turner's and Beard's — former colleague, Woodrow Wilson, regarding justice and liberty among the nations, which in fact was concerned only with the spoils.[53] Beard accompanied Becker down the slope of relativism, reinforced by Mannheim's sociology of knowledge, to which his attention was probably drawn by his wife and collaborator, Mary Beard, and culminating in his ironic commentary in his presidential address to the American Historical Association in 1935, on the "noble dream" of objectivity — which was also, according to Peter Novack, "the founding myth of the historical profession" — upsetting news to many Americans but an old problem for European scholars.[54] This apparent attack on impartiality, one of the cornerstones of history as an autonomous discipline, was another byproduct of the interdisciplinary enticements to which modern historians were exposed.

One of the greatest and most original contributors to the New History, though until recently seldom recognized as such, was Lucy Maynard Salmon, who studied with Charles Kendall Adams (student of Andrew Dickson White) at the University of Michigan. She became professor of history at Vassar and was the first influential woman in the American Historical Association. Salmon was a pioneering women's historian, but she was much more than that. An admirer of Robinson (whose textbook she used in her courses), she wanted to extend historical studies and the field of "progress" beyond the intellectually elitist innovations of Robinson and also beyond the geographical expansionism of Turner. Through her training and travels in Europe, she became in her own way devoted in the generation before World War I to "scientific" methods and ideals, to the seminar system, and to the collecting of original sources; but she carried this apparatus into another dimension of historical inquiry, that is, private space and the domestic world, which she investigated in a series of essays on, for example, "domestic service" (1897), "our kitchen" (1906), "democracy in the household" (1912), "history in a back yard" (1912), and "main street" (1915).[55] Like Turner she believed in the primacy of environment, but she applied the insight to smaller and more concrete living spaces and predicaments; like Robinson she rejected old-fashioned political preoccupations, wanting to expand, or to refocus, ideas of civilization beyond the sphere of public and national culture and discourse. She wanted to speak of cabbages as well as kings — to return in a sense to the "material culture" explored by earlier cultural historians and also, through her utilization of newspapers, to the practices of social historians like Macaulay. Like Turner and Robinson — and following Henry Adams's prophecy — she followed the lead of "democracy," but into the world not of high politics and culture but that of the household, its inhabitants, horizons, structures, and social problems; for "progress" had to include everyday and local humanity as well as the movers, the shakers, and the talkers.

Salmon also followed her interests in material culture and her "object-based epistemology" (as Nicholas Adams and Bonnie Smith call it) into the developing arena of museology. Museums devoted to the arts, to crafts, industry, mineralogy, ethnology, and biography all expanded the sources of history; and Salmon's trips to Scandinavia reinforced her insistence on the importance of this scientific and pedagogical institution for history, referring in particular to Thomsen's famous periodization of stone, bronze, and iron ages. "Sweden was the first country in Europe to collect its own antiquities, and its first effort in this direction date back to 1666," she wrote; today it was again in the lead with the new open-air museums; and "May it today soon come in America!"[56] Such were some of the new materials for historians of the future, including "our greatest historian," who — despite the valuable efforts of storytellers like Parkman and Motley, editors like Winsor, collectors like Andrew Dickson White and H. H. Bancroft, innovators like Turner, and excavators like Henry Charles Lea (who had all been presidents of the American Historical Association) — had not yet been honored as such. Maybe it would be a woman, and wouldn't that be a "new history"?

The New History continued to thrive under the leadership of Becker and Beard in the 1930s, when each delivered his message to the A.H.A., Becker in 1931 and Beard in 1933. Becker invoked Robinson directly, as he brought historical scholarship into the perspective of "Everyman." While acknowledging the value of the accumulation of erudition in recent times, he remarked also on the illusion of truth which dogmas of objectivity associated with Ranke and especially Fustel de Coulanges. Much historical writing was in fact uncritical as well as trivial, as Robinson had pointed out a generation before.[57] Becker's allegiance to the New History was apparent also in his Yale lectures given that year and dedicated to Haskins and Turner, which resurrected Glanvil's old phrase, "climates of opinion," and which found a counterpart to the New History in the conjectural history of the Enlightenment — itself a kind of secular recapitulation of the medieval impulse to philosophic system.[58] In his and his wife's textbook, published in 1927, Beard had celebrated the work of Turner and Robinson, under whose leadership "the narrow confines of Clio's kingdom were widened to include the history of the intellectual classes and the role of intelligence in the drama of mankind."[59] Two years after Becker's address, Beard reinforced his friend's line of argument, while at the same time grounding it more firmly in recent continental theories, including those of Croce, Mannheim, and Heussi. Beard denounced older ideas based on reductionism, organicism, and other products of a natural science model of interpretation. Yet like Becker, Beard was in effect declaring independence of European traditions — while remaining within conventions of national historiography.

La Nouvelle Histoire

French historians have repeatedly sought to distinguish themselves and their work from their antecedents through new and improved understanding of the past, especially the national past. From La Popelinière in the late sixteenth to Thierry in the early nineteenth century and down to the present, "new histories" have been announced and justified with invidious arguments deprecating prevailing conventions and fashions, and so it was also at the turn of the twentieth century in the early years of the historical profession in the Third Republic. Thierry's "new history" was directed against the inadequacies of the official histories of the Old Regime; the political and institutional histories of the following generation were directed against the Walter-Scottisée histories of the Romantic period and, like Renan and Taine, held up "science," in one sense or another, as the model for historical inquiry; and these productions were in turn superseded by new generations that sought still a more "scientific" formulation of historical reality and/or truth at just the time that Lamprecht and Robinson were seeking to renovate historical scholarship in Germany and America.

"Science" was a multivalent term which few scholars wanted to reject but for which they found it difficult to agree on a definition. Was it merely the determination of facts according to a constant method, or was it the derivation of general laws from these facts? The singular and even unique (idiographic) versus the universal and law-abiding (nomothetic)? Was it a matter of insisting on the autonomy of historical study, or of forming alliances with other disciplines, natural, perhaps, as well as social, cultural, and psychological sciences? Did history need to connect in any way with philosophy? Paul Lacombe and A.-D. Xénopol agreed that it should, but did not agree on how the connection is made. Lacombe wanted to move beyond the reality of fact to the higher truths found in historical patterns, similarities, and constants of human behavior; and though he acknowledged the role of the historian in his field of study and did not expect to go beyond probability in understanding humanity, to this extent he continued the rationalist tradition of Montesquieu, Voltaire, Turgot, and Condorcet.[60] For Xénopol, science treated phenomena in space while history traced them in time, and so he turned to biology and evolution for a better way of determining the succession of facts in the historical process.[61] Both sought the answers to historical inquiry outside of the old art and science of history itself and in what amounted to a philosophy of history.

The quest for historical "synthesis" culminated in the work of Henri Berr, whose contributions arose not from a university chair but from the *Revue de Synthèse historique,* founded in 1900, and later from the great series of volumes, *L'Evolution de l'Humanité,* begun in 1914, which are part both of the prehistory of the school of the *Annales,* founded in 1929, and so, in this same tradition of novelty, of still another and later "new history" in France.[62] Fustel's aphorism, that "one day of synthesis takes years of analysis," might be correct, wrote Berr in his manifesto for "synthetic history" and "history-science"; but the author of *The Ancient City* well knew the superior worth of the former. The nineteenth was "the century of history," but the mighty advance of erudition, of "history-discipline," as illustrated by the ordered bibliographies and the historiographical handbooks of Berhheim and Seignobos-Langlois, left many theoretical questions in its wake that the old philosophy of history could not resolve.[63] The purpose of Berr's review was precisely to address such questions, generally ignored by professional journals devoted to specialized scholarship.

Berr's review became an interdisciplinary forum for many of the debates of the day in the human sciences: questions of objectivity, methodology, race, of cultural history, of the "history of ideas," of the relationship of history with sociology and geography, and of the classification of sciences; and in the first two years he published statements by Lamprecht, Durkheim, Croce, Gentile, Villari, and others — as well as reviews of many of the important books in the human sciences. Xénopol wrote on the state of the "fact," Lacombe on history as a science, and, most controversially, François Simiand on "historical method and social science," in which he attacked Lacombe and Seignobos for their unscientific view of contingency. Rejecting the fetish of chronology displayed by Seignobos in his *Historical Method Applied to the Sciences* (1901), Simiand, following Durkheimian sociology, insisted that for the "new generation" the business of social science was to explain according to laws.[64]

Berr himself rejected the scientistic views deriving from Durkheim and his followers, who, in the spirit of old-fashioned philosophy of history, subordinated the particularities of history to a homogenizing and universalizing-nomothetic sociological framework; instead, he wanted synthetic history to incorporate the study of economic behavior as well as mentalities. As Renan had written on "the future of science," so Berr wrote on "the future of history," hoping to transcend the old art-versus-science contest — and to do this by drawing on the labors of earlier scholars. Here he cited the dictum of Goethe cited by Droysen: "What you have inherited from your fathers, take over and possess for yourself." He also went on to comment on the insights of Nietzsche on "the use and abuse of history" and the need to raise history above the level of mere science and draw it into human life and the similar (!) drift of American pragmatism.[65] Berr also, though he was very critical of German *Geschichts-wissenschaft*, referred favorably to the contemporary "new history" represented by Karl Lamprecht, who indeed offered a programmatic statement of *Kulturgeschichte* for Berr's journal.[66]

One phenomenon of history that seemed alien to natural science was that of contingency, although Emil Boutroux's subversive thesis of 1874, cited by Berr, insisted on this even for the hard sciences. "It is act that explains essence" rather than vice versa, he argued, in terms which to modern ears sound almost existentialist: "It is not, then, the 'nature of things' that should be the final object of our scientific investigations, it is their history."[67] All the more so since, Boutroux wrote, "he would be a bold man who would affirm that some particular conception had a future before it, while some other had had its day."[68] Others saw similar problems in history, such as Eduard Meyer's "hazards," Rickert's "singular phenomena," Croce's "facts," Xenophon's "facts of succession," and Windelband's idiographic method; and Berr, while affecting no real originality, hoped to build on these distinctions without giving up the ideal of "law" in some way appropriate to history. As in the eighteenth century, history was poised "between philosophy and erudition," so in the next century it stood between erudition and sociology, and Berr wanted to bridge the gap; for "historical synthesis must itself be a science—a true and full science."[69]

Berr's own contributions to this project were only theoretical (and rhetorical), but younger scholars—the "generation of 1905"—would carry on his ideals in a much more concrete and fruitful fashion. Of these the most prominent were Lucien Febvre and Marc Bloch (who also studied for a year in Germany), who both began their studies before World War I in the Ecole Normale Supérieure, and who both taught at the University of Strasbourg before coming to Paris—Febvre to the Collège de France in 1933 and Bloch to the Sorbonne in 1936. Febvre had studied with Paul Vidal de la Blache, Antoine Meillet, Lucien Levi-Bruhl, Henri Bremond, and Emile Mâle; Bloch with both Seignobos and Durkheim as well as his father Gustav Bloch. From the beginning they had interdisciplinary leanings—geography, especially in the manner of Vidal de la Blache (who also published in Berr's *Revue* even after founding his own *Annales de Géographie*), sociology, anthropology, linguistics, and (following Durkheim in a limited way) comparative methods; and like Lamprecht their first researches were in local history. Febvre's thesis on

Phillip II and Franche-Comté, dedicated to Monod, appeared in 1911, Bloch's on the Ile-de-France in 1913.[70] In 1920 they became friends at the University of Strasbourg, where Bloch taught medieval and Febvre modern history, and from then on their collaboration became closer. Febvre's book, published in 1911, opened with a rich geographical introduction to this "double province" (whose origins, however, were historical, not geographical) and went on to treat the conflict between nobility and bourgeoisie and the coming of the Reformation down to the eve of the Revolution. Bloch's work, published in part in Berr's review, considered the emancipation of serfs in the area around Paris. His study of French royalty led him to a deeper, more sensitive, and more anthropological view of the monarchy in his path-breaking work on thaumaturgic kings, which appeared in 1924.

This was the time of the incubation of Bloch's and especially Febvre's own brainchild, the *Annales d'histoire économique et sociale,* which was modelled on Berr's journal but had more professional goals for the "science," not of humanity in general, but of history more particularly. The trajectory "from the *Revue de Synthèse* to the *Annales*" can be traced in detail in the correspondence between Febvre and Bloch and especially between Febvre and Berr, beginning in 1911, at the time of the publication of both Febvre's thesis and Berr's *La Synthèse en histoire,* which gave Febvre "great pleasure" and reinforcement in his own views, especially of the relation between history and the self-promoting sciences — twin determinisms — of sociology and geography.[71] (Bloch reviewed Febvre's book on Franche-Comté and agreed that local history was valuable, though only when connected to general questions, but he was critical of Febvre's careless use of evidence and his pretentious style.) In 1912, Febvre agreed to do the volume on the geographical introduction to history, or "geohistory," as he called it, following the coinage of Jean Bodin — for Berr's "Evolution of Humanity."[72] In this book, which he discussed at great length with Berr after the war, he reviewed current literature, including that of Vidal de la Blache, Friedrich Ratzel, and "the astonishing Simiand"; and worked out his own ideas between two extremes: "Human geography or social morphology, geographical method or sociological method," he wrote: "the choice must be made" — and yet history was too complex to be reduced to either.[73] Reviewing the earlier, pre-scientific history of geography (Hippocrates, Galen, Polybius, Ptolemy, Lucretius, Bodin, Montesquieu, etc.), Febvre analyzed questions of borders, frontiers, climate, and race, and rejected conventional Rousseauist ideas of primitive humanity accepted in effect even by Fustel de Coulanges.[74] The concept of "nation" was also misused, and so was "state," a historical not a natural creation. From a geographical point of view, moreover, history was the action not of individuals but of collectivities.

In this correspondence Febvre also became deeply involved in the planning of the *L'Evolution de l'Humanité* series, whose categories also overlapped with his ideas for a "new historical," but also interdisciplinary, journal devoted to the science, not of "synthesis," but of history. As early as 1921 Bloch joined his colleague in this plan.[75] Febvre's first choice for a title was *L'Evolution générale des sociétés humaines,* and he intended to cover the following topics: prehistory, language, geography, psychology, religious belief, rational ideas, literature and the arts, economics, law and politics, and civilizations.[76] By late 1928, however, he was writing to Berr under the letterhead of *Annales d'histoire économique et social,* and this new periodical, modelled after the *Vierteljahrschrift für Sozial- und Wirtschaftsgeschichte* (one of whose editors was Lamprecht's old nemesis, Georg von Below) and conceived in the interdisciplinary spirit of the *Revue de Synthèse Historique,* Vidal de la Blache's *Annales de Géographie,* and Durkheim's *Année Sociologique,* began to appear in January 1929, including not only leading French scholars on its masthead but also such eminent foreign names as Pirenne, Ganshof, Sanchez-Albornoz, and Tawney.[77] Thus was created the "Annales paradigm," another brand of "new history" which, in one form or another, was to be a dominant presence in the historical inquiry, thought, and writing in both the Old World and the New.

Although aimed primarily at historians, the *Annales* was almost aggressively, though not uncritically, interdisciplinary, as were their primary editors. Following his work on geography, Febvre turned to problems of culture and mentality — first to the religion of Rabelais and criticism of the "strange thesis" of Abel Lefranc concerning Rabelais as a pioneering freethinker and atheist, and then to Luther. "But how difficult it is!" Febvre wrote to Berr: "Intellectual history, the history of ideas and beliefs, and as impassioned as it is difficult to write.[78] Bloch was ahead of Febvre in his interest in questions of *mentalité* — the term taken from Lucien Lévy-Bruhl (whom Bloch asked to review his book on the thaumaturgic kings). *The Royal Touch,* conceived before the First World War, took up the old question that troubled historians — that of miracles, in this case the royal power to heal scrofula — and the conflict between modern common sense and the need to accept recorded testimony. Bloch's solution was to save rationality by recourse to the anthropological notion of miracles as "collective error," but nonetheless a mighty presence in history.[79] Like Febvre, Bloch was enough of a Durkheimian to advocate comparative method, and indeed Henri Brunschwig recalled that he recommended abandoning history: "Study law, prepare for your archeology degree, learn German, anything," he advised, "it will give you a basis for comparison."[80] Just after the founding of the *Annales,* Bloch carried this message to the International

Historical Congress in Oslo, where he met Berr, who was still arguing his "synthetic" thesis.[81] But he was no less resistant than Febvre to the imperialism of theory, since, as he later wrote, history had to adapt its classifications "to the very contours of reality."[82]

The grand tradition of French historical writing was not forgotten by Febvre and Bloch, especially in the geohistorical emphasis, which was shared not only by Michelet but also by Montesquieu and indeed by Bodin, all writing, Febvre recalled, before geography existed as a science. Michelet was perhaps the greatest icon, and in fact Febvre devoted a course to his work on the Renaissance; but of course they had a sense of professional superiority; and as Bloch remarked, "Between you and me, he wasn't good at history."[83] Yet they admired his intellectual breadth and, at least tacitly, his literary style. They shared with economic historians suspicions about political history, and Bloch criticized Below and Flach for their nationalist and statist exaggerations. About German scholarship they had mixed feelings, though Lamprecht was to some extent an exception. They rejected both the mindless pedantry of positivism and the abstractions of conjectural history, and like Acton, they thought history should be not about periods but problems — *histoire-problème*. To that end, too, they both adopted a limited (Eurocentric, not global, like the speculative anthropology of Fraser) sort of comparative method. Most of all, perhaps, to judge from their career moves and correspondence, they saw in the historical profession a field of competition and power. In this enterprise they were finally successful beyond all their rivals and forebears; and their legacy, though transformed by three generations of criticism, is still with us.

Huizinga and Cultural History

Like Burckhardt and Lamprecht, Johan Huizinga was attracted to cultural history by his interests in art and literature and his impulse to expand history beyond its political, military, and economic focus to more creative and emotional aspects of human behavior.[84] Huizinga began as a Sanskrit scholar and retained the broad, linguistic, and aesthetic horizons of his studies of Indian culture. Through the influence of his *Doktorvater*, P. J. Blok, he became a professor of Dutch history at the University of Groningen in 1905, when his sights were already set on cultural history, as apparent from his review of the sixth volume of Lamprecht's German history. Ten years later he moved to the University of Leiden, where he began, or resumed, correspondence with Henri Pirenne.[85] His great study of late medieval Burgundy appeared in 1919 and his follow-up work on Erasmus in 1924. In this connection he also published work on the "problem of the Renaissance" and its relation to the Middle Ages, the methods of cultural history, and the meaning of history more generally, as well as broader commentaries on contemporary questions and his meta-anthropological masterpiece, *Home Ludens* (1938).

Huizinga followed Heinrich Rickert's distinction between the natural and the cultural sciences, and his view of history deviated from the natural science model that fascinated even as subtle an author as Henry Adams. With Burck-hardt he accepted the demands and the invitations of the historian's "point of view," which put him in the position more of an artist than of a scientist. "The knowledge of history is always sheerly potential not only because no one knows all details but because each sees it differently," he wrote.[86] "History is always an imposition of form upon the past, and cannot claim to be more," he wrote, associating himself with Ernst Cassirer's philosophy of symbolic forms.[87] More formally: "History is the intellectual form in which a civilization renders account to itself of its past" (*Geschiedenis is de geestelijke vorm, waarin een cultur zick rekenschap geeft van haar verleden*). More precisely, it was an "intellectual form" dependent ultimately on aesthetic judgment, imagination, and storytelling and picture-making, citing Michelet's formula of "resurrection" as an example of this ideal expressed in the work of Herodotus and Thucydides, Machiavelli and Villani, Voltaire, Macaulay, and Motley. Huizinga did not deny the insights brought by archeology, anthropology, history of art, literature, etc., but he believed that overemphasis on economic factors had undercut historical (as well as political) understanding; and more generally he also held out the hope that "a coming generation will win back the classic form of history."[88]

Huizinga's own contribution to this effort of antiquitization came with his classic study of fifteenth-century Burgundian culture (1919), which served as an essential supplement (and in some ways a corrective) to Burckhardt's equally interpretive *Civilization of the Renaissance in Italy*. Huizinga minimized the contrast between medieval and Renaissance attitudes toward honor and fame and emphasized the persistence of aristocratic values, though his opposition to Burckhardt's enthusiasms were indirect and moderate, and his impressionist (or, in Huizinga's case, post-impressionist) methods were similar, if not derivative.[89] Like Burckhardt (and Barante a century earlier) Huizinga turned to the chroniclers, especially Froissart, Commines, Monstrelet, La Marche, Basin, and Chastellain, to evoke the emotions and values, the colors and sounds, the ceremonial and superstitions, which illustrated the mentality of Dutch and French civilization in a period of religious crisis before the Reformation. Like Burckhardt, too, Huizinga resisted the nationalist enthusiasm of the war years, especially Pirenne's notion that Burgundy was Belgium *avant la lettre,* created by the great line of dukes in full rivalry with

France. Relying especially on Chastellain, who was "the best mirror of the thought of the time," Huizinga held that Burgundy had never broken with the nation of its origin, or reached the level of a state. He also warned against the inadequacy of the efforts of modern historians to explain the division of parties in terms of economic-political causes.[90] The history of culture had to deal with dreams and illusions as well as material facts uncovered "by the researcher who traces the development of the state and of economics in the documents" in search of "the real history of the late medieval period."

Huizinga portrayed the late medieval history in chiaroscuro terms, full of contradictions between the sacred and the profane, brutality and piety, eroticism and idealized love, pride and humility, asceticism and greed, the knightly and the priestly, the active and the contemplative life, the contrasting dances of life and of death, "blood and roses." As Burckhardt had emphasized "the dignity of man," so Huizinga recalled the parallel (and symmetrical) theme of human misery (*de contemptu mundi*) and played down individual liberty and the bourgeois values celebrated by nineteenth-century historians, French, German, and British alike. Like Burckhardt, Huizinga displayed a disregard for the artificial narratives demanded by chronology and tied his arguments to cultural patterns, styles, and human desires and anxieties. He celebrated the pleasures of life, which are, "now as before, reading, music, fine arts, travel, the enjoyment of nature, sports, fashion, social vanity (knightly orders, honorary offices, gatherings), and the intoxication of the senses";[91] but he also elaborated on the sorrows and evils of the human condition in that remote, premodern world of religious and chivalric sensibilities. To fill in his portrait, Huizinga drew not only on chronicles, poems, sermons, and painting but also on emblems, proverbs, mottos, and the language of symbolism, which was reincarnated as mythology in the Renaissance, when new forms of life and culture made their appearance.

The "problem of the Renaissance" occupied much of Huizinga's thought in his work on fifteenth-century Burgundy and on Erasmus, and he traced the history of the idea of the Renaissance from its sixteenth-century origins down to his own time — Amyot, Valla, Machiavelli, Vasari, Bayle, Voltaire, Guizot, Michelet, Georg Voigt, and Burckhardt, who referred to "the so-called Renaissance" as early as 1838 and whose great book, published in 1869, had a "stream" of reissues from 1897 to 1919.[92] As a counterbalance, Huizinga referred to Troeltsch's identification of Protestantism as the preparation (*Anbahung*) of the modern world. Against these views and Lamprecht's notion of a "typical age," Huizinga argued for more complexity and overlap, for in fact there had been individualism in the medieval (*Middeleeuwscher*) period, as in the cases of Abelard, Guibert de Nogent, Bertrand de Born, Chrétien de

Troyes, Wilhelm von Eschenbach, and hundreds of others; and of course there had been forerunners (*voorloopers*) such as Dante and Petrarch, who was an "Erasmus *avant la lettre*" before the fifteenth century. Similarly, Burckhardt's hyperbolic identification of the Renaissance with modernity was controverted by the persistence of medieval characteristics in Savonarola, Luther, Müntzer, and others. Huizinga did not join what Wallace Ferguson called "the revolt of the medievalists," but he did undermine the arguments of the champions of modernizing humanism and preservers of a naive antithesis — necessary as it was for shorthand reference — on both sides of the false periodization that denied that St. Francis was also part of the "Renaissance." So the movement from medieval to modern times was not a single great change (like Panofsky's "something happened") but "that of succession of waves coming to shore, each of them breaking at different places and different times."[93] Such was the character of cultural transformation.

The mixture of elements that appeared in the late medieval and early Renaissance periods is strikingly illustrated in the career of Erasmus, who was himself a product of Burgundian culture and whose ego-centered career Huizinga surveyed with characteristic subtlety and breadth of vision. Beginning as an Augustinian and ending up as a popular modern author, Erasmus displayed to an extreme degree the tensions of a scholar caught between the classics and Christian devotion, between a literary and a religious calling, between pagan erudition and "the light of theology," in this age of world crisis. He was an individualist, yet bowing always to authority; he affirmed the value of life, yet he was "shy and a little stiff and, above all, very intellectual."[94] Following Erasmus in his travels around the courts, cities, and universities of Europe, Huizinga stopped his chronological narrative long enough to devote three central chapters of his book to Erasmus's life and character. Like More and Montaigne, Erasmus was "steeped in the essence of antiquity," but more connected with medieval ideals than he was aware.[95] His goal was a spiritual one, cleansed of and liberated from the materialism and tyranny of his greedy, warlike, and most un-Christian age. A moderate, a man of the center, and yet an idealist, he was not strong enough for his age, not decisive enough to resist or to move it. He was not a "hero of history," being too full of contradictions and too concerned with "public opinion," and yet his influence was nonetheless lasting, representing the best of Dutch tradition and drawing, finally, the largest part of the Christian church to himself, beyond the militant reformers and counter-reformers.

Huizinga continued to reflect on the nature of cultural studies and its terminology — not only culture, but civilization, civility, and the Dutch *beschaving* — and "the task of cultural history," which he distinguished especially from the economic and political varieties, and he continued to argue for the primacy of imagination. Though he was deeply concerned with life forms and in that sense "morphology," he rejected the naive evolutionism of "new historians" like Lamprecht and Robinson (and H. G. Wells and Hendrik Van Loon) and in general the hunt for underlying, mechanical causes. "The chief task of cultural history," he declared, "is the morphological understanding and description of the actual, specific course of civilization" ("morphology" was Oswald Spengler's term, too, for macro-historical development).[96] The aim of the cultural historian was to determine human meaning—not giving meaning to the meaningless (*Sinngebung des Sinnlosen*), but determining the meaning of what was significant (*Sinndeutung des Sinnvollen*). The limits of this operation were those of culture itself, for "the historical discipline is [itself] a cultural process."[97] And: "Every culture must create its own form of history."

In *The Autumn of the Middle Ages*, Huizinga—like Burckhardt before him—pursued the forms of culture beyond the normal territory of the mainstream, national or universal, historian, leading him to questions, from birth to death, of social psychology, anxiety, eroticism, sexuality, symbolism, rhetoric, ceremony, witchcraft, irrationalism, madness, festivals, sense of time, and popular entertainments. It also led him to uncover, or to infer, a wide range of emotions that registered very differently from those of his own age—for the past was indeed a "foreign country." In this he anticipated not only the supposedly novel investigations of more recent cultural history but also a belief in the primacy of "representation"—which appears not only in the "passionate intensity of life" and efforts to make it more beautiful, but also in the visual, ceremonial, and literary ways of coping with hardship, death, and evil. But representation, even in the works of the chroniclers, was largely a product of the imagination, and so modern historians had to employ the same techniques in restoring the past.

In keeping with his early interests in Indo-European civilization, Huizinga continued to broaden his horizons until his most original effort of historical, or rather metahistorical, anthropology, which was dedicated to expanding the understanding of human nature and thus adding to classical analysis of man as a political, social, economic, technological, predatory, religious, linguistic, and symbolic animal (*homo politicus, homo economicus, homo faber,* etc.). *Homo Ludens,* published in "the demented world" of 1938, presented a picture of humanity in terms of the play element—"older than culture," Huizinga remarked—and, for all the jocular, tongue-in-cheek tone, literary virtuosity, and irony, he does so in the most earnest way. He criticized Burckhardt in his lectures on Greek cultural history (given before the maturity of anthropology and sociology) for limiting the "agonistic" to Greece, when Semitic and Indo-

European civilizations displayed similar patterns. For Huizinga, play involved sport, entertainment, a sense of the comic, acting, performing, and "fun," among other things; but it was also essential to most other aspects of civilization, including language, politics, law, war, philosophy, literature, art, myth, and indeed religion. Philosophy and other disciplines could themselves be regarded as games. Moreover, play was not just a kind of behavior but a point of view (*sub specie ludi*) from which to examine the whole human condition, humanity in its "freest" state. "The play-concept as such is a higher order than is seriousness," Huizinga argued (and not just playfully). "For seriousness seeks to exclude play, whereas play can very well include seriousness."[98] Certainly this was the case for the serious games that historians had, from the beginning, played.

The Crisis of Historicism

"Historicism, which analyzes itself and seeks to understand its own beginnings," wrote Friedrich Meinecke, "is a serpent that bites its own tail."[99] "Historicism" — German *Historismus*, French *historisme*, but Italian *storicismo* — is a word carelessly thrown about in recent times. The term is Romantic in origin, appearing first, it seems, in "fragments" left by Novalis and Friedrich Schlegel. In the course of a very miscellaneous listing of methods or systematic approaches to thought (Fichte's, Kant's, chemical, mathematical, artistic, etc.), Novalis produces the neologism "historism," associating it, perhaps pejoratively, with mysticism and "the system of confusion."[100] Contemporaneously, Schlegel associated "Historismus" with the modern science of philology.[101] The term was also sometimes used in philosophical polemics, for example in 1835, when the young Hegelian Ludwig Feuerbach contrasted it with unhistorical Kantian idealism;[102] a generation later Felix Dahn argued that "historicism is above all a methodological moment, not a speculative principle . . . ; its goal is [not philosophy but] life";[103] and in a similar vein Christlieb Julius Braniss opposed it specifically to the reductionist and deterministic philosophy of naturalism.[104] In 1879, Karl Werner applied the phrase "philosophical historicism" to the work of Vico, a connection later popularized by Croce, Meinecke, Erich Auerbach, and many Vichians.[105] And in 1895, Lord Acton pointed to "that influence for which the depressing names historicism and historical-mindedness have been devised" — "all things," for him, including law, theology, science, and philosophy itself.[106]

From a general way of designating a historical method, the term "historicism" had, by the later nineteenth century, acquired a largely pejorative meaning, suggesting a dangerous conceptual fallacy, especially that old devil

Relativism.[107] Who, in these prewar years, was afraid of "historicism," and why? Those who felt most threatened were the theologians, the philosophers, and the economists; and the reason was that this cast of mind threatened three of the absolutes of Western culture, namely, religion, reason, and the free market. The suggestion that history was in any way a "foundational" discipline was an affront to the status of the human as well as the natural sciences. "For philosophy, historicism is even more dangerous than naturalism," Heinrich Rickert argued, since "every historicism ends in relativism, even in nihilism."[108] Some even wanted to make Kant "historical," that is, "eliminate him from the philosophical controversy of the present." "Ennervating historicism," as Rudolph Eucken called it in 1910,[109] imperilled both the superstructure and the material base of European society and led to that cultural "crisis" — *Krisis des Historismus* — which he, Troeltsch, Heussi, Husserl, Heidegger, Meinecke, and others lamented and struggled to overcome.[110] The "crisis" was worldwide, and, reinforced by the process of professionalization, it also invaded Russian thought at this time.[111]

The attack had begun not in philosophy, however, but in the newly professionalized field of economics, with Karl Menger's liberal assault of 1883 on "the errors of historicism," that is, the irrational methods of Gustav Schmoller and members of the so-called younger historical school of economics.[112] Twenty years later the aimless pedantry of Wilhelm Roscher and the older historical school was attacked on similar grounds by Max Weber in his quest for a universal, "value-free" science of society. In a sense this war of methods (*Methodenstreit*) recapitulated the struggles between the historical and philosophical schools in the early nineteenth century, but now with the weaponry of modern positivism and quantitative methods. The rejection of historicism, indeed of historical method in general, has persisted in many areas of social sciences and the humanities, as in Russian Formalism, structural linguistics, and the New Criticism.

In theology the errors of historicism were equally offensive. In the prewar years, religious controversies raged around various forms of "Modernism," which had been denounced in Pius IX's "Syllabus of Errors" of 1864, accompanied by a whole list of other secularizing "-isms." Positivism, Psychologism, and Historicism all posed threats not only to traditional moral values but also to the validity of both reason and revelation. The historicizing of Christianity was the avowed aim of the historical school of religion (*religionsgeschichtliche Schule*) headed by Weber's friend Troeltsch, whose classic work, *The Social Teachings of the Christian Churches* (1912), marked the intersection of the socioeconomic and theological problematics of historicism; and it, too, was carried on with heavy anxiety about questions of traditional norms. In *Histor-*

icism and Its Problems (1922), Troeltsch, like Braniss, opposed "historicism" to "naturalism" and traced this struggle of methods back to the seventeenth century, with special reference to Vico's attack on Cartesianism.[113] Troeltsch celebrated historicism for removing the "dead hand" of dogma, but he also feared the threat it posed to philosophical and moral tradition. Following Troeltsch, Karl Heussi distinguished among "history for the sake of history" (*l'histoire pour l'histoire*), relativism, radical evolutionism, and speculative philosophy of history, and analyzed them all under the rubric "the crisis of historicism."[114]

If religion fell to historicism, could formal philosophy be safe? In 1910, Husserl denounced historicism as the enemy of "philosophy as a rigorous science"; and Heidegger, following Nietzsche's famous critique of "the use and abuse of history," contrasted it with true historicity (*Geschichtlichkeit*), grounded in contemporary existence. The tension between historicism and historicity was already implicit in Hegel, spelled out by his biographer, Rudolf Haym, who contrasted "illusory historicism" (*illusorische Historismus*) with true historicity (*wirkliche Geschichtlichkeit*), and was employed as well by Dilthey and Yorck.[115] Dilthey was himself formed intellectually by the forces which converged on the University of Berlin in the nineteenth century, including Mommsen and Ranke, who was "like a mighty organism assimilating chronicles, Italian politicians, ambassadors, historians, Niebuhr, Fichte, and, not least, Hegel."[116] "To these great influences," he acknowledged, "I owe the direction of my thought." Moreover, Dilthey accepted the principle of historicity, and he committed himself to the tradition of hermeneutics, which developed out of philological virtuosity to the level of historical understanding. Despite his ambition to expand the Kantian critique to include historical reason, he rejected the relativism implied by contemporary historicism. Yet Troeltsch, who regarded himself as a student of Dilthey, saw him as the best representative of pure historicism.[117]

Among historians Otto Hintze took up this issue in a review of Troeltsch's work, and though he realized that Troeltsch wanted "to overcome history through history," he reduced historicism in effect to just another "mode of thought," another philosophy of history tied to ideas of development and "biological organism."[118] For Hintze, as for Rickert and Weber, the central question was that of values and their historical conditions, and here indeed arose a potential innovation: "Troeltsch's theory represents a shift in historical thought comparable to the change Einstein's theory of relativity represents in science." Yet neither Einstein nor Troeltsch "opened the way to unlimited relativism." Troeltsch sought to understand the moral and cultural "standards" of the past, but in fact he clung to a kind of absolutism, a "leap" beyond history, derived from his religious orientation and "individual consciousness." As a practicing historian, however, Hintze rejected the "metaphysical assumption" by which history is interpreted as "the activity of the divine spirit."

Historicism, beyond parochial concerns of unreflective historians, represented a problem for all the human sciences; and indeed, for Karl Mannheim it had become, in the wake of evolutionary ideas, a *Weltanschauung* beyond the level of conscious reflection or ideology, so that history itself was caught in its net.[119] It was a view, or set of assumptions, that needed to be confronted as Socrates had confronted the Sophists in Athens. It served the modern dynamic world as "timeless reason" had served a more static world. As a counterpart to the older faith in reason, now itself historicized, historicism also needed to be the object of critical theory. Yet it was not absolute, only bound to assumptions of spatial, temporal, and material conditions which had undercut universalist conceptions. According to Mannheim, "Historicism is . . . the only solution of the general problem of how to find *material* and concretely exemplified standards and norms for a world outlook which has become dynamic." The virtue of historicism for Mannheim was that it set dynamism at the center of its conceptualizations instead of relativizing it as in "the old static system," and so made it "the Archimedean lever" for the modern worldview and life-experience, that is, made it in effect the condition of human, historical, and indeed philosophical understanding.

Benedetto Croce, following his interpretation of Vico and Hegel, thought that the Germans had not pushed historicism far enough. Grounding his thought in deep studies of Italian and European historiography, Croce rejected the claims of modern social science, such as those of Weber and Durkheim, to universal status, regarding them all as open to contingency and subject to historical conditions. So indeed were human values, and Croce had no fear that relativism was a major threat, since for him historicism was "a logical principle . . . , the very category of logic."[120] In Germany (Croce agreed with Meinecke), historicism was as much a revolution as the Reformation and was reinforced especially by the philosophy of Hegel and other philosophers, and again by that of Troeltsch, who linked history with liberty. Moreover, historicism was the reigning condition of contemporary thought and life—and according to his famous aphorism, "Every true history is contemporary history"[121]—and philosophy itself was "absolute historicism."[122] In short, historicism was not the source of the intellectual crisis of the twentieth century but rather its potential solution. Yet Croce, too, assimilated historicism to philosophy, denying (against Cassirer and others) the importance of erudition and criticism of evidence for historicism in the Enlightenment.[123] Croce's views and prejudices were carried over into the Anglophone world by Colling-wood, who translated his work and followed his interpretation of historio-graphical tradition, also limited to its philosophical dimensions, and who turned back to the classical (Herodotean) view of history as a form of "in-quiry" into human behavior, proceeding through the interpretation of evi-dence and aimed ultimately at "human self-knowledge."[124]

In this tradition, historicism reached its culminating expression in the long career of Friedrich Meinecke, who began as editor of the *Historische Zeitschrift* and keeper of the Rankean, or neo-Rankean, flame (Ranke died just three days after Meinecke's doctoral examination).[125] In his first major work, published in 1907, he followed Ranke's idea of nationality within the framework of European — and universal — history (nationalism and cosmo-politanism).[126] For Meinecke, Germany had become a "culture-nation" in the eighteenth century through literature and philosophy, and then through the development, seen by Luden and others during the Wars of Liberation, from nation to state. The rise of a new "great power" was apparent in the emergence of Prussia and its development into a more broadly German state. Ranke's genius was to establish the individuality of the state between the poles of Hegelian idealism and the political reality expressed in scientific history; and Meinecke, too, followed this duality, which he found in the pairing, for exam-ple, of Fichte and Stein, and of Ranke himself and Bismarck. In the 1915 edi-tion, Meinecke expressed gratification that the new Germany had the power and morale to defend itself against other nations.

In his study of "reason of state" (1924), Meinecke broadened his horizons and moved further into the mode of intellectual history (*Ideengeschichte*) and cultural history — "history is nothing else but *Kulturgeschichte*," he remarked — and in this way softened his political views.[127] *Staatsräson, raison d'état, ragione di stato* was the "vital principle" of the state, its "first law of motion," and investigating the career of this concept, or practice, was a way of gaining access to history as a mean between the ideal and the real in the modern contest between the great powers.[128] The shift from the ideals of utopian politics to the realities of the Italian and European state systems was first and best expressed in the life and works of Machiavelli — as well as in the anti-Machiavellian backlash of the later sixteenth century. Bodin ex-tended Machiavelli's arguments by focusing on the question of the legitimacy of power, while in the seventeenth century Pufendorf and others carried the arguments into natural law, as Frederick the Great later joined the issues with practical politics. Reason of state came late to Germany and took an exagger-ated form because of the disappointing experience of 1848. Meinecke carried his dualistic story through the contributions of Hegel, Fichte, Ranke, and Treitschke, who, identifying power as the essence of the state, went too far in shifting morality from the individual to the state.

Meinecke's last major work, *The Rise of Historicism* (1936), completes the circle by reviewing — and to some extent inventing — the tradition from which he had, more or less unreflectively, emerged. Croce (following Hegel) thought the book premature because historicism was still a living mode of thought, and he also objected to the irrationalism of the "pure historian" Meinecke.[129] But Meinecke felt no such philosophical constraints. In this book, he gave systematic form to the Rankean principles of individuality and development, and detached them from the hard political realism of his earlier books. He granted a place for cultural history — as in Vico, Voltaire, Ferguson, Winckelmann, and Herder — and indeed he ended with a detailed assessment of Goethe, "Herder's pupil," down to the breakthrough of the fundamental ideas, though not to its "full evolution."[130] What Goethe represented was the synthesis of the four main ingredients of historicism: the pre-Romantic need to investigate primitive times, Pietist subjectivism, the new understanding of ancient art, and "the old Platonic–Neo-Platonic world of ideas," seen first in Leibniz and Shaftesbury. This shift from the material to the ideal, the collective to the individual, the political to the cultural, ended with Meinecke's taking a different, chastened view of German politics and its "catastrophe," and with his leaning away from Ranke and toward Burckhardt as his historicist ideal.[131] So from the grave, one might say, Lamprecht overcame his old foe.

As for "historicism," its later semantic history has become increasingly muddled because of misappropriations of the word for philosophical or ideological but quite un- (or even anti-) historical purposes, beginning with Karl Popper's *Poverty of Historicism* (1957), which identifies historicism with naive biological determinism (precisely the opposite of the view of Braniss) and a total innocence of history, experience, and even common sense.[132] Another instance is the book of Maurice Mandelbaum, who writes, "Historicism is a belief that an adequate understanding of the nature of any phenomenon and an adequate assessment of its value are to be gained through considering it in terms of the place which it occupied and the role which it played within a process of development."[133] He admits that the philosophical term "development" is open to correction in this connection but retains it in a form that conflates romantic and evolutionist conceptions, and that allows him to focus on purely theoretical rather than empirical concepts of "history," especially Marxism, utopian socialism, and social Darwinism. A still more egregious example is the book on Hegel and Heidegger by Michael Gillespie, who thinks historians go "critically astray" in tracing the source of historicism to the attitudes associated with historical scholarship, especially that of early modern Europe. Instead he places history wholly in philosophical tradition and so in a theoretical conversation that contradicts the original and sustaining premises of historicism and continues the tendency of modern philosophy to disassociate itself from the problems and practices of positive knowledge and inquiry — the original and enduring terrain of historicism.[134]

It is too late in the day to undo the working of the semantic history of this much-abused H-word, but it may be now in order to make, or to repeat, a small revisionist point. Historically speaking, "historicism" has little to do with philosophy, except in a negative and critical way, and nothing to do with the claims of universal science and scientism. On the contrary, it was an alternative to conventional philosophy and to scientific naturalism, and it flourished in the rich soil of literary and antiquarian learning and in the teachings of the historical schools.[135] It was much closer to the formulation of Erich Auerbach, who identified "historicism" with cultural relativism and with a "realization that epochs and societies are not to be judged in terms of a pattern concept that is desirable absolutely speaking . . . but rather in terms of their own premises."[136] In fact, historicism has been cast in opposition to the scientisms which evaded questions of point of view, perspective, cultural context, and the necessity of interpretation in posing questions about a past that is not only a "foreign country," but also largely inaccessible except through traces and testimonies which happen to have survived and must be expressed in the language and conditions of the present — a present that is itself soon on its way to becoming a past.

The New Hermeneutics

There is another H-word that, converging with historicism, has shaped and given critical standing to modern historical inquiry: hermeneutics had, by the twentieth century, produced philosophical as well as theological, legal, and literary branches. From this time-honored tradition were produced concepts of horizon, temporal as well as spatial, point of view, prejudice, and interpretation, not only in historiography but even in supposedly neutral source materials. Hermeneutics posed the problem not only of the role of the subject in a field of observation but also of the subject itself, being prey to weakness or distortion of memory, to inertial forces of the linguistic medium, to forestructures of understanding, to unconscious factors, and in general to its own historicity. From a hermeneutical standpoint, however, these are not obstacles to but rather conditions and possibilities of historical study and the pursuit of historical meaning.[137]

Classically, historians were masters of their discipline, whether artists or
scientists (or historicists); and though they made their inquiries locally, in
terms of specific sources, they fashioned their narratives *sub specie aeternitatis*, explained the processes of cause and effect, and often showed readers
what lessons could be derived from their stories. The territory of their explorations was "the past," or some part of antiquity, or even periods of origins; and
its accessibility was seldom questioned — except by uncaring skeptics who
rejected the historical enterprise altogether. Yet the past was long gone, and its
surviving records, traces, and remnants had to be deciphered and interpreted
in a present that was itself rapidly passing. Historians themselves, moreover,
even as they strove, self-consciously, to be impartial and "objective," were
products and inhabitants of a culture often remote from the object of their
study; and their creations were subject to the same sort of explanatory and
analytical treatments that they imposed on their materials. With the accumulation of historiographical tradition, the accounts of later historians were the
last in a long series of interpretations that had no ultimate foundations. Like
the serpent of historicism, the serpent of hermeneutics chased its own tail, but
without ever catching it — another version, perhaps, of the "hermeneutical
circle" imagined by Friedrich Ast.[138]

In retrospect, Nietzsche represents both a hermeneutical moment and a
critique of the scientific view of history that prevailed in his day. The "introduction of meaning is not a matter of rational, unhistorical explanation," but
rather "in most cases a new interpretation over an old interpretation that
has become incomprehensible, that is itself only a sign."[139] And: "History,
conceived as pure science and become sovereign, would constitute a final
closing out of the accounts of life for mankind."[140] Nietzsche was both an anti-
philosopher and an anti-historian, and yet he opened up crucial perspectives
on both traditions. Following the objections of earlier historians to "fatalism,"
he insisted that "necessity is not a fact but an interpretation" — and so indeed
(despite a "world system of egoism" in the nineteenth century) is the subject,
the ego, the "I," actual or implied, of the historian's narrative.[141] So the old
hermeneutical search for the "Thou" in the "I," the past in the present, was
compounded. Nietzsche was also, with Husserl, important for introducing the
metaphor of "horizon" into philosophical and historical discourse.[142]

Nietzsche protested against the "indigestible knowledge" that passed for
"culture" and, among historians, for "science," accompanied by a "flooding,
numbing, violent historicizing" and a conception of history which was in fact
a "disguised theology" that threatened future life and thought.[143] There was
a "surfeit of history" in his generation, Nietzsche warned, which not only
"weakens the personality," impairs the instincts of a people and the matura-

tion of the individual, encourages a debilitating belief of being a latecomer and an epigone (no poetry, only "criticism," as in the case of contemporary German, "overloaded heirs and epigones"), but with its fetish of "objectivity" it induces a paralyzing kind of irony and even cynicism, if not nihilism.[144] There was a time for forgetting as well as for remembering: a sense of history without restraints, a crude "historical audit," destroys illusions and ideals; history aimed at "a final closing of accounts" brings not life but death, that is, conventional answers but, fatal to history, no further questions.

Regarding the phenomenon of historicism, Nietzsche made his own crude audit, recognizing, in general, three types of history: the monumental, which looked to the past for great deeds and edifying lessons; the antiquarian, which venerated tradition and honored ancestors; and the critical, which struggled to liberate itself from the burden of the past and prepare people for action. Nations all need each of these perspectives at different moments in their experience, but now, argued Nietzsche, is the time for the last of these, the time not for "the historical men" but for "the superhistorical men" (it is too late for unhistorical men), whose vision included the future as well as the past—in short, the time (or almost the time, for Nietzsche's ideas were still "untimely") for prophets like Nietzsche to bring a new and forward-looking sort of self-knowledge, which remained the purpose of history. What Nietzsche wanted above all was to bring history into the twentieth century, for—another version of Croce's aphorism that all history is contemporary history—"Only from the standpoint of the highest strength of the present may you interpret the past."[145]

Nietzsche was not alone in his critique of the burden of history associated with vulgar historicism, especially in the intellectual crisis surrounding the First World War. Walter Benjamin spent his apprenticeship in Marxist revisionism and in fact never extricated himself from it: "Historicism rightly culminated in universal history," he wrote, and—a remarkably historicist judgment—was no less rightly followed by materialist historiography.[146] Yet Benjamin agreed with Nietzsche that the attribution of cause and effect was not "telling the sequence of events like the beads of a rosary" but was always made in retrospect, and so was interpretive. Making his own "Copernican revolution" from a dead past to a living present, not Romantic "empathy" but "making things present," he concluded that historical meaning was always established "posthumously." The Rankean aim of describing past events "as they really were," he commented, "was the most potent narcotic of the century."[147] In this judgment Benjamin was again in agreement with Nietzsche, though here, too, he remained closer to Marx.

Husserl incorporated a similar attitude toward historicism, bringing the

Rankean cliché into phenomenological arguments, casting doubt on a point of view possessing "little receptivity for a depth of inquiry which goes beyond the usual factual history."[148] Conventional historicism uncritically assumes a universal horizon of "implicit certainty" in determining causes and effects despite the "background-indeterminacy" interfering with historical judgments. Yet, Husserl adds, "what is historically primary in itself is our present." The "horizon-certainty" of historicism is to be found not in the answers historians derive from their sources but in the preexisting world of experience within a horizon "toward which all questions tend." "Historicism" here seems reduced to the idea of the historicity of the human — and the historian's — condition, within which a "science" of historical inquiry can be constructed, though how, Husserl does not venture to say.

Heidegger, proceeding from Husserlian phenomenology, was more attentive to the factor of time, to the question of history and its eponymous byproducts — historicality (*Geschichtlichkeit*), historiology (*Geschichtswissenschaft, historische Forschung*), historicity (*Historizität*), and historicism (*Historismus*).[149] Rejecting metaphysics, Heidegger nonetheless makes a fundamental ontological turn, or return, where Being is seen against the horizon of temporality — and the meaning of history is seen as derivative of the meaning of Being. Behind Heidegger's terminology is a subtle evocation of the individual human condition, "Dasein," in the dimension of time. Dasein is humanity in the world, and the historian is just one form of Dasein, and likewise understood not as an isolated psyche but as a subject formed under the imprint of historicity, a "being-in-the-world" and in the forestructures (a philosophical sort of "prejudice") of Dasein's life-world. As a form of Dasein — being as thought — the historian seeks meaning and illumination by self-projection, with the assistance of language, which is a sort of codification of tradition, of the given world, including the historical world. As relation and accommodation to the world is a mode of "caring," of intentional involvement with the world, so even more deliberately is the act of writing history.

Like Husserl, Heidegger was concerned in his own way with the crisis of historicism and with the problems that historical inquiry and quest for historical understanding brought to modern thought; and for him, with his obsession with existence, this meant confronting the question of time. Time gone by, however, cannot be recaptured except in the most Romantic and figurative sense; time is not a process that can be traced, or retraced, but is a condition of human existence — "historicity." And historicism, which arises from this Romantic dream, is likewise bound by this historicity, as are the scholars who practice the art of history in this spirit; it is present only in the forestructures and fore-conceptions of life and thought. As Nietzsche had also argued, historical research and understanding, like historical writing, must be accomplished in the present—and so the historian's task is to render the past "present"—to create a "caring" narrative that finds meaning within the horizons of today, with its memories and anticipations. The historian's own historicity, though it does not give him access to the essentialized, or hypostasized, "past" as such, furnishes the grounds for the science of history he practices through his sources and self-projection, which "lights up the world" of history as well as of being, and which allows him (or her) to explore the cultural "tradition" which is codified especially in language. What is clarified and given meaning, however, is not the fabled past but the challenging present into which we have been thrown. How, following these insights of Heidegger, can scholars move from their own inherited historicity to historical—or what some call historicist—knowledge? Here the other H-word comes into play, as Heidegger, in the spirit of Nietzsche and Dilthey, brings out his own idea of hermeneutics and the "hermeneutical situation," with the associated concept of language as the "house of being."[150] Already understood in a sense, interpretation and circumspection of the horizons of the world bring fuller meaning and awareness of historical forestructures. Because of the relationship between fore-understanding and meaning arising from interpretation, the hermeneutical process is circular in a deeper sense than that of Ast and earlier champions of hermeneutics. Historical scholarship finds this feature of hermeneutics to constitute a "vicious circle," and prefers a historical science, Heidegger writes, "which would be as independent of the standpoint of the observer as our knowledge of Nature is supposed to be."[151] But this is to misunderstand understanding itself and the conditions of historical knowledge—the error of the old historicism.

These considerations represent the end, or another turning, in the long road from eighteenth-century reflections on historical inquiry and interpretation. Hermeneutics was partially received by historians like Droysen but then, in a frenzy of scientific, or scientistic, enthusiasm, was rejected as a deviation from objectivity and certainty, only to be revived by a more reflective generation. Now although an invitation to interpretation could be a license for partisanship and prejudice in an unenlightened way, more responsibly, it brought intellectual honesty and maturity to the practice and theory of history. The spurious objectivism and explanatory claims that were staples in the rhetoric of scientific historians were exposed as illusions or products of a drive to intellectual and disciplinary hegemony. What historians of the school of Ranke, the persuasion of Fustel, and the hubris of Freeman—if not the subjectivist indulgence of Michelet, the dark perspective of Burckhardt, and the ironic self-awareness of Adams—would reject as philosophical obscurantism was actually a more critical and productive view of the limits and potential of historical research and writing, and indeed of other disciplines subject to historical interpretation. This was "historicism" in the best sense.

What would a hermeneutical outlook yield? Optimists like Jürgen Habermas (and in another direction, Sigmund Freud), preserving Marxist, or Marxoid, aspirations, hope to unveil the interests hidden behind the language and actions of social groups — hope, that is, to apply hermeneutics (and a "historicist critique of meaning") to the "critique of ideology," as in a cruder way Marx had tried to do in his materialist science of society.[152] So the "knowing subject" triumphs again over the aporia of the human condition and finds a way to decipher the real meaning behind the words of an ideological façade. In contrast to a "hermeneutics of suspicion," which evades the difficulties of prejudice (foreknowledge), historicism, and historicity, is a "hermeneutics of tradition," which Gadamer, carrying on in many ways the arguments of Heidegger, has maintained at length.[153] The debate over these questions extends into many areas of philosophy and the human sciences, but for purposes of historical inquiry the cautions and insights of Gadamer seem more to the point. What he proposes is a "fusion of horizons," in which the remnants of the past are given meaning in the present. Habermas seeks in effect a metacritique beyond language, but, as Gadamer points out, "Reality does not happen 'behind the back' of language," for "reality happens precisely *within* language," and so indeed does history.[154] Like Nature (in Galileo's famous metaphor), History, too, is a book — "the great dark book, the collected work of the human spirit, written in the languages of the past, the text of which we have to understand."[155] This is the task begun haltingly by Herodotus and Thucydides and carried on, more reflectively but no less haltingly, by their epigones within the horizons of a present which itself changes too fast to be captured. But the inquiry continues.

Conclusion

*For behold, I create new heavens and a new earth, and the former shall
not be remembered, nor come into mind.*

— Isaiah 65:17

· Claims of novelty and the rhetoric of innovation grew ever more insistent in the age of modernism, with "new histories" appearing in Germany, France, and the United States; and indeed this habit has persisted down to the present. History has ever to be rewritten and the errors of our elders not only corrected but edited out of our stories. What is old must be revered and studied, but out-of-date historiography must be replaced, or anyway historicized, into conceptual irrelevance — unless it is vouchsafed classic status. The old name for this was progress; the newer name is revisionism, and we are all victims of the process. As always, the Ancients may protest, but they will be drowned out by the Moderns — and the Moderns, perhaps, by the Postmoderns (although the Postmodern Age, according to Toynbee, dates from 1870).

So despite claims of novelty, after the long nineteenth century, from the French Revolution to the Great War, historical inquiry continued in many ways in the channels cut by the previous twenty-two centuries, and the faces of Herodotus, Thucydides, Eusebius, and other ancient models remained present, though overlaid and transformed by many generations of modern practice and theory. Continuities abound, and discussions of the art of history preserve common features from the Italian *artes historicae* and Bodin's *Methodus* (1566) to the handbooks of Bernheim, Langlois and Seignobos, and Charles Kendall Adams in the late nineteenth century. In a long perspective, many of the essential questions and some of the answers have remained constant: What is history (inevitably invoking Herodotus's coinage)? What are the main types of history (biographical, local, national, universal)? How does history differ from fiction (poetry)? Is history a "science" or an "art" (or both or something else)? What is the relation of human history to natural and divine history (philosophy of history)? What are the best "authorities" (sources)? How are they to be employed critically (*ars critica, Quellenkritik, documents pour servir à . . .*)? What disciplines may be drawn on for assistance (beginning with geography and chronology)? How can one approach questions of the origins of nations and, more concretely, of later periodization (especially the beginning of our "modern" age)? Who were the major historians in European tradition (the history of historiography)? Finally, what is the purpose of history? — the answer from the time of Cicero to that of Bodin to that of Collingwood, who all cite Herodotus, being usually some sort of human self-knowledge.

Consciously or not, historians have been locked into traditions, schools, discipleships, disciplinary habits, doctrines, and ideologies, but above all they have been subject to the constraints of language. What bound European historians to their predecessors above all was the vocabulary — commonplaces, metaphors, figures, epithets, comparisons, methods of interpretation, lines of argument, and formal tactics and strategies — developed over some twenty-four centuries of the life of the historiographical genre (through Greek, Latin, and the vernaculars). Linguistic and rhetorical convention weighed heavily not only on historical writers, even when they claimed (the humility topos) to fall below the level of their great "precursors"; this "burden of the past" weighed not only on those who repeated, imitated, or plagiarized from their disciplinary ancestors, but also on those who anxiously sought to escape their influence and to find an original way of understanding the past.[1] With this linguistic and rhetorical inheritance came a sense of irony and of separation from the process of history reflected in the sources — building perhaps on the opposition between Ancients and Moderns — whether through a naive faith in the possibility of "objectivity" by taking a view *sub specie aeternitatis* (Ranke's principle that all ages are equal in the sight of God), or through an awareness of the "point of view" to which all human authors are fated (Burckhardt's "to each eye . . ." and Nietzsche's "horizon").[2] Either way the historian's task entailed inferring meaning and making judgments, whether moral, political, or cultural, whether explicit or implicit. Even if efforts were limited to the uncovering and publication of records, questions of selection, arrangement, and interpretation (not to speak of biases embedded in the texts) undercut claims of objectivity.

The most insightful and influential discussion of the rhetorical dimensions of historical writing remains that of Hayden White, who offers an elaborate and systematic analysis of the tropes, figures, and modes of emplotment of some of the master historians of the nineteenth century.[3] Critical discussion of the work of Ranke, Michelet, Tocqueville, and Burckhardt in terms of literary theory, that is, Northrop Frye's — ultimately Aristotle's — four modes (romantic, comic, tragic, satiric) and corresponding modes of argument and "ideological implications" offer novel explorations of the deep structures of these selected narratives. The problem here is that White's interest is admittedly in the "philosophy of history," and not in historical inquiry and interpretation. What he (deliberately) ignores is the heuristic dimension of historical writing and the problematic role of sources in historical narrative — the question of how finished, and in many ways derivative, narratives are related to primary sources, and so how history has been constructed in the first place out of materials not gathered for a sophisticated or even academic readership. In other words, the "historical imagination" is not like the poetical imagination, since it depends in a literal way on a previous reality — on "the thing that happened," in Aristotle's proto-Rankean words, and not "a kind of thing that might happen."[4] Following this line of inquiry may not cast light on the larger literary strategies of writers of texts (and textbooks) working with, in effect, predigested materials, but it is necessary for understanding more immediate confrontations between scholars and the raw materials of history before incorporation into conventional stories, plots, arguments, and ideological discourses.

Yet language and its conventions are always intermediaries between historical inquiry and historical expression. There is no access to "what really happened," except by way of what witnesses (first-, second-, or third-hand) said happened; and even so, the leap to larger patterns of explanation or interpretation can be made only with the assistance of the resources of language. In whatever literary mode, it is easy enough for historians to describe the words, actions, and interactions of individual agents, to link them with other occurrences, and to infer consequences; but when dealing with social groups, institutions, collective actions, cultural phenomena, and national life, they necessarily have recourse to more figurative language — metaphors, similes, analogies, personifications, "objective correlatives" — and other ways of expressing the equivalents to Hegel's concrete universals. The same problems arose with attempts to establish the contexts of thought and action, which likewise had to be constructed out of a range of sources. As with nouns and substantives, so with verbs and copulas, so that the effort to connect such essentialist representations in causal and explanatory ways required a shift from simple psychological motivation to more complex and problematic linkages on the level of collective behavior — with the help of concepts from political science, economics, sociology, anthropology, and archeology. To these strategies the modes of romance, comedy, tragedy, and satire can only be superadditives — or literary preconceptions or forestructures brought to materials which, as some scholars have testified, have the power to change assumptions, prejudices, and even plots.

The claim to fame of history in the nineteenth and early twentieth centuries was its rise to the level of "science," whether in the sense of simple accuracy or of determination of large-scale "laws" of development on the analogy of natural, and especially biological, science; and many historians shared with their Enlightenment predecessors the ideal of an "end of myth" — a bequest of the Enlightenment which Hans Blumenberg regarded as another and later, if not last, myth.[5] In spite of the continued fascination with origins and prehistory, many historians continued to be suspicious of prehistorical inquiries (Thucydides' "archeology") that went beyond the documents and human testimony to conjectures based on comparative mythology and philological (even philosophical) speculation. Yet this was also the period of the emergence of new, or renewed, myths, including those that made historical interpretations attractive or usefully invidious, and especially those that enhanced notions of national identity or antiquity as well as modern superiority. Among the constructions or inventions that qualify as modern myths are "revolution" (as expanded semantically beyond the macrohistorical phenomena of 1688, 1789, and 1848), "feudalism" (as a coherent social system and a term of abuse), the "constitution" (in the English and German, not the French and American sense), ideas of race (extended to Indo-European and "Aryan"), shifting views of the point of departure of "modern history" (beginning with Charlemagne, or Charles VIII, or Napoleon?), and the resurgence of the conflict between Romanists and Germanists (not to speak of Celticists) over the question of European origins. There are ideological aspects — and rich prehistories — to all of these terms and issues; but under cover of science, or the rhetoric of "science," they all invaded and in many ways distorted historical interpretations. Indeed they seemed to thrive in the heyday of history's pretensions to scientific status and public power.

As historians have been drawn by a weighty past, so they have also been captive of their own cultural and political presents. From the Persian and Peloponnesian wars down to the Renaissance and to the nineteenth century, times of crisis had always inspired reexamination of the past, and so it was, on a massive scale, with the Revolution, when ideology came to the fore. For some, history came to a stop in 1789, with prospects of a new and better-managed future; for others, their world destroyed, it went underground, or into exile, until it could be restored and returned to the old ways. Such revolutionary and counterrevolutionary visions, however distorted by resentment or utopian motives, also shaped the interpretations of historians — the "new historians" — who, after 1815, had to make sense of the world-shaking experiences and the larger context of universal history. So words like "revolution," "liberty," "progress," and "ideology" became common labels to attach to selected aspects of the European past, and especially the medieval past. But the stock of "revolution" fell after 1848, at least in the West, and the rhetoric of national expansion and rivalry took its place, and with it (to adapt White's terminology) a shift from a comic to a tragic mode, as decadence, national conflict, imperialism, colonialism — political expressions of the Darwinian struggle for existence — seemed to express the trajectory of European history in the later nineteenth century. The First World War represented another world crisis, more destructive and perhaps more "revolutionary" than the paradigmatic events of 1789–1815, and called again for a review and re-evaluation of European political and cultural traditions. As Goethe said, every age (perhaps every generation?) has to write its own history. And moreover, every historian who ventures to publish is subject to review and revision, if not oblivion. *Veritas filia termporum* — but also *Tempus edax rerum*.

These are some of the conditions of the emergence of those casts of mind associated with historicism and hermeneutics. "Historicism," a neologism of the late eighteenth century, is not, in the sense that was originally intended and that has been suggested here, a particular conception of the past; rather it is a critical concern with the stories underlying the presence of a particular phenomenon of human creation (rather than with the analysis of their supposed natures). "Hermeneutics," which has a richer prehistory in theology and law, arises from the problem of understanding a text, a "source," written by another, perhaps unknown, author. Understanding an argument was one thing, as Chladenius pointed out, but understanding a statement by another required an understanding both of viewpoint and of difference in psychological, cultural, and so historical, context. Both historicism and hermeneutics imply relativism, but not a theoretical or philosophical relativism; for they merely recognized the conditions of human understanding and exchange. "For the very reason that no man is identical to any other man," Diderot wrote, "we never understand precisely, we are never precisely understood; our speech never goes beyond or it falls short of the sensation itself."[6] "What really happened" is the *Ding an sich* of the historian, and while the sources might permit approximation to this state, historical narrative can never presume to be more than one layer of interpretation — and indeed an updated sort of "conjectural history."

Yet in the nineteenth century, historians had come to occupy an important place in the public sphere — not only as "court historians" and ideologists (this is an old story), but as prophets of the state and educators of the people. What enhanced their power, of course, was the vast expansion of their institutional base and of the media of publicity and influence. Not only the publication of books but also university chairs, public education on lower levels, control of journals, founding of societies and international "schools" and networks all contributed to make history an industry as well as a pedagogical political calling — and indeed an "establishment" in its own right. More than that, the profession of history was often an apprenticeship to entrance into the corridors of power and leadership — Guizot, Thiers, Theodore Roosevelt, Woodrow Wilson, and Jean Jaurès being some of the more conspicuous examples. Here history appears as neither art nor science but as power — as the associate neither of Clio nor Minerva but of Mars and his devotees — and its prestige continues even now to profit from this company.

But besides such extensions of the Herodoto-Thucydidean canon, what is the meaning and use of history for its writers and readers? At this point the continuity of historical inquiry and the persistence of its rhetoric are strikingly apparent — and this despite perennial and almost generational claims of novelty and innovation over the discredited efforts of intellectual ancestors. Regardless of the grandiose claims of scholars across the ages that history teaches us how live, that it reveals God's plan, that it shows unending Progress to be the secular version of this plan, that it leads to a comprehensive understanding of humanity, that it affords a way to predict the future, that it liberates us from the past, that it represents the "history of liberty," or that it is equivalent to modern consciousness, modern historians have hardly changed the rhetoric of history since Cicero's extravagant but vague pedagogical formulas, which were still being repeated in the early years of the twentieth century. Perhaps the best that can be said of the value of history is still that it offers not only learning relevant to general culture and perhaps to professional life but also one route to what used to be called wisdom, except that it is limited to knowledge of "things human" — "things divine" being left to the philosophers of history. Philosophers of history, however, like public figures who leave the study of history for the practice of power, are in search of answers (and how many times have they been found to be wrong?), while historians, following the ancient trail of Herodotus, keep finding new questions and so new doubts.

"New histories" continued to be proclaimed, or denounced, in the early twentieth century, though without much in the way of innovation, to the extent that complaints about fixation on political and military history and calls for attention to cultural and social matters had been voiced for generations since the time of Herder and Voltaire. Deep prehistorical perspectives were being opened up, but history was still regarded as essentially a unified, or unifiable, process that could be described and even explained in linear time. In the Romantic period, history and literature were strongly interconnected, but at the turn of the twentieth century historians seemed untouched by modernist literature and art.[7] There were movements toward more pluralist and relativist views, but hardly beyond conventional recognition of point of view, cultural difference, and the role of imagination in historical narrative. More conspicuous was the rise of specialties such as economic, social, diplomatic history, and even psychohistory, as well as the histories of particular disciplines; but these, too, developed in the inertial context of an institutional matrix tied in many ways to the state (if not to oppositional ideologies), to the values and the rhetoric of empirical science, and in that connection, to the huge weight of records and a historiographical canon that was growing in a dialogical, or dialectical, way. The effect of the First World War was mainly to enhance these forces of tradition and the inclination of historians to national ideologies, and to eschatological philosophies of history, to replace the discredited myth of unending Progress, if not to restore it in more complex terms. These were the foundations on which the modern discipline of history would continue to be built and rebuilt into the present millennium.

Notes

Preface

1. I have recently published a parallel study of a more specialized aspect of Western historiography: *The Descent of Ideas: The History of Intellectual History* (London, 2002).

Chapter 1: Enlightened History

1. Hazard, *La Crise de la conscience européenne (1680–1715)* (Paris, 1935).

2. Becker, *The Heavenly City of the Eighteenth-Century Philosophers* (New Haven, 1932), 71.

3. Gay, "Carl Becker's Heavenly City," in *The Party of Humanity* (Princeton, 1959), 188–210, leading to his own *The Enlightenment: An Interpretation*, 2 vols. (New York, 1966–1969).

4. See, e.g., Axel Honneth et al., eds., *Philosophical Interventions in the Unfinished Project of Enlightenment* (Cambridge, Mass., 1992); and Max Horkheimer and Theodore Adorno, *Dialectic of Enlightenment*, trans. John Cumming (New York, 1991); also James Schmidt, ed., *What Is Enlightenment? Eighteenth-Century Answers and Twentieth-Century Questions* (Berkeley, 1996).

5. See, e.g., Mark Lilla, *G. B. Vico: The Making of an Anti-Modern* (Cambridge, Mass., 1993), esp. 3–6, continuing the thesis of Isaiah Berlin (article following "Enlightenment" in *Dictionary of the History of Ideas*).

6. J. G. A. Pocock, *Barbarism and Religion*, vol. 1, *The Enlightenments of Edward Gibbon, 1737–1764* (Cambridge, 1999).

7. Cassirer, *The Philosophy of the Enlightenment*, trans. Fritz C. A. Koelln and James P. Pettegrove (Princeton, 1951).

8. Dilthey, "Das achtzehnte Jahrhundert und die geschichtliche Welt," in *Gesammelte Schriften*, vol. 3 (Leipzig, 1927), 210–268.

9. Dilthey, *Introduction to the Human Sciences*, ed. Rudolf A. Makkreel and Frithhof Rodi (Princeton, 1989), 99ff.

10. Luigi Marino, *Praeceptores Germaniae: Göttingen, 1770–1820* (Göttingen, 1995), trans. from the Italian edition (1975); Hans Erich Bödeker, Georg G. Iggers, Jonathan B. Knudsen, and Peter Hanns Reill, eds., *Aufklärung und Geschichte: Studien zur deutschen Geschichtswissenschaft im 18. Jahrhundert* (Göttingen, 1886); Karl Hammer and Jürgen Voss, *Historische Forschung im 18. Jahrhundert: Organisation, Zielsetzung, Ergebnisse* (Bonn, 1976); Carlo Antoni, *La Lotta contro la ragione* (Florence, 1968); Jonathan B. Knudsen, *Justus Möser and the German Enlightenment* (Cambridge, 1986); Joachim Streisand, ed., *Die deutsche Geschichtswissenschaft vom Beginn des 19. Jahrhunderts bis zur Reichseinigung von oben* (Berlin, 1965); Joist Grolle, *Landesgeschichte in der Zeit der deutschen Spätaufklärung: Ludwig Timotheus Spittler (1752– 1810)* (Göttingen, 1963); Josef Engel, "Die deutsche Universitäten und die Geschichtswissenschaft," *Historische Zeitschrift*, 189 (1959), 223–378.

11. Wachler, *Geschichte der historischen Forschung und Kunst seit der Wiederherstellung der litterarischen Cultur in Europa* (Göttingen, 1812–1816), and Wegele, *Geschichte der deutschen Historiographie seit dem Auftreten des Humanismus* (Munich, 1885). See Lord Acton, "German Schools of History," *Selected Writings of Lord Acton*, vol. 2, *Essays in the Study and Writing of History*, ed. J. Rufus Fears (Indianapolis, 1985), and especially, Horst Walter Blanke, *Historiographiegeschichte als Historik* (Stuttgart, 1991), and Hans-Jürgen Pandel, *Historik und Dialektik als Problem der Distribution historiographisch erzeugten Wissens in der deutschen Geschichtswissenschaft von der Spätaufklärung zum Frühhistorismus (1765–1830)* (Stuttgart, 1990).

12. Cited by Blanke, *Historiographiegeschichte*, 159.

13. Nicholas Boyle, *Goethe: The Poet and the Age*, vol. 2 (Oxford, 2000), 401.

14. Konrad H. Jarausch, "The Institutionalization of History in Eighteenth-Century Germany," in Bödeker et al., *Aufklärung und Geschichte*, 26; Friedrich Meinecke, *Historism: The Rise of a New Historical Outlook*, trans. J. E. Anderson (London, 1972).

15. Meinecke, *Historism*, 237; cf. Paul Requadt, *Johannes von Müller und der Frühhistorismus* (Munich, 1929); *Johannes von Müller — Geschichtsschreiber de Goethezeit*, ed. Christoph Jamme and Otto Pöggler (Schaffhausen, 1986); and Friedrich Meinecke, *Zur Theorie und Philosophie der Geschichte*, ed. Eberhard Kessel (Stuttgart, 1959), 204.

16. J. C. L. Sismondi, *Lettres inédites de J. C. L. Sismondi*, ed. Saint-René Taillendier (Paris, 1865), 134.

17. Reill, *The German Enlightenment and the Rise of Historicism* (Berkeley, 1975).

18. Windelband, "Geschichte und Naturwissenschaft," in *Präludien*, vol. 2 (Tübingen, 1921[7]), 142–145; and Heinrich Rickert, *The Limits of Concept Formation in Natural Science*, trans. Guy Oakes (Cambridge, 1986). Superscript number refers to edition.

19. But see Frederick C. Beiser, "Hegel's Historicism," *The Cambridge Companion to Hegel*, ed. Frederick C. Beiser (Cambridge, 1993), 270–300.

20. Popper, *The Poverty of Historicism* (Boston, 1957), ix–x; and from another angle,

Carl Page, *Philosophical Historicism and the Betrayal of First Philosophy* (University Park, Pa., 1995). See Chapter 12, below.

21. Muhlack, *Geschichtswissenschaft im Humanismus und in der Aufklärung: Die Vorgeschichte des Historismus* (Munich, 1991); Blanke, *Historiographiegeschichte;* and Friedrich Jäger and Jörn Rüsen, *Geschichte des Historismus* (Munich, 1992); also the series, *Geschichtsdiskurs,* ed. W. Küttler, J. Rüsen, and E. Schulin (1993–).

22. Donald R. Kelley, *Faces of History: Historical Inquiry from Herodotus to Herder* (New Haven, 1998), 265–269.

23. Berlin, *The Roots of Romanticism* (Princeton, 1999), ix.

24. On the four-stage theory of Turgot, Smith, Goguet, and others, see Ronald L. Meek, *Social Sciences and the Noble Savage* (Cambridge, 1976), and also his *Smith, Marx, and After* (London, 1977).

25. In general, see Eduard Fueter, *Geschichte der neueren Historiographie* (Berlin, 1936³); James Westfall Thompson, *A History of Historical Writing,* 2 vols. (Chicago, 1942); G. P. Gooch, *History and Historians in the Nineteenth Century* (London, 1952²).

26. See especially Karl Hamme and Jürgen Voss, *Historische Forschung,* and Bödeker et al., *Aufklärung und Geschichte.*

27. See Wegele, *Geschichte.*

28. See Lewis White Beck, ed., *Kant on History* (New York, 1963).

29. Michael Albrecht, *Eklektik: Eine Begriffsgeschichte mit Hinweisen auf die Philosophie und Wissenschaftsgeschichte* (Stuttgart, 1994), 46–49.

30. Donald R. Kelley, ed., *Versions of History from Antiquity to the Enlightenment* (New Haven, 1991), epitaph.

31. See Kelley, *Faces,* 246–249.

32. Herder, *Sämtliche Werke,* vol. 3 (Vienna, 1851), 281; "Metaphysics of the Purism of Reason," in Gwen Griffith Dickson, *Johann Georg Hamman's Relational Metacriticism* (Berlin, 1995), 284.

33. Herder, *Metakritik,* in *Sämtliche Werke,* vol. 37 (Stuttgart, 1853), 291.

34. Herder, ibid., 17.

35. Hausen, "Von der Theorie der Geschichte," in Horst Walter Blanke and Dirk Fleischer, eds., *Theoretiker der deutschen Aufklärungshistorie,* vol. 1 (Stuttgart, 1990), 301.

36. See Kelley, *Faces,* chapter 5.

37. See Donald R. Kelley, "The Theory of History," in *The Cambridge History of Renaissance Philosophy,* ed. Charles Schmitt et al. (Cambridge, 1988), 746–761.

38. Kelley, *Faces,* chapter 9.

39. Blanke and Fleischer, *Theoretiker,* and Pandel, *Historik und Dialektik,* 156–180.

40. Cicero, *De Oratore,* trans. E. W. Sutton (Cambridge, 1988), 2.9, 2.15.

41. Baumgarten, "Über die eigentlihe Beschaffenheit und Nutzbarkeit der Historie" (1744), in Blanke and Fleischer, *Theoretiker,* vol. 1, 178.

42. Reinhard Koselleck, *Futures Past: On the Semantics of Historical Time,* trans. Keith Tribe (Cambridge, Mass., 1985), 21–38 ("Historia Magistra Vitae").

43. Gatterer, "Räsonnement über die jetzige Verfassung der Geschichtskunde in Teutschland" (1772), in Blanke and Fleischer, *Theoretiker,* vol. 2, 716.

44. See Jean Jehasse, *La Renaissance de la critique: l'essor de l'Humanisme érudit de 1560 à 1614* (Saint-Etienne, 1976).

45. See Giuseppe D'Alessandro, *L'Illuminismo dimenticato: Johann Gottfried Eichhorn (1752–1827) e suo tempo* (Göttingen, 2000), 159ff.

46. Bierling, "De Fide historica," and "Über die historische Gewissheit," in Blanke and Fleischer, *Theoretiker,* vol. 1, 167: "Non inconcinne igitur veritates Historicis cum veritatibus Physicis comparare licebit"; and 168: "Nicht von ungefähr wird es also erlaubt sein, die historischen mit den naturwissenschaftlichen Wahrheiten zu vergleichen."

47. See Georges Gusdorf, *Les Origines de l'herméneutique* (Paris, 1988); Joachim Wach, *Das Verstehen* (Tübingen, 1926); and Pandel, *Historik und Dialektik,* 323–332.

48. Chladenius in *The Hermeneutics Reader,* ed. Mueller-Vollmer, 56; and see Reill, *The German Enlightenment,* 105–112.

49. Christoph Friedrich, *Sprache und Geschichte: Untersuchungen zur Hermeneutik von Johann Martin Chladenius* (Meisenheim, 1978).

50. Eckermann, *Gespräche mit Goethe in den letzten Jahres seines Lebens,* ed. C. H. Beck (Munich, 1984), 390; *Conversations,* trans. John Oxenford (London, 1930), 383.

51. Certeau, *Heterologies: Discourse on the Other,* trans. Brian Massumi (Minneapolis, 1986).

52. Hegel, *Introduction to the Lectures on the History of Philosophy,* trans. T. M. Knox and A. V. Miller (Oxford, 1985), 11.

53. See George Boas, *Primitivism and Related Ideas in the Middle Ages* (Baltimore, 1948), and, with Arthur O. Lovejoy, *Primitivism and Related Ideas in Antiquity* (Baltimore, 1935).

54. Kelley, *Faces,* 32.

55. Andreas Kraus, *Vernunft und Geschichte: Die Bedeutung der deutschen Akademien für die Entwicklung der Geschichtswissenschaft im späten 18. Jahrhundert* (Freiburg, 1963).

56. *Historisches Journal von Mitgliedern der königlichen historischen instituts zu Göttingen* (Göttingen, 1772), Vorrede: "Die reine lautere Wahrheit halter für uns das Wesen der Geschichte." And see Giuseppe D'Alessandro, "Recencire e fare storia a Gottinga: il caso di Gatterer e Heeren," *La recensione: Origini, splendori e declino della critica storiografia,* ed. Massimo Mastrogregorio (Pisa, 1997), 129–147.

57. Friedrich Wilhelm Nettberg, *Kirchengeschichte Deutschlands* (Göttingen, 1846), 5, referring all to the parallel *Gallia Sacra* (1656), *Anglia Sacre* (1691), *Italia Sacra* (1717), *España Sagrada* (1754), and *Illyricum Sacrum* (1751).

58. Notker Hammerstein, *Jus und Historie: Ein Beitrag zur Geschichte des historischen Denkens an deutschen Universitäten im späten 17. und 18. Jahrhundert* (Göttingen, 1972).

59. See Notker Hammerstein, "Reichs-Historie," in Blanke and Fleischer, *Aufklärung und Geschichte,* 98.

60. A. G. Dickens and John M. Tonkin, *The Reformation in Historical Thought* (Cambridge, Mass. 1985), and John Stroup, "Protestant Church Historians in the German Enlightenment," in Blanke and Fleischer, *Aufklärung und Geschichte,* 169–192.

61. Melanchthon, *Chronica Carionis* (Wittenberg, 1580), preface (1558).

62. C. A. Patrides, *The Grand Design of God* (London, 1972).

63. See Adolph Harnack, *A History of Dogma,* vol. 1, trans. Neil Buchanan (New York, 1958), 26.

64. *An Ecclesiastical History, Antient and Modern,* trans. Archibald Maclaine (London, 1765); and see Karl Heussi, *Die Kirchengeschichtschreibung Johann Lorenz von Mosheims* (Gotha, 1904), and Florian Neumann, "Mosheim und die westeuropäische Kirchengeschichtsschreibung," *Johann Lorenz Mosheim (1693–1755): Theologie im Spannungsfeld von Philosophie, Philologie und Geschichte,* ed. Martin Mulsow et al. (Wiesbaden, 1997), 111–146.

65. Stroup, "Protestant Church Historians," 190.

66. See Friederike Fürst, *August Ludwig von Schlözer, ein deutsche Aufklärer im 18. Jahrhundert* (Heidelberg, 1928).

67. Donald R. Kelley, *The Human Measure: Western Social Thought and the Legal Tradition* (Cambridge, Mass., 1990), 121–127.

68. Paolo Rossi, *The Dark Abyss of Time: The History of the Earth and the History of Nations from Hooke to Vico,* trans. Lydia G. Cochrane (Chicago, 1984).

69. Ludwig Wachler, *Versuch einer Allgemeinen Geschichte der Literatur* (Lemgo, 1793), reviews the whole tradition, going back to Polydore Vergil and including B. G. Struve, *Introductio in notitiam rei literariae et usum bibliothecarum* (Jena, 1710); J. F. Reimann, *Versuch einer Einleitung in die historiam literariam antediluvianum* (Halle, 1709); C. A. Heumann, *Conspectus Reipublicae litterariae sive via ad historiam literariam iuventuti studiosae* (Hannover, 1718); Gottlieb Stolles, *Anleitung zur Historie der Gelahrheit* (Jena, 1727), and his *Introductio in historiam litterarium* (Jena, 1728); Nicholas Gundling, *Historie der Gelahrheit* (Frankfurt, 1734), accompanied by a vast amount of journal literature; and his was succeeded by such later reference works as that of J. G. Eichhorn, *Geschichte der Litteratur von ihrem Anfang bis auf die neuesten Zeiten* (Göttingen, 1797).

70. See Kelley, *Faces,* chapter 4.

71. See Wegele, *Geschichte,* 472–489, 783. But how many have disappeared (the fate of most popular textbooks)?

72. *An Universal History from the Earliest Accounts to the Present Times,* vol. 1 (London, 1779), advertisement.

73. Berkenmeyer, *Poëtische Anleitung zur Universal-Historie* (Hamburg, 1724).

74. Colmar, *Die Welt in einer Nuss oder kurzer Begriff der merkwürdigsten Welt-Geschichte* (Wittenberg, 1730).

75. Eichhorn, *Weltgeschichte,* vol. 2 (Göttingen, 1804), 5; and see D'Alessandro, *L'Illuminismo dimenticato,* 201ff.

76. Geoffroy Atkinson, *Les nouveaux Horizons de la Renaissance française* (Paris, 1935), and Raymod Schwab, *The Oriental Renaissance: Europe's Rediscovery of India and the East, 1680–1880,* trans. Gene Patterson-Black and Victor Reinking (New York, 1984).

77. See Michael Carhart, "Anthropologie und Statistik in the Göttingisches Historisches Magazin (1787–94)," *Historians and Ideologues: Essays in Honor of Donald R. Kelley,* ed., Anthony T. Grafton and J. H. M. Salmon (Rochester, 2001), 327–349.

78. J. A. Burrow, *The Ages of Man: A Study in Medieval Writing and Thought* (Oxford, 1986).

79. Cellarius, *Historia antiqua* (1685), *Historia medii aevi* (1688), and *Historia nova* (1696); and see Wallace K. Ferguson, *The Renaissance in Historical Thought: Five Centuries of Interpretation* (Cambridge, Mass., 1948), 75–77.

80. Freyer, *Nähere Einleitung zur Universalhistorie* (Halle, 1736³).

81. Donald J. Wilcox, *The Measure of Times Past: Pre-Newtonian Chronologies and the Rhetoric of Relative Times* (Chicago, 1987).

82. Gatterer, *Versuch einer allgemeinen Weltgeschichte bis zur Entdeckung Amerikens* (Göttingen, 1792).

83. Kubler, *The Shape of Time: Remarks on the History of Things* (New Haven, 1962); and see below, Chapter 9.

84. Richard H. Popkin, *Isaac La Peyrère (1596–1676): His Life, Work and Influence* (Leiden, 1987), 26ff.

85. Jaroslav Malina and Zdenek Vasicek, *Archeology Yesterday and Today* (Cambridge, 1990), 29.

86. *Vorlesung über Universalgeschichte (1805–1806)*, ed. Jean-Jacques Anstett, in *Kritische Friedrich-Schlegel-Ausgabe*, vol. 16, ed. Ernst Behler (Paderborn, 1960), 28.

87. Schlegel, *A Course of Lectures on Modern History*, trans. Lyndsey Purcell and R. H. Whitelock (London, 1878), 1–2.

88. Schlegel, Review of Condorcet's *Esquisse*, in *Werke in zwei Bänden*, vol. 1 (Berlin, 1980), 187–195.

89. Rotteck, *General History of the World* (Philadelphia, 1840), 23; and see Gooch, *History and Historians*, 105; Srbik, 343, and George G. Iggers, *The German Conception of History* (Middletown, Conn., 1983²), 98. In Germany alone, according to the English preface, this work sold more than 100,000 copies.

90. Rotteck, *History of the World*, 9.

91. Woodruff D. Smith, *Political and the Sciences of Culture in Germany, 1840–1920* (Oxford, 1991), 13.

92. Pölitz, *Die Weltgeschichte für gebildete Leser und Studierende* (Leipzig, 1824).

93. Iselin, *Die Geschichte der Menschheit*, vol. 2 (Carlsruhe, 1770²), 215.

94. Robertson, *The History of America*, vol. 1 (Dublin, 1797 [1777]), 401–402. Bracketed dates refer to first edition.

95. Irwing, *Versuch über die Kultur des Menschen überhaupt* (1779), in *Erfahrungen und Untersuchungen über den Menschen*, vol. 3 (Munich, 1799), 88: "die allgemeine Theorie der Kultur der Menschen überhaupt."

96. C. D. Beck, *Anleitung zur Kenntniss der allgemeinen Welt-und Völker-Geschichte für Studierende* (Leipzig, 1787).

97. Donald R. Kelley, "The Old Cultural History," *History and the Human Sciences* (1996), 101–126, and Jög Fisch, "Zivilization, Kultur," *Geschichtliche Grundbegriffe*, vol. 7. *Aufklärung, Bildung,* and *Kultur* were all new words in the Enlightenment, remarks Franco Venturi, in "Towards a Historical Dictionary," in *Italy and the Enlightenment*, trans. Susan Corsi (New York, 1972), 33. And see now D'Alessandro, *L'Illuminismo dimenticato*, 245ff.

98. According to Moses Mendelssohn, "On the Question 'What Is Enlightenment?' " *What Is Enlightenment?* ed. James Schmidt, 53, the terms culture, enlightenment, and education were all neologisms in 1784.

99. Andres, *Historical View of the Literature of the South of Europe,* trans. Thomas Roscoe (London, 1908), 32. See Andres, *Dell'Origine, progressi e stato attuale di ogni letteratura* (Venice, 1830 [1782]), prefazione, and Denina, *An essay on the Revolutions of Literature* (1761), trans. John Murdoch (London, 1771).

100. Pölitz, *Geschichte der Kultur der Menschheit, nach kritischen Principien* (Leipzig, 1795), 76.

101. Jenisch, *Universalhistorischer Ueberblick der Entwickelung des Menschenge-schlechts als einer fortbildenden Ganzen* (Berlin, 1801), 391.

102. Ibid., 9.

103. Meiners, *Historische Vergleichung der Sitten und Verfasssungen, des Gesetz und Gewerbe, des Handels, und der Religion, der Wissenschaften, und Lehranstalten des Mittelalters mit denen unsers Jahrhunderts in Rücksicht auf die Vorteile und Nachteile der Aufklärung,* vol. 2 (Hannover, 1793), 465.

104. Meiners, *Grundriss der Geschichte der Menschheit* (Lemgo, 1793³), 13.

105. Heeren, "Über Quellenstudium, Raisonnement und historische Kritik," in Blanke and Fleischer, *Theoretiker,* vol. 2, 515.

106. Eichhorn, *Allgemeine Geschichte der Cultur und Litteratur des neueren Europa* (Göttingen, 1796), vi.

107. Ibid., 78.

108. On the earlier background, see my "Writing Cultural History in Early Modern France: Christoph Milieu and His Project," *Renaissance Quarterly,* 52 (1999), 342–365.

109. Baumgarten, in Blanke and Fleischer, *Theoretiker,* 176, 301.

110. Walckenaer, *Essai sur l'histoire de l'Espèce humaine* (Paris, 1798).

111. Irwing, *Erfahrungen,* vol. 3, 123.

112. Other works on cultural history before 1800 include those by D. G. Herzog, J. F. Reitemeier, A. F. W. Crome, H. W. A. Marees, J. D. Hartmann, Friedrich Maier, J. G. Heynig, various anonymous publications, and the German translation of Arthur Young's travels in France (1795). See the bibliography in Volker Hartmann, *Die deutsche Kultur-geschichtschreibung von ihren Anfängen bis Wilhelm Heinrich Riehl* (diss., Marburg, 1971), 145–146; also Friedrich Jodl, *Die Culturgeschichtschreibung: Ihre Entwicklung und ihr Problem* (Halle, 1878); Ernst Schaumkell, *Geschichte der deutschen Kultur-geschichtschreibung* (Leipzig, 1905); and *Geschichtliche Grundbegriffe,* vol. 7, "Ziviliza-tion."

113. *Zeitschrift für Kulturgeschichte: Bilder und aus den Leben der deutschen Volkes,* founded in 1856 and edited by Johannes Müller and Johannes Falke.

114. See below, Chapter 10.

Chapter 2: History between Research and Reason

1. Adolf Harnack, *Geschichte der königlich preussische Akademie der Wissen-schaften zu Berlin,* (Berlin, 1900), 1: 421: "Qu'est-ce qui a fait de la langue française la langue universelle de l'Europe?"

2. See Chantal Grell, *L'Histoire entre érudition et philosophie: étude sur la con-naissance historique de l'âge des lumières* (Paris, 1993), and Peter Stadler, *Geschicht-schreibung und historisches Denken in Frankreich, 1789–1871* (Zurich, 1958).

3. Henri Griffet, *Traité des différentes sortes de preuves qui servent à établir la vérité de l'histoire* (Liege, 1769), 7; and see Lenglet de Fresnoy, *L'Histoire justifié contre les romans* (Paris, 1735).

4. Volney, *Leçons d'histoire prononcées à l'école normale, en l'an III* (Paris [1800]), iii; and see Denise Brahimi, "Les 'Leçons d'histoire' de Volney (1795)," *L'Histoire au XVIIIe siècle* (Aix-en-Provence, 1908), 405–427, and Jean Gaulmier, *L'Idéologue Volney, 1757–1820* (Geneva, 1980).

5. François Fossier, "A propos du titre d'historiographe sous l'ancien régime," *Revue d'histoire moderne et contemporaine*, 32 (1985), 361–417.

6. See Abel Lefranc, *Histoire du Collège de France* (Paris, 1893), 387, and Orest Ranum, *Artisans of Glory* (Chapel Hill, 1980).

7. Velly, *Histoire de France depuis l'établissement de la Monarchie jusqu'au regne de Louis XIV*, vol. 1 (Paris, 1775), viii.

8. Martin Staum, *Minerva's Message: Stabilizing the French Revolution* (Montreal, 1996), and Sophie-Anne Leterrier, *L'Institution des Sciences Morales [1795–1850]* (Paris, 1995).

9. Dacier, *Rapport historique sur les progrès de l'histoire et de la littérature ancienne depuis 1789* (Paris, 1810); and see June K. Burton, *Napoleon and Clio: Historical Writing, Teaching, and Thinking during the First Empire* (Durham, 1979).

10. Charles Villers, *Rapport fait à la Class d'Histoire et de littérature ancien de l'Institut de France: Sur l'état actuel de la littérature ancienne et d'histoire en Allemagne* (Paris, 1809).

11. *Catalogue de l'histoire de France* (Paris, 1968 [1855]), vol. 1; and Pin den Boer, *History As a Profession: The Study of History in France, 1818–1914*, trans. Arnold J. Pomerans (Princeton, 1998), 5.

12. Chantall Grell, *L'Histoire entre érudition et philosophy*, 291–298.

13. Chantereau, *Science de l'histoire* (Paris, an XI [1803]).

14. John Kent Wright, *A Classical Republican in Eighteenth-Century: The Political Thought of Mably* (Stanford, 1997), 145.

15. Montesquieu, *De l'Esprit des lois*, vol. 6, 18; and see Robert Morrissy, *L'Empereur à la barbe fleurie: Charlemagne dans la mythologie et l'histoire de France* (Paris, 1997); and Robert Folz, *Le Souvenir et la légende de Charlemagne dans l'empire germanique médiéval* (Paris, 1950).

16. Knowles, *Great Historical Enterprises* (London, 1962), 55.

17. D. R. Kelley, *Historians and the Law in Postrevolutionary France* (Princeton, 1984), 56ff.

18. Krzysztof Pomian, "Les Archives," *Les Lieux de mémoire*, vol. 3, *Les France*, 3. *De l'Archive à l'emblème* (Paris, 1992), 162–233.

19. D. R. Kelley, "Jean Du Tillet, Archivist and Antiquary," *Journal of Modern History*, 38 (1966), 337–354, and *Foundations of Modern Historical Scholarship: Language, Law, and History in the French Renaissance* (New York, 1970), 215–240.

20. See especially Blandine Kriegel, *L'Histoire à l'âge classique*, vol. 4 (Paris, 1988).

21. Baker, "Controlling French History: The Ideological Arsenal of Jacob-Nicolas Moreau," *Inventing the French Revolution* (Cambridge, 1990), 59–85.

22. D. R. Kelley, "Ancient Verses on New Ideas: Legal Tradition and the French Histor-

ical School," *History and Theory,* 26 (1987), 319–338, and *Historians and the Law,* 68–69, also in D. R. Kelley, *The Writing of History and the Study of Law* (London, 1997); Harold A. Ellis, *Boulainvilliers and the French Monarchy: Aristocratic Politics in Early Eighteenth-Century France* (Ithaca, 1988); and J. Q. C. Mackrell, *The Attack on 'Feudalism' in Eighteenth-Century France* (London, 1973).

23. Lézardière, *Théorie des lois politiques de la monarchie française* (Paris, 1844).

24. Portalis, *Du Devoir de l'historien* (Paris, an VIII [1800]), 129.

25. Griffet, *Traité des différentes sortes, de preuves qui servent à établir la vérité de l'histoire* (Liege, 1769); and cf. Lenglet du Fresnoy, *L'Histoire justifiée contre les romans* (Paris, 1735).

26. Kelley, *Faces,* 188–97.

27. Rollin, *The Ancient History* (New York, 1825), introduction.

28. "History," in the *Encyclopédie,* in D. R. Kelley, *Versions of History,* 442–446; and see Kelley, *Faces,* 241–244.

29. Voltaire, "History," from the *Philosophical Dictionary,* in *The Age of Louis XIV and Other Selected Writings,* trans. J. H. Brumfitt (New York, 1963), 324.

30. See Mark Hulliung, *The Autocritique of Enlightenment: Rousseau and the Philosophes* (Cambridge, Mass., 1994), 52–78.

31. *Turgot on Progress, Sociology, and Economics,* trans. Ronald L. Meek (Cambridge, 1973); and see Meek, *Social Science and the Noble Savage* (Cambridge, 1976), and *Smith, Marx, and After* (London, 1977).

32. Sergio Moravia, *Il Tramonto dell'illuminismo: filosofia e politica nella società francese (1770–1810)* (Bari, 1968); F. Picavet, *Les Idéologues* (Paris, 1891); and B. W. Head, *Ideology and Social Science: Destutt de Tracy and French Liberalism* (Dordrecht, 1985).

33. Condorcet, *Esquisse d'un tableau historique des progrès de l'esprit humain* (Paris, 1988), 265ff.

34. Volney, *The Ruins; or, A Survey of the Revolutions of Empires,* Eng. trans. (London, 1811⁵); and see Sergio Moravia, *Il tramonto dell'illuminismo,* 163.

35. Volney, *Leçons d'histoire* (Paris, 1795), 145ff.

36. Ibid., 183.

37. See Robert Morrissey, *L'Empereur à la barbe fleurie,* 349.

38. Michaud, *The History of the Crusades,* trans. W. Robson, vol. 1 (New York, n.d.), 20.

39. Ibid., vol. 1, 259.

40. Ibid., vol. 3, 256.

41. Chateaubriand, *Génie du Christianisme,* bk. III, chapter 1.

42. Chateaubriand, *Mémoires d'outre-tombe,* vol. 1 (Paris, 1951), 461.

43. Patricia B. Craddock, *Young Edward Gibbon: Gentleman of Letters* (Baltimore, 1982), 107.

44. *Lettres inédites de J. C. L. de Sismondi,* ed. Saint-René Taillandier (Paris, 1863), 143.

45. Madame de Staël, Charles de Villers, Benjamin Constant, *Correspondence,* ed. Kurt Kloocke (Frankfurt, 1993), 17; and see Simone Balayé and Jean-Daniel Candaux, eds., *Le Groupe de Coppet* (Geneva, 1977); also Gioacchio Gargallo di Castel Lentini,

Storia della storiografia moderna, vol. 3 (Rome, 1985), Etienne Hofman and Anne-Lise Decrétaz, eds., *Le Groupe de Coppet et la révolution française* (Lausanne, 1988).

46. De Staël, *Considérations sur les principaux événements de la révolution françoise* (1818), in *Oeuvres complètes,* vol. 12 (Paris, 1820), 139–161.

47. Constant, *Oeuvres,* vol. 5, 8.

48. De Staël, *De lâ Littérature considérée dans ses rapports avec les institutions sociales* (1800), trans. in part by Morroe Berger, *Madame de Staël on Politics, Literature and National Character* (London, 1964), 218, 245, etc.

49. De Staël, *De l'Allemagne,* chapter 11.

50. Wellek, *History of Modern Criticism: 1750–1950,* vol. 2, *The Romantic Age* (New Haven, 1955), 224.

51. Villers, letter to de Staël (June 25, 1802), in de Staël et al., *Correspondence,* 17.

52. Villers, *Essai sur l'esprit et l'influence de la Reformation de Luther* (Paris, 1851⁵), 50, 36–37.

53. Sismondi, *La Littérature du midi de l'Europe* (Paris, 1813); trans. Thomas Roscoe, *Historical View of the Literature of the South of Europe* (1813), 28–30. See Jean-R. de Salis, *Sismondi, 1773–1842: la vie et l'oeuvre d'un cosmopolite philosophe* (Paris, 1932).

54. Ibid., 440.

55. Sismondi, *Histoire des Républiques italiennes du moyen age* (Paris, 1838⁵).

56. De Salis, *Sismondi,* 103; and on Müller, see Fueter, *Geschichte der neueren Historiographie,* vol. 2 (Berlin, 1936³), 82.

57. Sismondi, *Fall of the Roman Empire,* vol. 1 (London, 1834), 3.

58. Sismondi, *New Principles of Political Economy: Of Wealth in Its Relation to Population,* trans. Richard Hyse (New Brunswick, 1991), 21.

59. *The Spirit of Conquest and Usurpation in their Relation to European Civilization* and "The Liberty of the Ancients Compared with That of the Moderns," in *Political Writings,* trans. Biancamaria Fontana (Cambridge, 1988).

60. See *The French Revolution and the Creation of Modern Political Culture,* vol. 1, ed. Keith Baker (Oxford, 1987), and vol. 2, ed. Colin Lucas (Oxford, 1988), also my review in *Journal of Modern History,* 63 (1991), 392–396; and Linda Orr, *Headless History: Nineteenth-Century Historiography of the Revolution* (Ithaca, 1990).

61. La Hode, *Histoire des révolutions de France. Où l'on voit comment dette Monarchie s'est formée, et les divers changemenss qui y sont arrivez par a rapport à son Etendue et à son Gouvernement* (The Hague, 1738), from Clovis to the death of Louis XIV.

62. D. R. Kelley, "Men of Law and the French Revolution," *Politics, Ideology and the Law in Early Modern Europe,* ed. Adrianna E. Bakos (Rochester, 1994), 127–146; also in Kelley, *Writing of History.*

63. See D. R. Kelley, *The Beginning of Ideology* (Cambridge, 1981), 1–3.

64. *Archives parlementaires,* vol. 8, 440ff. See also F. A. Aulard, *Les Orateurs de L'Assemblée Constituante* (1882), and G. Guatherot, *L'Assemblée Constituante, Le Philosophisme en action* (1914), as well as A. Lameth, *Histoire de l'Assemblée Constituante* (1828–1829), and individual biographies. Bernardi published an "Essai sur les révolutions du droit français" in 1785; see also J. M. Goulemot, "Le mot Révolution et la formation du concept de Révolution politique (fin XVII siècle)," *Annales historiques de la révolution française,* 39 (1967), 417–444.

65. Désodouard, *Histoire philosophique de la révolution française* (Paris, 1801⁴), 1.

66. J. Q. C. Mackrell, *The Attack on "Feudalism,"* 35–41.

67. Ibid., 38–39.

68. Chartier, *The Cultural Origins of the French Revolution,* trans. Lydia G. Cochrane (Durham, 1991).

69. Rabaut de Saint-Etienne, *The History of the Revolution of France,* trans. James White (London, 1792).

70. Barnave, *Introduction à la Révolution* (Paris, 1792).

71. *Mémoires pour servir à l'histoire du Jacobinisme* (Paris, 1973), 345–369; see also Maxim Leroy, *Histoire des idées sociales en France,* vol. 1 (Paris, 1946), 345ff., and James L. Osen, *Royalist Political Thought during the French Revolution* (Westport, Conn., 1995).

72. Mallet du Pin, *Considerations on the Nature of the French Revolution; and on the Causes which Prolong its Duration* (London, 1793), and Mounier, *De l'Influence attribuée aux Franc-Maçons et aux Illuminés sur la Revolution de France* (Tübingen, 1801).

73. Acton, *Lectures on the French Revolution* (London, 1910), 345–346.

74. Daunou, *Cours d'études historiques,* vol. 1 (Paris, 1842), preface; and see Fr. Picavet, *Les Idéologues* (Paris, 1891), 399ff.

75. D. R. Kelley, "The Theory of History," *Cambridge History of Renaissance Philosophy* (Cambridge, 1988), 746–762.

76. Sismondi, *The French under the Merovingians,* trans. William Bellingham (London, 1850), xxxii.

77. Frank E. Manuel, *The Prophets of Paris* (Cambridge, Mass., 1962).

78. Kant's review in *Kant on History,* ed. Lewis White Beck (New York, 1963), 27.

79. Henri Tronchon, *La Fortune intellectuelle de Herder en France* (Paris, 1920).

80. Stewart, *Histoire abrégée des sciences metaphysiques, morales et politiques depuis la renaissance des lettres,* trans. J. A. Buchon (Paris, 1820), ded. to Cousin.

81. Herder, *Idées sur la philosophie de l'histoire de l'humanité* (Paris, 1834), ded. to Friedrich Creuzer; and see Richard Howard Powers, *Edgar Quinet: A Study in French Patriotism* (Dallas, 1957).

82. *Essais de palingénésis sociale,* vol. 2 (Paris, 1829), 49–109; and see A. J. George, *Pierre-Simon Ballanche, Precursor of Romanticism* (Syracuse, 1945).

83. Cournot, *Considérations sur la marche des idées et des événements dans le temps modern* (Paris, 1868), chapter 14.

84. See Robert Flint, *History of the Philosophy of History* (New York, 1894), 655.

85. Flint, *Historical Philosophy in France, French Belgium, and Switzerland* (London, 1893), and the article by Flint's French translator Ludovic Carrau, "La Philosophie de l'histoire et la loi du progrès d'après de récens travaux," *Revue des deux mondes,* 45 (5) (1875), 568–586; and D. R. Kelley, "Robert Flint, Historian of Ideas," *Storiografia,* 27 (1995), 1–17, repr. in *Writing of History.*

86. Schlegel, *The Philosophy of History,* trans. James Burton Robertson (London, 1890), preface.

87. Ibid., 413.

88. Ibid., 86.

89. Hegel, *Philosophy of History*, trans. J. Sibree (New York, 1944), 72.

90. Ibid., 104.

91. D. R. Kelley, "The Metaphysics of Law: An Essay on the Very Young Marx," *American Historical Review*, 83 (1978), 350–367; repr. in *History, Law, and the Human Sciences*.

92. D. R. Kelley,"The Science of Anthropology: An Essay on the Very Old Marx," *Journal of the History of Ideas*, 45 (1984), 245–262; repr. in *Writing of History*.

93. See M. M. Bober, *Karl Marx's Interpretation of History* (New York, 1927).

94. Manuel, *Shapes of Philosophical History* (London, 1965), 130.

95. Balbo, *Meditazioni storiche* (Florence, 1855³), and La Fuente, *Historia ecclesiástica de España* (Madrid, 1873²), 3.

96. Molitor, *Philosophie der Geschichte* (Münster, 1857); Rougement, *Les Deux Cités: La Philosophie de l'histoire aux différents ages de l'humanité* (Paris, 1874); Lasaulx, *Philosophie der Geschichte* (Munich, 1952 [1856]); Ferrari, *Essai sur les principes et les limites de la philosophie de l'histoire* (Paris, 1843); Gustav Biedermann, *Philosophie de l'histoire* (Prague, 1884); also Konrad Hermann, *Zwölf Vorlesungen über Philosophie der Geschichte* (Leipzig, 1863); Hugh M. P. Doherty, *Philosophy of History and Social Evolution* (London, 1884); and Shedd, *Lectures upon the Philosophy of History* (Andover, 1873).

Chapter 3: Expanding Horizons

1. Hegel, *The Phenomenology of Mind*, trans. J. B. Baillie (New York, 1967), 229.

2. Raynal, *Histoire philosophique et politique des Etablissements et du Commerce des Européens dans les deux Indes* (Paris, 1762); and see Michèle Duchet, *Anthropologie et histoire au siècle des lumières* (Paris, 1771), 170–180.

3. D. R. Kelley, "The Archeology of Wisdom," *The European Legacy*, 1 (1996), 2037–2054.

4. Raymod Schwab, *The Oriental Renaissance: Europe's Rediscovery of India and the East 1680–1880,* trans. Gene Patterson-Black and Victor Reinking (New York, 1984).

5. *An Historical Disquisition Concerning the Knowledge which the Ancients Had of India* (London, 1791).

6. Degérando, *Histoire comparée des systèmes de philosophie relativement aux principes des conaissances humaines*, 3 vols. (Paris, 1804), and vol. 4 (Paris, 1847), and Cousin, *Course of the History of Philosophy*, vol. 1, trans. O. W. Wight (New York, 1860), 365.

7. Acton, *Essays in the Study and Writing of History*, ed. J. Rufus Fears (Indianapolis, 1985), 327 ("German Schools of History").

8. Heine, *The Romantic School*, trans. S. L. Fleischman (New York, 1882), 81.

9. Schlegel, *The Philosophy of History*, trans. James Burton Robertson (London, 1890), 153; and *Lectures on the History of Literature, Ancient and Modern* (London, 1876), 107ff.

10. See Thomas R. Trautman, *Ayrans and British India* (Berkeley, 1997).

11. Ibid., 41.

12. Ibid., 289.

13. Stephen G. Alter, *Darwinism and the Linguistic Image: Language, Race, and Natural Theology in the Nineteenth Century* (Baltimore, 1999).

14. W. H. C. Frend, *The Archeology of Early Christianity* (London, 1996), 37.

15. Jean Lacouture, *Champollion: une vie de lumières* (Paris, 1988); also Johannes Friedrich, *Extinct Languages*, trans. Frank Gaynor (New York, 1957), and P. E. Cleator, *Lost Languages* (New York, 1959).

16. Chateaubriand, *Essai sur les révolutions* and *Génie du christianisme*, ed. Maurice Regard (Paris, 1978), 136.

17. Ibid., 473.

18. Ibid., 843.

19. Ibid., 471.

20. George Stocking, "French Anthropology in 1800," *Race, Culture and Evolution* (Chicago, 1968), 13–41; and see Robert Sole, *Les Savants de Bonaparte* (Paris, 1998).

21. See D. R. Kelley, "Mythistory in the Age of Ranke," *Leopold von Ranke and the Shaping of the Historical Profession*, ed. G. Iggers and J. Powell (Syracuse, 1989), 3–20 and 181–185; also Heinz Gockel, *Mythos und Poesie: Zur Mythosbegriff in Aufklärung und Frühromantik* (Frankfurt, 1981), and the texts in Burton Feldman and Robert D. Richardson, trans., *The Rise of Modern Mythology, 1680–1860* (Bloomington, 1972).

22. Herder, "On the Modern Usage of Mythology," *Selected Early Works*, trans. Ernest A. Menze (University Park, Pa., 1992), 227.

23. Schelling, *Einleitung in der Philosophie der Mythologie*, trans. in *The Rise of Modern Mythology*, 327.

24. Fontenelle, *De l'Origine des fables*, ed. J. R. Carré (Paris, 1932); and Rosalba di Napoli, "La *Histoire des Oracles* di Fontenelle e la critica alla superstizione: Polemiche e prima recenzione (1680, 1707)," *Studi filosofici*, 16 (1993), 89–121. See also Joachimus Hasenmüllerus, *Disputatio Philosophica de Fabulis et Mythologica* (n.p., 1705), bound in the British library copy with other dissertations concerning mythology.

25. Banier, *The Mythology and Fables of the Ancients Explain'd from their History*, translation (London, 1739), x, 56.

26. *The New Science of Giambattista Vico*, trans. T. G. Bergin and M. H. Fisch (Ithaca, 1948), par. 347.

27. Burnett, *Archeologiae philosophicae sive doctrina de rerum originibus* (London, 1692), 94.

28. Brosses, *Du Culte des dieux fétiches* (1760), trans. in *The Rise of Modern Mythology*, 170.

29. Blackwell, *An Enquiry into the Life and Writings of Homer* (London, 1735), 233.

30. Schelling, *System of Transcendentalism*, in *The Rise of Modern Mythology*, 322.

31. A. L. Heeren, *Christian Gottlieb Heyne biographisch dargestellt* (Göttingen, 1813), 185; and see Peter G. Bietenholz, *Historia and Fabula: Myths and Legends in Historical Thought from Antiquity to the Modern Age* (Leiden, 1994), 280–288.

32. Ibid., 197–198.

33. Cited in K. O. Müller, *Introduction to a Scientific System of Mythology*, trans. J. Leitsch (London, 1844), 256.

34. Heyne, "An Interpretation of the Language of Myths . . . ," in *The Rise of Modern Mythology*, 223.

35. Hermann, *Handbuch der Mythologie aus Homer und Hesiod* (Berlin, 1787–1795).

36. Wolf, *Prolegomena to Homer (1795)*, trans. A. Grafton, G. Most, and J. Zetzel (Princeton, 1985), 155.

37. Creuzer, *Die historische Kunst der Griechen* (Leipzig, 1803); and see Momigliano, "Friedrich Creuzer and Greek Historiography," *Studies on Modern Scholarship* (Berkeley, 1994), 1–14; Manfred Frank, *Der kommende Gott: Vorlesungen über die neue Mythologie* (Frankfurt, 1982), 88–95; and Andrew von Hendy, *The Construction of Myth* (Bloomington, 2002).

38. Creuzer, *Symbolik und Mythologie der alten Völker, besonders der Griechen* (Leipzig, 1810–1812).

39. Opening sentence of *Young Joseph*.

40. Michelet, *Origines du droit français*, in *Oeuvres complètes*, vol. 3, ed. P. Viallaneix (Paris, 1973), 604ff; and see D. R. Kelley, "Ancient Verses on New Ideas: Legal Tradition and the French Historical School," *History and Theory*, 26 (1987), 319–338; also in *The Writing of History*.

41. Chassan, *Essai sur la symbolique du droit, précédé d'une introduction sur la poésie du droit primitif* (Paris, 1847), xxiii.

42. Ibid., cxxiii.

43. Müller, *Comparative Mythology*, ed. A. Smyth Palmer (New York, 1909), 140; *Life and Letters of the Right Honorable Friedrich Max Müller*, vol. 1 (London, 1902), 184; and see Trautmann, *Aryans and British India*, 172.

44. Dilthey, "Schleiermacher's Hermeneutical System in Relation to Earlier Protestant Hermeneutics," *Hermeneutics and the Study of History*, trans. Rudolf A. Makkreel and Frithjof Rodi (Princeton, 1996), 61.

45. Reimarus, *Fragments*, ed. Charles H. Talbert (Philadelphia, 1970); and Albert Schweizer, *The Quest of the Historical Jesus: A Critical Study of Its Progress from Reimarus to Wrede*, trans. W. Montgomery (Baltimore, 1998).

46. *Heterodoxy, Spinozism, and Free Thought in Early-Eighteenth-Century Europe: Studies on the Traité des trois importeurs*, ed. Silvia Berti, Françoise Charles-Daubert, and Richard H. Popkin (Dordrecht, 1996).

47. Anna-Ruth Löwenbrück, "Johann Michael Michaelis et les débuts de la critique biblique," *Le siècle des Lumières et la Bible*, ed. Yvon Belaval and Dominique Bourel (n.p., n.d.).

48. Wolf, *Prolegomena to Homer (1795)*, 227; and see Giuseppe D'Alessandro, *L'Illuminismo dimenticato: Johann Gottfried Eichhorn (1752–1827) e il suo tempo* (Naples, 2000).

49. Ibid., 25.

50. Schleiermacher, *Luke: A Critical Study*, trans. Connop Thirlwall (Lewiston, n.d.), 2.

51. Friedrich Meinecke, *Historicism: The Rise of a New Historical Outlook*, trans. J. E. Anderson (London, 1972), 204; and see especially Christian Hartlich and Walter Sachs, *Der Ursprung des Mythosbegriffes in der modernen Bibelwissenschaft* (Tübingen, 1952).

52. Strauss, *The Life of Jesus Critically Examined*, trans. George Eliot (London, 1982), preface.

53. Baur, *Symbolik und Mythologie oder die Naturreligion des Alterthums* (Stuttgart, 1824); and see Richard S. Cromwell, *David Friedrich Strauss and His Place in Modern Thought* (Fair Lawn, N.J., 1974).

54. See John Edward Toews, *Hegelianism: The Path toward Dialectical Humanism, 1805–1841* (Cambridge, 1980), 165–175, 255–287.

55. Strauss, *The Christ of Faith and the Jesus of History,* ed. and trans. Leander E. Keck (Philadelphia, 1977), 20.

56. Ibid., 61.

57. Grote, *Greece,* vol. 1 (New York, 1899), viii and 351.

58. A. G. Dickens and John M. Tonlin, *The Reformation in Historical Thought* (Cambridge, Mass., 1985), and on *historia sacra,* Friedrich Wilhelm Nettberg, *Kirchengeschichte Deutschlands* (Göttingen, 1846).

59. Ranke, *History of the Reformation in Germany (1839–47),* trans. Sarah Austin (London, 1905), 263.

60. Janssen, *History of the German People at the Close of the Middle Ages,* vol. 13, trans. A. M. Christie (London, 1909), 423–470.

61. Janssen, *An meine Kritiker, nebst Ergänzungen und Erläuterungen zu den ersten drei Bänden meiner Geschichte des deutschen Volkes* (Freiburg, 1891²).

62. Möhler, *Symbolism, or Exposition of the Doctrinal Differences between Catholics and Protestants as Evidenced by Their Symbolical Writings,* trans. James Burton Robertson (London, 1906⁵).

63. Joseph Fitzer, *Moehler and Baur in Controversy, 1832–38: Romantic-Idealist Assessment of the Reformation and Counter-Reformation* (Tallahassee, 1974).

64. Ferdinand Christian Baur, *On the Writing of Church History,* ed. and trans. Peter C. Hodgson (Oxford, 1968).

65. Neander, *History of the Planting and Training of the Christian Church by the Apostles,* vol. 1, trans. J. E. Ryland (London, 1859), vi (preface of 1832).

66. Harnack, *History of Dogma,* trans. Neil Buchanan, 6 vols. (New York, 1958), 1: 34.

67. Ibid., vol. 7, 274.

68. Döllinger, *Addresses on Historical and Literary Subjects,* trans. Margaret Warre (London, 1894), 15, 42.

69. Acton, "Döllinger's Historical Work," in *Essays in the Study and Writing of History,* ed. J. Rufus Fears (Indianapolis, 1985), 418.

70. Johann Sebastian Drey, *Brief Introduction to the Study of Theology with Reference to the Scientific Standpoint and the Catholic System,* trans. Michael J. Himes (Notre Dame, 1994).

71. Acton, "Döllinger's Historical Work," 428.

72. Döllinger, *Addresses,* 210–242.

73. Oliver Elton, *Frederick Powell: A Life,* vol. 2 (Oxford, 1906), 27.

74. Döllinger, *Fables Respecting the Popes of the Middle Ages,* trans. Alfred Plummer (London, 1871).

75. Döllinger, *Studies in European History,* trans. Margaret Warre (London, 1890), 75.

76. Ibid., 144.

77. See Owen Chadwick, *Acton and History* (Cambridge, 1998), 73.

78. Acton, manuscript cited in *Essays in Religion,* 621.

79. Meiners, *Geschichte der Entstehung und Entwickelung der hohen Schulen unsers Erdtheils* (Göttingen, 1802), 1.

80. Thomas Cooper, *Thesaurus linguae Romanae et Brittanicae* (London, 1565): "*Literatura:* Grammar: learning writing: cunning." In general, see Adrian Marino, *The Biography of the Idea of Literature from Antiquity to the Baroque,* trans. Virgil Stanciu and Charles M. Carlton (Albany, 1996).

81. Jonsius, *De Scriptoribus historiae philosophiae libri I* [1659] (Jena, 1716); and see also B. G. Struve, *Introductio in notitiam rei literariae et usum bibliothecarum* (Jena, 1710); J. F. Reimann, *Versuch einer Einleitung in die historiam literariam antediluvianum* (Halle, 1709); C. A. Heumann, *Conspectus Reipublicae litterariae sive via ad historiam literariam iuventuti studiosae* (Hannover, 1718); Gottlieb Stolles, *Anleitung zur Historie der Gelahrheit* (Jena, 1727) and *Introductio in historiam litterarium* (Jena, 1728); Nicholas Gundling, *Historie der Gelahrheit* (Frankfurt, 1734); Ludwig Wachner, *Versuch einer Algemeinen Geschichte der Literatur* (Lemgo, 1793), who points to Polydore Vergil and especially Konrad Gesner as the pioneers of this genre; cf. also Gabriel Naudé, *Advice on Establishing a Library* [1627] (Berkeley, 1950); and on public opinion, Susan Crane, *Collecting and Historical Consciousness in Nineteenth-Century Germany* (Ithaca, 2000), 170.

82. C. S. M. Rademaker, *Life and Works of Gerardus Joannis Vossius (1577–1649)* (Assen, 1981).

83. Schlegel, *Lectures on the History of Literature,* 6.

84. Boureau-Deslandes, *Histoire critique de la philosophie* (Amsterdam, 1737), iii. In general, see Jean Dagen, *L'Histoire de l'esprit humain dans la pensée française de Fontenelle à Condorcet* (Strasbourg, 1977).

85. See Ulrich Johannes Schneider, *Philosophie und Universität: Historisierung der Vernunft im 19. Jahrhundert* (Hamburg, 1999), and "The Teaching of Philosophy at German Universities in the Nineteenth Century," *History of Universities,* 12 (1993), 197–338.

86. For example, J. C. Sturm (1679), J. Esperus (1695), A. A. Dysing (1698), and F. Gotter (1730).

87. See Hauspeter Marti, *Philosophische Dissertationen deutscher Universitäten* (Munich, 1982).

88. See especially Arno Borst, *Der Turmbau von Babel: Geschichte der Meinungen und Vielfalt der Spranchen und Völker,* 4 vols. (Munich, 1957–1963).

89. Borrichius, *De Causis diversitatis linguarum dissertatio* (Jena, 1704).

90. Adolf Harnack, *Geschichte der königlich preussische Akademie der Wissenschaften zu Berlin,* vol. 1 (Berlin, 1900), 409, 414.

91. Jean Sgard, ed., *Condillac et les problèmes du langage* (Geneva, 1982), and Pierre Juliard, *Philosophies of Language in Eighteenth-Century France* (The Hague, 1970); also Ronald Grimsley, *Sur l'Origine du langage* (Paris, 1971), including texts by Maupertuis, Turgot, and Maine de Biran.

92. Condillac, *Philosophical Writings,* trans. Franklin Philip (Hillsdale, N.J., 1982), *Treatise on Sensations,* vol. 3, ii, 3.

93. Hans Aarsleff, *From Locke to Saussure* (Minneapolis, 1983), 163; Isabel F. Knight, *The Geometric Spirit: The Abbé Condillac and the French Enlightenment* (New Haven, 1968).

94. Michaelis, *A Dissertation on the Influence of Opinions on Language and of Language on Opinions* (London, 1769), 2, 39.

95. Ibid., 12.

96. Hermann J. Cloeren, *Language and Thought: German Approaches to Analytical Philosophy in the Eighteenth and Nineteenth Centuries* (Berlin, 1988), 14.

97. Herder, *Selected Early Works,* 102 ("On Recent German Literature: First Collection of Fragments" [supplement to "Briefe über die neueste Literatur"; in *Deutsche Bibliothek*]); and see Ulrich Gaier, *Herders Sprachphilosophie und Erkenntniskritik* (Stuttgart, 1986).

98. Herder, ibid., 30 ("On Diligence in the Study of Several Learned Languages" [1764]), and 215 ("On the Modern Usage of Mythology").

99. Coleridge, *Aids to Reflection* (London, 1825), 6n.

100. Müller, *A History of the Literature of Ancient Greece,* vol. 1, trans. J. W. Donaldson (London, 1859), 4.

101. Hand Arens, *Sprachwissenschaft: Der Gang ihrer Entwicklung von der Antike bis zur Gegenwart* (Freiberg, 1969).

102. Humboldt, *On Language: The Diversity of Human Language-Structure and Its Influence on the Mental Development of Mankind,* trans. Peter Heath (Cambridge, 1988), 21.

103. Ibid., 63, 64.

104. Gervinus, *Grundzüge der Historik* (Leipzig, 1837), and Wachsmuth, *Entwurf einer Theorie der Geschichte* (Halle, 182); also Horst Blanke, *Historiographiegeschichte als Historik* (Stuttgart, 1991), 232, 235, and Ulrich Muhlack, "Universal History and National History: Eighteenth- and Nineteenth-Century German Historians and the Scholarly Community," *British and German Historiography: Traditions, Perceptions, and Transfers,* ed. Benedikt Stuchtey and Peter Wende (Oxford, 2000), 42.

105. Montesquieu, *De l'Esprit des lois,* vol. 30, 2.

106. Otto Gierke, *Natural Law and the Theory of Society, 1500 to 1800,* trans. Ernest Barker (Cambridge, 1934); Hans Thieme, "Der Zeit der späten Naturrechts," *Zeitschrift der Savigny- Stiftung für Rechtsgeschichte,* Ger. Abt., 56 (1936), 202–263; and Peter Stein, *Legal Evolution: The Story of an Idea* (Cambridge, 1980).

107. Peter Hanns Reill, *The German Enlightenment and the Rise of Historicism* (Berkeley, 1975), 184; and see Herbert Butterfield, *Man on His Past* (Cambridge, 1955).

108. Cambacérès, *Discours sur la science social* (1789); and see Georges Gusdorf, *Les Sciences humaines,* vol. 8 (1978), 401; Sergio Moravia, *Il Pensiero degli Idéologues: Scienza e filosofia in Francia (1780–1815)* (Florence, 1974), 746; and B. W. Head, *Ideology and Social Science: Destutt de Tracy and French Liberalism* (The Hague, 1985), 109; also D. R. Kelley, *Historians and the Law in Postrevolutionary France* (Princeton, 1984).

109. James Q. Whitman, *The Legacy of Roman Law in the German Romantic Era: Historical Vision and Legal Change* (Princeton, 1990), 205–206; Theodore Zilkowski, *Roman Romanticism and Its Institutions* (Princeton, 1990); and see Giuliano Marino, *L'Opera di Gustav Hugo* (Milan, 1969).

110. Treitschke, *History of Germany in the Nineteenth Century,* trans. Eden and Cedar Paul, ed. Gordon Craig (Chicago, 1975), 19.

111. Dilthey, "Friedrich Christoph Schlosser and the Problem of Universal History" (1862), in *Hermeneutics and the Study of History,* ed. Rudolf A. Makkreel and Frithjof Rodi (Princeton, 1966), 323, 298.

112. Heeren, *A Manual of the History of the Political System of Europe and Its Colonies* (1809; Eng trans. London, 1833, 1846), and *Historical Researches,* 57.

113. Heeren, *Historical Researches into the Politics, Intercourse, and Trade of the Carthaginians, Ethiopians, and Egyptians* (Eng. trans. Oxford, 1832), xvi (preface 1825).

114. Creuzer, *Die historische Kunst der Griechen,* ed. J. Keyser (Leipzig, 1845²), 175.

115. Ulrici, *Characteristik der antiken Historiographie* (Berlin, 1833), Vorrede.

Chapter 4: British Initiatives

1. Hume, "Of the Study of History," in *Versions of History from Antiquity to the Enlightenment,* ed. D. R. Kelley (New Haven, 1991), 459.

2. Robertson, *History of the Reign of Charles V,* in Kelley, *Versions of History,* 471.

3. Hutcheson, *On Human Nature,* ed. Thomas Mautner (Cambridge, 1993), "An Augural Lecture on the Social Nature of Man," 147.

4. Dunbar, *Essays on the History of Mankind in Rude and Cultivated Ages* (Dublin, 1782), 94; and cf. the less optimistic view of Gilbert Stuart, *View of Society in Its Progress from Rudeness to Refinement* (Edinburgh, 1792); also J. G. A. Pocock, "Cambridge Paradigms and Scotch Philosophers: A Study of the Relations between the Civic Humanist and the Civil Jurisprudential Interpretation of Eighteenth-Century Thought," in *Wealth and Virtue: The Shaping of Political Economy in the Scottish Enlightenment,* ed. Istvan Hont and Michael Ignatieff (Cambridge, 1983), 235–252; and David Spadafora, *The Idea of Progress in Eighteenth-Century Britain* (New Haven, 1990).

5. Ferguson, *An Essay on the History of Civil Society,* ed. Fania Oz-Salzberger (Cambridge, 1995), 161–163; and see Malcolm Jack, *Corruption and Progress: The Eighteenth-Century Debate* (New York, 1989).

6. Robertson, *The History of America,* vol. 1 (Dublin, 1777), 401.

7. Colin Kidd, *Subverting Scotland's Past: Scottish Whig Historians and the Creation of an Anglo-British Identity* (Cambridge, 1993), and J. G. A. Pocock, *Barbarism and Religion,* vol. 2, *Narratives of Civil Government* (Cambridge, 1999), 258–305.

8. Robertson, *The History of Scotland,* vol. 1 (Philadelphia, 1811⁵), 146.

9. Whitaker, *The Genuine History of the Britons Asserted in a Full and Candid Refutation of Mr. Macpherson's Introduction to the History of Great Britain and Ireland* (Cambridge, 1772), 7.

10. Robertson, *History of Scotland,* 173.

11. Ronald L. Meek, *Social Sciences and the Noble Savage* (Cambridge, 1976), and *Smith, Marx, and After* (London, 1977).

12. Smith, *Lectures on Jurisprudence,* ed. R. L. Meek, D. D. Raphael, and P. G. Stein (Oxford, 1978), 201, 459.

13. John Millar, *The Origin of the Distinction of Ranks* (London, 1779 [1771]), and William Russell, *The History of Ancient Europe with a View of the Revolutions in Asia and Africa* (London, 1793), 11; and in general Ronald L. Meek, *Social Science and the Noble Savage.*

14. Ferguson, *An Essay,* 75.

15. Millar, *The Origin of the Distinction of Ranks,* 4.

16. Monboddo, *Of the Origin and Progress of Language* (Edinburgh, 1773), vol. 1, 189ff; vol. 2, 262ff.

17. See Ian Simpson Ross, *Lord Kames and the Scotland of His Day* (Oxford, 1972); William C. Lehman, *Henry Home, Lord Kames, and the Scottish Enlightenment* (The Hague, 1971); and David Lieberman, "The Legal Needs of a Commercial Society: The Jurisprudence of Lord Kames," *Wealth and Virtue: The Shaping of Political Economy in the Scottish Enlightenment,* ed. Istvan Hont and Michael Ignatieff (Cambridge, 1983), 203–234.

18. Kames, *Historical Law-Tracts* (Edinburgh, 1861²).

19. Monboddo, "Of the Introduction of the Feudal Law into Scotland," in *Essays upon Several Subjects concerning British Antiquities* (London, 1799²).

20. Stewart, "Dissertation First: Exhibiting a General View of the Progress of Metaphysical, Ethical, and Political Philosophy since the Revival of Letters in Europe," in *Works,* vol. 1, ed. William Hamilton (Edinburgh, 1854); and see Knud Haakonssen, "From Moral Philosophy to Political Economy: The Contribution of Dugald Stewart," *Philosophers of the Scottish Enlightenment,* ed. V. Hope (Edinburgh, 1984), 211–232; and Nicholas Phillipson, "The Pursuit of Virtue in Scottish University Education: Dugald Stewart and Scottish Moral Philosophy in the Enlightenment," *Universities, Society, and the Future,* ed. N. Phillipson (Edinburgh, 1983), 82–101.

21. Stewart, "Dissertation First," 14–18.

22. Ibid., 28.

23. See J. H. J. Van Der Pot, *De Periodisierung der Geschiedenis: en Overzicht der Theorieën* (The Hague, 1951).

24. Wilfried Nippel, "Gibbon and German Historiography," *British and German Historiography: Traditions, Perceptions, and Transfers,* ed. Benedikt Stuchtey and Peter Wende (Oxford, 2000), 68–69.

25. Apthorp, *Letters on the Prevalence of Christianity* (1778), 25.

26. Chelsum, *Remarks on the Two Last Chapters of Mr. Gibbon's History,* vol. 1 (1778), xiii, and *A Reply to Mr. Gibbon's Vindication* (1785), 146.

27. Gibbon, *The History of the Decline and Fall of the Roman Empire,* vol. 2, ed. William Smith, with notes by Milman, Guizot, and Wenk (New York, n.d.), 72.

28. Ibid., 112, 131.

29. Milman, *History of Latin Christianity* (London, 1872³), vi.

30. Milman, *The History of the Jews* (London, 1863³), xxx.

31. Merivale, *A General History of Rome B.C. 753–A.D. 425* (New York, 1875), x.

32. Hare, *Guesses at Truth by Two Brothers* (London, 1847), 169; and see Klaus Dockhorn, *Der Deutsche Historismus in England: Ein Beitrag zur Englischen Geistesgeschichte des 19. Jahrhunderts* (Göttingen, 1950), 17ff.

33. *Letters Literary and Theological of Connop Thirlwall,* ed. J. J. S. Perowne and L. Stokes (London, 1881), 49; and see John Connop Thirlwall, Jr., *Connop Thirlwall: Historian and Neologian* (London, 1936).

34. Macaulay, *Selected Letters,* 147 (Dec. 13, 1834). Neither Thirlwall nor Hare is listed in the biographical directory of W. C. Lubenow, *The Cambridge Apostles, 1820–1914* (Cambridge, 1998).

35. Hare, *A Vindication of Niebuhr's History of Rome from the Charges of the*

Quarterly Review (Cambridge, 1829), 31, 34; in general, see Dockhorn, *Der Deutsche Historismus,* and Norman Vance, "Niebuhr in England: History, Faith, and Order," *British and German Historiography,* ed. Stuchtey and Sende, 87ff.

36. Arnold, *The History of Rome* (New York, 1861 [1840]), preface; and see Duncan Forbes, *The Liberal Anglican Idea of History* (Cambridge, 1952).

37. *Letters of the Right Hon. Sir George Cornwell Lewis* (London, 1870), 312.

38. Mitford, *The History of Greece* (London, 1829²), 119.

39. Hare, *Guesses at Truth,* 71.

40. Grote, *Greece,* vol. 1 (New York, 1899), viii; and see Arnaldo Momigliano, "George Grote and the Study of Greek History," *Studies on Modern Scholarship* (Berkeley, 1994), 15–31; also M. L. Clarke, *George Grote: A Biography* (London, 1962).

41. Ibid., 351.

42. Ibid., 423.

43. See Johann Friedrich, *Extinct Languages,* trans. Frank Gaynor (New York, 1957), and P. E. Cleator, *Lost Languages* (New York, 1959).

44. Heeren, *Historical Researches into the Politics, Intercourse, and Trade of the Principal Nations of Antiquity,* English translation (London, 1847), 125.

45. Rawlinson, *The Five Great Monarchies of the Ancient Eastern World* (New York, n.d.).

46. Daniel, *The Origins and Growth of Archeology* (Harmondsworth, 1967), 126.

47. See below, Chapter 10.

48. Glynn Daniel and Colin Renfrew, *The Idea of Prehistory* (Edinburgh, 1988), 32; John Reader, *Missing Links: The Hunt for Earliest Man* (New York, 1981), and Peter J. Bowler, *The Invention of Progress: The Victorians and the Past* (Oxford, 1989).

49. Kelley, *Faces,* 182–187.

50. R. J. Smith, *The Gothic Bequest: Medieval Institutions in British Thought, 1688–1863* (Cambridge, 1987); and see Hugh A. MacDougall, *Racial Myth in English History: Trojans, Teutons, and Anglo-Saxons* (Montreal, 1982).

51. Bridget Hill, *The Republican Virago: The Life and Times of Catharine Macaulay, Historian* (Oxford, 1992), 31.

52. Priestley, *Lectures on History and General Policy* (London, 1826), 234.

53. Henry, *The History of Great Britain,* vol. 1 (London, 1815 [1788]), xxxiv.

54. Ibid., 201.

55. Kelley, *Versions of History,* 465.

56. Turner, *The History of the Anglo-Saxons from the Earliest Period to the Norman Conquest* (Philadelphia, 1841).

57. Ibid., 37.

58. Ibid., 75.

59. Ibid., 112.

60. Donald F. Shea, *The English Ranke: John Lingard* (New York, 1969), and Edwin Jones, *The English Nation: The Great Myth* (Thrupp, Stroud, 1998), 168–217.

61. Smith, *The Gothic Bequest,* 136.

62. Lingard, *History of England from the First Invasion by the Romans* (Paris, 1840⁵), preface.

63. See Thomas Coonan, "John Lingard (1771–1851)," in *Some Modern Historians of Britain,* ed. Herman Ausubel et al. (New York, 1951), 11.

64. Lingard, *History of England,* 28.

65. Jones, *The English Nation,* 179.

66. Allen, *Inquiry into the Rise and Growth of the Royal Prerogative in England* (London, 1830); in general, see P. B. M. Blass, *Continuity and Anachronism: Parliamentary and Constitutional Development in Whig Historiography and in the Anti-Whig Reaction between 1890 and 1930* (The Hague, 1978).

67. Francis Palgrave, *The History of Normandy and of England* (London, 1951), 30; and see Smith, *The Gothic Bequest,* 164, and G. P. Gooch, *History and Historians in the Nineteenth Century* (London, 1952²), 164, 286.

68. Lappenberg, *A History of England under the Anglo-Saxon Kings,* vol. 1, trans. Benjamin Thorpe (London, 1845), 86; and see Elard Hugo Meyer, *Johann Martin Klappenberg: Eine biographische Schildering* (Hamburg, 1867), and more generally, Charles E. McClelland, *The German Historians and England: A Study in Nineteenth-Century Views* (Cambridge, 1971).

69. *John Mitchell Kemble and Jakob Grimm: A Correspondence, 1832–1852,* ed., trans. Raymond A. Wiley (Leiden, 1971); also Dockhorn, *Der Deutsche Historismus in England,* 125–131.

70. *Letters of William Stubbs, Bishop of Oxford, 1825–1901* (London, 1904), 77 (to Freeman, Dec. 1859); and Burrow, *A Liberal Descent: Victorian Historians and the English Past* (Cambridge, 1981), 162; also his *Evolution and Society: A Study in Victorian Social Theory* (Cambridge, 1966).

71. Kemble, *The Saxons in England: The History of the English Commonwealth till the Period of the Norman Conquest,* vol. 1 (London, 1876²), chapter 2, and appendix A.

72. See Steven Blackmore, *Burke and the Fall of Language: the French Revolution as Linguistic Event* (Hanover, 1988).

73. Hallam, *Constitutional History of England* (London, 1827), 1; and see Timothy Lang, *The Victorians and the Stuart Heritage: Interpretations of a Discordant Past* (Cambridge, 1995), 23 ff.

74. Hallam, *Constitutional History of England,* preface.

75. Macaulay, *Critical, Historical and Miscellaneous Essays and Poems,* vol. 1 (New York, n.d.), 312; and see John Clive, *Macaulay: The Shaping of the Historian* (New York, 1973).

76. Macaulay, *Essays,* 340, 344; and cf. *The History of England from the Accession of James II* (New York, n.d.), 340, 344.

77. Macaulay, *Essays,* 11 n. 29.

78. Hallam, *View of the State of Europe during the Middle Ages,* 2 vols. (New York, 1904), 2:521–522, 525; and see Lang, *Victorians,* 54.

79. Hallam, *Middle Ages,* vol. 2, 919.

80. Hallam, ibid., vol. 1, 110.

81. Hallam, ibid., vol. 2, 581 ff; cf. Herodotus, 3.80.

82. Stubbs, *Select Charters* (Oxford, 1921⁹), 235.

83. Hallam, *Middle Ages,* vol. 2, 1084.

84. Ibid., 596.

85. Ibid., 698.

86. Ibid., 858–859.

87. Scott, *Chronicles of the Canongate,* introduction (Oct. 1, 1827).

88. Scott, *Waverly* (last rev. ed.), general preface.

89. See Scott, *Kenilworth,* n. 1.

90. Scott, *The Antiquary.*

91. Scott, *Waverly,* general preface; and chapter 21.

92. Scott, *The Antiquary,* advertisement.

93. Scott, *Ivanhoe,* dedicatory epistle.

94. A. Dwight Culler, *The Victorian Mirror of History* (New Haven, 1985), 20ff, and Ann Rigney, *Imperfect Histories: The Elusive Past and the Legacy of Romantic Historicism* (Ithaca, 2001).

95. Meinecke, *Historicism: The Rise of a New Historical Outlook,* trans. J. E. Anderson (London, 1972), 202.

96. Scott, *Ivanhoe,* dedicatory epistle ("1817").

97. Wardour, like Dryasdust and his friend and also antiquarian, Jonathan Oldbuck, figure as characters in Scott's *Antiquary,* all three modeled no doubt on acquaintances of Scott.

98. Culler, *Victorian Mirror of History,* on Scott and Macaulay in particular.

99. Carlyle, "Walter Scott," in *Critical and Miscellaneous Essays* (New York, 1901), vol. 4, 22.

100. *Lettres inédites de J. C. L. de Sismondi,* ed. Saint-René Taillandier (Paris, 1863), 305.

101. *Ecrits de jeunesse* (Paris, 1959), 315.

102. George Otto Trevelyan, *The Life and Letters of Lord Macaulay* (London, 1886²), 21; and see Clive, *Macaulay.*

103. Trevelyan, *Life and Letters,* 95.

104. Macaulay, "History" (1828), in Macaulay, *Essays,* 270–309.

105. Macaulay, *History,* 191; and see Hamburger, *Macaulay and the Whig Tradition* (Chicago, 1976), and H. A. L. Fisher, "The Whig Historians," *Pages from the Past* (Oxford, 1939), 40–92.

106. Clive, *Macaulay,* 478; Trevelyan, *Life and Letters,* 404 (to T. F. Ellis, June 12, 1841); 319 (to Ellis, Dec. 30, 1835).

107. Trevelyan, *Life and Letters,* 528 (diary, July 1, 1849).

108. Ibid., 387.

109. Macaulay, *Essays,* vol. 1, 310 (review of Hallam's *Constitutional History*).

110. Ibid., 307.

111. Trevelyan, *Life and Letters,* 142, 316.

112. Ibid., 533, 689.

113. Macaulay, *History,* vol. 1, 5.

114. Ibid., 20.

115. Ibid., 36.

116. Ibid., 103.

117. Cited in Hamburger, *Macaulay,* 44.

118. Macaulay, *History,* vol. 1, 253.

119. Ibid., 316; and see I. Bernard Cohen, *Revolution in Science* (Cambridge, Mass., 1987), note citing Macaulay's comment.

120. Macaulay, *History,* vol. 1, 333.

121. See Charles Firth, *A Commentary on Macaulay's History of England* (London, 1938), 35, 285.

122. John Kenyon, *The History Men: Macaulay, Carlyle, Buckle, Acton Stubbs, Namier, Tawney, Elton* . . . (London, 1983), 73; and *Acton in America: The American Journal of Sir John Acton, 1853,* ed. S. W. Jackman (Shepardstown, 1979), 65.

123. Mahon, *History of the War of the Spanish Succession* (London, 1833), reviewed by Macaulay; *History of England, Comprising the Reign of Queen Anne until the Peace of Utrecht* (London, 1870); *History of England from the Peace of Utrecht to the Peace of Versailles, 1713–1783* (London, 1836–1853).

124. *The Selected Letters of Thomas Babington Macaulay,* ed. Thomas Pinney (Cambridge, 1974), 53.

125. Kenyon, *The History Men,* 72.

126. *Letters of Lord Acton to Mary, Daughter of the Right Hon. W. E. Gladstone* (London, 1904), 210 (April 1885).

Chapter 5: German Impulses

1. Schlegel, *A Course of Lectures on Modern History,* trans. Lindsey Purcell and R. H. Whitelock (London, 1878), 1.

2. Wolf, *Prolegomena to Homer 1795,* trans. Anthony Grafton, Glen W. Most, and James E. G. Zetzel (Princeton, 1995), 137, etc.; Anthony Grafton, "Prolegomenon to Friedrich August Wolf," in *Defenders of the Text: The Traditions of Scholarship in an Age of Science, 1450–1800* (Cambridge, Mass., 1991), 214–243, 308–319.

3. Treitschke, *History of Germany in the Nineteenth Century,* 7 vols., trans. E. and C. Paul (London, 1915–19), 2: 70, 313.

4. Suzanne L. Marchand, *Down from Olympus: Archeology and Philhellenism in Germany, 1750–1996* (Princeton, 1996), 43; and see George Grote, *Greece,* 2 vols. (New York, 1899), 1: 24–41.

5. Boeckh, *Encyclopädie und Methodologie der philologischen Wissenschaften,* ed. Ernst Bratuscheck (Leipzig, 1886).

6. Arnaldo Momigliano, "K. O. Müller's *Prolegomena zu einer wissenschaftlichen Mythologie* and the Meaning of Myth," *Settimo Contributio alla storia degli studi classici e del mondo antiquo* (Rome, 1984), 271–286; and "A Return to Eighteenth-Century 'Etruscheria': K. O. Müller," *Studies on Modern Scholarship* (Berkeley, 1994), 302–314.

7. Müller, *A History of the Literature of Ancient Greece,* trans. J. W. Donaldson (London, 1858), 1: 4.

8. Ibid., 1: 352ff, 2: 118.

9. Marchand, *Down from Olympus,* 77–91.

10. David A. Traill, *Schliemann of Troy: Treasure and Deceit* (New York, 1995); and see William M. Calder, III, "A New Picture of Heinrich Schliemann," in *Myth, Scandal, and History,* ed. William Calder and David Traill (Detroit, 1986).

11. Marchand, *Down from Olympus,* 122–123.

12. Droysen, letter to Welcker, cited by Helmut Berve, introduction to Droysen, *Geschichte Alexanders des Grossen* (Stuttgart, 1941³), xviii; and see Felix Gilbert, "Johann Gustav Droysen," in *History: Choice and Commitment* (Harvard, 1977), 17–38; Benedetto Bravo, *Philologie, histoire, philosophie de l'histoire: étude sur J. G. Droysen, historien de l'antiquité* (Wroclaw, 1968); and Jean Grondin, *Introduction to Philosophical Hermeneutics*, trans. Joel Weinsheimer (New Haven, 1994), 79.

13. Boeckh, *Enzyklopädie und Methodologie der philologischen Wissenschaften,* in *The Hermeneutics Reader,* ed. Kurt Mueller-Vollmer (Oxford, 1986), 138.

14. Droysen, *Grundriss der Historik* (Leipzig, 1875), 26; E. Benjamin Andrews, trans., *Outline of the Principles of History* (Boston, 1897), 32; and see Chr. D. Pflaum, *J. G. Droysens Historik in ihrer Bedeutung für die moderne Geschichtswissenschaft* (Gotha, 1907), and Jörn Rüsen, "Die sittliche Macht de Geschichte — Johan Gustav Droysen," in *Konfigurationen des Historismus* (Frankfurt, 1993), 226–275.

15. Droysen, *Grundriss der Historik,* 9.

16. Ibid., 38, 49.

17. Ibid., 38.

18. Bunsen, *Egypt's Place in Universal History,* trans. Charles H. Cottrell (London, 1848), 1: xi.

19. Duncker, *History of Greece,* trans. S. E. Alleyne (London, 1883).

20. Meyer, *Geschichte des Altertums* (Stuttgart, 1925⁵), 1: 1.

21. Treitschke, *History of Germany,* 2: 60.

22. *The Life and Letters of Barthold Georg Niebuhr,* trans. Susanne Winkworth (London, 1852²), 493.

23. Franz X. von Wegele, *Geschichte der deutschen Historiographie seit dem Auftreten des Humanismus* (Munich, 1885), 995; and Leonard Krieger, *Ranke: The Meaning of History* (Chicago, 1977), 3.

24. See especially Gerrit Walther, *Niebuhrs Forschung* (Stuttgart, 1993), and Gerhard Wirth, ed., *Barthold Georg Niebuhr: Historiker und Staatsmann* (Bonn, 1984); also Emery Neff, *The Poetry of History* (New York, 1947).

25. Winkworth, *Life and Letters,* 48.

26. Niebuhr, *The History of Rome,* trans. Julius Charles Hare and Connop Thirlwall (London, 1851), 1: 100.

27. Ibid., 240.

28. Niebuhr, *Lectures on Ancient History,* trans. Leonhard Schmitz (Philadelphia, 1852), 1: 37.

29. Niebuhr, *History of Rome,* 1: 2, 132.

30. Ibid., 1: 1.

31. Niebuhr, *Ancient History,* 1: 99.

32. Ibid., 1: 92.

33. Niebuhr, *History of Rome,* 1: 389.

34. Schlegel, review of Niebuhr's two volumes (1811–1812), in *Sämmtliche Werke* (Leipzig, 1847), 444–512.

35. Winkworth, *Life and Letters,* 501–502.

36. Ibid., 2: 244.

37. Arnaldo Momigliano, "Perizonius, Niebuhr, and the Early Roman Tradition," in

Essays in Ancient and Modern Historiography (Oxford, 1977), 231–251; and Renate Bridenthal, "Was There a Roman Homer? Niebuhr's Thesis and Its Critics," *History and Theory,* 11 (1972), 193–213.

38. Niebuhr, *History of Rome,* 1: 4.

39. Ibid., 1: 187.

40. Ibid., 1: 194.

41. Ibid., 1: 218.

42. Ibid., 1: 244, 310.

43. Ibid., 1: 223.

44. Ibid., 1:42.

45. Lewis, *An Inquiry into the Credibility of Early Roman History,* 2 vols. (London, 1855), 1: 230.

46. Toynbee, *A Study of History* (New York, 1962), 1: 4.

47. Mommsen, letter to Gustav Freytag (1877), cited by Alfred Heuss, "Theodor Mommsen als Geschichtsschreiber," in *Deutsche Geschichtswissenschaft um 1900,* ed. Notker Hammerstein (Stuttgart, 1988), 42.

48. Mommsen, *Reden und Aufsätze* (Berlin, 1905), 36 ("Antrittsrede" 1858). See Alfred Heuss, *Theodor Mommsen und das 19. Jahrhundert* (Kiel, 1956), and especially Lothar Wickert, *Theodor Mommsen: Eine Biographie,* 3 vols. (Frankfurt/a/M, 1959–1969).

49. Mommsen, *The History of Rome,* trans. William Purdie Dickson, 5 vols. (New York, 1908), 1: 52.

50. Ibid., 1: 106.

51. Ibid., 1: 188.

52. Ibid., 2: 102.

53. Mommsen, *The Provinces of the Roman Empire,* trans. T. Robert S. Broughton (Chicago, 1968), 6.

54. Mommsen, *History of Rome,* 3: 89.

55. Ibid., 4: 247.

56. Ibid., 5: 4.

57. Ibid., 5: 99.

58. Ibid., 2: 522.

59. Ibid., 5: 102.

60. Lionel Gossman, *Orpheus Philologus: Bachofen versus Mommsen on the Study of Antiquity,* American Philosophical Society, *Transactions,* 73.5 (1983), 21.

61. P. F. Stuhr (1838), cited by Bravo, *Philologie, histoire,* 167; and see the exaggerated argument of Martin Bernal, *Black Athena: The Afroasiatic Roots of Classical Civilization* (New Brunswick, 1987), 31, 308–318.

62. Nietzsche, *The Birth of Tragedy,* trans. Walter Kaufmann (New York, 1967), 41.

63. Bachofen, *Myth, Religion, and Mother Right,* trans. Ralph Manheim (Princeton, 1967), 13 ("My Life in Retrospect," written for Savigny); and see Peter G. Bietenholz, *Historia and Fabula: Myths and Legends in Historical Thought from Antiquity to the Modern Age* (Leiden, 1994), 350–368.

64. Strauss, *The Life of Jesus Critically Examined,* trans. George Eliot (London, 1892), 81.

65. Treitschke, *Politics,* trans. Blanche Dugdale and Torben de Bille (New York, 1916), 1: xxxiii. In general, Heinrich Ritter von Srbik, *Geist und Geschichte vom deutschen Humanismus bis zur Gegenwart,* 2 vols. (Munich, 1964), and Stefan Berger, *The Search for Normality: National Identity and Historical Consciousness in Germany since 1800* (Providence, 1997), 1–55.

66. Lamprecht, "Die Entwicklung der deutschen Geschichtswissenschaft vornehmlich seit Herder," *Alternative zu Ranke* (Leipzig, 1988), 320.

67. Acton, "The German Schools of History," in *Essays in the Study and Writing of History,* ed. J. Rufus Fears (Indianapolis, 1985), 326; and see von Srbik, *Geist und Geschichte,* 1: 222, with emphasis on the Austrian schools and on cultural history.

68. Hermann Heimpel, "Geschichtsvereine einst und jetzt," *Geschichtswissenschaft und Vereinswesen im 19. Jahrhundert,* ed. Hartmut Bookmann, et al. (Göttingen, 1972), 45–73; Susan Crane, *Collecting and Historical Consciousness in Early Nineteenth-Century Germany* (Ithaca, 2000), 15.

69. Meinecke, *Cosmopolitanism and the National State,* trans. Robert B. Kimber (Princeton, 1970), 79.

70. Dahlmann, *The Life of Herodotus,* trans. G. V. Cox (London, 1845), 25.

71. Droysen, *Vorlesungen über das Zeitalter der Freiheitskriege* (Gotha, 1886²), 13.

72. Theodore Ziolkowski, *German Romanticism and Its Institutions* (Princeton, 1990), 269.

73. Treitschke, *History of Germany,* 4: 136.

74. *Einige Worte über das Studium der vaterländischen Geschichte* (1810), 5; and see Crane, *Collecting,* 32–33.

75. Karl Obermann, "Heinrich Luden," in *Die deutsche Geschichtswissenschaft von Beginn des 19. Jahrhunderts bis zur Reichseinigung von oben* (Berlin, 1969), 95; Franz Herrmann, *Die Geschichtsauffassung Heinrich Ludens im Lichte der gleichzeitingen geschichtsphilosophischen Strömmingen* (Gotha, 1904); and Srbik, *Geist und Geschichte,* 1: 222.

76. K. G. W. Stenzel, *Gustav Adolf Harald Stenzels Leben* (Gotha, 1897).

77. Wegele, *Geschichte der deutschen Historiographie,* 1011.

78. Harry Bresslau, *Geschichte de Monumenta Germaniae Historiae* (Hannover, 1921); David Knowles, *Great Historical Enterprises* (London, 1962), 63–98; and Crane, *Collecting,* 81–91.

79. Ulrich Muhlack, "Universal History and National History: Eighteenth- and Nineteenth-Century German Historians and the Scholarly Community," in *British and German Historiography: Traditions, Perceptions, and Transfers,* ed. Benedikt Stuchtey and Peter Wende (Oxford, 2000), 37.

80. Gangolf Hübinger, *Georg Gottfried Gervinus: Historische Urteil und politische Kritik* (Göttingen, 1985), and Jonathan F. Wagner, *Germany's Nineteenth-Century Cassandra: The Liberal Federalist Georg Gottfried Gervinus* (New York, 1955).

81. For a list of historical journals (though without dates) see Crane, *Collecting,* 179–180.

82. Krieger, *Ranke,* 3; and see *Leopold von Ranke and the Shaping of the Historical Discipline,* ed. Georg G. Iggers and James Powell (Syracuse, 1990); *Leopold von Ranke*

und die moderne Geschichtswissenschaft, ed. Wolfgang Mommsen (Stuttgart, 1988); Srbik, *Geist und Geschichte,* 1: 239–292.

83. Ranke, *The Secret of World History,* ed. Roger Wines (New York, 1981), 48.

84. Ranke, *Tagebücher,* ed. Walther Peter Fuchs (Munich, 1964), 1: 110; see Carl Hinrichs, *Ranke und die Geschichtstheologie der Goethezeit* (Göttingen, 1954), and "Rankes Lutherfragment von 1817 und der Ursprung seines universalhistorischen Anschauung," in *Festschrift für Gerhard Ritter* (Tübingen, 1950), 299–321.

85. *Historisch-politische Zeitschrift* (Hamburg, 1832), 1: 1.

86. Ranke, *Tagebücher,* 241.

87. Ibid., 233 (1816–1817).

88. Ranke, *History of the Latin and Teutonic Nations from 1494 to 1514,* trans. Philip A. Ashworth (London, 1887), 173, 224.

89. Ranke, *Universal History,* ed. G. W. Prothero (New York, 1885), preface, xi.

90. Ranke, *Zur Kritik neuerer Geschichtschreiber* (Leipzig, 1824), on Guicciardini, Beaucaire, Mariana, Sleidan, Giovio, Commines, Seyssel, Pasquier, Machiavelli, and many others.

91. Ranke, *Secret of World History,* 76.

92. Konrad Repgen, "Über Rankes Diktum von 1824: 'Bloss sagen wie es eigentlich gewesen,'" *Historisches Jahrbuch,* 102 (1982), 439–449.

93. Preface to *The Histories of the Latin and Germanic Nations,* in Ranke, *The Theory and Practice of History,* ed. Georg G. Iggers and Konrad von Moltke (New York, 1973), 137; and see Bonnie G. Smith, *The Gender of History* (Cambridge, Mass., 1998), 116.

94. Ranke, *Theory and Practice of History,* 44, 42.

95. Ranke, *History of the Latin and Teutonic Nations.*

96. *A History of Serbia and the Serbian Revolution,* trans. Mrs. Alexander Kerr (London, 1848²).

97. Ranke, *The History of the Popes during the Last Four Centuries,* 3 vols., trans. Mrs. Foster (London, 1907), 1: 26.

98. Ranke, ibid., 2: 105.

99. Ibid., 2: 13.

100. Ranke, *History of the Reformation in Germany,* trans. Sarah Austin (London, 1905), ix.

101. Cf. Sleidan, *The General History of the Reformation of the Church,* trans. Edward Bohun (London, 1689), preface: "In the history of religion I would not omit what concerned the civil government because . . . they are interwoven with the other, so that it is not possible to separate them."

102. John B. Roney, *The Inside of History: Jean Henri Merle d'Aubigné and Romantic Historiography* (Westport, Conn., 1996).

103. Ranke, *Reformation,* 130, 132.

104. Ranke, *Memoirs of the House of Brandenburg and History of Prussia,* trans. Sir Alexander and Lady Duff Gordon (London, 1849), 1: 6.

105. Ranke, *Civil Wars and Monarchy in France in the Sixteenth and Seventeenth Centuries,* trans. M. A. Garvey (New York, 1853).

106. Ibid., 285.

107. Ranke, *A History of England Principally in the Seventeenth Century,* trans. G. W. Kitchin and C. W. Boase (Oxford, 1875).

108. Andrew Zimmerman, *Anthropology and Antihumanism in Imperial Germany* (Chicago, 2001), 39.

109. Ranke, *Universal History,* preface.

110. Fulvio Tessitore, "Ranke's 'Lutherfragment' und die Idee der Universalgeschichte," in *Leopold von Ranke,* ed. W. Mommsen, 37–71.

Chapter 6: French Novelties

1. Pim den Boer, *History as a Profession: The Study of History in France, 1818–1914,* trans. Arnold J. Pomerans (Princeton, 1998).

2. "L'Avenir de la science," in *Oeuvres complètes de Ernest Renan,* vol. 3, ed. Henriette Psichari (Paris, 1849), 834.

3. Chateaubriand, *Oeuvres complètes,* ed. Sainte-Beuve (Paris, 1861), vol. 9, *Etudes historiques,* 30; and cf. Thierry, *Dix ans d'études historiques* (Paris, 1868[11]), 20.

4. *Lettres inédites de J. C. L. de Sismondi,* ed. Saint-René Taillandier (Paris, 1863), 117.

5. Chateaubriand, *Considérations sur l'histoire de France* (Paris, 1840), 181.

6. Jullian, *Extraits des historiens français du XIXe siècle* (Paris, 1896[10]), xxxvi.

7. Jouffroy, "How Dogmas Come to an End," in *Specimens of Foreign Standard Literature,* vol. 2, ed. George Ripley (Boston, 1838), 121–142; and see Alan B. Spitzer, "Victor Cousin and the French Generation of 1820," in *From Parnassus: Essays in Honor of Jacques Barzun,* ed. Dora B. Wiener and William R. Keylor (New York, 1976), 177–194.

8. See B. Réizov, *L'Historiographie romantique française 1815–1830* (Moscow, n.d.); Jo Tollenbeek, *De Illusionisten: Geschiedenisen cultur in de Franse Romantiek* (Louvain, 2000); Ceri Crossley, *French Historians and Romanticism* (London, 1993); Jean Walch, *Les Maîtres de l'histoire 1815–1850* (Geneva, 1986); Stanley Mellon, *The Political Uses of History: A Study of Historians in the French Restoration* (Stanford, 1958); and Friedrich Engel-Janosi, *Four Studies in French Romantic Historical Writing* (Baltimore, 1955).

9. Eric Fauquet, *Michelet* (Paris, 1990), 159.

10. See Jean-Jacques Goblot, *La jeune France: le Globe et son groupe littéraire 1824–1830* (Paris, 1995).

11. See Douglas Johnson, *Guizot: Aspects of French History, 1787–1874* (London, 1963); Charles-H. Pouthas, *La Jeunesse de Guizot (1787–1814)* (Paris, 1936); Gabrielle de Broglie, *Guizot* (Paris, 1990); and Karl J. Weintraub, *Visions of Culture* (Chicago, 1966), 75–114.

12. Guizot, *Memoirs to Illustrate the History of My Time,* vol. 1, trans. J. W. Cole (London, 1858), 11.

13. Letter of Chateaubriand to Guizot (May 12, 1809); ibid., 361.

14. Chateaubriand, *Etudes historiques,* 1: 90.

15. Montalembert, *The Monks of the West from St. Benedict to St. Bernard,* Eng. trans. (New York, n.d.)

16. Guizot, *Memoirs*, vol. 1, 154.

17. Guizot, *History of the Origin of Representative Government in Europe*, trans. Andrew R. Scroble (London, 1852), 2.

18. Guizot, *Memoirs*, 377.

19. Guizot, *Representative Government*, 7.

20. Ibid., 3.

21. Guizot, *Memoirs*, vol. 1, 294.

22. Ibid., 323.

23. Ibid., 385.

24. Ibid., 387; Guizot, *Representative Government*, 12.

25. Guizot, *Representative Government*, 13–16.

26. Ibid., 302.

27. Ibid., 77.

28. Guizot, *The History of Civilization in Europe*, 3 vols., trans. William Hazlitt (London, 1997), 32.

29. Ibid., 11–12.

30. Ibid., 37.

31. Ibid., 48.

32. Ibid., 54.

33. Ibid., 66.

34. Ibid., 104.

35. Ibid., 109.

36. Ibid., 127.

37. Ibid., 112.

38. Ibid., 143.

39. Ibid., 207.

40. Guizot, *History of the English Revolution*, trans. William Hazlitt (London, 1846).

41. Guizot, *History of Civilization*, vol. 2, 182.

42. Ibid., 120.

43. Ibid., 147.

44. Ibid., vol. 3, 11.

45. Ibid., vol. 2, 4.

46. Jullian, *Extraits*, xiv.

47. Laurent Theis, "Guizot et les institutions de mémoire," in *Les Lieux de mémoire*, vol. 2, ed. Pierre Nora, *La Nation*, vol. 1 (Paris, 1984), 569–592.

48. Rulon Naphi Smithson, *Augustin Thierry: Social and Political Consciousness in the Evolution of a Historical Method* (Geneva, 1973), with further bibliography; Lionel Gossman, "Augustin Thierry and Liberal Historiography," in *Between History and Literature* (Cambridge, Mass., 1990), 83–151; and Ann Rigney, *Imperfect Histories: The Elusive Past and the Legacy of Romantic Historicism* (Ithaca, 2001), 83–88.

49. Thierry, *Lettres sur l'histoire de France* (Paris, 1868), preface.

50. Smithson, *Thierry*, 64.

51. Thierry, *Dix ans*, 13.

52. Thierry, *Lettres*, 65.

53. Ibid., 3.

54. Thierry, *Dix ans,* 9.

55. Thierry, *Tales of the Early Franks,* trans. M. F. O. Jenkins (University, Ala., 1977), 23.

56. Thierry, *Lettres,* 8; and see ibid.

57. Thierry, *Histoire de la conquête de l'Angleterre par les Normands,* vol. 1 (Paris, 1825), xi.

58. Thierry, *Essai sur l'histoire de la formation et des progrès du tiers état* (Paris, 1866⁴).

59. Thierry, *Lettres,* 204.

60. Thierry, "Notes sur quatorze historiens antérieurs à Mézeray," in *Dix ans,* 335–393.

61. See Charles Rearick, *Beyond the Enlightenment: Historians and Folklore in Nineteenth-Century France* (Bloomington, 1974), 62–81.

62. Thierry, *History of the Conquest of England by the Normans,* vol. 1, trans. William Hazlitt (London, 1847), xx.

63. Thierry, *Conquest of England,* 53.

64. Scott, *Ivanhoe,* chapter 1.

65. Guizot, *Memoirs,* vol. 2, 17.

66. Thierry, *Essai sur l'histoire . . . du tiers état* (Paris, 1866⁴), 87, 73.

67. Ibid., 182.

68. Ibid., 219.

69. Ibid., 128, 152.

70. Amédée Thierry, *Histoire des Gaulois depuis les temps les plus reculés jusqu'à l'entière soumission de la Gaule à la domination romaine* (Paris, 1827).

71. Mignet, *De la Féodalité, des institutions de Saint Louis* (Paris, 1821), 192, cited by Yvonne Kniebiehler, *Naissance des sciences humaines: Mignet et l'histoire philosophique au XIXᵉ siècle* (Paris, 1973), 32.

72. Michelet, *Journal,* vol. 1, ed. Paul Viallaneix (Paris, 1959), 357 (1841).

73. Roland Barthes, *Michelet,* trans. Richard Howard (New York, 1987), 17. In general, see Arthur Mitzman, *Michelet, Historian: Rebirth and Romanticism in Nineteenth-Century France* (New Haven, 1990); Lionel Gossman, "Jules Michelet and Romantic Historiography," *Between History and Literature,* 152–200; Eric Fauquet, *Michelet, ou la gloire du professeur d'histoire* (Paris, 1990); Gabrielo Monod, *La Vie et la pensée de Jules Michelet, 1798–1852* (Paris, 1923); Paul Villaneix, *La Voie royale: Etude sur l'idée de peuple dans l'oeuvre de Michelet* (Paris, 1959), and *Michelet, les travaux et les jours 1798–1874* (Paris, 1998).

74. Michelet, *Histoire de France,* preface of 1869, in *Oeuvres complètes,* vol. 4, ed. Paul Viallaneix (Paris, 1971), 11.

75. Michelet, *Journal,* vol. 1, ed. Paul Viallaneix (Paris, 1959), 116 (June 1834).

76. Michelet, *Cours au Collège de France,* 2 vols. (Paris, 1995), 1:416.

77. Michelet, *Ecrits de jeunesse* (Paris, 1959), 75.

78. Michelet, *Histoire romaine,* introduction, chapter 2, *Oeuvres complètes,* vol. 2, ed. Paul Viallaneix (Paris, 1972).

79. Michelet, *Journal,* vol. 1, 358 (1841).

80. Michelet, "Journal des idées," in *Ecrits de jeunesse* (Paris, 1959), 228.

81. Michelet, *Ecrits de jeunesse,* 229 (1824). Stewart, *Histoire abrégée des sciences metaphysiques, morales et politiques depuis la renaissance des lettres,* trans. J. A. Buchon (Paris, 1820), ded. to Cousin; see Michelet, *Oeuvres complétes,* vol. 1 (Paris, 1971), for his trans. of Vico's *La Science nouvelle* (1827).

82. Michelet, *Correspondance générale,* vol. 1, ed. Louis Le Guillou (Paris, 1994), 147.

83. Ibid., 215 (to Sismondi, 16 Sept. 1825).

84. Michelet, *Cours d'études historiques,* vol. 1 (Paris, 1842), xvi.

85. Michelet, *Correspondance,* vol. 1, 365 (May 27, 1827).

86. Michelet, *Journal,* 56; *Cours,* vol. 1, 84; *Correspondance,* vol. 4, 111 (article of Heine); and see Paul Viallaneix, *Michelet: Les travaux et les jours (1798–1874)* (Paris, 1998), 174.

87. Michelet, *Correspondance générale,* vol. 2, 548; and the similar criticism of Théodore Jouffroy, ibid., vol. 1, 613.

88. Michelet, *Correspondance,* vol. 2, 575.

89. Michelet, *Oeuvres complètes,* vol. 2, 679; and *Histoire romaine,* in ibid., 322.

90. Michelet, *Histoire romaine,* 379.

91. Ibid., 641.

92. Michelet, *Cours,* vol. 1, 359.

93. *Oeuvres choisies de Vico,* avant-propos, in *Oeuvres complètes,* vol. 1, 280; *Histoire romaine,* avant-propos; *Journal,* vol. 1, 388 (1842).

94. Michelet, *La Renaissance,* iii, alluding to Sallust (?), "faber est suae quisque fortunae."

95. Chateaubriand, *Etudes historiques* (Paris, 1831), preface.

96. Michelet, *Oeuvres complètes,* vol. 2, 217.

97. Michelet, *Journal,* vol. 1, 353.

98. Michelet, *The People,* trans. G. H. Smith (New York, 1846), 25; *Le Peuple* (Paris, 1979), 73.

99. Michelet, *Journal,* vol. 1, 161 (Oct. 1834).

100. Chateaubriand, *Etudes historiques* (Paris, 1831), preface.

101. Michelet, *Journal,* vol. 2, 211.

102. Michelet, "Rapport au ministre de l'instruction publique sur les bibliothèques et archives des départements du sud-ouest de la France," in *Oeuvres complètes,* vol. 3, 539–564.

103. Michelet, *Cours,* vol. 1, 483; cf. *Journal,* vol. 1, 52.

104. Michelet, *Cours,* vol. 2, 393.

105. Michelet, *Histoire de France,* preface of 1869.

106. Jullian, *Extraits,* lii.

107. Michelet, *Histoire de France,* in *Oeuvres complètes,* vol. 4, 11.

108. Michelet, letter to Charles Labitte (1841), in *Correspondance,* vol. 3, 487, referring to the *Imitation of Christ* as well as the career of "La Pucelle."

109. Michelet, *Histoire de France,* vol. 4, 1.

110. Michelet, *Cours,* vol. 1, 153; ibid., 73, 85.

111. Ibid., 108.

112. Michelet, *Journal,* vol. 1, 307 (July 1839).

113. Michelet, letter to Sainte-Beuve (1840?) in *Correspondance,* vol. 3, 216.

114. Michelet, *Journal,* vol. 1, 362 (June 1841).

115. Ibid., 384 (March 1842).

116. Michelet, *Cours,* vol. 2, 205–206.

117. Michelet, *Journal,* vol. 1, 392 (April 1842).

118. Ibid., 385 (1842).

119. Michelet, *Cours,* vol. 2, 144, "Or l'historien est prophèt (Richard Simon)."

120. Michelet, *Journal,* vol. 1, 326 (1840, a year in which only two undated entries appear).

121. Ibid., 516; and ibid., 517: "Adieu Eglise, adieu ma mère et ma fille; *adieu douces fontaines que me fûtes si amères. Tout ce que j'aimai et connu, je le quitte pour l'infine inconnu, pour la sombre profondeur d'où je sens, sans le savoir, le Dieu nouveau de l'avenir.*"

122. Michelet, *Cours,* vol. 2, 144.

123. Michelet, *Journal,* vol. 1, 506.

124. Michelet, *Spiritual Direction and Auricular Confession: Their History, Theory and Consequences* (Philadelphia, 1845), trans. of *Du Prêtre, de la femme, de la famille,* vii.

125. Michelet, *Cours,* vol. 1, 594–595.

126. Michelet, *Journal,* vol. 1, 290 (1839); *Cours,* vol. 1, 83 (1838).

127. Michelet, *Journal,* vol. 1, 657 (November 21, 1846).

128. Michelet, *Histoire de la révolution française,* vol. 1 (Paris, 1979), 43 (preface of 1868).

129. Michelet, *Historical View of the French Revolution,* trans. C. Cocks (London, 1848), 55.

130. Michelet, *French Revolution,* vol. 1, 217, 383.

131. Ibid., 11, 200.

132. Michelet, *Journal,* vol. 2, 43 (April 24, 1849); cf. ibid., vol. 1, 693 (26 June 1848).

133. Michelet, *Bible de l'humanité* (Paris, 1864).

134. Michelet, *Journal,* vol. 2, 154 (March 1851).

135. Ibid., 152.

136. Michelet, letter of April 5, 1540, in *Correspondance,* vol. 3, 221.

137. See Paul Bénichou, *Le Temps des prophètes: Doctrines de l'âge romantique* (Paris, 1977), 454–564.

138. Michelet, *Journal,* vol. 2, 226; *Oeuvres complètes,* vol. 16, ed. P. Viallaneix (Paris, 1980), 569ff.

139. Michelet, *Journal,* vol. 2, 242.

140. Michelet, *Histoire de France,* preface.

Chapter 7: German Ascendancy

1. In general, see Alphons Lhotsky, *Österreichische Historiographie* (Wien, 1962).

2. *Historisches Jahrbuche,* sponsored by the Görres-Gesellschaft and edited by Georg Hüffer.

3. Häusser, *Ueber die teutschen Geschichtschreiber vom Anfang des Frankenreichs bis auf die Hohenstaufen* (Heidelberg, 1830).

4. Dahlmann, *The Life of Herodotus*, trans. G. V. Cox (London, 1895 [1845]).

5. Cited in James Westfall Thompson, *A History of Historical Writing*, vol. 2 (New York, 1942), 188; and see Bonnie G. Smith, *The Gender of History* (Cambridge, Mass., 1998), 105.

6. See Wolfgang Weber, *Priester der Klio: Historisch-Sozialwissenschaftliche Studien zur Herkunft und Karriere deutsche Historiker und zur Geschichte der Geschichtswissenschaft 1800–1970* (Frankfurt, 1987); Stefan Berger, *The Search for Normality: National Identity and Historical Consciousness in Germany since 1800* (Providence, 1997); and Fritz K. Ringer, *The Decline of the German Mandarins: The German Academic Community, 1890–1933* (Cambridge, Mass., 1969), 97ff.

7. Thompson, *History*, vol. 2, 190.

8. Andreas Dorpalen, *Heinrich von Treitschke* (New Haven, 1957); Walter Bussmann, *Treitschke: Sein Welt- und Geschichtsbild* (Göttingen, 1952); and Hans Schleier, *Sybel und Treitschke: Antidemokratismus und Militarismus im historisch-politischen Denken grossbourgeoisen Geschichtsideologen* (Berlin, 1965).

9. Treitschke, *History of Germany in the Nineteenth Century*, 7 vols., trans. E. and C. Paul (London, 1915–1919), 2: 62.

10. Ibid., 4: 247.

11. Ibid., vol. 1, dedication to the ancient historian Max Duncker.

12. Ibid., 4: 312.

13. Sybel, *The History and Literature of the Crusades*, trans. Lady Duff Gordon (London, n.d.), 1; and see Volker Dotterweich, *Heinrich von Sybel: Geschichtswissenschaft in politischen Absicht (1817–1861)* (Göttingen, 1978).

14. Treitschke, *History of Germany*, vol. 1, preface.

15. Sybel, *The Founding of the German Empire by William I*, trans. Marshall Livingston Perrin (New York, 1890), 37.

16. *Historische Zeitschrift*, vol. 1, ed. Heinrich von Sybel (1859), 21.

17. Fritz Stern, ed., *The Varieties of History from Voltaire to the Present* (New York, 1972), 171; and see Walter A. Ricklinger, *Heinrich von Sybel und die Historische Zeitschrift* (Munich, 1936).

18. Seignobos, *Etudes de politique et d'histoire* (1881) (Paris, 1934), 105.

19. *Jahresberichte der Geschichtswissenschaft im Auftrage des Historischen Gesellschaft zu Berlin*, ed. F. Abraham, J. Hermann, and Edm. Meyer (Berlin, 1880).

20. See Christian Daniel Beck, *Anleitung zur Kentniss der allgemeinen Welt- und Völker-Geschichte* (Leipzig, 1878), which represented fundamental and pragmatic history as concerned not with the *Welt* but with the *Volk*.

21. Droysen, *Historik: Vorlesung über Enzyklopädie und Methodologie der Geschichte*, ed. Rudolph Hübner (Munich, 1958), 324.

22. Humboldt, "On the Historian's Task" (1821), in Ranke, *The Theory and Practice of History*, ed. Georg G. Iggers (Indianapolis, 1973), 5.

23. In general, see *Su Federico Carlo di Savigny, Quaderni fiorentini per la storia del pensiero giuridico moderno*, 9 (1980); Giuliano Marini, *Friedrich Karl von Savigny*

(Milan, 1978); and Friedrich Meinecke, *Cosmopolitanism and the National State,* trans. Robert B. Kimber (Princeton, 1970), 158–159.

24. *On the Vocation of Our Age for Legislation and Jurisprudence,* trans. A. Hayward (London, 1831), 18.

25. Ibid., 71.

26. Ibid., 136.

27. Puchta, *Das Gewohnheitsrecht* (Marburg, 1828), and Beseler, *Volksrecht und Juristenrecht* (Berlin, 1843).

28. Grimm, "Von der Poesie im Recht," in Savigny's *Zeitschrift für geschichtliche Rechtswissenschaft,* 2 (1816), 22–99; and D. R. Kelley, *Historians and the Law in Postrevolutionary France* (Princeton, 1984), 82.

29. Grimm, *Weisthümer* (Göttingen, 1840), on which see Dieter Werkmüller, *Über Aufkommen und Verbreitung der Weistümer nach der Samlung von Jakob Grimm* (Berlin, 1972); also *Deutsche Rechtsalterthümer* (Leipzig, 1899⁴); and Wilhelm Ebel, *Jacob Grimm und die deutsche Rechtswissenschaft* (Göttingen, 1963); Ulrich Wyss, *Die wilde Philologie: Jacob Grimm und der Historismus* (Munich, 1979), 197ff; James Q. Whitman, *The Legacy of Roman Law in the German Romantic Era* (Princeton, 1900), 201.

30. Bancroft, *History of the United States of America,* vol. 4 (Boston, 1876), 568.

31. See David F. Lindenfeld, *The Practical Imagination: The German Sciences of State in the Nineteenth Century* (Chicago, 1997), 154, and Woodruff D. Smith, *Politics and the Sciences of Culture in Germany, 1840–1920* (New York, 1991), 174.

32. Thompson, *History,* 2: 410–428.

33. Georg von Below, *Die deutsche Geschichtschreibung von den Befreiungskriegen bis zu unsern Tagen* (Berlin, 1924), 165ff; and *Probleme der Wirtschaftsgeschichte* (Tübingen, 1926).

34. Kelley, *Historians and the Law,* 85ff.

35. Ibid., 93–112.

36. Lézardière, *Théorie des lois politiques de la monarchie française* (Paris, 1844 [1792]); and see also *Ecrits inédits de Mlle de Lézardière,* ed. E. Carcassonne (Paris, 1927).

37. Blanke, *Historiographiegeschichte als Historik* (Stuttgart, 1991), 25–36; and, e.g., Rüsen, *Konfigurationen des Historismus* (Frankfurt, 1993), 340.

38. Bernheim, *Lehrbuch der historischen Methode und der Geschichtsphilosophie* (Leipzig, 1908⁶), 22.

39. Ibid., 2: 750.

40. Quoted by Friedrich Meinecke, *Autobiographische Schriften,* ed. Eberhard Kessel (Stuttgart, 1969), 141.

41. Blanke, *Historiographiegeschichte.*

42. *Geschichte der deutschen Historiographie seit dem Auftreten des Humanismus* (Munich, 1885), 2: 1081.

43. D. R. Kelley, "De Origine Feudorum: The Beginnings of an Historical Problem," *Speculum,* 34 (1964), 207–228; repr. *History, Law, and the Human Sciences* (London, 1984).

44. D. R. Kelley, "Tacitus Noster: The *Germania* in the Renaissance and Reformation," in *Tacitus and the Tacitean Tradition,* ed. T. J. Luce and A. Woodman (Princeton, 1993), 152–167; repr. *The Writing of History and the Study of Law* (London, 1997).

45. Friedrich Meinecke, *Historism: The Rise of a New Historical Outlook,* trans. J. E. Anderson (London, 1972), 250–294; more generally, Charles E. McClelland, *The German Historians and England: A Study in Nineteenth-Century Views* (Cambridge, 1971).

46. Meinecke, *Zur Theorie und Philosophie der Geschichte,* ed. Eberhard Kessel (Stuttgart, 1959), 244.

47. Dopsch, *The Economic and Social Foundations of European Civilization,* trans. M. G. Beard and N. Marshall (New York, 1937), 11, with a critical sketch of the later fortunes of the theory.

48. Garabed Artin Davoud-Oghlou, *Histoire des législations des anciens germains* (Berlin, 1845).

49. Maurer, *Einleitung zur Geschichte der Mark-, Hof-, Dorf- und Stadtverfassung* (Vienna, 1896 [1854]), and later elaborations, including *Geschichte der Markenverfassung* (Erlangen, 1856), *Geschichte der Dorfverfassung in Deutschland* (1865–1866); see also Karl Dickopf, *Georg Ludwig von Maurer 1790–1872: Eine Biographie* (Munich, 1960), and Carl Stephenson, *Borough and Town: A Study of Urban Origins in England* (Cambridge, Mass., 1933), 3ff.

50. Jakob Grimm, *Deutsche Rechtsalterthümer* (Göttingen, 1828).

51. Engels, "The Mark," in *The Peasant War in Germany* (Moscow, 1956), 162.

52. Burrow, *A Liberal Descent: Victorian Historians and the English Past* (Cambridge, 1981), 110, 124.

53. Sybel, *Entstehung des Deutschen Königthums* (Frankfurt, 1881²), 3.

54. John W. Burgess, *Reminiscences of an American Scholar* (New York, 1934), 105.

55. Dahlmann, *Die Politik* (Frankfurt, 1968), "Einleitung."

56. Waitz, *Deutsche Verfassungsgeschichte* (Kiel, 1880³), 32.

57. Ibid., 1: 453.

58. Giesebrecht, *Geschichte der deutschen Kaiserzeit,* vol. 1 (Braunschweig, 1863³), 338, 773.

59. Carlheinrich Brühl, *Deutschland und Frankreich: Die Geburt Zweier Völker* (Cologne, 1990), 8.

60. The texts are presented in *Universalstaat und Nationalstaat: Macht und Ende des Ersten deutschen Reiches,* ed. Friedrich Schneider (Innsbruck, 1943²). See also Heinrich Hostenkamp, *Die mittelalterliche Kaiserpolitik in der deutschen Historiographie seit v. Sybel und Ficker* (Berlin, 1934); Julius Jung, *Julius Ficker: Ein Beitrag zur ein deutschen Gelehrter* (Innsbruck, 1907), 307–354; Gottfried Koch, "Der Streit zwischen Sybel und Ficker und die Einschätzung der mittelalterliche Kaiserpolitik in der modernen Historiographie," *Die deutsche Geschichtswissenschaft vom Beginn des 19. Jahrhunderts bis zur Reichseinigung von oben,* ed. Joachim Streisand (Berlin, 1969), 311–338; Srbik, *Geist und Geschichte vom deutschen Humanismus bis zur Gegenwart* (Munich, 1950), 2: 33–37; and Blanke, *Historiographiegeschichte,* 354ff; also Raoul Manselli and Josef Riedmann, eds., *Federico Barbarossa nel dibattito storiografico in Italia e Germania* (Bologna, 1982).

61. Berger, *Search for Normality,* 29.

62. In general, see Thomas Brechenmacher, *Grossdeutsche Geschichtsschreibung im neunzehnten Jahrhundert: Die erste Generation (1830–1848)* (Berlin, 1996), pointing out the *kleindeutsch* distortions of Acton, Fueter, Gooch, and even Srbik; also Gerhard

Schilfert, "Die kleindeutsche Schule," in Streisand, *Die deutsche Geschichtswissenschaft*, 271–310, and Srbik, *Geist und Geschichte*, 355–400.

63. Schneider, *Universalstaat und Nationalstaat*, 265.

64. Roth, *Geschichte des Beneficialwesens* (Erlangen, 1850).

65. Gaupp, *Die germanische Ansiedlunger in den Provinzen des römischen Reiches* (Breslau, 1884).

66. Fustel de Coulanges, *Recherches sur quelques problèmes d'histoire* (Paris, 1894), 319–356 ("De la Marche germanique").

67. See the translation by Mary Fischer in Anthony Black in *Community in Historical Perspective* (Cambridge, 1990), 21, 99, 101, 124.

68. Inama-Sternegg, *Deutsche Wirtschaftsgeschichte bis zum Schluss der Karolingenperiode* (Leipzig, 1879), 3; and see Edwin Seligman, *The Economic Interpretation of History* (New York, 1902).

69. Burckhardt, *Reflections on History*, trans. M. D. Hottinger (Indianapolis, 1979), 54.

70. See Felix Gilbert, *History: Politics or Culture?* (Princeton, 1990), 46–92; Karl J. Weintraub, *Visions of Culture* (Chicago, 1966), 115–160; Wolfgang Hardtwig, "Jakob Burckhardt: Trieb und Geist — Die neue Konzeption von Kultur," *Deutsche Geschichtswissenschaft um 1900*, ed. Notker Hammerstein (Stuttgart, 1988), 97–112; Peter Gay, *Style in History* (New York, 1974), 139–182; Alan S. Kahan, *Aristocratic Liberalism: The Social and Political Thought of Jacob Burckhardt, John Stuart Mill, and Alexis de Tocqueville* (Oxford, 1992); John R. Hinde, *Jacob Burckhardt and the Crisis of Modernity* (Montreal, 2000); Thomas Albert Howard, *Religion and the Rise of Historicism: W. M. L. de Wette, Jacob Burckhardt, and the Theological Origins of Nineteenth-Century Historical Consciousness* (Cambridge, 2000); the standard biography by Werner Kaegi, *Jacob Burckhardt, eine Biographie*, 7 vols. (Basel, 1947–1982); and see now Lionel Gossman, *Basel in the Age of Burckhardt: A Study in Unseasonable Ideas* (Chicago, 2000).

71. Werner Kaegi, *Burckhardt*, 3: 647.

72. Ibid., 3: 567.

73. Burckhardt, *Reflections*, 180.

74. Burckhardt, *The Letters of Jacob Burckhardt*, trans. Alexander Dru (New York, 1955), 145–146 ("New Year's Eve, 1870").

75. Burckhardt, *Reflections*, 21.

76. Burckhardt, *Letters*, 45.

77. Ibid., 129–130

78. Burckhardt, *Reflections*, 327.

79. Burckhardt, *Judgments on History and Historians*, trans. Harry Zohn (Indianapolis, 1999), 160.

80. Burckhardt, *The Greeks and Greek Civilization*, trans. Sheila Stern (New York, 1998), 7.

81. Burckhardt, *The Civilization of the Renaissance in Italy*, trans. S. G. C. Middlemore (London, 1950), 1.

82. Burckhardt, *Greeks*, 7.

83. See Alfred von Martin, *Nietzsche und Burckhardt: Zwei geistige Welten im Dialog* (Basel, 1945).

84. Burckhardt, *Letters*, 212.

85. Burckhardt, *Reflections*, 32.

86. Burckhardt, *Letters*, 73.

87. Burckhardt, *Reflections*, 50.

88. Ibid., 106.

89. Ibid., 104.

90. Burckhardt, *Judgments*, 112.

91. Ibid., 122.

92. Ibid., 66.

93. Burckhardt, *Letters*, 58; cf. Burckhardt, *Reflections*, 55, 265.

94. Burckhardt, *Reflections*, 63, 67.

95. Ibid., 56.

96. Burckhardt, *Judgments*, 171.

97. Burckhardt, *Greeks*, 136; Burckhardt, *Letters*, 87.

98. Burckhardt, *Greeks*, 364.

99. Ibid., 36.

100. Ibid., 81.

101. Ibid., 8.

102. Ibid., 95.

103. Burckhardt, *The Age of Constantine the Great,* trans. Moses Hadas (New York, 1949), 11.

104. Ibid., 129.

105. Ibid., 290.

106. Ibid., 203.

107. Burckhardt, *Civilization,* 2.

108. Kaegi, *Burckhardt,* 3: 589 (citing a manuscript source), and 647.

109. Burckhardt, *Reflections,* 69.

110. Ibid., 93–94.

111. Ibid., 105.

112. Ibid., 213ff.

113. Ibid., 251.

114. Ibid., 293.

115. Burckhardt, *Letters,* 97.

Chapter 8: French Visions

1. Pim den Boer, *History As a Profession: The Study of History in France, 1818–1914,* trans. Arnold Pomerans (Princeton, 1998).

2. *L'Histoire en France depuis cent ans* (Paris, 1914), 57; and see R. Howard Block, *God's Plagiarist: Being an Account of the Fabulous Industry and Irregular Commerce of the Abbé Migne* (Chicago, 1994).

3. *Catalogue de l'histoire de France,* vol. 1 (Paris, 1895), 83–102; and see Den Boer, *History As a Profession,* 149.

4. Guizot, *France,* trans. Robert Black (New York, n.d.), 103, 113, 181.

5. Den Boer, *History As a Profession,* 14.

6. Cited by Stanley J. Jaki, *Uneasy Genius: The Life and Work of Pierre Duhem* (The Hague, 1984), 55.

7. Duruy, *Histoire des Grecs*, vol. 1 (Paris, 1887–89), 1.

8. Duruy, *History of Rome and the Roman People,* vol 1, trans. W. J. Clarke (Boston, 1883), 137.

9. See William R. Keylor, *Academy and Community: The Foundation of the French Historical Profession* (Cambridge, Mass., 1975), 36.

10. *Revue des Questions Historiques,* vol. 1 (1866), 5; the first article concerned the massacres of St. Bartholomew, still the center of confessional and historiographical controversy.

11. Lavisse, *Souvenirs* (Paris, 1912), 284.

12. Lavisse, *Etudes de politique et d'histoire* (Paris, 1934), 16, 105; and see Den Boer, *History As a Profession,* 295–300.

13. Seignobos, *Les Archives de l'histoire de France* (Paris, 1891).

14. Langlois, *La Vie en France au moyen age* (1903–1928); and see Den Boer, *History As a Profession,* 300–304.

15. Martin, *Histoire de France,* vol. 1 (Paris, 1861¹), xi.

16. Ibid., viii–ix.

17. Among other competitors for public attention in the second and third quarters of the century were the surveys of Dupressoir (1850, 5 vols.), Bordier and Charton (1859, 2 vols.), Lavallée (1864–73, 7 vols.), Rognon (1863–65, 5 vols.), Gouet (1865–69, 6 vols.), and Dareste de la Chavanne (1868–73, 8 vols.), who also wrote histories of administration (1848) and agrarian classes in France (1854).

18. Sismondi, *Histoire de France,* vol. 2, 121; and see Peter Stadler, *Geschichtsschreibung und historisches Denken in Frankreich, 1789–1871* (Zurich, 1958), 89.

19. Mignet, *De la Féodalité* (Paris, 1822).

20. Laferrière, *Histoire du droit civil de Rome et du droit Français* (Paris, 1846). On these pioneering legal historians see D. R. Kelley, *Historians and the Law in Postrevolutionary France* (Princeton, 1984).

21. Giraud, *Essai sur l'histoire du droit français au moyen age* (Paris, 1846) and *Notice sur Etienne Pasquier* (Paris, 1848); and in general see D. R. Kelley, *Foundations of Modern Historical Scholarship: Language, Law, and History in the French Renaissance* (New York, 1970).

22. *De l'Enseignement du droit en France* (Paris, 1839), 10.

23. Klimrath, *Travaux sur l'histoire du droit français,* ed. L. A. Warnkoenig (Paris, 1843), esp. vol. 1, 1–62, "Importance scientifique et sociale d'une histoire du droit français."

24. *De l'Etablissement des Francs dans la Gaule, du gouvernment des premiers mérovingiens jusqu'à la mort de Brunehaut* (Rennes, 1838), his thèse; and *Histoire des institutions mérovingiennes* (Paris, 1843) and *Histoire des institutions carolingiennes* (Paris, 1843). See Arthur de la Borderie's biographical notice in Lehuërou, *Histoire de la constitution anglaise depuis l'avènement de Henri VIII jusqu'à la mort de Charles I* (Nantes, 1863), i–cxx.

25. Lehuërou, *Histoire,* 3.

26. Lehuërou, *Institutions carolingiennes*, 67.

27. Dareste de la Chavanne, *Histoire de l'administration en France et des progrès du pouvoir royal depuis le règne de Philippe Auguste jusqu'à la mort de Louis XIV* (Paris, 1848).

28. Dareste de la Chavanne, *Histoire de France depuis les origines jusqu'à nos jours* (Paris, 1884²).

29. Cheruel, *Histoire de l'administration monarchique en France: Depuis l'avènement de Philippe-Auguste jusqu'à la mort de Louis XIV* (Paris, 1855).

30. Cheruel, *Dictionnaire historique des institutions, moeurs et coutumes de la France* (Paris, 1855).

31. Ibid., 1: lxx.

32. Boutaric, *La France sous Philippe le Bel: Etude sur les institutions politiques et administratives du moyen age* (Paris, 1861).

33. Ibid., 1: 437.

34. Monod, *Etudes critiques sur les sources de l'histoire mérovingienne*, vol. 2 (Paris, 1872), 37.

35. Glasson, *Histoire du droit et des institutions de la France*, 8 vols. (Paris, 1887–1903), 2: 58.

36. Ibid., 1: 77.

37. Viollet, *Histoire des institutions politiques et administratives de la France*, 3 vols. (Paris, 1890–1903).

38. Flach, *Les Origines de l'ancienne France: Le Régime seigneuriale X et XIe siècles* (Paris, 1880), 2.

39. Ibid., 1: 146.

40. Ibid., 1: 472.

41. Fustel de Coulanges, *The Ancient City: A Study on the Religion, Laws, and Institutions of Greece and Rome*, Eng. trans. (Garden City, N.J., 1955). See also François Hartog, *Le XIXe siècle et l'histoire: Le Cas de Fustel de Coulanges* (Paris, 1988), and Arnaldo Momigliano, "The Ancient City of Fustel de Coulanges," in *Essays in Ancient and Modern Historiography* (Middletown, Conn., 1982), 325–344.

42. Keylor, *Academy and Community*, 30.

43. Fustel, *Polybe, ou la Grèce conquise par les Romains* (Amiens, 1858), 1.

44. Fustel, *Histoire des institutions politiques de l'ancienne France* (Paris, 1891 [1875]), 1: xi; 2: 225.

45. Ibid., 2: xi.

46. Fustel, "De la manière d'écrire l'histoire en France et en Allemagne depuis cinquante ans," cited in Hartog, *Le XIXe siècle et l'histoire*, 392.

47. Fustel, "De l'analyse des textes historiques (1887)," cited in Hartog, *Le XIXe siècle et l'histoire*, 349–350.

48. Fustel, "Le Problème des origines de la propriété foncière," in *Questions historiques*, ed. Camille Jullian (Paris, 1893), 115.

49. Hartog, *Le XIXe siècle et l'histoire*, 351.

50. Fustel, *Histoire des institutions politiques de l'ancienne France* (Paris, 1891), 2: 228, 240; and 3: 6, remarking that the modern works of Monod and others on Gregory add little to the magisterial study of Ruinart (1699).

51. Fustel, "De la manière d'écrire l'histoire en France et en Allemagne depuis cinquante ans," in Jullian, *Questions historiques,* 3–16.

52. Martha Hanna, *The Mobilization of Intellect: French Scholars and Writers during the Great War* (Cambridge, Mass., 1996), 88–91, 190.

53. Albert Grenier, *Camille Jullian: Un Demi-siècle de science historique et de progrès français, 1880–1930* (Paris, 1944); Toynbee, *Study of History,* 12 vols. (Oxford, 1934–61), 1: 12.

54. Mary Pickering, *Auguste Comte: An Intellectual Biography,* vol. 1 (Cambridge, 1993), 178; and see Robert Flint, *Historical Philosophy in France and French Belgium and Switzerland* (New York, 1994), 394ff.

55. Buchez, *Introduction à l'histoire de l'histoire* (Paris, 1833); see Barbara Patricia Patri, *The Historical Thought of P.-J.-B. Buchez* (Washington, D.C., 1958), and Gaston Castilla, *Buchez historien: Sa théorie du progrès dans la philosophie de l'histoire* (Freiburg, 1909).

56. Comte, *Cours de philosophie positive* (Paris, 1949), 1: 7.

57. Bourdeau, *L'Histoire et les historiens: Essai critique sur l'histoire considérée comme science positive* (Paris, 1888).

58. Lacombe, *L'Histoire considérée comme science* (Paris, 1894); and see Keylor, *Academy and Community,* 116–121.

59. Renan, *L'Avenir de la science,* in *Oeuvres complètes,* ed. Henriette Psichari (Paris, 1949), 3: 864.

60. Lewis Freeman Mott, *Ernest Renan* (New York, 1921), 61.

61. Renan, *The Life of Jesus,* Eng. trans. (New York, 1927), 65.

62. Taine, *History of English Literature,* trans. H. Van Laun (New York, 1883), 1: 17; and see François Leger, *Monsieur Taine* (Paris, 1986), and Regina Pozzi, *Hippolyte Taine: Scienze umane e politica nell'Ottocento* (Venice, 1993).

63. Taine, *History of English Literature,* 1: 6.

64. Sainte-Beuve, *Les grands écrivains français, XIX*ᵉ *siècle, Philosophes et essayistes* (Paris, 1930), 3: 213 ("Hippolyte Taine").

65. Langlois and Seignobos, *Introduction to the Study of History,* trans. G. G. Berry (London, 1898); and see Keylor, *Academy and Community,* 75; also Fritz Ringer, *Fields of Knowledge: French Academic Culture in Comparative Perspective, 1890–1920* (Cambridge, 1992), 265ff, and *Toward a Social History of Knowledge* (New York, 2000), 225.

66. Goncourt, *Journal, Mémoires de la vie littéraire,* 3 vols., ed. Robert Ricatte (Paris, 1989); and see *Préfaces et manifestes littéraires,* ed. Hubert Juin (Paris, 1926).

67. *Histoire de la société française pendant la révolution* (Paris, 1864), 1: 187.

68. Françoise Dosse, *New History in France,* trans. Perter V. Conroy, Jr. (Urbana, Ill., 1994), 19.

69. B. Reizov, *L'Historiographie romantique française, 1815–1830* (Moscow, n.d.), 353ff.

70. Mignet, *Oeuvres* (Paris, 1949), 1: 157, 143.

71. Laferrière, *Histoire des principes, des institutions, et des lois, pendant la révolution française (1789–1804)* (Paris, 1851–52⁶), xxiii.

72. Lamartine, *History of the Girondists,* trans. H. T. Ryde (London, 1848), 1: 1.

73. Ibid., 1: 41.

74. Blanc, *Histoire de la Révolution française* (Paris, 1869⁷), preface of 1868.

75. Paul Viallaneix, *Michelet: Les travaux et les jours, 1798–1874)* (Paris, 1998), 309.

76. Michelet, *Histoire de la Révolution française* (Paris, 1979), 1: 198.

77. Ibid., preface of 1847.

78. Quinet, *La Révolution* (Paris, 1865), 21.

79. Carlyle, *The French Revolution: A History* (New York, n.d.), 173, 169.

80. Ibid., 669.

81. Sybel, *Geschichte der Revolutionszeit von 1789–1800*, 10 vols. (Stuttgart, 1897–1900⁸).

82. Acton, *Lectures on the French Revolution* (London, 1910), 370.

83. Tocqueville, *Democracy in America*, trans. Henry Reeve (New York, 1838), xiv.

84. Tocqueville, *The Old Regime and the Revolution*, trans. Alan S. Kahan (Chicago, 1898), 1: 86.

85. Tocqueville, *Democracy in America*, 431.

86. Tocqueville, *The Old Regime*, 145.

87. Taine, *Les Origines de la France contemporaine*, 6 vols. (Paris, 1898⁹), 1: 11; *The Origins of Contemporary France*, ed. Edward T. Gargan (Chicago, 1974), 81. See also Pieter Geyl, "French Historians for and against the French Revolution," in *Encounters in History* (Cleveland, 1961), 67–142, and Paul Farmer, *France Reviews Its Revolutionary Origins: Social Politics and Historical Opinion in the Third Republic* (New York, 1944).

88. Taine, *Les Origines*, 294.

89. Mona Ozouf, "La Révolution française et l'idée de l'homme nouveau," in *The Political Culture of the French Revolution*, ed. Colin Lucas (Oxford, 1988), 2: 213–232.

90. See Linda Orr, *Headless History: Nineteenth-Century Historiography of the Revolution* (Ithaca, 1990).

Chapter 9: English Observances

1. To these may be added Charles Kingsley (b. 1819), Goldwin Smith (b. 1823), Thomas Hodgkin (b. 1831), and James Bryce (b. 1838); and see John Kenyon, *The History Men: Macaulay, Carlyle, Buckle, Acton, Stubbs, Namier, Tawney, Elton . . .* (London, 1983).

2. Philippa Levine, *The Amateur and the Professional: Antiquarians, Historians and Archaeologists in Victorian England, 1836–1886* (Cambridge, 1886), 101–134, and Rosemary Jann, *The Art and Science of Victorian History* (Columbus, Ohio, 1985).

3. David Knowles, *Great Historical Enterprises* (London, 1862), 134.

4. Levine, *The Amateur and the Professional*, 135–163.

5. W. R. W. Stephens, *The Life and Letters of Edward A. Freeman* (London, 1895), 2: 389; and see Deborah Wormell, *Sir John Seeley and the Uses of History* (Cambridge, 1980), 14, and Sheldon Rothblatt, *The Revolt of the Dons: Cambridge and Society in Victorian England* (New York, 1968), 155–180.

6. Newman, *An Essay on the Development of Christian Doctrine* (Garden City, N.J., 1960), 417.

7. Cited by Waldo Hilary Dunn, *James Anthony Froude: A Biography* (Oxford, 1961), 2: 305.

8. Froude, *Nemesis of Faith, or the History of Markham Sutherland* (London, 1903), xxiii.

9. Kingsley, *The Limits of Exact Science as Applied to History* (Cambridge, 1860), 71.

10. *Letters of John Richard Green,* ed. Leslie Stephen (London, 1901), 103 (to W. Boyd Dawkins, 11 Sept. 1862) and 24 (1858).

11. Smith, *Lectures on the Study of History* (New York, n.d.), 29, 138, 145.

12. Stubbs, *Seventeen Lectures on the Study of Medieval and Modern History* (New York, 1967), 6.

13. Green, *Letters,* 64.

14. Ibid., 118 (to Dawkins, 24 Mar. 1863).

15. Stubbs, *Seventeen Lectures,* 12; and see Klaus Dockhorn, *Der Deutsche Historismus in England: Ein Beitrag zur Englischen Geistesgeschichte des 19. Jahrhunderts* (Göttingen, 1950).

16. Arthur Penrhyn Stanley, *The Life and Correspondence of Thomas Arnold* (London, 1858⁵), 45; and see Duncan Forbes, *The Liberal Anglican Idea of History* (Cambridge, 1952), and Dockhorn, *Deutsche Historismus,* 35.

17. Stephens, *Edward A. Freeman,* 1: 199; *Historical Essays* (New York, 1873), 2: 234, 266; and see the critique of Toynbee, *A Study of History* (New York, 1935²), 1: 339 ("E. A. Freeman's conception of 'the Unity of History'").

18. Lewis, *Letters . . . to Various Friends* (London, 1870), 80 (to Head, 1837), 312 (to Twisleton, 1856), and 93 (to his father, 1837).

19. See Dockhorn, *Deutsche Historismus,* 72–78, 115–122.

20. Freeman, *The Methods of Historical Study* (London, 1886), 118.

21. Stephens, *Edward A. Freeman,* 1: 238.

22. Ibid., 2: 87.

23. Freeman, *Methods,* 270.

24. Freeman, *Essays,* 2: 155.

25. Stephens, *Edward A. Freeman,* 1: 346 (1866) and 2: 88 (1874).

26. Green, *Letters,* 426.

27. Ibid., 193.

28. Stubbs, *Seventeen Lectures,* 9.

29. Ibid., 12.

30. Green, *Letters,* 425 (to Freeman, 26 Feb. 1876).

31. Green, *Letters,* 235 (to Freeman, Nov. 1869); and cf. *A Short History of the English People* (New York, 1884), 48.

32. Freeman, "The Mythical and Romantic Elements in Early English History," in *Historical Essays* (London, 1871), 2.

33. Ibid., 3–16.

34. Stubbs, *Constitutional History of England* (Oxford, 1883⁴), 1: 5ff.

35. Ibid., 1: 33; and see J. W. Burrow, *A Liberal Descent: Victorian Historians and the English Past* (Cambridge, 1981), 189.

36. Freeman, *History of Federal Government from the Foundations of the Achaean League to the Disruptions of the United States* (London, 1867) and *Comparative Politics* (London, 1873).

37. Stephens, *Edward A. Freeman,* 1: 178–179.

38. Green, *Letters,* 369.

39. Stephens, *Edward A. Freeman,* 1: 292.

40. Green, *Letters,* 360.

41. Stephens, *Edward A. Freeman,* 1: 125.

42. Stubbs, *Seventeen Lectures,* 15.

43. Louise Creighton, *Life and Letters of Mandell Creighton by His Wife* (London, 1906), 1: 287.

44. Ibid., 1: 331.

45. Green, *Letters,* 175; cf. Stubbs, *Seventeen Lectures,* 14.

46. Green, *Letters,* 248, 41.

47. Freeman, *Methods,* preface, 82.

48. Creighton, *Mandell Creighton,* 1: 338.

49. Raymond Schwab, *The Oriental Renaissance,* trans. Gene Patterson-Black and Victor Reinking (New York, 1984), 47, citing Salomon Reinach that "Bopp, Schlege, Lassen, Rosen, and Burnouf studied Sanskrit in England."

50. Creighton, *A History of the Papacy from the Great Schism to the Sack of Rome* (London, 1907), 1: 53; and see Arthur Milman, *Henry Hart Milman* (London, 1900).

51. Creighton, *Mandell Creighton,* 218.

52. Louise Creighton, *Life and Letters of Thomas Hodgkin* (London, 1917).

53. H. A. L. Fisher, *James Bryce* (New York, 1927), 2: 239.

54. Bryce, *Holy Roman Empire* (New York, n.d. [1873]), 3.

55. Ibid., 48.

56. Ibid., 376.

57. Ibid., 386.

58. Stubbs, *Seventeen Lectures,* 13; cf. Freeman, *Methods,* 21.

59. Stubbs, ibid., 208.

60. Stubbs, *Constitutional History,* 1: 1.

61. Ibid., 1: 230; 3: 4.

62. Ibid., 1: 35, 74, 180, 269.

63. Ibid., 1: 142, 300, 400.

64. Ibid., 1: 35; and see Charles Petit-Dutaillis, *Studies and Notes Supplementary to Stubbs' Constitutional History,* trans. W. E. Rhodes (Manchester, 1911), 4.

65. Stubbs, *Constitutional History,* 1: 281.

66. Ibid., 1: 571–579; 2: 1.

67. Stubbs, *Select Charters* (Oxford, 1921⁹), 116, 291–302.

68. Stubbs, *Constitutional History,* 1: 668, 674.

69. Ibid., 1: 681.

70. Ibid., 2: 172, 305.

71. Ibid., 198, 207.

72. See the learned but hostile and small-minded attack in H. G. Richardson and G. O. Sayles, *The Governance of England from the Conquest to Magna Carta* (Edinburgh, 1963), 1–21.

73. Freeman, *The History of the Norman Conquest of England, Its Causes and Results* (Oxford, 1970²), 1: 2.

74. Ibid., 1: 16.

75. Freeman, *Comparative Politics*, 335, 497n.

76. Ibid., 11, 16, 302; and see Alan Diamond, ed., *The Victorian Achievement of Sir Henry Maine* (Cambridge, 1991).

77. Freeman, *Comparative Politics*, 55.

78. Freeman, *The History of Sicily from the Earliest Times* (London, 1863).

79. Green, *Letters*, 62.

80. Green, *A Short History of the English People* (New York, 1984), 86.

81. Ibid., 153, 194.

82. Ibid., 488.

83. Maine, *Ancient Law* (London, 1861); and John W. Burrow, "Henry Maine and Mid-Victorian Ideas of Progress," in *The Victorian Achievement of Sir Henry Maine*, ed. Alan Diamond (Cambridge, 1991), 61; also Alan D. J. Macfarlane, "Some Contributions of Maine to History and Anthropology," ibid., 111–142.

84. Maine, *Lectures on the Early History of Institutions* (New York, 1888), 3.

85. C. H. S. Fifoot, *Frederic William Maitland: A Life* (Cambridge, Mass., 1971); and H. E. Bell, *Maitland: A Critical Examination and Assessment* (London, 1965); also Dockhorn, *Der Deutsche Historismus*, 177–182.

86. *Selected Historical Essays of F. W. Maitland*, ed. Helen M. Cam (Cambridge, 1957), 97.

87. Pollock and Maitland, *History of English Law before the Time of Edward I*, 2 vols. (Cambridge, 1895), 1: 151.

88. Ibid., 2: 556.

89. Ibid., 1: 203.

90. Ibid., 1: 65.

91. Maitland, *Selected Historical Essays*, 117.

92. Trevelyan, "Clio: A Muse," in Stern, *Varieties of History*, 227–245.

93. Carlyle, *English and Other Critical Essays* (London, 1915), 80.

94. Bury, "The Science of History," in Stern, *Varieties of History*, 209; cf. Barzun, *Clio and the Doctors* (Chicago, 1974).

95. G. P. Gooch, *History and the Historians in the Nineteenth Century* (London, 1952²), 324.

96. John Clive, introduction to his edition of Carlyle, *History of Friedrich II of Prussia Called Frederick the Great* (Chicago, 1969), xxiii.

97. Carlyle, "On Heroes, Hero-Worship, and the Heroic in History," in Fritz Stern, *The Varieties of History* (New York, 1973²), 101; and see Perez Zagorin, "Thomas Carlyle and Oliver Cromwell," in *Historians and Ideologues: Essays in Honor of Donald R. Kelley* (Rochester, 2001), 231–256.

98. Carlyle, "On History Again," in *Critical and Miscellaneous Essays* (Philadelphia, 1852), 425.

99. Carlyle, "History as Biography," in Stern, *Varieties of History*, 91.

100. Buckle, *History of Civilization in England* (New York, 1884), 1: 29.

101. Froude, *History of England from the Fall of Wolsey to the Defeat of the Spanish Armada* (London, 1910), 1: 61.

102. Ibid., 1: 189; 3: 205.

103. Dunn, *James Anthony Froude*; and Herbart Paul, *The Life of Froude* (New York, 1906); also Jeffrey Paul van Arx, *Progress and Pessimism: Religion, Politics, and History in Nineteenth-Century Britain* (Cambridge, Mass., 1985), 173–200.

104. Froude, *History of England,* 1: 206.

105. Ibid., 3: 175.

106. Ibid., 1: 71.

107. Ibid., 1: 62.

108. Ibid., 3: 130.

109. Stephens, *Freeman,* 2: 302; Paul, *Life of Froude,* 147; and see Langlois and Seignobos, *Introduction to the Study of History,* trans. G. G. Berry (London, 1898), 125.

110. Froude, *History of England,* 3: 40.

111. Ibid., 1: 129, 510; 6: 96.

112. Ibid., 2: 271.

113. Ibid., 2: 348.

114. Ibid., 4: 276.

115. Ibid., 4: 349–350.

116. Ibid., 1: 337.

117. Ibid., 1: 178.

118. Ibid., 12: 502.

119. Froude, "The Science of History," *Short Studies on Great Subjects* (New York, 1968), 13.

120. Froude, "On Progress," *Short Studies,* second series (New York, 1871), 269–270.

121. Froude, "Scientific Methods Applied to History," *Short Studies,* second series, 470.

122. Oliver Elton, *Frederick York Powell: A Life* (Oxford, 1906), 1: 169.

123. Gardiner, *History of England* (London, 1985), 2: 78.

124. Timothy Lang, *The Victorians and the Stuart Heritage: Interpretations of a Discordant Past* (Cambridge, 1995), 167.

125. Ibid., 139.

126. Seeley, *Expansion of England* (London, 1899), 193; and see Wormell, *Sir John Seeley.*

127. Seeley, *Expansion of England,* 2.

128. Ibid., 44.

129. *A Memoir of the Right Hon. William Edward Hartpole Lecky by his Wife* (London, 1909), 101.

130. Ibid., 28, 122.

131. Ibid., 28, 90.

132. Ibid., 248.

133. Roland Hill, *Lord Acton* (New Haven, 2000); Daniel McElrath, *Lord Acton: The Decisive Decade, 1864–1874* (Louvain, 1970); Gertrude Himmelfarb, *Lord Acton: A Study in Conscience and Politics* (Chicago, 1952); and the earlier works of Ulrich Noack.

134. *Döllinger-Acton Briefwechsel, 1850–1890,* vol. 1, ed. Victor Conzemius (Munich, 1963), 47ff (1855).

135. Acton, "Döllinger's Historical Work," in *Essays in the Study and Writing of History,* vol. 2, ed. J. Rufus Fears (Indianapolis, 1985), 419.

136. MS cited by McElrath, *Lord Acton,* 127.

137. Acton, "Ultramontanism," in *Essays in Religion, Politics, and Morality*, vol. 3, ed. J. Rufus Fears (Indianapolis, 1988), 149–194.

138. Acton, review of Ranke's English history in *Home and Foreign Review*, 1863, in *Essays in the Study of Writing*, 169.

139. Review of a volume of Brewer's *Letters and Papers*, in *Quarterly Review*, 1877, in *Essays in the Study of Writing*, 259.

140. McElrath, *Lord Acton*, 140 (Acton's MS "Notes on archival researches, 1864–68").

141. *The Correspondence of Lord Acton and Richard Simpson*, vol. 1 (Cambridge, 1971), 141.

142. Acton, *Essays on Church and State*, ed. Douglas Woodruff (London, 1952), 353–373; and cf. Owen Chadwick, *Acton and History* (Cambridge, 1998), 16.

143. "Fra Paolo Sarpi," in *Essays on Church and State*, 256; cf. Hill, *Lord Acton*, 184.

144. *Briefwechsel*, 1: 128 (17 Feb. 1858).

145. Acton, *Correspondence*, 1: 21; and see his review in *Rambler*, 1858, in *Essays in Religion*, 443–459.

146. Acton, *Essays*, 2: 198.

147. See especially the documentary materials in McElrath, *Lord Acton*.

148. Acton, letter of 16 June 1882, cited in Hugh A. MacDougall, *The Acton-Newman Relations: The Dilemma of Christian Liberalism* (New York, 1962), 142.

149. Hill, *Lord Acton*, 275; also Hugh Tulloch, *Lord Acton* (London, 1988), 49, and George Watson, *Lord Acton's History of Liberty: A Study of His Library, with an Edited Text of His History of Liberty Notes* (Aldershot, 1994).

150. Toynbee, *A Study of History*, 1: 46; 10: 38.

151. Acton, *Essays in the Study of Writing*, 79.

152. Acton, "Political Causes of the American Revolution," in *Essays in the History of Liberty*, 216–262.

153. See, e.g., Julia Stapleton, *Englishness and the Study of Politics: The Social and Political Thought of Ernest Barker* (Cambridge, 1994), 98.

154. Hill, *Lord Acton*, 67.

155. Michelet, *Histoire de France*, preface of 1868.

156. Acton, *Lectures on Modern History* (London, 1950), 315.

157. Acton, *Essays*, 3: 621.

158. Acton, "The Study of History," in ibid., 2: 543.

159. Acton, *Essays in Religion*, 3: 624.

160. Acton, *Essays in the Study of Writing*, 2: 504–552.

161. Acton, *Essays in Religion*, 3: 620.

162. Acton, *Essays in Religion*, 3: 641; and see Butterfield, *Man on His Past* (Boston, 1955), 622ff.

Chapter 10: Beyond the Canon

1. Kant, *Anthropology from a Pragmatic Point of View*, tr. Mary J. Gregory (The Hague, 1974), 120.

2. Degérando, *The Observation of Savage Peoples*, tr. F. C. T. Moore (London, 1969), 63.

3. Dankovsky, *Die Griechen als-Stamm- und Sprachverwandte der Slawen historisch und philologisch dargestellt* (Pressburg, 1828).

4. See T. K. Penniman, *A Hundred Years of Anthropology* (New York, 1974); J. O. Brew (ed.), *One Hundred Years of Anthropology* (Cambridge, Mass., 1968); Glynn Daniel, *A Hundred and Fifty Years of Archaeology* (London, 1975²) and *The Origins and Growth of Archaeology* (Harmondsworth, 1967); Bruce G. Trigger, *A History of Archaeological Thought* (Cambridge, 1989); and Alain Schnapp, *The Discovery of the Past,* trans. Ian Kinnes and Gilliam Varndell (New York, 1997).

5. James Cowles Pritchard, *Researches into the Physical History of Man,* ed. George W. Stocking (Chicago, 1973 [1813]).

6. Gérard Lacaze-Duthiers, *Philosophie de la préhistoire* (Paris, 1931), 347.

7. Boucher de Perthes, *Pre-Historic Times as Illustrated by Ancient Remains and the Manners and Customs of Modern Savages* (London, 1890⁵), 1–2; and see Peter J. Bowler, *The Invention of Progress: The Victorians and the Past* (Oxford, 1989).

8. Herbert Kühn, *Geschichte der Vorgeschichteforschung* (Berlin, 1976); Glen Daniel and Colin Renfrew, *The Idea of Prehistory* (Edinburgh, 1988); Jaroslav Malina and Zdenek Vasicek, *Archaeology Yesterday and Today: The Development of Archaeology in the Sciences and Humanities* (Cambridge, 1990); and Philip L. Kohl and Clare Fawcett (eds.), *Nationalism, Politics, and the Practice of Archaeology* (Cambridge, 1995).

9. John Lubbock, *Pre-Historic Times* (New York, 1913⁷), preface.

10. See *Towards a History of Archaeology,* ed. Glynn Daniel (London, 1981), especially the papers of Ole-Klindt-Jensen, Kristian Kristiansen, Bo Gräslund, and Judith Rodden.

11. Daniel, *Origins and Growth,* 90ff.

12. *Primeval Antiquities of Denmark,* tr. William J. Thoms (London, 1849).

13. Worsaae, *Pre-History of the North based on contemporary memorials,* trans. H. F. Morland Simpson (London, 1886), 7.

14. Worsaae, *The Pre-History of the North,* 2.

15. Worsaae, *The Pre-History of the North,* 4.

16. Worsaae, ibid., 181.

17. Eric Gustave Geijer, *The History of the Swedes,* tr. J. H. Turner (London, 1845); and cf. Henry Wheaton, *History of the Northmen, or, Danes and Normans from the earliest times to the conquest of England by William of Normandy* (London, 1831), drawing on Scandinavian scholarship.

18. Keyser, *The Private Life of the Old Norsemen,* tr. M. R. Barnard (London, 1868).

19. Munch, *Det norske folks historie* (Christiana, 1852), and *Nordens aelteste Historie* (Christiana, 1872).

20. C. F. Allen, *Histoire de Danemark depuis les temps les plus reculés jusqu'à nos jours,* trans. E. Beauvois (Copenhagen, 1878²).

21. Figuier, *L'Homme primitif* (Paris, 1870), preface.

22. Allen, *On Nationality and Language in the Duchy of Sleswick* (Copenhagen, 1848).

23. In general see Benedetto Croce, *Storia della storiografia italiana nel secolo decimonono* (Bari, 1930²), and Luigi Bulferetti, *La storiografia italiana dal romanticismo a oggi* (Milan, 1957).

24. See J. G. A. Pocock, *Barbarism and Religion,* II, *Narratives of Civil Government* (Cambridge, 1999), 29–71.

25. See Max Fisch's introduction to *The Autobiography of Giambattista Vico,* trans. Fisch and Bergin (Ithaca, 1944), 63ff.

26. Cosimo Ceccuti, "Gino Capponi: dall'Antologia al nuova antologia," *Gino Capponi: storia e progresso nell'Italia dell'ottocento,* ed. Paolo Bagnoli (Florence, 1994), 111–124.

27. Balbo, *Della Storia d'Italia dalle origini fino ai nostri tempi sommario,* ed. Giuseppe Talamo (Milan, 1962).

28. Croce, I, 83; and see Paolo Pavesio, *Carlo Botta e le sue opere storiche* (Florence, 1874), and Michael Kraus and David D. Joyce, *The Writing of American History* (Norman, Okla., 1985), 88.

29. Botta, *History of Italy during the Consulate and Empire of Napoleone Buonaparte,* Eng. trans. (London, 1828).

30. *Storia d'Italia continuate da quella di Guiciardini fino al 1789* (Capolago, 1835 [1832]), I, 7.

31. Colletta, *Storia del reame di Napoli,* ed. Anna Bravo (Turin, 1975), and Capponi, *Storia della repubblica di Firenze* (Florence, 1875).

32. Micali, *Storia degli antichi popoli italiani* (1822) and *Monumenti per servire all'storia degli antichi popoli italiani* (1832).

33. *History of Rome,* 100.

34. See Manzoni, *Discorso sopra alcuni punti della storia lombardica* (Lecce, 1971–72).

35. See Troya, *Del veltro allegorico di Dante* (1826), and Balbo, *The Life and Times of Dante Alighieri,* trans. J. Bunbury (London, 1852 [1839]).

36. Balbo, *Dalla Storia d'Italia dalle origini fino ai nostri tempi sommario,* ed. Giuseppe Talano (Milan, 1962), xiii; and see Giovanni Battista Scaglia, *Cesare Balbo: Il Risorgimento nelle prospetta storica del "progresso cristiano"* (Rome, 1975).

37. Balbo, *Storia d'Italia,* 850 (letter to Troya, 19 Nov. 1830).

38. Balbo, "Dell'utilità presente di una storia generale d'Italia" (1832), and "Studi di farsi sulla storia d'Italia" (1832), in *Storia d'Italia,* 85–102, 107–127.

39. Troya, *Storia d'Italia del medio-evo* (Naples, 1839), 48, citing Gregor Dankowsky, *Die Griechen als Stamm- und Sprachverwandte der Slawer.*

40. Balbo, *Della Speranza d'Italia* (Florence, 1855[5]).

41. Balbo, *Meditazioni storiche* (Florence, 1855[3]), 18.

42. Cantù, *Dalla Indipendenza italiana* (Turin, 1877); and see *Carteggio Montalembert-Cantù 1842–1868,* ed. Frencesca Kaucisvili Melzi d'Eril (Milan, 1969).

43. *La Réforme en Italie: Les Précurseurs,* tr. Anicet Digard and Edmund Martin (Paris, 1867); and cf. *Storia di cento anni 1750–1850* (Florence, 1855[3]), on free thought and the Jesuits.

44. Cantù, *Histoire des Italiens,* tr. Armand Lacombe (Paris, 1859).

45. Cantù, *Histoire universelle,* tr. Eugène Aroux (Paris, 1865[3]), 127; and *Gli ultimi trent'anni: continuazione della storia universale* (Turin, 1880[2]) — 1846: "Viva Pio IX."

46. Amari, *History of the War of the Sicilian Vespers,* trans. Earl of Ellesmere (London, 1850), iv; *La Guerra del Vespro siciliano* (Milan, 1886[2]).

47. Tosti, *Storia della Badia di Montecasino* (Rome, 1841–43).

48. *History of Pope Boniface VIII and His Times,* tr. Eugene J. Donnelly (New York, 1911).

49. Ferrari, *Vico et l'Italie* (Paris, 1839), 376.

50. Ferrari, *Teoria dei periodi politici* (Milan, 1874). Alan Spitzer, "Victor Cousin and the French Generation of 1820," *From Parnassus: Essays in Honor of Jacques Barzun* (New York, 1976), 177–194. The phrase "nouvelle génération" is Sainte-Beuve's in *Les grands écrivains,* II, *XIXe* siècle, 221.

51. See especially Volker Hartmann, *Die deutsche Kulturgeschichtsschreibung von ihren Anfängen bis Wilhelm Heinrich Riehl* (Ph.D. diss., Marburg, 1971), and Hans Schleier, "Kulturgeschichte im 19. Jahrhundert," in *Geschichtsdiskurs,* ed. Wolfgang Küttler, Jörn Rüsen, and Ernst Schulin, III (Frankfurt, 1997) *Die Epoche der Historisierung,* 424–446.

52. Tylor, *Researches into the Early History of Mankind and the Development of Civilization* (1865), ed. Paul Bohannan (Chicago, 1964), 1. Woodruff Smith, *Politics and the Sciences of Culture,* 60; and George Stocking, "Matthew Arnold, E. B. Tylor, and the Uses of Invention," in *Race, Culture, and Evolution* (Chicago, 1968), 69–90.

53. Honegger, *Allgemeine Kulturgeschichte* (Leipzig, 1882); and Tylor, *Researches into the Early History of Mankind and the Development of Civilization* (1865), ed. Paul Bohannan (Chicago, 1964), 1.

54. Penneman, *A Hundred Years of Anthropology,* 97.

55. Schlosser, *Universalhistorische Ubersicht der Geschichte der alten Welt und ihrer Cultur* (Frankfurt, 1826); Wachsmuth, *Allgemeine Culturgeschichte* (Leipzig, 1850); Wirth, *Fragmente zur Culturgeschichte* (Kaiserslautern, 1826²); Lorentz, *Die allgemeine Geschichte der Völker und ihrer Cultur* (Elberfeld, 1837–40); Klemm, *Allgemeine Cultur-Geschichte der Menschheit* (Leipzig, 1843); Kolb, *Geschichte der Menschheit und der Kultur* (Pforzheim, 1843); Apelt, *Die Epochen der Geschichte des Menschheit: Ein historisch-philosophische Skizze* (Jena, 1845); Drumann, *Grundriss der Cultur-Geschichte* (Königsberg, 1847).

56. Taylor, *The Natural History of Society in the Barbarian and Civilized State* (New York, 1841); MacKinnon, *History of Civilisation* (London, 1846); Alison, *The Philosophy and History of Civilisation* (London, 1860); Dean, *The History of Civilization* (Albany, 1860).

57. Draper, *The Intellectual Development of Europe* (New York, 1876); Hittell, *A History of the Mental Growth of Mankind* (New York, 1893); Allen, *The Prehistoric World: Europe-America* (Cincinnati, 1887); Wilson, *Prehistoric Man: Researches in the Origin of Civilisation in the Old and the New World* (London, 1865).

58. See Eno Beuchelt, *Ideengeschichte der Völkerpsychologie* (Mersenheim, 1974), and Ivan Kalmar, "The *Völkerpsychologie* of Lazarus and Steinthal and the Modern Concept of Culture" *Journal of the History of Ideas,* 48 (1987), 671–690.

59. Geiger, *Contribution to the History of the Development of the Human Race,* trans. David Ashe (London, 1880), 32, 4.

60. See Stefan Haas, *Historische Kulturforschung 1880–1930* (Cologne, 1994), 49.

61. Freytag, *Bilder aus der deutschen Vergangenheit* (Leipzig, 1859).

62. Wachsmuth, *The Historical Antiquities of the Greeks,* trans. Edmund Woolrych (Oxford, 1837).

63. Riehl, *Die Naturgeschichte des Volkes als Grundlage einer deutschen Sozial-Politik* (Stuttgart, 1862–69); *The Natural History of the German People,* tr. David J. Diephouse (Lewiston, N.Y., 1990).

64. *Zeitschrift für deutsche Kulturgeschichte: Bilder und Züge sus den Leben des deutschen Volkes* (Nürnberg, 1856).

65. Jodl, *Die Kulturgeschichtschreibung* (Halle, 1878).

66. *Catalog der culturhistorischen Sammlung des verstorbenen Hofrath Dr. Gustav Klemm* (Dresden, n.d.), copy received by the American Philosophical Society in 1868 and known to the founders of the Smithsonian Institution; see also Klemm, *Allgemeine Culturwissenschaft: Die materiellen Grundlagen menschlichen Cultur* (Leipzig, 1854), and Susan A. Crane, *Collecting and Historica Consciousness in Nineteenth-Century Germany* (Ithaca, 2000), 135.

67. Klemm, *Allgemeine Cultur-Geschichte,* 1.

68. Kolb, *Kulturgeschichte der Menschheit* (Leipzig, 1884[3]).

69. Kolb, ibid., 53.

70. Hellwald, *Kulturgeschichte in ihrer natürlichen Entwicklung bis zur Gegenwart* (Augsburg, 1883[3]), 223.

71. Kolb, *Kulturgeschichte der Menschheit,* I, 21.

72. Grün, *Kulturgeschichte des sechzehnten Jahrhunderts* (Leipzig, 1872); Honegger, *Allgemeine Kulturgeschichte* (Leipzig, 1882); Lippert, *Kulturgeschichte der Menschheit in ihrem organischen Aufbau* (1886) and *The Evolution of Culture,* trans. G. P. Murdoch (New York, 1931); and for further bibliography Hartmann, *Die deutsche Geschichtschreibung,* 145–159.

73. Henne am Rhyn, *Die Kultur der Vergangenheit, Gegenwart und Zukunft* (Danzig, 1890[2]), 133, and "Einleitung" to Hellwald, *Kulturgeschichte,* 9.

74. Roger Chickering, *Karl Lamprecht: A German Academic Life (1856–1915)* (Atlantic Highlands, N.J., 1993), 88.

75. Spengler, *The Decline of the West,* trans. Charles Francis Atkinson (New York, 1932); and see H. Stuart Hughes, *Oswald Spengler* (New Brunswick, 1992[2]), Alexander Demandt and John Farrenkopf (ed.), *Der Fall Spengler: Eine kritische Bilanz* (Cologne, 1994), and now John Farrenkopf, *Prophet of Decline: Spengler on World History and Politics* (Baton Rouge, 2001).

76. Bonnie G. Smith, "The Contribution of Women to Modern Historiogrraphy in Great Britain, France, and the United States, 1750–1940," *American Historical Review,* 89 (1994), 709–732.

77. Herder, *Outlines,* 484.

78. Snyder, *Global Mini-Nationalisms: Autonomy or Independence* (Westport, Conn., 1982). See Harry Elmer Barnes, *A History of Historical Writing* (New York, 1962[2]), 220–229, 257–259; and Matthew A. Fitzsimmons et al., *The Development of Historiography* (Port Washington, N.Y., 1954), 286–349.

79. Anderson, *Imagined Communities: Reflections on the Origin and Spread of Nationalism* (New York, 1991[2]); C. A. Macartney, *National States and National Minorities* (Oxford, 1934); Eric Hobsbawm and Terence Ranger, *The Invention of Tradition* (Cambridge, 1983); see also Tony Kellen, *Die Luxemburgische Geschichtsschreibung: Ein*

Rückblick und ein Ausblick (Luxemburg, 1933), and Kerim K. Key, *An Outline of Modern Turkish Historiography* (Istanbul, 1954).

80. G. P. Gooch, *History and Historians in the Nineteenth Century* (London, 1952²), 425, and J. W. Thompson, *A History of Historical Writing* (Chicago, 1942), 2: 595.

81. D. R. Woolf (ed.), *A Global Encyclopedia of Historical Writing* (New York, 1998), entries on: Byron J. Nordstrom, "Scandinavian Historiography," Pekka Kalevi Hämäläinen, "Finnish Historiography"; Oscar J. Falnes, *National Romanticism in Norway* (New York, 1933); and Sven Tägil (ed.), *Ethnicity and Nation Building in the Nordic World* (Carbondale, Ill., 1995).

82. See Knut Gjerset, *History of the Norwegian People* (New York, 1915), II, 495.

83. Geijer, *The History of the Swedes*, tr. J. H. Turner (London, [1845]), and Allen, *Histoire de Danemark* (Copenhagen, 1878).

84. Max Engman, "Finns and Swedes in Finland," in Tägil, 179–216.

85. Aira Kemiläinen, *Finns in the Shadow of the "Aryans": Race Theories and Racism* (Helsinki, 1998).

86. Articles by Gunnar Karlsson, Hans Jacob Debes, and Axel Kjaer Sorensen in Tägil, op cit., 33–105.

87. *American Historical Review,* 97 (1992), 1011–1117, "Historiography of the Countries of Eastern Europe": Piotr S. Wandycz, "Poland"; Jiri Koralka, "Czechoslovakia"; István Déak, "Hungary"; Keith Hitchins, "Romania"; Ivo Banac, "Yugoslavia"; and Maria Todorova, "Bulgaria"; also Woolf, op cit., articles on historiography: Antoon de Baets, Belgium; Robert Stallaerts, Croatia and Serbia; Anita Shelton, Czechoslovakia; Toivo U. Raun, Estonia; Attila Pók, Hungary; Andreijs, Latvia; J. Dainauskas and J. Rackauskas, Lithuania; Ewa Domanska, Poland; S. Remny, Romania — both with further bibliography.

88. Jerzy Jedlicki, *A Suburb of Europe: Nineteenth-Century Polish Approaches to Western Civilization* (Budapest, 1999), 33; and see Joan S. Skurnowicz, *Romantic Nationalism and Liberalism: Joachim Lelewel and the Polish National Idea* (New York, 1981), and more generally the contributions on Poland, Czechoslovakia, Hungary, Romania, Yugoslavia, and Bulgaria in *American Historical Review,* 97 (1992), 1011–1117.

89. Lelewel, *Considérations sur l'état politique de l'ancienne Pologne et sur l'histoire de son peuple* (n.p., 1836).

90. See Steven Bela Vardy, *Modern Hungarian Historiography* (New York, 1976), and Tibor Baráth, *L'Histoire en Hongrie (1867–1935)* (Paris, 1936).

91. K. Sklenár, "The History of Archaeology in Czechoslovakia," *Towards a History of Archaeology,* 150–158.

92. Palácky, *A History of the Czechs and Slovaks* (Hamden, Conn., 1965), 176; and see Richard Georg Plaschka, *Von Palácky bis Pekar: Geschichtswissenschaft und Nationalbewusstsein bei den Tschechen* (Cologne, 1955).

93. Xénopol, *La Théorie de l'histoire* (Paris, 1908²).

94. E. g., Iorga, *Essai de synthèse de l'histoire de l'humanité* (Paris, 1926); *Le Caractère commun des institutions du Sud-Est de l'Europe* (Paris, 1929); *A History of Roumania,* trans., Joseph McCabe (London, 1925); and other volumes on Romanian history.

95. R. W. Seton-Watson, *The Southern Slav Question and the Habsburg Language* (London, 1911), 29.

96. Ibid., 134; and see Prince Lazarovich-Hrebelianovich, *The Servian People, Their Past Glory and Their Destiny* (New York, 1910), 386–87, listing the Serbian historians.

97. See K. A. Jusaitis, *The History of the Lithuanian Nation and Its Present National Aspirations* (Philadelphia, 1918).

98. Besides Gooch and Thompson, see Ignacio Pieró Martin, *Los Guardianes de la historia: la historiografia académica de la Restauracion* (Zaragoza, 1995); also Woolf, op cit., entries on Portugal (Luís Reis Torgal) and Spain (Ignacio Olábarri).

99. Lea, *A Critical History of the Inquisition of Spain* (Williamstown, Mass., 1967 [1823]), xvii; and see the introduction by Gabriel H. Lovett.

100. B. Sanchez Alonso, *Historia de la historiografia española* (Madrid, 1950), III, 191.

101. Menéndez y Pelayo, *Historia de los heterodoxes españoles* (Madrid, 1880–81).

102. Manuel Moreno Alonso, *Historiografia romántica española* (Seville, 1979), 230.

103. Moreno Alonso, ibid., 184.

104. Moreno Alonso, ibid., 185.

105. Georg von Wyss, *Geschichte der Historiographie in der Schweiz* (Zurich, 1895).

106. Fueter, *Geschichte der neueren Historiographie* (Berlin, 1936^3 [1911]), with translations into French and Italian but not English; also "Geschichte der gesamtschweizerischen historischen Organisation," *Hundert Jahre Historische Zeitschrift 1859–1959,* ed. Theodor Schieder (Munich, 1959), 449–505.

107. Jo Tollebeek, *De Toga van Fruin: Denken over geschiedenis in Nederland sinds 1860* (Amsterdam, 1990), 26, and P. A. M. Geurts and A. E. M. Janssen (eds.), *Geschied-schrijving in Nederland* (The Hague, 1981).

108. See Bryce Lyon, *Henri Pirenne: A Biographical and Intellectual Study* (Ghent, 1974), 131.

109. Pirenne, *Early Democracies in the Low Countries: Urban Society and Political Conflict in the Middle Ages and the Renaissance,* tr. J. V. Saunders (New York, 1963), 156; introduction by John Hine Mundy.

110. Pirenne, *Medieval Cities: Their Origins and the Revival of Trade* (Princeton, 1948), trans. Frank D. Halsy, 213; and see *Economic and Social History of Medieval Europe,* trans. I. E. Clegg (New York, n.d.).

111. *Mahomet and Charlemagne,* trans. Bernard Miall (New York, 1939); and see Lyon, op cit., 441–56.

112. Vico, *Scienza nuova,* par. 127.

113. See especially Carlrichard Brühl, *Deutschland-Frankreich: die Geburt Zweier Völker* (Vienna, 1990).

Chapter 11: American Parallels

1. Kelley, *Faces of History: Historical Inquiry from Herodotus to Herder* (New Haven. 1998), 156–161.

2. *De Origine rerum Americanarum dissertatio* (Paris, 1642).

3. Winsor (ed,), *Narrative and Critical History of America* (Boston, 1889), 1 (part 1): 59.

4. Ibid., 1 (part 1): 86; and see *The Literary Memoranda of William Hickling Prescott* (Norman, Okla., 1961), 2: 43.

5. Priest, *American Antiquities and Discoveries in the West* (Albany, 1833³), 127.

6. Bradford, *American Antiquities and Researches into the Origin and History of the Red Race* (New York, 1841), preface.

7. Ibid., 435.

8. Winsor, 1 (part 1): 83.

9. Translations in North Ludlow Beamish, *The Discovery of America by the Northmen in the Tenth Century* (London, 1841), and B. F. de Costa, *The Pre-Columbian Discovery of America by the Northmen* (Albany, 1890²).

10. Winsor, 1 (part 1): 89.

11. Ibid., 106.

12. White, *A History of the Warfare of Science with Theology in Christendom* (New York, 1907), 1: 86, 303.

13. Winsor, 1 (part 2): 437.

14. See Gordon R. Willey and Jeremy A. Sabloff, *A History of American Archaeology* (San Francisco, 1980²), and Willey, "One Hundred Years of American Archaeology," *One Hundred Years of American Anthropology,* ed. J. O. Brew (London, 1968), 35.

15. *Proceedings of the American Antiquarian Society 1812–1849* (Worcester, 1912), 28.

16. Bureau of Ethnology, *First Annual Report to the Secretary of the Smithsonian Institution 1879–80* (Washington, D.C., 1881).

17. Prescott, *The Conquest of Mexico* (London, 1909), 2: 375.

18. In general see John Higham, Leonard Krieger, and Felix Gilbert, *History: The Development of Historical Studies in the United States* (Englewood Cliffs, N.J., 1965); Michael Kraus and David D. Joyce, *The Writing of American History* (Norman, Okla., 1985), 88; Bert James Loewenberg, *American History in American Thought* (New York, 1972); and Harvey Wish, *The American Historian* (Oxford, 1960).

19. Herbert B. Adams, *The Life and Writings of Jared Sparks* (Boston, 1893).

20. See Orie William Long. *Literary Pioneers: Early American Explorers of European Culture* (Cambridge, Mass., 1935), and also Van Wyck Brooks, *The Flowering of New England 1815–1865* (New York, 1937).

21. *Life, Letters, and Journals of George Ticknor* (Boston, 1877), 1: 18; Robinson, *Diary, Reminiscences, and Correspondence* (Boston, 1869).

22. Russel B. Nye, *George Bancroft, Brahmin Rebel* (New York, 1944), and Mark DeWolfe Howe, *The Life and Letters of George Bancroft* (New York, 1908), 1: 47; also David Levin, *History as Romantic Art: Bancroft, Prescott, Motley, and Parkman* (Stanford, 1959).

23. Bancroft, *History of the United States of America from the Discovery of the Continent* (Boston, 1876), 2: 544.

24. A. H. L. Heeren, *A Manual of the History of the Political System of Europe and Its Colonies* (London, 1857), reviewed by Bancroft in *The North American Review* (1826).

25. Bancroft, *History,* 1: 3.

26. Bancroft, *History,* 3: 7.

27. Bancroft, *History,* 2: 175.

28. Bancroft, *History,* 3: 311.

29. Bancroft, *History,* 2: 461.

30. Ticknor, *Life of William Hickling Prescott* (Philadelphia, 1875), 67; and see Richard Kagan, "Prescott's Paradigm: American Historical Scholarship and the Decline of Spain," *Imagined Histories: American Historians Interpret the Past,* ed. Anthony Molho and Gordon S. Wood (Princeton, 1998), 324–348.

31. Holmes, *John Lothrop Motley: A Memoir* (London, 1878), 61; and Brooks, *Flowering,* 111.

32. C. Harvey Gardiner, *William Hickling Prescott: A Biography* (Austin, 1969), 67.

33. Irving, *The Life and Voyages of Christopher Columbus,* ed. John Harmon McElroy (Boston, 1981).

34. *The Literary Memoranda of William Hickling Prescott,* ed. C. Harvey Gardiner (Norman, Okla., 1961), 1: 90, 135, 190.

35. Ticknor, *Life,* 77; and see letter to Bancroft (16 Nov. 1826) in *The Papers of William Hickling Prescott,* ed. C. Harvey Gardiner (Urbana, 1964), 46, and the many to Pascual de Gayangos in *The Correspondence of William Hickling Prescott 1833–47,* ed. Roger Wolcott (Boston, 1925).

36. Prescott, *History of the Reign of Ferdinand and Isabella the Catholic* (Philadelphia, 1837), 2: 153.

37. Prescott, *The Conquest of Mexico* (London, 1909), vol. 1, preface.

38. Ibid., 2: 373–402.

39. Motley, *The Rise of the Dutch Republic: A History* (Philadelphia, n. d.), vol. 1, preface.

40. Introduction to the anthology, *John Lothrop Motley,* ed. Chester Penn Higby and B. T. Schantz (New York, 1939).

41. *The Correspondence of John Lothrop Motley,* ed. George William Curtis, 2 vols. (New York, 1889), 1: 211.

42. Ibid., 1: 318.

43. Ibid., 1: 292.

44. Motley, *Rise of the Dutch Republic,* 3: 388.

45. Ibid., 3: 546.

46. Ibid., 3: 671.

47. Mason Wade, *Francis Parkman, Heroic Historian* (New York, 1942), and Charles Haight Farnham, *A Life of Francis Parkman* (Boston, 1902).

48. Parkman, *The Conspiracy of Pontiac* (New York, 1991), 429, 846.

49. Parkman, *La Salle and the Discovery of the Great West* (New York, 1962), 118, 335.

50. On the institutional vehicles see Winsor, vol. 1, with bibliographies and critical notes.

51. Palfrey, *History of New England during the Stuart Dynasty* (Boston, 1890³), 1: vii, 33, 5.

52. Hildreth, *History of the United States* (New York, 1882), vi.

53. Hildreth, *Theory of Politics* (New York, 1877), 267.

54. See Daniel T. Rogers, "Exceptionalism," *Imagined Histories,* 21–40.

55. Draper, *History of the Intellectual Development of Europe* (New York, 1976⁶), 1: 2, 17; and see Donald Fleming, *John William Draper and the Religion of Science* (Philadelphia, 1950).

56. Ibid., ii, 147.

57. Ibid., 1: 166; 2: 201.

58. Ibid., 2: 319.

59. White, *Autobiography* (New York, 1907), 1: 39, 260, 381.

60. White, *A History of the Warfare of Science with Theology in Christendom* (New York, 1907), 1: 312.

61. Ibid., 1: 312.

62. Ibid., 2: 395.

63. Milton Berman, *John Fiske: The Evolution of a Popularizer* (Cambridge, Mass., 1961); and John Spencer Clark, *The Life and Letters of John Fiske* (Boston, 1917).

64. Fiske, *Excursions of an Evolutionist* (Boston, 1891¹²), 88.

65. Ibid., 88.

66. Ibid., 201.

67. Ibid., 369.

68. Fiske, *The Discovery of America* (Boston, 1892).

69. Fiske, *American Political Ideas from the Standpoint of Universal History* (Boston, 1911), 5.

70. Rhodes, *Historical Essays* (New York, 1909), 4, 7.

71. Ibid., 49.

72. Ernest Samuels, *The Young Henry Adams* (Cambridge, Mass., 1948); *Henry Adams: The Middle Years* (1958); *Henry Adams: The Major Phase* (1964); and J. C. Levenson, *The Mind and Art of Henry Adams* (Cambridge, Mass., 1957).

73. Becker, *Everyman His Own Historian: Essays in History and Politics* (New York, 1935), 162.

74. *The Education of Henry Adams* (New York, 1918), 33.

75. Ibid., 91.

76. Ibid., 303.

77. Adams, *Essays in Anglo-Saxon Law* (Boston, 1876), 1; Samuels, *Young Henry Adams*, 247, and Levenson, *Henry Adams*, 43.

78. Adams, Review of Maine's "Village Communities," in *Sketches for the North American Review* (Hamden, Conn., 1986), 47.

79. Letter of 2 Jan. 1873, *The Letters of Henry Adams*, ed. J. C. Levenson et al. (Cambridge, Mass., 1982), 2: 155.

80. Bert James Loewenberg, *American History in American Thought*, 446–447.

81. Adams, *History of the United States during the Administrations of Thomas Jefferson* (New York, 1986), 66.

82. Levenson, *Henry Adams*, 191; Adams, *Education*, 382.

83. Adams, *Letters*, 2: 563.

84. Samuels, *The Middle Years*.

85. Adams, *Education*, 314, 395, 497.

86. Ibid., 410.

87. Ibid., 16, 472.

88. Samuels, *The Major Phase*, 214.

89. Adams, *Mont-Saint-Michel and Chartres* (New York, 1961), 42.

90. Ibid., 193, 102.

91. Edward Sculley Bradley, *Henry Charles Lea: A Biography* (Philadelphia, 1931).

92. Herman Ausubel, *Historians and Their Craft: A Study of the Presidential Addresses of the American Historical Association 1884–1945* (New York, 1950), and Molho and Wood, *Imagined Histories.*

93. Gordon S. Wood, "A Century of Writing Early American History: Then and Now Compared; or How Henry Adams Got It Wrong," *American Historical Review,* 100 (1995), 679; and see Adams, "The Tendency of History," *The Great Secession Winter of 1860–61 and Other Essays,* ed. George Hochfield (New York, 1958), 415–424.

94. Adams, *Education,* 505.

95. Cited by Levenson, *Henry Adams,* 126.

Chapter 12: New Histories

1. Hervé Contau-Begarie, *Le Phénomène "nouvelle histoire"* (Paris, 1983), and Ignacio Olábarri Gortázar, " 'New' New History: A *Longue Durée* Structure," *History and Theory,* 34 (1995); Jacques Le Goff, "Antique (Ancient) Modern," *History and Memory,* trans. Steven Rendell and Elizabeth Claman (New York, 1992), 21–50.

2. Bezold, "Die neue historische Methode," *Historisches Zeitschrift,* 81 (1898), 193–273 (he had reviewed Lamprecht's first two volumes five years earlier in *Historisches Zeitschrift*) and the later treatment in *Die deutsche Geschichtschreibung von den Befreiungskriegen bis zu unsern Tagen* (Munich, 1924), 95; and Earle W. Dow, "Features of the New History: Apropos of Lamprecht's 'Deutsche Geschichte,' " *American Historical Review,* 3 (1898); also Ernst Breisach, *American Progressive History: An Experiment in Modernization* (Chicago, 1993), 29.

3. Lamprecht, *Deutsche Wirtschaftsleben in Mittelalter: Unterzuchung über die Entwicklung der materiellen Kultur des platten Landes auf Grund der Quellen* (Leipzig, 1885–86), and *Deutsche Geschichte* (Leipzig, 1891–1909).

4. Roger Chickering, *Karl Lamprecht: A German Academic Life (1856–1915)* (Atlantic Highlands, NJ, 1993), 88; also Horst Walter Blanke, *Historiographiegeschichte als Historik* (Stuttgart, 1991), 439–474, Stefan Haas, *Historische Kulturforschung in Deutschland 1880–1930* (Cologne, 1994), 98–105, Karl J. Weintraub, *Visions of Culture* (Chicago, 1966), 161–207, Gerald Diesener, *Karl Lamprecht weiterdenken: Universal- und Kulturgeschichte heute* (Leipzig, 1993), and Thompson, *History of Historical Writing,* 2: 422–428.

5. Schäfer, *Das eigentliche Arbeitsgebiet der Geschichte* (Jena, 1888), and *Geschichte und Kulturgeschichte* (Jena, 1891); also Haas, *Historische Forschung,* 98ff, and Blanke, *Historiographiegeschichte,* 391ff.

6. Gothein, *Die Aufgaben der Kulturgeschichte* (Leipzig, 1889); and see Peter Alter, "Eberhard Gothein," in *Deutsche Historiker,* ed. H.-U. Wehler (Göttingen, 1982), 3: 40–55.

7. Ibid., 11.

8. Ibid., 48.

9. Ibid., 35.

10. See Friedrich Albert Lange, *The History of Materialism and Criticism of Its Present Importance,* trans. E. C. Thomas, 3 vols. (New York, 1925³), from the Sophists to Darwin.

11. Haas, *Historische Kulturforschung,* 55; and see Beloch, *Die Bevölkerung der griechisch-römischen Welt* (Lepizig, 1886).

12. Lamprecht, *Alternative zu Ranke: Schriften zur Geschichtstheorie,* ed. Hans Schleier (Leipzig 1988), 256.

13. Ibid., 137.

14. Meinecke, *Zur Geschichte der Geschichtsschreibung,* ed. Eberhard Kessel (Munich, 1968), 321–330; Meinecke's and Lamprecht's letters in Theodor Schieder (ed.), *Hundert Jahre Historische Zeitschrift* (Munich, 1959), 81ff; and see Fulvio Tessitore, *Friedrich Meinecke storico delle idee* (Florence, 1969), 61–67.

15. Meinecke, letter to Below (18 Jan. 1899), *Ausgewählte Briefwechsel,* ed. Ludwig Dehio and Peter Classen (Stuttgart, 1962), 16; 67 (3 Aug. 1915); and 84, to Goetz (30 July 1915).

16. Below, *Die deutsche Geschichtsschreibung*; and Otto Gerhard Oexle, "Ein politische Historiker (1858–1927)," *Deutsche Geschichtswissenschaft um 1900,* ed. Notker Hammerstein (Stuttgart, 1988), 283–312.

17. *Histoire et historiens depuis cinquante ans,* ed. M. Bataillon et al. (Paris, 1927), 19.

18. Lamprecht, *What Is History?* (New York, 1905), 19.

19. Lamprecht, *Alternative,* 165; and see 307–332 ("Die Entwicklung der deutschen Geschichtswissenschaft vornehmlich seit Herder").

20. Lamprecht, "Was ist Kulturgeschichte?" *Alternative zu Ranke,* 215; see also Smith, *Politics and the Sciences of Culture,* 115.

21. On the seminar see Bonnie G. Smith, *The Gender of History* (Cambridge, Mass., 1998), chapter 4.

22. Haas, *Historische Kulturforschung,* 229–242.

23. Chickering, *Lamprecht,* 412.

24. See, e. g., Max Verworn, *Die biologischen Grundlagen der Kulturpolitik* (Jena, 1915), Georg Simmel, *Die Konflikt der modernen Kultur* (Munich 1918), and Emil Utitz, *Die Kultur der Gegenwart* (Stuttgart, 1921).

25. See, e.g., G. Hamilton MacLeod, *The Blight of Kultur* (London, 1918).

26. Steinhausen, *Geschichte der deutschen Kultur* (Leipzig, 1904, 1913, 1920, 1936), lavishly illustrated; and see Haas, *Historische Kulturforschung,* 166ff.

27. Steinhausen, *Der Aufschwung der deutschen Kultur vom 18. Jahrhundert bis zur Weltkrieg* (Leipzig, 1920), 176.

28. Steinhausen, *Geschichte der deutschen Kultur* (Leipzig, 1936), 536.

29. Wolf Stuyterman von Langewende, *Kultur ist Dienst am Leben* (Berlin, 1937).

30. See Felix Gilbert, *History: Politics or Culture: Reflections on Ranke and Burckhardt* (Princeton, 1990).

31. See note 96, below.

32. *The Letters of Henry Adams,* ed. J. C. Levenson et al. (Cambridge, Mass., 1982), 2: 558 (26 November), 562 (21 December).

33. Ernest A. Breisach, *American Progressive History: An Experiment in Modernization* (Chicago, 1993), 30; also John Higham, with Leonard Krieger and Felix Gilbert, *History: The Development of Historical Studies in the United States* (Englewood Cliffs, N.J., 1965).

34. Chickering, *Lamprecht,* 347.

35. Ernst Breisach, *American Progressive History: An Experiment in Modernization* (Chicago, 1993), and David Noble, *Historians against History: The Frontier Thesis and the National Covenant in American Historical Writing since 1830* (Minneapolis, 1965).

36. Jameson, *An Historian's World,* ed. Elizabeth Donnan and Leo F. Stock (Philadelphia, 1956), 104 (letter of 31 Jan. 1907).

37. Jameson, *The History of Historical Writing in America* (Boston, 1891), 141; and *An Historian's World,* 105 (letter to James Bryce, 17 April 1907).

38. Hofstadter. *The Progressive Historians: Turner, Beard, Parrington* (New York, 1968), 5.

39. Benson, *Turner and Beard: American Historical Writing Reconsidered* (New York, 1960), 83.

40. Ray Allen Billington, *Frederick Jackson Turner: Historian, Scholar, Teacher* (New York, 1973), 65, 162.

41. Turner, "The Significance of History," in Harvey Wish, ed., *American Historians: A Selection* (New York, 1962), 289.

42. Turner, *The Frontier in American History* (New York, 1920), 2–3, 24.

43. Ibid., 323.

44. Robinson, *The New History: Essays Illustrating the Modern Historical Outlook* (New York, 1912), 46.

45. Ibid., 43.

46. Ibid., 83.

47. Ibid., 86–87.

48. Ibid., 91.

49. Barnes, *History of Historical Writing* (Norman, Okla., 1937), 373.

50. See Ellen Nore, *Charles A. Beard: An Intellectual Biography* (Carbondale, Ill., 1983); Burleigh Taylor Wilkins, *Carl Becker: A Biographical Study in American Intellectual History* (Cambridge, Mass., 1961); Cushing Strout, *The Pragmatic Revolt in American History: Carl Becker and Charles Beard* (New Haven, 1958); and Peter Novick, *That Noble Dream: The "Objectivity Question" and the American Historical Profession* (Cambridge, 1988).

51. Nore, *Carl Becker,* 63.

52. Becker, *Everyman His Own Historian: Essays in History in Politics* (New York, 1935), 227.

53. Becker, *"What Is the Good of History?" Selected Letters of Carl Becker 1900–1945,* ed. Micheal Kammen (Ithaca, 1973), to William E. Dodd, 17 June 1920.

54. Novick, *That Noble Dream: The "Objectivity Question" and the American Historical Profession* (Cambridge, 1988), 268.

55. See Salmon, *Selected Essays,* ed. Nicholas Adams and Bonnie G. Smith (Philadelphia, 2001).

56. Ibid., 204, 208.

57. Herman Ausubel, *Historians and Their Craft: A Study of the Presidential Addresses of the American Historical Association, 1884–1945* (New York, 1950).

58. Becker, *The Heavenly City of the Eighteenth-Century Philosophers* (New Haven, 1932).

59. Beard, *The Rise of American Civilization* (New York, 1937), 2: 795.

60. Lacombe, *De l'Histoire considérée comme science* (Paris, 1894), and his review of Xénopol in *Revue de Synthèse historique*, 1 (1900), 28–51; and see Keylor, *Academy and Community*, 125–140.

61. Xénopol, *Les Principes fondamentaux de l'histoire* (Paris, 1899).

62. Berr, *La Synthèse de connaissance et l'histoire* (Paris, 1898), followed by another manifesto, *La Synthèse en histoire* (Paris, 1911), 217, citing Lamprecht; Martin Siegel, "Henri Berr's *Revue de Synthèse historique,*" *History and Theory,* 9 (1970), 322–334; and *Henri Berr et la culture du XXᵉ siècle: Histoire, science et philosophie,* ed. Agnès Biard, Dominique Bourel, and Eric Brian (Paris, 1997); also, on the *Annaliste* school, Jacques Le Goff, Jacques Revel and Roger Chartier, eds., *La Nouvelle Histoire* (Paris, 1978); Luciano Allegra, *La Nascità della storia sociale in Francia: Dalla comune alle "Annales"* (Turin, 1977); François Dosse, *New History in France: The Triumph of the Annales,* trans. Peter V. Conroy, Jr. (Urbana, 1994); Philippe Carrard, *Poetics of the New History: French Historical Discourse from Braudel to Chartier* (Baltimore, 1992); Peter Burke, *The French Historical Revolution: The Annales School 1929–89* (Stanford, 1990); Traian Stoianovich, *French Historical Method: The* Annales *Paradigm* (Ithaca, 1976); Georg G. Iggers, *New Directions in European Historiography* (Middletown, Conn., 1984²); H. Stuart Hughes, *The Obstructed Path: French Social Thought in the Years of Desperation 1930–1960* (New York, 1966); Roger Chartier, "Intellectual History and the History of *Mentalités,*" *Cultural History,* trans. Lydia G. Cochrane (Ithaca, 1988), 19–52.

63. Berr, *La Synthèse en histoire: son rapport avec la synthèse générale* (Paris, 1953), preface of 1911.

64. *Revue de Synthèse,* 6 (1903), 1–22, 129–157; and see Jacques Revel, "Le Moment Berr," in *Henri Berr et la culture du XXᵉ siècle,* 168; also Fritz Ringer, *Fields of Knowledge: French Academic Culture in Comparative Perspective 1890–1920* (Cambridge, 1992).

65. Berr, *La Synthèse en histoire,* 225.

66. Peter Schöttler, "Henri Berr et l'Allemagne," in *Henri Berr et la culture du XXᵉ siècle,* 194.

67. Boutroux, *The Contingency of the Laws of Nature,* trans. Fred Rothwell (Chicago, 1916), 166; and see Richard Horner, "A Pragmatist in Paris: Frédéric Rauh's 'Task of Dissolution,'" *Journal of the History of Ideas,* 58 (1997), 289–308.

68. Boutroux, *Historical Studies in Philosophy,* tr. Fred Rothwell (Port Washington, N.Y., [1912]), 5.

69. Berr, *La Synthèse historique,* 23.

70. Febvre, *Philippe II et la France-Comté* (Paris, 1970 [1912]); Bloch, *The Ile-de-France: The Country around Paris,* trans. J. E. Anderson (Ithaca, 1966 [1912]); also *Rois et serfs: une chapitre d'histoire capétienne* (Paris, 1996 [1920]).

71. Febvre, *De la* Revue de Synthèse *aux* Annales: *Lettres à Henri Berr 1911–1954,* ed. Gilles Candar and Jacqueline Pluet-Despatin (Paris, 1997), 3; and Bloch and Febvre, *Correspondance,* ed. Bertrand Müller, vol. 1, *La Naissance des* Annales *1928–33* (Paris, 1994).

72. Febvre, *A Geographical Introduction to History* (London, 1925), the French original of which, planned for 1915, appeared in 1922; and see *Pour un Histoire à part entière* (Paris, 1962), 147; also Susan W. Frieman, *Marc Bloch, Sociology, and Geography: Encountering Changing Disciplines* (Cambridge, 1996), 44.

73. Febvre, *Geographical Introduction,* 36; repeated in letter to Berr (18 Jan. 1914), *Lettres,* 26.

74. Ibid., 162.

75. Carole Fink, *Marc Bloch: A Life in History* (Cambridge, 1989), 130.

76. Febvre, *Lettres,* 306–309 (17 Dec. 1927).

77. Bloch and Febvre, *Correspondance,* 44–45.

78. Febvre, *Lettres,* 125 (August 1926).

79. Bloch, *The Royal Touch: Sacred Monarchy and Scrofula in England and France,* trans. J. E. Anderson (London, 1973), 243.

80. Etienne Bloch, *Marc Bloch: une biographie impossible* (Limoges, 1997), 62.

81. Bloch and Febvre, *Correspondance,* 48 (Bloch to Febvre, 8 Aug. 1928); and see Karl Dietrich Erdmann, *Die Ökumene der Historiker: Geschichte det Internationalen Historikerkongresse und der Comité Internationale des Sciences Historiques* (Göttingen, 1987), 124.

82. Bloch, *The Historian's Craft,* trans. P. Putnam (New York, 1962 [1949]), 189.

83. Cited by H. Stuart Hughes, *The Obstructed Path,* 21.

84. See W. E. Krul, *Historicus tegen de tijd: Opstellen over Leven en Werk van J. Huizinga* (Groningen, 1990); Christoph Strupp, *Johan Huizinga: Geschichtswissenschaft als Kulturgeschichte* (Göttingen, 2000); and Karl J. Weintraub, *Visions of Culture* (Chicago, 1966), 208–246.

85. Huizinga, *Briefwisseling,* ed. Leon Hanssen, W. E. Krul, and Anton van der Lem (Veen, 1989), 1: 76 (to H. Th. Colenbrander, 22 Nov. 1905); 200ff (to Pirenne, March 1917).

86. *Men and Ideas: History, the Middle Ages, the Renaissance,* trans. James S. Holmes and Hans van Marle (Princeton, 1984), 21; *Culturhistorische Verkenningen* (Haarlem, 1929).

87. Huizinga, "Over een Definitie van het Begrip Geschiedenis," *Culturhistorische Verkenningen,* 156–168; "A Definition of the Concept of History," in *Philosophy and History: Essays Presented to Ernst Cassirer,* ed. Raymond Klibansky and H. J. Paton (New York, 1963), 5, 9.

88. Huizinga, "History Changing Form," *Journal of the History of Ideas,* 4 (1943), 223; repr. *The History of Ideas: Canon and Variations,* ed. D. R. Kelley (Rochester, 1990), 221.

89. Huizinga, "Het Probleem der Renaissance," *Tien Studien* (Haarlem, 1926); 289–344; and see Wallace K. Ferguson, *The Renaissance in Historical Thought* (Boston, 1948), 373–376.

90. *The Autumn of the Middle Ages* , trans. Rodney J. Payton and Ulrich Mimmitzsch (Chicago, 1996), 17, 103.

91. Huizinga, *Autumn,* 40.

92. Huizinga, "Het Probleem der Renaissance," 305.

93. Huizinga, *Autumn,* 37.

94. Ibid., 32.

95. Huizinga, *Erasmus of Rotterdam,* tr. F. Hopman (London, 1952), 104.

96. Huizinga, "De Taak der Culturgeschiedenis," *Culturhistorische Verkenningen,* 1–85; *Men and Ideas,* 51; and *In the Shadow of Tomorrow,* trans. J. H. Huizinga (New York, 1936), 39.

97. Huizinga, *In the Shadow of Tomorrow,* 22; and see Theodor Lessing, *Geschichte als Sinngebung des Sinnlosen* (Hamburg, 1927).

98. *Home Ludens: A Study of the Play Element in Culture,* trans. from the German (Boston, 1950), 45.

99. Meinecke, "Aphorismen," in *Zur Theorie,* 215.

100. *Schriften,* ed. J. Minor (Jena, 1907), 190. See *Handwörterbuch der Philosophie,* and Erich Rothacker, "Das Wort Historismus," *Zeitschrift für deutsche Wortforschung,* 16 (1960), 3–8.

101. Novalis, *Fragmente zur Poesie und Literatur,* kritische Ausgabe (Paderborn, 1981), 35.

102. Feuerbach, *Werke,* ed. W. Bolen, vol. 8 (1960²), 1, 43.

103. Dahn, *Philosophische Studien* (1882).

104. See Gunter Scholtz, *"Historismus" as speculative Geschichtsphilosophie: Christian Julius Braniss (1792–1873)* (Frankfurt, 1973).

105. Werner, *Giambattista Vico als Philosoph und gelehrter Forscher* (Vienna, 1879).

106. *Essays in the Study and Writing of History,* ed. J. Rufus Fears (Indianapolis, 1985), 543.

107. See Pieto Rossi, *Lo storicismo tedesco contemporaneo* (Turin, 1956), and Giuseppe Cacciatore, *La lancia di Odino: Teorie e metodi della storia in Italia e Germania tra '800 e '900* (Milan, 1994).

108. Rickert, *The Limits of Concept Formation in Natural Science,* trans. Guy Oakes (Cambridge, 1986), 18, 99.

109. Eucken, *Main Currents of Modern Thought,* tr. M. Booth (New York, 1912), 316.

110. Heussi, *Die Krisis des Historismus* (Tübingen, 1932); Meinecke, "Von der Krisis des Historismus," in *Zur Theorie und Philosophie der Geschichte,* ed. Ebehard Kessel (Stuttgart, 1959), 196–204; Gustav Schmidt, *Deutscher Historismus und der Übergang zur parlamentarische Demokratie* (Lübeck, 1964); Georg G. Iggers, *The German Conception of History: The National Tradition of Historical Thought from Herder to the Present* (Middletown, Conn., 1982²), 124–173; and Charles R. Bambach, *Heidegger, Dilthey, and the Crisis of Historicism* (Ithaca, 1995).

111. Edward C. Thaden, *The Rise of Historicism in Russia* (New York, 1999).

112. See Franco Bianco (ed.), *Il dibatto sullo storicismo* (Bologna, 1978), and *Storicismo e ermeneutica* (Rome, 1974); also Wilhelm Hennis, "A Science of Man: Max

Weber and the Political Economy of the German Historical School," in *Max Weber and His Contemporaries,* ed. Wolfgang J. Mommsen and Jürgen Osterhammel (London, 1987), 5–58.

113. Troeltsch, *Historismus und seine Probleme* (Tübingen, 1922); and see Robert J. Rubanowice, *Crisis in Consciousness: The Thought of Ernst Troeltsch* (Talahassee, 1982), and Kurt Nowak, "Historische oder dogmatische Methode? Protestantische Theologie im Jahrhundert des Historismus," in *Geschichtsdiskurs,* ed. Wolfgang Küttler, Jörn Rüsen, and Ernst Schulin, III *Die Epoche der Historisierung* (Frankfurt, 1997), 282–297.

114. See Karl Heussi, *Die Krisis,* opposing also "Psychologismus" and "Aesthetizismus."

115. Haym, *Hegel und seine Zeit* (1857), 467; and see Leonhard von Renthe, *Geschichtlichkeit: Ihre terminologischen und begrifflichen Ursprung bei Hegel, Haym, Dilthey, und Yorck* (Göttingen, 1968²).

116. Dilthey, "Reminiscences of the University of Berlin" (1903), trans. Patricia van Tuyl, in *Hermeneutics and the Study of History,* ed. Rudolf A. Makkreel and Frithjof Rodi (Princeton, 1996), 389.

117. Theodore Plantinga, *Historical Understanding in the Thought of Wilhelm Dilthey* (Toronto, 1980), 123.

118. Hintze, "Troeltsch and Problems of Historicism: Critical Studies," *The Historical Essays of Otto Hintze,* ed. Felix Gilbert (New York, 1975), 368–421.

119. Mannheim, "Historicism," *Essays on the Sociology of Knowledge,* trans. Paul Kecskemeti (London, 1952), 84.

120. Croce, *History as the Story of Liberty,* tr. Sylvia Sprigge (New York, 1941), 78.

121. Croce, *History, Its Theory and Practice,* trans. Douglas Ainslie (New York, 1960), 12.

122. Croce, "Il concetto della filosofia come storicismo assoluto," in *Filosofia, poesia, storia* (Milan, 1951), 13–29; and see David Roberts, *Benedetto Croce and the Uses of Historicism* (Berkeley, 1987).

123. Croce, *History as the Story of Liberty,* 70.

124. *The Idea of History* (Oxford, 1946), 9–10.

125. Meinecke, *Autobiographische Schriften,* Eberhard Kessel (Stuttgart, 1969⁷), 76.

126. Meinecke, *Cosmopolitanism and the National State,* tr. Robert B. Kimber (Princeton, 1970); and see Richard W. Sterling, *Ethics in a World of Power: The Political Ideas of Friedrich Meinecke* (Princeton, 1958), and Henry Pachter, *Weimar Etudes* (New York, 1982), 135–170.

127. Meinecke, "Kausalitäten und Werte in der Geschichte," *Historische Zeitschrift,* 124 (1928), 23.

128. Meinecke, *Machiavellism: The Doctrine of Raison d'Etat and Its Place in Modern History,* trans. Douglas Scott (New Haven, 1957).

129. Croce, *History,* 313–314; *History and the Story of Liberty,* 66; and see Robert A. Pois, *Friedrich Meinecke and German Politics in the Twentieth Century* (Berkeley, 1972), 59–60.

130. Meinecke, *Historism: The Rise of a New Historical Outlook,* trans. J. E. Anderson (London, 1972), 492.

131. See Felix Gilbert, *History: Politics or Culture? Reflections on Ranke and Burckhardt* (Princeton, 1990).

132. Popper, *The Poverty of Historicism* (Boston, 1957), ix.

133. Mandelbaum, *History Man and Reason: A Study in Nineteenth-Century Thought* (Baltimore, 1971), 42.

134. Michael Allen Gillespie, *Hegel, Heidegger, and the Ground of History* (Chicago, 1984). See also Carl Page, *Philosophical Historicism and the Betrayal of First Philosophy* (University Park, PA, 1995).

135. Popper, *The Poverty of Historicism.*

136. Auerbach, *Mimesis: the Representation of Reality in Western Literature,* trans. Willard Trask (Princeton, 1953); and see "Vico and Aesthetic Historicism," in *Scenes from the Drama of European Literature* (New York, 1959).

137. Hans-Georg Gadamer, *Truth and Method,* trans. Garrett Barden and John Cumming (New York, 1982), and a vast literature, for which see now *The Philosophy of Hans-Georg Gadamer,* ed. Lewis Edwin Hahn (Chicago, 1997).

138. *The Hermeneutical Tradition from Ast to Ricoeur,* ed. Gayle L. Ormiston and Alan D. Schrift (Albany, 1990), 45.

139. Nietzsche, *The Will to Power,* trans. Walter Kaufmann and R. J. Hollingdale (New York, 1967), 327.

140. Nietzsche, *On the Advantage and Disadvantage of History for Life,* trans. Peter Preuss (Indianapolis, 1980), 14; and see Hayden White, "The Burden of History," *Tropics of Discourse: Essays in Cultural Criticism* (Baltimore, 1978), 27–50.

141. Nietzsche, *The Will to Power,* 327, 297; and in a large literature, Alan D. Schrift, *Nietzsche and the Question of Interpretation: Between Hermeneutics and Deconstruction* (New York, 1990).

142. Gadamer, *Truth and Method,* 269; and Nicholas Davy, "Hermeneutics and Nietzsche's Early Thought," in *Nietzsche and Modern German Thought,* ed. Keith Ansell-Pearson (London, 1991), 88–118.

143. Nietzsche, *On the Advantage,* 41, 56.

144. Ibid., 28.

145. Ibid., 3.

146. Benjamin, "Theses on the Philosophy of History," in *Critical Theory and Society,* ed. Stephen Eric Bronner and Douglas MacKay Kellner (New York, 1989), 261–262.

147. John McCole, *Walter Benjamin and the Antinomies of Tradition* (Ithaca, 1993), 289.

148. Husserl, *The Crisis of European Sciences and Transcendental Phenomenology,* trans. David Carr (Evanston, 1970), 373.

149. Heidegger, *Sein und Zeit* (Tübingen, 1986), esp. 19ff, 372ff, 395ff. These are the awkward English equivalents in the standard translation of *Sein und Zeit* by John Macquarrie and Edward Robinson (New York, 1962), who give "historizing" for happening (*Geschehen*) and in general neglect Heidegger's play on *Geschehen-Geschichte,* as well as the distinction between what happens (*Geschichte*) and what is interpreted (*Historie*).

150. Ibid., 188.

151. Ibid., 152.

152. Habermas, *Knowledge and Human Interests,* tr. Jeremy J. Shapiro (Boston,

1971), and *The Theory of Communicative Action,* I, *Reason and the Rationalization of Society,* trans. Thomas McCarthy (Boston 1981), 130–136; see also Thomas McCarthy, *The Critical Theory of Jürgen Habermas* (Cambridge, Mass., 1981), 187–193.

153. See Paul Ricoeur, "Hermeneutics and the Critique of Ideology," in *Hermeneutics and the Human Sciences,* tr. John B. Thompson (Cambridge, 1981), 63–100.

154. Gadamer, *Philosophical Hermeneutics,* 35.

155. *Truth and Method,* 156.

Conclusion

1. See W. Jackson Bate, *The Burden of the Past and the English Poet* (Cambridge, Mass., 1970), and Harold Bloom, *The Anxiety of Influence: A Theory of Poetry* (Oxford, 1973).

2. See Ernst Behler, *Irony and the Discourse of Modernity* (Seattle, 1990).

3. White, *Metahistory: The Historical Imagination in Nineteenth-Century Europe* (Baltimore, 1973); and see the critical and often discipular comments by seventeen authors in two issues of *Storia della storiografia,* 24 (1993) and 25 (1994).

4. Aristotle, *Poetics,* 1451; Kelley, *Versions of History,* 62.

5. Blumenberg, *Work on Myth,* trans. Robert M. Wallace (Cambridge, Mass., 1985), 263.

6. Diderot, *Oeuvres complètes,* ed. J. Assézat and M. Tourneaux, 20 vols. (Paris, 1875–77), 180–181.

7. Frederick R. Karl, *Modern and Modernism: The Sovereignty of the Artist 1885–1925* (New York, 1988), 75, but mentions only Dilthey and Croce.

Index